COMPARATIVE CRIMINAL JUSTICE SYSTEMS

GLOBAL AND LOCAL PERSPECTIVES

SHAHID M. SHAHIDULLAH,

Professor and Chair
Department of Criminal Justice, Sociology, and Social Work
Elizabeth City State University—University of North Carolina

JONES & BARTLETT
LEARNING

World Headquarters
Jones & Bartlett Learning
5 Wall Street
Burlington, MA 01803
978-443-5000
info@jblearning.com
www.jblearning.com

Jones & Bartlett Learning books and products are available through most bookstores and online booksellers. To contact Jones & Bartlett Learning directly, call 800-832-0034, fax 978-443-8000, or visit our website, www.jblearning.com.

Substantial discounts on bulk quantities of Jones & Bartlett Learning publications are available to corporations, professional associations, and other qualified organizations. For details and specific discount information, contact the special sales department at Jones & Bartlett Learning via the above contact information or send an email to specialsales@jblearning.com.

Production Credits

Publisher: Cathleen Sether
Acquisitions Editor: Sean Connelly
Editorial Assistant: Caitlin Murphy
Production Assistant: Leia Poritz
Marketing Manager: Lindsay White
Rights & Photo Research Assistant: Ashley Dos Santos

Manufacturing and Inventory Control Supervisor: Amy Bacus
Composition: Laserwords Private Limited
Cover Design: Michael O'Donnell
Cover Image: © Kamaga/iStockphoto, Inc.
Printing and Binding: Edwards Brothers Malloy
Cover Printing: Edwards Brothers Malloy

Library of Congress Cataloging-in-Publication Data
Shahidullah, Shahid M., 1950-
  Comparative criminal justice systems : global and local perspectives / Shahid Shahidullah.
    p. cm.
  Includes bibliographical references and index.
  ISBN 978-1-4496-0425-7 (pbk.) — ISBN 1-4496-0425-0 (pbk.)
1. Criminal justice, Administration of. I. Title.
  K5001.S53 2012
  364—dc23

2012017799

6048

Printed in the United States of America
16 15 14 13 12   10 9 8 7 6 5 4 3 2 1

To my wife Sufia and our daughter Ashley

Contents

Foreword

I must question whether anyone can fully comprehend criminal justice in the United States or in any other jurisdiction without a command of comparative criminal justice. I speak from personal experience. When I began my studies for a law degree in 1972, I embarked on a strikingly parochial undertaking. As I recollect, even references to the mother of common law, England, were fleeting. Surely Islamic jurisprudence went unnoticed. This held true when I later undertook a graduate degree in criminal justice. It wasn't until I attended Oxford University for a postgraduate law degree that I was introduced to, and eventually immersed in, comparative criminal justice. As I wrote in my Oxford thesis, "comparisons can reveal underlying premises and challenge accepted truths." In my study of comparative criminal justice, I have found guidance and inspiration that I might have not otherwise acquired.

Comparative criminal justice initially received an indifferent reception in the United States. It now deserves better—and for good reason: it is ready to join the traditional canon of criminal justice subject matter. No better case can be made for its readiness than Professor Shahidullah's *Comparative Criminal Justice Systems: Global and Local Perspectives*. This book's coverage is truly global. It profiles criminal justice not only in the West, but also in Asia, Africa, Latin America, and the Middle East. Equally important, *Comparative Criminal Justice Systems: Global and Local Perspectives* establishes the identity of comparative criminal justice by delineating its research traditions as well as its theoretical and methodological perspectives.

The reach and depth of *Comparative Criminal Justice Systems: Global and Local Perspectives* represent a signal contribution to criminal justice as an academic discipline.

James E. Robertson, JD, MA, Dipl. in Law
Distinguished Faculty Scholar & Professor of Corrections
Minnesota State University

Preface

Comparative criminal justice is currently one of the fastest growing areas of interest in criminal justice. It is the study of not only the nature and evolution of criminal justice across the world's societies, but also the similarities and differences in their perceptions of crime and criminality, as well as their pursuit of law and justice. Although the issues of crime, law, and justice are as old as civilizations, criminal justice is one of the youngest academic specialties. Criminal justice as a recognized academic specialty in the United States and Europe is barely three decades old. In contrast, the academic specialty of criminal justice in most of the world's developing countries, such as Asia, Africa, and Latin America, is known only through assorted criminal justice reform activities of the United Nations and other international assistance organizations.

In the United States and Europe, even though criminal justice is a young academic specialty, it has grown very quickly concerning the rising complexities of governing crime, law, and justice in the high-tech global information society and the knowledge economy that has been rapidly engulfing the world from the beginning of the 1970s. What is intellectually challenging, however, is that the field of criminal justice has been evolving quickly in terms of its scope of interest, theoretical development and diversities, and methodology of studying diverse rates and patterns of crime and criminality. In the 1970s—in the initial phase of its academic evolution—criminal justice was perceived primarily as the study of the police, courts, prisons, parole, and probation. The approach was primarily intrasystemic in nature. In the 1980s and 1990s, interest in criminal justice began to expand to issues of penology, punishment, politics of crime control, equal justice, crime and poverty, systemic management, and the integration of science and ICT (information and communication technology) into criminal justice.

This shift to some of the more macro issues of criminal justice in the 1980s and 1990s generated a new interest in comparative criminal justice. Curiosity about the nature of criminal justice in different countries of the world—particularly in the countries of the West—began to emerge. From the late 1990s to the early 2000s, comparative criminal justice started to become more global in nature. This trend reflected the intensification of modernization and globalization processes across the world's societies following the end of the Cold War in the mid-1980s. The dream of a "new world order" devoid of wars, crises, and conflicts went unrealized after the end of the Cold War, but a global movement for the spread of development and democracy started to expand all across the world's societies from that time. With this, a more global approach to understanding crime and justice began to grow. Criminal justice experts, development professionals, and political leaders began to express interest in understanding the world's diverse patterns of crime and criminality, and divergent systems of law and justice. It is from this focus, and from the perspective of modernization and globalization, that *Comparative Criminal Justice Systems: Global and Local Perspectives* was written.

Any work on comparative criminal justice must be seen from a global perspective—a perspective of diverse countries, creeds, cultures, and civilizations, and the processes that shape their specific nature and articulations. Modernization and globalization are spreading many homogenizing sets of institutions and cultural codes across the world's societies in almost all domains of life, including law and justice. As a result, global perspectives on organizing the world's polities and shaping the nature of their law, justice, and governance have emerged. Increasingly across the world's societies, there are similar demands for the criminalization of domestic violence, child abuse, corporal punishment, dating violence, genital mutilation, honor killing, torture, and sexual harassment. There are also growing demands for the decriminalization of abortion, homosexuality, alternative faiths and lifestyles, and various kinds of reproductive rights and behaviors. Different groups of individuals—including women, children, religious minorities, and LGBT groups—are demanding a system of criminal justice that is sensitive to their specific locations in a society and their specific life situations. At the same time, these groups demand a system based on some of the universal principles of equal justice, fairness, and human rights.

Similarly, there is also a vision across the world's societies of developing a system of criminal justice that is compatible with modernity. The search for modernity in criminal justice is pursued not just to obtain the latest technology of force and surveillance for the police and prisons, but also to design a new system of law and justice based on modernist values of secularization, due process of law, and policy-making for crime control and prevention on the basis of science, reason, and rationality. With the advancement of global crimes, different societies of the world are facing similar problems and predicaments. There is hardly any society today that has not been touched by the invisible hand of transnational organized criminal groups that are roaming across the world's continents, trafficking anything that can be economically profitable (from sex to human organs). Transnational organized criminal groups in societies around the world are not only bringing new challenges for their criminal justice systems, but also posing formidable threats to their development and democracy. Many failed states of the world today—from Somalia, to Guatemala, to Pakistan—are the hotspots of transnational organized crimes. In any serious comparative analysis of criminal justice, these global and local issues and their nexus need to be addressed in terms of the dynamics of modernization and globalization.

The processes of modernization and globalization are not creating a single world civilization. There are many forces and possibilities of "civilizational clash" and "intercivilizational" debates and disputes with respect to what constitutes the nature of a "good society," a "good government," or a "good system of criminal justice." Therefore, one must take a systemic, historical, and holistic approach to pursuing comparative criminal justice. A country's criminal justice system is an extension of its instrumentality of the state and governance. The nature and the health of a state define the nature and the health of its criminal justice. A number of world reports and studies, such as the World Bank's *Governance Indicators*, the World Justice Project's *The Rule of Law Index*, and the Economic Intelligence Unit's *Index of Democracy*, have shown that countries ranking low in democracy and rule of law also rank low in the efficiency of their criminal justice systems and have high rates of violent crimes (e.g., murder).

In exploring comparative criminal justice around the world's societies, analysis of the nature of polities, political ideologies, and political elites is very important. Pakistan is a good case-in-point. Pakistan was born with a vision of a modern society under the leadership of highly educated modernist elite in the sub-continent of India in 1947. The criminal justice system of Pakistan was solidly built on the foundations of modern law and legal institutions imported to India by the British colonial government. This legacy was completely overthrown in the late 1970s when political leadership was taken over by the military, who introduced a Shari'a system of law and justice in Pakistan—a country that did not have any historical legacy of an educated Islamic clergy capable of understanding and interpreting the intricate laws and rules of Islamic jurisprudence.

China is another case-in-point. Modernization of China's criminal justice system began at the behest of the imperial rule in the late 19th century. In 1940, criminal justice in China was built on some major institutions of modern law and law enforcement, but in the 1950s and 1960s, under communist government ideology and the leadership of Mao Zedong, China's modern institutions of criminal justice were deliberately and completely destroyed. The same is true for Iran. Until 1979, Iran's criminal justice was firmly based on modern law and legal institutions. A secular system of justice had been growing in Iran since the beginning of the Safavid dynasty in the 16th century. Under the rule of Reza Shah Pahlavi in the 1950s and 1960s, the foundation for a modern criminal justice system was firmly established. However, this was completely destroyed when the Shi'ite clergy captured the political power of Iran and introduced its own version of Shari'a Law.

Understanding the nature of the state, state ideologies, and political elites is equally relevant for understanding comparative criminal justice in the West. In almost all Western countries, the rise and expansion of new penology (e.g., the "get tough" approach) from the mid-1970s was closely associated with the rise to power of a new generation of conservative political elites, such as Richard Nixon and Ronald Reagan in the United States, Brian Mulroney and Stephen Harper in Canada, Margaret Thatcher and David Cameron in the United Kingdom, and John Howard in Australia. Although political elites of all brands of ideologies like the new penology's rhetoric, it is a particularly popular perspective on crime control and prevention among conservative political elites in the West. Such political and ideological perspectives take us to Chapter 1 of this text, which argues that an analysis of comparative criminal justice must be both intrasystemic and extrasystemic in nature. The intrasystemic nature of criminal justice in a country—the police, courts, and prisons, and the way they have evolved over time—needs to be examined in the larger context of that country's political evolution, and evolution of the state, state elites, and ideologies. Therefore, modernization and globalization, discussed in Chapter 2, are relevant as overarching processes and forces of connectivity that have been shaping the nature and dynamics of Western societies since the Renaissance and Age of Enlightenment, and developing worlds such as Asia, Africa, and Latin America since the days of colonialism.

This book is divided into two parts. Part I contains four chapters that define and describe the nature, theories, and methods of comparative criminal justice. One of the objectives of these chapters is to provide an understanding of how the problem of comparison is to be conceptualized and theorized—that is, how different societies of the world are connected and what forces shape that connectivity. This section examines four theoretical perspectives: Modernization Theory, Civilization Theory, World-Systems Theory, and Globalization Theory. Chapter 3 (on methodology) describes the nature and sources of data on crime trends and patterns, and the performance indicators for criminal justice systems in different countries. It also examines national crime surveys of the United States, Canada, the United Kingdom, Germany, and Japan; describes the various regional crime surveys in Europe; and characterizes the nature of various international crime surveys, such as the United Nations Surveys on Crime Trends (UN-CTS) and the International Crime Victimization Survey. Chapter 4, which is one of the major chapters of this book, describes and characterizes the nature and profile of modern criminal justice in terms of its core institutions and values. An argument has been made in this chapter that since the beginning of the 19th century, a modern system of criminal justice has been evolving within the framework of a modern state based on democracy and the rule of law. The institutions and values of the modern system of criminal justice are the benchmarks of comparison—benchmarks of studying the nature and evolution of criminal justice across the world's societies.

Part II comprises eight chapters organized in terms of four models or types of criminal justice systems: modern systems (e.g., the United States, Canada, the United Kingdom, European Countries, and Australia); modernizing systems (e.g., Asia, Africa, and Latin America); traditional systems (e.g., Saudi Arabia and Iran); and dual systems (e.g., China, Pakistan, Malaysia, Indonesia, and Nigeria). The major dividing line among these four models of criminal justice is between secular and sacred traditions of law. The modern and modernizing criminal justice systems are based on secular legal traditions (e.g., English common law and continental civil law). The traditional systems of criminal justice are based on religious law (i.e., Shari'a Law in both Saudi Arabia and Iran). The dual criminal justice systems exist in countries that try to adopt modern institutions and values of criminal justice within the framework of either their traditional religion (e.g., Shari'a Law and English common law in Pakistan, Malaysia, and Nigeria; and Shari'a Law and civil law in Indonesia), or traditional politics (e.g., China's modernization of criminal justice within the framework of a socialist polity).

Chapters 5 and 6 (on modern systems of criminal justice) examine the nature of police reforms in the United States, the United Kingdom, Germany, and the European Union; the growing trends of homogenization in sex offender registration laws in the United States, Canada, and the United Kingdom; and the growing trends of homogenization in sentencing laws (e.g., the rise of new penology) in the United States, Canada, the United Kingdom, and Australia. Chapters 7 and 8 are on modernizing systems of criminal justice. Chapter 7 examines the nature of colonial legacies in criminal justice; the problem of the rule of law, democracy, and criminal justice; and the problems and predicaments of criminal justice systems in the failed and fragile states of Africa and Central America, as well as in the postauthoritarian states of South America. Chapter 8 examines the problem of police reforms in India, Kenya, Bangladesh, and Brazil; the new demands for the criminalization of sexual harassment, domestic violence, and child sexual exploitation in different countries of Asia, Africa, and Latin America; new movements for the decriminalization of homosexuality; and progress of reforms in criminal procedural laws in Indonesia, Chile, and Nigeria. One of the key observations made in this section is that a vast number of countries in Asia, Africa, and Latin America are slowly but surely reforming their criminal justice systems under the impact of modernization and globalization. Chapter 9 (on the nature and evolution of Islamic jurisprudence and Shari'a Law) intends to provide an understanding of the intricate laws and rules of Islamic criminal justice. The chapter describes the meaning and sources of Shari'a Law; the nature of *Hudud*, *Qisas*, and *Ta'zir* crimes and punishments; and the nature of due process in Islamic criminal justice. As an example of how Islamic criminal justice depends on the nature of the state and the ideology of the state elites, this chapter presents some historical examples related to the implementation of Shari'a Law during the Ottoman Empire of the Turks (1300–1920) and the Mughal Empire of India (1526–1757). Chapter 10 further examines the nature and implementation of Shari'a Law and Islamic criminal justice in the context of two contemporary states: Saudi Arabia and Iran. One of the key observations from Chapters 9 and 10 is that the central point of debate and discourse in Islamic criminal justice is the extent to which *ijtihad* (logic and analytical reasoning) and *ijma* (judicial consensus) can be applied in the interpretation of the Quran and the Sunna—the sources of Shari'a Law. Modernists within Islamic jurisprudence, based primarily on the Hanafi School of Islamic jurisprudence, argue that Islamic criminal justice can be made compatible with varying times and spaces through the use of *ijtihad* and *ijma*. The ultra-traditionalists, on the other hand, assert—primarily on the basis of the Hanbali School of Islamic jurisprudence—that there is no scope for the use of human reason, logic, and rationality in the interpretations of the divine sanctions of the Quran and Sunna. A close examination reveals that there are tensions within Islamic criminal justice in Saudi Arabia. The monarchy of Saudi Arabia represents the modernist version of Islamic jurisprudence, but the Islamic clergy, who are not a part of the monarchy and the ruling elite, represent the ultra-traditionalist perspective (e.g., the Wahhabist perspective) of Islamic jurisprudence. In Iran, unlike Saudi Arabia, the Islamic clergy are in political power, and they represent their own version of radical and ultra-orthodox interpretation of Islamic jurisprudence. They have deliberately destroyed secular and modern systems of law and justice in pursuit of their vision of an ideal Islamic state based on an ideal system of Islamic criminal justice. For the radical ultra-orthodox Shi'ite clergy of Iran, modern criminal justice is incompatible with Islam.

A considerable number of countries in Asia, Africa, and the Middle East have systems of criminal justice that are dualistic in nature. China and Pakistan are two examples, and are examined in Chapters 11 and 12, respectively. China has been pursuing modernization in criminal justice within the political framework of a socialist state, while Pakistan has been pursuing Islamic criminal justice within the framework of a modern state and modern law and justice.

I have searched for an understanding of how, in the context of modernization and globalization, criminal justice systems in varying societies are performing and pursuing changes and reforms. Curiosity is basic to science and it is at the core of comparative methodology. In reading this book, I hope students develop a genuine sense of curiosity about criminal justice in different countries, cultures, and civilizations. I have gone back and forth in my analysis of criminal justice workings, from micro to macro and macro to micro issues. I have described the nature and the plights of the failed states in Africa and Central America; how reforms in pretrial detention are underway in Nigeria; the legal traditions of imperial China; and police reforms in India, Bangladesh, Kenya, Brazil, the United States, the United Kingdom, and Germany.

This book is substantially different from existing literature on comparative criminal justice. It relies mostly on primary materials—such as different countries' constitutions, legislative documents, court cases, governmental crime reports, and studies by the United Nations and the world's leading think-tanks on crime and development—in order to examine how criminal justice systems of disparate countries and cultures are performing and reforming in the context of modernization and globalization. Although this book is deliberately broad and deeply historical, it focuses on issues of criminal justice that are mundane and pragmatic, such as the rule of law and democracy; criminalization of sexual harassment, intimate partner violence and child sexual abuse; decriminalization of abortion and homosexuality; due process of law in China; human rights issues in Iran; judicial reform in Saudi Arabia; and issues of equal justice in Pakistan. Understanding the nature and dynamics of both intrasystemic and extrasystemic characteristics of criminal justice across the world's societies in terms of the vicissitudes of modernization and globalization form the core of comparative criminal justice.

About the Author

Shahid M. Shahidullah, PhD is a Professor in the Criminal Justice Program of the Department of Criminal Justice, Sociology, and Social Work at Elizabeth City State University, North Carolina. Before joining Elizabeth City State University—one of the 16 campuses of the University of North Carolina System—Dr. Shahid taught at St. John's University in New York, Virginia State University, and Christopher Newport University in Virginia. He received his MPIA (Master of Public International Affairs), and MA and PhD in Sociology from the University of Pittsburgh. His major research interests include crime policy in America, comparative criminal justice, transnational organized crime, global terrorism, and criminal justice system in South Asia.

Westview Press published Dr. Shahid's first book, *Capacity Building in Science and Technology in the Third World*, in 1991. His next book, *Globalization and the Evolving World Society* (with P. K. Nandi), was published in 1998 by E. J. Brill, the Netherlands. In 2008, American University Press published his book, *Crime Policy in America: Laws, Institutions, and Programs*. Dr. Shahid has also authored and coauthored numerous journal articles that were published in *Global Crime*; *Criminal Law Bulletin*; *Aggression and Violent Behavior: Future Research Quarterly*; *Knowledge: Creation, Diffusion, and Utilization*; *International Journal of Sociology and Social Policy*; *Knowledge in Society: International Journal of Knowledge Transfer*; *Journal of Developing Societies*; and *Virginia Social Science Journal*. Dr. Shahid has worked as a member of the Editorial Board of *Victims and Offenders: International Journal of Evidence-Based Theory and Practice*, and the *Journal of Developing Societies*, published by E. J. Brill, the Netherlands. He was also the President of Virginia Social Science Association in 2008–2009. Dr. Shahid lives in Chesapeake, Virgina with his wife, Sufia B. Shahid, MD, and daughter, Ashley Shahid.

Acknowledgments

The project of writing this book on comparative criminal justice began with Sean Connelly, Acquisitions Editor at Jones & Bartlett Learning. After the publication of my book *Crime Policy in America: Laws, Institutions, and Programs* in 2008, I was not immediately poised to start another major book project. However, I was certainly exploring some of the emerging issues in criminal justice in the context of globalization, particularly on the nature and threats of transnational crimes. In early January 2010, Sean called and asked me whether I would be interested in writing a book on comparative criminal justice. I agreed and the project began to evolve. I am therefore truly thankful to Sean for making this book possible. I am also thankful to the manuscript reviewers for their thoughtful comments and remarks on the book prospectus and proposal. Their views and comments helped me to sort out and organize my thoughts. One reviewer commented that the "key strengths of this book are its theoretical sophistication and its emphasis on historical transformation." These two perspectives, in fact, run throughout this book, with one of the core arguments being that comparative criminal justice is not merely a process of comparing cops, courts, and prisons of different societies. Rather, it must be theoretically grounded and historically relevant to time and space; it must be global in perspective, but at the same time, emphatically local in perception, insight, and sensitivity.

I consider myself fortunate for having had some of the world's renowned criminologists and criminal justice experts read the manuscript and write reviews. I am truly grateful to Professor Freda Adler of the University of Pennsylvania, President of the American Society of Criminology in 1995, for reading the manuscript and writing a testimonial for the book. As one of America's early pioneers in comparative criminal justice, her thoughts and opinions touched the core themes of this book. Professor Jianhong Liu, President of the Asian Society of Criminology and Editor-in-Chief of the *Journal of Asian Criminology*, was extremely gracious in offering to read the manuscript, particularly from the perspective of the developing world. I am thankful for his very inspirational reviews and comments. Professor James Robertson, Editor-in-Chief of *Criminal Law Bulletin*, is one of our country's distinguished criminologists, with expertise in comparative law and comparative corrections. I thank him for taking the time to write a foreword for this book.

The research for this book was supported by a generous grant from Elizabeth City State University (ECSU). I am grateful to the existing leadership of the university for its focus on making ECSU one of the great institutions of research and learning in the 21st century. Provost Ali Khan and Dean Murel Jones greatly aided this project by allowing me to take some time away from my responsibilities as Chair of the Department of Criminal Justice, Sociology, and Social Work in order to do research and writing for this book. Dr. Brenda Norman, Professor and Director of the Social Work Program, was very generous in shouldering some of the responsibilities of the Chair while I was working on this project. Thanks also to all of my colleagues in the Department of Criminal Justice, Sociology, and Social Work for their kind support and cooperation. Joyce Shaw, my Administrative Support Associate, not only helped in the completion of the day-to-day operations with utmost sincerity and competence, but she also urged me to sleep well after burning the midnight oil.

Dr. Elizabeth Byrne, Associate Professor of English in ECSU's Department of Language, Literature, and Communication, has done a remarkable job in editing the manuscript. Her interests in globalization and fostering in readers a deeper understanding of the perspective of post-colonialism, as well as her wide familiarity with the writings of some of the giants of social science, including Karl Marx, Max Weber, Sigmund Freud, Charles Darwin, Jeremy Bentham, and Michel Foucault, greatly helped her delve deeply into some of the more complex concepts in social science and criminology and edit the manuscript with the utmost care and competence. Dr. John Luton, Professor in the Department of Language, Literature, and Communication, had a chance to read some of the earlier chapters. His reviews and comments were truly inspirational. Cheryl Leigh, ECSU's Inter-Library Loan Specialist in the G. R. Little Library, facilitated my reading of some of the discipline's rare books by bringing them in from all over the country for the past two-and-a-half years. Thank you so very much, Cheryl, for all of your research expertise. At Jones & Bartlett Learning, Leia Poritz, Ashley Dos Santos, Caitlin Murphy, Lindsay White, and many others have done tremendous work to complete the production process of this manuscript on time. Their professionalism and prudent advice have greatly enriched the quality of this book.

Last, but not the least, is my utmost gratitude to my family. My wife Sufia and my 15-year-old daughter Ashley endured hundreds of hours of isolation and loneliness, even when I was in the same house and eating in the same kitchen. My complete immersion in this project for almost two-and-a-half years has brought many moments of silence in the family, but I was never deprived of support, help, and excitement as the project was evolving. I am truly grateful to my wife and my daughter Ashley. The book is dedicated to both of them.

Now a few words, not about what I completed, but about the "incompleteness" of this book. Elizabeth Byrne from ECSU, and the whole crew from Jones & Bartlett Learning worked hard with me to reach a high level of perfection in the quality and the production of this book. However, I believe that there still remain some mistakes, though none of the individuals cited above are responsible for those mistakes both in terms of the data and the nature of the arguments. For those mistakes, only I am to blame. At the same time, I also believe in Nobel Laureate Herbert Simon's theory of bounded rationality. Human brains, he theorized, are not fully grown and competent enough to be absolutely certain and rational in making a decision or making an argument. There is always an element of uncertainty in the understanding of a given reality from nature, to life, to society. This is also what is at the core of Noble Laureate's Werner Heisenberg's principal of "indeterminacy," or broadly, of quantum physics. Most philosophers of science believe that the process of doing science is like searching for a black cat in a dark room. We know it is there, but we are not absolutely certain of its existence at a given point of time. All data and arguments, particularly in social science, criminology, and criminal justice, need to be comprehended with some amount of doubt and humility.

I would also like to thank the following people for reviewing the text:

Bakhitah B. Abdul-Ra'uf, Radford University
Martha Earwood, University of Alabama, Birmingham
Luca Follis, Lancaster University
Shannon Hankhouse, Tarleton State University
J. D. Jamieson, Texas State University
Anthony LaRose, University of Tampa
Rafael Rojas, Jr., Southern New Hampshire University
Larry Salinger, Arkansas State University at Jonesboro
Colby Lynne Valentine, Florida State University
W. Jesse Weins, Dakota Wesleyan University

Comparative Criminal Justice: Theory, Methods, and Benchmarks of Comparison

PART

I

Comparative Criminal Justice: Nature, Scope, and Research Traditions

▶ CHAPTER OUTLINE

■ Introduction

Comparative criminal justice is the study of how criminal justice is perceived, practiced, and pursued in different countries. There are about 195 countries in the world currently recognized by the United Nations, and they belong to disparate regions, different cultures, and diverse civilizations of the East and the West. The patterns of crime and criminality, the nature of law and legal traditions, the organization of law enforcement, the composition of the judiciary, and the pursuit of justice and punishment widely vary among these countries. However, there are also many similarities among these countries in the way they are challenged by new forms of crime and criminality, new needs for criminalization and decriminalization, new claims for accountability and ethicality in law enforcement and the judiciary, and new demands for reforms in criminal justice compatible with international standards in law, justice, and human rights.

Enormous variations exist around the world in the way crimes are defined and law and justice are pursued. In the United States and in almost all countries of the Western world, cohabitation between unmarried partners is not a crime. Among some groups, it may be morally problematic, but in the wider society it is legally protected, socially recognized, and culturally legitimate. In most of the Muslim countries such as Saudi Arabia, Iran, Pakistan, United Arab Republic, and Kuwait, cohabitation is a high crime punishable by law. In most of the Asian, African, and Latin American countries, cohabitation between unmarried partners is seen at best as a deviance, but it is not a crime.

Abortion is a crime punishable by law in about 41 countries of Latin America and the Caribbean region, even though various feminist groups in these countries have been demanding its decriminalization for almost 4 decades (see **Box 1-1**). In most of the countries of the West, however, abortion is defined as a right, not a crime. The U.S. Supreme Court, through its decision in *Roe v. Wade*, legalized and decriminalized abortion in 1973. In the United States, placing obstructions to legal abortion is a crime punishable by law. In 2010, a Kansas judge sentenced Scott Roeder, the killer of an abortion doctor, to life in prison without any possibility of parole for at least 50 years.

Adultery is still a high crime in many countries, particularly in Muslim countries such as Saudi Arabia, Iran, and Pakistan. In the Islamic criminal justice systems of these countries, adultery is a crime punishable by stoning to death. In India, adultery is a crime, but it is defined mainly as a male criminality. Women cannot be legally punished in India for involvement in adulterous relations. In 1996, the Constitutional Court in Turkey declared its law against adultery unconstitutional because it was disproportionately applied to women. In the United States, there are laws against adultery based on English common law, but they are hardly applied. In Virginia, adultery is a misdemeanor crime and is punishable by a fine of $250. In Maryland, adultery carries a fine of $10.

Homosexual relations are also dealt with in varying ways in different countries. In 2005, as shown in **Figure 1-1**, two boys were publicly executed in Iran for having homosexual relations. In 2010, in the African country of Malawi, two youths were sentenced to 10 years in prison for gay relationships. In the same year, as shown in **Box 1-2**, the country of Morocco became widely divided as to whether Elton John, a British homosexual celebrity, was to be

BOX 1-1

"A" for Abortion: Latin America's Scarlet Letter

Abortion is a crime in most of the Latin American countries and the countries of the Caribbean region, except in the case of rape, incest, and serious fetal disorders. Statistics show that about 4 million illegal abortions are done every year under clandestine conditions, and about 4,000 women die every year trying to get an abortion. Examples are not few and far between where women are prosecuted for using illegal drugs and alcohol during pregnancy, giving birth to stillborn babies, miscarrying a fetus, or failing to abstain from sexual intercourse during pregnancy. There are criminal laws in many states that restrict women's access to family planning goods and services and surgical methods of contraception. But the waves of modernization have already reached the shores of the region. At the 5th Annual Latin American and the Caribbean Feminist Meeting in Argentina, thousands of women gave birth to a new movement for the decriminalization of abortion and the end of "sexual slavery." This movement, which was born in 1990 and named the "September 28th Campaign" to mark the end of slavery in Brazil in 1888, is now swiftly spreading across the region, demanding the decriminalization of abortion and the restoration of women's rights of reproductive freedom compatible with the promises and principles of the 1979 United Nations Convention on the Elimination of All Forms of Discrimination Against Women (CEDAW). The spread of this movement is obviously opposed by leaders of Catholic and evangelical churches, but "almost all of the Latin American countries are currently immersed in projects of modernization, scratching and clawing to do away with old injustices" and old definitions of crime and criminality.

Source: El País (Spain) I Editorial. (2009, October 26). Retrieved from www.truthout.org.

Figure 1-1 Two Gay Teens Were Executed in Iran in July 2005
Source: © STR/AP Photos.

BOX 1-2

The Blurred Boundaries of Hate and Crime: Elton John Will Play in Morocco: Festival Chief

In most countries of the world, particularly in the Muslim majority countries of the world, people of the LGBT (gays, lesbians, bisexuals, and transgenders) community are hated, abused, despised, and dehumanized. Homosexuality in most of those countries is not just a crime punishable by law. Homosexuals are also deliberately debased and marginalized. With the growing sense of homophobia around the world, the boundaries between hate and crime are becoming increasingly blurred. The waves of modernization are also spreading among the world's societies for the decriminalization of discriminations on the basis of sexual orientation. But with the spreading of the waves of modernization, the issues of the LGBT community are also becoming intensely political. A good case in point is a debate that arose in Morocco in 2010 in the wake of the visit of Elton John, a British pop star, to play a concert in Rabat's Mawazine festival. One of the major political parties in Morocco, the Islamist Justice and Development Party, galvanized a movement not to allow Elton John to play a concert because of his declared homosexual orientation. The leaders of the Islamist party argued that John's concert "had a risk of encouraging homosexuality in Morocco." However, festival chief and artistic director Aziz Daki declared that John would play in Morocco. He claimed that banning the festivity because of sexual orientation would "undermine the respect and privacy and breach certain values that the international Mawazine festival is based on." The global and local perspectives collide with the eventual triumph of the global perspective for the respect of privacy and human rights around the world.

Source: CBC News. (2010, May 11). *Elton John will play in Morocco: Festival chief.* Retrieved from http://www.cbc.ca/news/arts/music /story/2010/05/11/elton-john-morocco.html; photo © anyamuse/ShutterStock, Inc.

allowed to perform in a concert. Homosexuality is a crime punishable by law in some of the major Muslim countries, including Saudi Arabia, Iran, Sudan, Northern Nigeria, and Yemen. It was a crime punishable by death during the Taliban regime in Afghanistan.

Most of the Western countries during the last few decades, on the other hand, have decriminalized homosexuality. In the United States, gay marriage has become legal through judicial decisions and legislation in the District of Columbia, Connecticut, Iowa, Massachusetts, New Hampshire, New York, and Vermont. The Matthew Shepard and James Byrd, Jr. Hate Crimes Prevention Act, passed by Congress and signed into law by President Obama in 2009, made it a federal crime in the United States to hate, hurt, or discriminate against someone on the basis of his or her sexual orientation. In 2005, Canada, through the enactment of the Civil Marriage Act, which followed a decision by the Supreme Court of Canada, legalized same-sex marriage. Same-sex marriage is legal in the Netherlands, Belgium, and Spain.

Because of the diverse definitions of crime, the nature of legal systems, the nature and philosophy of justice, the nature of punishment, and the rate of incarceration, as **Box 1-3** suggests, also widely vary from country to country. The United States has been fighting the modern drug war for almost 40 years, and thousands of drug offenders are in federal and state prisons for drug offenses. There are mandatory sentencing laws for drug offenses in the United States, but usually they do not carry a death penalty. Today, drug trafficking carries the death penalty in 32 countries, including Bahrain, Bangladesh, China, Egypt, India, Indonesia, Iran, Iraq, Kuwait, Libya, Malaysia, Myanmar, North Korea, Oman, Pakistan, Qatar, Saudi Arabia, Singapore, South Korea, Sri Lanka, Sudan, Syria, Taiwan, Thailand, United Arab Emirates, Vietnam, and Yemen (International Harm Reduction Association, 2010). In Malaysia, 36 executions were carried out for drug trafficking between 2004 and 2005. In 2003, Saudi Arabia executed 26 individuals in public for drug trafficking. Vietnam executes about 100 people by firing squad every year for drug trafficking. China uses June 26—the United Nations International Day Against Drug Abuse and Illicit Drug Trafficking—as the day for public executions for drug offenses. In 2005, 55 people were publicly executed in China to observe the day (International Harm Reduction Association, 2007). In 2008, "Iran executed at least 96 people for drug offences. That number rose sharply in 2009 to an estimated 172" (International Harm Reduction Association, 2010, p. 12).

The drug laws in the United States do not have the death penalty for drug trafficking, but the United States has one of the highest rates of incarceration in the world. In 2008, based on an estimated population of 305.8 million, the U.S. incarceration rate reached 753 people per 100,000 population. This is much higher than that of several other countries per 100,000 population, including the United Kingdom (154 in 2010), China (119 in 2005), France (96 in 2008), Germany (88 in 2009), Japan (63 in 2008), and India (32 in 2007; International Centre for Prison Studies, 2010).

There are wide variations in the way crimes and punishments are defined and devised in different countries. But under the contemporary processes of modernization and globalization, countries are also facing similar issues and challenges in governing their criminal justice systems. Some of these issues and challenges are a higher rate of crime and criminality, growth

BOX 1-3

U.S. Rate of Incarceration: A Global Perspective

Since the dominance of the philosophy of "new penology" in America's criminal justice system in the beginning of the 1970s, incarceration has remained the dominant mode of crime control and crime prevention. The liberal philosophy of humanization began to enter into almost all domains of human acts, rights, and culture in America, but not in the domain of criminal justice. Then came the end of the era of "progressive penology." Although the boundaries of the principle of due process began to expand from that time, the boundaries of criminalization and incarceration also began to widen under the impact of such laws and crime control strategies as mandatory sentencing, truth in sentencing, three-strikes laws, "Jessica's law," "Aimee's law," Project Exile, and "Rockefeller drug laws." Prison population in the United States was about 218,000 in 1974. In 2000, the number jumped to about 1.3 million. At the end of 2010, prison population in local, state, and federal prisons reached about 2.4 million. In addition, more than 7 million people were under some kind of correctional supervision. It is estimated that the population in state prisons increased 708% between 1972 and 2008. In 1980, there were 600 state prisons. In 2000, the number of state prisons reached about 1,000—a growth rate of about 70%. In 2008, federal, state, and local governments spent about $75 billion on corrections. Research shows that "crime rates do not account for incarceration rates. For some crimes, the U.S. has higher crime rates than other countries, but not at levels that explain the high rates—and costs—of its current use of incarceration . . . even controlling for crime categories that are defined in the most consistent ways internationally, the U.S. still locks up more people per incident than any other nation. The one exception is incarceration for robbery in Russia."

Source: Hartney, C. (2006). *U.S. rate of incarceration: A global perspective.* Washington, DC: National Council on Crime and Delinquency (NCCD).

of new global crimes, and the emergence of a new breed of transnational organized crime groups. At the same time, there are new demands for criminal justice reforms compatible with democracy, equality (see **Box 1-4**), and human rights. In all countries, except a very few in the Middle East, political leaders, legal communities, criminal justice professionals, civil society groups, and human rights activists are pressing for criminal justice reforms and modernization in terms of the international standards of law and justice. Hundreds of international organizations and think tanks today are also engaged in advancing reforms and modernization in criminal justice in various countries.

For a student of comparative criminal justice, diversities in the way criminal justice is presently pursued in different countries around world stand in puzzling contrast to the

BOX 1-4

Religious Police in Saudi Arabia Arrest Mother for Sitting with a Man

The Kingdom of Saudi Arabia, a country with vast physical infrastructures of modern technology and huge architectural wonders of the 21st century, has one of the most traditional forms of criminal justice in the world. Under Saudi Arabia's Shari'a Law, cohabitation, fornication, homosexuality, and mingling of unrelated men and women are crimes. The Kingdom's religious police (Mutaween), under the direction of the Saudi Commission for the Promotion of Virtue and the Prevention of Vice, are responsible for the enforcement of the Shari'a code of conduct. The religious police, described also as "virtue police" or "morality police," are responsible particularly to see whether the Shari'a injunctions with respect to the conduct of women are being strictly observed in public. In recent years, the abuse of power by religious police has become a major concern for Saudi women and tourists and foreigners living in Saudi Arabia. There are many examples when men and women were harassed and beaten in public, arrested without any warrant, and detained for an indefinite period without charges. The event of the death of 14 girls in an all-girl school in Saudi Arabia in 2002 shocked the world. When fire broke out in the school, the religious police prevented the male firefighters from entering the school to put out the fire. As a result, 14 girls burned to death in front of the whole world. The ordeal of an American businesswoman who was harassed and arrested for having a cup of coffee with a man in Starbucks in Riyadh in 2008 is another case in point about the abusive nature of religious police in Saudi Arabia. The *Times* of London reported: "A 37-year-old American businesswoman and married mother of three is seeking justice after she was thrown in jail by Saudi Arabia's religious police for sitting with a male colleague at a Starbucks coffee shop in Riyadh. Yara . . . was bruised and crying when she was freed from a day in prison after she was strip-searched, threatened, and forced to sign false confessions by the Kingdom's 'Mutaween police.'" Here again, global and local norms are colliding, and modernization is slowly but surely creeping into the Kingdom of Saudi Arabia. The religious police are directly under the command of the King of Saudi Arabia. In January 2012, King Abdullah fired the chief of the religious police with a definite promise of its reform and modernization.

Source: Verma, S. (2008, February 6). Religious police in Saudi Arabia arrest mother for sitting with a man. *The Times (U.K.)*. Retrieved from http://www.religionnewsblog.com/20554/islamic-extremism-42.

similarities of the issues and challenges the same countries face. It is with these puzzles that the field of comparative criminal justice is concerned.

Why do systems of crime and justice differ so greatly from one country to the next?

How are those differences related to political, social, and cultural diversities that exist among those countries (see **Figure 1-2**)?

Figure 1-2 Criminalization of Driving by Women in Saudi Arabia

Source: © Lynsey Addario/VII/Corbis.

How did colonialism affect the crime and justice systems of the colonies, and how do those legacies still shape postcolonial realities?

How are the world's societies increasingly becoming similar in terms of their structures of law and justice, definition of criminalization and decriminalization, and demands and challenges for reforms in criminal justice?

What effect do modernization and globalization have on those processes of change and transformation?

These and similar questions and puzzles are at the core of comparative criminal justice.

■ Comparative Criminal Justice: Compare What?

Criminal justice is the totality of the roles, institutions, organizations, and norms and values in a society that are related to defining crime and deviance, developing laws and sanctions, and devising justice and punishment. In every society, there is a system of criminal justice, as there are systems of politics, economy, family, education, and faith and beliefs. In every society, criminal justice is one of the core institutions of politics and governance. In the 195 countries of the world, there are 195 different systems of criminal justice. Each of these systems is independent of the others. The United States, for example, cannot change decisions made by the Supreme Court of India or the Supreme People's Court of China. In the same way, neither India nor China can force a decision on the Supreme Court of the United States. The sovereignty of the criminal justice system of a country is an integral part of its political sovereignty. The world's various criminal justice systems are more than just politically sovereign. They are also unique, because they are the by-products of their country's specific historical, ideological, and cultural structures and dynamics (e.g., the public hanging in Iran in **Figure 1-3**). The task of comparing different criminal justice systems of the world is therefore hugely

Figure 1-3 Public Executions in Iran: Five People Were Hanged in the Northeastern Religious City of Mashhad in August 2007 on Charges of Rape and Kidnapping

Source: © Reuters/Landov.

complex. To simplify the task, students of comparative criminal justice need to explore three questions:

1. What is it that we want to compare?
2. How do we compare them?
3. Why do we want to compare them?

These questions can be addressed in terms of two levels of analysis: intrasystemic comparison and extrasystemic comparison.

Intrasystemic Comparison: Criminal Justice Structures and Organizations

Internally, a criminal justice system is the totality of the institutions and organizations related to three sectors of governance: police, court, and corrections. There is no country without a system of policing, a system of justice, and a system of prison and other correctional institutions, however archaic those institutions may be. The criminal justice system of a country also does not grow overnight. In all countries, the evolution of criminal justice is intimately connected to the evolution of its politics, economy, culture, and ideology. From the perspective of intrasystemic comparison, we study how law enforcement institutions, judicial structures, and prison and correctional systems have evolved in different countries. If we compare, for example, how policing is structured in the United States and Japan, how judicial bodies vary between China and the United Kingdom, or how correctional centers and prisons are organized in India and Nigeria, we pursue an intrasystemic structural comparison. The nature and pursuit of crime and justice in a country significantly depend on how these three core sectors of criminal justice are structured and organized.

One of the key structural issues is whether criminal justice in a country is unitary or dualistic in nature. In countries characterized by a unitary form of government (e.g., England, China, Japan, France, Iran, Indonesia, the Philippines, and Singapore), there is only one form of criminal justice system based on a centralized structure of law enforcement, court, and prison. In countries based on a federal system (e.g., the United States, Canada, Germany, Australia, and Brazil), there are dual systems of criminal justice. In the United States, there is a federal system of criminal justice composed of federal crimes, criminal laws, law enforcement, courts, and prisons (e.g., Bureau of Prisons). In addition to its federal system,

BOX 1-5

Global Expenditure on Criminal Justice

In almost all countries of the world, criminal justice—police, courts, and prisons—occupies a significant portion of public expenditure. In all countries of the world, the cost of crime control has also been rapidly growing. The total direct expenditure on police, courts, and prisons in the United States in 1980, according to data from the U.S. Department of Justice, was about $36 billion. In 2006, it increased to about $214 billion. Between 1980 and 2006, the direct expenditure increased 420% for police, 660% for corrections, and 503% for the judiciary. According to data from the U.S. Department of Justice's Bureau of Justice Statistics published in 2007, the per capita expenditure for criminal justice in the United States that year was about $633. Out of this amount, $279 was for police, $225 was for corrections, and $129 was for the judiciary. The same trend is observed in the United Kingdom (England and Wales). According to data published by the U.K.'s Centre for Crime and Justice Studies in 2010, between 1999 and 2009, police expenditure in England and Wales increased from 9.83 billion pounds to 14.55 billion pounds. In 2004, the total expenditure for prison and probation services was about 3.6 billion pounds. In 2008–2009, it increased to about 4.91 billion pounds. The first systematic research on global expenditure on criminal justice was published by the European Institute for Crime Prevention and Control in 2004. The research, based on data provided by the governments of 70 countries, shows that in 1997, the global expenditure on criminal justice was about $424 billion in 2004 prices, "of which 62 percent was spent on policing, 3 percent on prosecutions, 18 percent on courts, and 17 percent on prisons." The study concluded that "at the country level there is a strong relationship between the level of available public money and expenditure upon public policing, courts, prosecution and prisons."

Source: Farrell, G., & Clark, K. (2004). *What does the world spend on criminal justice?* (HEUNI Paper No. 20). Helsinki, Finland: European Institute for Crime Prevention and Control.

the United States also has a state system of criminal justice that includes state laws, crimes, law enforcement, courts, and prisons. In Australia, as in the United States, the states and territories are constitutionally empowered to develop their respective systems of criminal justice with their respective laws and law enforcements (see **Box 1**-**5**).

Another core structural component of criminal justice that can be compared across countries is their legal traditions. The evolution of criminal justice in different countries is intimately connected to the evolution of their legal traditions (Glenn, 2004). There are three major legal traditions in the world: English common law, continental civil law, and religious law. Most countries that were under British colonialism follow the English common law tradition (Glendon, Gordon, & Carozza, 1999). Some of the major common law countries include the United States, Australia, India, Canada (English speaking), Jamaica, New Zealand, and the United Kingdom. All of these countries were colonies ruled by the British for centuries. Some of the major countries where the criminal justice system is based on continental civil law include Austria, Belgium, Germany, France, Norway, Denmark, Hungary, Italy, and the Netherlands (Merryman & Perez-Perdomo, 2007). The criminal justice systems of Latin American countries that were ruled by the Spaniards and the Portuguese (Brazil), as well as the Asian and African countries that were ruled by the Dutch, French, and German colonial powers, are also based on the continental civil law tradition. In the Middle East, criminal justice systems of Saudi Arabia and Iran are exclusively based on religious law—Islamic Shari'a Law. The legal traditions of other Middle East countries including Algeria, Egypt, Iraq, Libya, Syria, and Tunisia are based on both civil law and Islamic law. In many countries, the legal systems are rooted in both common law and customary law, as in Ghana, Malawi, Tanzania, Uganda, and Zambia. Alternatively, common law is combined with both religious law and customary law in countries such as Gambia, Kenya, Malaysia, Nigeria, and Pakistan. Along with the unique combination of competing legal traditions, the global variety of legal traditions makes comparison of laws and legal structures across countries one of the intriguing issues in comparative criminal justice.

English common law is a body of laws and legal procedures that (1) have evolved in England over a period of centuries and (2) are based on local, customary conceptions of crime and criminality, right and wrong, and justice and punishment (Holmes, 1881/1991). It is a body of legal paradigms and procedures that are also based on centuries of judge-made laws, case laws, and judicial precedents in England. The governance of the British colonies in the New World and Asia and Africa was primarily based on the rules and institution of English common law. The civil law tradition, on the other hand, is based on Roman law and the Justinian tradition. It is a body of statutes made not by judges, as in common law, but by legislatures and executives. The civil law tradition evolved over a long period of time in medieval continental Europe through the development of statutes made by royal legislatures and promulgated by imperial decrees. There are two major schools of civil law in continental Europe: the French Napoleonic Code and the German Civil Code. The French Napoleonic Code has been dominant in shaping criminal justice in the Netherlands, Belgium, Luxembourg, Italy, and Spain. In the 19th and early part of the 20th century, the development of criminal justice systems in the French colonies of the New World (Haiti, Quebec, and Louisiana),

Middle East (Algeria and Morocco), and Africa (Chad, Mauritania, Niger, Senegal, Gabon, Republic of the Congo, and Madagascar) were largely shaped by the tradition of French civil laws (Napoleonic Code). The German Civil Code was dominant in Austria, Switzerland, Denmark, Sweden, Norway, and Finland. Outside continental Europe, the German Civil Code spread only to Japan and to the German colonies of East Africa. In comparing these varying legal traditions and their effect on criminal justice systems in different countries across the world today, one needs to explore the extent to which historical traditions are being changed and reformed through judicial interventions and statutory developments in law and legal procedures. Among the major common law countries, the United States, Australia, and Canada have substantially changed and reformed many common law definitions of crime and criminal procedures through statutory developments and judicial laws (L. M. Friedman, 2005). On the other hand, in the countries of South Asia (e.g., India and Bangladesh), criminal law and criminal justice institutions are still predominantly based on common law.

Equally significant for intrasystemic structural comparisons of criminal justice across countries is the exploration of the nature of different judicial systems. The United States, England, and Canada have an adversarial system of justice. The adversarial model is structurally different from a judiciary based on the inquisitorial model of Germany, France, Italy, Spain, and other European countries. These two models differ significantly from each other in terms of judicial rules and trial procedures. In an adversarial system, the judges are merely referees and moderators, and jurors play no role in fact finding and courtroom debates and disputes. The prosecutors and defense attorneys primarily play the battles to search and select evidence and witnesses, and to settle the arguments. The accused in an adversarial system cannot be legally forced to testify. In an inquisitorial system of justice, on the other hand, judges play a key role in selecting and searching for evidence, questioning witnesses, and rendering judicial decisions. The accused in an inquisitorial system is legally obligated and can be legally compelled to testify in the court of trial. The pretrial and trial rules and procedures, nature of adjudications, nature of plea bargaining, prosecutorial roles and responsibilities, role of the jurors, roles and responsibilities of the defense attorneys, and posttrial decision making in the delivery of justice widely vary in the countries characterized by these competing models of justice.

Around the world, the division of criminal justice into two structures—adult and juvenile justice systems—is increasingly becoming a major area of demand for reforms in criminal justice. This division of criminal justice in terms of age can also be an important topic for cross-national comparison. The United Nations Standard Minimum Rules for the Administration of Juvenile Justice (the Beijing Rules) state: "Juvenile justice shall be conceived as an integral part of the national development process of each country, within a comprehensive framework of social justice for all juveniles, thus, at the same time, contributing to the protection of the young and the maintenance of a peaceful order in society" (United Nations Organization, 1985, p. 2). The international comparison of how juvenile justice systems are organized in different countries, how juveniles and juvenile delinquency are defined in their criminal law, how juvenile rights to due process of law are protected, what special legal procedures exist for adjudicating juveniles, and how juvenile sentencing and punishments are imposed can be significant in comparative criminal justice. All modern systems of criminal justice in the West maintain a separate system of juvenile justice with a separate body of laws and statutes; separate styles and forms of law enforcement; separate systems of courts and judicial interventions; and different methods and types of sentencing, sanctions, jails, and prisons. In most countries of Asia, Africa, and Latin America, there are no separate systems of juvenile justice (United Nations Children's Fund, 2006). There are no separate courts and institutions for the trial and adjudication of juveniles, and they share the same jails and prisons with adults. In Iran, law permits the execution of juveniles under the age of 17 in violation of the Beijing Rules.

Intrasystemic Comparison: Criminal Justice Processes

The intrasystemic comparison of criminal justice structures and organizations can be complementary to the intrasystemic comparison of criminal justice processes across societies. Although the intrasystemic comparison of structures is a comparison of different types, forms, and structures of criminal justice institutions at a given point of time, intrasystemic comparison of processes is a comparison of how those types, forms, and structures work and function over time across different societies. If, for example, we examine the nature of crime and criminality and of criminalization and decriminalization, as well as the crime trends and patterns across societies, we conduct an intrasystemic comparison of criminal justice processes. For a more historically, politically, and culturally grounded analysis in comparative criminal justice, the intrasystemic comparison of processes can be more significant than a mere understanding of different structures and organizations of criminal justice at a given point of time. It is through the comparison of processes that we can develop an important understanding of the changes and reforms in criminal justice in different countries, the types of challenges these countries face in terms of the growth of crime and criminality, and the directionality of their criminal justice systems in terms of modernization and globalization.

One of the crucial tasks of intrasystematic comparison of processes is to explore the rate of crimes in different countries and understand their trends and patterns over time. The nature of crimes and crime trends vary across societies depending on a society's economic growth, political development, culture, and demography. Research has shown that a high rate of crime is related to poverty and a high rate of economic growth. The societies of the Asia-Pacific region that have experienced high rates of economic growth during the last 3 decades have also experienced high rates of crime and violence during the same time. It is observed that between 1981 and 2001, "The overall crime rate [in China] more than quadrupled . . . . Some crimes have increased more dramatically than others: robbery jumped from just over 20,000 cases in 1981 to a staggering 530,000 in 2001, a 17-fold increase in 20 years" (Bakken, 2004, p. 1). On the basis of crime data available from the *United Nations Surveys on Crime Trends and the Operations of Criminal Justice Systems,* another study has found that between 1980 and 2000, overall reported crime rates in most of the world's regions and countries, except the United States, Canada, and some countries of the European Union, have consistently increased "from 2,300 incidents per 100,000 people in 1980 to just over

3,000 in 2000. Worldwide, problems of crime have become worse over the past decades" (Shaw, Van Dijk, & Rhomberg, 2003, p. 41).

The countries of Latin America, the Caribbean region, Eastern Europe, the Commonwealth of Independent States, Southeast Asia, and the Arab region have shown high volumes of recorded crime during the same period (Shaw et al., 2003). The countries and the regions that have experienced high volumes of reported crime also experienced high rates of homicides (around 25 cases per 100,000 population) and robbery (around 60 incidents per 100,000 population). The countries that have experienced political instability, ethnic conflicts, and political transitions during the same period (e.g., the Russian Federation, the countries of Eastern Europe, South Africa, and some of the countries of the Caribbean) also experienced high volumes of reported homicides, robberies, and other violent crimes (Shaw et al., 2003). In its 2004 study on the international homicide rate, the United Nations Office on Drugs and Crime found the highest rate of homicides (low estimate per 100,000 population) in El Salvador (56.4), Colombia (45.5), South Africa (39.5), Burundi (35.4), Sudan (28.6), and Brazil (26.2). The regions with highest rates of homicide per 100,000 population include Latin America (more than 25), Southern Africa (more than 25), and East and West Africa (about 20–25) (United Nations Office on Drugs and Crime, 2004). In any comparative study of crime trends and patterns across countries, what is important, however, is not just the gathering of data on how crime rate varies across countries and regions, but also the explanation of the economic, political, and social forces that contribute to different rates and patterns of crime in different countries.

The criminal justice systems of all countries seem to follow some universal processes in devising justice and punishment. These processes include arrest, pretrial detentions, pretrial investigations, search and seizure, evidence collection, preliminary hearing, bail and plea bargaining, arraignment, trial and adjudications, and conviction and sentencing. Although these processes are more or less universal, the way they work and function vary widely among countries. The power of law enforcement, styles of policing, limits of search and seizure, protection of self-incrimination rights, exclusionary rules, doctrine of reasonable doubt, doctrine of presumption of innocence, and many other intrasystemic processes in criminal justice are not valued and practiced in the same way in every country. In many countries, there are modern structures of policing based on modern methods of operation, use of information technology, division of work and authority, hierarchical organization, and professional training. But those countries widely practice torture and brutality in seeking confessions, and there are no legal and constitutional protections against unusual searches and seizures, self-incrimination, and cruel and unusual punishment. In many countries, particularly those that are based on the inquisitorial system of justice, the prosecutors do not play any significant role in pretrial investigation and indictment. In India, charging and indictment are the functions not of the prosecutors, but of the police, and this is one of the reasons why police corruption and police brutality are widespread in India. In Chile, until the beginning of criminal procedural reforms in the 1990s, the doctrine of presumption of innocence and the principle of exclusionary rules were not valued and applied. The meaning of the *Miranda* rights is not the same in the United States, Canada, and the United Kingdom

(Skinnider, 2005). In 2010, the Canadian Supreme Court said that the Canadian Charter of Rights and Freedoms, Section 10(*b*) "does not mandate the presence of defence counsel throughout a custodial interrogation . . . . Moreover, the purpose of §10(*b*) does not demand the continued presence of counsel throughout the interview process" (*R. v. Sinclair*, 2010). In the United Kingdom, the police are required in terms of the Police and Criminal Evidence Act of 1984 to caution suspects of their rights to remain silent, but are not legally obligated as in the United States (Ma, 2007). These and various other differences in criminal procedural laws in different countries are of intriguing interest for research in comparative criminal justice (Bradley, 2007; Vogler, 2005). Why these processes of devising justice and punishment vary widely is a question of enormous complexity. It is related to the historical evolution of the criminal justice system in a country and the political, ideological, cultural, and civilizational context within which it evolves.

Extrasystemic Comparison: The Social Ecology of Criminal Justice

Criminal justice systems of the world's societies need to be seen not just in terms of how they are internally structured and organized, but also how they are shaped and molded by a host of factors, forces, and institutions that are external to the system of criminal justice. Criminal justice is a unique institution. It grows in a society over a long period of time in the context of a variety of other social institutions. It is located at the crossroads of different sectors of society, such as the economy, politics, and government. The nature of criminal justice in a society is intimately connected with the nature and growth of its economy and the nature and ideology of its government. Criminal justice in a society is also located at the crossroads of different sectors of knowledge based on different grounds of evidence and different forms of validity, such as religion, philosophy, morality, law, and science. There is hardly any institution of modern society that is so connected to politics and government and is based on the confluence of so many facets of knowledge. The economy, politics, law, religion, culture, ideology, and philosophy of a society form the social ecology of its criminal justice.

The nature of crime and criminal justice in a predominantly agricultural economy will be very different from their nature in more technologically advanced economies, such as the United States, Canada, Germany, and Japan. In technologically advanced economies, for example, there are more concerns for cyber crimes, money laundering, human trafficking, global illegal drug trades, and global terrorism. These are the crimes that are mostly connected to the globalization of the world economy and the rise of information technology. They are more prevalent in the countries that are the key participants in the global economy. Research has shown that in all advanced economies, economic crimes including identity theft, credit card fraud, banking fraud, healthcare fraud, securities fraud, mail and wire fraud, and telecommunications fraud have dramatically increased since the 1990s (Glenny, 2009; Kshetri, 2010). Identity theft in the United States between 2007 and 2008 increased 22%. About 8.1 million Americans were victims of identity theft in 2007. The number increased to 9.9 million in 2008. The U.S. Federal Trade Commission (FTC) received 31,400 complaints of identity theft in 2000. In 2008, the number of complaints received by the FTC increased to 313,982 (Finklea, 2010). To control and combat the emerging economic crimes, the U.S. Congress enacted three major pieces of legislation between 1998 and 2008. They include the Identity Theft and Assumption Deterrence Act of 1998 (PL 105-318), the Identity Theft Penalty Enhancement Act of 1998 (PL 108-275), and the Identity Theft Enforcement and Restitution Act of 2008 (Title II of PL 110-326). The Identity Theft and Assumption Deterrence Act of 1998 defined identity theft as a federal crime punishable by law. The Federal Bureau of Investigation (FBI) has several task forces to work for the investigation and prosecution of identity theft crimes in the United States (Finklea, 2010).

Identity theft is also rapidly growing in the United Kingdom. In 2002, the United Kingdom reported a loss of 1.3 billion pounds per year through identity theft. In 2006, the number increased to 1.9 billion pounds per year. In 2002, the United Kingdom's Credit Industry Fraud Avoidance System reported 32,000 people as victims of identity fraud. In 2003, the number of victims jumped to 42,000 (Meulen, 2006). The U.K.'s Fraud Prevention Service (CIFAS) has reported that compared to 2009, identity fraud increased about 20% in 2010. To control and combat identity theft and other economic crimes, the British Home Office created two new organizations to aid the United Kingdom's criminal justice system: the Identity Fraud Steering Committee (IFSC) and the Identity Fraud Forum in 2003. The U.K. Parliament enacted a new fraud control law, the Identity Cards Act, in 2006 (Meulen, 2006). Similar laws and criminal justice institutions are being created in many economically advanced countries as a way to control and combat the new economic crimes. Studying these crimes across countries has become an important task for students of comparative criminal justice.

In addition to the study of relations between crime and economics in terms of new economic crimes, one can also explore relations between crime and economic growth. There are a number of hypotheses in criminal justice that are related to crime and economics, including relations between crime and poverty, crime and unemployment, crime and income inequality, crime and urbanization, and crime and industrialization. There is no linear relationship between crime and poverty. Not all people who live in poverty commit crime, and not all nations that are poor have high crime rates. Poverty, however, is more than just the lack of income or employment. The effect of poverty is multidimensional (Sen, 2000). It reduces or constrains the capability of an individual to have access to basic necessities of life, including food, housing, health, and education. Poverty also reduces life opportunities by limiting access to law, justice, and fairness. Poverty dehumanizes people and destroys their sense of dignity, morality, responsibility, and loyalty to law and authority. It makes people depressed, powerless, and alienated. Volumes of research have shown that in all countries, developed and underdeveloped, the cities and communities that are poor and economically disadvantaged are more likely to have high rates of crime and violence. Relatedly, the people who live in poverty are more likely to be victimized by street, gun, and drug crimes, and they are less likely to report crimes to law enforcement. They are also more likely to be deprived of justice because of their lack of access to legal services and resources. The effect of poverty on crime and violence is particularly intense when it is associated with institutional inequality, racial and ethnic conflicts, political turmoil, and large-scale economic dislocations and transitions (Demombynes & Özler, 2003; Richardson & Kirsten, 2005).

As defined by the World Bank (2012), about 1.2 billion people in the world live in extreme poverty—living on less than $1.25 a day. In 2005, according to the World Bank (2012), about 16.8% of the people in East Asia and the Pacific, 3.7% in Europe and Central Asia, 8.2% in Latin America and the Caribbean, 3.6% in the Middle East and North Africa, 40.3% in South Asia, and 50.9% in sub-Saharan Africa lived on less than $1.25 a day. If the poverty headcount ratio is increased to $2.00 a day, the number of people who lived in poverty in 2005 was 73.9% in South Asia and 72.9% in sub-Saharan Africa (World Bank, 2012). The poorest region of South Asia includes the countries of India, Pakistan, Bangladesh, Nepal, Bhutan, and Sri Lanka. The poorest region of sub-Saharan Africa is a region composed of about 47 countries, including Angola, Benin, Burundi, Cameroon, Chad, Republic of the Congo, Ethiopia, Ghana, Kenya, Malawi, Mali, Nigeria, Rwanda, Senegal, Sierra Leone, South Africa, Sudan, Tanzania, Uganda, and Zambia. How crime rates and crime patterns are related to extreme poverty in these countries, how increased crime and violence stress and strain their systems of criminal justice, and how their criminal justice systems respond to increased crime and violence are significant issues in comparative criminal justice.

The expansion of industrialization, urbanization, and globalization in most countries in the 20th century has caused significant economic developments. These expansions have also caused significant economic dislocations in many countries and regions of the world. The beginning of the development of a market economy in the countries of the Russian Federation, Eastern Europe, and Baltic Region after the end of the Cold War in the 1990s caused many economic dislocations. Those economic dislocations, in turn, produced a new generation of transnational organized crimes, a new breed of transnational criminal syndicates, and a new set of challenges for criminal justice systems (Jackson, 2007). The relations between the rise of global organized crime and the expansion of market economy and globalization across countries and regions are intriguing issues in comparative criminal justice.

Another core component of the social ecology of criminal justice in a country is the nature of its government and political authority (Newburn & Sparks, 2004). The patterns of crime and crime trends and the nature of criminal justice in a country are connected to its form of government and the nature of its political authority, political legitimacy, political development, and political culture. The nature of criminal justice in liberal democracies (e.g., the United States, Canada, the United Kingdom, Germany, France, and Japan) is qualitatively different from that of authoritarian governments (e.g., Taiwan and Singapore) or monarchical regimes (e.g., Saudi Arabia and Jordan) or a theocracy (e.g., Iran). The advanced democracies of the world are characterized by modern systems of criminal justice. In advanced democracies, criminal justice is a relatively autonomous institution with independent judiciaries, professionalized groups of judges and jurists, and professional bodies of law enforcement. A democracy's principles of the separation of power and checks and balances guide and control the relations among the three core sectors of governance—the executive, the legislative, and the judicial. In authoritarian governments and monarchical regimes, the constitutional controls on separation of power and checks and balances do not always work. The criminal justice systems in such countries and regimes are usually controlled to serve the interests of the political entity in power at the time. Law enforcement is used for suppressing political dissidents, whereas the process of law making is executively controlled, and the independence of the judiciary is always violated (Ginsburg & Moustafa, 2008). As a result, the criminal justice systems of the authoritarian governments and monarchical regimes are overtly dominant, coercive, and oppressive in nature. In theocracies, such dominance, coercions, and oppressions are legitimated on the ground of the sanctity of the laws emanating from the sacred texts. In any comparative study of criminal justice, the understanding of the nature of government and political authority within which criminal justice grows and expands is vitally important.

Outside the world's major democracies, authoritarian states, monarchical regimes, and theocracies, there are huge numbers of states in Asia, Africa, and Latin America that do not clearly fit any one of the four traditional categories of states. Some of them are ruled by military dictators, some of them are struggling for democracy, and some are in crisis for legitimacy because of protracted racial, ethnic, and religious conflicts. In the literature of political development and international diplomacy, some of these states are defined as failed or fragile states. Most of the failed and fragile states are in South Asia, sub-Saharan Africa, and the Caribbean region—regions that are also the economically poorest in the world. The failed states are characterized by extreme poverty, political underdevelopment, extreme centralization of authority, weak delivery of public services, widespread violation of human rights, arbitrary application of the rule of law, and extreme fractionalization in politics. Some of the major failed states in sub-Saharan Africa include Somalia, Zimbabwe, Sudan, Chad, Republic of the Congo, Central African Republic, Kenya, Nigeria, Ethiopia, Yemen, Uganda, Burundi, Rwanda, and Sierra Leone (African Human Security Initiative, 2009). In South Asia, Pakistan is one of the major failed states. In Latin America and the Caribbean region, Colombia, Bolivia, Honduras, Guatemala, and Nicaragua are referred to as major failed states (Brands, 2010; Marshall & Cole, 2009). The failed states are hot spots for global illegal drug trades, human trafficking, trafficking of illegal weapons, and global terrorism. Criminal justice in failed states is deliberately coercive and oppressive when it comes to the restoration of law and order and securing political legitimacy for their governments. Police torture and brutality, militarization of the police force, politicization in police and judicial recruitments, police and judicial corruption, alliances between politics and organized crime, and gross violation of human rights are some of the endemic features of criminal justice in the failed states (Shettima & Chukwuma, 2002). An understanding of these endemic features of criminal justice in failed states will be much clearer if they are seen through the eyes of comparative criminal justice.

Beyond economy and politics, the social ecology of criminal justice in a country is also formed by its ideology (i.e., liberalism versus conservatism), religion (e.g., modern jurisprudence versus Islamic jurisprudence), and different philosophical perspectives about law and justice, such as the philosophy of Confucianism in China, South Korea, and Vietnam. The nature of a country's criminal justice, in other words, is intimately connected to its larger cultural framework. The economy and the nature of political development form the structural contexts of criminal justice. The cultural framework is the constellation of a country's styles, themes, models, and modalities of organizing criminal justice. Volumes of research have shown the

TABLE 1-1 Comparative Criminal Justice: Compare What?

Intrasystemic Issues and Problems	Extrasystemic Issues and Problems
Crime types, patterns, and trends	Due process versus crime control models
Process of criminalization	Crime policy-making process across countries
Process of decriminalization	Colonial effects on modern criminal justice
Evolution of policing	Crime, criminal justice, and poverty connections
Nature and types of policing	Crime, criminal justice, and economic transitions
Women in law enforcement	Crime and the growth of market economy
Models of judicial systems	Global market economy and global crimes
Evolution of court and court structures	Criminal justice in democratic states
Judicial selections, accountability, and corruption	Criminal justice in authoritarian states
Nature and evolution of prison systems	Criminal justice in failed states
Incarceration rates	Criminal justice in theocratic regimes
Sentencing types and philosophy	Criminal justice and human security issues
Nature and evolution of criminal law	Culture, criminology, and criminal justice
Criminal justice in common law countries	Crime, religion, and criminal justice
Criminal justice in civil law countries	Law, philosophy, and indigenous criminal justice
Due process comparison	Global criminal justice knowledge system
Miranda rights comparison	Criminal justice and modern technology
Comparison of exclusionary principles	Evolution of global crimes
Presumption of innocence doctrine comparison	

effect of religion (Islamic Shari'a Law) on criminal justice systems in the Middle East and other Muslim countries; the effect of the philosophy of Confucianism on criminal justice systems in China, South Korea, and Vietnam; the role of informal social control in the criminal justice system in Japan; and the effect of indigenous traditions of law and justice in Africa (African Human Security Initiative, 2009). Studies have also shown how religion plays a role in the criminalization and decriminalization of abortion in the United States and Latin America; in the legalization of the death penalty in the United States; and in the decriminalization of homosexuality in various countries, including the secular and liberal democracies of the United States, Canada, and the countries of the European Union. **Table 1-1** captures some of the significant problems and issues in comparative criminal justice. These can be seen in terms of two levels of analysis: intrasystemic comparison and extrasystemic comparison.

■ Comparative Criminal Justice: Compare How?

Research in comparative criminal justice begins with a question of what it is that we want to compare. This is a question primarily about the unit or the focus of analysis. What we learned previously is that the issues and problems of comparison are both internal and external to the system of criminal justice. The second question that immediately emerges is about the strategies of comparison or the perspectives of comparison: Compare how? The nature of the field of comparative criminal justice demands the use of multiple analytical strategies.

Historical Perspective: The Evolution of Criminal Justice Systems

For comparative criminal justice, one strategy of analysis involves looking at the evolution of criminal justice systems from a historical perspective (Shelley, 1981a). Criminal justice systems in different countries have evolved in the context of their different historical times and different social and cultural settings. Before the rise of the nation states in the 19th and 20th centuries, most of the world's societies had been ruled for centuries by different monarchies, kingdoms, and colonial powers. Those monarchies, kingdoms, and colonial powers created different systems of law and justice for governance. With the rise and demise of a country's monarchy, there came changes and transformations in its crime and justice. With the advent of colonial power, there came new models of law and justice in the colonies. The Portuguese, Dutch, French, German, Spanish, and British colonial powers brought their respective models of law and justice to their colonies in Asia, Africa, South America, and North America. Any systematic understanding of criminal justice across the world's societies today requires a serious analysis of changes and mutations in law and justice; of particular interest are the evolutions brought about by their respective monarchies, kingdoms, and colonies. The British East India Company and the British colonial power, for example, ruled India for almost 3 centuries. The present criminal justice system in India is largely the creation of the British colonial government. The Indian Police Act of 1861, the Indian Penal Code of 1862, and the Code of Criminal Procedure of 1882 introduced by the colonial government are still the bedrocks of criminal justice in India (as well as Pakistan and Bangladesh). In the United States, however, the colonial penal code based on English common law has been largely replaced with federal and state statutes and judicial laws (L. M. Friedman, 2005). In most of the English colonies in Asia and Africa, this trend of transformation from colonial to postcolonial modernization in law and justice has remained limited. Limited transformation is also true of the Spanish colonies of Latin America. Many African scholars argue that the criminal justice system imposed by colonial powers in Africa was incompatible with indigenous systems of law and justice, and that is the reason criminal justice systems in most of the countries in Africa today are in shambles (Elechi, 2004; Saleh-Hanna & Affor, 2008). They believe that even after centuries of dominance of the European criminal justice systems in Africa, "the African systems persist" (Okafo, 2007, p. 5). A historical understanding of the evolution of criminal justice in different countries, particularly in postcolonial societies, where indigenous law and justice systems were so affected for centuries by European systems of law and justice, is enormously significant.

Systems Perspective: The Need for a Holistic Analysis

Like a historical perspective, a systems perspective in comparative criminal justice is equally significant. A systems perspective requires an understanding of both the macro and micro institutions of criminal justice and the way they are connected in an integrated system. It requires an understanding of the themes, thoughts, ideas, and ideologies that bind criminal justice as an integrated sector within the structure of the government of a country. The themes and thoughts of criminal justice in Saudi Arabia, Iran, and Pakistan, for example, are certainly different from those of the United States, Canada, the United Kingdom, and Germany. Without the understanding of the systemic properties of criminal justice in a country, we will not know why, for example, due process of law is not a significant part of criminal justice in Iran and Pakistan; why the method of incarceration is incompatible within the indigenous systems of community justice in Africa; or why the Japanese do not comprehend the sense and sensibilities of the Second Amendment and gun control in America.

A country's criminal justice system, like its economic system, may be predominantly traditional or modern, largely centralized or decentralized, primarily formal or informal, and highly oriented toward science and technology or commonsense knowledge and traditions. The criminal justice system in America today, for example, is highly formal, professionalized, bureaucratized, autonomous, decentralized, and science and technology intensive. Even though there have been many projects and discourses for strengthening the role of informal institutions of social control, community justice, and restorative justice in America's criminal justice system, it has remained highly formal and legalistic, unlike that of Japan (Jiang, Lambert, & Wang, 2007). It is generally believed that Japan has the lowest crime and incarceration rate among the most industrialized countries, mainly due to the strength of its institutions of informal control—family, parents, friends, relatives, neighborhoods, communities, schools, and religious institutions. In Japan, these informal institutions are legitimately expected to intervene in crime situations and exert behavioral controls on individuals and clients. Crime control is largely seen in Japan as a group responsibility (Foote, 1992; Haley, 1991). If there is any violence in a school, the whole school is put to shame and made responsible for failing to control the violent behavior of its students—a cultural process called the reintegration of shaming (Braithwaite, 1989). In America, bystanders are not culturally and legally expected to intervene in crime situations; they are expected at best to call 911. In Japan, the surveillance on crime and criminality is seen more as a collective responsibility. One Japanese scholar in criminal justice rightly described Japan as a society uniquely characterized by "socio-cultural conditions of mutual surveillance" (Fujieda, 1989, p. 65). The American use of parole, probation, GPS tracking, home incarceration, drug court, and other community-based corrections and treatments are seen as efforts to revitalize the institutions of informal control. However, in America's formal and legalistic system of criminal justice, the nature and functions of informal institutions are highly formalized (Pildes, 2003; Shahidullah, 1994). One American legal scholar observed: "Compared to other economically advanced democracies, American civil life is more deeply pervaded by legal conflict and controversy about legal processes. The United States more often relies on lawyers, legal threats, and legal contestation in implementing public policies" (Kegan, 2003, p. 1).

The American system is based on the model of crime control within the framework of the due process of law. Even though there is a high rate of crime and violence in America, and a high incarceration rate, the system strongly safeguards the laws and principles of due process. In *In re Gault* in 1967, the United States Supreme Court ruled that due process of law is equally applied to adult and juvenile justice systems. In *Miranda v. Arizona* in 1966, the U.S. Supreme Court ruled that pretrial investigation of an alleged offender by a police officer, without informing that alleged offender about his or her rights to keep silent without the help of an attorney, violates the Fifth Amendment rights of protection against self-incrimination and the right to counsel—the rights that are now commonly known in the United States as the *Miranda* rights. In *Escobedo v. Illinois* in 1964, the U.S. Supreme Court made a decision that a defendant has the right to counsel even before his or her indictment for a crime. In a number of landmark cases, the Supreme Court ruled that confessions and evidence collected in violation of the Fourth Amendment protection against unusual search and seizure are not admissible in state and federal courts (*Weeks v. United States,* 1914; *Mapp v. Ohio,* 1961; *Boyd v. United States,* 1986). These decisions and many laws in America will not be adequately understood unless they are examined in the context of America's overall system of criminal justice (see **Box 1-6**), which is based on the due process model of crime control.

Similarly, the working of a country's institutions of criminal justice—police, courts, and prisons—depends significantly on whether they enjoy some autonomy from politics and the executive branch in decision making. Criminal justice is an integral part of a government. It is an organ of a government for the preservation of law and order and the protection of public security. However, a modern system of criminal justice enjoys a significant amount of autonomy from the encroachment and infringement of politics. One of the most common complaints about criminal justice systems in developing countries is that they are highly politicized (Naim, 2006). Because of their excessive politicization, police brutality, police corruption, and judicial corruption, as well as torture and violence in prisons and correctional institutions, are all endemic (Van Dijk & del Frate, 2011). There is hardly any developing country where law enforcement or the judiciary can independently initiate legal investigations and proceedings against political corruption or white collar crime. This lack of autonomy leads to the erosion of the legitimacy of criminal justice. The study of the extent of the political autonomy of criminal justice across countries is an interesting issue in comparative criminal justice.

Relativistic Perspective: Global and Local Challenges

In every country and region of the world, there is something called a local perspective or an indigenous model of what is and is not crime, what kinds of behavior should and should not be brought into the public sphere, what kinds of behavior should not be publicly condoned, how justice should be pursued, and how punishment should be served. Conversely, there is also a global or modern perspective on how these issues should be perceived and defined. What is happening in today's world is that all local systems of criminal justice, including those of advanced industrialized countries, are being challenged by a relatively modern set of values and expectations about crime and justice (Jaishankar, 2009). A comparative analysis of criminal justice across countries needs to examine the local characteristics of criminal justice in a country and the way they conflict and converge with those of global and modern demands in criminal justice. Comparative criminal justice should explore how local perceptions about crime are changing across time and how and whether

BOX 1-6

What Will Criminal Justice Look Like in the United States in 2050?

America's criminal justice system in 2012 is vastly different from what it was 50 years ago. In the 1960s, there was no separate office within the Department of Justice for organizing the nation's institutions of crime and justice. The Office of Justice Programs that is now the center of federal policy making in crime and justice was created in 1984. In the 1960s, the federal government did not have any major involvement in organizing juvenile justice. Today, the Office of Juvenile Justice and Delinquency Prevention (OJJDP), created through the Juvenile Justice and Delinquency Prevention Act of 1974, is the major federal agency for overseeing the growth of a national system of juvenile justice. Most of the other federal institutions and agencies that now constitute the foundation of modern criminal justice in America, such as the National Institute of Justice, Bureau of Justice Assistance, Bureau of Justice Statistics, Drug Enforcement Administration, Office of National Drug Control Policy, Office for Victims of Crime, Office on Violence Against Women, and Federal Law Enforcement Training Center were created between the 1970s and 1990s. The period from the 1960s to the 1990s saw the enactment and development of some of the major federal crime legislation (e.g., Omnibus Crime Control and Safe Streets Act of 1968, Comprehensive Crime Control Act of 1984, and the Violent Crime Control and Law Enforcement Act of 1994), and Supreme Court decisions (e.g., *Mapp v. Ohio*, 1961, *Griswold v. Connecticut*, 1965, *Miranda v. Arizona*, 1966, *In re Gault*, 1967, *Katz v. United States*, 1967, and *In re Winship*, 1970, that vastly transformed the America's landscape of criminal justice. How America's criminal justice will look in 2050 cannot be exactly ascertained, but some predictions can definitely be made on the basis of some emerging trends. America's criminal justice will be increasingly science-intensive, technologically driven, and global in nature. Criminal justice in the future will be increasingly engaged in local control and containment of global crimes through the use of science-based "super-technology" such as DNA, crime mapping, predictive policing, GPS tracking, and biometrics. The debate for a balance between "progressive penology" and "new penology" will also continue to expand. "The search for a balance between progressive penology and new penology—between offender rehabilitation and systemic control—in America's crime policy will continue. But it will continue within the contexts and realities of crimes [emerging from the forces of globalization] in the 21st century."

Source: Shahidullah, S. M. (2008). *Crime policy in America: Laws, institutions, and programs* (p. 284). Lanham, MD: University Press of America; Farrell, G., & Clark, K. (2004). *What does the world spend on criminal justice?* European Institute for Crime Prevention and Control (HEUNI Paper No. 20). Retrieved from www-staff.lboro.ac.uk/~ssgf/PDFs/GlobalCJSpending.pdf.

local laws and statutes are changing in response to global demands and international standards for reforms in criminal justice (Sheptycki, 2005).

There are three key areas with respect to local and global challenges in criminal justice in different countries. The first is the issue of criminalization and decriminalization—what should and should not be defined as a crime. The different countries do not think alike about the nature of crime and criminality. In criminal justice, many are highly amazed about the strength and the role of institutions of informal social control and group responsibility for crime and justice in Japan. In the Japanese system, however, there is a great reluctance to bring issues related to family, marriage, sex, intimacy, and sexuality into the realm of public crime and justice (Fujieda, 1989). The World Health Organization's (2005), Multi-Country Study on Women's Health and Domestic Violence Against Women found that 15% of women in Japan who had ever partnered had experienced physical or sexual violence or both. In 2002, the Cabinet Office of Japan published its first major survey on the nature and prevalence of domestic violence in Japan. The survey was based on mailed questionnaires sent to 4,500 people randomly selected for participation. In the survey, 2,888 or 64.6% of females responded. The survey shows that "15.5 percent of women have suffered physical assault from their spouse or boyfriend, 5.6 percent have suffered frightening threats from their spouse or boyfriends, and 9 percent have suffered sexual coercion from their spouse or boyfriend in their life time" (Government of Japan, 2002, p. 1). Domestic violence in Japan even today, however, is not clearly criminalized. Japan, for the first time, passed a new law against domestic violence in 2001, the Act on the Prevention of Spousal Violence and the Protection of Victims. However, the new law, as one scholar observed, "does not make domestic abuse a crime in a society in which, by tradition, men are considered superior to women, violence is a man's prerogative, and domestic abuse is a private affair and no business of the policy and the criminal justice system" (Rice, 2001, pp. 1–2). The Japanese laws on domestic violence are very different from those of the United States, which were enacted through such legislation as the Violence Against Women Act (VAWA) of 1994, the Victims of Trafficking and Violence Protection Act of 2000, the Violence Against Women and Department of Justice Reauthorization Act of 2005, and related legislation such as the PROTECT Act of 2003 and the Unborn Victims of Violence Act of 2004 (Shahidullah & Derby, 2009).

In most of the world's societies today, demands are growing for the criminalization of domestic violence, intimate partner violence, dating violence, stalking, sexual harassment, female genital mutilation (FGM), child abuse, hate crimes, and corporal punishment (Jejeebhoy, Shah, & Thapa, 2005). In Bangladesh, for example, there are movements growing for the criminalization of domestic violence, sexual harassment, and cyber stalking (eavesdropping). Bangladesh's Women and Children Repression Prevention Act of 2000 and the Acid Crime Control Act of 2002 are two of the most stringent laws on domestic and interpersonal violence in the world. The Women and Children Repression Prevention Act of 2000 provided the death penalty for 12 offenses, including causing death by corrosive substance, causing permanent bodily injury by corrosive substance, rape, rape with murder, rape with attempted murder, gang rape, gang rape with murder, dowry death, and woman trafficking (Monsoor, 2006). The Supreme Court of Bangladesh recently ruled that forcing a woman to wear a religious veil or a man to wear a religious cap is a crime in Bangladesh. The Supreme Court also criminalized the offering of *fatwa* (i.e., mandatory religious instructions given by religious leaders).

Since the 1970s, a world movement has been growing for the criminalization of female genital mutilation (FGM)—a practice widely prevalent in about 30 countries of Africa and the Middle East. FGM is also prevalent among the African and Middle Eastern immigrants in the United States, England, Canada, and European countries (Walker & Parmar, 1996). FGM is widely prevalent in the African countries of Somalia (98%), Mali (94%), Sudan (90%), Sierra Leone (90%), Burkina Faso (70%), Gambia (60–90%), Nigeria (60–90%), Guinea (60–90%), Egypt (85–90%), and Ethiopia (70–90%). After decades of international debates and discussions, publication of a number of United Nations Human Rights related research studies, and intensive lobbying by local advocates, laws have been enacted in many countries of Africa and the Middle East to criminalize FGM (Center for Reproductive Rights, 2008). Criminal legislation has been enacted in Benin (2003), Burkina Faso (1996), Chad (2003), Egypt (2008), Ethiopia (2004), Ghana (1994), Kenya (2001), Niger (2003), Nigeria (2002), Senegal (1999), South Africa (2005), and Tanzania (1998). FGM is a federal crime in the United States. In 1996, the U.S. Congress passed the Criminalization of Female Genital Mutilation Act (PL 104-208). The Act states that "whoever knowingly circumcises, excises, or infibulates the whole or any part of the labia majora or labia minora or clitoris of another person who has not attained the age of 18 years of age shall be fined under this title or imprisoned not more than five years, or both" (United States Code of Criminal Law, 2002, p. 1). Laws to criminalize FGM have also been enacted in Australia (Female Genital Mutilation Act of 1996), Belgium (Article 29 of the Belgian Criminal Code, 2000), Canada (Section 268 of the Canadian Criminal Code, 1997), Denmark (Law No. 490 of the Penal Code, 2003), France (Penal Code Decree No. 95-1000, 1995), Norway (Law No. 74 of the Penal Code, 2009), Spain (Organic Law No. 11, 2003), Sweden (Law No. 360 of the Penal Code, 1982), and the United Kingdom (Female Genital Mutilation Act of 2003).

Along with the progress of criminalization, demands are also growing in many countries for the decriminalization of behaviors related to love and intimacy, body adornment, sexual freedom, reproductive freedom, and abortion. In most Latin American countries, for example, the number of movements for the decriminalization of abortion is growing. Internationally, movements for the decriminalization of homosexuality are also growing. In 2008, the United Nations, celebrating the 60th anniversary of the Universal Declaration of Human Rights, appealed to the world's nations to decriminalize homosexuality and protect the human rights of gays, lesbians, bisexuals, and transsexuals. The 2008 Universal Declaration of Human Rights states: "We are deeply concerned by violations of human rights and fundamental freedoms based on sexual orientation or gender identity" (Permanent Mission of the Kingdom of the Netherlands to the United Nations, 2008, p. 1). The issue of decriminalizing homosexuality is hotly debated in the countries of Africa, the Middle East, and Asia. It has created many sharply divided groups and opinions. Therefore, the dynamics of criminalization and decriminalization across countries is an object of genuine curiosity in comparative criminal justice.

The second issue with respect to local and global challenges is one concerning global demands for changes and reforms in criminal justice. Increasingly today, development experts and international assistance organizations are recognizing that effective control of crime and corruption, legal protection of human rights, and effective delivery of justice are central to economic growth, democracy, and good governance. Today's global demand, in other words, is for changes and reforms in criminal justice (United Nations Development Programme, 2009). Since the 1990s, the United Nations Development Programme (UNDP), United Nations Office on Drugs and Crime (UNODC), World Bank, European Union, United States Agency for International Development (USAID), Canadian International Development Agency (CIDA), U.K. Department for International Development, Danish International Development Agency, and many other nongovernmental international organizations such as the International Police Training Institute and the American Bar Association (ABA) have been supporting hundreds of criminal justice reform programs in Asia, Africa, and Latin America. The UNDP has been supporting a number of programs for police and judicial reforms in several countries in Asia and Africa. The World Bank has been funding a number of programs to improve criminal justice capacity and judicial competence in countries of Asia, Africa, and Latin America. These programs include the Judicial Reform Learning Program in Francophone, Africa (2005); Judicial Reform for Improving Governance in Anglophone, Africa (2005); the Judicial Reform Learning Program in Turkey (2004); Judicial Reform for Improving Governance in Latin America (2004); Judicial Reform Project for Malawi (2006); and Judicial Reform for Guatemala (2006) (World Bank, 2010).

The ABA has a major program for reforms in criminal justice in Asia, Africa, Latin America, and Eastern and Central Europe called the Rule of Law Initiative. The Rule of Law Initiative, introduced in 1990, is a public service project dedicated to promoting the rule of law around the world. The Rule of Law Initiative embodies the belief that rule of law promotion is the "most effective long-term antidote to the pressing problems facing the world community today, including poverty, economic stagnation, and conflict" (American Bar Association, 2010). For 12 years (1995–2007), the CIDA supported a number of projects, through the Vancouver-based International Centre for Criminal Law Reform and Criminal Justice Policy (ICCLR), for criminal justice reforms in China (ICCLR, 2007). In comparative criminal justice, the study of how global demands and challenges for reforms in criminal justice are locally seen, perceived, and pursued is hugely important.

The third issue with respect to local and global challenges is the rise of a new generation of global crimes and their effect on local systems of law and justice. Today, the criminal justice system of almost every country is being challenged by the growth of transnational organized crimes such as drug trafficking, human trafficking, global sex trade, trading of conventional military weapons, money laundering, trafficking of cultural properties, cyber crime, and global terrorism. One of the United Nation's reports, *The Globalization of Crime: A Transnational Organized Crime Threat Assessment* (United Nations Office on Drugs and Crime, 2010a), cautioned that "crime has internationalized faster than law enforcement and world governance" (Costa, as quoted by Kemp, 2010, p. 3). The traditional frameworks of law and justice in most countries today are inadequate to face the new challenges of transnational crimes. There is a great need for understanding the nature and magnitudes of these crimes for developing new laws and statutes; for establishing effective regional and international cooperation; and for new training of law enforcement, prosecutors, and judges. It is impossible today for a nation to combat global crimes by remaining in isolation and working within the traditional framework of law and justice. The aforementioned report of the United Nations therefore asserted that "Stopping the operations of transnational organized crime has thus become a matter of international priority. Translating political will into concrete results will mean achieving two difficult goals: understanding transnational organized crime and integrating national responses into international strategies" (United Nations Office on Drugs and Crime, 2010a, p. 1). It is primarily in the context of transnational organized crime that internationalization is becoming a new demand for reforms in crime and justice among the world's societies. How transnational organized crimes are locally defined and perceived in different countries, what new laws and statutes are being developed to combat transnational organized crime, and how regional and international commissions, conventions, and protocols related to transnational crimes are affecting local criminal justice systems are issues of great interest in comparative criminal justice. These issues can be more systematically explored if comparative criminal justice is based on a perspective of understanding local and global challenges for crime and justice among the world's societies.

Cultural Perspective: Moral and Philosophical Issues

In cross-national analysis of criminal justice, an understanding of the history of criminal justice in a country, an understanding of its systemic features, and an understanding of its local and global challenges are important. Equally important is an understanding of the moral and philosophical contexts of criminal justice in different countries. The philosophical and ideological notions of liberalism, conservatism, democracy, secularism, individualism, and collectivism bring competing visions of organizing law and justice in a society. The religious worldviews of Protestantism, Catholicism, Buddhism, Judaism, Hinduism, and Islamism also bring competing moral visions about crime, justice, and punishment. The due process model of crime and criminal justice, for example, is based on the philosophy of liberalism. The philosophy of liberalism, in turn, is based on the philosophical notions of the Renaissance and the Age of Enlightenment. Both these philosophical movements, which developed in Europe between the 13th and 18th centuries, gave birth to the idea of organizing a polity and a system of law and justice on the basis of humanism, reason, science, and rationality. The birth of the modern state and the philosophy of liberalism also brought the birth of modern criminal justice.

In any cross-cultural comparison of criminal justice, these philosophical contexts need to be explored. Countries belonging to the non-European world did not go through indigenous cultural movements like those of the Renaissance and the Age of Enlightenment before their rise to the modern world in the 20th century. Most were colonies under European rule for centuries. Some of the institutions of modern law and justice were established under colonial rule. In postcolonial societies, the structures of law and justice created by the colonial rulers remained, but their underlying themes, thoughts, and philosophies are largely misunderstood and misinterpreted, and oftentimes ignored. For example, the continuing criminalization of abortion in Latin America, and of homosexuality in Africa and most countries of the Middle East, is also deeply rooted in the religious and moral contexts of these cultures and regions. In 2010, the second Pan-African Bishops' Conference in Uganda renewed the call to keep homosexuality as a crime in the African Anglican Church. The African College of Bishops of the United Methodist Church in 2010 called on all African political leaders to continue a ban on homosexuality. For those who advocate for the criminalization of homosexuality, the spirit of the Bill of Rights in the American Constitution or the essence of the Matthew Shepard and James Byrd, Jr. Hate Crimes Prevention Act of 2009 will be hard to comprehend. However, even in the United States, the passing of the Matthew Shepard and James Byrd, Jr. Hate Crimes Prevention Act stalled for a decade and raised many moral and religious debates and disputes. As President Obama said in the signing ceremony of the bill in October 2009, "After more than a decade of opposition and delay, we've passed inclusive hate crimes legislation to help protect our citizens from violence based on what they look like, who they love, how they pray, or who they are" (Weiner, 2010, p. 1).

At about the same time, the High Court of Delhi in India decriminalized homosexuality: "In their decision, Chief Justice A. P. Shah and Justice S. Muralidhar declared Section 377, as it pertains to consensual sex among people above the age of 18, in violation of important parts of India's Constitution" (Timmons & Kumar, 2009, p. 1). They ruled that "Consensual sex amongst adults is legal, which includes even gay sex and sex among the same sexes" (Timmons & Kumar, 2009, p. 1). The judges further added that Section 377 of the Indian Penal Code "violates Article 14 of the Constitution, which guarantees all people 'equality before the law;' Article 15, which prohibits discrimination 'on grounds of religion, race, caste, sex or place of birth'" (Timmons & Kumar, 2009, p. 1). In repealing Section 377 of the Indian Penal Code that criminalized homosexuality, the High Court of Delhi upheld the notion of equality enshrined in the secular and liberal constitution of India. In comparative criminal justice, revealing the moral and philosophical underpinnings of different systems of law and justice is therefore critically important.

■ Comparative Criminal Justice: Compare Why?

Comparative criminal justice is one of the rapidly expanding specialties in academic criminal justice in the United States and Europe, and is also spreading in other regions of the world. Comparative criminal justice is sometimes referred to as international or global criminal justice. There are, however, some major differences between comparative criminal justice and international or global criminal justice (Sheptycki & Wardak, 2005). International or global criminal justice seeks to study the emergence and formation of international criminal law, of international criminal law enforcement organizations (e.g., INTERPOL), and of the International Criminal Court (ICC) located in The Hague in the Netherlands. The ICC is at the core of international criminal justice, and was established on the basis of the Rome Statute of the International Criminal Court promulgated in 1998. As of 2009, about 110 countries had ratified the ICC. The core function of the ICC is to prosecute and punish the world leaders responsible for genocide, war crimes, and crimes against humanity. An emerging series of laws and statutes centering on the ICC are the subjects of international and global criminal justice (Boister, 2003; International Centre for Criminal Law Reform and Criminal Justice Policy, 2001; Sheptycki, 2011; Turner, 2007).

Comparative criminal justice, on the other hand, is a specialty in criminal justice that seeks to study criminal justice systems of different countries and explore their similarities and differences. The core of the quest for comparative criminal justice is how countries are different from or similar to one another in terms of their perceptions about crime, the practice of law, and justice. Although international criminal justice begins from above—national compliance to international laws related to genocide, war crimes, and crimes against humanity—comparative criminal justice begins from below—the localities of the world—and explores their competing systems of criminal justice. The rapid growth of the field of comparative criminal justice in recent years has obviously raised questions about the need and the significance of comparative study in criminal justice—compare why.

Comparative Method in Social Science

The comparative method is at the core of modern science. It is widely used in astronomy, physics, chemistry, geology, biology, medicine, sociology, and psychology. Astronomers compare the nature of different planets and galaxies; physicists compare the nature of different atomic particles; biologists compare the genetic composition of different species; neurologists compare the functions of the different regions of the brain; epidemiologists compare disease patterns in different countries, races, and ethnic groups; sociologists compare cultures and social structures of different countries; and psychologists compare human and animal behavior. In 1543, Copernicus discovered the heliocentric conception of the Earth—the conception that the Earth is not at the center of the universe. The Earth is just another planet, like Mars or Venus, that centers on the sun. With the discovery of the heliocentric conception of the Earth came the birth of modern science. Copernicus reached his heliocentric conception of the universe through a comparative understanding of the orbits of the sun, moon, and planets. In 1898, Edward Jenner made one of the major discoveries in medicine—the discovery of the smallpox vaccine—through the use of the comparative method. The word *vaccine* comes from the Latin word *vacicinus*, meaning cow. Jenner compared smallpox in cows, horses, and pigs (Beveridge, 1973). The comparative method or the evolutionary approach to science reached a new level of scientific legitimacy with the publication of Charles Darwin's *Origin of Species* in 1859. Darwin empirically established his theory of natural selection by comparing the genetic composition and the adaptive capacity of different species.

Biology's tradition of comparative method and the evolutionary approach came to social science in the middle of the 19th century. The comparative method, in fact, was at the center of the birth of modern social sciences such as economics, political science, sociology, anthropology, and psychology. Adam Smith, the father of modern economics, compared nations in terms of their labor productivity in his *The Wealth of Nations* published in 1776. In his *Theory of Moral Sentiments,* published in 1759, Smith surprisingly appeared as one of the precursors of comparative criminology. He said that the perception of the people of a given country "regarding what degree of this or that quality is either blameworthy or praiseworthy vary according to the degree that is usually blamed or praised in their own country" (Bennett, 2010, p. 108).

Niccolo Machiavelli, one of the fathers of modern political science, developed his political theory in the context of his life and comparative understanding of the ancient Republic of Rome and the rise of absolutist feudal monarchies in Europe. "The *Prince* deals with the monarchies or the absolute governments, and the *Discourses* deals with the expansion of the Roman republic" (Sabine, 1973, p. 311). Among all political philosophers of the Age of Enlightenment in the 18th century, comparative methods received their most elegant justification from Baron de Montesquieu. In his *The Spirit of Laws*, published in 1734, Montesquieu said that there were no immutable natural laws of crime and justice. A country's principles of law and justice grow in the context of its social milieu, "which require comparison of institutions on a wide scale" (Sabine, 1973, p. 508). After *The Spirit of Laws,* many classical works on comparative method came from a new generation of intellectuals in the early 19th century. A study of that time that can be called the precursor of comparative criminal justice is Alexis de Tocqueville's *Democracy in America,* published in 1835. In 1821, de Tocqueville and his friend Gustave de Beaumont were sent to the United States by the French government to study the prison system in America. *Democracy in America,* which describes the novelty not just of the prison system in America, but also of the whole gamut of social and cultural institutions of the New Republic, is still regarded as one of the major classics in social science in general and comparative criminal justice in particular.

After economics and political science, comparative method in the 19th and early 20th centuries was widely used in classical sociology and anthropology. The core of the project of classical sociology was to understand the rise and the directionality of modernity in the 19th century. Almost all classical sociologists—Auguste Comte, Karl Marx, Max Weber, Emile Durkheim, Georg Simmel, and Ferdinand Tönnies—theorized and hypothesized on the basis of comparison between tradition and modernity. They developed typologies and classifications of traditional and modern institutions and examined the social and cultural forces responsible for their transition from tradition to modernity. Marx's writings in *British Rule in India* (1853); Weber's *The Protestant Ethic and the Spirit of Capitalism* (1904–1905), *Sociology of Religion* (1921), and *Economy and Society* (1921–1922); Durkheim's *The Division of Labor in Society* (1893) and *Suicide* (1897); and Tönnies's *Gemeinschaft and Gesellschaft* (1887) are some of the most enduring contributions in comparative sociology or comparative methodology. Along with classical sociology, the comparative method was widely used in anthropology. Some of the remarkable works on comparative methods in anthropology come from the writings of Henry Maine (1872), Lewis Henry Morgan (1877), Bronisław Malinowski (1926/1989), Alfred R. Radcliffe-Brown (1922/1964), Ruth Benedict (1934/2005), Margaret Mead (1935/2001), and Claude Lévi-Strauss (1968).

Following the tradition of classical social science, the use of the comparative method vastly expanded in modern social science in the middle of the 20th century, particularly in the context of decolonization and the emergence of new nations in Asia, Africa, and Latin America. Currently, there exists a huge volume of literature on comparative sociology, comparative politics, comparative law, comparative education, comparative linguistics, and comparative development. Some of the most notable studies on comparative sociology and comparative politics in the 20th century were conducted by Karl Polanyi (1944/2001), Joseph Needham (1947), Talcott Parsons (1966/1993), Barrington Moore (1966/1993), Robert Bellah (1985), Theda Skocpol (1979), Clifford Geertz (1971), Immanuel Wallerstein (1979), and Charles Tilly (1984/2006).

Comparative Method in Classical Criminology and Criminal Justice

It is in this context of the traditional use of comparative method in social science that the specialty of comparative criminal justice is currently experiencing rapid growth. Criminal justice as an academic specialty did not fully emerge until the middle of the 1970s, but the origin of criminology and the vision for an ideal criminal justice system can be traced back to the time of social science's birth in the 19th century. From the beginning of the 19th century, criminology and criminal justice began to use the comparative perspective. The present expansion of comparative methodology in criminal justice came from both the tradition of comparative method in social science in general and the 19th century classical school of criminology and criminal justice in particular. The spirit of the comparative method was at the core of the writings of the two founding fathers of criminology and criminal justice—Cesare Beccaria (1738–1794) and Cesare Lombroso (1835–1909).

Beccaria (1764/2009), in his *On Crimes and Punishments,* created the first vision for a modern system of criminal justice. Beccaria's vision of an ideal criminal justice system came out of his perspective on what was lacking in the criminal justice of his time and what was deeply anchored in the past (e.g., in the medieval culture of demonology, inquisitions, and the institutions of torture, executions, and exorcism). Beccaria did not draw comparisons between different countries but two different systems of criminal justice—the one that he saw during his lifetime in late medieval Italy and the one that came out of his vision of modernity. His vision of comparative criminology and criminal justice evolved in the context of the emerging changes and transformations in Europe during the Age of Enlightenment.

Whereas Beccaria's comparative criminal justice came from a philosophical vision about crime and justice, Lombroso's comparative criminology was based on a purely scientific perspective. In his *Criminal Man,* Lombroso (1876/2006) developed a biological theory of criminality. He theorized that criminal men and women are human species of different kinds and that they are morphologically and anatomically different from normal individuals. He established his theory through systemic comparison of the anatomical features of normal individuals and criminal offenders. Some of his hypotheses suggested that criminal individuals have long arms, excessive dimensions in the cheekbones, asymmetric facial characteristics, and asymmetric functions of the hemispheres of the brain. Modern biological theories of crime and criminality have largely rejected the ideas of Lombroso, but his methodology of morphological comparison between normal and criminal individuals is still an intriguing issue in criminology. He also compared two categories of offenders: life-course persistent offenders and adolescent-limited offenders (Rafter, 2005). Lombroso's typology of offender characteristics is the precursor of modern developmental criminology or life-course criminology.

The birth of comparative criminal justice can also be traced back to the research of Adolphe Quetelet (1796–1874), a Belgian mathematician who was a strong advocate of the use of comparative method in the study of social and moral issues. Quetelet is sometimes regarded as the father of modern social science. Using empirical crime data, Quetelet made a comparative study of crime patterns and crime trends in France from 1826 to 1829. In his comparative study of data from different regions of France, he noticed that "young males, the poor, [and] those with less education . . . in lowly occupations or without employment were more likely to be apprehended in, or accused of, committing crime and to be convicted" (Sheptycki, 2005, p. 72). He further observed that crime rates in France varied by region, and that "poverty in itself did not cause crime . . . neither the prevalence of poverty nor the lack of formal education was the key causal factor in predicting crime rates" (Sheptycki, 2005, p. 72). Quetelet theorized that relative deprivation can explain the "rise and fall of crime over time" (Sheptycki, 2005, p. 72). Even though Beccaria and Lombroso used the method of comparison, Quetelet was the "first . . . to make generalized comparisons concerning crime rates across different populations" (Sheptycki, 2005, p. 71).

Comparative Method in Contemporary Criminal Justice

The current explosion of interest in comparative criminal justice that began in the 1960s and 1970s is the outgrowth of five different but interrelated intellectual and developmental trends: (1) decolonization and the rise of new movements for change and transformation in the new nations of Asia, Africa, and Latin America in the 1960s; (2) the engagement of social science in the new nations in the context of the Cold War in the 1970s; (3) the rise of academic criminal justice and criminology in the United States in the 1970s; (4) the post–Cold War changes, crises, and transformations of the 1980s; and (5) the rise of globalization and the spread of a new generation of transnational crimes in the 1990s.

The Effect of Decolonization

By the end of the 1960s, there emerged a huge number of independent countries in Asia, Africa, and Latin America as a result of decolonization and the end of World War II. Decolonization in North America began with the triumph of the American Revolution in 1783 and in South America with the triumph of the Mexican Revolution in 1910. Most of the Spanish colonies in South America became independent by the 1930s. The process of decolonization in Asia, Africa, and the Caribbean, however, did not begin until the 1950s and 1960s. The 1960s saw the emergence of a huge number of independent countries in Asia, Africa, and the Caribbean. These countries were restless to enter the community of world nations with pride, progress, and dignity. It was particularly in that context that social science in the 1960s began to study the process of modernization and state building in the new nations. That was also the time when criminology and criminal justice began to draw interest in law and justice in postcolonial societies; these societies were simultaneously developing interest in learning more about Western forms of law and justice.

In 1957, the United Nations Educational, Scientific, and Cultural Organization (UNESCO) prepared a report for the introduction of criminology in the new nations and emphasized the need for comparative research in criminal justice. In response to UNESCO's call, many universities in developing countries introduced criminology as an academic discipline, and India probably took the lead. The formal teaching of criminology in India began at the Tata Institute of Social Sciences in 1952. The first academic department of criminology and forensic science in India was established at Saugar University in 1959. In Africa, one of the major centers for comparative research in criminal justice—Abidjan Institute of Criminology, Ivory Coast—was established in the late 1960s with the help of the Canadian International Development Agency (CIDA) and the McGill University's International Centre for Comparative Criminology. Some of the other major international initiatives that began to promote research on comparative criminal justice in the new nations at that time include the creation of the United Nations Congress on the Prevention of Crime and the Treatment of Offenders in 1950, the United Nations Asia and Far East Institute for the Prevention of Crime and the Treatment of Offenders (UNAFEI) in 1961, the United Nations Interregional Crime and Justice Research Institute (UNICRI) in 1968, and the Latin American Institute for the Prevention of Crime and the Treatment of Delinquency in 1975.

The Effect of the Cold War

In the wake of the rise of new nations and the end of World War II in 1945, there began a new global process called the Cold War between the East (the Union of Soviet Socialist Republics including Hungary, Poland, Romania, Bulgaria, and the Czech Republic) and the West. For almost 4 decades, the world was polarized by the demands of two competing worldviews—socialism and Western liberal democracy. During the Cold War, social science remained engaged with the developing countries of Asia, Africa, and Latin America for creating an intellectual and scientific base for development and liberal democracy. In the context of the Cold War, interest in comparative criminal justice continued to grow especially as related to creating the infrastructures of modern law and justice in developing countries. In the 1970s and 1980s, comparative criminal justice began to expand mostly as a part of modernization and international development efforts (Bayley, 1985; Clinard & Abbott, 1973; Otterbein, 1988; Shelley, 1981b).

Some of the major international initiatives created to promote comparative criminal justice at that time were the National Institute of Justice (NIJ) within the U.S. Department of Justice in 1969; the *World Criminological Directory* by the UNICRI in 1974; the *United Nations Surveys on Crime Trends and the Operations of Criminal Justice Systems* in 1978; and the program on criminal justice in different countries—*World Factbook of Criminal Justice Systems*—at the Bureau of Justice Statistics of the U.S. Department of Justice in the late 1980s. The NIJ was created to promote policies relevant to comparative research on criminal justice in different countries. The major goal of the *United Nations Surveys on Crime Trends* was "to collect data on the incidence of reported crime and the operations of criminal justice systems with a view to improving the analysis and dissemination of that information globally" (United Nations Office on Drugs and Crime, 2010b, p. 1).

The Bureau of Justice Statistics began to collect data on criminal justice systems in different countries around the world. As of 2012, there are profiles of the criminal justice systems of 45 countries in its *World Factbook of Criminal Justice Systems. The World Criminological*

Directory is the storehouse for descriptions of the world's leading institutes of crime and justice, and as of this writing, there are descriptions of more than 500 institutes representing about 90 countries.

The Birth of Modern Criminal Justice in the United States

The historical processes of decolonization and the rise of the Cold War created vast interest in all fields of social science for understanding the emerging world and its diversities in politics, creeds, and cultures, including crime, law, and justice. Contemporary scholarly works on comparative criminal justice, however, did not systematically begin until the growth of criminology and criminal justice in the academic world of the West. The present rapid expansion of criminology and criminal justice has been happening in the context of a variety of world events. But one of the most significant forces has been the birth of modern criminal justice and its rapid expansion in the United States from the beginning of the 1970s. The growth of ideas for modernization in criminal justice in the United States began in the late 1920s. Serious policy deliberations for a modern system of criminal justice began at the time of the presidency of Herbert Hoover (1929–1933). Hoover "was the first president to assemble a team of practitioners and scholars to comprehensively investigate the conditions under which federal, state, and local governments administered justice" (Calder, 1993, p. 3). In 1929, Hoover appointed the National Commission on Law Observance and Enforcement. George W. Wickersham, Attorney General under President William H. Taft, chaired the commission (Shahidullah, 2008). The Wickersham Commission was "the first occasion in thirty administrations on which a federal commission was formed to examine comprehensively federal criminal justice" (Calder, 1993, p. 77). The Wickersham Commission Report, released in 1931, contained 14 volumes of information on reforms in crime and justice. One of the major recommendations was to conceptualize justice administration as a system of interconnected and interdependent federal, state, and local justice institutions. The commission, formed after the growth of the classical and positivist schools of criminology in Europe, strongly recommended the use of a scientific approach to design and reform the institutions of justice (Shahidullah, 2008). The commission's report, *The Causes of Crime,* "marked the coming-of-age of American criminology" (Walker, 1997, p. 3). The two-volume report "played a major role in shaping the development of the field of criminology in the United States" (Walker, 1997, p. 3).

The Wickersham Commission "presented a blueprint of ideas about the architecture of modern criminal justice. But the transformation of the commission's ideas into policy-making did not systematically begin until Lyndon Johnson took over the Presidency" (Shahidullah, 2008, p. 64). In 1964, President Johnson appointed the Commission on Law Enforcement and Administration of Justice to recommend measures to overhaul the nation's crime and justice system (Shahidullah, 2008). The commission's report, *The Challenge of Crime in a Free Society,* "was published in 1967—a year before the assassinations of Martin Luther King Jr. and Robert Kennedy. The Wickersham Commission recommended thinking of crime and justice as a 'system.' The President's Commission recommended the 'system approach' as a new paradigm for crime and justice administration" (Shahidullah, 2008,

p. 65). It is generally recognized today that "America's vastly complex system of crime and justice with hundreds of federal, state, and local organizations, interconnected through information technologies, owes its origin to the system paradigm recommended by President Johnson's Commission" (Shahidullah, 2008, p. 65). From the birth of modern criminal justice in the United States in the 1970s, academic criminology and criminal justice began to rapidly grow in American universities. This led, in turn, to the further growth of systematic academic research on comparative criminal justice in Europe and the world as a whole (Shahidullah, 2008; Stamatel, 2009).

Post–Cold War Changes, Crises, and Transformations

After the end of the Cold War in the middle of the 1980s, new global events and realities began to emerge and affect the growth of interest in criminal justice in general and comparative criminal justice in particular (Nelken, 2011). Two competing global forces emerged after the end of the Cold War. One is a global movement for reforms in crime and justice in the former communist countries, particularly in China, Soviet Russia, newly independent countries in Eastern Europe (Poland, Hungary, Czech Republic), Baltic Republics (Estonia, Latvia, and Lithuania), and Ukraine, Uzbekistan, Turkistan, and Georgia. In fact, once the Cold War ended, movements for democracy and demands for reforms in law and justice began in almost all countries of Asia, Africa, and Latin America. These post–Cold War events of change and transformation contributed to the rise of new interest in comparative criminal justice.

Another set of events that began to unfold after the end of the Cold War—events that gravely shocked and surprised the world—was the rise of new ethnic conflicts, violence, and tribalism. The rise of ethnic war and violence in the 1990s in Bosnia, Rwanda, Burundi, Sudan, and many parts of the former communist countries brought a new sense of urgency for the study of crime, law, and justice in those countries. The international development assistance community found a new domain of interest in crime, law, and justice in the failed and fragile states of Asia, Africa, and Latin America. The number of scholarly works comparing crime and justice in different countries, cultures, and civilizations saw tremendous growth (Daniels, Haleem, & Shariff, 2003; Fennell, Harding, Jörg, & Swart, 1995; Goodman, 2008; Lu, 1995; Meadows, 2010; Mühlhahn, 2009; Nethercott, 2009; Thornton & Endo, 1992; Tonry, 2007).

The Rise of New Global Crimes

The end of the Cold War in the mid-1980s and the collapse of the possibility of an alternative world system of socialism led to a new era of globalization. In this new era, the world's societies began to experience an intense process of movement of people, culture, and goods and services from one society to another and from one region of the world to another. Globalization led to the expansion of democracy, growth, and prosperity. The opening of China, Russia, and the countries of Eastern Europe to the West after the end of the Cold War brought global progress and stability. The birth of modern information technology in the 1990s furthered the progress of globalization.

In the first decade of the 21st century, there was hardly any region of the world that was not touched by the invisible hands of transnational organized crime (United Nations Office on Drugs and Crime, 2007). This rise of transnational organized crime brought the study of comparative criminal justice to a new sense of urgency. The progress of research and interest in comparative criminal justice came to yet another turning point after the events of September 11, 2001—events that were a wake-up call for the world's nations to rise to a new age of global uncertainty (Farah, 2004; R. I. Friedman, 2000; Glenny, 2009; Lilley, 2003; Naim, 2006).

■ Significance of Comparative Criminal Justice

Scholars in criminology and criminal justice firmly believe that "Any criminology worthy of the name should contain a comparative dimension . . . . most of the important points made by leading scholars in criminology are comparative in nature" (Hardie-Bick, Sheptycki, & Wardak, 2005, p. 1). Comparison of the study of crime and justice, in one sense, is as old as Beccaria's *On Crimes and Punishments* (1764/2009), or Quetelet's study of patterns of crime and criminality in France in 1826, or de Tocqueville's *Democracy in America* (1835). In another sense, comparative criminal justice is of recent origin—it emerged in the contexts of decolonization in Asia, Africa, and Latin America in the 1950s and 1960s, and of the rise of academic criminology and criminal justice in the West, particularly in the United States, in the 1970s. The end of the Cold War, the expansion of globalization, and the growth of a new generation of transnational crimes in the 1980s and 1990s created a vast scope for research and interests in comparative criminal justice in almost all countries (Adler, 1983; Shelley, 1981b). The academic significance of comparative criminal justice, however, can be understood in terms of four major research traditions or strategies within the specialty.

Tradition of Research on Crime and Victimization Patterns

One of the most compelling reasons for why comparative criminal justice is significant is the scientific curiosity about the nature of crime and criminality among societies. Recent years have seen the growth of a considerable number of comparative studies on crime and victimization trends among the world's societies (Hall & Mclean, 2009; Mares, 2009; Neapolitan, 1999, 2001, 2003). In his 1999 study, for example, criminologist Neapolitan compared the nature of violent crimes in 12 nations and generalized about the role of social and cultural factors in producing or reducing violent crimes. He compared six nations with a low level of violent crimes (Chile, Uruguay, Indonesia, Mauritius, Ghana, and Nepal) to six nations with a high level of violent crimes (Angola, Colombia, El Salvador, Sri Lanka, the Philippines, and Uganda). On the basis of his data, Neapolitan generalized that the nations exhibiting economic stress, high levels of social disorganization, higher incidence of child abuse, high rates of corruption, low levels of competence of the criminal justice system, and political approval of violence are more likely to have higher levels of violent crime. In another study, on the basis of data collected from the *International Crime Victims Survey,* Neapolitan (2003) examined whether victimization is primarily related to income or culture. He found that there is "a strong negative association" between income and victimization. The theory that people with lower income are more likely to be victimized is not always true. As he said, "It has always been assumed that poor people are the primary victims of street crime, yet this research found no difference between people below and above the median income in terms of percentages of people victimized in most nations" (p. 85). The study (Neapolitan, 2003) concludes that culture mediates the rate of victimization, particularly in Asian countries. In their comparative study of homicide rates in Western Europe and the United States during the period of the rise of globalization and the expansion of the free market economy in the 1980s and 1990s, Hall and Mclean (2009) found that homicide rates in the countries of Western Europe remained lower than those of the United States. Interest in comparative criminal justice has grown in the context of similar research on crime and victimization patterns among the world's societies (Hartjen, 2008; Hartjen & Priyadarsini, 2012; Shaw, Van Dijk, & Rhomberg, 2003; Van Dijk & del Frate, 2011; WHO, 2005).

Tradition of Research for Theory Development and Validation

Scientific progress in any specialty is a process of evolution from one paradigm to another, or from one set of theories to another that has more explanatory power and strength. In general, theory development and theory validation in social science are achieved primarily through intersocietal comparisons. There are a number of theoretical schools and theories that seek to explain the nature of crime and criminality, such as the social disorganization theory, control theory, social bond theory, rational choice theory, differential association theory, strain theory, life-course theory, labeling theory, and conflict theory. In recent years, much progress has been made in criminology and criminal justice to examine these and other theories of crime based on cross-national comparisons (Alanezi, 2010; Cao, 2007; Kim & Pridemore, 2005; Nivette, 2011; Ozbay & Ozcan, 2006; Pratt & Godsey, 2002; Vazsonyi, Pickering, Junger, & Hessing, 2001; Zhao, 2008; Zhao & Cao, 2010).

In the early 1980s, Freda Adler (1983) conducted a comparative analysis of why the crime rate is lower in some countries than others. Based on data collected from the *First United Nations Survey on Crime Trends and the Operations of Criminal Justice Systems* in 64 of the world's societies in 1975–1976, Adler selected 10 low-crime countries from 5 regions of the world: Switzerland and Ireland from Western Europe; Bulgaria and the German Democratic Republic from the European socialist countries; Costa Rica and Peru from Latin America; Algeria and Saudi Arabia from North Africa and the Middle East; and Japan and Nepal from Asia. Adler observed that these 10 countries were widely divergent in terms of their legal traditions and economic and political structures. Their criminal justice systems were also vastly different from one another. The only commonality was that in all of them, the crime rate was relatively low in comparison to other countries of the world that participated in the United Nations Survey. Adler theorized, based on analysis of the informal social control mechanisms of those countries, that the low rate of crime is strongly associated with what Durkheim called "social solidarity," or "collective consciousness." Countries with strong informal social control mechanisms are more likely to have low rate of crimes. "Among those social control systems," Adler observed, "there is, above all, the family. Most of the countries under study have seen little disruption of their strong family systems" (1983, p. 130). Adler further stated: "It is noteworthy that among our sample of ten countries, family controls have been maintained even in the wake of modernization" (1983, p. 131).

Gottfredson and Hirschi (1990), in their book *A General Theory of Crime*, theorized that individuals with a low level of self-control are more likely to commit crimes. Individuals with a low level of self-control are driven by passions and pleasure and are insensitive to the long-term consequences of deviance and criminal activities. The authors claim that the relationship between the lack of self-control and criminal behavior is universal across genders, countries, and cultures. "Cultural variability," they claim, "is *not* important in the causation of crime," and "a single theory of crime can encompass the reality of cross-cultural differences in crime rates" (1990, p. 175). They further argued that the "definition of crime should be derived from a conception of human nature that transcends social groupings (whether within or across societies)" (1990, p. 175). In 2001, Vazsonyi, Pickering, Junger, and Hessing conducted a major comparative study to test the validity of the self-control theory across countries. They collected data from a sample of 8,417 adolescents in four countries (Hungary, the Netherlands, Switzerland, and the United States) and found that "the self-control and deviance relationship appears to be tenable for all adolescents from the four countries in the study" (p. 120). Their comparative study further increased the validity of the self-control theory of crime (or the General Theory of Crime) developed by Gottfredson and Hirschi.

Another example of the significance of comparative study in theory development and theory validation is Pratt and Godsey's (2002) study of homicide rates in 46 countries based on data from the World Health Organization and the United Nations. Their objective was to test the hypothesis that violent crime in a country (homicide rate) is related to its social support system, which includes characteristics such as social altruism, social cohesiveness, social network, and shared cultural values of helping one another in times of need. The quality of social support in a country is measured in terms of its percentage of gross domestic product (GDP) spent on health care and education. The authors found that cross-national data confirmed an inverse relationship between social support systems and crime rates, and concluded that investment in health care and education can reduce crime rates (2002).

In 1994, Steven Messner and Richard Rosenfeld wrote a book titled *Crime and the American Dream*. The thesis of the book is that the American dream of material success contributes to the high crime rate in America. They compared crime data of 16 developed countries in their revised version of the book in 1997, but the thesis remained unchanged. Chamlin and Cochran, in their 2007 study, challenged the institutional anomie theory of Messner and Rosenfeld. On the basis of official crime data (homicide rate per 100,000 population) from a sample of 73 countries collected from the *Seventh United Nations Survey on Crime Trends and the Operations of Criminal Justice Systems, 1998–2000*, Chamlin and Cochran observed that crime rates in the United States "are not exceptional" (p. 46). They reported, "The results are clear. When compared to a larger and more heterogeneous (with respect to economic development) sample of countries, we find no evidence of support of Messner and Rosenfeld" (p. 53).

In his study of crime in transitional China, Zhao (2008) used Merton's anomie theory to explain the rising rate of crime and its relation to recent economic growth and modernization in China. Merton's anomie theory is based on the hypothesis that when there is a gap between rising expectations and the socially legitimate ways to translate them into reality, individuals are more likely to be frustrated, and crimes are more likely to increase. Groups and individuals who experience blocked social and economic opportunities feel deprived. The deprivations generate strain and stress, and strain and stress generate crime. The expansion of a market economy and of modernization in China, Zhao argued, has raised expectations for better social and economic opportunities. But the growth of the market economy within the framework of an authoritarian socialist state has blocked many social and economic opportunities and generated a sense of deprivation for millions of Chinese. Zhao, however, proposes a revised version of the anomie theory—institutional discrepancy-anomie theory—to capture the peculiarities of the growth of the market economy within the framework of socialism and authoritarianism in China. The revised institutional discrepancy-anomie theory claims that "the institutional discrepancies generated by coexistence of China's market-oriented economy and authoritarian polity contribute significantly to the dramatic increase in crime rates" (Zhao, 2008, p. 137). Comparison of crime and criminality among societies is thus a way of theory development and theory validation in criminology and criminal justice.

Tradition of Systemic Comparison

Research on the understanding of crime and victimization patterns among societies, as well as research on theory development and theory validation on crime causation, fall primarily within the scope of comparative criminology. There is a growing amount of literature that is focused on the comparative understanding of criminal justice systems across countries. Research on law, legal traditions, policing, and judicial systems in different countries began during the days of colonialism, and its needs were considerably recognized in the context of the beginning of modernization in the 1960s and 1970s. In the 1970s, there began a more systematic process of understanding the nature of criminal justice in different countries in the context of the rise of academic criminal justice in the West; the emergence of new ethnic wars and conflicts in many areas of the world after the Cold War; and the rise of transnational organized crimes in the wake of globalization in the 1990s. The new impetus to explore the nature of criminal justice in different countries also came in the context of the human development approach that the United Nations and other international organizations began using in the 1990s (United Nations Development Programme, 2011). From that point on, a comparative approach to criminal justice was necessary for a more systemic understanding of criminal justice across the world's societies (Nelken, 2011; Sheptycki & Wardak, 2005). Literature also began to focus on the role of extrasystemic factors such as religion, ideology, culture, and democracy in shaping criminal justice systems in different countries (Daniels et al., 2003; Pieris, 2009; Tonry, 2007).

Tradition of Comparison for Reforms and Modernization

The reasons comparative criminal justice is significant can be broadly divided into two sets of arguments. One set of arguments is about its theoretical significance for the science of criminology and criminal justice. It contributes to the scientific understanding of crime trends, crime patterns, and crime causation across cultures and countries. Comparative criminal justice explores how criminal justice has evolved in different countries and how its various institutional configurations are formed and shaped in various countries by culture, ideology, politics, and philosophy. The second set of arguments is applied in nature, which is that knowledge of comparative criminal justice is needed for change, reforms, and modernization in criminal justice (Berman & Fox, 2010). There is hardly any country in the world today that does not have an agenda for changes and reforms in criminal justice. Reforms in criminal justice are now being increasingly seen as vital for development, democracy, and transparent and effective governance (see **Box 1-7**). There is a serious need for research-based and evidence-based knowledge about the best practice methods and strategies of crime control and prevention in all countries, particularly in developing countries. One report from the United Nations Office on Drugs and Crime (2011) clearly recognized the multi-dimensional nature of reforms and modernization in criminal justice. The report states: "Criminal justice and crime prevention is not purely a 'technical' legal matter. It has a political, social, cultural, and anthropological dimension that should be fully addressed and never under-estimated" (2011, p. 10). The report further adds that "criminal justice reformers should keep in mind . . . that criminal justice reform is both a project for institution-building and a cultural project of shaping attitude and commitments," and that criminal justice reforms is a long-term process, "sometimes spanning generations" (United Nations Office on Drugs and Crime, 2011, p. 10).

The global agenda for reforms in criminal justice has taken research and studies on comparative criminal justice to a new level of familiarity and significance (Armytage, 2011; Armytage & Metzner, 2009; Nelken, 2011). Today, almost all international organizations, including the United Nations, the World Bank, the European Union, the United States Agency for International Development (USAID), the Canadian International Development Agency (CIDA), the U.K. Department for International Development, the Asian Development Bank (ADB), the Inter-American Development Bank (IDB), the Inter-American Commission on Human Rights, and the Organization of African Unity (OAU) have systematic programs for reform and modernization in criminal justice in the countries of Asia, Africa, and Latin America (see **Table 1-2**). One study on judicial reform in Latin America and the Caribbean finds that "starting in the 1980s, and accelerating through the 1990s, international financial centres (IFCs), non-governmental organizations (NGOs), and development agencies funneled considerable resources into judicial reform and rule of law programmes in virtually every Latin American and Caribbean country" (Wilson, Cordero, & Handberg, 2004, p. 507). The third annual report of the U.N. Secretary-General on United Nations rule of law activities states that: "The United Nations provide rule of law assistance in over 150 Member States spanning every region of the world. Three or more United Nations entities engage in rule of law activities in at least 70 countries" (United Nations Organization, 2011a, p. 1).

BOX 1-7

World Criminal Justice System Found Wanting

A comparative study of the criminal justice systems of the world's societies is a formidable task. There are 195 major countries of the world recognized by the United Nations. There are also 195 systems of criminal justice in the world. A comparative understanding of the nature and the performance of these countries in the governing of crime and criminal justice is a daunting task because crimes are not defined and classified in similar ways, crime data are not collected with the same methodology, criminal laws are not made and applied with the same procedures, and punishments are not perceived and devised in the same way in different countries. The different societies of the world are economically, politically, socially, and culturally very different from one another. They belong to different traditions of law and justice, and judges and jurisprudence. The United Nations Organization is a great provider of global data on a variety of areas in economic growth and development, but not in crime and law and justice. The lack of democratic political systems and the rule of law, economic poverty, and widespread corruption in governance have left the criminal justice systems of most of the countries of the developing world in shambles. Corruption in policing and the judiciary are endemic in the countries of the developing world. This has been further worsened by the rise of global crimes in almost all countries of the world. The transnational criminal gangs and mafias are not only weakening the criminal justice systems, but also destabilizing the prospect of democracy in the developing world. The Twelfth United Nations Congress on Crime Prevention and Criminal Justice held in Salvador, Brazil in 2010 addressed these challenges of the world criminal justice system and discussed the role of the United Nations in responding to them. The theme of the congress was "Comprehensive strategies for global challenges: crime prevention and criminal justice systems and their development in a changing world." The congress urged the member states to develop policies based on four principal strategies: "Establishing . . . the criminal justice system as a central pillar in the rule of law architecture; Highlighting the pivotal role of the criminal justice system in development; Emphasizing the need for a holistic approach to criminal justice system reform . . . [and] Identifying emerging forms of crime that pose a threat to societies . . . and exploring ways to prevent and control them."

Source: United Nations Information Service. (2010). *Twelfth United Nations congress on crime prevention and criminal justice.* New York, NY: United Nations; United Nations Organization. (2010). *Twelfth United Nations congress on crime prevention and criminal justice.* New York, NY: Department of Public Information, United Nations.

Some of the major examples of international programs for reform in criminal justice include the United Nations Development Programme's (UNDP's) Police Reform initiatives in Afghanistan, India, Bangladesh, Haiti, and Kyrgyzstan in Central Asia; the UNDP's Gender-Sensitive Police Reform programs in Kosovo, Liberia, and Sierra Leone; the UNDP's Judicial Reform Programs in Africa, Asia, Latin America, and the Arab region; USAID's

TABLE 1-2 Selected Criminal Justice Reform Programs in Developing Countries Supported by the United Nations Office on Drugs and Crime, 2008–2013

Country/Region	Duration	Program Title or Aim
Afghanistan	2003–2010	Criminal law and criminal justice capacity building
Afghanistan	2007–2011	Criminal justice capacity building extensions to the provinces
Brazil	2009–2012	Prevention of violence and strengthening citizenship
Brazil	2010–2013	Expressive Youth: Citizenship, access to justice and peace
Colombia	2010–2012	Strengthening public security policies
Eastern Africa	2010–2011	Justice sector reforms
Egypt	2003–2009	Strengthening legislative and capacity for juvenile justice
Guinea Bissau	2008–2011	Strengthening justice and security sector reform
India	2008–2010	Reducing children's vulnerability to abuse
Indonesia	2008–2010	Strengthening judicial integrity and capacity
Iran	2005–2009	Reforming the judiciary and prison system
Kenya	2009–2011	Strengthening the integrity and the capacity of the court system
Libya	2007–2010	Support to the process of criminal justice reform
Middle East	2008–2010	Increasing access to justice and legal aid
Nigeria	2009–2011	Prison reform through adherence to international standards
Southeast Asia	2010–2013	Towards Asia-Just
Southern Africa	2008–2011	Effective law enforcement response to violence against women
Sub-Region Africa	2009–2009	Access to legal aid

Source: Data from United Nations Office on Drugs and Crime. (2011). *Crime prevention and criminal justice reform, 2010–2011.* Vienna, Austria: Author.

Justice Reform Program in Latin America; CIDA's Legal Reform Project in the Baltic countries; World Bank's Governance and Anti-Corruption Reforms in developing countries (World Bank, 2010); ADB's Governance and Criminal Justice Modernization Program in South Asia (Asian Development Bank, 2006); and the IDB's Judicial Reform Programs in Latin America and the Caribbean. The UNDP launched the Accelerating Access to Justice for Human Development program in 2009. The program "supports rule of law, justice and security programmes—including legal empowerment of the poor—in over 90 countries worldwide" (United Nations Organization, 2011b, p. 1).

These and hundreds of other rule of law and criminal justice reform programs that were designed and funded by international development organizations from the beginning of the 1990s in developing countries have made significant effects on the progress of academic research and studies on comparative criminal justice. In the mid-1990s, literature on academic research on comparative criminal justice focusing on reforms and modernization in criminal justice in Asia, Africa, and Latin America began to grow at a tremendous rate (Nelken, 2011; Peerenboom, 2009; Pino & Wiatrowski, 2006; Sheptycki & Wardak, 2005; Wong, 2009).

■ Summary

Comparative criminal justice is the study of criminal justice systems in different countries and regions of the world. It is the study of how and why the patterns of crime and victimization are different in different societies; how and why various societies of the world define crime and criminality in different ways; and how the organization of policing, courts, and prisons varies across societies. It uses cross-country and cross-cultural analysis in the understanding of the intrasystemic characteristics of criminal justice such as the law and legal traditions, judicial models, due process laws, nature of police power and investigation, and nature of sentencing and convictions. Comparative criminal justice is also an analysis of extrasystemic characteristics such as the role of politics, ideology, and culture in the shaping of criminal justice. It is historical, systemic, relativistic, and cultural in nature, exploring how crime and justice have evolved in the context of historical settings in different countries; examining whether a criminal justice system is predominantly traditional or modern, formal or informal, and centralized or decentralized in terms of organization; and exploring local and global institutions of law and justice and examining how the processes of modernization and globalization are creating many homogenized structures of law and justice among the world's societies. The origin of comparative criminal justice, in one sense, goes back to the days of Cesare Beccaria's *On Crimes and Punishments*, Cesare Lombroso's *Criminal Man*, and Alexis de Tocqueville's *Democracy in America*. In another sense, comparative criminal justice is barely half a century old. It has emerged in the context of decolonization and the spread of modernization in Asia, Africa, and Latin America; the rise and expansion of academic criminology and criminal justice in the West; and the growth of transnational organized crime in the wake of the spread of globalization. The significance of comparative criminal justice can be drawn from its four different but interrelated research traditions: research on cross-national understanding of the patterns of crime and victimization, cross-national research for theory development, cross-national understanding of different systems of criminal justice, and cross-national analysis of evidence-based research for reforms and modernization in criminal justice.

■ Discussion Questions

1. What are the major intrasystemic institutions of criminal justice? Choose two intrasystemic institutions of the U.S. criminal justice system and compare and contrast them to those of England or Germany. (Hint: adversarial versus inquisitorial system of justice and common law versus civil law.)

2. What are some of the extrasystemic factors and forces that shape and mold the U.S. criminal justice system? Discuss in this context the role of conservative and liberal approaches to gun control and the debate on the legalization of same-sex marriage and marijuana.

3. How is the definition of crime different from the process of criminalization, and how is the process of criminalization different from the process of decriminalization? Describe some of the acts and behaviors that have recently been criminalized and some of the

acts and behaviors that have been decriminalized in the United States. (Hint: criminalization of domestic violence and child abuse, and decriminalization of abortion and homosexuality.)

4. What are the key analytical strategies for pursuing comparative criminal justice? What does it mean to say that comparative criminal justice must be historical and systemic in nature? How is the federal system of criminal justice in the United States different from the criminal justice system of the United Kingdom based on the unitary form of government? Give examples.

5. How are some of the contemporary issues in the U.S. criminal justice system related to globalization, and how are local and global issues being debated in the U.S. criminal justice system? (Hint: the debate on whether terrorist suspects should be tried in the military or civilian courts and whether they should be given the right of protection usually given to U.S. citizens.)

6. What are the various historical and developmental forces that have contributed to the growth and expansion of the field of comparative criminal justice since the 1970s? How have the academic growth of criminal justice in the 1970s and the events related to the end of the Cold War in the mid-1980s affected the growth of the field of comparative criminal justice? Give examples.

7. Scholars in criminology and criminal justice firmly believe in the following statement: "Any criminology worthy of the name should contain a comparative dimension. The contents of cultural meanings that are loaded into the subject of criminology are too variable for it to be otherwise" (Hardie-Bick et al., 2005, p. 1). Explain the statement with examples.

8. Why is the study of comparative criminal justice significant for a student in criminology and criminal justice? Cite and briefly summarize some of the major theories of criminology that have been cross-nationally examined and tested for further validation and empirical justifications. (Hint: cross-national testing of Hirschi's social bond theory and Gottfredson and Hirschi's general theory of crime.)

■ References ■

Adler, F. (1983). *Nations not obsessed with crime*. Littleton, CO: Fred B. Rothman and Company.

African Human Security Initiative. (2009). *The theory and practice of criminal justice in Africa*. Addis Ababa, Ethiopia: Institute of Security Studies.

Alanezi, F. (2010, Spring). Juvenile delinquency in Kuwait: Applying social disorganization theory. *Digest of Middle East Studies*, pp. 68–81.

American Bar Association. (2010). *Rule of Law Initiative 1990–2010*. Washington, DC: Author.

Armytage, L. (2011). Judicial reform in Asia: Case study of ADB's experience: 1990–2007. *Hague Journal on the Rule of Law, 3*, 70–105.

Armytage, L., & Metzner, L. (Eds.). (2009). *Searching for success in judicial reform: Voices from the Asia Pacific experience*. New York, NY: Oxford University Press.

Asian Development Bank. (2006). *Strengthening the criminal justice system*. ADB Regional Workshop, Dhaka, Bangladesh. Manila, the Philippines: Author.

Bakken, B. (2004). Moral panics, crime rates and harsh punishment in China. *Australian and New Zealand Journal of Criminology*. Retrieved from www.highbeam.com/doc/1G1-129364748.html.

Bayley, D. (1985). *Patterns of policing: A comparative international analysis*. New Brunswick, NJ: Rutgers University Press.

Beccaria, C. (2009). *On crimes and punishments*. Lexington, KY: Seven Treasures Publications. (Original work published in 1764.)

Bellah, R. N. (1985). *Tokugawa religion: The cultural roots of modern Japan*. New York, NY: Free Press. (Original work published in 1964.)

Benedict, R. (2005). *Patterns of culture*. New York, NY: Houghton Mifflin Company. (Original work published in 1935.)

Bennett, J. (2010). *The theory of moral sentiments: Adam Smith*. Retrieved from www.earlymoderntexts.com/pdfbits/stms56.pdf

Berman, G., & Fox, A. (2010). *Trial and error in criminal justice reform: Learning from failure*. Washington, DC: Urban Institute Press.

Beveridge, W. I. B. (1973). *Frontiers in comparative medicine*. Minneapolis, MN: University of Minnesota Press.

Boister, N. (2003). Transnational criminal law? *European Journal of International Law, 14*(5), 953–976.

Boyd v. United States, 116 U.S. 616 (1886).

Bradley, C. (Ed.). (2007). *Criminal procedure: A worldwide study* (2nd ed.). Durham, NC: North Carolina Academic Press.

Braithwaite, J. (1989). *Crime, shame, and reintegration*. Cambridge, MA: Cambridge University Press.

Brands, H. (2010). *Crime, violence, and the crisis in Guatemala: A case study in the erosion of the state*. Carlisle, PA: Strategic Studies Institute, U.S. Army College.

Calder, J. D. (1993). *The origins and development of federal crime control policy: Herbert Hoover's initiatives*. Westport, CT: Praeger.

Cao, L. (2007). Returning to normality: Anomie and crime in China. *International Journal of Offender Therapy and Comparative Criminology, 51*(1), 40–51.

Center for Reproductive Rights. (2008). Female genital mutilation (FGM): Legal prohibitions worldwide. Retrieved from www.reproductiverights.org/en/document/female-genital-mutilation-fgm-legal-prohibitions-worldwide.

Chamlin, M. B., & Cochran, J. K. (2007). An evaluation of the assumptions that underlie institutional anomie theory. *Theoretical Criminology, 11*(1), 39–61.

Clinard, M. B., & Abbott, D. J. (1973). *Crime in developing countries: A comparative perspective*. New York, NY: John Wiley & Sons.

Daniels, K., Haleem, M. A., & Shariff A. O. (2003). *Criminal justice in Islam: Judicial procedure in the Shariʼah*. London, England: I. B. Tauris.

Demombynes, G., & Özler, B. (2003). *Crime and local inequality in South Africa*. (World Bank Policy Research Working Paper No. 2925). Washington DC: The World Bank.

Elechi, O. O. (2004, August). *Human rights and the African indigenous justice system*. Paper presented at the Eighteenth International Conference of the International Society for the Reform of Criminal Law, Montreal, Canada.

Escobedo v. Illinois, 378 U.S. 478 (1964).

Farah, D. (2004). *Blood from stones: The secret financial network of terror*. New York, NY: Broadway Books.

Fennell, P., Harding, C. C., Jörg, N., & Swart, B. (Eds.). (1995). *Criminal justice in Europe: A comparative study.* New York, NY: Oxford University Press.

Finklea, K. M., for the Congressional Research Service. (2010). *Identity theft: Trends and issues.* Washington, DC: Government Printing Press.

Foote, D. H. (1992). The benevolent paternalism of Japanese criminal justice. *California Law Review, 80,* 317–390.

Friedman, L. M. (2005). *A history of American law* (rev. ed.). New York, NY: Touchstone.

Friedman, R. I. (2000). *Red mafiya: How the Russian mob has invaded America.* New York, NY: Little, Brown.

Fujieda, M. (1989). Some thoughts on domestic violence in Japan. *Review of Japanese Culture and Society, 3*(1), 60–66.

Geertz, C. (1971). *Islam observed: Religious development in Morocco and Indonesia.* Chicago, IL: University of Chicago Press.

Ginsburg, T., & Moustafa, T. (Eds.). (2008). *Rule by law: The politics of courts in authoritarian regimes.* Cambridge, MA: Cambridge University Press.

Glenn, H. P. (2004). *Legal traditions of the world: Sustainable diversity in law.* New York, NY: Oxford University Press.

Glendon, M. A., Gordon, M. W., & Carozza, P. G. (1999). *Comparative legal traditions in a nutshell.* St. Paul, MN: West Publishing Company.

Glenny, M. (2009). *McMafia: A journey through the global criminal underworld.* New York, NY: Knopf.

Goodman, C. F. (2008). *The rule of law in Japan: A comparative analysis.* Dordrecht, the Netherlands: Kluwer Law International.

Gottfredson, M., & Hirschi, T. (1990). *A general theory of crime.* Palo Alto, CA: Stanford University Press.

Government of Japan. (2002). *Domestic violence in Japan.* Tokyo: The Cabinet Office of Japan.

Haley, J. O. (1991). *Authority without power: Law and the Japanese paradox.* New York, NY: Oxford University Press.

Hall, S., & Mclean, C. (2009). A tale of two capitalisms: Preliminary spatial and historical comparisons of homicide rates in Western Europe and the USA. *Theoretical Criminology, 13*(3), 313–339.

Hardie-Bick, J., Sheptycki, J., & Wardak, A. (2005). Transnational and comparative criminology in a global perspective. In J. Sheptycki & A. Wardak (Eds.), *Transnational and comparative criminology* (pp. 1–18). London, England: Glasshouse Press.

Hartjen, C. A. (2008). *Youth, crime, and justice: A global inquiry.* Piscataway, NJ: Rutgers University Press.

Hartjen, C. A., & Priyadarsini, S. (2012). *The global victimization of children: Problems and solution.* New York, NY: Springer.

Holmes, O. W., Jr. (1991). *The common law.* Mineola, NY: Dover Publications.

In re Gault, 387 U.S. 1 (1967).

International Centre for Criminal Law Reform and Criminal Justice Policy. (2001). *The changing face of international criminal law* (selected papers). Vancouver, BC, Canada: Author.

International Centre for Criminal Law Reform and Criminal Justice Policy. (2007). *Promoting criminal justice reform: A collection of papers from the Canada-China cooperation symposium.* Vancouver, BC, Canada: Author.

International Centre for Prison Studies. (2010). *World prison brief—Highest to lowest.* London, England: Kings College.

International Harm Reduction Association. (2007). *The death penalty for drug offenses: A violation of international human rights Law.* London, England: Author.

International Harm Reduction Association. (2010). *The death penalty for drug offences: Global overview 2010.* London, England: Author.

Jackson, R. J. (2007). *Organized crimes in postcommunist regimes* (Dissertation). Chapel Hill: University of North Carolina.

Jaishankar, K. (Ed.). (2009). *International perspective on crime and justice.* New Castle, England: Cambridge Scholars Publishing.

Jejeebhoy, S. J., Shah, I., & Thapa, S. (Eds.). (2005). *Sex without consent: Young people in developing countries.* London, England: Zed Books.

Jiang, S., Lambert, E. & Wang, J. (2007). Correlates of formal and informal social/crime control: An exploratory study. *Journal of Criminal Justice, 35*(3), 261–271.

Kegan, R. A. (2003). *Adversarial legalism: The American way of law.* Cambridge, MA: Harvard University Press.

Kemp, W. (2010). Organized crime has globalized and turned into a security threat (Press Release). Vienna, Austria: United Nations Office on Drugs and Crime.

Kim, S., & Pridemore, W. A. (2005). Social change, institutional anomie and serious property crime in transitional Russia. *British Journal of Criminology, 45*(1), 81–97.

Kshetri, N. (2010). *The global cybercrime industry: Economic, institutional, and strategic perspectives.* New York, NY: Springer.

Lévi-Strauss, C. (1968). *The savage mind.* Chicago, IL: The University of Chicago Press.

Lilley, P. (2003). *Dirty dealing: The untold truth about global money laundering, international crime, and terrorism.* New York, NY: Kogan Page Business Books.

Lombroso, C. (2006). *Criminal man* (M. Gibson & N. H. Rafter, Trans.). Durham, NC: Duke University Press. (Original work published in 1876.)

Lu, Y. (1995). *China's legal awakening: Legal theory and criminal justice in Deng's era.* Hong Kong: Hong Kong University Press.

Ma, Y. (2007). A comparative view of the law of interrogation. *International Criminal Justice Review, 17*(1), 5–26.

Maine, H. (1872). *Village-communities in the East and West.* London, England: John Murray.

Malinowski, B. (1989). *Crime and custom in savage society.* Lanham, MD: Rowman & Littlefield. (Original work published in 1926).

Mapp v. Ohio, 367 U.S. 643 (1961).

Mares, D. M. (2009). Civilization, economic change, and trends in interpersonal violence in western societies. *Theoretical Criminology, 13*(4), 419–449.

Marshall, M. G., & Cole, B. R., for the Center for Global Policy. (2009). *Global report 2009: Conflict, governance, and state fragility.* Arlington, VA: George Mason University.

Mead, M. (2001). *Sex and temperament: In three primitive societies.* New York, NY: Harper Perennial. (Original work published in 1935).

Meadows, R. J. (2010). *What price for blood? Murder and justice in Saudi Arabia.* New York, NY: Robert Reed Publishers.

Merryman, J. H., & Perez-Perdomo, R. (2007). *The civil law tradition: An introduction to the legal systems of Europe and Latin America.* Palo Alto, CA: Stanford University Press.

Messner, S. F., & Rosenfeld, R. (1994). *Crime and the American dream.* Belmont, CA: Wadsworth.

Meulen, N. V. (2006). *The challenge of countering identity theft: Recent developments in the United States, United Kingdom, and the European Union* (report commissioned by National Infrastructure Cyber Crime Program). Tilburg, the Netherlands: International Victimology Institute.

Miranda v. Arizona, 384 U.S. 436 (1966).

Monsoor, T. (2006). *Justice delayed is justice denied: Women and violence in Bangladesh.* Retrieved from www.thedailystar.net/law/2006/03/02/index.htm.

Moore, B. (1993). *Social origins of democracy and dictatorship: Lord and peasant in the making of the modern world*. New York, NY: Beacon Press. (Original work published in 1966.)

Morgan, L. H. (1877). *Ancient society*. London, England: MacMillan & Company.

Mühlhahn, K. (2009). *Criminal justice in China: A history*. Cambridge, MA: Harvard University Press.

Naim, M. (2006). *Illicit: How smugglers, traffickers, and copycats are hijacking the global economy*. New York, NY: Doubleday.

Neapolitan, J. L. (1999). A comparative analysis of nations with low and high levels of violent crime. *Journal of Criminal Justice, 27*(3), 259–274.

Neapolitan, J. L. (2001). An examination of cross-national variation in punitiveness. *International Journal of Offender Therapy and Comparative Criminology, 45*(6), 691–710.

Neapolitan, J. L. (2003). Explaining variation in crime victimization across nations and within nations. *International Criminal Justice Review, 13*, 76–89.

Needham, J. (1947). *Science and civilisation in China* (reprinted in 2009). London, England: Cambridge University Press.

Nelken, D. (2011). *Comparative criminal justice and globalization*. Surrey, England: Ashgate Publishing.

Nethercott, F. (2009). *Russian legal culture before and after communism: Criminal justice, politics, and the public sphere*. Abingdon, England: Routledge.

Newburn, T., & Sparks, R. (Eds.). (2004). *Criminal justice and political cultures: National and international dimensions of crime control*. London, England: Willan Publishing.

Nivette, A. (2011). Cross-national predictors of crime: A meta-analysis. *Homicide Studies, 15*(2), 103–131.

Okafo, N. (2007, May 20–23). Law enforcement in post-colonial Africa: Interfacing indigenous and English policing in Nigeria. *International Police Executive Symposium* (working paper No. 7). Vienna, Austria: the European Union and the International Police Executive Symposium.

Otterbein, K. (1988). *The ultimate coercive sanction: A cross-cultural study of capital punishment*. New Haven, CT: Human Relations Area Files Press.

Ozbay, O., & Ozcan, Y. Z. (2006). A test of Hirschi's social bonding theory: Juvenile delinquency in the high schools of Ankara, Turkey. *International Journal of Offender Therapy and Comparative Criminology, 50*(6), 711–726.

Parsons, T. (1966). *Societies: Evolutionary and comparative perspectives* (A. Inkeles, ed.). Upper Saddle River, NJ: Prentice Hall.

Peerenboom, R. (2009). *Judicial independence in China: Lesson for global rule of law promotion*. Cambridge, MA: Cambridge University Press.

Permanent Mission of the Kingdom of the Netherlands to the United Nations. (2008). *Human rights: Statement on human rights, sexual orientation and gender identity at high level meeting*. Retrieved from www.netherlandsmission.org.

Pieris, A. (2009). *Hidden hands and divided landscapes: A penal history of Singapore's plural society*. Honolulu, HI: The University of Hawaii Press.

Pildes, R. H. (2003). Conflicts between American and European views of law: The dark side of legalism. *Virginia Journal of International Law, 145*, 45–166.

Pino, N., & Wiatrowski, M. D. (Eds.). (2006). *Democratic policing in transitional and developing countries*. London, England: Ashgate Publishing.

Polanyi, K. (2001). *The great transformation: The political and economic origins of our time*. New York, NY: Beacon Press. (Original work published in 1944).

Pratt, T. C., & Godsey, T. W. (2002). Social support and homicide: A cross-national test of an emerging criminological theory. *Journal of Criminal Justice, 3*(6), 589–601.

R. v. Sinclair, 2010 SCC 35, [2010] 2 S.C.R. 310.

Radcliff-Brown, A. R. (1964). *The Andaman islanders.* New York, NY: Free Press. (Original work published in 1922).

Rafter, N. (2005). Cesare Lombroso and the origins of criminology: Rethinking of criminological tradition. In S. Henry & M. Laner (Eds.), *The essential criminology reader.* Boulder, CO: Westview Press. Retrieved from www.farum.it/publifarumv/n/01/pdf/Rafter.pdf.

Rice, M. (2001). *Japan adopts tough domestic violence law.* Retrieved from http://womensenews.org /story/crime-policylegislation/011202/japan-adopts-tough-domestic-violence-law.

Richardson, L., & Kirsten, A. (2005). *Armed violence and poverty in Brazil.* Bradford, England: University of Bradford, Centre for International Cooperation and Security.

Sabine, G. H. (1973). *A history of political theory* (4th ed.). Hinsdale, IL: Dryden Press.

Saleh-Hanna, V., & Affor, C. (2008). *Colonial systems of control: Criminal justice in Nigeria.* Ottawa, ON, Canada: University of Ottawa Press.

Sen, A. (2000). *Development as freedom.* Harpswell, ME: Anchor Publishing Company.

Shahidullah, S. M. (1994). Emerging trends in crime policy in America: Problems of returning to gemeinshaft. *Proceedings of the New York State Sociological Association.* Fort Worth, TX: Cyberspace Publications.

Shahidullah, S. M. (2008). *Crime policy in America: Laws, institutions, and programs.* Lanham, MD: American University Press.

Shahidullah, S. M., & Derby, C. N. (2009). Criminalisation, modernisation, and globalisation: The U.S. and international perspectives on domestic violence. *Global Crime, 10*(3), 196–223.

Shaw, M., Van Dijk, J., & Rhomberg, W. (2003). Determining trends in global crime and justice: An overview of results from the United Nations Surveys of Crime Trends and Operations of Criminal Justice Systems. *Forum on Crime and Society, 3*(1–2), 35–63.

Shelley, L. I. (1981a). *Crime and modernization: The impact of industrialization and urbanization on crime.* Carbondale, IL: Southern Illinois University Press.

Shelley, L. I. (1981b). *Readings in comparative criminology.* Carbondale, IL: Southern Illinois University Press.

Sheptycki, J. (2005). Relativism, transnationlisation, and comparative criminology. In J. Sheptycki & A. Wardak. (Eds.). *Transnational and comparative criminology* (pp. 69–90). London, England: Glasshouse Press.

Sheptycki, J. (2011). Transnational and comparative criminology reconsidered. In D. Nelken (Ed.), *Comparative criminal justice and globalization* (pp. 145–162). Surrey, England: Ashgate Publishing.

Sheptycki, J., & Wardak, A. (Eds.). (2005). *Transnational and comparative criminology.* London, England: Glasshouse Press.

Shettima, K., & Chukwuma, I. (2002, October). *Crime and human rights in Nigeria.* Paper presented at the Seminar on Crime: Managing Public Order in Countries in Transition, New York, NY.

Skinnider, E. (2005). *The art of confessions: A comparative look at the law of confessions—Canada, England, the United States, and Australia.* Vancouver, BC, Canada: International Centre for Criminal Law Reform and Criminal Justice Policy.

Skocpol, T. (1979). *States and social revolutions. A comparative analysis of France, Russia and China.* Cambridge, MA: Cambridge University Press.

Stamatel, J. P. (2009). Contributions of cross-national research to criminology at the beginning of the 21st century. In M. D. Krohn, A. J. Lizotte, and G. P. Hall (Eds.), *Handbook on crime and deviance* (pp. 3–22). London, England, and New York, NY: Springer.

Thornton, R.Y., & Endo, K. (1992). *Preventing crime in America and Japan: A comparative study*. New York, NY: M. E. Sharpe.

Tilly, C. (2006). *Big structures, large processes, huge comparisons*. New York, NY: Russell Sage Foundation Publications. (Original work published in 1984.)

Timmons, H., & Kumar, H. (2009, July 2). India court overturns gay sex ban. *New York Times*, p. 2. Retrieved from www.nytimes.com/2009/07/03/world/asia/03india.html.

Tonry, M. H. (2007). *Crime and justice: Crime, punishment, and politics in comparative perspectives*. Chicago, IL: University of Chicago Press.

Turner, J. I. (2007). Transnational networks and international criminal justice. *Michigan Law Review, 105,* 985–1032.

United Nations Children's Fund (UNICEF). (2006). *Juvenile justice in South Asia: Improving protection for children in conflict with the law*. Kathmundi, Nepal: Author.

United Nations Development Programme. (2009). *Globalization with a human face* (Human development report). New York, NY: Author.

United Nations Development Programme. (2011). *Human development report, 2011*. New York, NY: Author.

United Nations Educational, Scientific, and Cultural Organization. (1957). *The university teaching of social science-criminology*. Paris, France: Author.

United Nations Office on Drugs and Crime. (2004). *International homicide statistics (HIS)*. Retrieved from www.unodc.org/documents/data-and-analysis/IHS-rates-05012009.pdf.

United Nations Office on Drugs and Crime. (2007). *An assessment of transnational organized crime in Central Asia*. Vienna, Austria: Author.

United Nations Office on Drugs and Crime. (2010a). *The globalization of crime: A transnational organized crime threat assessment*. Vienna, Austria: Author.

United Nations Office on Drugs and Crime. (2010b). *United Nations surveys on crime trends and the operations of criminal justice systems*. Vienna, Austria: Author.

United Nations Office on Drugs and Crime. (2011). *Crime prevention and criminal justice reform, 2010–2011*. Vienna, Austria: Author.

United Nations Organization. (1985). *United Nations standard minimum rules for the administration of juvenile justice*. New York, NY: Author.

United Nations Organization. (2011a). *Third annual report on strengthening and coordinating United Nations rule of law activities: Report of the secretary-general*. New York, NY: United Nations Rule of Law Initiative.

United Nations Organization. (2011b). *United Nations Development Programme (UNDP)*. New York, NY: United Nations Rule of Law Initiative.

Van Dijk, J., & del Frate, A. A. (2011). *Criminal victimization and victim services across the world: Results and prospects of the International Crime Victims Survey*. Vienna, Austria: United Nations Office on Drugs and Crime.

Vazsonyi, A. T., Pickering, L. E., Junger, M., & Hessing, D. (2001). An empirical test of a general theory of crime: A four-nation comparative study of self-control and the prediction of deviance. *Journal of Research in Crime and Deviance*, 38(2), 91–131.

Vogler, R. (2005). *A world view of criminal justice*. Surrey, England: Ashgate Publishing Limited.

Walker, A., & Parmar, P. (1996). *Warrior marks: Female genital mutilation and the sexual blinding of women.* Orlando, FL: Harcourt Brace and Company.

Walker, S. (1997). *Record of the Wickersham commission on law observance and enforcement.* Retrieved from www.lexisnexis.com/academic/upa_cis/group.asp?g=256.

Wallerstein, I. (1979). *The capitalist world-economy.* Cambridge, MA: Cambridge University Press.

Weeks v. United States, 232 U.S. 383 (1914).

Weiner, R. (2010). Hate crime bill signed into law 11 years after Matthew Shepard's death. *The Huffington Post.* Retrieved from www.Huffingtonpost.com/2009/10/28/hate-crimes-bill-to-be -si_n_336883.html.

Wilson, B. M., Cordero, J. A. R., & Handberg, R. (2004). Judicial reform in Latin America: Evidence from Costa Rica. *Journal of Latin American Studies, 35,* 507–531.

Wong, K. C. (2009). *Chinese policing: History and reform.* New York, NY: Peter Lang Publishing Group.

World Bank. (2010). *Legal and judicial reform. Governance and anti-corruption.* Washington, DC: Author.

World Bank. (2012). *Poverty and equity data.* Retrieved from http://povertydata.worldbank.org.

World Health Organization. (2005). *WHO multi-country study on women's health and domestic violence against women.* Geneva, Switzerland: Author.

Zhao, L. S. (2008). Anomie theory and crime in a transitional China (1978–). *International Criminal Justice Review, 18*(2), 137–157.

Zhao, R., & Cao, L. (2010). Social change and anomie: A cross-national study. *Social Forces, 88*(3), 1209–1229.

Comparative Criminal Justice: Theoretical Perspectives

■ Introduction

The criminal justice systems of the world's 195 countries represent diverse ways in which crime, law, and justice are pursued and perceived around the world. At the same time, these systems have similar issues and challenges. Such diversities and similarities raise many scientific curiosities and theoretical puzzles. Why are the world's systems of criminal justice different from one another? How are those differences historically, politically, and culturally created and embedded? How are the world's systems of criminal justice also becoming more and more similar? Why are they increasingly facing similar challenges? The core theoretical question is: How are the world's different systems of criminal justice connected? What are the overarching cultural, civilizational, and global processes that are making these systems connected and integrated, and how is that connectivity shaping the thoughts, ideas, and philosophies about crime, law, and justice among the world's societies today? This chapter will describe four theoretical perspectives that explain this connectivity among the world's systems of criminal justice: modernization theory, civilization theory, world-systems theory, and globalization theory.

■ Modernization Theory and Comparative Criminal Justice

Modernization is one of the most dominant theoretical perspectives in contemporary social science, including sociology, political science, anthropology, comparative law, comparative education, development economics, and comparative criminal justice. Modernization theory has generated an enormous amount of literature in the last 5 decades in all branches of social science. The roots of modernization theory go back to the days of the development of social science in the middle of the 19th century in Europe, when different branches of social science emerged to bring the scientific method into social analysis. One of the first projects of social scientific analysis was to theorize about the social, economic, and cultural transformations that were unfolding in Europe in the wake of the disintegration of feudalism and monarchical political systems. Modernization theory emerged in the context of that time of great transformations in Europe to theorize about the nature of the emerging modern society and the future of humanity's search for a good society. The classical theorists of modernization developed a number of hypotheses that are still at the core of social science, including criminology and criminal justice.

Crime and Modernization: The Classical Ideas

One of the major hypotheses of modernization theory is that with the progress of modernization, societies are more likely to change from agricultural to industrial economies. With this change in the economy, politics is more likely to move from monarchy and absolutism to democracy. With the transition to industrialization, urbanization, and democracy, crime is more likely to grow. However, as industrialization advances and democracy matures, the crime rate is more likely to drop. The second hypothesis is that modernization is primarily a process of cultural change from tradition to modernity. Modernity is not just an industrial economy or a huge process of urbanization. It is a complex set of cultural values that put a premium on democracy, individualism, secularization, equality, science, reason, and rationality.

The modernization theorists of 19th century classical sociology and social science in general, such as Karl Marx (1818–1883), Gabriel Tarde (1843–1904), Emile Durkheim (1858–1917), Georg Simmel (1858–1918), Ferdinand Tönnies (1855–1936), and Max Weber (1864–1920), theorized about relations between crime and modernization. Marx was excited to see the disintegration of feudalism and the birth of capitalism in front of his eyes in Europe in the middle of the 19th century. But in his analysis of the structure of the capitalist economy in his *Das Kapital* (1867/2007), Marx theorized that it is inherently an exploitative economic system. Under capitalism, crime would be endemic among the working class because of their pauperization, alienation, powerlessness, and dehumanization.

Of all the classical sociologists of the 19th century, Tarde was one who was formally regarded in his time as a criminologist. He was the director of criminal justice at the Ministry of Justice in France, which published his ideas about crime and justice in *Comparative Criminality* in 1886 (New World Encyclopedia, 2008). Tarde (1912) theorized that crime is not a biological phenomenon, but that it is social in origin. He hypothesized that the crime rate will be higher in societies where the strategic and ruling elites fail to maintain a balance between modernity (innovations) and tradition (the maintenance of cultural patterns). Tarde's idea that crime is a learned behavior, learned from peers and in association with others, predates Edwin Sutherland's differential association theory.

German sociologist Simmel, in his *The Metropolis and Mental Life* (1903/1971) theorized that modern cities and modern life are more likely to generate crimes because of conflicts between the demands of radical individualism and the demands of collectivity. In his *The Philosophy of Money* (1978), Simmel predicted the negative effect of consumerism on crime and deviance in modern societies. From the same generation of German sociologists, Tönnies (1957) theorized that with modernization, societies are more likely to move from gemeinschaft (community) to gesellschaft (society). Whereas gemeinschafts are characterized by the dominance of informal social relations and informal social control institutions, gesellschafts are rational organizations dominated by formal laws and formal social control institutions. The crime rate is more likely to be higher, according to Tönnies, in societies that have lost the influence and the power of their informal social control mechanisms.

Max Weber, another leading theorist of modernity who came from Germany, claimed that societies undergoing modernization are more likely to develop rational-legal authority and rational bureaucracy in all spheres of life, including law and justice. The societies experiencing modernization are more likely to develop a political regime based on the rule of law and rational-legal authority. In a modern state, Weber claimed, the monopolized use of physical force must be based on legitimate and rational-legal systems. In a rational-legal system, laws are formulated by legitimate governmental authorities, and they are not affected by charisma or religion. The states that are based on charismatic authority or traditional authority and traditional legal systems are less likely to progress toward modernity. For Weber, a modern criminal justice system based on the rule of law cannot emerge in a state based on traditional authority and traditional legal systems (Gerth & Mills, 1958).

French sociologist Durkheim, in his books *Division of Labor in Society* (1893/1964), *Suicide* (1897/1951), and *The Rules of Sociological Method* (1895/1964), elaborated a noble conception of crime and justice. Durkheim theorized that crimeless society is not possible, nor is it desirable. It is because of crime that there exists a system of law and justice in society, and a system of law and justice is the foundation of social order and social solidarity. According to Durkheim, individuals in a society must be socialized to conform to its moral and normative standards. However, because socialization always remains incomplete, individuals must be controlled through laws and penal sanctions to conform. The function of criminal justice is thus imperative for the maintenance of social order. Durkheim hypothesized that with modernization, societies are more likely to move from a stage of mechanical solidarity dominated by collectivism and repressive laws to organic solidarity dominated by individualism and restitutive laws. He predicted that societies undergoing industrialization and urbanization are more likely to produce a high rate of crime because of the rise in anomie—a state of economic and social disorganization. The classical thinkers in social science in general, and sociology in particular, were therefore skeptical about the directionality of modernity and the effect of the death of traditionalism on social order (Etzioni, 1996; Nisbet, 1969; Shils, 2006). Most of them hypothesized that modernity is more likely to generate a high rate of crime because of the breakdown in informal social control mechanisms and too much reliance on legalism, formalism, professionalization, and bureaucratization.

Crime and Modernization: The Contemporary Ideas

The first generation of modernization theorists of the 19th century theorized and hypothesized about the nature of change from tradition to modernity and the predicament of crime and justice in the context of change and transformation. Modernization theorists of the second generation—social scientists and sociologists in the 1960s and 1970s—such as Talcott Parsons, Marion J. Levy, Daniel Lerner, Alex Inkeles, Shmuel N. Eisenstadt, Neil J. Smelser, and Robert Bellah theorized and hypothesized about how modernization is possible. Who are the agents of change, and what are the driving forces of change from tradition to modernity? Some of the theories and hypotheses of the second generation of modernization theorists are also relevant for cross-national analyses in crime and justice. The progress of modernization, as viewed by most modernization theorists, is a process of gradual change and evolution. In the process of modernization, a society's institutions are more likely to go through a process of differentiation, integration, and institutionalization. The differentiation process implies the emergence of a certain amount of autonomy for all social institutions, for example, the autonomy of the economy from politics, politics from the economy, and politics from religion. The process of differentiation and autonomy creates, in turn, the need for integration and institutionalization. Institutionalization is the process of sustained institutional growth within the cultural framework of modernity. In most traditional societies, for example, criminal justice is highly politicized and is used as a means of imposing political controls and deriving political legitimacy. In most countries of Asia, Africa, and Latin America, criminal justice is not a highly differentiated and autonomous institution of law and justice. The lack of judicial independence is a widely prevalent fact of law and justice in developing countries. Because of the lack of autonomy and differentiation from politics, and in some cases from religion, criminal justice systems in most developing countries are unable to integrate and institutionalize the norms and values of modernity.

The possibility of modernization, according to the second generation of modernization theorists, depends on both internal and external forces of transformation. Internally, the need for a cultural transformation often comes through the leadership of modernizing elites. The Tokugawa elites in Japan after the Meiji Restoration in 1868, for instance, made deliberate decisions to modernize their law and justice system, particularly through the importation of modern law enforcement strategies from Germany. In the late 1970s, in the wake of China's expanding market economy, the Chinese Communist Party elites, under the leadership of Deng Xiaoping, made deliberate decisions to modernize the Chinese criminal justice system by developing a new code for criminal law and criminal procedure. Externally, the modernization process can advance through a process of diffusion from relatively more modern societies. The process of diffusion of the values and the institution of modern criminal justice in developing countries began to expand during the spread of colonialism in the 18th and 19th centuries—the first wave of modernization. The second wave of modernization began during the 1990s, after the end of the Cold War and at the beginning of a new process of globalization.

One of the strongest hypotheses originating with the second generation of modernization theorists is that the social institutions undergoing modernization are more likely to have a higher level of legitimacy, adaptability, competence, and performance. A modern social institution such as a state, a system of education, or a system of criminal justice is more likely to depend on science, innovations, and evidence-based knowledge. A modern legal system is more likely to be dominated by professional jurists trained and educated in modern law and theories of jurisprudence. A social system is likely to move from a lower to a higher level of adaptive capacity with the development of new cultural values. More importantly, the modernization theorists claim, the societies undergoing modernization will be increasingly homogeneous with respect to their dominant economic, political, and social structures, including law and justice.

Crime and Modernization: Some Empirical Evidence

In recent decades, a considerable amount of literature has grown to test some of the hypotheses of modernization theory with cross-national crime and justice data, particularly from developing countries (Heiland, Shelley, & Kato, 1991; Shelley, 1981a). There are three major sets of empirical literature (1) literature on economic modernization, transitions to a market economy, and crime trends; (2) literature on political modernization, democracy, and crime trends; and (3) literature on cultural modernization and criminal justice. Many social historians who examined the relations between crime and the rise of industrialization and urbanization in Europe in the 19th century found that, when taking a long-term historical perspective, the rise of modernization is associated with a remarkable decline in violent crimes. A considerable number of recent empirical studies, however, have shown that during the time of economic modernization (rapid industrialization and urbanization), the crime rate has increased in all advanced countries of the West. Industrialization and urbanization, in their formative stage of expansion in a country, are more likely to produce a state of social disorganization characterized by poverty, unemployment, income inequality, neighborhood disintegration, community breakdown, and family disruption. Social disorganization is related to a high rate of crime and delinquency (Shaw & McKay, 1969; Thomas & Znaniecki, 1918–1920). Although industrialization and urbanization began in Western countries in the mid-19th century, these accelerated after World War II, particularly from the early 1960s. The crime rate in Western countries also began to climb from that time of accelerated pace of industrialization and urbanization. As Levinson (2002) found: "During the thirty years spanning 1962 to 1995, the more economically developed and industrialized countries of the world, as measured by gross domestic product (GDP), have had higher crime rates than the less developed ones" (p. 1716).

Based on data collected from the United Nations World Crime Surveys (developed and underdeveloped countries, 1970–1994), Fajnzylber, Lederman, and Loayza (2001) conducted a cross-national study of what causes violent crime. Their study revealed that income inequality is positively related to a high level of violent crimes. Using data drawn from INTERPOL and the World Health Organization, Messner (1989) examined the relations between homicide rates and economic discrimination and found that "indicators of economic discrimination against social groups are significantly and positively related to homicide rates" (p. 597).

Since the 1980s, scholars in comparative criminology and criminal justice have been closely observing developments in the area of crime, law, and justice in China. These developments have been observed in the context of China's transition to a market economy and modernization that began in the late 1970s under the leadership of Deng Xiaoping. Since then, China has rapidly moved from predominantly agricultural to predominantly manufacturing and service industries. Between 1980 and 1993, China's GDP grew at a rate of 9.6%. China is aggressively becoming a market economy based on the growing dominance of its private sector (Zhang, 1996). What is intriguing, however, is that the total crime rate in China has also gone up during the time of modernization (Zhao, 2008). One of the recent empirical studies (Liu, Messner, & Zhang, 2001) that examined the patterns of crime in China based on a large volume of official crime data found that "the total crime rate tripled from 55.91 per 100,000 population in 1978 to 163.19 per 100,000 population in 1998" (Liu et al., 2001, p. 10) and that the "increasing trends in Chinese crime rates evidently apply to both violent and property offenses" (Liu & Messner, 2001, p. 18). The researchers concluded their study by saying, "Our analysis demonstrates the utility of applying the modernization theory to the explanation of recent developments in crime in China" (Liu & Messner, 2001, p. 18). Other studies have shown that modernization in particular has brought new types economic crimes such as bribery, contract corruption, party corruption, tax evasion, smuggling, and embezzlement to China (Liu, 2005; Schultz, 1989).

Similar developments in crime, particularly in economic crimes, are observed in the transitional and modernizing economies of Russia, the countries of Eastern Europe, and the Baltic Republic (Kim & Pridemore, 2005; Pridemore, 2005; Zhao, 2008). Kim and Pridemore (2005) conducted an empirical study of crime trends in Russia at the time of its transition to a market economy. Using data collected from the Russian Ministry of Interior and an index of socioeconomic change, they found that the "late 1980s and the transition years of the 1990s produced dramatic increases in Russian crime rates. Data . . . show that property crime rose steeply, though not as much as homicide" (Kim & Pridemore, 2005, p. 83).

In his study of the characteristics of homicide trends, victims, and offenders in transitional Russia, Pridemore (2007) found that the "Russian homicide rate doubled during the 1990s and is now among the highest in the world. During this same period, Russian citizens experienced swift, widespread, and meaningful political, economic, and social change"

(p. 331). Similar crime trends are also observed in the countries of Central and Eastern Europe, including Bulgaria, Croatia, Hungary, Poland, Romania, Slovakia, and Slovenia. During the late 1980s and the 1990s—the time of the transition to a market economy—the homicide rate, theft, and other economic crimes increased in all Central European countries. The reported homicide rate increased about 39% in Hungary and about 9% in Romania in the beginning of the economic transition in the late 1980s. During the same period, reported motor vehicle theft increased 15% in Poland and 6% in Hungary. According to one study, "Data from the International Criminal Police Organization (ICPO) from 1990 to 1997 indicate that crime rates in many Central European countries may indeed be stabilizing at levels higher than pre-transition years" (Stamatel, 2002, p. 641).

Even though a considerable amount of empirical literature has shown a correlation between economic modernization and high crime rates in Western societies during the initial period of their economic modernization, and in postcommunist societies at the time of their transition to a market economy in the 1980s and 1990s, such correlations are highly complex and multifaceted. As Shelley (1981a) observed: "The relationship between industrialization and urbanization and changes in levels and forms of criminality is shown never to be [a] simple linear one . . . . [A] complex relationship exists among different variables associated with the process of development and . . . crime" (p. xv).

Using data collected from INTERPOL, Arthur (2002) conducted a study of crime trends in 11 African countries. He found that violent crime decreased in those countries during the time of their economic modernization between 1961 and 1984. He claimed that the "impact of development on crime was positive" except for minor property crimes (p. 499). Studies have also found that economic modernization in the countries of East Asia including Japan, South Korea, Taiwan, and Hong Kong in the 1980s and 1990s was not associated with higher levels of crime (Rushton & Whitney, 2002). Japan maintained one of the lowest rates of homicide in the world during its past 5 decades of modernization (Leonardsen, 2005; Roberts & Lafree, 2006). "Japan's homicide rate dropped 70% in the last 50 years, and the nation now has one of the lowest homicide rates in the world" (Johnson, 2008, p. 146). Crime rates and patterns and modernization are connected, but there are no linear relations.

The modernization theorists have also hypothesized that countries undergoing modernization are more likely to move from authoritarian to democratic political systems, and the progress of democracy is more likely to be associated with lower levels of crime. The hypothesis, in other words, is that the crime rate is likely to be lower in countries characterized and governed by democratic political systems, but higher in countries with authoritarian systems and failed states (Prillaman, 2003). The countries with democracies are more likely to have low levels of crime, homicides, and corruption. Crime trends are more likely to be controllable under democratic political systems because of effective resource distribution, limits to extreme deprivations and discriminations (Pridemore & Trent, 2010), inclusive politics, wide levels of political participation, institutionalization of effective and transparent governance, and effective and independent law enforcement and judicial systems (Halim, 2006; Lin, 2007). Analyzing the United Nations data, Sung (2006) observed that "In authoritarian states, criminal justice systems rely on a larger law enforcement–punishment apparatus for order maintenance and produce higher rates of arrests, prosecution, conviction, and incarceration" (p. 311). He further observed that "By contrast, in liberal democracies, justice is sought as the defense of civil liberties, through the due process of law, which . . . leads to a higher rate of case attrition in criminal justice process" (p. 311).

Empirical evidence also exists about relations between crime and democracy. According to the Economist Intelligence Unit's (EIU's) 2006 and 2008 global studies, there are only about 30 countries in the world that are full democracies (Kekic, 2007). Of the world's 30 full democracies, the top 15, in order of their rank, are Sweden, Norway, Iceland, the Netherlands, Denmark, Finland, New Zealand, Switzerland, Luxembourg, Australia, Canada, Ireland, Germany, Austria, and Spain. The 30 full democracies include about 17% of the world's countries and only 13% of the world's 7 billion people (2012 estimate). These top democracies are also the countries that have the lowest total crime rate, particularly the lowest homicide rate, in the world. In the top 15 countries, the homicide rate is less than 1.5 per 100,000 population (United Nations Office on Drugs and Crime, 2009). According to the EIU's Democracy Index, the top 14 authoritarian states include the African states of Chad, Mauritania, Egypt, Morocco, Rwanda, Burkina Faso, Nigeria, Niger, Angola, Algeria, Swaziland, Gabon, Zimbabwe, and Togo. These are also the countries that have the highest rates of homicide in the world. Their homicide rates are more than 20 per 100,000 population (United Nations Office on Drugs and Crime, 2009).

The relations between democracy and crime trends can also be understood in terms of the nature and extent of public corruption in a country. Transparency International, based in Berlin, Germany, and Global Integrity, based in Washington, D.C., are two of the major international research organizations that measure the growth of public corruption in all major countries. According to the Corruption Perceptions Index of 2009 published by Transparency International, the world's top 10 countries since 2002 that had the lowest rate of corruption include New Zealand, Denmark, Singapore, Sweden, Switzerland, Finland, the Netherlands, Australia, Iceland, and Norway. With the exception of Singapore, these countries are at the top of the EIU's Democracy Index.

Studies have also shown that public perceptions about crime and justice are strongly related to the progress of democracy. The people of a country with high crime and violence rates are more likely to have a low level of support and legitimacy for their progress (Perez, 2003). Democracy, in other words, cannot succeed in a country with high levels of crime, corruption, and violence. In a cross-national study conducted on the basis of 2003 data from Afrobarometer and Latinobarometer, Fernandez and Kuenzi (2006) found that victimization and perception of crime influence citizens' attitudes toward democracy. Analyzing data from four countries (Chile, Nicaragua, Nigeria, and Malawi), they observed that "a citizen's perception of public safety is as important [a] factor as any socio-economic variable in predicting support for and satisfaction with democracy" (p. ii). A report from the African Human Security Initiative (2009) similarly observed that the "Legitimacy of the legal system in Africa has become fundamental to the establishment of the rule of law and the resultant efficacy of regimes and criminal justice systems" (p. 3).

For the modernization theorists, cultural modernization is a precondition for economic and political modernization. A shift in core values, choices, and preferences related to a particular institution must precede structural and institutional changes and transformations. It is the framework of culture that binds a structure together. Democratic political institutions in a country are less likely to grow and evolve without a democratic political culture. Similarly, a modern institution of criminal justice, the modernization theorists would claim, cannot grow and evolve without developing a new set of core values about modern law and justice. The modernization theories thus bring three major analytical directions for comparative criminal justice: the effect of industrialization and urbanization on crime types and trends; the effect of political modernization and democracy on criminal justice; and the growth of cultural modernity in criminal justice. The focus of analysis is not on any particular society or on a particular country's system of criminal justice, but on the institutional and cultural processes of modernity in criminal justice among all of the world's societies. The modernization theory makes it imperative to examine how criminal justice systems of different countries grow and change in response to the choices and challenges of modernity (Shelley, 1981b).

■ Civilization Theories and Comparative Criminal Justice

The notion of civilization has been at the center of social science discourses since the birth of social science in the 19th century. Before the birth of modern states in the 18th century, civilization was the frame of reference for understanding different groups, races, cultures, and religions among the world's societies. Marx's study of British colonial rule in India and of the Asiatic Mode of Production; Comte's theory of the coming of an era of industrialism and the dominance of science; and Weber's study of the rise of modern capitalism and the nature of the world religions (Judaism, Hinduism, and Islam) were all conceptualized in the context of the rise and dynamics of modern Western civilization. The 195 countries of the present world belong to different civilizations that traveled different routes of social and political evolutions, and different trajectories of history.

The earliest human civilizations arose about 10,000 years ago with the invention of agriculture and rudimentary farming technology. Then civilizations spread into the river valleys of India, China, and Egypt. With the progress of civilization, there has been progress in human knowledge and technology and the modalities of culture. The earlier civilizations of Greece and Rome and the Islamic civilization of the 11th and 12th centuries not only created complex systems of law, bureaucracy, and governance, but also began the evolution of civilized human manners and behaviors. In the beginning of the 13th century, the dynamics of world civilization began to move to the West. The Renaissance in the 13th century, the Reformation in the 16th century, the growth of modern science in the 17th century, and the Age of Enlightenment in the 18th century created a unique civilization in the West. It is this unique civilization, as Weber claimed, that created the notions of a modern rational capitalist economy, a modern rational state, a modern system of rational law, a modern system of rational science, and a modern system of rational bureaucracy. A vast trajectory of modern social science theory has been in the direction of understanding the nature and peculiarities of modern Western civilization. With respect to the civilization frame of reference in comparative criminology and criminal justice, there are three competing perspectives, including the theory of the civilizing process developed and expanded by Norbert Elias (1939/1994), the theory of the clash of civilizations developed by Samuel Huntington (1996), and the theory of civilizational complexes and intercivilizational encounters developed by Benjamin Nelson (1981).

Theory of the Civilizing Process: Norbert Elias

Norbert Elias's theory of the civilizing process presents a broad macrohistorical perspective about the gradual decline of crime and violence in Western civilization (Fletcher, 1997). Elias theorized that the rise of modern states from the womb of the feudal absolutist monarchies is the reason crime and violence declined in most areas of Western civilization. He said that "a wealth of contemporary observations suggest that the structure of civilized behavior is closely interrelated with the organization of Western societies in the form of states" (1939/1994, p. xii). Modern states have a complete monopoly on using the physical force of violence in order to control and contain violence. His hypothesis is that crime and violence are more likely to decline with the birth of the modern state. In his view, in a modern state, "the whole apparatus which shapes individuals, the mode of operation of the social demands and prohibitions which mould their social habitus, and above all the kinds of fear that play a part in their lives are decisively changed" (Elias, Dunning, Goudsblom, & Mennell, 2000, p. xiii).

The modern states emerged, Elias further theorized, as a result of the evolution of civilizing processes—evolution in the manners and behaviors of people. He argued that with the growth of civilizing processes in the West, people internalized a sense of self-control. People learned to control impulsivity and to restrain what Freud called the blind forces of instinctual gratification (e.g., the Id). Social control became more a matter of self control. People had, in Elias's word, a *psychogenetic* evolution in manners and behaviors, and this affected the rate of violence in the whole civilization. He further theorized that with the development of civilizing processes, people also go through a process of "sociogenetic" transformations. Whereas the psychogenetic process involves the evolution of an internalized sense of social control (what Freud defined as the superego), the process of sociogenetic evolution, according to Elias, involves the birth of a shaming structure that defines the boundaries of morality and normative standards of behavior and decency in a society. Modern states emerged in the context of these dual civilizing processes of evolution in the behavior of people. As Elias said: "The sociogenetic and psychogenetic investigation sets out to reveal the order underlying historical changes, their mechanics and mechanisms" (Elias et al., 2000, p. xiii). He did not, however, claim that the Western "civilized mode of behavior is the most advanced of all human possible modes of behavior" (Elias et al., 2000, p. xiv). The core of his theory is that the control and containment of violence in a society must proceed with the progress of civilizing processes—strong states and social and psychological transformations in the manners and behaviors of people. With the progress of civilizing processes and the decline of violence, the modes and modalities of punishment are also likely to be civilized in nature.

A considerable number of studies in recent years have been conducted, particularly by historians of crime and justice, to examine Elias's thesis of civilizing processes in the context of the history of violence in Western civilization (Eisner, 2003; Fletcher, 1997; Gurr, 1981; Johnson & Monkkonen, 1996; Mennell, 2007; Monkkonen, 2006). In his study of the historical trends in violent crime in Europe, Gurr (1981) found that "typical [homicide] rates may have been about twenty homicides per 100,000 population in the High and late Middle ages, dropping to ten around 1600, and ending after an extended downsizing at about one in the twentieth century" (as quoted in Eisner, 2003, p. 84). Gurr claimed, as shown in **Box 2-1**, that this trend is a "manifestation of cultural change in Western society, especially [the] growing sensitization to violence and the development of increased internal and external control on aggressive behavior" (Gurr, 1981, p. 295, as quoted in Eisner, 2003, pp. 84–85).

Theory of Civilizational Clash: Samuel Huntington

Modernization theorists have a vision that the world under modernization will be increasingly homogenous in terms of its core values and institutions. The people of different countries will not be eating the same food, wearing the same kind of clothes, and believing in the same God, but they will be increasingly similar in their aspirations for liberal democracy, equality, individualism, and a system of justice compatible with human rights and dignity. After the Cold War, the proponents of modernization believed that the world had begun the construction of a liberal civilization of a global nature (Fukuyama, 1993). In the mid-1990s, when the democracy movement was swiftly engulfing the world and many were dreaming of a new world order of peace and progress for the world's societies, Harvard political scientist Samuel Huntington (1996) presented a new vision of conflict among the world's nations—a new paradigm of a clash of civilizations. He was not offering a theory on comparative criminal justice, but his theory of the clash of civilizations is relevant for any cross-national analysis of social and cultural institutions, particularly criminal justice, which is at the crossroads of a society's politics, ideology, faith, morality, and culture.

Huntington begins with the assumption that the unit of analysis for understanding changes and transformations in the world today is not a nation-state but a civilization. There are, in his view, eight major civilizations: Western, Chinese, Japanese, Hindu, Islamic, Orthodox (Russian), African, and Latin American. The world's nations are divided into these eight civilizations. Each of these civilizations is primarily, according to Huntington, a cultural entity that has grown over a long period of time. Each civilization has a culture that understands and interprets politics, authority, ideology, equality, freedom, law, and justice differently. Each civilization has a broad cultural perspective of what is moral and immoral, what is good and bad, and what is just and unjust. Each civilization is based on certain underlying moral and philosophical themes, thoughts, and ideologies that justify the way people do the things they do. There are some economic and technological similarities among these civilizations, yet culturally, Huntington believes, they are far apart. Some of these civilizations are becoming increasingly modern but not Western in cultural terms. There are major cultural differences, he claims, between the civilizations of the West and the rest, particularly between Islam and the West. Modernization will not result in a westernization

BOX 2-1

Global Homicide Rates and the Levels of Human and Economic Development

The 2011 *Global Study on Homicide: Trends, Contexts, Data* conducted by the United Nations Office on Drugs and Crime (UNODC) found that among the world's societies, violent crime and development are connected; violent crime retards human development and economic growth; and gender-based violence affects a large number of women around the world. The study observed that in some regions of the world, such as Central America, the rates and trends of violent crime are related to the rise of gangs, guns, drug trafficking, and other forms of transnational crime. In other regions, they are connected to family and intimate partner violence. In 2010, the highest numbers of homicides were found in the African region. Out of 468,000 homicides in 2010 in the world as whole, about 36% occurred in Africa, 31% in the Americas, 27% in Asia, 5% in Europe, and 1% in Oceania. Among the world regions, the highest rate of homicide was found in the African region. The average global rate of homicide was about 6.9 per 100,000 population. The average rate in the African region was about 17 per 100,000 population—more than double the global average. Since 1995, the homicide rate has consistently decreased in North America, Europe, and Asia, but it has alarmingly increased in Central America and the Caribbean region. The UNODC study confirmed the hypothesis that homicide rates and human and economic developments (i.e., advance of civilization) are connected, saying that high levels of homicides "are associated with low human and economic development. The largest shares of homicides occur in countries with low levels of human development, and countries with high levels of income inequality are afflicted by homicide rates almost four times higher than more equal societies. Homicide and property crime were affected by the global financial crisis of 2008/2009, with increases in homicides coinciding with drops in Gross Domestic Product (GDP)." The World Bank's *World Development Report 2011* similarly confirmed that high rates of homicides and low rates of economic growth are connected: "New poverty data reveal that poverty is declining for much of the world, but countries affected by violence are lagging behind. For every three years a country is affected by major violence (battle deaths or excess deaths from homicides equivalent to a major war), poverty reduction lags behind by 2.7 percentage points."

Source: United Nations Office on Drugs and Crime. (2010). *Global study of homicide: Trends, contexts, data.* Vienna, Austria: Author; The World Bank. (2012). *World development report 2011.* Washington, DC: Author.

of the rest of the world. Conflicts and clashes of ideas and ideologies between the West and the rest, and between Islam and the West are inevitable and unavoidable. Huntington says that the major origin of "conflict in this new world will not be primarily ideological or primarily economic. The great divisions among humankind and the dominating source of conflict will be cultural. The fault lines between civilizations will be battle lines of the future" (1993, p. 1).

In a cross-national analysis of crime and justice, there are many cultural issues that can be examined from the clash of civilizations theory. How and to what extent are ideas such as the rule of law, due process of law, equal justice, judicial independence, and protections against cruel and unusual punishment culturally valued and understood in different countries? How can these processes of modern criminal justice grow from within the cultural milieu of the countries under reform and transition? Why should some forms of facts and behaviors such as interpersonal violence, genital mutilation, child abuse, sexual harassment, or stalking be criminalized irrespective of the contexts of culture and civilization? How do modern ideas of reforming criminal justice conflict with those of indigenous cultures? Why are many international organizations becoming interested in revitalizing indigenous systems of community justice in many developing countries, particularly in Africa? Why do the Japanese have problems understanding Americans' fatal attraction to guns and the Second Amendment? Relatedly, why are Americans unable to comprehend how shaming can be such a strong force for social control in Japan? Why in many developing countries, even today, do people find it an act of supreme pleasure to participate in public lynching and vigilante justice? Huntington's theory of the clash of civilizations can help to frame many of these questions and issues that are at the core of comparative criminal justice.

Theory of Civilizational Complexes and Intercivilizational Encounters: Benjamin Nelson

Huntington gave us a theory that suggests using civilization as a frame of reference for the analysis of contemporary social and political events, including the problem of modernization in the world's societies. He claimed that the cultural boundaries of different civilizations are unique and that there are more differences than similarities among these civilizations, especially between the West and the rest. But Huntington gives us neither a theory about what a particular civilization possesses that contributes to its specific shape and specific boundaries of meaning and values, nor a theory about what is so unique to the West that renders it so incompatible with that of the rest. Benjamin Nelson's (1981) theory of civilizational complexes and intercivilizational encounters attempted to answer the questions about Huntington's theory. Nelson asked the same question that was at the core of the beginning of modern social science in the 19th century: Why did modernity come to the West and the West alone? Almost all civilizations had remarkable achievements in science, technology, art, literature, knowledge, and philosophy before the beginning of modernity in the 13th and 14th century. But still, why were the modern universalized notions of state, bureaucracy, science, law, and justice born only in the West? What was at the core of the cultural progress of Western civilization that gave its meaning and uniqueness as a universalizing civilization? Nelson theorized that a rationalization and universalization process remains at the core of Western civilization's progress. As Nelson noted, "From the twelfth century forward in western Europe, universalities and universalizations came to play an increasing part in all sorts of central settings and structures, especially in the most decisive spheres of theology, philosophy, law, and science" (1981, p. 8).

Nelson first begins his analysis with the development of the *structure of consciousness* concept. The structure of consciousness is at the core of the culture of a civilization.

The structure of consciousness is the totality of the moralities, logics, and rationalities that shape and drive human actions and that build the trajectories of symbolic culture and expression. What is the logic of reading the *Miranda* rights in a modern system of crime and justice? What is, for example, the logic of decriminalizing or criminalizing abortion? What is the logic of criminalizing marital rape? The culture of modern criminal justice can therefore be defined as a totality not just of some criminal laws and penal institutions, but also, at a higher level of generality, of the moralities, logics, and rationalities of some specific kinds of such laws and institutions. It is this totality of logics and rationalities that, according to Nelson, is the structure of consciousness. One needs to understand, Nelson argues, "what explains how people conduct and comport themselves; what explains the suppositions they apply in defining their patterns of interaction; what explains the ways in which they affiliate and organize [and] the way they map their world" (1981, p. 233).

Nelson described the following three structures of civilizational consciousness: "sacromagical" (type 1), faith (type 2), and rationalized (type 3). A civilization dominated by a sacromagical structure of consciousness is dedicated to preserving its collective harmony with utmost authoritative control on individuals. Its logic is the preservation of collective harmony and the collective consciousness. The ancient civilizations of China, India, Israel, Greece, and Rome, Nelson says, were based primarily on the sacromagical structure of consciousness. The faith-structures type of consciousness, according to Nelson, is primarily the structure of consciousness of the great world religions. It is also the consciousness of different mystical groups such as the Sufis of Islam. In Nelson's words: "The key to the faith-structures of consciousness is that individuals committed to faith feel themselves to be part of the truth, a manifestation of the divine in expression of the universal will or sovereign design" (1981, p. 95).

Civilization advances from one structure of consciousness to another, not primarily because of growth in the economy and technology, but, according to Nelson, because of certain historical predicaments—the turns and twists of history. This means that "people everywhere . . . inexorably find themselves in the midst of predicaments which call forth urgent responses in the way of passions, actions, efforts to achieve mastery and control through multiple forms of affiliation, organization, imposition, and imputation" (Nelson, 1981, p. 231).

Nelson subsequently theorized that only the Western civilization has been able to develop a rationalized and universalized structure of consciousness. The ancient civilizations of China, India, Israel, Greece, and Rome, and the early medieval civilization of Islam had the potential to evolve to a rationalized and universalized structure of consciousness. But it happened only in the West because of certain historical predicaments created by the Renaissance in the 14th century, the Reformation in the 16th century, the birth of modern science in the 17th century, the Age of Enlightenment in the 18th century, and the spread of industrialization in the 19th century. These historical events and movements created in the West a unique cultural perspective—a rationalized and universalized structure of consciousness—that is not seen as a dominant feature of any other civilization in the world. This rationalized and universalized structure of consciousness embodies the logic of modern science; a modern sense of humanity, of a rational state, and of secularism; and a modern notion of individualism, of natural law, and of a rational system of law and justice.

It is in the sense of the structure of consciousness that Nelson used the concepts of civilizational complexes and intercivilizational encounters. The concept of civilizational complexes implies the existence of multiple structures of consciousness within the bounds of a civilization. In the West, the modern rationalized structure of consciousness is dominant, but there also exist other structures of consciousness (sacromagical and faith-structure consciousness) that compete and conflict with the dominant structure of consciousness. Competing and conflicting structures of consciousness—competing and conflicting moralities and logics of action—are also seen in other civilizations. With the progress of modernization, the rationalized and universalized structure of consciousness has been spreading in the civilizations of the non-West. The intercivilizational encounters began during the days of colonialism and produced intense intracivilizational debates and disputes about competing logics and rationalities of actions and expressions in all domains of life, including law and justice. In Nelson's view, the progress of modernization in any social and cultural sphere of a civilization can be understood by examining the debates and disputes that are expressed about the competing structures of consciousness. Nelson did not elaborate on his views of modernization in developing countries, but made some intriguing observations. He said that the developing countries "will not find it possible or desirable to preserve order or create newer civilizational cultural structures . . . . The new nations are unlikely to have structures defending the judicial rights of individuals, whoever they may be, against the powers of government" (Nelson, 1973, p. 102).

The theories of the civilizing process by Elias, the clash of civilizations by Huntington, and civilizational complexes and intercivilizational encounters by Nelson are macrohistorical perspectives about the nature and complexity of modernity and modern social, economic, and cultural institutions. What is common to all three perspectives is the notion that institutions of modernity, including law and justice, developed in the West, but they developed with the universalized logics and rationalities that are applicable to all of humanity, not just the humanity of the West. The process of modernization therefore is a process of the globalization of modernity, and it is an irreversible process of change and transformation in the whole world. But the universalizing logics and rationalities of modern institutions are not easily compatible with those of the countries belonging to other civilizations. For cross-national analyses in criminal justice, therefore, it is imperative to examine the logics and rationalities of different systems of law and justice in different countries, and the debates and disputes that arise in the context of their modernization.

■ World-Systems Theory and Comparative Criminal Justice

The modernization and civilization theories are primarily cultural in nature. They applied to the distinct nature and evolution of modern culture in the West and presented a cultural analysis of the problem of modernization. The world-systems theory, developed by Immanuel Wallerstein (1979), is based on an economic analysis of the problem of culture and modernization. It is based on the premise that all societies and regions of the world presently belong to a single world system of capitalism—a capitalist world economy (Wallerstein, 2000). The modern capitalist world economy, which has been spreading in Europe, in Wallerstein's views, since the 16th century, presently engulfs the whole world. Today, the economic production structure and the division of labor in all the world's societies and regions are formed and shaped by the logics and necessities of the world capitalist economy. In countries such as Sri Lanka, Cambodia, and Bangladesh, for example, women are working in garment factories and sweatshops because these countries are now producing for the world market. There is now a global market for all commodities, and all countries are fiercely competing to participate in the global market.

The Analytical Framework and Key Hypotheses

The proponents of world-systems theory claim that in social science, the unit of analysis is no longer a particular country, society, or civilization. The world capitalist system should be the unit of analysis and frame of reference in intersocietal and intercivilizational analysis of development and modernization. The political, legal, and cultural dynamics of the world's societies are shaped and framed by their specific location in the capitalist world economy (Chase-Dunn & Grimes, 1995). The world system of capitalism is asymmetrical. There is a capitalist core comprised of countries of the developed world, including the United States, Canada, Germany, France, and Japan. A large number of countries in Asia, Africa, and Latin America belong to the periphery of the world capitalist system. A sizable number of countries also belong to the semiperiphery of the world system. These are the newly industrialized countries of Asia and the Pacific and Latin America, including South Korea, Singapore, Taiwan, Thailand, Mexico, Argentina, and Brazil. World-systems theorists would include China, India, and Russia in the semiperiphery of the world capitalist economy.

World-systems theorists hypothesized that countries that belong to the peripheries are more likely to be economically exploited by the countries at the core of the capitalist world economy. A process of unequal exchange within the world economy is at the core of capital accumulation on a global scale. Because of the process of unequal exchange, the countries in the peripheries are structurally constrained to pursue economic production in terms of their own goals and necessities. The core countries control the ability of the peripheral countries to access the global market and high technology. Uneven development is an endemic feature of the modern world capitalist system (Goldfrank, 2000).

It is through this notion of the inevitability of uneven development that the world-systems theory becomes relevant for cross-national analysis of crime and justice. The uneven development and exploitation of the peripheries are more likely to be associated with social disorganization, anomie, urban poverty, income inequality, discrimination, and deprivation—the factors that are strongly correlated with high levels of crime and violence. One of the major contributions of the world-systems theory is that it presents a perspective that suggests that a country's microsocietal issues, such as crime and justice, must be examined in the context of its larger economic status and location within the world system. Economic context has always been one of the central analytical directions in understanding the causes of crime, as well as crime trends and patterns. Social disorganization theory (Shaw & McKay, 1969), anomie theory, institutional anomie theory, strain theory (Agnew, 1992; Cloward & Ohlin, 1960), and critical theory (Quinney, 2001) are all economy oriented in explaining crime trends and patterns. Many of these traditional theories of criminology explain the economic context of crime in terms of industrialization, urbanization, poverty, unemployment, income inequality, and economic deprivation. These traditional theories, however, do not present a perspective on how economic contexts can be integrated within a broader framework of cross-national analysis. World-systems theory presents an argument that the effect of industrialization, urbanization, social disorganization, and social class and power on crime and criminality across nations can be more systematically examined in the context of the nature and dynamics of the world capitalist economy.

Crime Trends in the Core and the Peripheries

From 1980 to about 2008—for almost 3 decades—the world economy consistently expanded. The countries of the peripheries and semiperipheries became more integrated in the world economy in terms of international trade, private capital flow, and foreign direct investment from the core countries. "From 1980 through 2007, the world's financial assets—including equities, private and public debt, and bank assets—nearly quadrupled in size relative to world gross product (WGP). Similarly, global capital flows surged" (United Nations Organization, 2010, p. 76). The annual average net private capital flows to developing countries in 1996–1999, for example, was $120 billion. It increased to $403 billion in 2008. In Africa, the average annual net private capital flows in 1996–1999 was $5.3 billion. It increased to $15.3 billion in 2008. In East Asia and South Asia, annual average net private capital flows in 1996–1999 was $30.3 billion. It increased to $160.8 billion in 2007. In Latin America and the Caribbean, the annual average net private capital flows in 1996–1999 was $68 billion. In 2007, it increased to $112.2 billion. In the transitional economies of Eastern Europe and the Baltic Republic, the annual average net private capital flows in 1996–1999 was $1.6 billion. In 2007, it increased to $142.5 billion (United Nations Organization, 2010). New research has shown that with the advance of the world capitalist economy, the total crime rate has increased. During the same time period (1980–2008) of the rapidly expanding world economy, a United Nations study showed that "total recorded crime increased from 2300 to 3000 crimes for every 100,000 people" (UN-HABITAT, 2007, p. xvvii). The total reported crime rate, however, increased in the peripheral economies of Asia, Africa, and Latin America, although it declined in the core countries of North America. The 2007 UN-HABITAT report found that "In North America and Western Europe total crimes rates fell significantly over the two decades whereas in Latin America and the Caribbean, Eastern Europe, and Africa, total crime rates increased" (p. xvvii).

Crime Trends in the World System of Capitalism: Some Empirical Evidence

Research has shown that many countries of the periphery, which are becoming rapidly integrated into the world system in terms of trade and business, are also the countries that have a higher level of economic crime and corruption. The top 11 exporters of services among developing countries from 1990 to 2008 included (according to their rank in 2008) China, India, Hong Kong, Singapore, South Korea, Taiwan, Thailand, Turkey, Malaysia, Brazil, and Mexico. During the same period, crime rates rapidly increased in all these countries. Crimes rates also increased in countries that are at the bottom of the peripheries but are desperately trying to participate in the world economy. Cambodia, for example, is one of the Asian countries that is becoming rapidly integrated into the world system through its manufacturing and export of garments. One of the International Labour Organization's (2010) studies shows that garment "exports [from Cambodia] grew from nothing in 1994 to $1.9 billion in 2004. Roughly, two-thirds of sales are to the United States, and most of the remainder to the European Union" (2010, p. 1). The report also noted, "Garments make up almost 80 percent of all of Cambodia's exports, and almost 66 percent of its manufacturing workforce" (2010, p. 1). During the same period, crime and corruption rapidly increased in Cambodia. According to Transparency International's Corruption Perceptions Index of 2008, Cambodia ranks 166 out of 180 countries included in the survey. According to Transparency International's Global Corruption Barometer of 2009, Cambodia is one of the countries in Asia where people perceive that their public officials and civil servants (scores 3.5 out of 5, with 5 being extremely corrupt) and the judiciary (4.0 out 5) are highly corrupt. Similar inverse relations between a country's economic performance within the world system and its level of crime and corruption exist for many countries belonging to the peripheries and the regions that are in transition to market economies. In comparative criminal justice, an analysis of how a country's poverty (see **Box 2-2**), income, unemployment, and other economic conditions are affected by its location in the world system, and how these conditions generate social disorganization, unequal power relations, strains, and many challenges for criminal justice, has a great import.

■ Globalization Theory and Comparative Criminal Justice

Globalization theory is a perspective that integrates the key ideas of modernization theory, civilization theory, and world-systems theory into a single framework of analysis of the contemporary world. Modernization theory explains the nature of modernity and its worldwide expansion, particularly from European to non-European societies. It presents a sense that the countries and cultures of many civilizations are the passive and uncritical receptors of modernity. The modernization theorists, many critics argue, do not adequately recognize the strength and versatilities of the people, language, culture, and philosophy of the societies yet to embark on a journey to modernity. Civilization theories describe the uniqueness of the West's culture as a crucial divide between the West and the rest. Norbert Elias theorized this in terms of the rise of modern states and the concomitant social and psychological transformations in the minds of western individuals. Benjamin Nelson explained it in terms of the rational and universalized structure of consciousness. World-systems theory conceptualized

BOX 2-2

A Lost Decade in the Fight Against Poverty

During the last decade, the global trade and the world economy had rapidly expanded around the world. Today, there is hardly any country in the world that is not a part of the global economy in some way or another. But this progress of the global economy has not been associated with concomitant progress in the reduction of global poverty. The World Bank's *World Development Report 2000–2001*, the United Nations Development Programme's (UNDP's) *Human Development Report 2005*, the United Nations report on *the World Social Situation 2011*, and a number of other global reports and studies have shown that global poverty is on the rise. The World Bank's data show that in 1990, there were about 1.9 billion people in the developing world who lived on $1.25 a day. In 2008, the number increased to about 1.29 billion. The World Bank's *World Development Report 2000–2001: Attacking Poverty: Opportunity, Empowerment, and Security* found that during the time of rapid development of wealth for many countries, about 2.8 billion people in the world, mostly from the developing world, lived on $2 a day, and about 1.2 billion lived on $1 a day. According to a World Bank study published in 2002, "The richest 50 million people in Europe and North America have the same income as 2.7 billion poor people" (Milanovic, 2002). The UNDP's 2005 report *Human Development Reports 2005: International cooperation at a crossroads: Aid, trade and security in an unequal world* reported that income inequality is highest (Gini coefficients above 50) in the countries of Latin America and sub-Saharan Africa. (These are also the regions with high levels of homicides.) The report further observed: "Of the 73 countries for which data are available, 53 (with more than 80% of the world's population) have seen inequality rise, while only 9 (with 4% of the population) have seen it narrow." The United Nations report *World Social Situation 2011: The Global Social Crisis* warned that pursuing economic policies without any regard to the reduction of poverty and improvement in social situations could lead major crises. The report said: "It is essential that Governments take into account the likely social implications of their economic policies . . . economic policies considered in isolation from their social outcomes can have dire consequences for poverty, employment, nutrition, health and education, which, in turn, adversely affect long-term sustainable development. The disconnect between economic policies and their social consequences can create a vicious circle of slow growth and poor social progress."

Source: Milanovic, B. (2002, January). True world income distribution, 1988 and 1993: First calculation based on household surveys alone. *The Economic Journal, 112,* 51–92 (published for The World Bank); United Nations, Department of Economic and Social Affairs. (2011). *World social situation 2011: The global social crisis.* New York, NY: Author; United Nations Development Programme. (2006). *Human development reports 2005: International cooperation at a crossroads: Aid, trade and security in an unequal world.* New York, NY: Author; The World Bank. (2000–2001). *World development report 2000-2001: Attacking poverty: Opportunity, empowerment, and security.* Washington, DC: Author.

the world in terms of the world capitalist economy, but kept the whole trajectory of human culture out of its analytical scope. Civilization theorists presented a unidirectional analysis of the contemporary world and did not adequately theorize about the inner strength and dynamism of other cultures and civilizations and their contributions to the creation of modern science, art, music, literature, language, architecture, law, and philosophy. Confucianism, Hinduism, Buddhism, and Sufism are just some examples, without which an understanding of the modern philosophy of rationalism or objectivism is bound to remain incomplete.

The Analytical Framework and Key Hypotheses

Globalization theory is an analytical framework within which all countries, cultures, and civilizations, as well as their contemporary journeys toward economic and cultural modernity, can be examined in terms of the effect of both global and local peculiarities. The theory of globalization becomes relevant in comparative criminal justice because of its wider analytical scope of examining the connectivity between crime, law, and justice, and the vicissitudes of the modern world economy and culture. The core of the globalization idea is the notion of connectivity among the world's nations and civilizations. The process of globalization, in fact, has brought a new dimension in our approach to comparative criminology and criminal justice. "Traditional comparative criminology focused on the comparison of isolated and self-contained cultures and arrangements. However, globalization has altered states of isolation and self-containment to produce spheres of interaction. That provides a challenge to the comparative method" in cross-national analyses of crime and justice (Pakes, 2010, p. 17). There have always been some forms of economic, political, and cultural connectivity among the world's nations and civilizations. But globalization has been emerging as a major transformative force in the modern world, particularly since the spread of colonialism in the 17th and 18th centuries (Lechner & Boli, 2000; Nandi & Shahidullah, 1998; Waters, 1995). Colonialism was not only a process of economic and political domination of the colonized countries, but also a process of creating new structures and new cultures of intercivilizational connectivity—a global process of modernization. Globalization theorists claim that modernization is irreversible and bound to be global (Giddens, 1991). However, the contemporary globalization process, with a new sense of meaning and expression and an unprecedented degree of intense connectivity among the world's nations, has been emerging only since the end of the Cold War in the mid-1980s.

In the context of a cross-national analysis of crime, law, and justice, three hypotheses of globalization theory need to be explored. The first is the hypothesis of world-systems theory, which is that the world's societies are increasingly becoming a part of the modern world capitalist economy, which is increasingly becoming global and integrated. For comparative criminal justice in this context, it is important to explore whether the integration within the global economy is related to a low or high rate of crime. What are the rates and trends of crimes in the countries that are more highly or more loosely connected to the global economy? How did the global economy affect global poverty and global socioeconomic conditions, particularly in the cities that are the centers of global economic activities? Is the increasing expansion of the global economy related to the contemporary rise of transnational organized crime and, if so, how?

The second hypothesis of globalization theory is about political globalization—increasing demand for sustainable development, human security, democracy, human rights, equal justice, and transparent governance all over the world. Because of political globalization, nation-states are being increasingly challenged by transnational issues (Waters, 1995). These transnational economic and political issues are being increasingly addressed by and within international and regional political organizations such as the United Nations (UN), European Union (EU), World Trade Organization (WTO), Association of Southeast Asian Nations (ASEAN), Organization of African Unity (OAU), Inter-American Development Bank (IDB), Organization of Islamic Cooperation (OIC), South Asian Association for Regional Cooperation (SAARC), and Gulf Cooperation Council (GCC). The idea of political globalization is the spread of choice, challenges, and possibilities of liberal democracy in the world's societies. For comparative criminal justice in this context, it is important to explore the challenges that nation-states are facing because of the spread of a new notion of political culture. How are the global ideas of human rights, human security, and governance affecting criminal justice reforms in societies around the world? How are the rise of global organized crimes and transnational organized crime groups shaping and constraining the nature and performance of criminal justice systems in the world's societies? How are transnational organized crime groups affecting the nature and progress of worldwide democracy? These and many other related questions can form a vital research agenda for comparative criminal justice.

The third hypothesis is about cultural globalization. A group of globalization theorists claim that globalization is essentially a cultural process (Featherstone, 1990; Robertson, 1992). It is a process of the emergence of a new global culture that is emerging not merely because of the diffusion of Western culture, but also the globalization of the culture of all countries and civilizations into a new form of symbolism and expression. This new global culture is emerging as a result of the global cross-fertilization of the ideas and creativity of all peoples and cultures in the realm of knowledge, technology, art, music, literature, language, and philosophy. Cultural globalization is also seen as the progress of modernization at a global scale—the progress of what Norbert Elias called a civilizing process and Benjamin Nelson described as the advance of a universalized and rationalized structure of consciousness. The advance of global culture has broken the boundaries between universalism and particularism, society and community, and formal and informal rules and expressions (Waters, 1995). The advance of global culture has created a new sense of understanding, empathy, and reflexivity about different cultures and civilizations. People are not rejecting the legacy of traditional culture in the name of modernity, but rather are in the process of globalizing the locality and localizing the globality (Robertson, 1992). A new sense of reflexivity about local and global cultures is one of the defining features of contemporary globalization (Giddens, 1991). The expansion of global culture is not merely the expansion of Western culture. As Nobel Laureate Amartya Sen says, "To see globalization as merely Western imperialism of ideas and beliefs (as the rhetoric often suggests) would be a serious and costly error" (2000, p. 17).

The Extent and the Intensity of Globalization

Since the beginning of the 1990s, the rise of modern information technology, the birth of a knowledge economy, and the rapid expansion of the Internet around the world have been creating a new virtual global culture characterized by intense curiosity about human acts and creations in different lands and civilizations. Statistics show that the number of Internet users in the world between 2000 and 2010 increased 440.8%. During the same period, the number of users grew 2,357.3% in Africa, 621.8% in Asia, 352.0% in Europe, 1,825.3% in the Middle East, 143.3% in North America, and 1032.8% in Latin America and the Caribbean (Internet World Stats, 2010). The world's Internet penetration rates in 2010 were 77.4% for North America, 61.3% for Oceania and Australia, 58.4% for Europe, 34.5% for Latin America and the Caribbean, 29.8% for the Middle East, 21.5% for Asia, and 10.8% for Africa (Internet World Stats, 2010). In 2010, the ratio of Facebook users in relation to the total number of Internet users was highest in North America (56.0%) followed by Oceania and Australia (54.5%), the Caribbean (39.0%), Latin America (35.0%), Europe (34.1%), the Middle East (18.5%), Africa (15.9%), and Asia (11.3%). About 162.1 million people in Europe, 149.1 million in North America, 93.6 million in Asia, and 68.2 million in Latin America were regular users of Facebook in 2010 (Internet World Stats, 2010). About 90% of the user traffic for the Internet and other telecommunication devices in the world today is done through the use of submarine cables that connect the world through the oceans (United Nations Environmental Programme's World Conservation Monitoring Centre, 2009). The fiber-optic highway is the critical infrastructure of globalization. "Today more than a million kilometres of state-of-the art submarine fibre-optic cables span the oceans, connecting continents, islands, and countries around the world" (Thiaw, Hutton, & Green, 2009, p. 3). It is on the basis of these modern information and communication technologies that the world is economically, politically, and culturally becoming a single global planet of diverse countries, cultures, and civilizations—a planet in which goods, people, ideas, and cultures travel (Zwingle, 1999) with a speed and intensity never seen in any other period of human history, creativity, and achievement. The social scientists therefore describe globalization as an irreversible process of changes and transformations. Globalization is not a matter of choice; it is a stark reality of progress in the present world of the 21st century.

The Effect of Globalization on Criminal Justice

As a result of globalization, the nature and dynamics of economics, politics, and culture of the world's societies are not only rapidly changing, but also being increasingly challenged to change (Nelken, 2011; Sheptycki & Wardack, 2005). In the area of law and justice, political and cultural modernization has had many positive effects. The countries are being increasingly challenged to modernize their criminal justice in ways that are compatible with the global values of democracy, human rights, human security, and equal justice. Within the global culture of human rights and equal justice, the practice of a barbaric and medieval system of criminal justice has no legitimacy. The punishment of public executions for homosexuality and widespread tortures by religious police in Iran; execution by beheading in Saudi Arabia; caning in Singapore; and stoning to death for the crimes of rape and adultery in Pakistan and Afghanistan are today widely condemned. This condemnation by world opinion comes not only from the West but also from the East. The crimes of genital mutilation and Albino killing in Africa, honor killings in the Middle East, and the practice of extrajudicial killings by a militarized police force in many countries of Africa and Asia are seen as major aberrations in the global system of law and justice. The nation-states within global politics and global culture will be increasingly challenged to modernize their systems of law and criminal justice as a part of their global vision of transition to democracy.

The problem of the effect of economic globalization on crime and justice, however, is more complex. Economic globalization has brought positive changes for some countries in the world in terms of industrialization, urbanization, increased participation of women in the workforce, scientific and technological development, increased labor productivity, growth of the private sector, and growth in income and employment. These effects, however, have remained highly asymmetrical among the world's nations. What is more alarming is that, as indicated earlier, economic globalization in many countries has produced high levels of crime and violence, particularly in urban areas. It has also brought, as shown in **Box 2-3**, a new generation of global crimes and created a new breed of transnational organized crime groups. The growth in urban crime and violence and the rise of global crimes in the context of economic globalization is a big puzzle that demands an analysis in comparative criminal justice.

The UN-HABITAT's *Global Report on Human Settlements 2007: Enhancing Urban Safety and Security* found that urban crime has risen in countries that experienced rapid economic growth since the late 1970s. The study found that in "Latin America . . . the rapidly expanding metropolitan areas of Rio de Janeiro, Sao Paulo, Mexico City, and Caracas account for over of half of the violent crimes in their respective countries" (UN-HABITAT, 2007, p. xxvii). The study also found that in "Africa, cities such as Lagos, Johannesburg, Cape Town, Durban, and Nairobi account for a sizeable proportion of their nation's crime. Urban areas in Africa also have the highest reported level of burglary" (UN-HABITAT, 2007, p. xxviii). The UN-HABITAT's report (2009), *Urban Safety and Poverty in Asia and the Pacific*, indicated that about 35 million people in the Indian cities of "Delhi, Mumbai and Bangalore together accounted for more than one third of all crimes" (p. 13). The report further stated that Delhi, the capital of India, "records the highest in crimes against women. Delhi is the most crime prone city with 51,010 cases (comprising both economic and non-economic offences) . . . Mumbai, with 31,432 cases, took the second spot followed by Hyderabad (29,355), and Bangalore (29,042)" (p. 13).

The last 3 decades of rapid globalization has also seen the rapid development of a new generation of global crimes and transnational organized crime groups. A report from the United Nations Office on Drugs and Crime recognized that "as globalization has expanded

BOX 2-3

Globalization of Crime: A Transnational Organized Crime Threat Assessment

The progress in the globalization of the world economy, the rise and expansion of the new information and communication technology, and the new "openness to the West" that came in the wake of the Cold War in the mid-1980s, created an intense process of globalization and connectivity between and among the world's societies. The process of globalization created unprecedented opportunities for social and economic progress, the advancement of global science and technology, and the development and strengthening of the rule of law and democratic political orders for all societies of the world. But with the progress of globalization, there also emerged a new generation of transnational criminal groups and gangs in almost all regions of the world. By the end of the 1990s, such global crimes as drug trafficking, human trafficking, money laundering, sex trade, cyber crime, and illegal trading of conventional weapons became major concerns for further advancement of globalization. In Latin America and the Caribbean region, drug cartels and criminal gangs are spreading violence and corruption; in Central Africa and South Asia, insurgents and organized criminal groups are engaged in fueling and exporting global terrorism; in Southeast Asia, criminal groups have created a new world of sex trade and sex tourism and are exporting their services to Europe and North America; in Western Africa, Eastern Europe, and Latin America, a new age of modern slavery has emerged through the smuggling of migrants and the trafficking of women and children; a new band of young and educated cyber criminals has been continuously threatening to disrupt, damage, and destroy the world's "information superhighway;" and there is a new age of piracy rapidly emerging in the Horn of Africa. The transnational organized crime groups are threats not only for the rise of crime and corruptions, but also for the diminution of the progress of democracy and the rule of law around the world. The 2010 report produced by the United Nations Office on Drugs and Crime, *The Globalization of Crime: A Transnational Organized Crime Threat Assessment*, rightly asserted that "Globalization has progressed faster than our collective ability to regulate it, and it is in the unregulated areas created by this disjuncture that organized crime opportunities have grown. Bringing the rule of law to the international flow of goods and services is essential if the problems of organized crime are to be uprooted."

Source: United Nations Office on Drugs and Crime. (2010). *The globalization of crime: A transnational organized crime threat assessment.* Vienna, Austria: Author.

international trade, so the range of organized crime activities has broadened and diversified" (United Nations Office on Drugs and Crime, 2010a, p. 1).

With the progress of economic globalization, the illegal drug trade, global sex trade, trafficking of women and children, illegal trading of conventional weapons, money laundering, maritime piracy, and crimes in cyberspace have rapidly increased all over the world (United Nations Office on Drugs and Crime, 2010b). Cross-national analysis of the extent and intensity of transnational organized crimes; the nature and the characteristics of different transnational organized crime groups; the effect of transnational organized crime activities on national economy, politics, and culture; and the evolving nature of national laws and strategies to combat transnational organized crime are vitally important in comparative criminal justice.

■ Summary

The core of comparative criminal justice is the analysis of why the nature of crime and criminality and the institutions of criminal justice vary widely among the world's societies. Comparative criminal justice is also the analysis of similarities in crime trends and patterns and in criminal justice systems of different countries. There are four theoretical perspectives that are relevant for cross-national analysis of crime and justice. These perspectives are modernization theory, civilization theory, world-systems theory, and globalization theory. These theories are different from traditional theories of criminology such as social disorganization theory, anomie theory, strain theory, differential association, developmental criminology, rational choice theory, and critical theory. Theories of modernization, civilization, world systems, and globalization are primarily macrohistorical and macrostructural in nature. They help to conceptualize and analyze the intersocietal issues in crime and justice from the broader perspective of historical, social, economic, political, and cultural changes and transformations. Through these macrohistorical and macrostructural perspectives, we are able to understand the similarities and differences not just in crime trends and patterns but also in the nature and evolution of criminal justice in the world's societies (see **Table 2-1**).

Modernization theory suggests that cross-national analyses of crime and justice need to be pursued in the broader context of modernization—a process of change in societies from tradition to modernity. In the beginning of modernization, because of sudden economic and social dislocations associated with industrialization and urbanization, crime is likely to increase. But as industrialization and democracy mature, the crime rate is more likely to decrease, and crime trends are more likely to stabilize. Modernization in criminal justice means an increase in adaptive capability. It is more likely to grow with the institutionalization of the rule of law, democracy, and the due process of law; the increasing autonomy of the system of criminal justice (i.e., away from politics and religion); the growth of professionalization in law and legal practice; and the increased use of modern science and technology.

The civilization theory presents three different ways to conceptualize intersocietal relations with respect to crime and justice. The theory of the civilizing process developed by Norbert Elias presents an argument that with the birth of modern nation-states in Europe—the states that had a complete monopoly on using law and physical force—crime and violence significantly declined. The birth of nation-states and concomitant social and psychological changes in manners and behaviors of people in Europe were associated with the rise of new civilizing processes, which contributed to a sharp decline of crime and violence in Europe.

TABLE 2-1 Theoretical Perspectives in Comparative Criminal Justice

Theories	Assumptions and Hypotheses	Relevance to Comparative Criminal Justice
Modernization theory Economic modernization Political modernization Cultural modernization	Modernization and industrialization are connected; modernization and urbanization are connected; modernization and democracy are connected; and modernization and cultural change are connected.	Crime rates and patterns are connected to industrialization; crime rates and patterns are connected to urbanization; and crime rates and patterns are connected to political modernization.
Civilization theory Civilizing process Civilizational clash Civilizational complexes and intercivilizational encounters	The nation-states belong to different civilizations; different civilizations have different cultures; civilizations differ in logic, morality, and action; and Western civilization is based on rationalized and universalized structure of consciousness.	Civilizing processes and crime control are connected; crime control and strong states are connected; Western values of organizing criminal justice may not be compatible with those of other civilizations; and cross-national analyses of criminal justice must study intercivilizational debates and disputes related to modernization in criminal justice
World-systems theory	The world's societies belong to a single world capitalist system; within the world capitalist system, some countries belong to the core, some belong to the semiperiphery, and some belong to the periphery; and the countries belonging to the world capitalist system are characterized by asymmetrical economic relations.	Poverty and social economic dislocations are more likely to be endemic in the countries belonging to the periphery of the world economy; and crime rates are more likely to be higher in the peripheries.
Globalization theory Economic globalization Political globalization Cultural globalization	The world's societies are economically, politically, and culturally increasingly connected; globalization is an expansion of the process of modernization on a global scale; globalization is an irreversible process of change; the world's societies are being increasingly challenged by economic globalization; political globalization brings new challenges for traditional and authoritarian political regimes; and cultural globalization is universalizing the values of modernity related to individualism, human rights, equality, freedom, justice, and democracy.	Economic globalization has increased urban poverty; urban poverty is related to the rise of urban crime and violence; economic globalization is also related to the rise of many global crimes; political and cultural globalization demands modern reforms in criminal justice compatible with the notions of human rights, human security, and due of process law.

In his theory of the clash of civilizations, Huntington claims that the culture and the institutional nature of Western civilization are qualitatively different from those of other non-Western civilizations. Western civilization's conceptions of law, morality, and justice are fundamentally different from other civilizations. A cross-national understanding of crime and justice, from the perspective of the clash of civilizations, needs to be based on a broader understanding of the nature and peculiarities of respective civilizations. Benjamin Nelson theorizes that Western civilization is characterized by the dominance of a rationalized and universalized structure of consciousness rooted in the cultural and philosophical ideas of the Renaissance, Reformation, and Age of Enlightenment. Because of its rationalized and universalized structure of consciousness, Western civilization is bound to expand to other civilizations and create foci of cultural conflicts, debates, and disputes. From this perspective, what is thus imperative in comparative criminal justice is to understand and examine those intercivilizational debates and disputes with respect to crime, law, and justice.

According to world-systems theory, one of the dominant characteristics of the world's societies today is that they all belong to a modern world capitalist economy. Within the world capitalist economy, however, all countries do not have the same level of development. The countries at the peripheries of the world capitalist system are more likely to be in poverty and experience various forms of economic and social dislocations. They are also more likely to have higher levels of crime and violence. Globalization theory presents a more integrative perspective by combining some of the core ideas of the theories of modernization, civilization, and the world systems. Globalization theory presents a perspective that the world's societies are increasingly becoming a single world community—a community that is economically, politically, culturally, and psychologically connected. Within the world's community of nations, in terms of law and justice, it is imperative for nation-states to adhere to a set of global norms and values about human rights, democracy, and due process of law. The process of economic globalization, however, is associated with the rise of urban crimes in many countries and the growth of a new generation of global crimes and transnational organized crime groups. From the perspective of globalization, comparative criminal justice needs to examine how globalization is affecting crime rates and types in different countries, as well as the challenges of changes and reforms inherent in the modernization of their systems of criminal justice.

■ Discussion Questions

1. What are the key hypotheses of modernization theory? Discuss in this context the relations between crime and industrialization, citing examples from China and the countries of Eastern Europe that embarked on a transition to a market economy after the Cold War in the middle of the 1980s.

2. Examine the hypothesis of modernization theory related to crime and democracy. Discuss and examine in this context some of the empirical studies on crime and democracy connections, citing examples from North America, Western Europe, Asia, Latin America, and the Caribbean.

3. What are the key arguments of Norbert Elias's civilizing process theory? How is Elias's theory of civilizing process different from Samuel Huntington's theory of the clash of civilizations? Explain how the theories of a civilizing process and the clash of civilizations can be significant and meaningful in cross-national analyses of crime, law, and justice. Give examples.

4. What are the major arguments in Benjamin Nelson's theory of civilizational complexes and intercivilizational encounters? What are the issues in cross-national analyses of criminal justice that would be significant to explore from the perspective of the civilizational complexes and intercivilizational encounters theory? Discuss and examine in this context some of the contemporary intercivilizational debates and disputes related to crime and justice in the developing world.

5. What does it mean to say that all the world's nations today belong to a single world capitalist system? What are the key arguments of world-systems theory, and how can those arguments be applied in cross-national analyses of crime and justice? Give examples of crime rates and trends from some of the countries belonging to the core and some of the countries belonging to the peripheries of the world economy. (Hint: Compare homicide rates between a selected set of core and peripheral countries as defined by world-systems theory.)

6. How is globalization theory related to the theories of modernization, civilization, and world systems? Describe in this context the effect of economic globalization on urban crime in Asia and the Pacific based on the UN-HABITAT's 2009 report, *Urban Safety and Poverty in Asia and the Pacific*.

7. What does it mean to say that nation-states belonging to the modern world of globalization are being challenged not just by the rise of new crimes but also by new demands to change and reform their criminal justice systems in terms of the international standards of human rights, justice, and equality? (Apply your understanding of the theories of modernization, civilization, and globalization to discuss and examine this question.)

■ References

African Human Security Initiative. (2009). *The theory and practice of criminal justice in Africa* (Monograph No. 161). Addis Ababa, Ethiopia: Institute of Security Studies.

Agnew, R. (1992). Foundation for a general strain theory of crime and delinquency. *Criminology*, *30*(1), 47–87.

Arthur, J. (2002). Development and crime in Africa: A test of modernization theory. *Journal of Criminal Justice*, *19*(5), 499–513.

Chase-Dunn, C., & Grimes, P. (1995). World-systems analysis. *Annual Review of Sociology*, *21*, 387–417.

Cloward, R., & Ohlin, L. (1960). *Delinquency and opportunity*. New York, NY: Free Press.

Durkheim, E. (1951). *Suicide*. New York, NY: Free Press. (Original work published 1897.)

Durkheim, E. (1964). *The division of labor in society*. New York, NY: Free Press. (Original work published 1893.)

Durkheim, E. (1964). *The rules of sociological method*. New York, NY: Free Press. (Original work published 1895.)

Eisner, M. (2003). *Long-term historical trends in violent crime*. Chicago, IL: The University of Chicago Press.

Elias, N. (1994). *The civilizing process: Sociogenetic and psychogenetic investigations*. Oxford, England: Blackwell Publishers Ltd. (Original work published 1939.)

Elias, N., Dunning, E., Goudsblom, J., & Mennell, S. (2000). *The civilizing process: Sociogenetic and psychogenetic investigations.* Oxford, England: Blackwell Publishers Ltd.

Etzioni, A. (1996). *The new golden rule: Community and morality in a democratic society.* New York, NY: Basic Books.

Fajnzylber, P., Lederman, D., & Loayza, N. (2001). What causes violent crime? *European Economic Review, 48*(7), 1323–1357.

Featherstone, M. (1990). *Global culture: Nationalism, globalization, and modernity.* Thousand Oaks, CA: Sage Publications.

Fernandez, K. E., & Kuenzi, M. (2006). *Crime and support for democracy: Revisiting modernization theory* (Working paper No. 64). East Lansing, MI: Michigan State University.

Fletcher, J. (1997). *Violence and civilization: An introduction to the work of Norbert Elias.* Cambridge, UK: Polity Press.

Fukuyama, F. (1993). *The end of history and the last man.* New York, NY: Harper Perennial.

Gerth, H. H., & Mills, C. W. (1958). (Eds.). *From Max Weber: Essays in sociology.* New York, NY: Oxford University Press.

Giddens, A. (1991). *The consequences of modernity.* Stanford, CA: Stanford University Press.

Goldfrank, W. L. (2000). Paradigm regained? The rules of Wallerstein's world-system method. *Journal of World-Systems Research, 6*(2), 150–195.

Gurr, T. R. (1981). Historical trends in violent crime: A critical review of the evidence. In M. Tonry & N. Morris (Eds.), *Crime and Justice: An Annual Review of Research* (Vol. 3, pp. 295–350). Chicago, IL: University of Chicago Press.

Halim, N. (2006, November). *Democracy and crime: An empirical investigation.* Paper presented at the annual meeting of the American Society of Criminology. Los Angeles, CA.

Heiland, H., Shelley, L. I., & Kato, H. (1991). *Crime and control in comparative perspectives.* New York, NY: Walter de Gruyter.

Huntington, S. P. (1993). The clash of civilizations? *Foreign Affairs, 72*(3), 22–49.

Huntington, S. P. (1996). *The clash of civilizations and the remaking of world order.* New York, NY: Simon & Schuster.

International Labour Organization. (2010). *Cambodia: Facts and figures.* Geneva, Switzerland: Author.

Internet World Stats. (2010). *World Internet users and population stats.* Retrieved from www .internetworldstats.com/stats.htm.

Johnson, D. T. (2008). The homicide drop in postwar Japan. *Homicide Studies, 12*(5), 146–160.

Johnson, E. A., & Monkkonen, E. H. (Eds.). (1996). *The civilization of crime: Violence in town and country since the Middle Ages.* Champaign, IL: University of Illinois Press.

Kekic, L. (2007). *The Economist Intelligence Unit's Index of Democracy.* London, England: The Economist.

Kim, S., & Pridemore, W. A. (2005). Social change, institutional anomie, and serious property crime in transitional Russia. *British Journal of Criminology, 45*(1), 81–97.

Lechner, F. J., & Boli, J. (Eds.). (2000). *The globalization reader.* Oxford, England: Blackwell Publishing Company.

Leonardsen, D. (2005). *Japan as a low-crime nation.* London, England: Palgrave Macmillan.

Levinson, D., & Human Relations Area Files (Ed.). (2002). *Encyclopedia of crime and punishment* (Vol. 1). Thousand Oaks, CA: Sage Publications.

Lin, M. (2007). Does democracy increase crime? The evidence from international data. *Journal of Comparative Economics, 35*(3), 467–483.

Liu, J. (2005). Crime patterns during the market transition in China. *British Journal of Criminology, 45*(5), 613–633.

Liu, J., & Messner, S. E. (2001). Modernization and crime trends in China's reform era. In J. Liu, S.E. Messner, & L. Zhang (Eds.). *Crime and social control in a changing China* (pp. 3–21). Westport, CT: Greenwood Press.

Liu, J., Messner, S. E., & Zhang, L. (2001). (Eds.). *Crime and social control in a changing China.* Westport, CT: Greenwood Press.

Marx, K. (2007). *Das Kapital.* Washington, DC: Regnery Publishing, Inc. (Originally published in 1867.)

Mennell, S. (2007). *The American civilizing process.* London, England: Polity Press.

Messner, S. F. (1989). Economic discrimination and societal homicide rates: Further evidence on the cost of inequality. *American Sociological Review, 54*(4), 597–611.

Monnkkonen, E. (2006). Homicide: Explaining America's exceptionalism. *American Historical Review, 111*(1), 1–21.

Nandi, P. K., & Shahidullah, S. M. (1998). *Globalization and the evolving world society.* Leiden, the Netherlands: E. J. Brill.

Nelken, D. (2011). *Comparative criminal justice and globalization.* Surrey, England: Ashgate Publishing.

Nelson, B. (1973). Civilizational complexes and intercivilizational encounters. *Sociological Analyis.* Retrieved from www.socrel.oxfordjournals.org/content/34/2/79.full.pdf.

Nelson, B. (1981). *On the roads to modernity: Conscience, science, and civilizations.* Totowa, NJ: Rowman & Littlefield.

New World Encyclopedia. (2008, April). *Gabriel Tarde.* Retrieved from www.newworldencyclopedia.org/entry/Gabriel_Tarde.

Nisbet, R. (1969). *The quest for community: A study in the ethics of order and freedom.* New York, NY: Oxford University Press.

Pakes, F. (2010). The comparative method in globalised criminology. *Australian and New Zealand Journal of Criminology, 43*(1), 17–30.

Perez, O. J. (2003). Democratic legitimacy and public insecurity: Crime and democracy in El Salvador and Guatemala. *Political Science Quaterly, 118*(4), 627–624.

Pridemore, W. A. (Ed.). (2005). *Ruling Russia: Law, crime, and justice in a changing society.* Lanham, MD: Rowman & Littlefield.

Pridemore, W. A. (2007). Change and stability in the characteristics of homicide victims, offenders and incidents during rapid social change. *British Journal of Criminology, 47*(2), 331–345.

Pridemore, W. A., & Trent, C. L. S. (2010). Do the invariant findings of Land, McCall, and Cohen generalize to cross-national studies of social structure and homicide? *Homicide Studies, 20*(10), 1–40.

Prillaman, W. C. (2003). *Crime, democracy, and development in Latin America* (policy paper of the Americas, Vol. XIV). Washington, DC: Center for Strategic and International Studies.

Quinney, R. (2001). *The social reality of crime.* New Brunswick, NJ: Transaction Publishers.

Roberts, A., & Lafree, G. (2006). Explaining Japan's postwar violent crime trends. *Criminology, 42*(1), 179–210.

Robertson, R. (1992). *Social theory and global culture.* Thousand Oaks, CA: Sage Publications.

Rushton, J. P., & Whitney, G. (2002). Cross-national variation in violent crime rates: Race, r-k theory, and income. *Population and Environment, 23*(6), 502–511.

Schultz, C. (1989). Economic crimes in the People's Republic of China: A swinging door policy. *American University Journal of International Law and Policy, 5*, 161–206.

Sen, A. (2000). How to judge globalism. In F. J. Lechner & J. Boli (Eds.), *The globalization reader* (pp. 16–21). Oxford, England: Blackwell Publishing Company.

Shaw, C. R., & McKay, H. D. (1969). *Juvenile delinquency and urban areas*. Chicago, IL: The University of Chicago Press.

Shelley, L. I. (1981a). *Crime and modernization: The impact of industrialization and urbanization on crime*. Carbondale, IL: Southern Illinois University Press.

Shelley, L. I. (1981b). (Ed.). *Readings in comparative criminology*. Carbondale, IL: Southern Illinois University Press.

Sheptycki, J., Wardak, A. (Eds.). (2005). *Transnational and comparative criminology*. London, England: Glasshouse Press.

Shils, E. (2006). *Tradition*. Chicago, IL: The University of Chicago Press.

Simmel. G. (1971). The metropolis and mental life. In D. Levine (Ed.), *Georg Simmel* (pp. 324–339). Chicago, IL: University of Chicago Press. (Original work published 1903).

Simmel, G. (1978). *The philosophy of money* (trans. by T. Bottomore and D. Frisby). Abington, England: Routledge.

Stamatel, J. P. (2002). Europe, Central Eastern. In D. Levinson & Human Relations Area Files (Eds.). *Encyclopedia of crime and punishment* (Vol. 1, pp. 639–641). Thousand Oaks, CA: Sage Publications.

Sung, H. (2006). Democracy and criminal justice in cross-national perspective: From crime control to due process. *Annals of the American Academy of Political and Social Science, 605*(1), 311–337.

Tarde, G. (1912). *Penal philosophy* (trans. from the 4th French edition by R. Howel). Boston, MA: Little, Brown, and Company.

Thiaw, I., Hutton, J., & Green, M. (2009). Foreword. In United Nations Environmental Programme's World Conservation Monitoring Centre, *Submarine cables and the oceans: Connecting the world* (p. 3). Cambridge, England: UNEP and WCMC.

Thomas, W. I., & Znaniecki, F. (1918–1920). *The Polish peasant in Europe and America*. Chicago, IL: University of Chicago Press.

Tönnies, F. (1957). *Community and society*. East Lansing, MI: Michigan State University.

United Nations Environmental Programme's World Conservation Monitoring Centre. (2009). *Submarine cables and the oceans: Connecting the world*. Cambridge, England: Authors.

United Nations-HABITAT. (2007). *Global report on human settlements 2007: Enhancing urban safety and security*. Nairobi, Kenya: Author.

United Nations-HABITAT. (2009). *Urban safety and poverty in Asia and the Pacific*. Bangkok, Thailand: United Nations Economic and Social Commission for Asia and the Pacific.

United Nations Office on Drugs and Crime. (2009). *International homicide, rate per 100,000 population*. Vienna, Austria: Author.

United Nations Office on Drugs and Crime. (2010a). *Organized crime*. Retrieved from www.unodc.org/unodc/en/organized-crime/index.html.

United Nations Office on Drugs and Crime. (2010b). *The globalization of crime: A transnational organized crime threat assessment*. Vienna, Austria: Author.

United Nations Organization. (2010). *World economic situation and prospects 2010*. New York, NY: Department of Economic and Social Affairs, United Nations.

Wallerstein, I. (1979). *The capitalist world-economy: Essays by Immanuel Wallerstein*. Cambridge, England: Cambridge University Press.

Wallerstein, I. (2000). The rise and future demise of the world capitalist system: Concepts for comparative analysis. In F. J. Lechner and J. Boli (Eds.), *The globalization reader* (pp. 63–69). Oxford, England: Blackwell Publishing Company.

Waters, M. (1995). *Globalization*. London, England, and New York, NY: Routledge.

Zhang, A. (1996). *Economic growth and human development in China*. Retrieved from http://hdr.undp .org/en/reports/global/hdr1996/papers/amei_zhang.pdf.

Zhao, L. S. (2008). Anomie theory and crime in a transitional China (1978—). *International Criminal Justice Review, 18*(2), 137–157.

Zwingle, E. (1999). Global culture. *National Geographic, 196*(2), 12–39.

Comparative Criminal Justice: Methodological Perspectives

▶ CHAPTER OUTLINE

■ Introduction

Comparative analysis of crime, law, and justice is an attractive and a significant intellectual pursuit in criminal justice. It is also a task of enormous complexity. Theories of comparative criminal justice suggest the nature of the connectivity among the different systems of criminal justice around the world and provide an understanding of the economic, political, and cultural contexts of their growth and evolution. The theories help to generate questions and hypotheses and make us aware of key issues and contexts. It is to further examine these issues and contexts of criminal justice among the world's societies that we face the challenge of methodology. The challenge of methodology is the task of understanding the methods of collecting crime and justice data that will have cross-national meaning and reliability.

■ Methodology in Comparative Criminal Justice: Significance and Challenges

The problem of comprehending methodology in comparative criminal justice is significant first because crime is defined in different ways by different countries. The process of criminalization varies widely among countries. Child abuse, for example, is a serious issue in U.S. criminal justice. In U.S. criminal law, child abuse is broadly defined to include acts and behaviors against children (who are below the age of 18 or the age specified by the laws of the respective states). These acts and behaviors are not only physical (such as beating, biting, hitting, kicking, throwing, choking, and shaking) and sexual in nature (such as rape, sodomy, fondling of the genitals, production of child pornography, and indecent exposure), but also neglectful (denial of a child's basic necessities such as food, shelter, and clothing) and emotionally harmful (the denial of love and care and a consistent pattern of rejection, threat, and criticisms). According to a report from the United Nations Children's Fund (2012), about 1 billion of the world's children live in countries where physical abuse of children is not defined as a crime by law. Children who are physically abused are also the victims of sexual abuse, emotional abuse, and neglect. A global report called *Ending Legalised Violence Against Children,* published by Save the Children Sweden (2009), said that physical punishment of children at home is not defined as a crime in 172 countries. The inflicting of physical punishment on children at school is not a crime in 88 countries, and in 169 countries, physical punishment in alternative caregiving institutions is legal. In other words, about 96.8% of the children of the world are not protected by legislation against physical abuse at home, and about 96.2% are not protected by legislation against physical abuse in alternative caregiving institutions. Differences in the meaning and definition of crime exist in a wide variety of areas, and those in the process of criminalization limit the scope of generalization in comparative criminal justice.

The second most important methodological challenge in comparative criminal justice is the issue of crime typology and classification. Crimes are categorized and classified in different ways in different countries. Many countries, for example, do not have a separate system of collecting data on juvenile delinquency and juvenile justice. The U.S. juvenile justice system is more than 100 years old. The existing formal structure of the juvenile justice system in India, a country with about 300 million children, on the other hand, is barely a decade old. It came into being after the promulgation of the Juvenile Justice Act of 2000. The countries with separate juvenile justice systems define and perceive the mission of juvenile justice differently, and this limits cross-national studies on juvenile delinquency and cross-national reliability of juvenile justice data.

The classification of general crimes also varies widely around the world. Japan, for example, classifies and collects crime data in terms of the following six categories: felonies (such as murder, robbery, rape, and arson); violent offenses (such as the possession of dangerous weapons in unlawful public gatherings, aggravated assault, and extortion); larceny (such as burglary and auto theft); intellectual crimes (such as white collar crime, corruption, bribery, embezzlement, and forgery); moral crimes (including different kinds of sex crimes and the production and distribution of pornography); and miscellaneous crimes (including the possession of stolen property, negligent homicide, and destruction of property). The Penal Code of China, adopted by the Second Session of the Fifth National People's Congress in 1979, identifies crimes in terms of the following eight categories: crimes of counterrevolution; crimes of endangering public security; crimes of undermining the socialist economic order; crimes of infringing upon the rights of a person and the democratic rights of citizens; crimes of property violation; crimes of obstructing the administration of public order; crimes of disrupting marriage and family; and crimes of dereliction of duty.

In England and Wales, according to the British Home Office's National Standard for the Recording and Counting of Notifiable Offences, crime statistics are collected in terms of the following nine categories: violence against the person; sexual offenses; robbery; burglary; theft and handling special goods; fraud and forgery; criminal damage; drug offenses; and other offenses (such as violent disorder, treason, bigamy, perjury, kidnapping, and aiding suicide). In France, criminal offenses are categorized, in terms of their seriousness, into two categories: felony crimes and misdemeanor crimes. The French Penal Code defines the nature of felony and misdemeanor crimes and the forms of punishment that are to be imposed for those offenses. The Swedish Penal Code, adopted in 1965, categorizes crimes into 20 major categories. Some of the unique categories include crimes against life and health, liberty and peace, the family, public order, public activity, and national security. The Criminal Code of the Russian Federation, enacted in 1996, sorts crime into four categories: crimes of little gravity; crimes of average gravity; grave crimes; and especially grave crimes.

The Indian Penal Code has 22 categories of crimes. Some of the major categories include offenses against the state; offenses against public tranquility; offenses against public health, safety, convenience, decency, and morals; offenses by or relating to public servants; offenses affecting the human body; cruelty by husband or relatives of husband; offenses relating to marriage; and offenses relating to intimidation, insult, and annoyance.

In the United States, crimes are classified in multiple ways. In terms of the seriousness of the offense, crimes are grouped, like those of France, into two categories—felony crimes and misdemeanor crimes. In terms of offense type, crimes are classified into four categories: violent crime; property crime; drug-related crime; and public order crime. In terms of the victim–offender relationship, crimes are classified into two categories—stranger and non-stranger crimes (Bureau of Justice Statistics, 2010a). In Canada, there are police-recorded crimes and the Crime Severity Index (CSI). The CSI measures the seriousness of the crimes that are reported to law enforcement. It is because of the classification of crimes in terms of severity that Canadian crime data can suggest which part of the country is more or less violent in a given year and over time. The CSI of 2009, for example, shows that of all the Canadian provinces, the violent crime severity index in 2009 was lowest in Prince Edward Island (44.0) and highest in Manitoba (175.4; Statistics Canada, 2010a).

The UN-HABITAT's (2007) report, *Global Report on Human Settlements 2007: Enhancing Urban Safety and Security*, counts crimes in terms of three major categories: violent crimes, property crimes, and crimes against public order and welfare. The category of violent crime in the world is divided into political violence (state and nonstate crimes), institutional violence (such as extrajudicial killings by police and lynching of suspected criminals by community members), economic violence (such as organized crime and financial crime), and social violence (such as intimate-partner violence, sexual violence, child abuse, and other forms of family violence). These and other widely diverse systems of crime classification in different countries and by different international organizations make cross-national comparison of crime rates and trends a task of great complexity.

The third challenge for cross-national analyses in crime and justice is about the reliability of official crime statistics. The official crime statistics are primarily those that are reported to law enforcement and organized and collated by law enforcement agencies. But crime reporting widely varies from country to country. In no society are all crimes reported to law enforcement. In 2009, according to a report from the U.S. Bureau of Justice Statistics (2009), about 4.3 million violent crimes and 15.6 million property crimes were committed against persons 12 or older in the United States. The report found: "About half (49%) of all violent crimes and about 40% of all property crimes were reported to the police. Violent crimes against females (53%) are more likely to be reported than violent crimes against males (45%)" (p. 1). In 2003, the U.S. Bureau of Justice Statistics published a special report on the nature of crime reporting to law enforcement in the United States between 1992 and 2000. The report observed some increase, from 43% in 1992–1999 to 49% in 2000, in the reporting of violent crimes. The analysis of 8 years of crime reporting data, however, still showed that more than 50% of violent crimes in the United States are not reported to law enforcement. The report further observed that "in 2000, 39% of the approximately 25.4 million violent and property victimization against persons 12 and older were reported to the police" (Bureau of Justice Statistics, 2003, p. 2). In other words, about 61% of violent crimes were not reported to police in the United States in 2000.

Another recent report from the Bureau of Justice Statistics (2010b) shows that on average about 51% of violent crimes and 60% of property crimes were not reported to police in the United States in 2006–2007. Of all the different categories of crime, rape and sexual assault are least likely to be reported in all societies. The average reporting rate of rape and sexual assault in the United States between 1992 and 2000 was only 31%. The reporting of rape and sexual assault crimes in the United States is increasing, but it still remained below 50% in 2000 (Bureau of Justice Statistics, 2003). A 2002 report from the Bureau of Justice Statistics that analyzed the reporting of 8 years (1992–2000) of rape and sexual assault data found that "Sixty three percent of completed rapes, 65% of attempted rapes, and 74% of completed and attempted sexual assaults against females were not reported to the police" (p. 2).

The number and rate of crimes reported to police in the developing countries of Asia, Africa, and Latin America are much lower than those of developed countries. The UN-HABITAT's (2007) *Global Report on Human Settlements 2007: Enhancing Urban Safety and Security* clearly recognized that "crime reporting is related to the prevalence of law enforcement and to peoples' willingness to come forward, both of which vary by country—in virtually all jurisdictions, many crimes are not reported to authorities" (p. 52). A report published by the United Nations Office on Drugs and Crime (1999) titled *Global Report on Crime and Justice* found that in most developing countries, theft and burglary are more reported than violent crimes. About 80–85% of violent crimes in developing countries are not reported to police. The report found that "crime rates for every offence varied greatly by country. Arab states generally reported very low rates for nearly all types of crime" (Chapter 2). The 1999 report further observed: "There is no accepted methodology for collecting crime figures recorded by the police. Figures for a particular country depend on the country's state of development, the role of the police and the extent to which police use technology" (Chapter 2). A study commissioned by the European Institute for Crime Prevention and Control (Heiskanen, 2007) titled *International Statistics on Crime and Justice* made a similar observation about the problem of crime reporting to police around the world. The study has analyzed 10 years of crime data reported to police taken from the *United Nations Surveys on Crime Trends and the Operations of Criminal Justice Systems*. The study observed, "The country level results show that especially the latest data are from Western Europe, North America, and Oceania. A smaller number of countries are represented from Africa and Latin America" (Heiskanen, 2007, p. 21).

The crime data reported to police in most countries, particularly in developing countries, suffer from a lack of credibility (Van Dijk, 2008). Developing countries not only have a low level of crime reporting to police, but also have the problem of the credibility of police-recorded crimes (Heiskanen, 2007). In a major study on this issue, Van Dijk, Kesteren, and Smit (2007) observed that "Police forces across the world routinely present official statistics of crime as evidence of good performance. Recorded crime rates that are declining or that are lower than any other countries are presented by police chiefs as the result of effective policing" (p. 24). They further noted: "In the light of global ICVS (International Crime Victimization Survey) results . . . a severe verdict on comparability of international police statistics seems warranted. In our view, there is evidence for a strong systemic bias in police recorded crimes rates" (Van Dijk et al., 2007, p. 25).

The low level of crime reporting, and the presumed bias and lack of reliability in police-recorded crimes can be explained in terms of a variety of factors such as different definitions of crime; different levels of tolerance for criminal behavior; different crime reporting mechanisms; different levels of trust and confidence in police performance; and differences in the levels of modernization in various countries. It is perceived, for example, that Swedish culture has a great tolerance for rape. Sweden has the highest rate of rape among all the developed countries, and about 90% of rapes in Sweden are not reported to law enforcement. In Japan, incidents of interpersonal violence are rarely reported to law enforcement, first, because it is not defined by law as a crime, and second, because it is perceived mainly as a family and domestic issue. In most of the Asian countries, physical abuse of children by parents at home and in schools is not defined as a crime, and hence, it is not reported to police in the way it is in the United States and Canada. In developed countries, there are technology-based mechanisms for crime reporting such as 911 in the United States and 999 in the United Kingdom. In most developing countries, there are no specific reporting mechanisms for specific types of crimes such as the reporting of Internet crime, interpersonal violence, and sexual crime. The trust and confidence in police and police performance greatly affects crime reporting. Studies have shown that the level confidence in police performance in developing countries is low, which has a negative effect on crime reporting. One survey on crime reporting found that about 82% of people in North America, 78% in Oceania, and 61% in Western and Central Europe reported to have been very or fairly satisfied with the police performance in their countries (Van Dijk et al., 2007). The percentage of people who reported to have been very or fairly satisfied with police performance was 60% for Africa, 37% for Latin America, and 37% for Asia (regions that hold about 3.8 billion of the world's 7 billion people).

The wide divergence in definitions of crime, differences in crime classifications, low levels of crime reporting to police, and lack of reliability in police-recorded crimes, however, do not suggest that in cross-national comparisons, national crime data should not be explored and used. The Uniform Crime Reporting (UCR), the National Incident-Based Reporting System (NIBRS), and the National Crime Victimization Survey (NCVS) of the United States; UCR of Canada; and the British Crime Survey (an annual survey of criminal victimization in England and Wales) are some of the most reliable national models of crime statistics. Recently, the reporting and organizing of crime statistics have also considerably improved in many countries. What the worldwide differences in the definition and classification of crimes suggest is that there is a great need for triangulating national crime and justice data with those that are collected by regional and international organizations. There are a number of regional and international organizations that regularly collect such data. The data collected by these organizations—which use state-of-the-art methodological expertise and modern information technology—are relatively more reliable for cross-national analysis. The contemporary research on comparative criminal justice is predominantly based on cross-national surveys conducted by regional and international organizations. There are three types of these surveys: surveys on crime rates and trends based on crimes reported to police and law enforcement agencies, criminal victimization surveys based on both reported and unreported crimes, and self-report crime surveys based on data provided by offenders.

■ National Surveys on Crime Statistics

Crime Statistics in the United States

The collection of crime statistics in the United States is conducted by the following four major forms of national surveys: (1) the UCR program; (2) the NIBRS; (3) the NCVS; and (4) self-report crime surveys such as the Youth Risk Behavior Surveillance System (YRBSS) and Monitoring the Future (MTF) survey.

Uniform Crime Reporting System

The Uniform Crime Reporting (UCR) program is one of the oldest national surveys for collecting crime statistics. The idea of the UCR was first conceived by the International Association of Chiefs of Police in 1929. In 1930, Congress enacted a law (Title 28, Section 534 of the United States Code) that mandated the Department of Justice and the Attorney General to collect U.S. crime statistics. Since then, the Federal Bureau of Investigation (FBI) has been responsible for the implementation and development of the UCR program. The UCR methodology is primarily based on crimes reported to police and law enforcement agencies. Currently, about 18,000 local, state, and federal law enforcement agencies participate in the UCR program. In 2009, these law enforcement agencies "represented more than 295 million United States inhabitants—96.3% of the total population" (Federal Bureau of Investigation, 2009, p. 1). The UCR program collects information on two types of offenses: Part I and Part II offenses. Part I offenses include eight categories of violent crimes collectively identified as index crimes. These are murder, nonnegligent manslaughter, forcible rape, robbery, aggravated assault, burglary, auto theft, and arson. Part II offenses of the UCR include weapons possession, embezzlement, drug abuse violations, liquor law violations, minor sex offenses, driving under the influence, disorderly conduct, vandalism, gambling, fraud, and forgery and counterfeiting. The UCR collects information on reported offenses (index crimes) and persons arrested (Part II offenses), but does not include information on trials, convictions, and sentences.

The UCR's data on the eight categories of index crimes are gathered, organized, and analyzed in terms of a number of variables such as country profile, state profiles, regional variations, and variations in crime rate in metropolitan and nonmetropolitan cities and counties. In each of the eight categories of index crimes, data are again presented in terms of a number of specific variations. Over the years, the scope of the UCR program has considerably expanded. The Hate Crime Statistics Act of 1990, the Violent Crime Control and Law Enforcement Act of 1994, and the Matthew Shepard and James Byrd, Jr. Hate Crimes Prevention Act of 2009 mandate that the UCR program collects information on crimes that are motivated by hate based on race, religion, age, gender, ethnicity, physical and mental disabilities, and sexual orientation.

According to the UCR, between 1990 and 2009, the violent crime rate in the United States consistently and considerably declined. In 1990, the total violent crime rate in the United States was 729.6 per 100,000 population. By 2009, the violent crime rate had declined to 424.2 per 100,000 population. In 1990, the rate of murder and nonnegligent manslaughter was 9.4 per 100,000 population. The rate dropped to 5.0 per 100,000 population in 2009. The rate for forcible rape in 1990 was 41.2 per 100,000 population. In 2009, the rate decreased to 28.7 per 100,000 population (see **Table 3-1**). In 2008, the UCR reported a total of 7,783 hate crime incidents. Out of the 7,783 incidents, 3,992 incidents were reported as hate crimes based on racial bias; 1,519 incidents were reported as hate crimes based on religious bias; 1,297 incidents were reported as hate crimes based on bias of sexual orientation; and 78 incidents were reported as hate crimes based on bias against disability.

National Incident-Based Reporting System

From the middle of the 1980s, a new complementary system of police-recorded crime survey was added to the UCR system. The new system, called the National Incident-Based Reporting System (NIBRS), was introduced to improve and expand the UCR (Bureau of Justice Statistics, 2000). The NIBRS collected crime data in two major categories: group A offenses and group B offenses. Group A includes 22 offenses, and group B includes 12 offenses. The core of the NIBRS system is to collect crime data in 6 segments or data elements. These are the administrative, offense, property, victim, offender, and arrestee segments. Under each of the segments, a crime incident is described in terms of a number of variables. The FBI

TABLE 3-1 Some Selected U.S. Crime Index Data From the UCR, 1960–2009*

Year	Murder	Rape	Robbery	Aggravated Assault	Vehicle Theft
1960	5.1	9.6	60.1	86.1	183.0
1965	5.1	12.1	71.7	111.3	256.8
1970	7.9	18.7	172.1	164.8	456.8
1975	9.6	26.3	220.8	231.1	473.7
1980	10.2	36.8	251.1	298.5	502.2
1985	8.0	37.1	208.5	302.9	462.0
1990	9.4	41.2	257.9	424.1	657.8
1995	8.2	37.1	220.9	418.3	560.4
2000	5.5	32.0	145.0	324.0	412.2
2005	5.6	31.8	140.8	290.8	416.8
2009	5.0	28.7	133.0	262.8	258.8

*Per 100,000 population.

Source: Data from U.S. National Incident-Based Reporting System.

has an extended set of guidelines with descriptions of these segments and instructions on how to collect crime data following the NIBRS methodology (Federal Bureau of Investigation, 2000; Lynch & Addington, 2006). Currently, the UCR program, in addition to using its traditional method of summary reporting, includes information collected through the NIBRS methodology. The FBI's annual publication, *Crime in the United States,* presently includes information provided by both the UCR system and NIBRS reporting. NIBRS is a more comprehensive measure of crime statistics than the UCR because the UCR "measures the overall number of incidents for an index crime, [and] NIBRS measures both the overall number of incidents and the occurrence of each type of crime within each incident" (Bureau of Justice Statistics, 2003, p. 9).

National Crime Victimization Survey

The UCR reporting system and NIBRS are based primarily on crimes reported to and recorded by police. Because not all crimes are reported to police, there is always a problem of validity and reliability in police-recorded crimes. In order to address this issue, the U.S. Department of Justice convened a panel of experts from the National Research Council in 1976 to develop a set of recommendations for a comprehensive system of crime measurement through the eyes of victims. Based on the report presented by the National Research Council (1976), *Surveying Crime,* a new system of victimization survey was introduced by the Department of Justice for crime measurement in the late 1970s. The new system was renamed the National Crime Victimization Survey (NCVS) in 1992 (Groves & Cork, 2008). The NCVS system was introduced with the objectives to develop a system of crime measurement independent of crimes reported to police and police-recorded crimes and to enhance the understanding of the nature, causation, and typology of victimization (Cantor & Lynch, 2000). The NCVS data are obtained each year from a "sample of 76,000 households comprising nearly 135,300 persons on the frequency, characteristics and consequences of criminal victimization in the United States" (United States Census Bureau, 2012, p. 1). According to the Bureau of Justice Statistics (2010c), the NCVS estimates "the likelihood of victimization by rape, sexual assault, robbery, assault, theft, household burglary, and motor vehicle theft for the population as a whole as well as for segments of the population such as women [and] the elderly" (p. 1). The NCVS also collects information on public attitudes toward crime and criminal justice, school crime and violence, and workplace violence. The data on victimization from the sampled households and their individuals, age 12 or older, are gathered on the basis of both face-to-face and computer-assisted telephone interviews (CATIs). The survey is conducted by the U.S. Census Bureau on behalf of the U.S. Department of Justice (United States Census Bureau, 2012).

A report on criminal victimization in 2009 published by the Bureau of Justice Statistics (2010d) indicated that "in 2009, U.S. residents age 12 or older experienced an estimated 20 million violent and property victimizations . . . . These criminal victimizations included an estimated 4.3 million violent crimes, 15.6 million property crimes, and 133,000 personal thefts" (p. 1). The report, however, found that the "rates of violent and property crime in 2009 were at the lowest overall levels recorded since the survey's inception in 1972" (Bureau

TABLE 3-2 NCVS, 2009: Rates of Criminal Victimization and Percent Change by Type of Crime in the United States, 2000–2009

Type of Crime	Victimization Rate 2000	Victimization Rate 2009	Percent Change, 2000–2009
Violent crime	27.9	17.1	–38.7%
Rape and sexual assault	1.2	0.5	–56.9%
Robbery	3.2	2.1	–34.9%
Aggravated assault	5.7	3.2	–43.1%
Simple assault	17.8	11.3	–36.8%
Property crime	178.1	127.4	–28.5%
Household burglary	31.8	25.6	–19.4%
Motor vehicle theft	8.6	6.0	–30.5%
Theft	137.7	95.7	–30.5%
Personal theft	1.2	0.5	–56.6%

Source: Data from Bureau of Justice Statistics. (2010). *National crime victimization survey: Criminal victimization, 2009* (Bulletin by J. L. Truman & M. R. Rand). Washington, DC: Department of Justice.

of Justice Statistics, 2010d, p. 1). The report further observed that the "rate for every type of violent and property crime measured by the NCVS declined from 2000 to 2009. During the 10-year period, violent crimes declined by 39% and property crimes decreased by 29%" (see **Table 3-2**) (Bureau of Justice Statistics, 2010d, p. 1).

The 2009 criminal victimization report also reveals a number of other criminal victimization trends in the United States, such as the higher rate of violent crime victimization by males; higher victimization rate of Blacks than of persons of other races (Whites, Asians, and American Indians) by violent crime, robbery, aggravated assault, and rape and sexual assault; higher rate of property crime victimization of low income and larger households; and higher rate of victimization of females by known offenders (68% for females as opposed to 45% for males). The report found that during 2009, only about 49% of violent crime victimizations and 39% of property crime victimizations were reported to police. Criminal victimizations were reported to police at a higher level in cases of motor theft (85%), robbery (68%), and aggravated assault (58%; Bureau of Justice Statistics, 2010d).

Self-Report Crime Surveys

The NCVS is based on self-reporting of victimization. There is another form of survey that is based on self-reporting of crime and criminality, particularly self-reporting of crime and delinquency by juveniles. The core strategy in self-report methodology "is to ask individuals if they have engaged in delinquent or criminal behavior, and if so, how often they have done so" (Thornberry & Krohn, 2000, p. 33). The self-report methodology began to be used in delinquency studies in the beginning of the 1950s. It was pioneered particularly by Edwin Sutherland's study, *White Collar Crime,* in 1949 and Travis Hirschi's study, *Causes of Delinquency,* in 1969. In the 1970s and 1990s, the self-report methodology of delinquency studies began to be seen as significant in the development of the social learning theory of crime; the social bond theory of delinquency; the rise of developmental criminology or life cycle criminology; and the growing research on connections between crime and class (Thornberry & Krohn, 2000). From academic research, the self-report methodology began to play a part in governmental crime surveys in the 1970s, particularly through the development and funding of the MTF survey in 1975 by the National Institute on Drug Abuse, National Institutes of Health, and the U.S. Department of Health and Human Services; and the YRBSS survey in 1990 by the Centers for Disease Control and Prevention (CDC) and the U.S. Department of Health and Human Services.

The MTF survey is conducted annually by the University of Michigan's Institute for Social Research on behalf of the National Institute on Drug Abuse and the U.S. Department of Health and Human Services. It measures the rate of illicit drug use, primarily by the nation's school-going adolescents. Questions are administered during a regular class period to 8th-, 10th-, and 12th-grade students. The 2009 MTF report is based on the survey of 46,000 students of the nation's 400 secondary schools (Johnston, O'Malley, Bachman, & Schulenberg, 2009). The report found that among all three grades of students "after a decade of gradual decline, marijuana use has begun to tilt up" (Johnston et al., 2009, p. 5).

The YRBSS is a self-report biannual survey of measuring and assessing six categories of behavior among American youth. The respondents are sampled from the nation's public and private schools, and the survey is based on self-administered questionnaires handed out in class. The six categories of behavior are unintentional injuries and violence; use of tobacco; use of alcohol and other illicit drugs; sex and sexual behaviors that contribute to unintended pregnancy and sexually transmitted diseases, including HIV infection; unhealthy dietary behaviors; and obesity and physical inactivity. Out of these six categories, behaviors related to unintentional injuries and violence and the use of alcohol and illicit drugs are considered criminal and status offenses. The 2009 national YRBSS, based on 16,460 completed questionnaires from 158 schools in 42 states, shows that "during the 30 days before the survey, 28.3% of students had ridden one or more times in a car or other vehicle with a driver who had been drinking alcohol," and of those students, 30.0% were black, 30.0% were Hispanic, and 26.2% were white (CDC, 2009, p. 5). The YRBSS survey also indicates that "Nationwide, 17.5% of students had carried a weapon (e.g., a gun, knife, or club) on at least 1 day during the 30 days before the survey," and of those students, 26.5% were male and 7.1% were female; 29.3% of males who had carried a weapon were white, 21.0% were black, and 26.5% were Hispanic (CDC, 2009, p. 5). About 5.9% of students, according to the YRBSS data, "had carried a gun on at least 1 day during the 30 days before the survey" (CDC, 2009, p. 5). These and many other data on status offenses and criminality among the youth population in America is more systematically collected by surveys based on the self-report methodology. The Office of Juvenile Justice and Delinquency Prevention's (OJJDP) *Juvenile Offenders and Victims National Report Series,* which has been published annually since 1995, is one of the most comprehensive sources on juvenile crime statistics in the United States. It is based mostly on crimes reported to police and police-recorded crimes.

Crime Statistics in Canada

Canadian Uniform Crime Reporting Survey

There are four different types of crime surveys in Canada conducted and organized by Statistics Canada, the Canadian Centre for Justice Statistics (CCJS), and the National Justice Statistics Initiative (NJSI). These are: (1) the Uniform Crime Reporting Survey (UCR1), (2) the Incident-Based Uniform Crime Reporting Survey (UCR2), (3) the Canadian Criminal Victimization Survey, and (4) the Canadian Homicide Survey. Systematic crime reporting in Canada began almost half a century ago with the introduction of the UCR1 system in 1962. The UCR1 of Canada, like that of the United States, is based on a summary of crimes reported to police and police-recorded crimes. Data are collected monthly from the nation's police agencies by Statistics Canada on behalf of the CCJS. According to Statistics Canada (2010a), "The response rate in terms of police respondents complying with the UCR Survey is virtually 100%. There are more than 1,200 separate police detachments responding to the survey, comprising 204 different police forces" (p. 2). Unlike in the United States, participation of police agencies in the UCR1 in Canada is mandatory. Each police agency is responsible for the accuracy and the reliability of its data. Once a master file is completed, it is sent to each reporting police agency for a verification of data accuracy, and the agency is required to "sign off" (Statistics Canada, 2010a, p. 4). The UCR1 collects three categories of information: actual crime incidence, clearance record of each incidence, and persons charged. The UCR1 methodology of reporting crime incidence has three distinctive characteristics. First, the recording of violent offenses follows a rule different from recording nonviolent offenses. The recording of violent offenses is equal to the number of victims of violent offenses. For example, if someone murders three individuals and there are three victims in one incident, it is counted as three offenses. But for all other nonviolent crimes and crimes of robbery, the total number of offenses counted is equal to the number of crime incidents. The second characteristic is the most serious offense. Under the most serious offense, if a crime incident involves a number of offenses, the UCR1 will count only the most serious offense as declared by the Canadian Penal Code. The third characteristic is a new measure of crime reporting—a measure not seen in the crime reporting systems of the United States or any other country in the world. Introduced in 2009, it is known as the Crime Severity Index (CSI). Dauvergne and Turner explain that "the traditional crime rate and the Crime Severity Index (CSI) are complementary measures of police-reported crime. The crime rate measures the volume of crime reported to the police, while the Crime Severity Index measures the seriousness of crime" (2010, p. 6).

In the calculation of the CSI, a weight is assigned to a particular crime on the basis of the sentence it receives from the criminal courts. According to both the traditional system of reporting of the volume of crimes and the CSI, the crime rate is consistently falling in Canada. According to the CSI of 2009, the crime rate in Canada declined about 22% between 1999 and 2009. "The drop in crime severity over the past 10 years had occurred virtually right across the country" (Dauvergne & Turner, 2010, p. 4).

The UCR1 collects information about 100 individual criminal offenses but still does not represent all forms of crimes that are reported to police because of its selectivity principles in counting violent offenses and the most serious offenses. The CCJS introduced the UCR2 system as an improved methodology for crime statistics in 1988. It is an incident-based reporting system like that of the NIBRS of the United States. It is also based on crimes reported to police and police-recorded crimes, but it records more information about a crime incident than the UCR1. Like the NIBRS of the United States, the UCR2 of Canada creates a separate system of statistical records with respect to a crime incident including the characteristics of offenders and victims. The UCR2 has three versions: UCR2.0 introduced in 1988, UCR2.1 introduced in 1998, and UCR2.2 introduced in 2005. The UCR2.2 was introduced in the context of a number of new pieces of legislation that mandated the gathering of crime statistics on hate-motivated crime, cyber crime, organized crime, street gang crime, and genocide. As a result of the introduction of the UCR2.2, in 2006, hate crime statistics began to be recorded by police more systematically. A report from Statistics Canada (Walsh & Dauvergne, 2010) explained: "Near-national data on the incidence of police-reported hate crime were first available in Canada in 2006. In that year, police services covering 87% of the population identified 892 incidents that had been motivated by hate, representing a rate of 3.1 per 100,000 population" (p. 8). The report shows that there are many similarities in hate crimes in the United States and Canada. In both countries, the majority of the hate crimes are based on race and ethnicity bias (51% in the United States and 66% in Canada).

Canadian Criminal Victimization Survey

Canada's National Survey on Criminal Victimization began in 1988 with the purpose of understanding the nature of and measuring the number of crimes that are not reported to police, and to assess the public attitudes toward crime and the Canadian criminal justice system. Statistics Canada, on behalf of the CCJS, conducts a General Social Survey (GSS) on criminal victimization every 5 years. The survey is based on telephone interviews of about 25,000 individuals aged 15 years or older drawn from the households of all 10 provinces using random digital dialing. The survey measures self-reported victimization in the following eight areas: sexual assault, robbery, assault, breaking and entering, theft of personal property, theft of household property, theft of motor vehicles, and vandalism. The criminal victimization report of 2009, based on a survey of 19,500 respondents from all provinces, shows that "nearly 1.6 million Canadians, aged 15 and over in the 10 provinces, reported having been the victim of a violent crime, that is, a sexual assault, a robbery or a physical assault, in the 12 months before the survey" (Statistics Canada, 2010b, p. 2).

About 7.4 million Canadians (i.e., just over one quarter of the total population) experienced some form of victimization from a criminal incident. The survey also shows that about 69% of crimes and victimizations in general, and about 71% of violent crimes and victimizations in particular, were not reported to police in 2009 (Perrault & Brennan, 2010). The reporting of crime and victimization to police declined 3% between 2004 and 2009. "Over 9 in 10 Canadians (93%) said they were either satisfied or very satisfied with their personal safety from crime [and about] 90% of Canadians reported that they felt safe when walking alone in their neighborhood at night" (Statistics Canada, 2010b, pp. 7–8).

Canadian Homicide Survey

Statistics Canada and the CCJS conduct, in addition to the UCR1, UCR2, and the Criminal Victimization Survey, a separate homicide survey for collecting data on murder, manslaughter, and infanticide. It describes the nature of homicide incidents and the characteristics of the homicide offenders and victims. The Homicide Survey, started in 1961 and further expanded under the Statistics Act of 1985, is based on three types of questionnaires: the incident questionnaire (for data related to the context of the homicide incident such as date and geographical location, gang activity, and drug involvement); the victim questionnaire (for data related to the age, gender, marital status, and employment status of homicide victims, weapons used in the commission of a homicide, and victim–offender relationship); and charged/suspect-chargeable questionnaire (for data related to age, gender, marital status, and employment status of homicide offenders, including their mental health status, drug and alcohol related behavior, and history of family violence). The Homicide Survey also collects data on police officers and corrections officers killed in connection with homicide incidents. "The Homicide Survey represents a complete count of the number of homicides known and reported by police in Canada. Homicides are scored according to the year that they are reported by police to the Homicide Survey" (Dauvergne & Li, 2010, p. 10). The Canadian Homicide Survey measures some of the characteristics of homicide that are unique, such as the victims of spousal homicide and homicide against prostitutes and taxi drivers as a result of their professions—the characteristics that are rarely measured by crime or homicide surveys in other countries, including the United States. The 2010 report on homicide trends in Canada (Mahony, 2011) indicated that "following a decade of relative stability, homicides decreased substantially in 2010 . . . . The 2010 homicide rate fell to 1.62 per 100,000 population, its lowest level since 1966" (p. 1).

Crime Statistics in the United Kingdom

The United Kingdom has one of the longest traditions of collecting crime statistics. It began in the early 19th century through the collection of court proceedings and trial and conviction records (Mellaerts, 2000). In 1857, British surveys also began to collect data on different types of crime. Currently, the United Kingdom, like the United States, has three types of crime surveys, and they are conducted by the Home Office Research Development and Statistics of the Ministry of Justice—an organization equivalent to the Bureau of Justice Statistics in the United States. These surveys are the Police-Recorded Crime Survey, the British Crime Survey (BCS), and the Offending, Crime, and Justice Survey (OCJS).

Police-Recorded Crime Survey

The Police-Recorded Crime Survey of the United Kingdom is like the UCR systems of the United States and Canada. It is exclusively based on crimes reported to police and police-recorded crimes. Statistics are collected on the following nine categories of crimes: violence against the person, sex crime, robbery, burglary, drug offenses, criminal damage, arson, theft and handling of stolen goods, and other offenses. Under these categories, data on more than 400 different types of offenses are recorded. One of the major differences between the UCR of the United States and the United Kingdom's Police-Recorded Crime Survey is that in the United Kingdom, the survey is based on a more detailed recording of offenses in each category of crimes. In the United Kingdom's survey, the category of sex crimes, for example, records data on 96 different types of sexual offenses (see **Table 3-3**), and the category of violence against the person collects data on about 110 different types of violent offenses against the person. The UCR of the United States and the UCR1 and UCR2 of Canada do not collect data on so many different facets of sexual offenses and violence against the person. In the UCR systems of the United States and Canada, criminal damage is not a separate category for crime data collection. In the United Kingdom's system, under the category of criminal damage, data are collected on a number of offenses, such as arson endangering life, arson not endangering life, criminal damage to a dwelling, criminal damage to a dwelling based on religious or racial bias motivation, criminal damage to a vehicle, and criminal damage to a vehicle based on religious or racial bias motivation.

TABLE 3-3 Selected Indictable Sex Offenses in the United Kingdom's Police-Recorded Crimes

Selected Sex Offenses	
Sexual assault on a male	Familial sexual offenses (incest)
Assault on a male by penetration	Exploitation of prostitution
Assault of a male child under 13 by penetration	Keeping a brothel used for prostitution
Rape of female aged under 16	Controlling a prostitute for gain
Rape of female aged 16 or over	Sex with a female with a mental disorder
Rape of a male aged under 16	Sex with a male with a mental disorder
Rape of a male aged 16 and over	Sex in front of a person with a mental disorder
Attempted rape of a female under 16	Threatening a person with a mental disorder for sex
Attempted rape of a female aged 16 and over	Care workers: sex with a mentally disordered client
Rape of female child under 13 by a male	Abuse of children by engaging in prostitution
Rape of a male child under 13 by a male	Abuse of children: pornography
Sexual assault on a female by penetration	Trafficking for sexual exploitation
Sexual assault of a female child under 13	Abuse of trust: sexual offenses
Inciting a female child under 13 for sexual activity	Gross indecency with female children
Inciting a male child under 13 for sexual activity	Gross indecency with male children
Sexual activity in the presence of a child	Intercourse with an animal by a male
Causing a child to watch a sexual act	Intercourse with an animal by a female
Sex with a female without consent—penetration	Trespass with the intent to commit a sex act
Sex with a male with consent—penetration	Sexual penetration of a corpse

Source: Data from British Ministry of Justice. (2010). *Criminal statistics: England and Wales 2009.*

Data on police-recorded crimes are collected on the basis of the British Home Office's (2010a) Counting Rules for Recorded Crime and The National Crime Recording Standard (NCRS). The NCRS was developed by the British Association of Chief Police Officers and adopted in 2002 for attaining more consistency and reliability in recording crimes by about 43 different police agencies that work under the control of the British Home Office and the British Transport Police (British Home Office, 2010b). Based on the crime data collected and recorded by the British police, the British Ministry of Justice publishes every year a national crime report titled *Criminal Statistics: England and Wales.*

According to the 2009 report (published in 2010), the British police recorded 4.34 million crimes committed between 2000 and 2010, and the crime rate in the United Kingdom fell about 8% between and 2000–2010. During the same time period, all forms of crimes, except sexual crimes, showed a declining trend. The report observed: "Violent crimes against the person decreased four percent from 930,400 to 871,700. Violent crimes leading to injury decreased by five percent from 421,000 to 401,700," but "Sexual offences increased by six percent from 51,400 to 54,500. Rape of a female increased by 15 percent from 12,000 to 14,000" (British Ministry of Justice, 2010, p. 9).

British Crime Survey

The British Crime Survey (BCS), like the U.S. NCVS, is based on the goal of understanding the volume of crime, the nature and extent of criminal victimization, and public opinion on crime and justice on the basis of large nationally sampled household surveys. The BCS, started in 1981, "is a face-to face victimization survey in which people resident in households in England and Wales are asked about their experience of crime in the 12 months prior to the interview" (British Home Office, 2009, p. 3).

The BCS, which was a biannual survey up to 2001 but is presently an annual survey, records crime and victimization data, both reported and unreported, on the following nine categories of crimes: assault, attempted assault, sexual offenses, personal theft, burglary, theft, attempted theft, vandalism, and threats. The majority of the questions on the BCS are related to property crimes (Tseloni, Wittebrood, Farell, & Pease, 2004). In the survey, about 33% of the questions are related to theft, 26% to vandalism, 14% to vehicle-related theft, 7% to burglary, and 20% to all forms of violence except sexual offenses (British Home Office, 2009). One of the important characteristics of the BCS is that it seeks to understand people's perceptions about crime and the criminal justice system. The survey studies the perception of antisocial behavior in terms of questions related to noisy neighbors and loud parties, teenagers hanging around on the street, rubbish or litter lying around, vandalism, graffiti, people using or dealing drugs, people being drunk or rowdy in public places, and abandoned or burned-out cars (British Home Office, 2010b). The British Home Office (2009) report called *Crime in England and Wales 2008/2009* showed that there are some major differences in the way crime trends are reported by the BCS and police-recorded crimes. The BCS, for example, recorded 10.7 million crimes in 2008–2009. For the same period, police recorded only 4.7 million crimes (see **Table 3-4**).

However, the BCS data on 14 years of British crime trends show that between 1995 and 2008–2009, most BCS crime rates significantly dropped: vandalism was down 18%, domestic

TABLE 3-4 British Crime Trends, 2008–2009: The Two Surveys

British Crime Survey	Police-Recorded Crime
All BCS crime—stable (10.7 million crimes)	Police-recorded crime down 5% to 4.7 million
Violent crime—stable	Violent against the person down 6%
With injury—stable	With injury down 7%
Domestic burglary—stable	Domestic burglary up 1%
Vehicle theft—stable	Offenses against vehicle down 10%
Theft from the person up 25%	Theft from the person down 12%
Vandalism—stable	Criminal damage down 12%
Risk of being a victim of crime up 23%	Robbery down 5%

Source: Data from British Home Office. (2009). *Crime in England and Wales 2008/2009.*

burglary was down 58%, vehicle-related theft was down 68%, household theft was down 48%, bicycle theft was down 20%, other theft of personal property was down 47%, and all BCS violence was down 49% (British Home Office, 2009a, p. 3). The BCS data also show that the overall risk of victimization in the United Kingdom declined between 1981 and 2005–2006: "Twenty-eight percent of people had been victims of crime (any BCS crime) in 1981. However, less than a quarter (23%) were victims of crime in 2005/2006" (Jansson, 2010, p. 10). In response to the new technology crimes, the BCS has recently been extended to gather data on three more areas: mobile phone theft, fraud and technology crimes, and ID theft (Jansson, 2010). More refined questions are also being added on drug use and interpersonal and intimate-partner violence.

Offending, Crime, and Justice Survey

The Home Office of the British Ministry of Justice, in addition to the Police-Recorded Crime Survey and the BCS, also conducts a national longitudinal survey on crime and criminality among young people (aged 10 to 25) in England and Wales. This is the Offending, Crime, and Justice Survey (OCJS), and like the YRBSS in the United States, it is based on a self-report methodology. The survey measures 7 broad categories of crime, and those include 20 core offenses. These 7 crime categories include burglary, vehicle-related thefts, other thefts (from place of work or school, shoplifting, thefts from the person), criminal damage, robbery, assault, and selling drugs. The OCJS also includes fraud and technology crimes. The core objectives of the OCJS are to measure self-reported offending, the nature of repeat offending, antisocial behavior, and crime–drugs–alcohol connections. The OCJS draws a sample of about 5,000 young people from across the country, and they are interviewed using the computer-assisted personal interviewing methodology. The OCJS "has been designed as a 'rotating panel' which means that in each subsequent year, part of the previous year's sample is re-interviewed, and is augmented by a further 'fresh' sample to ensure a cross-sectional representative sample of young people" (Economic and Social Data Service, 2010, p. 1). The basic OCJS questions include modules on such areas as sociodemographic background, neighborhood conditions, engagement in antisocial behavior, engagement in technology crimes, nature and types of offending, domestic violence conditions, drinking behavior, and drug use (Economic and Social Data Service, 2010). The basic strategy for collecting data by OCJS is "the use of 'audio self completion,' in which the respondent listened through headphones to the question about offending and then entered his or her answer directly on a computer" (Hales, Nevill, Pudney, & Tipping, 2009, p. 5).

A British Home Office (Hales et al., 2009) report based on data from the OCJS collected between 2003 and 2006 shows that "offending behavior is common among young people in Britain" (p. 7). The report stated that "Nearly a quarter of the sample (23%) reported committing some sort of offences, which included some relatively minor incidents, in the previous 12 months" (p. 7). Over the period of 4 years, about 27% of respondents said they had offended and used drugs. During the same period, about 72% of respondents said they had some involvement in antisocial behavior (British Home Office, 2010a).

German Crime Statistics

Systematic efforts to collect official crime statistics began in Germany at the beginning of the Weimar Republic in the 1920s. During the late 1920s, Germany experienced significant social, economic, and cultural transformations. The rapid social and economic changes were associated with the rise of crime and that led to policy making for the development of national crime statistics in Germany. The development of crime statistics began under the guidance of the newly formed German Criminal Police Commission composed of law enforcement experts from different states and municipal authorities. However, from 1930 to 1970, Germany went through many political changes and much turmoil, and that severely affected the development of crime statistics.

German Police-Recorded Crime Statistics

Modern development of national crime statistics in Germany began in the 1970s in the context of the rise of a more stable, prosperous, and high-tech global German economy. The present system of national crime statistics in Germany is managed by the Federal Criminal Police Office—the *Bundeskriminalamt*—in cooperation with the German Criminal Police Commission. The *Bundeskriminalamt* is like the FBI of the United States and the Ministry of Justice of the United Kingdom. Every year, the *Bundeskriminalamt* publishes a report called *Police Crime Statistics—Federal Republic of Germany* on the basis of police records of crimes sent electronically by each of the 13 German states and 3 city-states (Berlin, Hamburg, and the State of Bremen). The system of data gathering and organization is highly computerized. As the 2006 *Police Crime Statistics* report noted, "The aggregate data for each German state, structured in accordance with the catalogue of offenses and statistical attributes, were compiled in cross tabular tables and sent to BKA [*Bundeskriminalamt*] on magnetic tape" (*Bundeskriminalamt*, 2006, p. 4).

The series of *Police Crime Statistics* began in 1971 with data on 105 different kinds of offenses. Currently, because of the development of many new criminal statutes, the number of recorded offenses has increased to 421. The 2006 *Police Crime Statistics* report indicated that a higher level of differentiation in the catalogue of criminal offenses and the greater complexity of law are "reflected in the larger quantity of key numbers—from 105 key numbers in the first computerized police crime statistics published in 1971 to 421 key numbers for the 2006 reporting period" (*Bundeskriminalamt*, 2006, p. 7).

The 2009 *Police Crime Statistics—Federal Republic of Germany* report shows that all 421 criminal offenses are categorized in terms of eight broad categories of crimes: offenses against life, offenses against sexual self-determination, acts of brutality and offenses against personal freedom, theft without aggravating circumstances, theft with aggravating circumstances, fraud-type property offenses, other criminal offenses, and offenses under supplementary criminal legislation. Each of these eight categories includes a number of related offenses. The category of sexual self-determination, for example, includes 36 different types of sexual offenses, and the category of acts of brutality and offenses against personal freedom includes 62 different types of offenses. According to the 2009 *Police Crime Statistics—Federal Republic of Germany* report (*Bundeskriminalamt*, 2009), the overall offense rate in Germany during 1993–2009 did not show any significant trend of decline like that of the United States and Canada. In 1993, the overall offense rate in Germany (except traffic offenses and offenses against state security) was 8,337 per 100,000 population. In 2009, the overall offense rate came down to 7,383 per 100,000 population. The 2009 report also shows that the German cities with high rates of crime included Berlin, Frankfurt, Hamburg, Köln, Magdeburg, and Stuttgart.

One of the important characteristics of the police records of crime statistics in Germany is that the records show crime trends by dividing the population into two groups—Germans and non-Germans. The 2009 report noted that among the non-German population in Germany, the crime rate is higher among people coming from Poland, Italy, Romania, Greece, France, the Netherlands, Bulgaria, Austria, the Czech Republic, and Portugal. The crime rate among the non-German population in Germany who are not from the European Union (EU) countries is higher among Turks, Serbians, and Russians. Among all of the non-German population in Germany, including the population from EU and non-EU countries, the crime rate is highest, according to the 2009 *Police Crime Statistics—Federal Republic of Germany* report, among the Turkish population in Germany (*Bundeskriminalamt*, 2009).

There are two other national reports, in addition to the *Police Crime Statistics* series, that also bring a wealth of information on the criminal justice system in Germany. These are the yearly report, the *Criminal Justice in Germany,* published by the Federal Ministry of Justice (Jehle, 2009) and the *Periodical Report on Crime and Crime Control in Germany* (PRC) published by the Federal Ministry of the Interior and the Federal Ministry of Justice (2001). The PRC is published to supplement official crime statistics with data and research collected from other governmental and nongovernmental sources. The First PRC, published in 2001, "included findings on research on undetected crime, especially victims surveys, and thus shifted the focus more on to the important, though rarely seen, victim's perspective. This approach put official crime situation reporting in Germany on a new path" (Federal Ministry of the Interior and the Federal Ministry of Justice, 2001, p. 3).

German Criminal Victimization Statistics

Until early 2000, no serious attention was given to include victimization statistics in the collection of official crime statistics in Germany. Criminal victimization statistics in

Germany, unlike those in the United States, Canada, and the United Kingdom, were not gathered by a separate system of surveys until 2000. Since 2000, victimization statistics began to be gathered as a part of the *Police Crime Statistics* series. In *Police Crime Statistics,* victimization is measured in terms of the following five categories of offenses: murder and manslaughter; offenses against sexual self-determination; robbery; bodily injury; and offenses against personal freedom. The 2009 report, *Police Crime Statistics—Federal Republic of Germany* (*Bundeskriminalamt,* 2009), shows that the victims of these five categories of offenses are predominantly male, and the victimization rate is much lower among those who are over the age of 60. Juvenile (between ages 14 and 18) victimization rates are higher in the categories of bodily injury (2,153.6 per 100,000 population), offenses against personal freedom (447.9 per 100,000 population), and sexual offenses (99.9 per 100,000 population). The report also shows that about 66% of murder and manslaughter and 50% of sexual offenses were committed by relatives or close acquaintances.

Crime Statistics in Japan

Japanese White Paper on Crime Series

One of the major sources of crime statistics in Japan is the *White Paper on Crime* series published by the Research and Training Institute of the Ministry of Justice in Japan. The *White Paper on Crime* series is based on the following six official crime surveys: *Criminal Statistics in Japan* published yearly by Japan's National Police Agency (NPA; 2007); the *Annual Report of Statistics on Prosecution* published by the Ministry of Justice; the *Annual Report of Judicial Statistics* published by the Supreme Court of Japan; the *Annual Report of Statistics on Corrections,* the *Annual Report of Statistics on Rehabilitation,* and the *Annual Report of Statistics on Civil Affairs, Litigation, and Civil Liberties* published by the Ministry of Justice. One of the most important sources for the *White Paper on Crime* in Japan, however, is the series on *Criminal Statistics in Japan,* published by the NPA—an agency that is the central coordinating agency of the police system in Japan and which is administered by the National Public Safety Commission of the Cabinet of Japan.

The annual *Criminal Statistics in Japan* report is based on crimes reported by all 47 prefectures of Japan, including the cities of Tokyo, Hokkaido, Osaka, and Kyoto. The reporting of criminal statistics is classified into the following two major categories: penal code offenses and special law offenses. The penal code offenses include the following six types of offenses: felonious offenses (murder, robbery, arson, and rape); violent offenses (assault, bodily injury, intimidation, and extortion); larceny offenses; intellectual offenses (embezzlement, counterfeiting, official corruption, and breach of trust); moral offenses (gambling, sexual offenses, indecent assault, and indecent exposure); and other penal code offenses. The special law offenses include violations of statutory laws such as the Road Traffic Act, Stimulus Control Act, Immigration Control and Refugee Recognition Act, Minor Offenses Act, Adult Entertainment Law, and Firearm and Sword Possession Control Law.

The *White Paper on Crime* in Japan series is like the PRC in Germany, but it is more descriptive and analytical. It is designed to increase public understanding of crime trends in Japan and facilitate the use of crime statistics in Japanese policy making for crime control and crime prevention. Each year, the *White Paper* is based on a specific theme for a more focused analysis of the emerging trends and issues in crime and justice in Japan. The 2002 *White Paper on Crime,* for example, was subtitled, "Economic Offenses: Current Situation and Countermeasures"; the 2003 *White Paper* was called, "Changing Nature of Heinous Crimes and Countermeasures Against Them"; and the 2006 *White Paper* was called "New Trends of Criminal Policy." Each *White Paper*, in addition to focusing on its theme, includes statistical information and descriptions of crime trends, treatment of offenders, trends in juvenile delinquency, treatment of juvenile offenders, and criminal victimization.

The 2007 edition of *Criminal Statistics in Japan*, published by the NPA, shows that in 2007, about 2.7 million penal code crimes were reported to police, and this was significantly lower than about 3.3 million reported in 2000. In 2007, out of 2.7 million penal code crimes, about 1.9 million were recorded as felonious offenses (homicide, robbery, arson, and rape). This was again significantly lower than the approximately 2.5 million felonious crimes reported in 2000. Between 2000 and 2007, the number of reported felonious crimes decreased in all categories (homicide, robbery, arson, and rape). In the same period, however, the reporting of violent offenses, bodily injury, and intimidation increased. In 2000, police recorded 13,225 violent offenses in Japan; in 2007, the number increased to 31,966. During the same period, all intellectual offenses (embezzlement, counterfeiting, and official corruption), except fraud, declined. In 2000, police recorded 44,384 fraud crimes (Ministry of Internal Affairs and Communications, 2009); in 2007, the number increased to 67,787. What is learned from the report on *Criminal Statistics in Japan,* 2007, in summary, is that between 1990 and 2000, Japan experienced an increased rate in homicide, robbery, arson, rape, and other violent offenses. Between 2000 and 2007, most of these trends in traditional crimes began to decline, but they were still high in comparison to those of the 1980s. At the same time, Japan, like other advanced industrialized countries, began to experience a rise in new economic crimes, technology crimes, and global organized crimes from the beginning of the 1990s. The 2006 *White Paper on Crime* in Japan confirmed the observation that the number of nontraffic penal code offenses, after hitting a peak in 2002, "has been on a downward trend, but still remains at a high level. This situation does not allow optimism, and the general public is seriously concerned about the deterioration of public safety" (Japan Ministry of Justice, 2008, p. 1).

Regional Crime Surveys: Surveys From Europe

Cross-national analysis of crime and justice can be done to compare and contrast two or more countries. It can also be done to compare and contrast different regions of the world, such as crime and justice in the countries of the European Union (EU), Caribbean and Latin America, East Asia, South Asia, Southern Africa, Western Africa, and the Baltic region. Recent years have seen the emergence of some of these regions as major actors in leading economic, political, and social development activities, both regionally and globally. The regional organizations not only direct and deliberate policy issues related to growth and development, but also work as major sources for social and economic data, including crime and justice data, for those regions. Out of all regional organizations, the EU and the Council of Europe are the oldest and most prominent in mobilizing regional and global activities. The EU is an organization of 27 European countries (Austria, Belgium, Bulgaria, Cyprus, the Czech Republic, Denmark, Estonia, Finland, France, Germany, Greece, Hungary, Ireland, Italy, Latvia, Lithuania, Luxembourg, Malta, the Netherlands, Poland, Portugal, Romania, Slovakia, Slovenia, Spain, Sweden, and the United Kingdom). It was formally launched on the basis of the Treaty on European Union, commonly called the Maastricht Treaty, which was signed in 1992 and came into force in 1993. The Maastricht Treaty created a new regional organization in Europe described as the European Union (EUROPA, 2007).

The Council of Europe is a regional organization of 47 European countries created in 1949. All member states of the EU are members of the Council of Europe, but all members of the Council of Europe are not members of the EU. With a separate parliament, a separate currency, and limited control on common defense, the EU is a legal entity that is more powerful than any other regional organization in the world. What is significant from the perspective of comparative criminal justice is that both the EU and the Council of Europe adhere to the perspective that the control and prevention of crime and the building of a criminal justice system in the countries of Europe based on the universal principles of human rights and dignity is a precondition for building a just and democratic civilization in Europe. Both the EU and the Council of Europe created a number of high-quality institutions for research and policy making in crime and justice. Some of these institutions conduct cross-national surveys on crime and justice and work as major data banks on comparative criminal justice in Europe. The most prominent of these surveys and data banks include European Police Office (EUROPOL), Statistical Office of the European Communities (EUROSTAT), *European Sourcebook of Crime and Criminal Justice Statistics*, European Crime and Safety Survey (EU ICS), *EU Terrorism Situation and Trend Report* (TE-SAT), Organised Crime Threat Assessment (OCTA), and European Monitoring Centre for Drugs and Drug Addiction (EMCDDA).

European Police Office

European Police Office (EUROPOL) is the central coordinating agency for issues related to crime and law enforcement in the 27 countries of the EU. With about 600 personnel and 121 liaison offices in the member countries, EUROPOL is the police office for about 500 million citizens of the EU. It is headquartered in The Hague of the Netherlands. Its core mission, according to Article 3 of the EUROPOL Convention, is to gather, organize, analyze, and exchange the crime data and intelligence of the countries of the EU. EUROPOL has an information system (IS) network through which it can access official crime data from all member countries of the EU. It "maintains state-of-the-art data bases and communication channels offering fast and secure facilities for storing, searching, visualizing, and analyzing link information" (European Police Office, 2010, p. 6). EUROPOL collects data, information, and intelligence on a number of key areas including drug trafficking, human trafficking, child sexual abuse, money laundering, fraud and counterfeiting activities, high-tech crime, terrorism, and maritime crime in Europe. In addition to publishing various crime threat assessment reports and annual reports, EUROPOL conducts two major annual surveys. These are the *EU Terrorism Situation and Trend Report* (TE-SAT) and the Organised Crime Threat Assessment (OCTA). The TE-SAT is mainly a trend analysis of terrorism activities in Europe on the basis of terrorism data supplied by the member states. The survey on OCTA is a trend analysis of various organized criminal activities in the EU countries in areas of drug trafficking, human trafficking, crimes against persons, fraud, and counterfeiting. The report explores and analyzes the hubs and the types of organized criminal activities and their origin and destinations in the countries of the EU.

Statistical Office of the European Communities

Crime data of the countries of the EU are also available from the *Statistical Office of the European Communities* (EUROSTAT)—the central statistical office of the European Union located in Luxembourg. Every year, EUROSTAT, in collaboration with the EU directorate-general for justice, freedom, and security, publishes a report on crime trends and criminal justice in the EU countries and in the region as a whole based on official crime data supplied by the member states. The 2009 EUROSTAT report on crime and justice (European Commission, 2009) included a crime trend analysis in the EU for the period of 1998–2007. The analysis shows that the crime rate in about half of the EU countries from 1998 began to climb and peaked in 2002. In 2002, about 17.5 million crimes were reported by the member countries of the EU compared to about 16.8 million in 1998. But crimes began to fall in 2003. In 2007, about 16.2 million crimes were reported by the member states of the EU. The crimes that were reported in the period 1998–2007 included violent crime (up 3%) and drug trafficking and robbery (both up 1%). The annual rate of homicide reported for big cities in the EU countries in the period 1998–2007 was 1.9 per 100,000 population. During the same period, the prison population in the member countries grew at a rate of 1% to 123 prisoners per 100,000 population (European Commission, 2009).

European Monitoring Centre for Drugs and Drug Addiction

The European Monitoring Centre for Drugs and Drug Addition (EMCDDA) was established by the EU in Lisbon, Portugal, in 1996 for drug crime statistics in Europe. The EMCDDA was created to "provide the EU . . . with a factual overview of European drug problems and a solid evidence base to support the drugs debate. Today it offers policymakers the data they need for drawing up informed drug laws and strategies" (European Monitoring Centre for Drugs and Drug Addiction, 2010a, p. 1).

The EMCDDA publishes a yearly report on the state of drugs and drug abuse in Europe based on self-report surveys of selected adult populations of 15–64-year-olds and schoolchildren (published in 22 languages of Europe). The adult populations are surveyed from selected households, whereas schoolchildren are surveyed from selected schools in each of the countries belonging to the EU; the survey is conducted through a self-administered questionnaires called a general population survey (GPS). There are five key indicators that form the core of the GPS: prevalence; distribution and consumption of drugs and sociodemographic characteristics of drug users and drug addicts; drug use, mental health, and lifestyles; perception of different groups toward drug use and addiction; and drug use and abuse trends across countries in the EU. The 2010 EMCDDA annual report noted that marijuana was used by about 22.5% of European adults (77.5 million) at least once in their lifetime, by 6.8% (23 million) within the last year, and by 3.5% (12 million) within the month before the survey. There is a sharp variation in the lifetime use of marijuana in the countries of the EU; it ranges from 0.4% to 15.4%. Other common illegal drugs used include cocaine, ecstasy, and methamphetamine (European Monitoring Centre for Drugs and Drug Addiction, 2010b). The 2011 EMCDDA report indicated that the overall prevalence levels of the use of illicit drugs in the EU countries remained stable, but "there are worrying indications of developments in the synthetic drugs market and, more generally, in the way drug consumers now use a wider set of substances" (European Monitoring Centre for Drugs and Drug Addiction, 2011, p. 11).

The EMCDDA annual report also presents data on drug-related criminal offenses, demand and supply trends, trends in drug seizures, and national drug control policies of the EU as a whole and of the individual member countries of the EU. The EMCDDA annual report is an important source for cross-national analysis of drug problems and drug policy strategies in the countries of the EU.

European Crime and Safety Survey

To complement the understanding of the problem of crime and justice through police-recorded crimes and victim reports, in 2005, the director general of research of the European Commission set up a new victimization survey, like the BCS and the NCVS. This new system of the victimization survey is known as the European Crime and Safety Survey (EU ICS)—another major source of data for comparative analysis of crime and justice in Europe. The EU ICS is conducted by a consortium composed of Gallup Europe located in Brussels, the Max Planck Institute for Foreign and International Criminal Law in Germany, the Centre for Population, Poverty and Public Policy Studies/International Network for Studies in Technology, Environment, Alternatives, Development (CEPS/INSTEAD) located in Luxembourg, and the United Nations Interregional Crime and Justice Research Institute. Like the BCS for the United Kingdom and the NCVS for the United States, the main purpose of the EU ICS is to expand understanding of the magnitude of crime and criminality in Europe and the perception and attitudes of Europeans on crime and justice in general and on issues of safety and security in particular. The EU ICS provides evidence-based knowledge on crime and security trends that are used in policy making for crime and justice in the EU (EU ICS, 2010).

The first EU ICS was conducted in 2005, and it included 18 EU member countries. The survey was based on an average of 2,000 samples of households (with people aged 16 and over) drawn from each country on the basis of random digital dialing. About 40,000 interviews were conducted mainly through the use of computer-assisted telephone interviewing technology. A research report titled, *The Burden of Crime in the EU* (EU ICS, 2005), produced on the basis of the 2005 EU ICS, noted that victimization through common crimes such as burglaries, thefts, robberies, and assaults among the adult population in the EU countries increased in the 1990s. But starting in 2000, it began to decline. "The mean victimization rates of participating EU countries," the report observed, "went from 16.9 in 1988 to 21.6 in 1992 and to 21.6 in 1996. It fell slightly to 19.3 in 2000, and steeply decreased to 14.9 in 2004" (EU ICS, 2005, p. 2). According to *The Burden of Crime in the EU* (EU ICS, 2005), some forms of crime in 2004 went up because of the level of urbanization and the percentage of young people in the population in the United Kingdom, Ireland, and Estonia. The risks of being assaulted were high in 2004 in the United Kingdom, Ireland, the Netherlands, Belgium, Sweden, and Denmark. Women in Sweden, Ireland, Germany, and Austria reported a higher level of risk from sexual victimization. The respondents from Greece, Poland, Hungary, and Estonia reported an increased incidence of corruption and bribery, and the respondents from France, Denmark, and the United Kingdom—the countries with a high immigrant population—reported higher risks of victimization through hate crimes. The study found that "of those indicating to be immigrants, 10% report to have fallen victim to 'hate crime.' The victimization rate among non-immigrants is 2%" (EU ICS, 2005, p. 53). The respondents from Greece, Italy, France, Portugal, and the United Kingdom expressed more concerns about crime and safety than those from Finland, Denmark, Sweden, Austria, Germany, Hungary, and the Netherlands. Another significant observation made by the same report is that gun-related crimes are much lower in the EU countries than in the United States (EU ICS, 2005).

European Sourcebook of Crime and Criminal Justice Statistics

The *European Sourcebook of Crime and Criminal Justice Statistics* is another major source of data on comparative criminal justice in Europe. It is published every 4 years by the European Council. It started in 1993 with the formation of a European Committee on Crime Problems by a group of experts from France, Germany, Hungary, the Netherlands, Sweden, Switzerland, and the United Kingdom. The core methodology of organizing data is a system of national correspondents that mandates "that each country should have one person responsible for the collection and the initial checking of the data. Each correspondent would be an expert in crime and criminal justice statistics and act as a helpline" (Ministry of Justice, Research and Documentation, 2010, p. 14).

The national correspondents collect data from police agencies, prosecutorial services, court services, and correctional agencies. In creating the *Sourcebook,* the Ministry of Justice, Research and Documentation collects and uses data also from EUROPOL, EUROSTAT, the United Nations Office on Drugs and Crime (UNODC), the International Crime Victimization Survey (ICVS), and the International Self-Reported Delinquency Study. The compendium presents data in terms of the following four major categories: criminal offenses and offenders; prosecution; conviction and sentencing; and corrections, including noncustodial sanctions. The criminal offense category includes data on both traditional crimes and newer crimes such as money laundering, computer crime, drug trafficking, and corruption.

Some of the methodological challenges faced by the *Sourcebook* are common in cross-national analysis of crime and justice in general—the varying legal definitions of crime and criminality, different types of crime classification, and different rules and times of recording criminal offenses. In 2007, according to the 2010 *Sourcebook* (Ministry of Justice, Research and Documentation, 2010), the total offense rate (based on the number of offenses per 100,000 population) was highest in Sweden (14,465) followed by Iceland (11,134), Finland (10,368), Scotland (9,417), and England and Wales (9,158). In 2007, the lowest rate of total crime among the countries of the European Council (offenses per 100,000 population) was recorded for Albania (279), Armenia (284), and Moldova (445). In most of the countries of the European Council in 2007, the murder rate was between 1 and 2 per 100,000 population except in Lithuania (7.4), Estonia (7.1), and Albania (2.9).

In most European countries, the mean rate of rape is about 10 per 100,000 population. The mean, however, is higher in Iceland, Norway, Sweden, and the United Kingdom. In 2007, Sweden had the highest number of rapes per 100,000 population among all the countries of the European Council (53). Sweden was followed by Iceland (42 in 2006), Norway (23), England and Wales (23), and France (16). In 2003–2007, while the rate of rape decreased in most European countries, it increased 180% in Georgia, 84% in Sweden, 38% in Slovenia, and 29% in Norway. In terms of sexual abuse of minors, the highest rate based on 100,000 population in 2007 was found in Northern Ireland (34) followed by Sweden (28), Finland (14), and Latvia (11). During 2003–2007, the computer crime rate remained highest in Germany, Belgium, and Sweden. During the same period, computer crime increased 1,000% in Bulgaria, 695% in Slovenia, 504% in Estonia, 119% in Ireland, and 115% in Poland. Money laundering during the same period increased 1,000% in Finland and Russia, 530% in Estonia, 429% in Germany, and 425% in Romania (Ministry of Justice, Research and Documentation, 2010). One of the significant crime trends in Europe that is observed in the data presented by the 2010 *European Sourcebook of Crime and Criminal Justice Statistics* is that economic crimes such as money laundering, computer crime, corruption, and drug trafficking are growing in most European countries. They are rapidly growing particularly in the former communist countries of Eastern Europe, Russia, and the Baltic region. The Council of Europe, in addition to publishing the *European Sourcebook of Crime and Criminal Justice Statistics* every 4 years, also publishes a number of other reports on crime and justice in Europe. One of the most important of these reports is the *Council of Europe Annual Penal Statistics* (SPACE I and II).

Self-Reported Delinquency Surveys in Europe

For crime and delinquency data on young people, many major countries of Europe also conduct self-reported delinquency (SRD) surveys like the YRBSS of the United States and the OCJS of the United Kingdom. These studies are based on the same methodology as school-based surveys for understanding the nature and extent of delinquency and anti-social behavior among young people. It consists of personal interviews, computer-assisted personal interviews, computer-assisted self-administered interviews, and computer-assisted Web interviews. In Europe, although parents are informed that their children will be interviewed, the survey does not need explicit written authorization from the parents. The SRD surveys are conducted in a number of countries in Europe, including Belgium, Finland, France, Germany, Italy, Sweden, and the United Kingdom (Aebi, 2009). Some of the most notable of these studies have been conducted in the United Kingdom, such as the Cambridge Study in Delinquent Development (Farrington, 1994), the Edinburgh Study of Youth Transitions and Crime (Smith, McVie, McAra, Woodward, Flint, & Shute, 2001), and the Peterborough Adolescent and Young Adult Development Study (Wikström, Oberwittler, Treiber, & Hardie, 2012). These studies are comparable to some of the major longitudinal SRD surveys conducted in the United States, such as the Pittsburgh Youth Study (Browning & Loeber, 1999), the Rochester Youth Development Study (Browning, Thornberry, & Porter, 1999), and the Denver Youth Survey (Thornberry & Krohn, 2002).

■ International Crime Surveys

In addition to national and regional surveys, data on crime and criminal justice systems are also collected, organized, and analyzed by a number of international organizations, including the various agencies of the United Nations, the World Bank, INTERPOL, Transparency International, the Global Peace Index of the Australian Institute for Economics and Peace, and the Global Barometer Project. The United Nations, in particular, has a number of agencies and programs related to crime and justice (see **Table 3-5**). It funds and organizes some of the most comprehensive and reliable international surveys on crime and justice (see **Box 3-1**). Some of these include the United Nations Surveys on Crime Trends and the Operations of Criminal Justice Systems (UN-CTS) organized by the UNODC; the ICVS organized by the UNODC and the United Nations Economic Commission for Europe; the survey series, *International Statistics on Crime and Justice,* organized by the UNODC and the European Institute for Crime Prevention and Control (HEUNI); the World Health Organization's Study on Violence Against Women; United Nations Children's Fund's study on Violence Against Children; and United Nations Human Settlements Programme (UN-HABITAT). The United Nations and other international surveys and reports on crime data are relatively more reliable because of their methodological rigor, standardized questionnaires, research-based survey strategies, and greater access to national and regional data sources.

United Nations Surveys on Crime Trends

The United Nations Surveys on Crime Trends and the Operations of Criminal Justice Systems (UN-CTS) started in 1970 with the explicit purpose of developing a world data bank on crime and justice. Since the early 1980s, as a result of the development of new survey techniques and increased emphasis on crime and justice as a global development issue, the UN-CTS has vastly grown in scope and significance (United Nations Office on Drugs and Crime, 2012). Between 1970 and 2008, 11 surveys were completed (see **Table 3-6**), and by now a large amount of data has been accumulated to assess global trends in crime and justice. The UN-CTS is based on questionnaires sent to the member states. In each member state, there is a national coordinator designated by its government to complete the questionnaires on the basis of the crimes reported to police and police-recorded crimes. Data on crime, police, courts, and prisons are collected by the national coordinators from relevant governmental agencies. The U.N. survey includes a variety of questions on issues such as criminal justice resources, number of reported crimes, number of police personnel, crime in large cities, number of people arrested, number of people convicted and sentenced, prosecution by age

TABLE 3-5 United Nations Programs on Comparative Criminal Justice

Programs	Goals and Objectives
United Nations Commission on Crime Prevention and Criminal Justice	Developing, monitoring, and coordinating U.N. crime and justice-related activities as an advisory body. Priority areas include combating transnational crime, promoting the rule of law, reducing urban crime and violence, and capacity building in criminal justice systems of the member countries. Created in 1991.
United Nations Crime Prevention and Criminal Justice Programme Network	Assisting the U.N. programs on crime and justice through the funding and development of research-based knowledge. Some of the major institutions and programs within the network include the U.N. Office on Drugs and Crime (UNODC) in Vienna, Austria; United Nations Asia and Far East Institute for the prevention of crime and the treatment of offenders (UNAFEI) in Tokyo, Japan; European Institute for Crime Prevention and Control affiliated with the United Nations (HEUNI) in Helsinki, Finland; United Nations African Institute for the Prevention of Crime and the Treatment of Offenders (UNAFRI) in Kampala, Uganda; Australian Institute of Criminology, and the Korean Institute of Criminology.
United Nations Crime Congress	Meets every 5 years and brings criminal justice experts from all over the world to deliberate on critical crime and justice issues. The 12th U.N. Congress was held in Salvador, Brazil in 2010. Established in 1955.
United Nations Interregional Crime and Justice Research Institute (UNICRI)	Assisting and coordinating intergovernmental, governmental, and nongovernmental programs and activities related to crimes and justice. Some of the focused areas include global terrorism, justice reforms, human trafficking, and training in security governance. Established in 1967.
United Nations Surveys on Crime Trends and the Operations of Criminal Justice Systems (UN-CTS)	Compiling of crime and justice statistics from the member countries to assess global trends in crime and justice every 2–3 years. The 1st and 2nd U.N. surveys were completed in 1970 and 1980, respectively. The 11th U.N. Survey was completed in 2008.
United Nations Counter-Terrorism Implementation Task Force (UN CTITF)	Created in 2005 to coordinate U.N. activities for a global strategy to combat terrorism. In 2007, the UN CTITF launched its *Counter-Terrorism Online Handbook* for sharing terrorism information with all member states.

Source: Data from United Nations www.un.org/en/

and sex, average length of sentencing, structure of the judicial system, and number of prisons and prisoners.

Because of a wide diversity in the way crimes are defined by different countries, the U.N. survey questions include some standard definitions of the some of the major forms of crimes such as intentional homicide, rape, assault, robbery, arson, theft, kidnapping, and drug-related offenses. Questionnaires are sent to national coordinators of the member countries through

BOX 3-1

United Nations Manual for the Development of a System of Criminal Justice Statistics

The United Nations Organization is one of the world's leading institutions that systematically collects, analyzes, and disseminates criminal justice statistics of the various countries of the world. The first *Manual for the Development of Criminal Justice Statistics* was developed, on guidance of the United Nations General Assembly and the United Nations Congress on the Prevention of Crime and Treatment of Offenders, in the middle of the 1980s. The present manual, the *Manual for the Development of a System of Criminal Justice Statistics,* which presents the guidelines for the development of a national system of criminal justice statistics in all member countries of the United Nations, was drafted in 1997 and finalized in an expert group meeting in Buenos Aires in 2001. The manual also received opinions from experts from various countries of the world on developing criminal justice statistics. The manual has proposed that the collection of criminal justice statistics must be divided into three interrelated segments: administration, planning, and policy research and analysis. The United Nations suggests that the core requirements for the development of an efficient system of national criminal justice are: commitment of stakeholders; maintaining political neutrality and objectivity; effective utilization of technical and methodological sources; an integrated approach to crime and the collection of crime data; and fostering the evolution of the statistical program related to criminal justice data analysis. The manual is based on the vision that "comprehensive criminal justice statistics in countries is of immense importance to everyone involved with criminal justice, especially to the criminal justice administrator. Each component of the criminal justice system inevitably creates large quantities of records, but it is only when such raw information is transformed through purposeful collection and organization into statistical form that these records provide information valuable for criminal justice decision-making." In any comparative research on criminal justice in a country, it is imperative to examine how that country collects and organizes data on crime and criminal justice, and how it complies with some of the core requirements of the United Nations *Manual for the Development of a System of Criminal Justice Statistics.*

Source: United Nations Organization. (2003). *Manual for the development of a system of criminal justice statistics.* New York, NY: Department of Economic and Social Affairs, Statistics Division, United Nations Organization.

their permanent missions in the United Nations. The responses are coded and analyzed by the UNODC. The UNODC analyzed data from the 11th UN-CTS in terms of two major sectors: police-recorded crimes and victims, and responses on criminal justice. Under police-recorded crimes and victims, the data again are presented in terms of the following eight types of crimes: homicide, assaults, sexual violence, robbery, kidnapping, drug-related crimes,

TABLE 3-6 United Nations Surveys on Crime Trends and the Operations of Criminal Justice Systems (UN-CTS), 1970–2010

U.N. Surveys on Crime Trends	Years Surveys Taken
First United Nations Survey	1970–1975
Second United Nations Survey	1975–1980
Third United Nations Survey	1980–1985
Fourth United Nations Survey	1986–1990
Fifth United Nations Survey	1990–1994
Sixth United Nations Survey	1995–1997
Seventh United Nations Survey	1998–2000
Eighth United Nations Survey	2001–2002
Ninth United Nations Survey	2003–2004
Tenth United Nations Survey	2005–2006
Eleventh United Nations Survey	2007–2008
Twelfth United Nations Survey	2009–2010

Source: Data from United Nations Office on Drugs and Crime. (2012). *United Nations Surveys on Crime Trends and the Operations of Criminal Justice Systems (CTS).* Vienna, Austria: Author.

trafficking in person, and illegal trafficking of cultural property. Under criminal justice system response, data are presented in terms of person detained, person arrested, person prosecuted, person convicted, and criminal justice system resources.

Data on the rate of rape from the 11th U.N. survey analyzed by the UNODC shows that in 2008 it was highest in the Southern African country of Lesotho (91.6 per 100,000 population). It was followed by Sweden (53.1), New Zealand (30.9), the United States (28.6), Belgium (26.3), and England and Wales (24.1). In 2008, rape was lowest in Egypt (0.1), Azerbaijan (0.3), and Armenia (0.6). In terms of regional variations, rape was lowest in the countries of Eastern Europe, Western Asia, and South and Southeast Asia (United Nations Office on Drugs and Crime, 2010). According to the same U.N. survey, in 2008 the rate of robbery was highest in the countries of Eastern Europe, Western Europe, and Northern Europe (the robbery rate in Sweden was 96.8 per 100,000 population). It was also highest in some countries of Eastern Africa (Mauritius and Zimbabwe), North Africa (Morocco), and Central Asia (Kazakhstan and Kyrgyzstan). The rate of robbery in 2008 was lowest in Egypt (0.9 per 100,000 population). During the same year, drug-related crimes were higher in the countries of Northern Europe, Southern Europe, Eastern Europe, and North Africa. In 2008, drug-related crime was highest in Cyprus (90.6 per 100,000 population), Greece, (88.5), Morocco (81.8), and Montenegro (73.9).

International Crime Victimization Survey

Following the results, experience, and significance of the U.S. NCVS introduced in the late 1970s, the BCS created in the early 1980s, and general concerns about the limits of police statistics and police-recorded crime, the International Crime Victimization Survey (ICVS) was introduced in 1989 (see **Box 3-2**). It was first introduced and organized by a group of European experts on crime and justice interested in victimology—a specialization that began to grow in the academic field of criminology in the mid-1980s. The ICVS presently is one of the leading and most reliable international surveys on crime and justice. It is funded and

---

BOX 3-2

United Nations Manual on Victimization Surveys

Traditionally, crime rates, trends, and patterns are measured in terms of crimes reported to law enforcement. Police-recorded crimes occupy a significant portion of crime statistics in most countries of the world, particularly of the developing world. In the beginning of the 1970s, experts on criminology and criminal justice statistics began to realize that a much more fundamental understanding of crime and criminality in a country can be reached through victimization surveys—information from the victims who do not report their victimization to law enforcement. It became clear that victimization trends and patterns could yield valuable results about the nature of crime and criminal justice in a country. The growth of the specialty of victimization in the fields of criminology and criminal justice starting in the early 1970s spurred a new movement for the development of victimization surveys. In the United States, the National Criminal Victimization Survey began to collect data on household victimization in 1973. Australia started its first victimization survey in 1975. The British Crime Survey was introduced in 1981. By the end of the 1980s, victimization surveys became an integral part of criminal statistics in almost all countries of the West. The rise of national interest in victimization surveys also led to the rise of interest in international victimization surveys. The United Nations Organization took a leading role in developing a methodology for the designing of victimization surveys in all countries of the world. The United Nations Office on Drugs and Crime (UNODC) and the United Nations Interregional Research Crime and Justice Research (UNICRI) introduced the first International Crime Victimization Survey (ICVS) in 1989. The ICVSs "are now an important tool in helping governments and their public to understand their crime problems and how better to address them. Furthermore, in the last decades much attention has also been given to studying the subjective aspects of criminality: Fear of crime, worries, defense strategies are collected in the main victimization surveys." Between 2000 and 2006, 24 ICVSs were completed. For a comparative analysis of criminal justice around the world's societies, data from the ICVS are of immense value. The nature and level of participation of a country in the ICVSs will significantly suggest its level of growth and modernity in criminal justice.

Source: United Nations Office on Drugs and Crime and the United Nations Economic Commission for Europe. (2010). *Manual on victimization surveys.* Geneva, Switzerland: United Nations.

organized by the UNODC, the United Nations Interregional Crime and Justice Research Institute, the EU ICS, the HEUNI (affiliated with the United Nations), and governments and expert groups of more than 30 countries. After the first ICVS was conducted in 1989, "more than 140 surveys had been done in more than 78 different countries (nationwide in 37 countries). Over 320,000 citizens have been interviewed in the course of the ICVS so far" (Van Dijk et al., 2007, p. 21).

The ICVS methodology, like other victimization surveys, is based on self-report household surveys. From each country, or a city within a country, the landline phone numbers of about 2,000 households (adult members only) are randomly drawn by random digital dialing for both face-to-face and computer-assisted telephone interviews. The ICVS has a common set of questions on crimes including burglary, attempted burglary, theft of personal property and contract crimes (robbery, sexual offenses, and assault and threat), and vehicle-related crimes (theft of a car, theft from a car, and theft of a bicycle). Questions are also asked about street-level corruption, consumer fraud, hate crime, drug-related crime, fear of crime, satisfaction with law enforcement, and perception of punishment and sentencing (United Nations Office on Drugs and Crime and the United Nations Economic Commission, 2010).

Through the ICVS, a considerable amount of data on comparative crime and justice has been accumulated, and an improved understanding of the nature and operations of criminal justice in different countries has been achieved. One of the key findings from the ICVS of 2004–2005, for example, shows that "almost 16% of the people of 30 participating countries have been victims of a crime in 2004. The four countries with the highest overall prevalence of victimization rates in 2004 are Ireland, England and Wales, New Zealand, and Iceland" (Van Dijk et al., 2007, p. 42). The survey also shows high victimization rates for Estonia, the Netherlands, Denmark, Mexico, Switzerland, and Belgium. The nature of victimization in the aforementioned countries indicates that a high rate of victimization is positively related to a high rate of urbanization and a high degree of affluence (except Estonia and Mexico). The analysis of the data from the ICVS 2004–2005 "refutes conventional wisdom about poverty as the dominant root cause of common crime" (Van Dijk et al., 2007, p. 43). Between 1988 and 2004, victimization rates in North America, Australia, and nine European countries "show distinct downward trends" (Van Dijk et al., 2007, p. 46). The ICVS data from 2004–2005 show there was "an increase in general crime between 1988 and 1991 and a downward trend since 1996 or 2000 around the developed world" (Van Dijk et al., 2007, p. 102).

International Statistics on Crime and Justice

Along with the UN-CTS and the ICVS, the UNODC publishes, in collaboration with the HEUNI, a series called *International Statistics on Crime and Justice*. This is primarily based on analysis of data from the UN-CTS, but it also includes data gathered by the ICVS, EUROSTAT, UNICEF, and INTERPOL. Because its analysis is based on data collected by a number of international and regional crime and justice surveys, the UNODC series presents valuable information on global trends in crime and justice.

The 2010 *International Statistics on Crime and Justice* report, for example, noted that in 2004, the highest rates of intentional homicides were found in the countries of Southern Africa (about 35 per 100,000 population), the Caribbean region (about 29 per 100,000 population), and Central America (19 per 100,000 population). In the same year, the lowest rates of intentional homicides were observed in the countries of Western Europe, Southern Europe, Eastern Asia, and Oceania (less than 1 per 100,000 population). In North America, in 2004, the rate of intentional homicide was about 5 per 100,000 population (Harrendorf, Heiskanen, & Malby, 2010). The report also shows that, globally, traditionally violent crimes such as robberies and assaults increased during the period of 1996–2006, but property crimes including burglary and motor vehicle theft decreased. In 2005–2006, drug-related offenses were higher in Europe (about 30 per 100,000 population) and Africa (about 15 per 100,000 population). During the same time, the rates of drug trafficking were also higher in Europe and Africa. The data from the 10th UN-CTS show that human trafficking, counterfeit currency, corruption, and participation in organized criminal groups have increased in all participating countries (Harrendorf et al., 2010).

■ Comparative Criminal Justice: Innovative Methodological Strategies

The national, regional, and international crime surveys in recent years have generated a large amount of data on crime and justice. Data from the UN-CTS and the ICVS, particularly, are widely used by researchers in comparative criminal justice (see **Box 3-3**). The ICVS series has generated a large number of comparative studies on crime and justice in Europe, Asia, and Latin America (Stein, 2010; Tseloni et al., 2004). There are also many innovative methodological strategies that can be used in comparative research to complement the data available from various national, regional, and international crime surveys. Some of these are field research, ethnographic studies, observational studies, and panel studies. The goal of comparative research in criminal justice is not just the gathering of data on crime and justice in different countries. The more important task is the analysis of the social, economic, political, ideological, and cultural contexts of differences and similarities in crime and justice in different countries. The task is to examine the diversities in crime patterns and trends, as well as differences and similarities in the structuring and functioning of criminal justice in terms of such social processes as urbanization, industrialization, modernization, globalization, and traditionalism. This task demands that available data produced by national, regional, and international crime surveys are used within the framework of some innovative methodological strategies—strategies that are widely used in social science not only for empirically grounded analyses, but also historically, culturally, and theoretically grounded analyses. Almost all international crime surveys, for example, show data that the intentional rate of homicide is highest in the countries of Southern Africa, the Caribbean region, and Central America. This and other puzzles need to be examined in the context of economic, political, social, and cultural developments in these regions, particularly their specific articulations in terms of modernization and globalization.

BOX 3-3

Manual for the Measurement of Juvenile Justice Indicators

The development of a separate system of juvenile justice is one of the hallmarks of modern criminal justice. In the United States, a separate system of juvenile justice, particularly juvenile courts, began to develop through the Illinois Juvenile Court Act of 1899. In the United Kingdom, a separate juvenile courts system was established by the Children Act of 1908. Canada's juvenile justice system was created through the Juvenile Delinquents Act of 1908. In Germany, the Juvenile Welfare Act of 1922 and the Juvenile Justice Act of 1923 where the foundation of a separate system of juvenile justice. Juvenile justice systems have also been established in recent years in many developing countries of Asia, Africa, and Latin America. The international standards for the creation of a separate system of juvenile justice and the treatment of juveniles within the criminal justice system of a country are based on a number of United Nations rules and conventions, such as the United Nations Convention on the Rights of the Child, the United Nations Guidelines for the Prevention of Juvenile Delinquency, the United Nations Standard Minimum Rules for the Administration of Juvenile Justice, and the United Nations Rules for the Protection of Juveniles Deprived of Their Liberty. The United Nations Standard Minimum Rules for the Administration of Juvenile Justice ("The Beijing Rules"), adopted by the United Nations General Assembly in 1985, made it mandatory for all member states to develop separate systems of justice for juveniles. It was in this context that the United Nations Office on Drugs and Crime and the United Nations Children's Fund, in collaboration with a number of non-governmental agencies and many experts in juvenile justice, have created the *Manual for the Measurement of Juvenile Justice Indicators*. This manual includes guidelines for the collection and analysis of data on juvenile delinquency and juvenile justice. It provides "a framework for measuring and presenting specific information about the situation of children in conflict with the law. This information concerns both *quantitative* values . . . and the existence of relevant *policy*. The indicators . . . represent a basic dataset and comparative tool that offers a starting point for the assessment, evaluation and service and policy development." The manual is composed of 11 quantitative indicators and 4 policy indicators. Some of the quantitative indicators include number of children in conflict with the law per 100,000 child population; number of children in detention; number of children in presentence detention; time spent in detention by children before sentencing; and number of children sentenced receiving a custodial sentence. Some of the core policy indicators include the existence of a separate system of juvenile justice and a national plan for the prevention of juvenile crime.

Source: United Nations Office on Drugs and Crime and the United Nations Children's Fund. (2006). *Manual for the measurement of juvenile justice indicators*. Vienna, Austria: UNODC.

There is a long legacy of using field research, ethnographic studies, observational studies, and panel studies in crime and justice research. One of the classic works was by William Foote Whyte (1943) in his study, *Street Corner Society*. The research was conducted in Boston, Massachusetts, in the 1940s. Whyte lived 3 years in a Boston slum inhabited mostly by first- and second-generation Italian immigrants. In his study, Whyte, using participant observation methodology and ethnographic strategies, described how gangs were formed by "corner boys" and explained how social and economic contexts contributed to their participation in criminal activities. Many gang research experts suggest that an understanding of the contemporary phenomenon of organized gangs, both in developed and developing countries, need more involved methodologies of ethnography and participant observation (Hughes, 2005). Mendoza-Denton's (2008) *Homegirls: Language and Cultural Practice Among Latina Youth Gangs,* Laidler and Hunt's (2001) *Accomplishing Femininity Among the Girls in the Gang*, and Werdmolder's (1997) *A Generation Adrift: An Ethnography of a Criminal Moroccan Gang in the Netherlands* are some of the notable studies on the comparative understanding of youth gangs based on ethnography and participant observation strategies. Similarly, a considerable number of comparative studies in criminal justice have been done on the basis of panel studies. A panel study is a methodology of using expert informants. Some of the examples of the use of panel study in comparative criminal justice in recent years include *Criminal Justice in Europe: A Comparative Study,* edited by Fennell, Harding, Jörg, and Swart (1995); *International Handbook on Juvenile Justice,* edited by D. J. Shoemaker (1996); and *Coping with Overloaded Criminal Justice Systems: The Rise of Prosecutorial Power Across Europe,* edited by J. Jehle and M. Wade (2006). The latter presents research on the rise of new prosecutorial power that was conducted by a panel of judges and jurists from England and Wales, France, Germany, the Netherlands, Poland, and Sweden.

■ Summary

Cross-national analysis of crime and justice raises a number of methodological issues both because crimes are differently defined, perceived, and classified in different countries, and because criminal justice is organized and pursued differently in different societies. Presently, official crime statistics, in some form or another, are available in almost all countries. Official crime statistics, however, have many errors due to limited reporting of crimes to the police and bias in police-recorded crimes. In recent years, in addition to crime surveys conducted nationally, there has grown a vast number of national and regional crime surveys that produce a large number of cross-national data (see **Table 3-7**). Some of these national and regional surveys include the UN-CTS, ICVS, *International Statistics on Crime and Justice,* EUROPOL, EUROSTAT, EMCDDA, EU ICS, *European Sourcebook of Crime and Criminal Justice Statistics,* and Self-Reported Delinquency Surveys in Europe. Regional crime surveys are conducted also by the four United Nations regional crime and justice institutes. These include the United Nations Asia and Far East Institute for the Prevention of Crime and the Treatment of Offenders (UNAFEI), the United Nations African Institute for the Prevention of Crime and the Treatment of Offenders (UNAFRI), the United Nations Latin American Institute for the Prevention of Crime and the Treatment of Offenders (ILANUD), and the European Institute for Crime Prevention and Control (HEUNI).

TABLE 3-7 Comparative Criminal Justice: Some Selected National, Regional, and International Crime Surveys and Data Sources

Surveys and Data Sources	Types and Data and Statistics
Uniform Crime Reporting (UCR), USA	Official crime statistics
National Crime Victimization Survey (NCVS), USA	Self-reported data
National Incident-Based Reporting System (NIBRS), USA	Official crime statistics
Youth Risk Behavior Surveillance System (YRBSS), USA	Self-reported data
Uniform Crime Reporting Survey (UCR), Canada	Official crime statistics
British Criminal Statistics	Official crime statistics
British Crime Survey	Self-reported data
Police Crime Statistics, Germany	Official crime statistics
Periodical Report on Crime and Crime Control in Germany	Official crime statistics
Criminal Statistics in Japan	Official crime statistics
White Paper on Crime, Japan	Official crime statistics
EUROPOL	Official crime statistics
EUROSTAT	Official crime statistics
EMCDDA	Official crime statistics
European Crime and Safety Survey (EU ICS)	Self-reported data
European Sourcebook of Crime and Criminal Justice Statistics	Official crime statistics
UN-CTS	Official crime statistics
ICVS	Official crime statistics

There are three major ways in which crime statistics are produced by national, regional, and international organizations: crimes reported to police and police-recorded crimes based on the number of offenses and offenders; victimization reports based on self-report household surveys; and self-reported delinquency surveys. For a more balanced understanding of crime statistics and crime trends across countries, data from these and other sources need to be cross-examined and triangulated. What is even more important is to achieve a balance between the quantitative data and qualitative understanding of the context of crime, criminality, and criminal justice using such innovative methodologies as participant observation, ethnography, field research, and panel studies.

■ Discussion Questions

1. What are some of the methodological issues and challenges in comparative criminal justice and in the use of cross-national data? What are possible sources of errors in official crime statistics?

2. The United States, Canada, and the United Kingdom produce some of the most reliable sources of crime and justice data on their respective countries. Describe the nature and make a comparative study of official crime statistics in the United States, Canada, and the United Kingdom (focus particularly on how crimes are classified for the production of crime statistics).

3. Describe the nature and make a comparative study of the similarities and differences between the NCVS of the United States and the BCS. How are NCVS and BCS data qualitatively different from those of the UCR of the United States and the British Criminal Statistics?

4. Make a comparative study of different crime surveys used in Germany and Japan focusing particularly on the *Periodical Report on Crime and Crime Control in Germany* (PRC) and the *White Paper on Crime* in Japan. Comment in this context on the role of the *Bundeskriminalamt* of Germany and the National Police Agency (NPA) of Japan.

5. What are some of the major surveys used to generate crime statistics for the countries of the EU? Answer this question by focusing particularly on the nature and roles of EUROPOL, EUROSTAT, the EMCDDA, and the European Crime and Safety Survey.

6. Based on the crime statistics generated by EUROPOL and the European Crime and Safety Survey, describe the nature of violent crimes (for example, intentional homicide, rape, and robbery) in major European capitals. Which countries of the EU have the highest rates of rape and robbery? Develop an explanation in terms of urbanization, demography, and social and cultural values.

7. What is the role of the United Nations in the development of crime statistics in particular and the advancement in the comparative understanding of crime and justice in the world's societies in general?

8. Make a comparative study of the UN-CTS and ICVS, focusing particularly on their methodological strategies. Using data from the UN-CTS, summarized by the UNODC's 2010 *International Statistics on Crime and Justice*, describe the trends of intentional homicide in the countries of Southern Africa, Central America, and the Caribbean region.

■ References

Aebi, M. F. (2009). Self-reported delinquency surveys in Europe. In R. Zauberman (Ed.), *Self-reported crime and deviance studies in Europe* (pp. 11–49). Brussels, Belgium: Brussels University Press.

British Home Office. (2009). *Crime in England and Wales 2008/ 2009*. Retrieved on October 23, 2010, from http://rds.homeoffice.gov.uk/rds/crimeew0809ot.html.

British Home Office. (2010a). *Counting rules for recorded crime*. Retrieved on October 24, 2010, from http://rds.homeoffice.gov.uk/rds/countrules.html.

British Home Office. (2010b). *User guide to Home Office crime statistics*. Retrieved on October 24, 2010, from http://rds.homeoffice.gov.uk/rds/pdfs10/crimestats-userguide.pdf.

British Ministry of Justice. (2010). *Criminal statistics: England and Wales 2009*. Retrieved from www.justice.gov.uk/downloads/statistics/mojstats/criminal-statistics-annual.pdf/.

Browning, K., & Loeber, R. (1999). *Highlights of findings from the Pittsburgh Youth Study*. Washington, DC: Office of Justice Programs, U.S. Department of Justice.

Browning, K., Thornberry, T. P., & Porter, P. K. (1999). *Highlights of findings from the Rochester Youth Development Study*. Washington, DC: Office of Justice Programs, U.S. Department of Justice.

Bundeskriminalamt. (2006). *Police crime statistics 2006—Federal Republic of Germany*. Wiesbaden, Germany: BKA.

Bundeskriminalamt. (2009). *Police crime statistics 2009—Federal Republic of Germany*. Wiesbaden, Germany: BKA.

Bureau of Justice Statistics (2000). *Effects of NIBRS on crime statistics* (special report by R. R. Rantala and T. J. Edwards). Washington, DC: Department of Justice.

Bureau of Justice Statistics. (2002). *Rape and sexual assault: Reporting to police and medical attention, 1992–2000.* Washington, DC: Department of Justice.

Bureau of Justice Statistics. (2003). *Reporting crime to the police, 1992–2000* (special report by T. C. Hart and C. Rennison). Washington, DC: Department of Justice.

Bureau of Justice Statistics. (2009). *Criminal victimization.* Washington, DC: Department of Justice.

Bureau of Justice Statistics. (2010a). *Stranger and non-stranger crime.* Washington, DC: Department of Justice.

Bureau of Justice Statistics. (2010b*). Key facts at a glance: Crime reported to police.* Washington, DC: Department of Justice.

Bureau of Justice Statistics. (2010c). *National crime victimization survey (NCVS).* Washington, DC: Department of Justice.

Bureau of Justice Statistics. (2010d). *National crime victimization survey: Criminal victimization, 2009* (Bulletin by J. L. Truman & M. R. Rand). Washington, DC: Department of Justice.

Cantor, D., & Lynch, J. P. (2000). Self-report surveys as measures of crime and criminal victimization. In D. Duffee (Ed.), *Measurement and analysis of crime and justice: Criminal justice 2000* (pp. 85–138). Washington, DC: National Institute of Justice.

Centers for Disease Control and Prevention. (2009). *Youth risk behavior surveillance system—United States, 2009.* Atlanta, GA: Author.

Dauvergne, M., & Li, G., for Statistics Canada. (2010). *Homicide in Canada, 2005.* Ottawa, Canada: Statistics Canada..

Dauvergne, M., & Turner, J., for Statistics Canada. (2010). *Police-reported crime statistics in Canada, 2009.* Retrieved from www.statcan.gc.ca/pub/85-002-x/2010002/article/11292-eng.htm.

Economic and Social Data Service. (2010). *Guide to offending, crime and justice survey.* Essex, England: University of Essex.

European Police Office. (2010). *EUROPOL review: General report on Europol activities.* The Hague, the Netherlands: Author.

EU ICS. (2005). *The burden of crime in the EU: A comparative analysis of the European crime and safety survey.* Retrieved from www.europeansafetyobservatory.eu/downloads/EUICS%20-%20The%20 Burden%20of%20Crime%20in%20the%20EU.pdf.

EU ICS. (2010). *EU ICS consortium—Welcome.* Retrieved from www.europeansafetyobservatory.eu

EUROPA. (2007). *Treaty of Maastricht on European Union.* Brussels, Belgium: European Union.

European Commission. (2009). *Europe in figure—EUROSTAT yearbook, 2009.* Brussels, Belgium: Author.

European Monitoring Centre for Drugs and Drug Addiction. (2010a). *Mission: Background.* Retrieved from www.emcdda.europa.eu/about/mission.

European Monitoring Centre for Drugs and Drug Addiction. (2010b). *The state of the drugs problem in Europe.* Lisbon, Portugal: Author.

European Monitoring Centre for Drugs and Drug Addiction. (2011). *The state of the drugs problem in Europe.* Luxembourg, Belgium: Author.

Farrington, D. P. (1994). *Cambridge study in delinquent development.* Ann Arbor, MI: Interuniversity Consortium for Political and Social Research.

Federal Bureau of Investigation. (2000). *National incident-based reporting system* (Vol. 1. Data collection guidelines). Washington, DC: Department of Justice.

Federal Bureau of Investigation. (2009). *Crime in the United States.* Washington, DC: Department of Justice.

Federal Ministry of the Interior and the Federal Ministry of Justice. (2001). *First periodical report on crime and crime control in Germany* (abridged version). Berlin, Germany: Author.

Fennell, P., Harding, C., Jörg, N. M., & Swart, B. (1995). *Criminal justice in Europe: A comparative study.* Oxford, England: Clarendon Press.

Groves, R. M., & Cork, D. L. (2008). *Surveying victims: Options for conducting the national crime victimization survey.* Washington, DC: National Academies Press.

Hales, J., Nevill, C., Pudney, S., & Tipping, S., for the British Home Office. (2009). *Longitudinal analysis of the offending, crime and justice survey 2003–2006.* Retrieved from http://rds.homeoffice.gov.uk/rds/pdfs09/horr19c.pdf.

Harrendorf, S., Heiskanen, M., & Malby, S. (2010). *International statistics on crime and justice.* Geneva, Switzerland: UNODC and Helsinki, Finland: HEUNI.

Heiskanen, M. (2007). Trends in police recorded crime. In S. Harrendorf, M. Heiskanen, & S. Malby (Eds.), *International statistics on crime and justice* (pp. 21–47). Geneva, Switzerland: UNODC and Helsinki, Finland: HEUNI.

Hirschi, T. (1981). *Causes of delinquency.* New Brunswick, NJ: Transaction Publishers. (Originally published in 1969.)

Hughes, L. A. (2005). Studying youth gangs: Alternative methods and conclusions. *Journal of Contemporary Criminal Justice, 25,* 98–119.

Jansson, K. (2010). *British crime survey: Measuring crime for 25 years.* Retrieved from www.usak.org.tr/istanbul/files/bcs25.pdf.

Japan Ministry of Justice. (2008). *White paper on crime 2006: New trends of crime policy.* Tokyo, Japan: Author.

Jehle, J., for the Federal Ministry of Justice. (2009). *Criminal justice in Germany.* Berlin, Germany: Federal Ministry of Justice.

Jehle, J., & Wade, M. (2006). *Coping with overloaded criminal justice systems: The rise of prosecutorial power across Europe.* New York, NY: Springer.

Johnston, L. D., O'Malley, P. M., Bachman, J. G., & Schulenberg, J. E. (2009). *Monitoring the future: National results on adolescent drug use; Overview of key findings.* Ann Arbor, MI: University of Michigan and Bethesda, MD: National Institute on Drug Abuse.

Laidler, K. J., & Hunt, G. (2001). Accomplishing femininity among the girls in the gang. *The British Journal of Criminology, 1*(4), 656–678.

Lynch, J. P., & Addington, L. A. (Eds.). (2006). *Understanding crime statistics: Revisiting of the divergence of the NCVS and UCR.* Cambridge, England: Cambridge University Press.

Mahony, T. H., for Statistics Canada. (2011). *Homicide in Canada, 2010.* Ottawa, Canada: Statistics Canada.

Mellaerts, W. (2000). Criminal justice in provincial England, France, and Netherlands (1880–1905): Some comparative perspectives. *Crime, History, and Societies, 4*(2), 1–35.

Mendoza-Denton, N. (2008). *Homegirls: Language and cultural practice among Latina youth gangs.* Hoboken, NJ: Wiley-Blackwell.

Ministry of Internal Affairs and Communications. (2009). *Japan statistical yearbook.* Tokyo, Japan: Author.

Ministry of Justice, Research and Documentation. (2010). *European sourcebook of crime and criminal justice statistics.* The Hague, the Netherlands: WODC.

National Police Agency. (2007). *Criminal statistics in Japan in 2007.* Tokyo, Japan: Author.

National Research Council. (1976). *Surveying crime.* Washington DC: National Academy of Sciences.

Perrault, S., & Brennan, S., for Statistics Canada. (2010). *Criminal victimization in Canada, 2009.* Retrieved from www.statcan.gc.ca/pub/85-002-x/2010002/article/11340-eng.htm.

Save the Children Sweden. (2009). *Ending legalised violence against children: Global report 2009.* London, England: Global Initiative to End All Corporal Punishment of Children.

Shoemaker, D. J. (1996). *International handbook on juvenile justice.* Westport, CT: Greenwood Press.

Smith, D. J., McVie, S., McAra, L., Woodward, R., Flint, J. & Shute, J. (2001). *The Edinburgh Study of Youth Transitions and Crime: Key findings at ages 12 and 13.* Edinburgh, Scotland: University of Edinburgh Center for Law and Society.

Statistics Canada. (2010a). *Uniform crime reporting survey (UCR).* Retrieved from www.statcan.gc.ca/imdb-bmdi/3302-eng.htm.

Statistics Canada. (2010b). *General social survey-victimization (GSS).* Retrieved from www.statcan.gc.ca/imdb/p2SV.pl?Function=getSurvey&SDDS=4504&lang=en&db=imdb&adm=8&dis=2.

Stein, R. E. (2010). The utility of country structure: A cross-national multilevel analysis of property and violent victimization. *International Criminal Justice Review, 20*(1), 35–55.

Sutherland, E. H. (1983). *White collar crime.* New York, NY: Praeger. (Originally published in 1949.)

Thornberry, T. P., & Krohn, M. D. (2000). The self-report method for measuring delinquency and crime. In D. Duffee (Ed.), *Measurement and analysis of crime and justice: Criminal Justice 2000* (pp. 33–83). Washington, DC: National Institute of Justice.

Thornberry, T. P., & Krohn, M. D. (Eds.). (2002). *Taking stock of delinquency: An overview of findings from contemporary longitudinal studies.* New York, NY: Springer.

Tseloni, A., Wittebrood, K., Farell, G., & Pease, K. (2004). Burglary victimization in England and Wales, the United States and the Netherlands. *The British Journal of Criminology, 44*(1), 66–91.

United Nations Children's Fund. (2012). *The state of the world's children.* New York, NY: Author.

United Nations HABITAT. (2007). *Global report on human settlements 2007: Enhancing urban safety and security.* Nairobi, Kenya: Author.

United Nations Office for Drug Control and Crime Prevention. (1999). *Global report on crime and justice.* New York, NY: Oxford University Press.

United Nations Office on Drugs and Crime. (2010). *The eleventh United Nations survey on crime trends and the operations of criminal justice systems.* Vienna, Austria: Author.

United Nations Office on Drugs and Crime. (2012). *United Nations surveys on crime trends and the operations of criminal justice systems (CTS).* Vienna, Austria: Author.

United Nations Office on Drugs and Crime and the United Nations Economic Commission for Europe. (2010). *Manual on victimization survey.* Geneva, Switzerland: Author.

United States Census Bureau. (2012). *National crime victimization survey.* Washington, DC: Author.

Van Dijk, J. (2008). *The world of crime: Breaking the silence on problems of security, justice and development across the world.* Thousand Oaks, CA: Sage Publications.

Van Dijk, J., Van Kesteren, J., & Smit, P. (2007). *Criminal victimization in international perspective: Key findings from the 2004–2005 ICVS and the EU ICS.* The Hague, the Netherlands: Research and Documentation Centre, the Ministry of Justice.

Walsh, P., & Dauvergne, M., for Statistics Canada. (2010). *Police-reported hate crime in Canada, 2007.* Retrieved from www.statcan.gc.ca/pub/85-002-x/2009002/article/10844-eng.htm.

Werdmolder, H. (1997). *A generation adrift: An Ethnography of a criminal Moroccan gang in the Netherlands.* New York, NY: Springer.

Whyte, W. F. (1943). *The street corner society: The social structure of an Italian slum.* Chicago, IL: University of Chicago Press.

Wikström, P. H., Oberwittler, D., Treiber, K., & Hardie, B. (2012). *Breaking rules: The social and situational dynamics of young people's urban crime.* Oxford, England: Oxford University Press.

Profile of Modern Criminal Justice: The Benchmarks of Comparison

■ Introduction

The nature and extent of crime and criminality and the historiography of crime are issues of genuine interest in criminal justice. However, the nature and extent of crime and criminality in a country do not precisely define and describe its criminal justice system. Nor is the profile of criminal justice in a country defined and described by its rate and patterns of crime, its rate of incarceration, and the number of its police officers, courts, and prisons. The profile of criminal justice in a country is defined by the nature of its law and institutions and its values and beliefs for governing crime and punishment. Two of the most modern systems of criminal justice in the world exist in North America—the United States and Canada—but still, North America as a region is not known for having low crime and incarceration rates and a high number of police officers and judges. Rape is one of the worst forms of violent crime, and North America is among the world's regions with the highest rate of rape. Per 100,000 population in 2006, the average rate of rape in Canada was 68.2 and in the United States was 30.2. Asia, on the other hand, was one of the world regions with the lowest rate of rape in 2006 (India had a rate of 1.7). In North America, the average intentional homicide rate (cases per 100,000 population) is higher (about 5–6) than in Southern Asia (about 2–3), Northern Africa (about 1), and Eastern Asia (1–2). In North America, about 58% of homicides are committed with firearms in comparison to about 18% in Asia (2003–2008). The median rate of robbery in 2006 was higher in North America (about 146. 4 per 100,000 population) than in the regions of Southern Asia (less than 5 per 100,000 population) and East and West Asia (about 5 per 100,000 population). Many other crimes, such as burglary, motor vehicle theft, drug-related crime, organized crime, and cyber crime, are also higher in North America than other regions of the world.

In North America, the number of police and judges is lower than in many countries of the developing world where criminal justice is still very archaic. In North America, the number of police personnel is about 207.5 per 100,000 population. The world's highest number of police personnel is found in the countries of the Middle East and near East Asia (435.5 per 100,000 population regional average; Harrendorf, Heiskanen, & Malby, 2010). The median number of professional judges per 100,000 population is higher in the countries of Southeast Europe (196) than in the United States and Canada (8.6 average). Even North Africa has more professional judges (9.8 per 100,000 population) than the United States and Canada (Harrendorf et al., 2010). The United States has one of the highest rates of incarceration in the world, with "less than 5% of the world's population, but over 23% of the world's incarcerated people" (Hartney, 2006, p. 1).

These facts about crime and criminal justice are issues of definite interest in comparative criminal justice, but they do not present any clue about the nature and extent of modernity in a country's criminal justice. This necessitates, for pursuing comparative criminal justice, the development of a typology of different systems of criminal justice in the world's societies. There is an enormous amount of literature on comparative criminal justice, but macrostructural studies on different types of criminal justice are still very scanty. Currently, the typology developed by Herbert L. Packer (1968) in his book, *The Limits of the Criminal Sanction,* is the one that is widely used for systemic comparison between different types of criminal justice. Packer made a distinction between two types of criminal justice systems: the due process model (based on the dominance of the principles of the due process of law) and the crime control model (based on the dominance of the goal of crime control). The due process model is a liberal approach to governing crime and justice, and the crime control model is a conservative approach. Packer's twofold typology is useful in understanding the effect of politics and political ideologies on the shape of modern criminal justice. His typology, however, is limited to capturing the complexities of modern values and institutions of criminal justice and the problems and possibilities of their expansion among the world's societies. Packer's typology does not help to conceptualize and explain modernization as a global process or how modernization affects criminal justice systems in modernizing countries. It also does not present a perspective on how conflicts and convergences between modernity and tradition with respect to criminal justice among the world's societies and regions can be systematically comprehended.

The present study is based on a fourfold typology for cross-cultural comparison of criminal justice that compares modern, modernizing, traditional, and dual systems of criminal justice. The development of this typology is based on the assumption that since the advent of modernity, there is growing a modern system of criminal justice, just as there is growing a modern system of economy, state, education, family, bureaucracy, law, science, and cities. The understanding of the profile of this modern system of criminal justice, which has been progressing since the rise of the modern state in the 18th century, is the key to a comparative understanding of criminal justice among the world's societies. The institutions that form the core of modern criminal justice, and the values and beliefs that govern them, are the benchmarks of comparison of different systems of criminal justice in various countries and regions. This chapter develops a profile of a modern system of criminal justice in terms of some of its core institutional complexes and dominant values and beliefs about crime, law, and justice, primarily in the form of what German sociologist Max Weber called an *ideal type* (Shils & Finch, 2011). An ideal type is a conceptual abstraction. It never describes the whole truth and does not completely capture the whole gamut of a given reality. It is, rather, an attempt to approximate an empirical reality through the construction of a mental map. As sociologists Gerth and Mills (1958) noted: "The much-discussed 'ideal type,' a key term in Weber's methodological discussion, refers to the construction of certain elements of reality into a logically precise conception. The term 'ideal' has nothing to do with evaluations of any sort" (p. 59). The methodology of ideal type gave Weber the benchmarks for analysis, comparison, and comprehension of how different social institutions such as the economy, state, bureaucracy, law, religion, city, and science have been evolving in the societies of both the West and the East since the rise of modernity in the 18th and 19th centuries. It is from this perspective of an ideal type that this chapter describes the profile of modern criminal justice.

A modern system of criminal justice has been evolving from the beginning of modernization in Europe in the late 18th century. Modernization in criminal justice began around the same time that it began in all spheres of life—economy, politics, family, religion, science, culture, and ideology. With the advent of modernity in criminal justice, the boundaries of crime and criminality and the nature of law and justice began to be redefined. Today, there is hardly any country in the world where the political leadership does not want to modernize its criminal justice. There is hardly any international organization today that does not see the modernization of criminal justice in a country as an integral part of its efforts for improving governance. There is currently a growing global discourse on modernizing criminal justice among the world's societies. What are the characteristics of a modern system of criminal justice, and how are they different from those of premodern societies? What are the different trajectories for the evolution of modern criminal justice, and what is the nature of the modern state within which it has evolved? Why has modern criminal justice evolved in the West and the West alone? This chapter will address some of these questions and describe the profile—the core characteristics—of modern criminal justice, with examples from the United States.

■ Profile of Criminal Justice in Premodern Societies

Criminal justice in some form or another existed even in ancient civilizations. Some 2,000 years before the birth of Aristotle in 384 BC, a code of law for criminal justice was developed by and named after the third king of the Sumerian dynasty, Ur-Nammu. The Code of Ur-Nammu, established in 2050 BC, contained the ideas of judicial role and specialization, testimony under oath, and the notion of proportionality between crime and punishment. In 1700 BC, Babylonian King Hammurabi developed a code of law that contained the notions of retributive and restorative justice. Discovered by archeologists, the Code of Hammurabi is one of the most elaborate sets of criminal laws that came from the ancient world. The word *draconian* comes from an Athenian citizen, Draco (621 BC), who developed laws for criminal justice in the ancient city of Athens. Then came the birth of Roman law through the creation of the Twelve Tables in 450 BC and the Justinian Code in 529 AD. The word *justice* comes from the name of the emperor Justinian, who ruled the Byzantine Empire—the Eastern Roman Empire—in 527–565 AD.

Henry Maine (1861), in his classical work, *Ancient Law,* said that the "ancient Roman code belongs to a class of which almost every civilized nation in the world can show a sample" (p. 2). In primitive stages, societies were governed by customary laws. After some advancement, civilizations began to grow codes of law—the second stage of the evolution of criminal jurisprudence. As Maine commented: "From . . . Customary laws we came to another sharply defined epoch in the history of jurisprudence. We arrived in the era of Codes, those ancient Codes of which the Twelve Tables of Rome were the most famous specimen" (1861, p. 13). As civilizations advanced in Egypt, China, India, Greece, and other regions, criminal jurisprudence also advanced from customary laws to legal codes primarily aimed at strengthening the power and legitimacy of the kings and aristocracies. Beyond the development of legal codes, there were also traces of the development of the administration of justice in ancient civilizations. One of the classic examples is the statute of *Lex Calpurnia de Repetundis,* created by Lucius Calpurnius Piso Frugi in 149 BC in the Roman Empire. It introduced the law of jury trial in criminal proceedings. It was also through this statute that common people could bring charges against corruption by provincial governors (see **Table 4-1**).

TABLE 4-1 Selected Ancient Roman Criminal Laws

Laws	Related Goals and Procedures
Lex Acilia Repetundarum	Recovery of stolen property
Lex Acilia et Calpurnia	Exclusion from office in cases of electoral corruption
Lex Calpurnia de Repetundis	Permanent court to monitor the activities of the governors
Lex Cassia Tabellaria	Introduced secret ballot in court jury decisions
Lex Iulia de Adulteriis Coercendis	Made adultery a public as well as a private offense
Lex Porcia de Tergo Civium	Prohibited scourging of citizens without appeal
Lex Valeria de Provocatione	Granted legal right to appeal against a capital sentence
Lex Poetelia	Judgment by a court to authorize enslavement before execution

Source: Data from Index of Roman Law: www.unrv.com/government/index-of-roman-laws.php.

Between the gradual decline of ancient civilizations, dating from the Roman Empire's decline in the 5th century (an empire that ruled the West and the East for 500 years) and the rise of modern states in the late 18th century, the societies of Europe, Asia, Africa, and Latin America entered into an era referred to by historians as medieval times. For almost 1,000 years (800–1800), the medieval era was controlled and dominated by different monarchies, kingdoms, aristocracies, and dynasties. Medieval Europe, for example, was ruled, from 871 to 1603, by a number of kings and queens from the time of Alfred the Great (871–1016) to the time of Elizabeth I (1558–1603). Before Columbus discovered the New World in 1492 and arrived in the Island of Hispaniola, the countries that now belong to the continent of Latin America were successively ruled by the Mayan (300–900), Toltec (900–1100), Aztec (1100–1500), and Inca (1438–1535) empires. Medieval imperial China from 960 to 1911—for about 1,000 years—was ruled by 5 dynasties and 10 kingdoms, including such famous dynasties as the Han, Ming, Jin, and Shun. The period of medieval Japan began with the accession of power by the Kamakura emperor in 1185. From 1185 until the end of the Tokugawa period in 1867, medieval Japan was ruled by a number of successive emperors. The Tokugawa emperors ruled medieval Japan more than 250 years (1600–1867). Before medieval India was formally colonized by the British in the 18th century, it was ruled by successive Muslim dynasties from the days of the establishment of the Muslim sultanate in Delhi in 1192. Before slave trade and European colonialism began in Africa in the 16th century, medieval Africa was ruled by different empires and emperors from Ghana, Mali, Zimbabwe, and the Kingdom of Swahilis.

Historians of world civilizations have described the general nature of politics, economy, society, culture, and justice of these medieval empires and kingdoms as a system of feudalism. In recent years, the historiography of crime and criminal justice as a specialty has advanced considerably. Because of the advancement of this specialty, there is now a considerable amount of literature on medieval law, crime, and justice (Dean, 2007; Emsley & Knafia, 1996; Musson & Powel, 2009; Roth, 2001; Thome, 2001). In premodern societies, there were laws and legal traditions, judges and judiciaries, police and policing, and prison and corrections. The nature, themes, and ethos of these premodern institutions of criminal justice, however, were very different. Life in medieval societies was structured, predictable, and controlled. Medieval societies were not only hierarchical, but also deeply unequal. The roles and statuses of individuals in the medieval social and political landscape were legally defined, particularly in medieval Europe. The Middle Ages in Europe, as noted by one historian, "were remarkably litigious times," and this "era alone has bequeathed to us about 7,000 manuscripts on Roman law . . . and 8,000 manuscripts on canon law"(Janin, 2009, p. 5). It was further noted that in England in 1327–1328, "no fewer than 13,031 cases were brought in the court of common pleas" (Janin, 2009, p. 5). Criminal justice in medieval Europe was governed by a hugely complex set of local customary laws, secular laws, and canon laws. As James Brundage, a specialist in medieval canon law has pointed out, "Medieval laws came in abundance. Multiple legal systems coexisted within the same town or region . . . . Manorial law, feudal law, municipal law, royal law, maritime law, merchant law and canon law all nestled cheek by jowl with each other" (Brundage, as quoted in Janin, 2009, p. 7).

There was also a complex set of hierarchical court structures in medieval Europe. There were manorial courts, much like village courts in rural areas, to deal with small crimes including petty theft, assault, and public drunkenness. The manorial courts were mostly based on informal justice or on community justice based on customary laws. The judges were mostly the stewards—the representatives of the lords. The center of power in medieval society was the royal court. The royal courts were responsible for dealing with high crimes such as treason, murder, robbery, and other violent crimes. The royal courts in medieval Europe were mostly based on the common law tradition, and they had the authority to impose the death penalty. The judges in the royal courts were the kings themselves or their representatives. In the royal court of medieval England, called the Chancery court, the chief judge was the Lord Chancellor, appointed by the king. The medieval monarchies of China, Japan, and Mughal India were similarly based on the power and the supremacy of the royal courts.

In medieval Europe, the Roman Catholic Church was also a center of political and religious power, and there were ecclesiastical courts (church courts) throughout medieval Europe. The church courts were mainly based on canon law. "A uniform system of law came to be accepted throughout the Church in the West," as one historian observed, "based upon the decrees of the popes and church councils and upon the decisions rendered in the ecclesiastical courts, and called 'canon law'" (Thorndike, 1917, p. 295). The judges in the church courts were the bishops, deacons, priests, monks, and nuns. The church courts dealt mostly with moral crimes related to heresy, adultery, incest, rape, marriage, divorce, money lending, gambling, and witchcraft. The church courts did forbid and punish "a number of practices which were prohibited by the Bible or by the principles of Christianity . . . . Blasphemy is one example. Another is lending of money at interests by Christians, which was absolutely prohibited by medieval canon law" (Thorndike, 1917, p. 294).

Law enforcement in medieval criminal justice was primarily in the hands of local lords, knights, and vassals. A special cadre of people called *constables* responsible for law enforcement was developed in England and France. In France, another cadre of people called *marshals* was given military responsibilities for law enforcement. In medieval Spain, law enforcement task was in the hands of a special group called *hermandades* (a peacekeeping association of armed individuals). These groups were created by the royal authority in medieval Spain for keeping law and order in urban centers and municipal cities. Similarly, there were also prisons and incarcerations in medieval Europe. In his *The Medieval Prison: A Social History,* historian Geltner (2008) presented an enormous number of archival records, arguing that incarceration was widely practiced in medieval Europe as evidenced by prisons found in Venice, Florence, and Bologna in the 13th century. Historical records show that "from the 1270s on, the number of prisons in England and of imprisonable offenses increased rapidly. By 1520, there were 180 imprisonable offenses in the common law" (Peters, 1995, p. 34).

What these historical notes suggest is that there was a system of criminal justice in premodern medieval Europe and in all other kingdoms during the Middle Ages. The nature and the characteristics of this premodern system of criminal justice, however, were vastly different from what is defined and perceived as criminal justice in the 21st century. In premodern criminal justice, there were laws and legal systems, but there was no rule of law. There were judges and judiciaries, but no judicial autonomy and judicial accountability. There were rules and powers given to rulers, but there was no limit to the exercise of power and authority. There was no principle of due process of law. There were kings, queens, monarchs, and emperors who held the power, but their power was not legitimated by common people. Their power was legitimate on the basis of divine law. In the whole of medieval Europe, papal authority was the source of the legitimacy of the kings and queens for more than 1,000 years.

Premodern criminal justice systems were based on themes and ideas that exemplified the nature of medieval times and cultures. First, medieval criminal law was a blending of secular and canon law. Criminal justice was a complex mixture of secular and biblical justice. As a result of the dominance of canon law in medieval culture as a whole, crime and criminality were perceived primarily from the perspective of morality and demonology, and criminal investigations and procedures were based on the notions of confessions and redemptions. Canon law is "ordinance of faith, ordinatio fidei, not ordinance of reason, ordinatio rationis" (Beal, Coriden, & Green, 2000, p. 5). Second, premodern criminal justice was highly unequal. It was deliberately and legally unequal between the nobility and common people, men and women, and churchmen and laymen. Social inequalities within the feudal social hierarchy were legally defined. The due process of law that existed was not available for common people. The third is the nature of punishment in premodern criminal justice systems (see **Figure 4-1**). A variety of agencies existed to dispense justice and punishment, but "most prominent of all branches of separate jurisdiction was the church. It meted out justice through two types of institutions: courts that were dependent on ecclesiastical hierarchy and the Inquisition" (Spierenburg, 1995, p. 50). The institution of the Inquisition was one of the hallmarks of criminal justice in medieval Europe (Perez, 2006). It was created at the time of Pope Innocent III (1161–1216) to deal initially with the crime of heresy, but it eventually became

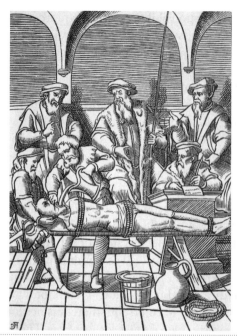

Figure 4-1 Medieval Method of Water Torture and Ordeal by Water

Source: © Universal History Arc/age fotostock.

one of the central strategies of criminal punishment for all kinds of crimes that came to the ecclesiastical courts. The Inquisition was a method of criminal trial without due process of law, without the right to counsel, and without even the need to have a definite accuser. It was primarily a method of torture for securing confessions (Pavlac, 2009). Historical records show that "in fact, Pope Innocent IV (1243–1254) oversaw the creation of machinery specifically designed for the torture of prisoners" (Schlager, 2002, p. 901), and the medieval church "defended its practice of torture by suggesting that the confessions that the clergy extracted as a result of torture might actually save the souls of the accused, rescuing them from eternal damnation" (Schlager, 2002, p. 902). Trial by ordeal was the core of criminal trial by the Inquisition method, and trial by ordeal, based on theology, was simply the use of a series of physical tortures for confessions (Bartlett, 1988). In an ordeal by hot iron, for example: "the accused was blindfolded . . . to walk over a path studded with . . . red-hot plowshares. At other times, without a blindfold, a man or a woman (when her chastity was at issue) had to hold a red hot iron" (Janin, 2009, p. 15). Cruel and unusual punishment was the hallmark of medieval criminal justice for almost 1,000 years. Hanging, execution, burning, decapitation, mutilation of breasts and genitals, amputation, flogging, banishment, bondage, branding, and public humiliation were legally prescribed by medieval judiciaries including manor courts, royal courts, and church courts. Public executions were held and dramatized with elaborate rituals and ceremonies. As one expert on medieval criminal justice put it, "Another theatrical element, the execution procession, sometimes figured into the drama. Smaller Dutch towns as well as large cities like London, Paris, and Seville marched prisoners through the streets" (Spierenburg, 1995, p. 55). In 17th century England, ". . . more than two hundred offenses were punishable by death. Condemned criminals were usually hanged, although occasionally they were quartered, or drawn (dragged along the ground by the tail of a horse)" (Gardner & Anderson, 2009, p. 158).

Throughout medieval Europe, homosexuals were beaten, burned, exiled, banished, or castrated by the makers and keepers of law and justice. One study on medieval sexuality noted that the "first documented execution [for homosexuality] in Western Europe is from 1277" (Bullough & Brundage, 1996, p. 75). Homosexuals were also subject to lifelong exclusion from the Christian community. "If a sodomite had been executed, and subsequently several times resuscitated," in the words of an Italian jurist in 1360, "each time he should be punished more severely if these were possible: hence those who practice this vice are seen to be enemies of God and nature" (Bullough & Brundage, 1996, pp. 173–174). From the beginning of the 13th century in medieval Europe, homosexuality was a grave crime not just in canon law but also in secular laws: "statutes against sodomy, with penalties ranging from fines to castration, exile, and death, enter secular law. The sacral offense moved from canon to civil law" (Bullough & Brundage, 1996, p. 75).

Similarly, witchcraft, which had become widespread in the 15th century, was seen as a heresy and was punishable by burning and execution. By the middle of the 15th century, "the learned inquisitors and secular judges," in medieval Europe, "particularly on the Continent, continued to conceive the fundamental crime of the witch as devil worship, the necessary act that empowered the witch to commit *maleficia*, evil acts against other humans" (Kors & Peters, 2000, p. 11). The medieval church, in response, criminalized witchcraft and empowered the inquisitors to bring them under control of canonical justice. "In 1258, Pope Alexander IV issues the first papal letter empowering the inquisitors of heretical depravity to deal with witchcraft. . . . Pope Alexander's letter was later reissued by other popes and became an official text of canon law" (Kors & Peters, 2000, p. 13). In 1484, Pope Innocent VIII formally approved (*Summis desiderantes affectibus*) the use of inquisition and execution of those, particularly women, who practiced witchcraft in Germany. It is estimated that about 80% of those who were burned, executed, and hanged for witchcraft in medieval Europe were women (see **Table 4-2**). For cross-national analysis of criminal justice, the understanding of some of these institutions and the culture of premodern medieval criminal justice is important.

■ The Rise of the Modern State and the Birth of Modern Criminal Justice

The rise of the modern state marks the beginning of modern criminal justice. With the rise of the modern state came the separation between church and state or state and religion. With the separation of state and religion, the foundation of medieval law and justice based on canonical laws finally crumbled. With modern states' birth and the disintegration of kingdoms and monarchies, the institution of parliament as the sole center for making laws for crime and justice emerged; the institution of modern professional bureaucracy evolved; and

TABLE 4-2 Women Convicted of High and Petty Treason in England (Old Bailey, 1750–1790)

Conviction	Name	Crime	Final Disposition
Jan. 1758	Alice Davis	HT—Coining	Strangled and burned
Jan. 1758	Margaret Larney	HT—Coining	Strangled and burned
Sept. 1773	Elizabeth Herring	PT—Murder of husband	Strangled and burned
Sept. 1779	Isabella Condon	HT—Coining	Strangled and burned
April 1786	Phoebe Harris	HT—Coining	Strangled and burned
July 1787	Henrietta Radbourne	PT—Murder of mistress	Hanged on special gallows
April 1788	Catherine Heyland	HT—Coining	Banishment for life
May 1788	Margaret Sullivan	HT—Coining	Strangled and burned
Sept. 1788	C. Murphy Bowman	HT—Coining	Strangled and burned
April 1790	Sophia Girton	HT—Coining	Banishment for life

Source: Data from Devereaux, S. (2005). The abolition of burning of women in England reconsidered. *Crime, History, and Societies, 9*(2), 73–98.

criminal justice as a system of modern bureaucracy for the maintenance of law and order became prominent. With the rise of the modern state, a new model of organizing power and authority based on of the principles of the separation of power, constitutionalism, judicial autonomy, the rule of law, equal justice, democracy, and respect for fundamental human rights were born. With the birth of the modern state, a new form of centralized and bureaucratized mechanism of formal social control emerged with the exclusive monopoly of the state as the sole agent for defining crime and justice, developing laws and statutes, and devising sanctions and punishments—a transformation described by Norbert Elias as the birth of a civilizing process. The birth of the modern state permanently buried the institution of the Inquisition as a mechanism of social control.

The Rise of Modern States

The institution of the modern state, the institution that emerged first in Western Europe, however, was not born in a day. It evolved over a long period of more than 400 years of changes and transformations in the medieval societies. The medieval societies and monarchical political systems in Europe began to slowly disintegrate from within at the beginning of the 14th century because of the effect of a series of changes and transformations in the realms of medieval power and politics, economy, knowledge and philosophy, and faith and beliefs. Historians have described these transformative forces primarily in terms of the rise of the Renaissance in the 14th century, the rise of the Reformation and the division of Christianity in the 16th century, the birth of the Scientific Revolution in the 17th century, the birth of the Enlightenment and the Age of Reason in the 18th century, and the rise of the Industrial Revolution in the 19th century. It is these forces that gave birth to the idea not just of a modern state on the basis of a sovereign parliament, but of modernity in all spheres of life and civilization in the West. The triumph of these forces was the triumph of modernity, and the triumph modernity is the triumph of the notions of science, reason, and rationality in all spheres of life including crime, law, and justice. However, the medieval kings, emperors, dukes, and knights, as well as the medieval Catholic Church that was at the height of domination and control for more than 1,000 years, did not abdicate their power on their own. They had to be forced to relinquish their power through political struggles and revolutions such as the Glorious Revolution of England and the birth of the modern English state in 1688, the American Revolution and the birth of the American republic in 1776, and the French Revolution and the birth of the modern French Republic in 1789–1799.

The concept of national sovereignty and of the modern international system of sovereign states began to grow, particularly after the Treaty of Westphalia was signed by almost all major European countries in 1648 in Westphalia, Germany. The Treaty of Westphalia formally ended the Thirty Years' War (1618–1648) between Catholics and Protestants in the whole of the medieval Roman Empire, particularly in Germany. The Holy Roman Empire's expansion, supported primarily by Spain and the Catholic princes of Germany during the Thirty Years' War, was opposed by France, Sweden, Denmark, and the Protestant princes of Germany (Bonney, 2002). After the end of the Thirty Years' War, the Holy Roman Empire began to disintegrate, and the Treaty of Westphalia paved the way for the rise of modern states in Germany, France, Spain, Sweden, Denmark, and the whole of Europe. The treaty "ended the Thirty Years War and opened the quest—which goes on to this day—to find a way for independent states" (Lynos & Mastanduno, 1995, p. 5).

A year after the Treaty of Westphalia, King Charles I of England was publicly tried and executed. His execution led to the Glorious Revolution in England (1688–1689). The Glorious Revolution brought an end to the English monarchy, abolished the House of Lords, and proclaimed the Republic. It created, for the first time in the medieval world, a new principle and new philosophy of freedom of religion for the English people. As one historian noted: "After 1660 Anglicanism was defended by parliament: the reality henceforth was parliamentary control of the Church" (Edwards, 2001, p. 401). The Glorious Revolution heralded the beginning of the evolution of modern states. Within 100 years after the Glorious Revolution, a new republic of the United States of America was created in the New World through the American Revolution in 1776, and a new French Republic was created through the French Revolution in 1789. The American republic was born by citizens overthrowing the power and control of the English monarchy, and the French Republic was born by citizens overthrowing the power of France's Bourbon monarchy. The rise of the new states in the 17th and the 18th centuries in Europe, however, did not immediately result in initiating the growth of liberal democracy on the basis of the ideals and principles of the Renaissance, Reformation, Scientific Revolution, and Age of Enlightenment (Nelson, 2006). The emerging states in Europe went through a long process of changes and transformations, from what one historian called absolutism to liberal democracy, for almost 100 years. "The classical liberal tradition, the outline of which are to be found in Hobbes and Locke," was not "fully developed until the early 19th century" (Nelson, 2006, p. 81).

When modern states were rising in Europe and creating the basis for a modern system of law and justice in the 17th, 18th, and 19th centuries, most of the non-Western world, except Japan and China, were controlled by the European colonial states of the Portuguese, Dutch, British, French, Spanish, and Germans. In Japan, the medieval Tokugawa monarchy was overthrown and the Meiji emperor created the foundation of a modern state in 1868. The rise of Meiji rule disintegrated the basis of feudalism in Japan. In China, imperial rule ended in 1912 through the Xinhai Revolution, and a new republic began through the creation of Kuomintang—the nationalist party of China—by Sun-Yat-sen. The modern People's Republic of China was born from a civil war between the supporters of Kuomintang and the Russian-backed Communist Party of China. The supporters of Kuomintang left for Taiwan and established another state—the Republic of China. In the rest of the non-Western world, modern states emerged after the end of colonialism. The era of colonialism began to wane in Latin America in the early 19th century and in Asia and Africa in the middle of the 20th century. In most of the Middle East, modern states emerged after the disintegration of the Ottoman Empire and the end of the First World War in the 1920s. The Ottoman Empire dominated the whole Middle East, including Syria, Iraq, Jordan, Yemen, Libya, and Algeria for almost 400 years (Owen, 2004). For a more historically grounded analysis of comparative criminal justice, understanding the history of the rise of modern states in different regions of the world is vitally important because the history of modern criminal justice is intimately connected to the rise of modern states in particular, and the rise of modernity in general.

The Birth of Modern Criminal Justice

It was in the context of the rise of modern states that modern ideas about criminal justice began to evolve in the beginning of the 18th century, particularly through the writings of Montesquieu (1689–1755), Cesare Beccaria (1738–1794), Jeremy Bentham (1748–1832), and Cesare Lombroso (1835–1909). Montesquieu's *The Spirit of Laws,* published in 1748; Beccaria's *On Crimes and Punishments,* published in 1764; and Bentham's *An Introduction to the Principles of Morals and Legislation,* published in 1789, were the classical works following the Magna Carta, the English Charter issued in 1215 by King John of England that contained some of the earliest ideas about modern criminal justice. The Magna Carta (Linebaugh, 2008), for the first time in the chronicles of human history, recognized the limits of power of the monarchy, admitted the centrality of the rule of law, and established the sacred duty of political authority to grant freedom and liberty to common people. The Charter declared that: "No freeman shall be taken, or imprisoned , or disseized, or outlawed, or exiled . . . nor will we go upon or send upon him—save by the lawful judgment of his peers or by the law of the land." The Charter further added, "To no one will we sell, to no one will we refuse or delay, right or justice."

The Magna Carta remained the foundation of the English Bill of Rights, introduced in 1689; the American Bill of Rights, introduced in 1789; and the French Bill of Rights

(The Declaration of the Rights of Man and of the Citizen), promulgated in 1793. The English Bill of Rights, introduced 100 years before the American Bill of Rights, contained the principle that "excessive bail ought not to be required, nor excessive fines imposed, nor cruel and unusual punishments inflicted." It also declared that "it is the right of the subjects to petition the king, and all commitments and prosecutions for such petitioning are illegal." The English Bill of Rights laid the foundation of a modern state on the basis of the supremacy of Parliament—a body of legislature to be freely elected by common people. It declared that "the pretended power of suspending the laws or the execution of laws by regal authority without consent of Parliament is illegal." More than 500 years after the promulgation of the Magna Carta, modern states began to grow, modern constitutions began to develop, and the notions of modern law and justice began to crystallize, particularly through the ideas of Montesquieu in France, Beccaria in Italy, and Bentham in England.

One of the ideas that was common to all three of these precursors of modern criminal justice is that a system of criminal justice is at the core of a modern state and of modernity. All three shared the idea that the principle of freedom and liberty—a principle that is the foundation of the modern state—is essentially a matter of personal security. "By liberty Montesquieu meant . . . the security of the individual so that life and property were not threatened either by others or by the state itself" (Burns & Hart, 1996, p. lxv). The basic protection of personal security through a system of criminal justice is therefore one of primary responsibilities of the modern state (Rahe, 2009). In his book, *The Spirit of Laws*, Montesquieu "offered the model of a government whose end was political liberty," and political liberty, in his view, "is the result of the separation of powers" (Cohler, Miller, & Stone, 1989, p. xxv). The nature and structure of government, for Montesquieu, "is the defense of liberty" (Cohler et al., 1989, p. xxv). What Montesquieu argued, in other words, is that the nature of a state and its function of defending the liberty of its citizens depend on the nature of its system of criminal justice—a system that is primarily responsible for the protection of personal security. Montesquieu's idea of the separation of power of the three branches of government—executive, legislative, and judicial—is still the foundation of the modern state. Montesquieu also argued that there are three forms of government (monarchical, despotic, and republic). These different forms are based on different sets of laws, institutions, and social environments. In a republic, Montesquieu said: "people can count on regularity in the rule . . . [and] relate to each other without fear in so far as they rely on the things they hold in common; they share something just other than fear of the ruler" (Cohler et al., 1989, p. xxvii). Montesquieu's *The Spirit of Laws* also pioneered the idea of what is, in modern jurisprudence, called legal positivism. *The Spirit of Laws* made sharp distinctions between law and morality, recognized the social contexts or nonlegal knowledge systems as a source of legal validity, and accepted the principle of judicial discretions. Legal positivism conceptually opened the door for doubts and uncertainty in legal reasoning (Samuel, 2003). The development of the U.S. Constitution and the framing of the Bill of Rights in the late

18th century were largely affected by Montesquieu's ideas: "Jefferson and Anti-Federalists took seriously Montesquieu's account of the social conditions that make republican government possible" (Cohler et al., 1989, p. xxiv).

Writing around the same time as Montesquieu, Cesare Beccaria, who is widely regarded as the founder of modern criminal justice, focused on the disintegration of feudalism, birth of the Age of Reason, and rise of modern states in Europe. Beccaria was deeply influenced by the thoughts and writings of Montesquieu on law and the nature of the modern state. However, whereas Montesquieu gave us an image of modern criminal justice by way of his theorizing about modern state and liberty, Beccaria (1764/2009), in *On Crimes and Punishments,* was directly engaged in theorizing about the nature of crime and criminality and describing a model or a profile of modern criminal justice. Beccaria "proposed a liberal theory of criminal justice" (p. xv). He theorized about human nature in terms of free will and rationality and proposed the rationalization of law, court, and punishment. He advocated that a rationally devised system of crime control and prevention should remain as one of the distinctive roles and rights of a modern government. Beccaria argued that criminal justice as a modern organization or a bureaucracy that is central to the functioning of a modern state must be based on certain fundamental principles such as the separation between secular and canon law, rational systems of law made by people's representatives, equal law and justice for all, equality of law enforcement, proportionality between crime and punishment, a humanized system of punishment, and protection against cruel and unusual punishment.

One author stated that Beccaria's goal was to produce "an entirely secular account of the origins and function of law" by avoiding "appeals to either revelation or natural law" and distinguishing "between God's justice . . . and terrestrial justice" (Bellamy, 1995, p. xv). In *On Crimes and Punishments*, Beccaria wrote that "the laws only can determine the punishment of crimes; and the authority of making penal laws can only reside with the legislator, who represents the whole society united by the social compact" (1764/2009, p. 13). In Beccaria's views, "A rational legal system required that laws be as precise as possible, with judicial discretions reduced to minimum, so that all citizens knew where they stood and could reason accordingly" (Bellamy, 1995, p. xvi). Like Hobbes and Montesquieu, Beccaria believed that the maintenance of social order is one of the essential functions of a modern state, and the maintenance of social order needs the inflicting of pain and punishment for those who break the rules. The right to punish is one of the fundamental rights of a modern state, and establishing that right "provided the key to our understanding of the whole legal and political system and consequently the starting point of Beccaria's theory" (Bellamy, 1995, p. xvii). For Beccaria, a state or a criminal justice system, however, does not have the right to inflict cruel and unusual punishment. Torture, he believed, "is both unjust and inefficient," because it involves "punishing someone before they had been proven guilty" (Bellamy, 1995, p. xxiv). Torture is not useful in reaching the true facts, and it is a gross violation of the "rights of the accused to self-defense" (Young, 1986, p. xiv). As Beccaria clearly articulated in *On Crimes and Punishments*: "No man can be judged a criminal until he be found guilty, nor can society take from him the public protection until it has been proved that he has violated the conditions on which it was granted" (1764/2009, p. 43).

Beccaria advocated against the retributive system of justice and claimed that a humane system of law and justice "is most in accord with basic human rights" (Young, 1986, p. xv). He concluded *On Crimes and Punishments* by stating that punishments "should be public, immediate, and necessary, the least possible in the case given, proportional to the crimes, and determined by the laws" (Beccaria, 1764/2009, p. 115). One author observed that Beccaria was the first major thinker coming from the late Medieval Age "to call for the abolition of the death penalty" (Young, 1986, p. xv).

Jeremy Bentham, who was writing around the same time as Beccaria, led the discourse on crime and justice more in the direction of theorizing about criminality. Bentham set the foundation of what is known as rational choice theory in modern criminology. In his view, humans are motivated by the principles of pain and pleasure. He began his book, *An introduction to the Principles of Morals and Legislation,* with the statement that "Nature has placed mankind under the governance of two sovereign masters, *pain and pleasure . . . .* They govern us in all we do, in all we say, [and] in all we think" (1789/1988, p. 2). He even went to the extent of developing laws and algorithms of universal human tendencies of behaving in terms of pain and pleasure. He believed that the goal of laws should be "to augment the total happiness of the community" (Bentham, 1789/1988, p. 170). The total happiness of a community, for him, is predicated on the nature of personal security. For Bentham, as for Montesquieu and Beccaria, "Security became a means to the end of happiness and a necessary condition for its maximization" (Burns & Hart, 1996, p. xxxvi). The fundamental task of a government is to protect and guarantee individual security, and hence, the fundamental need for a modern state is a modern system of criminal justice. "The business of government is to promote the happiness of the society, by punishing and rewarding" (Bentham, 1789/1988, p. 70). Bentham justified rationally devised prisons and punishment and a rational system of criminal justice because, in his view, it can bring the greatest benefit for the greatest number of people. Like Beccaria, Bentham was also a great advocate for the abolition of torture and the death penalty. As he stated, "Crimes are more effectively prevented by certainty, than the severity of punishment" (Burns & Hart, 1996, p. lxvi). He further said that "all punishment is mischief; all punishment is evil. Upon the principle of utility . . . it ought only to be admitted in so far as it promises to exclude some greater evil" (Bentham, 1789/1988, p. 170).

Bentham was also strongly opposed to "the intermingling of the ideas of crime and sin, and reserved for the former a narrow definition and a minimum range of punishment. As for the latter, sinful acts were not necessarily to be considered crimes at all" (1789/1988, p. lxvii). Bentham not only theorized about crime and criminality, but he was also a great advocate for reforms in laws, judicial systems, and penal systems. He advocated for judicial reforms such as decentralized court system, discovery of evidence, provision for cross-examination in criminal trials, open and fair trial, and judicial accountability. Bentham's model of a panopticon—a design of a prison that was based on his theory that observation is a deterrent for criminal behavior—is remarkably scientific and surprisingly modern. Modern criminal justice is significantly dependent on the model of surveillance as a deterrent.

■ The Profile of Modern Criminal Justice

The ideas of modern criminal justice found in the writings of Montesquieu, Beccaria, and Bentham did not remain sterile. During the past 200 years of the evolution of the state and modernity, those ideas have given birth to a profile of modern criminal justice. The most forceful expressions of this new profile of modern criminal justice began to appear in the 18th century through the evolution of the American Bill of Rights in 1789 and the French Bill of Rights in 1793. The incipient profile of modern criminal justice that was born through the Magna Carta in 1215 became an integral part of the institution of the modern state through the American and French Bills of Rights, which in turn gave birth to a new process of modernization in criminal justice all over the world. The ideas of Montesquieu, Beccaria, and Bentham remained at the core of modernity in criminal justice.

A modern system of criminal justice is not the description of criminal justice of any particular country. It is, rather, a profile or a set of ideas, values, and principles for organizing and governing criminal justice—the ideas, values, and principles that began to spread since the birth of modern states in the 18th century. The countries of the West approximate the modern profile of criminal justice more than those of other regions of the world. The benchmarks of the progress of modernization in criminal justice in a country are not defined by that country's volume of crime, crime trends, or rate of incarceration. A country with the lowest crime rate and lowest incarceration rate, such as Saudi Arabia or Singapore, may be far behind in creating a modern system of criminal justice. On the other hand, a country with a high volume of crime and high rate of incarceration, such as the United States and the United Kingdom, may have a modern system of criminal justice. The benchmarks of modern criminal justice are the laws, principles, and institutions in terms of which criminal justice is organized and governed within the structure of the state and the larger polity of a country. These benchmarks include the nature of the rule of law and democracy; separation between religion and politics; separation between canon law and secular law; dominance of the due process of law; separation between adult and juvenile systems of justice; and dominance of science and professionalism in criminal justice.

The Rule of Law and the Context of a Democratic Polity

From the beginning of the development of political philosophy and thinking about law and justice in ancient Greece, one of the central concerns has been the issue of the limits of power of the political authority. The central philosophical issue, in other words, has been the achievement of a balance between the powers of the authority and the individual, or between the ruler and the ruled. This has been a central concern in the whole chronicle of political philosophical thoughts and ideas that began from the days of Socrates in ancient Greece in the 5th century BC. It has been a central concern in the political and social philosophies of

Machiavelli (1469–1527), Hobbes (1588–1679), Locke (1632–1704), Montesquieu (1689–1755), Voltaire (1694–1778), and Rousseau (1712–1778). The limits of power and authority were also central in the framing of the Magna Carta in 1215, the English Bill of Rights in 1689, the American Bill of Rights in 1789, and French Bill of Rights in 1793. It is this notion of the limits of power and the search for a balance between the power of the ruler and the ruled that gave birth to the idea of the rule of law within the framework of the modern state. A country that does not have a modern state based on the rule of law cannot have a modern system of criminal justice.

The Rule of Law: Meaning and Definitions

The principle of the rule of law is based on the notion that "the king is not the law, law is the king" (Cass, 2001). Under the rule of law, each and every citizen of the state is to be governed by the same set of laws and rules enshrined in the constitution. The core of the concept of the rule of law is, as John Adams said in framing the Massachusetts Constitution (Bill of Rights, article 30, 1780) and in the Declaration of Rights, "a government of laws, not men" (Massachusetts Judicial Branch, 2010, p. 4). In a state governed by the rule of law, the parliament is the core institution for making laws and the judiciary is the protector of the laws made by the parliament. The supremacy of the parliament and the rule of law in the modern state was established more than 300 years ago by the English Bill of Rights. The English Bill of Rights (Levy, 2000) began with the following statement: "That the pretended power of suspending of laws, or the execution of laws, by regal authority, without consent of parliament, is illegal."

The World Justice Project (Agrast, Botero, & Ponce, 2010), an international think tank on the rule of law around the world, defines the concept of the rule of law in terms of four universal principles: accountability of the government under the law; protection of fundamental rights including the security of people and property; fair, efficient, accessible process of law making; and fair and equal access to justice. In 2010, after 3 years of research that included interviewing 41,000 people and 900 experts in 35 countries, the World Justice Project has developed a Rule of Law Index that includes 10 dimensions of the rule of law: limited powers; absence of corruption; clear and publicized law; order and security; fundamental rights; open government; regulatory enforcement; access to civil justice; effective criminal justice; and informal justice. These dimensions of the rule of law contain 3 core principles of modern criminal justice. The first is the notion of limited government. The notion of limited government means that the power of a government is limited by the constitution, parliament, adherence to the fundamental rights of its citizens, and the role of an independent judiciary. Under the dominance of the rule of law, a "government is embedded in a comprehensive legal framework, its officials accept that the law will be applied to their own conduct, and the government seeks to be law-abiding" (Carothers, 2006, p. 4). The second principle of the rule of law, which is also at the core of modern criminal justice, is recognition of fundamental human rights including equal treatment under the law, equal access to justice, and right to life and security of the person. The rule of law means that a state upholds the "political and civil liberties that have gained status as universal human rights over the last half a century" (Carothers, 2006, p. 4). The third important aspect of the rule of law is the establishment of a fair, effective, and impartial system of criminal justice on the basis of due process of law (Agrast et al., 2010).

The Rule of Law and Liberal Democracy

The principle of the rule of law is at the core of modern democratic states. "The relationship between the rule of law and liberal democracy is profound. The rule of law makes possible individual rights . . . . A government's respect for the sovereign authority of the people and a constitution depends on its acceptance of law" (Carothers, 2006, p. 5). A liberal democratic state is characterized by a configuration of principles that are crucial to develop a modern system of criminal justice. Some of these principles include constitutionalism, dominance of the parliament or the legislature, separation of powers, checks and balances, judicial review, representative politics, a multiparty system, and open and inclusive politics. In a liberal democratic state, the recognition of fundamental human rights and basic principles of governing criminal justice is not left in the hands the police, courts, and prisons. They are clearly enshrined in the constitution, known in some countries as the Bill of Rights. The basic structure of modern criminal justice in America, for example, was formed with the creation of the U.S. Constitution and the Bill of Rights (Levy, 2001). The Fourth, Fifth, Sixth, Seventh, Eighth, and Fourteenth Amendments of the Constitution are the foundations of the modern criminal justice system in America. The Fourth Amendment states that "the right of the people to be secure in their persons, houses, papers, and effects, against unreasonable searches and seizures, shall not be violated, and no Warrants shall issue, but upon probable cause, supported by Oath or affirmation" (Legal Information Institute, 2012a, p. 1). The Eighth Amendment states that "excessive bail shall not be required, nor excessive fines imposed, nor cruel and unusual punishments inflicted" (Legal Information Institute, 2012b, p. 1). Article X of the English Bill of Rights promulgated in 1689 established the same principle of modern criminal justice, which is that "excessive bail ought not to be required, nor excessive fines imposed; nor cruel and unusual punishments inflicted."

The basic structure of French criminal justice was created at the establishment of the First Republic and the 1789 promulgation of the French Bill of Rights (The Declaration of the Rights of Man and of the Citizen), which became an integral part of the French Constitution in 1791. Article I of the French Declaration of the Rights of Man and of the Citizen states that all "men are born and remain free and equal in rights; social distinctions can be established only for common benefit." Article VI states that "law is the expression of the general will. Every citizen has a right to participate personally, or through his representative, in its foundation. It must be the same for all, whether it protects or punishes." Articles VII, VIII, and XI of the French Declaration of the Rights of Man and of the Citizen are particularly focused on criminal justice. Article VII states: "No person shall be accused, arrested, or imprisoned except in the cases and according to the forms prescribed by law. Any one soliciting, transmitting, executing, or causing to be executed, any arbitrary order, shall be punished." Article VIII states that "the law shall provide for such punishments only as are strictly and obviously necessary, and no one shall suffer punishment except it be legally inflicted in virtue of a law passed and promulgated before the commission of the offense." Article XI brought the doctrine of innocence into the core of criminal law. It states that "as all persons are held innocent until they shall have been declared guilty, if arrest shall be deemed indispensable, all harshness not essential to the securing of the prisoner's person shall be severely repressed by law."

The basic profile of modern criminal justice was similarly established in Canada through the Canadian Charter of Rights and Freedoms that became a part of the Canadian Constitution in 1982. Sections 7 through 14 of the Canadian Charter of Rights and Freedoms are concerned with criminal justice. The Charter contained the provisions that everyone has the right to life, liberty, and security of the person (Section 7); right of protection against unusual search and seizure (Section 8); freedom from arbitrary detainment and imprisonment (Section 9); right to legal counsel (Section 10); right to be presumed innocent unless proven guilty (Section 11); right of protection against cruel and unusual punishment (Section 12); and right of protection against self-incrimination (Section 13). Section 52 of the Constitution Act of 1982 established the Canadian Charter of Rights and Freedoms as the supreme document governing law and justice in Canada.

The basic profile of modern criminal justice has been set up in a number of other modern states based on the structure of liberal democracy and the principle of the rule of law. Some of these liberal democracies in Europe are the United Kingdom, Germany, Spain, the Netherlands, Italy, Sweden, Denmark, Austria, Belgium, and Finland. In Asia, the foundation of modern criminal justice is relatively firmly established in Japan. Ten articles of the Japanese Constitution (Articles 31–40) explicitly describe the profile of modern criminal justice in Japan. Article 33 of the Japanese constitution states that "no person shall be apprehended except upon warrant issued by a competent judicial officer who specifies the offense with which the person is charged, unless he is apprehended, the offense being committed." Article 34 of the constitution states that "no person shall be arrested or detained without being at once informed of the charges against him or without the immediate privilege of counsel; nor shall he be detained without adequate cause." Article 35 of the Japanese Constitution includes the right of protection against unusual searches and seizures. It states that "the right of all persons to be secure in their homes, papers and effects against entries, searches and seizures shall not be impaired except upon warrant issued for adequate cause." The infliction of torture and cruel and unusual punishment by any criminal justice agents and agencies are absolutely forbidden by Article 36 of the Constitution of Japan.

A liberal democratic polity is also a precondition for the growth of modern criminal justice because of its adherence to the principles of the separation of powers, checks and balances, judicial review, representative politics, and open and inclusive political culture. The notions of the separation of power and of checks and balances are particularly crucial. Montesquieu, in Book XI of the *The Spirit of Laws,* said: "Democratic and aristocratic states are not in their own nature free. Political liberty is to be found only in moderate governments." Montesquieu further added that "constant experience shows us that every man invested with power is apt to abuse it . . . to prevent this abuse, it is necessary from the very nature of things that power should be a check to power." Imbibed with the same spirit, the French Declaration of the Rights of Man and of the Citizen stated that "any society in which the guarantee of rights is not assured or the separation of powers not settled has no constitution." In the U.S. constitution, the first three article describe the nature of the separation of power into the legislative, executive, and judicial branches. The U.S. Supreme Court, in a case decided in 1794, said: "When, in short, either branch of the government usurps that part of the sovereignty, which the Constitution assigns to another branch, liberty ends, and tyranny commences" (*Glass v. The Betsey*, 1794).

In any country with these three branches, criminal justice exists at the crossroads of all three branches. The legislative branch makes criminal statutes. The judicial branch applies the statutes in criminal trials, adjudications, convictions, and sentencing. The highest tier of the judicial branch also makes criminal laws in the way of applying and interpreting the constitution. The executive branch is responsible for organizing and maintaining the police, courts, and prisons—the system of criminal justice. A modern criminal justice system has evolved as a differentiated and an autonomous organization within the structure of a modern state, but its nature and autonomy are contingent on the nature and function of the principle of the separation of powers. If the principle of the separation of powers does not work in a state, and its checks and balances are violated, criminal justice will emerge as an instrument of authoritarian control and repressions. In authoritarian political regimes and governments, the first thing that is violated is the principle of the separation of powers and checks and balances. In most authoritarian regimes, the executive branch takes control of the legislative and the judicial branches. When the legislature and the judiciary are controlled by the executive, criminal justice is devoid of any autonomy (Moustafa & Ginsburg, 2008). When the judiciary is powerless, the police, on behalf of the executive, can unleash a reign of terror and grossly violate the basic principles of human rights. The history of criminal justice in most developing countries is a chronicle of torture, rape, extrajudicial killing, and other gross violations of human rights because they are mostly ruled by authoritarian governments. Judicial corruption and the lack of judicial accountability are also endemic in authoritarian political regimes. A modern system of criminal justice is unlikely to develop in a country without a democratic polity that is based on the principles of the rule of law, constitutionalism, separation of powers, and checks and balances.

One recent example that shows why a democratic polity based on the principle of the separation of powers and checks and balances is a precondition for modern criminal justice is a set of decisions made by the U.S. Supreme Court in 2004 and 2008 with respect to the constitutional rights of foreign terrorists in the United States. As of 2008, about 775 individuals, captured mostly in Afghanistan and Pakistan, were in detention at the U.S. Guantanamo Bay Naval Base. In 2002, two *habeas corpus* petitions were made to the Federal District Court of Washington, D.C., to challenge the legality of the Bush administration's policy of indefinite detention. The district court dismissed the cases on the grounds that it does not have jurisdiction because Guantanamo Bay is out of the sovereign territory of the United States. On appeal, the U.S. Court of Appeals for the District of Columbia Circuit affirmed the district court decision on the same grounds of lack of jurisdiction. In 2003, the cases were appealed to the U.S. Supreme Court. The Supreme Court in 2004 ruled (6–3 decision) that the "United States courts have jurisdiction to consider challenges to the legality of the detention of foreign nationals captured abroad in connection with hostilities and incarcerated at Guantanamo Bay" (*Rasul v. Bush,* pp. 4–17). The ruling further stated that "nothing in *Eisentrager* or any other of the Court's cases categorically excludes aliens detained in military custody outside the United States from that privilege [litigation]. United States courts have traditionally been open to nonresident aliens" (*Rasul v. Bush,* 2004, p. 2). Justice Stevens wrote "that the right to habeas corpus is not dependent on citizenship status. The detainees were therefore free to bring suit challenging their detention as unconstitutional" (Latimer, 2011, p. 299).

To deny the *habeas corpus* rights of the detainees, the U.S. Congress enacted the Detainee Treatment Act of 2005. The act not only made provisions for the CIA's use of a number of harsh interrogation techniques, but also denied the right to *habeas corpus* petition by foreign "enemy combatants" and the jurisdiction of the U.S. federal courts to hear those cases. In 2006, Congress enacted the Military Commissions Act, which "established procedures governing the use of military commissions to try alien unlawful enemy combatants engaged in hostilities against the United States." The Act was passed on the presumption that foreign enemy combatants are not entitled to the due process of law (including open trial in civilian courts) given to American citizens. The Act, under the Uniform Code of Military Justice, authorized the military commission both to try and to punish the enemy combatants including the imposition of the death penalty. The Act made a law "that no court, or justice, or judge, shall have jurisdiction to hear or consider an application for writ of habeas corpus filed by or on behalf of an alien detained by the United States." It also made a provision that "no court, justice, or judge shall have jurisdiction to hear or consider any other action against the United States or its agents relating to any aspect of the detention, transfer, treatment, trial, or conditions of confinement of an alien."

A number of Guantanamo detainees went to the federal court to challenge the constitutionality of the Detainee Treatment Act of 2005 and the Military Commissions Act of 2006. In 2008, in a landmark 5–4 decision in *Boumediene v. Bush*, the U.S. Supreme Court said that the detainees "have the constitutional privilege of habeas corpus.... [The] protection of the habeas privilege was one of the few safeguards of liberty specified in a constitution that at the outset had no Bill of Rights" (p. 3). The Court further said that "Once habeas corpus is abolished—as the Military Commissions Act sought to do—then we return to the pre-Magna Carta days where the Government is free to imprison people with no recourse" (Greenwald, 2008, p. 1). In a country without a democratic polity based on the rule of law, the judiciary is more likely to be controlled by the executive, and when the judiciary is under the control of the executive, the criminal justice system is more likely to be repressive in nature. Thus, in cross-national analysis of crime and justice, the understanding of the nature of the state is vitally important.

Secularization and Modern Criminal Justice

The second most defining characteristic of modern criminal justice is the notion of secularization in law and justice. In modern criminal justice, divine canonical laws and ecclesiastical courts and justice are deliberately kept separated from defining crime and criminality, delivering justice, and devising punishments. This trend of the growth of modern criminal justice began from the evolution of the modern state and modernity in the 18th century. The secularization of law and justice began in Europe as a part of the general philosophical transformations in thought and ideas associated with the rise of the Renaissance, the Reformation, and the Age of Enlightenment. It particularly began as one of the core principles of the rise of the modern state—the principle of the separation of church and state. The secularization process does not mean the abandonment of religion and the dethroning of God. What it precisely means is that the governing of worldly affairs within the framework of the modern state must be kept separated from religion. A modern state must preserve both the right to worship and the freedom of religion. It ought not, however, to be governed either by laws based on scriptures or by the hegemonic power of religious elites—popes, cardinals, bishops, priests, rabbis, monks, and imams. From ancient times to the modern age of the 21st century, millions of people have been burned, tortured, and mutilated in the name of God and religion. During the Middle Ages particularly, in the name of the Christ and the Church, millions were subjected to inquisitions, trials by ordeal, and exorcisms. The rise of modernity was a revolt against the domination of religion in which a political community is not legitimated on the basis of religion.

British philosopher John Locke (1689), in his *A Letter Concerning Toleration,* for the first time provided a profile of a modern secular state. In his letter, Locke said that a modern state (a commonwealth) is "a society of men constituted only for the procuring, preserving, and advancing their own civil interests" (p. 2). Civil interests, Locke said, are mainly the rights to life, liberty, and property. In a modern state, he said, "It is the duty of the civil magistrate, by the impartial execution of equal laws, to secure unto all the people in general . . . the just possession of these things belonging to this life" (1689, p. 3). The salvation of the soul or the advancement of religion must not be the task of a state authority. Additionally, Locke said that "the care of souls cannot belong to the magistrate" (1689, p. 3). As a result of the rise of the Renaissance, the Reformation, the Age of Enlightenment, and the writings of such philosophers as Locke, the principle of secularization—separation of the church and state—emerged as the core of modernity and basic to the formation of the modern state.

Church and State Separation and Modern Criminal Justice

The rise of modern states in Europe was firmly based on this principle of church and state separation. The English Bill of Rights of 1689 clearly stated: "That the commission for erecting the late court of commissioners for ecclesiastical causes, and all other commissions and courts of like nature are illegal and pernicious" (as cited in Garland & McGehee, 1898, p. 936).

The body of modern law must not be based on scriptures and holy texts. But the same secular law must preserve the fundamental right of freedom to pursue competing faiths and religions. The French Declaration stated, "No one shall be disquieted on account of his opinions, including his religious views, provided their manifestation does not disturb the public order established by law."

Canonical Law and Secular Law

In a modern system of criminal justice, located in a modern state based on the principle of the separation of church and state, there remains a separation between crime and sin. From the perspective of secularization, crime is not a sin, it is not evil, and it is not a transgression of the divine will (Örsy, 2000). It is a violation of criminal law. A crime is a crime if it is defined by law as a crime. If a certain type of behavior is not defined by law as a crime, then even if it is morally condemnable, it is not a crime. Sexual harassment, for example, is a crime in America because it is defined by law as a crime. Modern criminal law is primarily based on the doctrine of legal positivism. The legal positivists do not deny that certain kinds of acts and behaviors are universally wrong, morally condemnable, or even evil in the eyes of religion, but even those morally reprehensible behaviors are not crimes if they are not prohibited by law. The doctrine of legal positivism is based on the notion of *mala prohibita*, meaning that only those acts and behaviors that are prohibited by legal statutes and judicial laws are crimes. *Mala prohibita* is different from *mala in se*, meaning that certain acts and behaviors are intrinsically wrong. As one author on philosophy of criminal law states: "Crimes differ from extra-legal wrongs in that they are defined as wrongs by the law: they are not . . . wrongs in terms of . . . extra-legal social standards of morality" (Duff, 2008, p. 3). The body of secular criminal law is therefore a "distinctive kind of institution" (Duff, 2008, p. 6) that does not define crime in terms of divine or canonical laws. The degree of criminality in modern criminal justice has to be established in terms of the extent of harm caused and the degree of offender culpability. Crime in modern criminal law is also not a private matter. The offense against an individual is an offense against society. In modern criminal law, "the police act in the name and with the authority not just of the victim, but of the whole polity (Duff, 2008, p. 4). In divine and canonical laws, crimes are unchangeable and punishments are defined by the scriptures. In secular criminal justice, the definitions of crime and punishment change with social and cultural changes and transformations. In divine and canonical laws, crime and criminality are explained in terms of demonology—in terms of possession by demons or satanic evils. In secular criminal law, crime and criminality are scientifically explained from the perspectives of sociology, psychology, biology, neurology, or genetic markers. The rationality for criminalization, in divine law and justice, is that certain acts and behaviors are intrinsically evil, immoral, and sinful. The rationality for criminalization or decriminalization in modern secular criminal justice is based on a number of philosophical notions such as security, liberty, freedom, rights, justice, equality, fairness, responsibility, duty, harm, and obligations. In modern criminal justice, the evolving knowledge based on science and modern technology and the evolving standards of decency (Lyke, 2009) are used in justifying criminalization or decriminalization of many acts and behaviors.

Out of all domains of crime and criminality, those in the areas of sex and sexuality have historically been defined from a religious perspective. All major world religions, such as Hinduism, Judaism, Christianity, and Islam, have developed expansive codes of sexual ethics and morality. As one historian stated: "Virtually all histories of sexuality hold Christianity responsible for laying down the principle sexual norms that have guided behavior in the West to the present time" (Hull, 1996, p. 11). Christianity also created the primary disciplinary methods to uphold these standards: confession, penance, the ecclesiastical courts, and canon law (Hull, 1996, p. 11). In modern criminal justice, the growth of secular criminal law and criminalization and decriminalization are particularly prominent in this area of sex and sexuality. In almost all societies of the world today, in the wake of modernization and globalization, religious norms and mores on sex and sexuality are being increasingly challenged, whereas new secular laws are growing to define the related boundaries of criminalization and decriminalization.

Church and State Separation and the U.S. Constitution

The principle of the separation of church and state was at the core of the formation of the modern state and the writing of the Constitution in the United States. Thomas Jefferson was the architect of the American principle of the separation of church and state. In his *Notes on the State of Virginia*, Jefferson (1782) wrote: "Millions of innocent men, women and children, since the introduction of Christianity, have been burnt, tortured, fined and imprisoned; yet we have not advanced one inch towards uniformity." The First Amendment of the U.S. Constitution is about this fundamental notion of separation between church and state. It states that "Congress shall make no law respecting an establishment of religion, or prohibiting the free exercise thereof" (Legal Information Institute, 2012c, p. 1). In an 1802 letter written to the Danbury Baptist Association of Connecticut, Jefferson wrote, "I contemplate with sovereign reverence that act of the whole American people which declared that their legislature should 'make no law respecting an establishment of religion, or prohibiting the free exercise thereof'" (United States Constitution Online, 2012, p. 1).

The U.S. Congress has passed many statutes and the U.S. Supreme Court has rendered many judicial decisions that challenge the religious norms and ethos related to sex and sexuality. Until recently in the United States, most states had laws criminalizing homosexuality, adultery, fornication, and heterosexual sodomy. All of those laws are now being challenged or stand invalid in the context of the U.S. Supreme Court's (2003) landmark decision in *Lawrence v. Texas* (Viator, 2009). Before 2003, Texas, like many other states, had a law that criminalized intimate homosexual activity between two consenting individuals. In 1998, the Houston police found two men named John Lawrence and Tyron Garner engaged in homosexual activity in a Houston home. The police went to search the home in response to a false call about suspicious activities related to weapon possession. Lawrence and Garner were tried, found guilty, and convicted under the Texas sodomy statute. On appeal, the U.S. Supreme Court made a ruling in 2003 (6–3 decision) that the "Texas statute making it a crime for two persons of the same sex to engage in certain intimate sexual conduct violates the Due Process Clause" of the Fourteenth Amendment. The Texas sodomy statute, the Court argued, is a violation of the liberty clause of the Fourteenth Amendment. "The liberty protected by the Constitution," the Court said, "allows homosexual persons the right to choose to enter upon relationships in the confines of their homes and their own private lives and still retain their dignity as free persons" (*Lawrence v. Texas*, 2003). Neither the federal government nor the states have any constitutional authority to regulate "the most private human conduct, sexual behavior, and in the most private of places, the home" (*Lawrence v. Texas*, 2003). The Court further added: "The Texas statute furthers no legitimate state interest which can justify its intrusion into the individual's personal and private life" (*Lawrence v. Texas*, 2003). In giving the majority opinion, Justice Kennedy wrote that Lawrence and Garner's "right to liberty under the Due Process Clause gives them the full right to engage in their conduct without intervention of the government" (*Lawrence v. Texas*, 2003). The *Lawrence v Texas* decision, as one legal expert observed, "has called into question all state encroachments into the realm of sexual autonomy" (Cohen, 2010, p. 646).

The U.S. Supreme Court examines issues related to church and state separation and the First Amendment of the Constitution in terms of two clauses: the Establishment Clause and the Free Exercise Clause. The Establishment Clause prohibits preferential treatment to any religion in the United States. Under the Establishment Clause, the Supreme Court interprets whether any governmental actions have violated the separation of church and state principle. Under the Free Exercise Clause, the Court interprets whether the "right of American citizens to accept any religious belief and engage in religious rituals" has been violated (Legal Information Institute, 2012d, p. 1). The Clause "protects not just religious beliefs but actions made on behalf of those beliefs" (Legal Information Institute, 2012d, p. 1). In a number of decisions in recent times, the U.S. Supreme Court ruled in favor of criminalization or decriminalization of acts and behaviors that are based on religious faith and beliefs. However, one of the earliest of such decisions was made in the case of *Reynolds v. United States* in 1879 with respect to the criminalization of polygamy. Congress passed the Morrill Anti-Bigamy Act in 1862, particularly to put a ban on plural marriage practiced by Mormons, and it was signed into law by President Abraham Lincoln. Congress passed another act, the Edmunds Anti-Polygamy Act of 1882, and it made plural marriage a felony crime. In 1877, George Reynolds, the secretary to Mormon Church leader Brigham Young, was convicted by the Utah territorial District Court for violating the federal antibigamy statute. On appeal, the Utah territorial Supreme Court upheld the Utah District Court decision. Reynolds brought the case to the U.S. Supreme Court on the grounds that his conviction violated his First Amendment right of religious freedom. The U.S. Supreme Court in 1879 unanimously decided that Reynolds's conviction did not violate his First Amendment right. Chief Justice Morrison R. Waite, in declaring the unanimous opinion of the Court, said that federal statutes can criminalize any activity irrespective of its origin in religious faiths and beliefs.

In a number of other decisions, the Supreme Court decriminalized practices that are prohibited by religion, particularly by the Catholic faith. These include the decriminalization of the use of contraceptives by married women (*Griswold v. Connecticut,* 1965), the decriminalization of the use contraceptives by unmarried women (*Eisenstadt v. Baird,* 1972), and the decriminalization of abortion (*Roe v. Wade,* 1973). In *Roe v. Wade,* the U.S Supreme Court declared the criminal abortion statutes of Texas as unconstitutional. The first criminal abortion statute of Texas was enacted in 1854. By the middle of the 1950s, most states in the United States created statutes criminalizing abortion. The core issue in *Roe v. Wade* was whether a pregnant woman has the right to decide to terminate her pregnancy, and whether the Texas abortion statute is an infringement on that right. The Court rendered a decision that "a state criminal abortion statute of the current Texas type, that excepts from criminality only a lifesaving procedure on behalf of the mother . . . is in violation of the Due Process Clause of the Fourteenth Amendment" (*Roe v. Wade*, 1973).

Similar laws based on secular interpretations have been enacted by the U.S. Congress. In 2009, Congress passed the Matthew Shepard and James Byrd, Jr. Hate Crimes Prevention Act. The Act is named after Matthew Shepard, a 21-year old college student in Laramie, Wyoming, who was tied to a fence, tortured, and killed for his sexual orientation in 1998, and James Byrd, Jr., an African American, who was killed and decapitated by being dragged behind a pickup truck by two White supremacists in Jasper, Texas, in the same year. The act criminalized not only hateful behavior on the basis of sexual orientation, but also hateful behavior in terms of many other categories. As the text of the law states, "This Act applies to violent acts motivated by actual or perceived race, color, religion, national origin, gender, sexual orientation, gender identity or disability of a victim" (Matthew Shepard and James Byrd, Jr. Hate Crimes Prevention Act of 2009).

Thus, the dominance of secular law and statutes based on the principle of the separation of church and state and grounded on the philosophical notions of security, liberty, freedom, privacy, and equality is one of the major hallmarks of modern criminal justice. A secular system of criminal justice means that crime and criminality are not to be defined in terms of scriptures; criminalization is not to be perceived in terms of sin and evil; judges and justices are not to be appointed on grounds of religious roles and experience; trials and adjudications must not be based on religious law; and punishment must not be based on sacred scriptures. A secular system of criminal justice must also at the same time be responsible for the protection of the freedom of religion. The separation between church and state in modern criminal justice and modern secular criminal law have evolved over a long period of time, from the birth of the modern state in the 18th century. In comparative criminal justice, the study of this process of secularization in criminal justice is an intriguing issue. How religious issues intersect with the defining of crime and criminality, how secular criminal law evolves and conflicts with religious laws and morality, how judges and justices interpret secular criminal laws and statutes, and how the strategic elites of a society debate and dispute issues related to crime, morality, and religion are issues of vital significance in comparative criminal justice.

Due Process of Law and Modern Criminal Justice

The third defining feature of modern criminal justice is that it is based on the dominance of the due process of law. In a modern system of criminal justice, the laws that are made to define the boundaries of crime and criminality and the ways those laws are applied in criminal trials and investigations are governed by a defined set of laws and principles known as due process of law. Due process of law is the interior design of a modern system of criminal justice. It is a set of intrasystemic laws and rules that comprise the foundations of criminal justice. The history of due process of law goes back to the Magna Carta in 1215. Articles 39 and 40 of the Magna Carta stated: "No freeman shall be taken, or imprisoned, or disseized, or outlawed, or exiled . . . nor will we go upon or send upon him—save by the lawful judgment of his peers or by the law of the land." Since the beginning of the 18th century, the integration of the principle of the due process of law within the framework of a constitution remained fundamental to the evolution of the modern state. It remained at the core of the formulation of the English Bill of Rights and the rise of the nation-state in England, the rise of the American republic and the birth of the U.S. Bill of Rights, and the creation of the French Republic and the French Declaration of the Rights of Man and of the Citizen.

In the creation of modern criminal justice within the framework of a modern state, the due process of law has evolved in the following two directions: evolution of procedural due process and evolution of substantive due process. Procedural due process is related to those laws and principles that dictate how criminal arrests and detentions, searches and seizures, and trials and adjudications are to be pursued. Procedural due process defines the boundaries of the fundamental rights that are to be protected by the state. It brings limits on police power, it lays the rules of evidence, and it puts limits on sentencing and conviction by jurors and judges. Substantive due process, on the other hand, is related to the content of criminal law. It seeks to guarantee that no criminal law is made to abridge or made in violation of the fundamental rights of people. The whole perspective of the due process of law implies that criminal laws are to be made and criminal laws are to be applied on the basis of the recognition of some of the fundamental rights of people, including those who are brought into the system of criminal justice.

Procedural Due Process of Law: The U.S. Constitution

Modern procedural due process laws and principles emerged simultaneously with the modern state and the modern criminal justice system. There have been some kinds of procedural laws in criminal justice since the beginning of criminal justice in ancient societies. The Code of Hammurabi, developed in 1700 BC, contained a number of criminal procedures. As one of the procedural laws in the Code of Hammurabi stated: "If anyone brings an accusation of any crime before the elders, and does not prove what he has charged, he shall, if it be a capital offense charged, be put to death" (Horne, 2007). In the ancient Roman Code of Law developed in 450 BC—the Twelve Tables—Tables I, II, and VI were exclusively dedicated to establishing the procedures of criminal law. As Table I stated: "If he (plaintiff) summons him (defendant) into court, he shall go. If he does not go, (plaintiff) shall call witnesses. Then only he shall take him by force. If he refuses or flees, he (plaintiff) shall lay hands on him" (Scott, 2001). The method of the Inquisition discovered and used by the Catholic Church was a part of criminal procedure in medieval criminal justice. Modern criminal procedural laws did not emerge until the birth of the modern state and the expansion of the principle of due process. Modern criminal procedural due process of law has emerged to define the limits of governmental authority and the ways of protecting individual rights in the governance of criminal justice. Some of the key aspects of modern procedural due process include the right of protection against the suspension of *habeas corpus*, the right of protection against unreasonable searches and seizures, the right of protection against self-incrimination, the right to have counsel, the right to public trial, the right to a fair and speedy trial, and the right of protection against cruel and unusual punishment.

The Privilege of the Writ of **Habeas Corpus**   *Habeas corpus*, a Latin word meaning "you should have the body," is one of the fundamental rights that is protected in modern criminal justice. It means that anyone has the right to file a writ of *habeas corpus* to challenge the legality of arrest and detention. In other words, no one in a modern system of criminal justice can be detained for an indefinite period of time without legal reasons. The principle of *habeas corpus* is rooted in English common law and goes back to the time of the Magna Carta. From the time of King Henry VII (1485–1509), according to many historians, the notion of *habeas corpus* remained a major device to protect personal liberty. The British Parliament was the first to enact a law protecting the privilege of the writ of habeas corpus— the Habeas Corpus Act of 1679. The principle of *habeas corpus* has been subsequently integrated into the constitutions of all modern states, particularly those that are based on the tradition of the English common law. As Section 9 of Article I of the U.S. Constitution states: "The privilege of the writ of habeas corpus shall not be suspended, unless when in cases of rebellion or invasion the public safety may require it" (Legal Information Institute, 2012e, p. 1).

This provision of the constitution, known in jurisprudence as the suspension clause, denied Congress the power to suspend the privilege of the writ of *habeas corpus* except under extraordinary situations of rebellion or invasion when public safety is endangered (Halliday & White, 2008). The fact that the principle of *habeas corpus* was integrated into the U.S. Constitution before the integration of the Bill of Rights implies that it was considered by the framers of the constitution as vitally important for the protection of individual liberty. The privilege of the writ of *habeas corpus* is protected not only by the U.S. Constitution, but also by the U.S. Congress. Congress enacted the Judiciary Act of 1791 to create the structure of the federal judiciary and to describe its major roles and responsibilities. Section 14 of the Judiciary Act of 1791 states that all federal courts "shall have the power to issue . . . habeas corpus, and all other writs not specially provided for by statute, which may be necessary for the exercise of their respective jurisdictions, and agreeable to the principles and usages of law" (Library of Congress, 2011).

The writ of *habeas corpus* was suspended for the first time in American history by President Lincoln in the wake of the Civil War in 1861. Then–Chief Justice of the Supreme Court Roger Taney declared the suspension of the writ of *habeas corpus* by President Lincoln a violation of the Constitution. In a landmark ruling in *Ex parte Merryman* in 1861, Chief Justice Taney said that "if the authority which the constitution has confided to the judiciary department and judicial officers, may thus . . . be usurped by the military power . . . the people of the United States are no longer living under a government of laws." In response, Congress enacted the Habeas Corpus Act in 1863. The Act legalized the power of the president to suspend *habeas corpus* in a time of war. The Act declared that "during the present rebellion, the President of the United States, whenever, in his judgment, the public safety may require it, is authorized to suspend the privilege of the writ of habeas corpus." *Habeas corpus* privilege, according to the U.S. Supreme Court, "is one of the centerpieces of our liberty." The Supreme Court further confirmed in *Harris v. Nelson* (1969) that it "is the fundamental instrument for safeguarding individual freedom against arbitrary and lawless state action."

The Right of Protection Against Unreasonable Search and Seizure The right of protection against unreasonable search and seizure is another hallmark of modern criminal justice. Like arrests and detentions, search and seizure are two of the most vital functions of criminal justice. Law enforcement and criminal justice cannot work without collecting evidence. If the production and possession of marijuana or cocaine is a violation of law, the police must have the right to search and seize marijuana and cocaine even from the privacy of people's homes, cars, and backyards. If there is a murder in a home, the police must have the right to search the home for murder weapons. A vast number of violent crimes, sexual crimes, drug-related crimes, and cyber crimes are committed within the realm of the privacy of homes or in private spheres in general. With the aid of modern information and surveillance technology, law enforcement agents are now able to search homes and all realms of privacy without trespassing any physical boundaries. From the days of the Magna Carta and English common law, police search and seizure has been an important issue in criminal justice. In English common law, there is a saying: "Every man's house is his castle." The concern since then has been to achieve a balance between the need for evidence in criminal justice and the need for the protection of the privacy of individuals. In the Middle Ages, people were searched and their properties were seized by agents of the kings, queens, and barons without any regard to the protection of privacy and without any law and legal justification. The right of protection against unusual searches and seizures therefore became one of the fundamental human rights protected by modern states and modern systems of criminal justice. The Fourth Amendment of the U.S. Constitution protects the rights against unreasonable searches and seizures. It states that searches and seizures must be based on a valid warrant issued by a judge or a magistrate. The issuance of a warrant must be based on reasonable suspicion or probable cause, and it must specify what is to be searched, when, how, why, and by whom. The core idea of this due process principle of protection against unreasonable searches and seizures is to limit police power and to protect the fundamental right to privacy of individuals.

Because the right of protection against unreasonable searches and seizures is a constitutional right and the U.S. Supreme Court is the guardian and sole interpreter of the constitution, it is intriguing to see how the Supreme Court has interpreted the Fourth Amendment at different times in the history of the United States. One of the earliest cases in which the Supreme Court deliberated on this issue of search and seizure is the case of *Olmstead v. United States* in 1928. Olmstead and a number of other defendants were convicted by the District Court for the Western District of Washington for importing, transporting, and selling intoxicating liquors in violation of the Prohibition Act passed by Congress in 1919. FBI agents charged the defendants on the basis of tapped telephone conversations. The FBI agents placed wiretaps on the residential and office telephones of the defendants. The verdict of the district court was appealed to the Circuit Court of Appeals for the Ninth Circuit on the grounds of the violation of the defendant's Fourth Amendment right of protection against unusual search and seizure. The issue was whether the wiretapping of telephone conversations, where FBI agents did not physically trespass the homes and the offices of the defendants, was in violation of the Fourth Amendment. The Ninth Circuit affirmed the decision of the district court. On appeal again, the U.S. Supreme Court affirmed the decision of the Ninth Circuit by interpretating that the Fourth Amendment applies to physical search alone. Justice Taft, who wrote the majority opinion, said that the Fourth Amendment does not allow searches "to include telephone wires, reaching to the whole world from the defendant's house or office. The intervening wires are not part of his house or office, any more than are the highways along which they are stretched" (*Olmstead v. United States*, 1928).

The Supreme Court in recent years has broadened its definition of the Fourth Amendment, and it is now being interpreted mostly in terms of the doctrine of the reasonable expectation of privacy. In *Katz v. United States* in 1967, the Court rejected the trespass doctrine of *Olmstead v. United States*. Charles Katz was convicted by the District Court of the Southern District of California for sending gambling information over the phone across state lines. The evidence was collected, as in *Olmstead v. United States*, by putting wiretaps in public telephone booths used by the defendant. The conviction was appealed in the Court of Appeals of the Ninth Circuit. The Ninth Circuit Court upheld the conviction on the ground of the trespass doctrine used by the Olmstead court. It argued that the obtaining of information through wiretapping by FBI agents was not a violation of the Fourth Amendment because they did not trespass the physical space used by the defendant. On appeal, the U.S. Supreme Court reversed the decision of the Ninth Circuit Court on the basis of the doctrine of reasonable expectation of privacy. The Court argued that wiretapping of telephone conversations was a violation of privacy rights. "The Government's activities in electronically listening to and recording the petitioner's words violated the privacy upon which he justifiably relied while using the telephone booth" (*Katz v. United States*, 1967). The Fourth Amendment protects not only a physical space, but also people against unreasonable search and seizure.

Since *Katz v. United States*, the doctrine of the reasonable expectation of privacy has remained central to the Supreme Court's interpretations of the Fourth Amendment. The Court is of the opinion that the Fourth Amendment "only protects you against searches that violate your *reasonable expectation of privacy*. A reasonable expectation of privacy exists if 1) you actually expect privacy, and 2) your expectation is one that society as a whole would think is legitimate" (Electronic Frontier Foundation, 2011, p. 1).

The due process right of protection against unreasonable search and seizure is related to another due process principle called the exclusionary principle. What it means is that evidence collected in violation of the Fourth Amendment is not admissible in the court of law. It was first established by the U.S. Supreme Court in *Weeks v. United States* in 1918. Fremont Weeks was fined and imprisoned by the U.S. Western District Court of Missouri for sending lottery tickets and gambling information through the mail in violation of the gambling law of the state of Missouri. The conviction was appealed on the ground that Weeks's home was searched and evidence was collected without a warrant. In a unanimous opinion, the U.S. Supreme Court reversed the judgment of the lower court on the ground that evidence was collected "from the house of the accused by an official of the United States, acting under color of his office, in direct violation of the constitutional rights of the defendant" (*Weeks v. United States*, 1918). In *Weeks v. United States* (1918), the Court created a new principle of the exclusionary rule. In *Mapp v. Ohio* (1961), the Court argued that the exclusionary rule applied not only to federal but also to state criminal cases. The Court said, "All evidence obtained by searches and seizures in violation of the Federal Constitution is inadmissible in a criminal trial in a state court" (*Mapp v. Ohio*, 1961).

The Right of Protection Against Self-Incrimination The right of protection against self-incrimination is another core component of the due process of law. What it means is that an accused has the right to remain silent and to not respond to any questions asked by law enforcement without the help of an attorney. A suspect or an accused must not be forced or tortured to confess to a crime or to describe the circumstances that led to a criminal event that can later be used in his or her prosecution. The right of self-incrimination also implies that a police or law enforcement officer is obligated by law to let an accused or a suspect know his or her right of protection against self-incrimination—a law enforcement obligation known in U.S. criminal justice as the *Miranda* warning. If any confession is obtained and verbal statements are gathered in violation of the *Miranda* rights, they are not acceptable as evidence in the court of law. In the United States, the Fifth Amendment of the Constitution created this right of protection against self-incrimination. The Fifth Amendment states that no person "shall be compelled in any criminal case to be a witness against himself" (Legal Information Institute, 2012f, p. 1).

The right of protection against self-incrimination has become an integral part of the due process of law and modern criminal procedure since the institutionalization of the defense counsel's role in the 18th century's common law court. Before the 18th century, there was no role, in common law courts, for a defense counsel. In the common law courts of the 16th and the 17th centuries, the fundamental safeguard for the accused "was not the right to remain silent but rather the opportunity to speak" (Langbein, 1994, p. 1057). A different perspective that recognized the role of a defense counsel, however, began to emerge in English common law courts during the late 18th and early 19th centuries. With the emerging role of the defense counsel in criminal trials, the "privilege against self-incrimination entered common law procedure . . . . It was the capture of criminal trial by lawyers for prosecution and defense that made it possible for the criminal defendant to decline to be a witness against himself" (Langbein, 1994, p. 1048).

The right of protection against self-incrimination became firmly established as a part of modern criminal procedure and modern criminal justice in America, particularly on the basis of the U.S. Supreme Court decision in *Miranda v. Arizona* in 1966. In 1963, Miranda was convicted for kidnapping and rape and was sentenced to 20 years in prison. Miranda was convicted on the basis of his written confession to the police. The police did not inform Miranda of his right to keep silent under the Fifth Amendment. The conviction was appealed to the Arizona Supreme Court. The Arizona Supreme Court dismissed the appeal. The case was decided by the U.S. Supreme Court in 1966. The Supreme Court reversed the decision of the lower court on the grounds that it was based on evidence collected in violation of the Fifth Amendment right of protection against self-incrimination. The Court held that "the prosecution may not use statements, whether exculpatory or inculpatory, stemming from questioning initiated by law enforcement officers after a person has been taken into custody or otherwise deprived of his freedom of action in any significant way" (*Miranda v. Arizona*, 1966). The Court further added that "the privilege against self-incrimination, which has had a long and expansive historical development, is the essential mainstay of our adversary system" (*Miranda v. Arizona*, 1966). Since *Miranda*, the reading of the Fifth Amendment in custodial interrogation has become a legal obligation for police and law enforcement in America. However, in a recent case— *Berghuis v. Thompkins*—in 2010, the Supreme Court ruled that after the reading of the *Miranda* rights, the rights also have to be invoked by the defendant. The defendant must not just be silent after the *Miranda* warning is read to him or her by law enforcement. The defendant must explicitly tell law enforcement that he or she is taking the protection of the Fifth Amendment.

The Right to a Fair Trial   In a modern criminal justice system, the due process of law extends to all stages and phases of criminal trials and proceedings within the boundaries of the court. A modern criminal justice system is based on the recognition of the fundamental right to a fair trial. The concept of a fair trial includes a number of related rights and privileges such as the right to counsel, the right of indictment by a grand jury, the right to have a speedy trial, the right to have an open and impartial trial, the right to have a jury trial, the right to be presumed innocent, the right of protection against double jeopardy, and the right to equal justice. Most of these notions evolved from English common law.

In the U.S. Constitution, the Fifth and the Sixth Amendments guarantee these and other rights and principles related to the fundamental right of a fair trial. The Fifth Amendment states that: "No person shall be held to answer for a capital, or otherwise infamous crime, unless on a presentment or indictment of a grand jury" (Legal Information Institute, 2012f, p. 1). The Sixth Amendment states that in "criminal prosecutions, the accused shall enjoy the right to a speedy and public trial, by an impartial jury of the state and district wherein the crime shall have been committed, which district shall have been previously ascertained by law" (Legal Information Institute, 2012g, p. 1). The Sixth Amendment further states that a defendant has the right "to be informed of the nature and cause of the accusation; to be confronted with the witnesses against him; to have compulsory process for obtaining witnesses in his favor, and to have the assistance of counsel for his defense" (Legal Information Institute, 2012g, p. 1).

During the past 200 years, the U.S. Supreme Court has firmly protected the fundamental right to a fair trial within the federal and state criminal justice systems. In a landmark ruling in the case of *Gideon v. Wainwright* in 1963, the U.S. Supreme Court argued that the constitutional right to have a counsel extends to all capital and noncapital state felony cases. The Court held that "the right of an indigent defendant in a criminal trial to have the assistance of counsel is a fundamental right essential to a fair trial, and petitioner's trial and conviction without the assistance of counsel violated the Fourteenth Amendment" (*Gideon v. Wainwright*, 1963). In *Argersinger v. Hamlin* in 1972, the U.S. Supreme Court similarly argued that the Sixth Amendment right to have counsel is extended not only to felony but also to misdemeanor cases. The Court said that "no accused may be deprived of his liberty as the result of any criminal prosecution, whether felony or misdemeanor, in which he was denied the assistance of counsel" (*Argersinger v. Hamlin*, 1972). The Sixth Amendment right to counsel is extended also to all phases of criminal trials. In a number of cases, the Supreme Court established the right to counsel in pretrial arraignments (*Hamilton v. Alabama*, 1961), at preliminary hearings (*Coleman v. Alabama*, 1970), for trials (*Gideon v. Wainwright*, 1963; *Argersinger v. Hamlin*, 1972), in the sentencing phase (*Mempa v. Rhay*, 1967), and at the time of appeal (*Douglas v. California*, 1963). The right to a speedy trial is also one of the important components of the right to a fair trial established by the Sixth Amendment. The right to a speedy trial, however, is applied to cases only when someone has been formally charged. It is not applied in the phases of pretrial investigation and posttrial deliberations. In 1974, the U.S. Congress enacted the Speedy Trial Act. Title 1 of the Act specified the time limits for various phases in a federal criminal trial (Legal Information Institute, 2012).

The U.S. Supreme Court has also firmly established in a number of cases the fundamental right to a speedy trial. In *Klopfer v. North Carolina* in 1967, the Court made a ruling that "By indefinitely postponing prosecution on the indictment over petitioner's objection and without stated justification, the State denied petitioner the right to a speedy trial guaranteed to him by the Sixth and Fourteenth Amendments of the Federal Constitution" (*Klopfer v. North Carolina*, 1967). The Sixth Amendment of the Constitution also protects the fundamental right of a public trial by an impartial jury. Section II of Article III of the U.S. Constitution states that "the trial of all crimes, except in cases of impeachment, shall be by jury" (Legal Information Institute, 2012h, p. 1).

One of the core doctrines that forms the basis of a fair trial and that is also at the core of the due process of law is the doctrine of the presumption of innocence or the right of a defendant to be presumed innocent. The right of *habeas corpus*, the right of protections against unreasonable search and seizure, the right of protection against self-incrimination, and the right to a fair trial all are centered on the doctrine of the presumption of innocence. Roots of the presumption of innocence doctrine go back to ancient times. The Code of Hammurabi clearly stated, "If a man has accused another of laying a *nertu* . . . upon him, but has not proved it, he shall be put to death." Similarly, in ancient Roman law, the accuser had the burden of proof. The Roman law prohibited torture and punishment for those who are in custody. "A constitution of the Emperor Honorius and Theodose of A.D. 423 reminded consuls, praetors, senators, and tribunes of the people that defendants charged with a capital crime should not immediately be considered guilty merely because they had been accused" (Quintard-Morenas, 2010, p. 113).

In 1895, the U.S. Supreme Court, in its ruling in *Coffin v. United States* stated that "the principle that there is a presumption of innocence in favor of the accused is the undoubted law, axiomatic and elementary, and its enforcement lies at the foundation of the administration of our criminal law." The doctrine of the presumption of innocence created the following four major imperatives in modern criminal proceedings: (1) the defendant must not be punished before conviction; (2) the defendant must be presumed innocent unless proven guilty; (3) the burden of proof rests on the prosecution; and (4) guilt must be established by the jury, not on the basis of suspicion, but on the basis of evidence and the doctrine of beyond reasonable doubt.

The Right of Protection Against Cruel and Unusual Punishment   Among the various rights and principles included in the procedural due process of law, the right of protection against cruel and unusual punishment is an important evolution in modern criminal justice. In the United States, this right is protected by the Eighth Amendment of the Constitution. The Eighth Amendment states that "excessive bail shall not be required, nor excessive fines imposed, nor cruel and unusual punishments inflicted" (Legal Information Institute, 2012b, p. 1). The English Bill of Rights stated exactly the same principle in 1689: "That excessive bail ought not to be required, nor excessive fines imposed; nor cruel and unusual punishments inflicted." The French Declaration of the Rights of Man and of the Citizen includes the same principle. It states, "The law shall provide for such punishments only as are strictly and obviously necessary, and no one shall suffer punishment except it be legally inflicted in virtue of a law passed and promulgated before the commission of the offense" (Jellinek, 2009). It further stated that "if arrest shall be deemed indispensable, all harshness not essential to the securing of the prisoner's person shall be severely repressed by law." In a modern criminal justice system, people must not be subjected to torture and repression or such punishments as public execution, burning, crucifixion, banishment, public whipping, physical castration, and beheading. In defining cruel and unusual punishment and in applying the Eighth Amendment, the U.S. Supreme Court examines the methods of punishment, the amount and extent of punishment, and the proportionality between crime and punishment (*Rummel v. Estelle*, 1980; *Hutto v. Davis,* 1982). The court is of the opinion that punishment does not necessarily have to cause serious physical injury to be in violation of the Eighth Amendment. The use of excessive physical force, even if it does not cause serious physical injury, is a violation of the Eighth Amendment (*Hudson v. McMillian*, 1992). The violation of the Eighth Amendment includes not just physical injury but also the infliction of psychological pain such as the deprivation of the right of citizenship (*Hope v. Pelzer*, 2002). The Court has also argued that the executions of a mentally retarded person (*Atkins v. Virginia*, 2002) and a juvenile under the age of 18 (*Roper v. Simmons*, 2005) are violations of the Eighth Amendment. The Supreme Court, in a number of cases, held the opinion that an analysis of what is cruel and unusual punishment must be based on evolving societal standards of decency (*Gregg v. Georgia*, 1978; *Atkins v. Virginia*, 2002; and *Roper v. Simmons*, 2005).

Substantive Due Process of Law: U.S. Congress and the Constitution

In Anglo-American jurisprudence, one of the basic notions of substantive due process is that criminal legislation must not be enacted in violation of the natural law and customary rights based on common law. According to one legal expert, "On balance, the historical evidence shows that one widespread understanding of the due process clause of the Fifth Amendment in 1791 included judicial recognition and enforcement of unenumerated natural and customary rights against congressional action" (Gedicks, 2009, p. 669). The substantive due process is based primarily on the notion of the unalienable and self-evident right to life, liberty, and property—the rights that are rooted in human nature and universally valid among cultures and civilizations. The natural law tradition goes back to the writings of Aristotle, Aquinas, Hobbes, Locke, and Rousseau. The American Declaration of Independence "begins with the natural rights theory drawn from Locke's Second Treatise" (Gedicks, 2009, p. 622). In his *Second Treatise of Civil Government* (1690), Locke said that "the law of nature stands as an eternal rule to all men, legislators as well as others. The rules that they make for other men's actions, must . . . be conformable to the law of nature" (Ch. 11, § 135). Locke further added that "the legislative, or supreme authority, cannot assume to its self a power to rule by extemporary arbitrary decrees, but is bound to dispense justice, and decide the rights of the subject by promulgated standing laws" (1690, Ch. 11, § 135).

With respect to criminal law and criminal justice, the U.S. Supreme Court interprets the notion of substantive due process primarily in terms of the protection of the fundamental liberties. According to the Supreme Court, there are two "categories of fundamental liberties. The first category includes most of the liberties expressly enumerated in the Bill of Rights . . . [and the second] includes those liberties that are not expressly enumerated in the Bill of Rights" (*West's Encyclopedia of American Law*, 2011, p. 6). The Ninth Amendment states that the "enumeration in the Constitution, of certain rights, shall not be construed to deny or disparage others retained by the people" (Legal Information Institute, 2012i, p. 1). The Supreme Court derives these unenumerated liberties from the "common law, moral philosophy, and deeply rooted traditions of U.S. legal history" (*West's Encyclopedia of American Law*, 2011, p. 7). The Supreme Court opines that liberty interests cannot be simply described in terms of a long list of rights. Rather, the Court affirmed that it "must be viewed as a rational continuum of freedom through which every facet of human behavior is safeguarded from arbitrary impositions and purposeless restraints" (*West's Encyclopedia of American Law*, 2011, p. 7). In this light, the Supreme Court has observed that "the Due Process Clause protects very abstract liberty interests including the right to personal autonomy, bodily integrity, self dignity, and self-determination" and these liberty interests "often are grouped to form a general right to privacy" (*West's Encyclopedia of American Law*, 2011, p. 7).

The modern interpretation of the substantive due process of law in terms of the Supreme Court's ideas of liberty interests began in an expansive way from the 1960s, especially with *Griswold v. Connecticut* in 1965. In 1879, the state of Connecticut passed a law that criminalized the use of contraceptive information and devices. Under this law, the executive director of the Planned Parenthood League of Connecticut and its medical director, a licensed physician, were convicted for supplying contraceptive information and devices to married women. The Supreme Court of Connecticut affirmed the decision. The case was appealed to the U.S. Supreme Court in 1965. The U.S. Supreme Court, in a 7–2 decision, reversed the decision of the supreme court of Connecticut on the ground that the Connecticut statute was made in violation of the constitutionally protected right to privacy of a married couple. The majority opinion of the Court led by Chief Justice Earl Warren argued that "liberty protects those personal rights that are fundamental, and is not confined to the specific terms of the Bill of Rights" (*Griswold v. Connecticut*, 1965). Justice Arthur Goldberg said that the "Bill of Rights may not recognize some of the privacy and personal rights, but the Ninth Amendment justifies the incorporation of those rights" (*Griswold v. Connecticut*, 1965). The Court further added that "the language and history of the Ninth Amendment reveal that the Framers of the Constitution believed that there are additional fundamental rights, protected from governmental infringement" (*Griswold v. Connecticut*, 1965).

After *Griswold,* the U.S. Supreme Court incorporated a number of privacy rights and invalidated a number of state and federal statutes on the ground of liberty interests. One of the landmark cases decided in the 1960s on issues of liberty interests, after *Griswold*, is the case of *Loving v. Virginia,* 1967. In 1924, the Commonwealth of Virginia enacted the Racial Integrity Act that criminalized interracial marriage between Blacks and Whites. The Act stated that "If any white person intermarry with a colored person, or any colored person intermarry with a white person, he shall be guilty of a felony and shall be punished by confinement."

The U.S. Supreme Court struck down the Commonwealth's Racial Integrity Act on the ground of its violation of the equal protection and due process clauses of the Fourteenth Amendment. Other landmark decisions of the Supreme Court, with respect to the protection of liberty interests include decisions made in the cases of *Eisenstadt v. Baird*, 1972 (struck down a Massachusetts law that criminalized the use of contraceptive information and devices by unmarried women); *Roe v. Wade,* 1973 (struck down Texas's antiabortion statutes); *Moore v. City of East Cleveland,* 1977 (struck down an ordinance made by the City of East Cleveland that criminalized the keeping of grandparents and grandchildren in a single-family occupancy home; the Court invalidated the ordinance because of its violation of the due process of law of the Fourteenth Amendment); *Cruzan v. Director, Missouri Department of Health*, 1990 (the Court affirmed the Missouri Department of Health policy not to remove life support without clear and convincing evidence); *Atkins v. Virginia*, 2002 (the Court said that the execution of the mentally retarded is a violation of the Eighth Amendment); and *Hill v. McDonough*, 2006 (the Court affirmed the right of death row inmates to challenge the use of drugs in giving lethal injection for execution).

The U.S. Supreme Court has similarly upheld or invalidated a number of statutes and ordinances on the basis of the equal protection clause of the Fourteenth Amendment. One of the landmark decisions made by the U.S. Supreme Court on substantive due process of law argued from the perspective of the equal protection clause was in *Brown v. Board of Education of Topeka*, 1954. In *Brown v. Board of Education of Topeka,* the U.S. Supreme Court made a landmark ruling that segregated public school systems are in violation of the equal protection clause of the Fourteenth Amendment, saying that "the history of the Fourteenth Amendment is inconclusive as to its intended effect on public education" (1954). The Court added that the "segregation of children in public schools solely on the basis of race deprives children of the minority group of equal educational opportunities, even though the physical facilities and other 'tangible' factors may be equal" (*Brown v. Board of Education of Topeka*, 1954). The Court further added that the "'Separate but equal' doctrine [argued in *Plessy v. Ferguson* in 1896] has no place in the field of public education" (*Brown v. Board of Education of Topeka*, 1954). Some of the other landmark cases argued by the Supreme Court on the basis of the equal protection clause include *Faragher v. City of Boca Raton*, 1998, and *Burlington Industries Inc. v. Ellerth*, 1998 (employers are made liable for sexual harassment in the workplace; sexual harassment training was defined by the Court as an affirmative defense for employers), and *Oncale v. Sundowner Offshore Services,* 1998 (the Court criminalized same-sex harassment).

Juvenile Justice: A Structural Imperative in Modern Criminal Justice

A separate system of law and justice for juveniles is another distinctive characteristic of modern criminal justice. Juveniles in all eras and historical times committed crimes, and juvenile crimes in all eras and historical times were punished by laws. Before the birth of modernity, however, there was no separate system of law and justice for juveniles. In medieval criminal justice, juveniles were treated by the same laws applied to adults, subjected to the same kinds of punishments given to adults, and incarcerated in the same prisons built for adults. With the birth of modernity, there has been an emergence of the general notion of childhood and the specific idea of life stage known as adolescence. With the realization that childhood and adolescence are distinctive periods in human life, juvenile justice has become a separate realm of law in the modern states. In all modern states of the West, there are separate systems of juvenile justice with separate laws for juvenile arrests and detentions, trials and adjudications, convictions and sentencing, and incarcerations and corrections. In all modern states, in other words, there is a dual system of justice—one system of justice for the adults and another for the juveniles. There are three distinctive reasons for the growth and evolution of modern juvenile justice: the legal recognition of the rights of the children, the scientific recognition of the peculiarities of the brains and behaviors of the children, and the notion of the state's responsibility for the amelioration of the problems of delinquent and disadvantaged children.

Juvenile Justice and the Rights of Children

The evolution of the rights of children is intimately connected to the rise of modernity. The rise of modernity brought the notion of human rights in general to the center of law and justice and to the core of the formation of modern states. The recognition of the rights of children came as an extension of the recognition of human rights under modernity. Until the advent of modernity, children were seen primarily as properties of their fathers—properties that could be freely traded, bought, sold, or destroyed. One of the legal codes of Hammurabi stated: "If a son strike his father, his hands shall be [cut] off" (Horne, 2007/1915). Under the Roman legal doctrine of *patria potestas*—a doctrine that dominated not just the ancient world of the Romans, but also the whole of the Middle Ages in Europe—children did not have any separate rights. Their lives and rights were legally defined and controlled by their fathers—the patriarchs. One legal historian of ancient Roman law observed that in the Roman Republic, "The power of the father (patria potestas) over his dependent children was absolute. He might punish any of them in life and limb. He might sell his son into slavery" (Hunter, 1886, pp. 5–6). Table IV of the Roman code of law known as the Twelve Tables stated that "a dreadfully deformed child shall be killed" (Twelve Tables, tab. IV). Table IV also stated: "If a father surrenders his son for sale three times, the son shall be free" (Twelve Tables, tab. IV).

The advent of modernity brought a fundamental change in the notion of children's rights. Contemporary notions of children's rights are rooted in the Universal Declaration of Human Rights by the United Nations in 1948, the Declaration of the Rights of the Child by the United Nations in 1959, and the United Nations Convention on the Rights of the Child in 1989. Article III of the Universal Declaration of Human Rights states, "Everyone," including children, "has the right to life, liberty and security of person." Article V states that "no one," including children, "shall be subjected to torture or to cruel, inhuman or degrading treatment or punishment." The first principle of the Declaration of the Rights of the Child in 1959 declares that "the child shall enjoy all the rights set forth in this Declaration. Every child, without any exception whatsoever, shall be entitled to these rights." Principle IX states that "the child shall be protected against all forms of neglect, cruelty and exploitation. He shall not be the subject of traffic, in any form." In 1989, the United Nations developed a legally binding instrument of international law to protect the rights of children through the Convention on the Rights of the Child. The 54 Articles of the Convention on the Rights of the Child outlined the responsibility of the member states to develop legislative and organizational frameworks to apply and implement the rights of the children in all spheres of life including law and justice. Article XVI of the Convention on the Rights of the Child states that "no child shall be subjected to arbitrary or unlawful interference with his or her privacy, family, or correspondence, nor to unlawful attacks on his or her honour and reputation" and that "the child has the right to the protection of the law against such interference or attacks." Some of the institutions of modern juvenile justice such as juvenile courts and juvenile correction centers began to take shape long before these declarations and the conventions. These frameworks of international law, however, have greatly affected the expansion of those institutions and the rise of a new regime of criminal law related to the rights of children at a global scale.

Juvenile Justice and Modern Science

The advent of modernity brought the dominance of the perspective of scientific method and experiment. The modern growth of the science of early childhood greatly influenced the development of a separate system of juvenile justice. Even though development of juvenile justice institutions in the 19th century, such as reform schools and juvenile courts, began mostly in the context of social reforms, the growth of a modern science of early childhood development now provides the genuine rationale for a separate juvenile justice system. Scientific research in a number of areas including neurobiology, behavioral neurology, cognitive psychology, child psychology, child psychiatry, and sociology has shown that early childhood development is one of the most critical stages of the human life cycle. Research in neurology and behavioral neurology particularly has shown that children's brains are qualitatively different from those of adults. As a result, the capacities of adolescents to understand the boundaries of right and wrong, legal and illegal, and moral and immoral are different from those of the adults. One of the major discoveries in contemporary brain research is the notion of brain plasticity that means adolescent brains and adult brains are different in terms of brain structures, brain thickness, neural connectivity, and brain synapses. Because of these differences in brain development, adolescents are different from adults in rational reasoning, moral reasoning, emotional development, and impulse control. The existence of brain plasticity means that the human brain is an evolving and a living entity, and its growth and development are associated with early childhood experience and environment.

A study conducted by the Center on the Developing Child at Harvard University (2007) found that "although a great deal of brain architecture is shaped during the first three years, claims that the window of opportunity for brain development closes on a child's third birthday are unfounded" (p. 5). Research in behavioral neurology, child psychology, and child psychiatry has shown that juvenile delinquency is positively correlated with early childhood trauma and depression, exposure to stress and violence, sexual exploitation, and exposure to drugs and alcohol. Children who are exposed to early childhood trauma, depression, drugs, and violence are more likely to have abnormal growth of their brain. The abnormal growth of the brain, in turn, is more likely to be associated with low intelligence, lack of organized memory, high impulsivity, decreased coherence, low self-esteem, antisocial behavior, rigidity of thinking, obsessive thinking, and increased aggression—the factors that are positively correlated with juvenile delinquency. The study confirmed: "An abundance of scientific evidence clearly demonstrates that critical aspects of brain architecture began to be shaped by experience before and soon after birth, and many foundational aspects of that architecture are established well before a child enters school" (Center on the Developing

Child, 2007, p. 2). Modern juvenile justice is not merely a structure for the control of juvenile crimes and the punishment of juveniles. It has also grown as a system of law and justice for the prevention of juvenile delinquency, the criminalization of the behaviors that produce delinquency, and the rehabilitation of juveniles who are abused, neglected, and abandoned. Modern discoveries in the science of early childhood development provide a scientific rationale for organizing a separate system of law and justice for juveniles in all countries.

Juvenile Justice and the Doctrine of Parens Patriae

From the birth of the modern states in the 18th century, an idea began to crystallize that the welfare of children who are abused, neglected, and abandoned is a state responsibility. The advent of modernity brought some fundamental changes and transformations in family structure. The rise of industrialization, urbanization, nuclear families, and divorce rates has vastly affected the lives of children. With the progress of industrialization and urbanization, juvenile delinquency and child abuse vastly increased in almost all modernizing societies in the West. Although the advent of modernity brought recognition of childhood as a significant stage in human life, it also initiated the notion that modern states are responsible for protecting children from abuse, neglect, and abandonment. This notion of state responsibility for protecting the lives of children is embedded into the doctrine of *parens patriae*, which came from the English common law. The Latin meaning of the word is "the parent of the country," or "state is the father." In the 17th and 18th centuries, the English Chancery courts widely used the doctrine of *parens patriae* to justify state intervention in the lives of children who were poor, delinquent, neglected, and abandoned. The doctrine of *parens patriae* is at the core of the doctrine of the best interests of the child widely used by modern juvenile courts and modern juvenile justice.

The creation of a separate system of juvenile justice is one of the major benchmarks of modernity in criminal justice. The United States has one of the oldest and most developed juvenile justice systems. In the United States, there is a federal system of juvenile justice that includes the federal agencies, congressional acts and enactments, and judicial laws related to juvenile justice. There is also a separate department of juvenile justice in each of the states, such as the North Carolina Department of Juvenile Justice and Delinquency Prevention, the Florida Department of Juvenile Justice, the Georgia Department of Juvenile Justice, and the Maryland Department of Juvenile Services. In many states, juvenile justice is known under different titles, such as the Texas Youth Commission and the California Youth Authority. The major turning point in the modernization of juvenile justice in the United States came when the Juvenile Justice and Delinquency Prevention (JJDP) Act was passed by Congress in 1974. The JJDP Act mandated all 50 states to develop a separate system of juvenile justice within the broader scope of criminal justice (Shahidullah, 2008).

The JJDP Act of 1974 created the contemporary federal structure of juvenile justice that has enormously grown since then. The Act created a major federal juvenile justice agency, the Office of Juvenile Justice and Delinquency Prevention (OJJDP), within the Department of Justice. The OJJDP's major responsibilities are the administration and allocation of federal juvenile justice funds to state and local governments; dissemination of evidence-based research on juvenile delinquency and prevention; and the oversight of the state's compliance with federal juvenile justice laws and statutes. The JJDP Act of 1974 also created a separate office—the Coordinating Council on Juvenile Justice and Delinquency Prevention within the Executive Office of the President—as a national policy planning and advisory body on juvenile justice (Shahidullah, 2008). The JJDP Act also required the states to create similar policy-making and advisory bodies on juvenile justice. One of the most significant aspects of the JJDP Act is that it established the legal boundary of juvenile justice by developing a core set of requirements for dealing with juveniles within the state juvenile justice systems. These federally mandated requirements are: (1) the deinstitutionalization of status offenders; (2) the separation of juveniles from adult offenders; (3) adult jail and lockup removal; and (4) and the reduction of disproportionate minority conviction. The Act prohibited the states from imprisoning juveniles who commit status offenses and from housing them with adults.

In addition to the enactment of the JJDP, the Congress has enacted much legislation that criminalized child abuse, infanticide, child sexual abuse, corporal punishment, child labor, child trafficking, and child pornography. Congress also passed a number of enactments to protect the rights of children within the system of law and justice. Some of these enactments are the JJDP Act amendments of 1977, JJDP Act amendments of 1988, Crime Control Act of 1990, JJDP Act amendments of 1992, Violent Crime Control and Law Enforcement Act of 1994, Jacob Wetterling Crimes Against Children and Sexually Violent Offenders Registration Act of 1994, Sex Crimes against Children Prevention Act of 1995, Megan's Law of 1996, Pam Lychner Sexual Offender Tracking and Identification Act of 1996, Child Pornography Prevention Act of 1996, Child Online Protection Act of 1998, Children's Internet Protection Act of 2000, Victims of Trafficking and Violence Protection Act of 2000, Aimee's Law of 2000, the PROTECT Act of 2003, and the Adam Walsh Child Protection and Safety Act of 2006.

In addition to the aforementioned enactments by Congress, the U.S. Supreme Court has also rendered a number of landmark decisions on juveniles and juvenile justice. These decisions have firmly established the fundamental rights of children. The decisions also uphold the notion of childhood as a distinct phase in human life and vastly expand the role of the government in matters of juvenile justice. Some of these landmark decisions were made in the cases of *Kent v. United States* in 1966, *In re Gault* in 1967, *In re Winship* in 1970, *Breed v. Jones* in 1975, *New Jersey v. T.L.O* in 1985, *Yarborough v. Alvarado* in 2004, and *Roper v. Simmons* in 2005. Through these cases, the Supreme Court established that the constitutionally protected due process of law is applied not only to adults, but also to juveniles. In *In re Gault*, the Supreme Court argued that "neither the Fourteenth Amendment nor the Bill of Rights is for adults alone" (*In re Gault*, 1967). Juveniles, under the Fourteenth Amendment, have due process rights in all stages of juvenile justice (*Kent v. United States*, 1966). They have the constitutional rights of protection against unreasonable search and seizure (*New Jersey v. T.L.O.* 1985), self-incrimination (*Yarborough v. Alvarado*, 2004), double jeopardy (*Breed v. Jones,* 1975), and cruel and unusual punishment (*Roper v. Simmons,* 2005). In *In re Winship* in 1970, the Supreme Court ruled that the doctrine of beyond a reasonable doubt is an essential standard in the due process of law, and it is equally applied to juvenile justice.

■ Summary

A modern system of criminal justice has been evolving since the rise of modernity in the 19th century. Modern thoughts and ideas of reforming criminal justice began around the same time that modernization began in all spheres of life—economy, work, politics, power, family, faith, culture, and ideology—in the 19th century. Understanding the profile of this modern criminal justice system and its expansion among the world's societies is the core of comparative criminal justice. The nature of crime and criminality or the number of police officers, courts, and prisons in a country do not precisely define the profile of its criminal justice. The rate of crime and incarceration is much lower in many traditional and archaic systems of criminal justice because they are based on medieval systems of punishment, torture, and a culture of fear. A country's profile of criminal justice consists of the core characteristics of its institutions with respect to how crimes are defined and how law and justice are perceived and pursued.

In premodern societies, criminal justice was primarily an institution of punishment and repression based on the institutions of the Inquisition and trial by ordeal. Punishments such as public execution, burning, decapitation, mutilation of breasts and genitals, amputations, flogging, banishment, branding, and public humiliation were common throughout the Middle Ages. In medieval criminal justice, particularly under canonical law, crimes were defined and punishments were devised in terms of the dictates of the scriptures. Crime was seen as an evil and explained in terms of possession by demons. Demonology was the dominant perspective in crime and justice throughout the Middle Ages.

The advent of modernity, based on the rise of the Renaissance in the 15th century, the rise of the Reformation in the 16th century, the rise of modern science in the 17th century, and the Age of Enlightenment in the 18th century, brought a fundamentally new perspective in the understanding of crime and criminality and law and justice in the modern world. This new perspective was crystallized, particularly around the ideas contained in Montesquieu's *The Spirit of Laws,* Beccaria's *On Crimes and Punishments,* and Bentham's *An Introduction to the Principles of Morals and Legislation.* During the last 200 years, a new profile of criminal justice, based on these ideas, has been evolving and expanding in the West, and through modernization, expanding among the world's societies. Understanding this profile of modern criminal justice is therefore vitally important in comparative criminal justice.

Some of the core tenets that make up the profile of modern criminal justice include democracy and the rule of law, secularization in law and justice, the dominance of the due process of law, and a separate system of juvenile justice. The first and foremost characteristic of modern criminal justice is that it has grown with the modern state based on liberal democracy and the rule of law. The nature of the state defines and forms the nature of its system of criminal justice. A democratic polity is based on the principles of the rule of law, constitutionalism, limited government, the supremacy of the parliament, separation of powers, checks and balances, and judicial autonomy and accountability. A democratic polity upholds fundamental human rights, including equal treatment under the law, equal access to justice, and the rights to life, liberty, and property. These institutional features of a democratic polity form the architecture of modern criminal justice. A polity based on monarchy or authoritarianism is unlikely to grow a modern system of criminal justice. It may have the lowest rate of crime or the lowest rate of incarceration, but not a modern system of criminal justice.

Second, the growth of modern criminal justice is also predicated on the notion of the separation between politics and religion—separation between church and state. In medieval criminal justice, where the church and state were indistinguishable, crimes were defined and punishments were devised in terms of divine and canonical laws based on scriptures. In modern criminal justice, crimes are defined by secular laws and statutes. The rationality for criminalization in medieval criminal justice was that certain acts and behaviors are intrinsically evil, immoral, and sinful. The rationality for criminalization or decriminalization in modern criminal justice is based on such philosophical notions as security, liberty, freedom, rights, justice, equality, fairness, privacy, harm, responsibility, and obligations.

Third, modern criminal justice is characterized by the dominance of the due process of law. Procedural due process of law constitutionally protects the rights of the writ of *habeas corpus*, protection against unreasonable search and seizure, protection against self-incrimination, and protection against cruel and unusual punishment, as well as the right to counsel and to a fair trial. The substantive due process of law in modern criminal justice makes it certain that no criminal laws are made in violation of the rights to life, liberty, and property. The Fourth, Fifth, Sixth, Eighth, and the Fourteenth Amendments of the U.S. Constitution protect the rights of the due process of law within the American criminal justice system. During the past 200 years, the U.S. Supreme Court made a number of landmark decisions about how the due process of law must be applied within the American criminal justice system.

The fourth characteristic of modern criminal justice is its innovation of a separate system of juvenile justice. The need for a separate system of juvenile justice is grounded in the scientific notion of childhood as a distinctive phase in human life—a phase where the reasoning and rationalities and the minds and moralities of juveniles are markedly different from those of adults. The advent of modernity also brought the notion of protecting children's rights. The Universal Declaration of Human Rights in 1948, the United Nations Declaration of the Rights of the Child in 1959, and the United Nations Convention on the Rights of the Child in 1989 further strengthened the movement for the protection of the rights of children within the structure of the modern liberal democratic state. The growth of juvenile justice as a separate system is also rooted in the doctrine of *parens patriae*, which came from the English common law. In a number of landmark decisions, the U.S. Supreme Court argued that the due process of law is equally applied to juveniles. Within the U.S. Constitution, the Bill of Rights is not for adults alone. These four tenets—democracy and the rule of law, secularization in law and justice, the dominance of the due process of law, and a separate system of juvenile justice—define the profile of an ideal system of modern criminal justice, and they can be used as benchmarks in comparisons of criminal justice among the world's societies.

■ Discussion Questions

1. What were some of the major characteristics of criminal justice in medieval Europe? Describe in this context the role and the reasons for the dominance of the perspective demonology, canonical laws, and the method of the Inquisition in medieval criminal justice.

2. What are some of the major intellectual movements that contributed to the rise of modernity in the 19th century? How did they bring a new perspective on the organization of law and justice? Discuss the intellectual contributions of Montesquieu, Beccaria, and Bentham to the development of modern criminal justice.

3. Why is a modern state, based on the rule of law and democracy, a precondition for the growth of modern criminal justice? What are the characteristics of a modern state that form and shape the nature of modern criminal justice? Discuss in this context how the principles of the separation of powers, checks and balances, and church and state separation affect the organization of criminal justice in the Unites States. (Hint: Explain the Military Commissions Act of 2006 and the debate over the privilege of the writ of *habeas corpus* of the Guantanamo Bay detainees.)

4. Define and describe the nature and role of the due process of law in modern criminal justice. How is the procedural due process of law different from the substantive due process of law? Describe the role of the Fourth, Fifth, Sixth, Eighth, and Fourteenth Amendments of the Bill of Rights in the U.S. Constitution in shaping the nature of criminal justice in the United States. (Hint: Cite some decisions of the Supreme Court related to procedural due process in American criminal justice.)

5. Cite and explain some of the landmark decisions of the U.S. Supreme Court in the area of criminalization and decriminalization by applying the principles of the substantive due process of law. What implications do those decisions have with respect to the rights of liberty within the modern system of criminal justice? (Hint: *Griswold v. Connecticut,* 1965; *Loving v. Virginia,* 1967; *Roe v. Wade,* 1973; *Eisenstadt v. Baird,* 1972; *Atkins v. Virginia,* 2002; *Lawrence v. Texas,* 2003; and *Roper v. Simmons,* 2005.)

6. What are the major historical forces that contributed to the rise of a separate system of juvenile justice as an integral part of modern criminal justice? Why is the rise of juvenile justice as a separate system an important development in modern criminal justice? Explain in this context some of the landmark decisions of the U.S. Supreme Court related to the rights of juveniles. (Hint: *Kent v. United States,* 1966; *In re Gault,* 1967; *In re Winship,* 1970; *Breed v. Jones,* 1975; and *Roper v. Simmons,* 2005.)

7. Why is an understanding of the profile of modern criminal justice critical in comparative criminal justice? What are the core characteristics or benchmarks that define the nature of modern criminal justice, and what significance do they have in the study of comparative criminal justice among the world's societies? Develop a research agenda, on the basis of the benchmarks discussed previously, for a comparative study of criminal justice between the United States and Japan.

■ References

Agrast, M. D., Botero, J. C., & Ponce, A., for the World Justice Project. (2010). *Rule of law index.* Washington, DC: WJP.

Argersinger v. Hamlin, 407 U.S. 25 (1972).

Atkins v. Virginia, 536 U.S. 304 (2002).

Bartlett, R. (1988). *Trial by fire and water: The medieval judicial ordeal.* New York, NY: Oxford University Press.

Beal, J. P., Coriden, J. A., & Green, T. J. (Eds.). (2000). *New commentary on the code of canon law.* Mahwah, NJ: Paulist Press.

Beccaria, C. (2009). *On crimes and punishments* (E. D. Ingraham, Trans., 2nd American ed.). Philadelphia, PA: Seven Treasures Publication. (Originally published in 1764.)

Bellamy, R. (Ed.). (1995). *Beccaria: On crimes and punishments* (R. Davies, Trans). Cambridge, England: University of Cambridge Press.

Bentham, J. (1988). *An introduction to the principles of morals and legislation* (J. H. Burns & H. L. A. Hart, Eds.). Oxford, England: Clarendon Press. (Original work published 1789.)

Berghuis v. Thompkins, 560 U.S. (2010).

Bonney, R. (2002). *Thirty Years War 1618–1648.* London, England: Osprey Publishing Limited.

Boumediene v. Bush, 553 U.S. 723 (2008).

Breed v. Jones, 421 U.S. 519 (1975).

Brown v. Board of Education of Topeka, 347 U.S. 483 (1954).

Bullough, V. L., & Brundage, J. (Eds.). (1996). *Handbook of medieval sexuality.* London, England: Routledge.

Burlington Industries, Inc. v. Ellerth, 524 U.S. 742 (1998).

Burns, J. H., & Hart, H. L. A. (1996). *The collected works of Jeremy Bentham.* Oxford, England: Oxford University Press.

Carothers, T. (2006). *Promoting the rule of law abroad: In search of knowledge.* Washington, DC: Carnegie Endowment for International Peace.

Cass, R. A. (2001). *The rule of law in America.* Baltimore, MD: Johns Hopkins Press.

Center on the Developing Child. (2007). *Excessive stress disrupts the architecture of the developing brain* (working paper 3). Cambridge, MA: Harvard University Center on the Developing Child.

Cohen, A. D. (2010). How the establishment clause can influence substantive due process: Adultery bans after Lawrence. *Florida Law Review, 79,* 607–647.

Cohler, A. M., Miller, B. C., & Stone, H. S. (Eds.). (1989). *The spirit of the laws.* Cambridge, England: Cambridge University Press.

Coleman v. Alabama, 377 U.S. 129 (1964).

Coffin v. United States, 156 U.S. 432 (1895).

Cruzan v. Director, Missouri Department of Health, 497 U.S. 261 (1990).

Dean, T. (2007). *Crime and justice in late medieval Italy.* Cambridge, England: Cambridge University Press.

Devereaux, S. (2005). The abolition of the burning of women in England reconsidered. *Crime, History, and Societies, 9*(2), 73–98.

Douglas v. California, 372 U.S. 353 (1963).

Duff, A. (2008). Theories of criminal law. *Stanford encyclopedia of philosophy.* Retrieved from http://plato.stanford.edu/entries/criminal-law/.

Edwards, P. (2001). *The making of the modern English state.* London, England: Palgrave.

Eisenstadt v. Baird, 405 U.S. 438 (1972).

Electronic Frontier Foundation. (2011). Surveillance self-defense: Reasonable expectation of privacy. Retrieved from https://ssd.eff.org/your-computer/govt/privacy

Emsley, C., & Knafla, L. A. (Eds.). (1996). *Crime history and histories of crime: Studies in the historiography of crime and criminal justice in modern history.* Westport, CT: Greenwood Press.

Faragher v. City of Boca Raton, 524 U.S. 775 (1998).

Gardner, T. J., & Anderson, T. M. (2009). *Criminal law.* Belmont, CA: Thomson Publishing Company.

Garland, D. S., & McGehee, L. P. (Eds.). (1898). *The American and English encyclopedia of law.* Long Island, New York: Edward Thompson Company.

Gedicks, F. M. (2009). An originalist defense of substantive due process: Magna Carta, higher-law constitutionalism, and the Fifth Amendment. *Emory Law Journal, 58,* 585–670.

Geltner, G. (2008). *The medieval prison: A social history.* Princeton, NJ: Princeton University Press.

Gerth, H. H., & Mills, C. W. (1958). *From Max Weber: Essays in sociology.* New York, NY: Oxford University Press.

Gideon v. Wainwright, 372 U.S. 335 (1963).

Glass v. The Betsey, 3 U.S. 6 (1794).

Greenwald, G. (2008). *Supreme Court restores habeas corpus, strikes down key part of Military Commissions Act.* Retrieved from www.salon.com/2008/06/12/boumediene/

Gregg v. Georgia, 433 U.S. 584 (1978).

Griswold v. Connecticut, 381 U.S. 479 (1965).

Halliday, P. D., & White, G. E. (2008). The suspension clause: English text, imperial contexts, and American implications. *Virginia Law Review, 94,* 575–714.

Hamilton v. Alabama, 368 U.S. 52 (1961).

Harrendorf, S., Heiskanen, M., & Malby, S. (2010). *International statistics on crime and justice.* Geneva, Switzerland: UNODC and Helsinki, Finland: HEUNI.

Harris v. Nelson, 394 U.S. 286 (1969).

Hartney, C., for the National Council on Crime and Delinquency. (2006). *U.S. rates of incarceration: A global perspective.* Retrieved from www.caught.net/incarcerationRate.PDF.

Hill v. McDonough, 547 U.S. 573 (2006).

Hope v. Pelzer, 536 U.S. 730 (2002).

Horne, C. F. (2007). *The Code of Hammurabi* (trans. by L. W. King). Retrieved from http://www.forgottenbooks.org/info/The_Code_of_Hammurabi_1000914285.php. (Original work published 1915.)

Hudson v. McMillian, 503 U.S. 1 (1992).

Hull, I. V. (1996). *Sexuality, state, and civil society in Germany, 1700–1815.* Ithaca, NY: Cornell University Press.

Hunter, W. A. (1886). *A systematic and historical exposition of Roman law in the order of a code* (2nd ed.). London, England: Sweet & Maxwell Ltd (Google e-Book).

Hutto v. Davis, 454 U.S. 370 (1982).

In re Gault, 387 U.S. 1 (1967).

In re Winship, 397 U.S. 358 (1970).

Janin, H. (2009). *Medieval justice: Cases and laws in France, England and Germany, 500–1500.* Jefferson, NC: McFarland.

Jefferson, T. (1782). Notes on the state of Virginia. Retrieved from http://etext.virginia.edu/toc/modeng/public/JefVirg.html.

Jellinek. G. (2009). *The Declaration of the Rights of Man and of Citizens: A contribution to modern constitutional history* (trans. by M. Farrand). Franklin Park, IL: World Library Classics.

Katz v. United States, 389 U.S. 347 (1967).

Kent v. United States, 383 U.S. 541 (1966).

Klopfer v. North Carolina, 386 U.S. 213 (1967).

Kors, A. C., & Peters, E. (Eds.). (2000). *Witchcraft in Europe, 400–1700: A documentary history.* Philadelphia, PA: University of Pennsylvania Press.

Langbein, J. H. (1994). The historical origins of the privilege against self-incrimination at common law. *Michigan Law Review, 92,* 1047–1085.

Latimer, C. P. (2011). *Civil liberties and the state: A documentary and reference guide.* Santa Barbara, CA: ABC-CLIO.

Lawrence v. Texas, 539 U.S. 558 (2003).

Legal Information Institute. (2012a). *The Constitution of the United States of America: Amendment IV.* Ithaca, NY: Cornell University Law School.

Legal Information Institute. (2012b). *The Constitution of the United States of America: Amendment VIII.* Ithaca, NY: Cornell University Law School.

Legal Information Institute. (2012c). *The Constitution of the United States of America: Amendment I.* Ithaca, NY: Cornell University Law School.

Legal Information Institute. (2012d). *The Constitution of the United States of America: Free exercise clause.* Ithaca, NY: Cornell University Law School.

Legal Information Institute. (2012e). *The Constitution of the United States of America: Section 9 of Article 1.* Ithaca, NY: Cornell University Law School.

Legal Information Institute. (2012f). *The Constitution of the United States of America: Amendment V.* Ithaca, NY: Cornell University Law School.

Legal Information Institute. (2012g). *The Constitution of the United States of America: Amendment VI.* Ithaca, NY: Cornell University Law School.

Legal Information Institute. (2012h). *The Constitution of the United States of America: Section II of Article III.* Ithaca, NY: Cornell University Law School.

Legal Information Institute. (2012i). *The Constitution of the United States of America: Amendment IX.* Ithaca, NY: Cornell University Law School.

Legal Information Institute. (2012j). *The Speedy Trial Act of 1974.* Ithaca, NY: Cornell University Law School.

Levy, L. W. (2000). *Bill of Rights (English) (December 16, 1689).* London, England: Macmillan.

Levy, L. W. (2001). *Origins of the Bill of Rights.* New Haven, CT: Yale University Press.

Library of Congress. (2011). *Primary documents in American history: The Judiciary Act of 1789.* Washington, DC: Author.

Linebaugh, P. (2008). *The Magna Carta manifesto: Liberties and commons for all*. Berkeley: University of California Press.

Locke, J. (1689). *A letter concerning toleration* (trans. by W. Popple). Retrieved from www.constitution.org/jl/tolerati.htm.

Locke, J. (1690). *The second treatise of civil government*. Retrieved from www.constitution.org/jl/2ndtreat.htm.

Loving v. Virginia, 388 U.S. 1 (1967).

Lyke, S. B. (2009). Lawrence as an Eighth Amendment case: Sodomy and the evolving standards of decency. *William and Mary Journal of Women and the Law, 1*(3), 633–661.

Lynos, G. M., & Mastanduno, M. (1995). *Beyond Westphalia? State sovereignty and international intervention*. Baltimore, MD: Johns Hopkins University Press.

Maine, H. S. (1861). *Ancient law*. Boston, MA: Beacan Press.

Mapp v. Ohio, 367 U.S. 643 (1961).

Massachusetts Judicial Branch. (2010). *John Adams and the Massachusetts constitution*. Retrieved from www.mass.gov/courts/sjc/john-adams-b.html.

Matthew Shepard and James Byrd, Jr., Hate Crimes Prevention Act. (2012). In *Encyclopædia Britannica*. Retrieved from www.britannica.com/EBchecked/topic/1589109/Matthew-Shepard-and-James-Byrd-Jr-Hate-Crimes-Prevention-Act.

Mempa v. Rhay, 389 U.S. 128 (1967).

Miranda v. Arizona, 384 U.S. 436 (1966).

Montesquieu, C. (1989). *The spirit of laws* (edited by A. M. Cohler, B. C. Miller, and H. S. Stone). Cambridge, England: Cambridge University Press. (Originally published in 1784.)

Moore v. City of East Cleveland, 431 U.S. 494 (1977).

Moustafa, T., & Ginsburg, T. (2008). Introduction: The function of courts in authoritarian politics. In T. Ginsburg & T. Moustafa (Eds.) *Rule by law: The politics of courts in authoritarian regimes* (pp. 1–22). Cambridge, England: Cambridge University Press.

Musson, A., & Powel, E. (2009). *Crime, law, and society in the later Middle Ages*. Manchester, England: Manchester University Press.

Nelson, B. R. (2006). *The making of the modern state: A theoretical evolution*. New York, NY: Palgrave Macmillan.

New Jersey v. T.L.O., 469 U.S. 325 (1985).

Olmstead v. United States, 277 U.S. 438 (1928).

Oncale v. Sundowner Offshore Services, 523 U.S. 75 (1998).

Örsy, L. M. (2000). Theology and canon law. In J. P. Beal, J. A. Coriden, & T. J. Green. (Eds), *New commentary on the code of canon law* (pp. 1–10). Mahwah, NJ: Paulist Press.

Owen, R. (2004). *State, power, and politics in the making of the modern Middle East*. London, England and New York, NY: Routledge.

Packer, H. L. (1968). *The limits of the criminal sanction*. New York, NY: Oxford University Press.

Perez, J. (2006). *The Spanish Inquisition*. New Haven, CT: Yale University Press.

Pavlac, B. (2009). *Witch hunts in the Western world: Persecution and punishment from the Inquisition through the Salem trials*. Santa Barbara, CA: Greenwood Press.

Peters, E. M. (1995). Prison before the prison: The ancient and medieval worlds. In N. Morris & D. J. Rothman (Eds.), *The Oxford history of the prison: The practice of punishment in Western society* (pp. 3–47). New York, NY: Oxford University Press.

Plessy v. Ferguson, 163 U.S. 537 (1896).

Quintard-Morenas, F. (2010). The presumption of innocence in the French and Anglo-American legal traditions. *The American Journal of Comparative Law, 58,* 107–150.

Rahe, P. A. (2009). *Montesquieu and the logic of liberty.* New Haven, CT: Yale University Press.

Rasul v. Bush, 542 U.S. 466 (2004).

Reynolds v. United States, 98 U.S. 145 (1879).

Roe v. Wade, 410, U.S. 113 (1973).

Roper v. Simmons, 543 U.S. 551 (2005).

Roth, R. (2001). Homicide in early modern England 1549–1800: The need for a quantitative synthesis. *Crime, History, and Societies,* 5(2), 1–34.

Rummel v. Estelle, 445 U.S. 263 (1980).

Samuel, G. (2003). *Epistemology and method in law.* Burlington, VT: Ashgate Publishing Company.

Schlager, M. D. (2002). Inquisitorial justice. In D. Levinson & Human Relations Area Files (Eds.), *Encyclopedia of crime and punishment* (pp. 901–905). Thousand Oaks, CA: Sage Publications.

Scott, S. P. (2001). *The Civil Law: Including the Twelve Tables, the institutes of Gaius, the rules of Ulpian, the opinions of Paulus, the enactments of Justinian, and the constitutions.* Clark, NJ: The Law Book Exchange Ltd.

Shahidullah, S. M. (2008). *Crime policy in America: Laws, institutions, and programs.* Lanham, MD: The University Press of America.

Shils, E., & Finch, H. A. (Eds). (2011). *Methodology of social sciences: Max Weber.* New Brunswick, NJ: Transaction Publishers.

Spierenburg, P. (1995). Body and the state: Early modern Europe. In N. Morris & D. J. Rothman (Eds.), *Oxford history of the prison: The practice of punishment in Western society* (pp. 49–82). New York, NY: Oxford University Press.

Thome, H. (2001). Explaining long term trends in violent crime. *Crime, History, and Societies,* 5(2), 1–19.

Thorndike, L. (1917). *The history of medieval Europe.* Boston, MA: Houghton Mifflin and Company and Cambridge University Press.

United Nations Organization. (1948). *The universal declaration of human rights.* New York, NY: The United Nations.

United Nations Organization. (1959). *Declaration of the rights of the child.* New York, NY: The United Nations.

United Nations Organization. (1989). *Convention on the rights of the child.* New York, NY: The United Nations.

United States Constitution Online. (2012). *Jefferson's wall of separation letter.* Retrieved from www.usconstitution.net/jeffwall.html.

Viator, G. (2009). The validity of criminal adultery prohibitions after *Lawrence v. Texas. Suffolk University Law Review, 35,* 837–861.

Weeks v. United States, 245 U.S. 618 (1918).

West's Encyclopedia of American Law. (2011). Substantive due process. Retrieved from www.answers.com/topic/substantive-due-process.

Yarborough v. Alvarado, 541 U.S. 652 (2004).

Young, D. (1986). *Beccaria: On crimes and punishments.* Indianapolis, IN: Hackett Publishing Company.

Competing Models of Criminal Justice: Profiles of Criminal Justice Among the World's Societies

Modern Systems of Criminal Justice in the West: North America and the Countries of the European Union

■ Introduction

The description of the profile of modern criminal justice is based on a fourfold typology for cross-national comparison of criminal justice: a modern system, a modernizing system, a traditional system, and a dual system. Modern systems of criminal justice are those that have grown in the democratic states of the West based on the rule of law, separation of power, church–state separation, and constitutionally protected due process of law. Modern systems of criminal justice have been relatively firmly established in the democracies of North America, Western Europe, Northern Europe, Australia, and Oceania. One of the major characteristics of modern criminal justice systems in these regions is that they are becoming increasingly homogeneous in terms of defining crime and criminality; developing laws for criminalization and decriminalization; protecting the constitutional right to due process of law; creating equal justice and fair trials for all; devising separate systems of justice for adults and juveniles; and pursuing science, technology, and professionalism for crime control and criminal justice. The countries of the aforementioned regions have varied systems of legal traditions (e.g., English common law and civil law traditions); different forms of constitutions (written in the United States and unwritten in the United Kingdom); different types of government (presidential versus parliamentary forms); different types of courts and judicial systems (adversarial versus inquisitorial systems); and different ways of organizing policing and law enforcement (e.g., FBI of the United States versus the Royal Canadian Mounted Police of Canada versus Scotland Yard of the United Kingdom). They are, however, largely similar in terms of the basic foundations of modern criminal justice—the centrality of the rule of law, the dominance of the due process of law, the dominance of secularity in law and justice, and the constitutional guarantee of the right to life, liberty, and property.

The modernizing systems of criminal justice are those that are pursuing the path of modernity in criminal justice, but have not yet reached a threshold of certainty and stability. The modernizing systems are found in a vast number of countries in Asia, Africa, Latin America, and Eastern Europe. One of the defining characteristics of the countries with modernizing systems is that they do not have any strong indigenous legal traditions or religious traditions of law and justice that are sharply in conflict with the fundamental values and institutions of modern criminal justice. Most of the modernizing systems are in those countries that were under Western colonial rule for centuries and where some of the basic modern structural imperatives of modern criminal justice were implemented by colonial governments, such as a secular legal traditions (English common law or civil law tradition), structure of policing and law enforcement, structure of the judiciary, prisons, and legal education. In the countries with modernizing systems, the strategic societal elites and political leadership are open to the West, and seek to pursue modern reforms in criminal justice. But the progress of modernization is hindered because of the lack of democracy and the rule of law within the broader polity and the political culture of those countries. In many modernizing systems, there are constitutionally protected rights to the due process of law. Nevertheless, police repression and brutality, torture for confessions, extrajudicial killings, politicization of the judiciary, and the practice of unequal justice and judicial corruption are widespread. In modernizing systems, the problem of modernity in criminal justice is not primarily cultural or religious in nature. It is essentially a problem of the rule of law and the lack of a democratic polity.

The traditional systems of criminal justice are found in those societies that are deliberately opposed to modern criminal justice. The traditional systems are dominant mostly in the Islamic monarchies and theocracies of the Middle East that are opposed to values of democracy, secularization, separation of power, and due process of law. In traditional systems, criminal law is predominantly based on religious texts and scriptures. The process of criminalization and decriminalization is defined by the boundaries of religious law and morality. The court structure is dominated by religious judges, and law enforcement is controlled by religious police. The International Bill of Human Rights, which consists of the Universal Declaration of Human Rights, the International Covenant on Civil and Political Rights, and the International Covenant on Economic, Social and Cultural Rights, has no significant effect on traditional systems of criminal justice. The monarchical and theocratic political leadership of these countries deliberately keeps their systems of criminal justice outside the boundaries of international standards and protocols on human rights, due process of law, and rights of protection against torture and cruel and unusual punishment. In traditional systems, the crime rate is generally low because of a culture of fear about police torture and unusual punishment such as beheading, public execution, and flogging. In traditional systems of criminal justice, modern information and surveillance technologies are widely used in law enforcement, but there is not much recognition of the need for scientific analysis of crime and criminality. The dominant perspective of understanding crime in traditional systems is still the medieval perspective of demonology and the inviolable connection between crime and sin. Saudi Arabia and Iran are two of the classic examples of countries that have deliberately protected their systems of traditional criminal justice.

The dual systems of criminal justice are found in those countries where there are deliberate political and governmental efforts to combine modern institutions of criminal justice with those of religious or indigenous traditions of law and justice. Some of the countries that have dualistic systems of criminal justice include Pakistan (modern law and Islamic Shari'a law), Malaysia (modern law and Islamic Shari'a law), Indonesia (modern law and Islamic Shari'a law), Nigeria (modern law and Islamic Shari'a law), China (modern law, socialist law, and Confucianist social and political traditions), and Russia (socialist law and modern law). Some of the countries with dualistic systems began with the institutions of modernity in criminal justice in the middle of the 20th century (e.g., Pakistan and Malaysia), but they later implanted Islamic Shari'a law within their institutions of modernity. Some of the other countries, such as China and Russia, began in the early 20th century with the socialist legal tradition for organizing their systems of criminal justice. However, after the fall of communism and the collapse of the Union of Soviet Socialist Republics (USSR) in the mid-1980s, China and Russia began to take deliberate steps to implant the institutions of a modern legal tradition. A number of international assistance organizations have been working in those countries since the early 1990s to initiate modern reforms in criminal justice. The criminal justice systems of these countries are still dualist because their larger political systems and political cultures are still far from modern democracies. A system of criminal justice in a country is not dualistic simply because it wants to revitalize and preserve its systems of informal control, as does Japan. Most dualistic systems of criminal justice are characterized by political conflicts and tensions with respect to adherence to the due process of law and democratic polity and

TABLE 5-1 Competing Systems of Criminal Justice in the World's Societies: A Typology for Comparative Analysis

Criminal Justice Institutions	Modern Systems	Modernizing Systems	Traditional Systems	Dualistic Systems
Basic philosophy	Due process of law Rule of law Democracy	Due process of law Authoritarian political systems	Monarchical systems Theocratic systems No due process of law	Due process of law but within authoritarian or theocratic political systems
Law and legal traditions	Secular law Common law Civil law	Secular law Common law Civil law	Religious law No church and state separation	Secular law with religious law/traditional law
Policing	Professional police Police accountability Law enforcement technology Police ethics	Professional police Lack of police accountability Lack of police ethics Police brutality Police torture	Religious police Lack of police accountability Police brutality Police torture Control through a culture of fear	Professional police Religious police Lack of police accountability Police brutality Police torture
Judiciary	Modern jurisprudence Hierarchical court systems Judicial autonomy Judicial accountability Modern legal education	Modern jurisprudence Hierarchical court systems Lack of judicial autonomy Lack of judicial accountability Judicial corruption	Traditional jurisprudence based on scriptures Religious courts Religious judges Limited scope for judicial appeals Closed to modern legal education	Modern judiciary with religious judiciary Modern legal education with religious legal education Lack of judicial autonomy
Punishment and corrections	No cruel and unusual punishment Rehabilitation Prison-based treatment Prison reentry	Limited cruel and unusual punishment Incapacitation through incarceration	Cruel and unusual punishment Public execution Decapitation Flogging	Limited cruel and unusual punishment Modern prison systems
Examples of the countries and regions	United States, Canada, United Kingdom, European Union countries, Australia, and Japan	Countries of South Asia, Africa, and Latin America	Saudi Arabia and Iran	China, Russia, Pakistan, Malaysia, and Nigeria

governance. **Table 5-1** outlines these four criminal justice systems. This chapter examines some of the core homogenizing trends and characteristics of modern criminal justice in the United States, Canada, the United Kingdom, Germany, the countries of the European Union, and Australia.

■ Modern Criminal Justice and the Due Process of Law in Canada

Two of the world's most stable and developed democracies and most modern systems of criminal justice are in North America—the United States and Canada—but they are very different in terms of many of their social and political profiles. The United States is a country of about 313 million people (2012 estimate) of diverse races, nationalities, cultures, languages, and religions. In the United States, Hispanics, comprising about 15% of the population, and Blacks, comprising about 13% of the population, form the largest minority groups. Canada is a country of about 34 million people (2010 estimate). Two of the largest groups of minorities in Canada are South Asians (immigrants from India, Pakistan, Bangladesh, Sri Lanka, and Nepal), comprising about 5% of the population (2006 estimate), and Chinese (comprising about 3.7% of the population). In Canada, Blacks comprise about 2.5%, and Hispanics comprise only about 1% of the population. In 2009, about 10.9% of the people in Canada lived below the poverty line. In the United States, in 2009, about 13% of the population (about 44 million people) lived below the poverty line. Among some segments of Blacks and Hispanics, the percentage of people living in poverty in the United States is much higher (about 20–25%) than in Canada. Because of differences in demographic profiles and levels of poverty, the challenges of crime and criminality are very different in the United States and Canada.

   The United States and Canada also differ in terms of their political structures and the organization of their criminal justice systems. The United States has a presidential system of government; Canada has a parliamentary form of government. The political system of the United States is comprised of one federal government and 50 different states. In Canada, there is one federal government and 10 provinces. In the United States, there are federal courts and state courts. In Canada, there are federal courts and provincial courts. But in Canada, unlike in the United States, the federal government appoints the judges of the provincial courts. The constitution of the United States is more than 200 years old. The constitution of Canada was first enacted through the Constitution Act of 1867, after which Canada formally became independent from the United Kingdom. In 1982, the Constitution Act of Canada was amended and a new constitution called the *Canadian Charter of Rights and Freedoms* was created. Canada has been a democracy based on the rule of law since the enactment of the Constitution Act of 1867, but its democracy follows the British parliamentary model. The constitution is largely unwritten, and the parliament serves as the watchdog to oversee the working of the basic principles of the rule of law. The *Canadian Charter of Rights and Freedoms* brought the Canadian constitution close to that of the United States, particularly by giving the new power of judicial review to the Supreme Court of Canada.

TABLE 5-2 Modern Criminal Justice in Canada: The Canadian Bill of Rights

Life, liberty, and security of person	Everyone has the right to life, liberty, and security of the person and the right not to be deprived thereof except in accordance with the principles of fundamental justice.
Search or seizure	Everyone has the right to be secure against unreasonable search or seizure.
Detention or imprisonment	Everyone has the right not to be arbitrarily detained or imprisoned.
Arrest or detention	Everyone has the right on arrest or detention (1) to be informed promptly of the reasons therefore; (2) to retain and instruct counsel without delay and to be informed of that right; and (3) to have the validity of the detention determined by way of *habeas corpus* and to be released if the detention is not lawful.
Proceedings in criminal and penal matters	Any person charged with an offense has the right (1) to be informed without unreasonable delay of the specific offense; (2) to be tried within a reasonable time; (3) not to be compelled to be a witness in proceedings against that person in respect of the offense; (4) to be presumed innocent until proven guilty according to law in a fair and public hearing by an independent and impartial tribunal; (5) not to be denied reasonable bail without just cause; and (6) not to be denied a jury trial except for an offense under a military law and a trial before a military tribunal.
Treatment or punishment	Everyone has the right not to be subjected to any cruel and unusual treatment or punishment.
Self-incrimination	A witness who testifies in any proceedings has the right not to have any incriminating evidence so given used to incriminate that witness in any other proceedings, except in a prosecution for perjury or for the giving of contradictory evidence.

Source: Data from *The Canadian Charter of Rights and Freedoms.*

It is this *Canadian Charter of Rights and Freedoms* that outlines the profile of modern criminal justice in Canada and contains the Canadian Bill of Rights.

The *Canadian Charter of Rights and Freedoms* identifies six kinds of rights and freedoms for the Canadian: (1) fundamental rights; (2) democratic rights; (3) mobility rights; (4) legal rights; (5) equal rights; and (6) minority language educational rights. The fundamental rights and the legal rights are particularly related to criminal justice in Canada (see **Table 5-2**). Like the First Amendment of the U.S. Constitution, Articles I and II of the *Canadian Charter of Rights and Freedoms* outline the fundamental rights of freedom of conscience and religion; freedom of thought, belief, opinion, and expression, including freedom of the press and other media of communication; freedom of peaceful assembly; and freedom of association. Under legal rights, the *Charter* lists the right to life, liberty, and security; right of protection against unreasonable search and seizure; right of *habeas corpus;* right to counsel; right of protection against self-incrimination; and right of protection against cruel and unusual punishment—the rights that are protected in the U.S. Constitution by the Fourth, Fifth, Sixth, Eighth, and Fourteenth Amendments.

In a number of recent landmark decisions, the Supreme Court of Canada, like the Supreme Court of the United States, has firmly established that it works as a major watchdog for the application and protection of the due process of law in criminal justice. The strong position of the Canadian Supreme Court on preserving the due process of law in Canadian criminal justice has been expressed through decisions in a number of cases related to combating global terrorism in Canada. The Honorable Beverley McLachlin (2009), chief justice of Canada, wrote that terrorism "confronts democratic societies with a formidable challenge" (p. 2). She, however, also asserted that "states combating and prosecuting terrorists must remain true to the fundamental principles upon which democratic governance and a free society are based, including the presumption of innocence and a fair trial" (2009, p. 2).

After the destruction of the World Trade Center in New York City in September 2001, Canada enacted two major antiterrorism legislations: the Immigration and Refugee Protection Act of 2001 and the Anti-Terrorism Act of 2001. The Immigration and Refugee Protection Act of 2001 provided for a national security certification (certificates of inadmissibility) like the provision outlined in the national security letter introduced in the United States under the 2001 USA Patriot Act. Under the national certification provision, noncitizens of Canada who were certified as possible threats to Canadian national security were subject to detention and deportation. Hundreds of individuals were arrested and detained, without any criminal charges, under the national security certification provision introduced by the Immigration and Refugee Protection Act of 2001.

The Canadian Supreme Court in 2007 in *Charkaoui v. Canada* held that the national certification scheme was in violation of the due process of law guaranteed by Sections 7, 9, and 10 of the constitution—the *Canadian Charter of Rights and Freedoms.* In response to the Supreme Court decision, the Parliament of Canada amended the law and "introduced special advocates empowered to provide an independent perspective on the evidence against the detained person" (McLachlin, 2009, p. 4). Similarly, the Anti-Terrorism Act of 2001 made a number of provisions, like those of the 2001 USA Patriot Act, and allowed more police powers for preventive arrests, electronic surveillance, and detention without charges for more than 3 days. Under the Anti-Terrorism Act, knowingly giving or collecting funds for terrorist organizations, helping terrorist activities within the Canadian jurisdiction, inciting or leading terrorist activities, and harboring a terrorist became federal crimes. The Canadian Supreme Court and a number of Canadian federal courts found that some of these provisions were violations of the due process of law protected under the *Canadian Charter of Rights and Freedoms.* The Anti-Terrorism Act of 2001 defines terrorism as an act committed "for a political, religious or ideological purpose, objective or cause" (Parliament of Canada, 2012, p. 1). This motive clause was legally controversial, and in 2006, "a Superior Court judge struck down the motive clause, saying it violates the *Charter of Rights and Freedoms.* The judge was working on the case of Mohammed Mormin Khawaja, the first person charged under the new anti-terror provisions" (CBC News, 2007, p. 1).

The Supreme Court of Canada has also made a number of landmark rulings protecting the substantive due process of law related to privacy and liberty interests. One of famous case is related to the decriminalization of abortion. Before 1988, abortion was defined as a crime in the Criminal Code of Canada. In 1988, the Canadian Supreme Court ruled in the case of *R. v. Morgentaler*, as the U.S. Supreme Court ruled in *Roe v. Wade* in 1973, that the federal abortion law was in violation of a woman's right to choose under Section 7 of the *Canadian Charter of Rights and Freedoms* (*R. v. Morgentaler*, 1988). Section 7 of the *Charter*, the Court argued, guarantees the right to liberty. The right to liberty "guaranteed by s. 7 of the Charter gives a woman the right to decide for herself whether or not to terminate her pregnancy, does s. 251 of the Criminal Code violate this right? Clearly it does" (*R. v. Morgentaler*, 1988).

A similar case, but with respect to the liberty interest of same-sex couples, was argued by the Court of Appeal for Ontario in 2003. In *Halpern v. Canada* (2003), the Court of Appeal for Ontario ruled that the criminalization of same-sex marriage is a violation of the *Canadian Charter of Rights and Freedoms*. The court concluded "that the common law definition of marriage as 'the voluntary union for life of one man and one woman to the exclusion of all others' violated s. 15(1) of the *Charter*" (2003, p. 28). The court further stated that the "common law definition of marriage violates the Couples' equality rights on the basis of sexual orientation under s. 15(1) of the *Charter*" and that such violation "cannot be justified in a free and democratic society under s. 1 of the *Charter*" (*Halpern v. Canada*, 2003).

■ Policing and Modern Criminal Justice: The United States, the United Kingdom, and Germany

With the progress of the modern state on the basis of the rule of law and democracy, the due process of law, the principle of separation of church and state, and the dominance of modern science and technology, criminal justice as a system has been vastly modernized. With that modernization, the institution of policing has also been vastly transformed. The nature of modern criminal justice is largely defined by the nature and the characteristics of its policing. Policing is an intra-systemic institution of criminal justice that stands at the front end of criminal justice. The police are the gatekeepers of law and order. They are responsible for criminal arrests, detention, interrogation, and investigation. But the police are also the connecting link between criminal justice and its external institutions of politics, governance, economy, family, religion, and ideology. The profile of democracy and the rule of law in a state is indeed the profile of its policing. The nature of the modernity of a state and the progress of modernization in a society largely depend on the nature of its policing. Policing is one of the most visible components of criminal justice. In a comparative study of expenditures on various criminal justice components among the countries reporting to the Ninth United Nations Survey on Crime Trends, Shaw, Van Dijk, and Rhomberg (2003) found that "over half of all expenditure (56%) was on the police, while the cost of the courts (29%), and prosecution services (15%) made up the remainder" (p. 59). The researchers have found that "developing countries (particularly those with an authoritarian past) spend comparatively much more on policing and much less on the courts and prosecution services" (Shaw et al.,

2003, p. 60). But in developed countries, the expenditure breakdown is relatively more balanced. These researchers also noted that "in North America, the overall expenditure breakdown between the police, court and prosecution services is more balanced, 57 percent being spent on the police, 32 percent on the courts and 11 percent on the prosecution services" (Shaw et al., 2003, p. 60).

During the last 200 years of the evolution of the modern state and modern criminal justice, evolution in policing has been a long process. Policing has not evolved in the same way in different modern states and modern systems of criminal justice. The structure and organization of policing in the United States are different from those of Canada and the United Kingdom, and those of Canada and the United Kingdom are vastly different from those of Japan and Germany. However, a homogenizing set of characteristics of contemporary policing among modern societies has been emerging because their criminal justice systems are facing similar changes and challenges. Policing in all modern societies is increasingly becoming professionalized, diversified, internationalized, computerized, and innovative. The old style of policing on the basis of common sense, force, torture, brutality, and deception is becoming increasingly obsolete in the wake of the rise of high-tech global information societies, the appearance of new global crimes, the dawn of new surveillance societies, and the growth of a heightened public sense about rights, ethics, and equalities. How modern policing is evolving among the world's societies in the context of the local institutional peculiarities and the realities of the global world is a problem of enormous significance in comparative criminal justice. To shed some light on the nature of the evolving institution of policing in modern systems of criminal justice, the following sections will examine the nature of high-tech policing in the United States and the European Union, the emerging reforms for decentralization and neighborhood policing in the United Kingdom, and the emerging form of centralized "super policing" in Germany.

High-Tech Policing in the United States

The United States of America has a uniquely decentralized, but highly connected system of policing. There are four types of policing in the United States: federal, state, city or local, and county. Federal policing is responsible primarily for the investigation of federal crimes and the enforcement of federal laws. In the United States, even though crime control and prevention is mostly a state responsibility, there has evolved a huge body of federal criminal laws as a result of increased federalization in crime and justice. Two of the major federal law enforcement agencies are the U.S. Department of Justice and the U.S. Department of Homeland Security. The Department of Justice includes a number of law enforcement agencies such as the Federal Bureau of Investigation (FBI), the Drug Enforcement Administration (DEA), the U.S. Marshals Service, the Federal Bureau of Prisons, and the Bureau of Alcohol, Tobacco, Firearms, and Explosives. The Department of Homeland Security includes mainly the Secret Service, Immigration and Customs Enforcement, Customs and Border Protection, the Transportation Security Administration, and the Coast Guard. The Department of Justice and the Department of Homeland Security employ about 84% of federal law enforcement personnel. Each and every department of the federal government, including the Departments of State and Defense, also has an agency of policing and law enforcement. A federal law enforcement officer is defined as an employee "whose primary duties are the investigation, apprehension, or detention of individuals suspected or convicted of offenses against the criminal laws of the United States" (United States Government Accountability Office, 2010, p. 51). One report from the U.S. Government Accountability Office (2010) shows that between 2000 and 2008, the number of federal law enforcement personnel "increased 55 percent, from approximately 82,000 in September 2000 to approximately 127,000 in September of 2008. In addition, approximately 51,000 persons were employed in law-enforcement-related occupations as of September 2008" (p. 7). The FBI is one of the fastest-growing federal law enforcement agencies. In 2010, it had more than 33,000 law enforcement personnel with a budget of $7.9 billion (Mueller, 2009).

In addition to an expanding force of federal law enforcement, there are 50 state agencies of policing commonly called *state troopers*. The state troopers are responsible primarily for statewide enforcement of law and the promotion of peace and order. State troopers work for various state law enforcement agencies. In North Carolina, for example, state troopers work for the State Highway Patrol, the State Capitol Police, the North Carolina Department of Crime and Public Safety, the North Carolina Department of Justice, the North Carolina State Bureau of Investigation, the North Carolina Department of Transportation, the North Carolina Governor's Crime Commission, the North Carolina Department of Corrections, and the North Carolina Department of Juvenile Justice and Delinquency Prevention. In Texas, state troopers work for the Texas Attorney General, the Texas Commission on Law Enforcement, and the Texas Department of Public Safety. One of the recent trends found in most states is to organize state policing under a separate department of public safety for more centralized control and direction. Examples of this structure include the Texas Department of Public Safety, the Connecticut Department of Public Safety, the Alabama Department of Public Safety, and the Massachusetts Department of Public Safety. In 2004, there were about 58,000 sworn state law enforcement officers in the United States.

Most law enforcement officers in the United States, however, are employed by local governments, including cities and sheriff's offices. There are about 30,000 incorporated cities in the United States, and there are 250 cities with more than 100,000 people. A report from the Bureau of Justice Statistics (2007) of the Department of Justice noted that in 2004 there were more than 13,000 local (city) police departments, and about 3,067 sheriff's offices in the United States. The local law enforcement agencies in 2004 employed about 1.1 million people on a full-time basis, "including 732,000 sworn personnel (defined in the census as those with general arrest powers). Local police departments were the largest employer of sworn officers, accounting for 61% of the total. Sheriff's offices were next, accounting for 24%" (Bureau of Justice Statistics, 2007, p. 1).

One of the most remarkable changes in criminal justice in America in recent years has been the emergence of high-tech policing (National Institute of Justice, 1998; Stone & Travis, 2011; Weisburd & Neyroud, 2011). The increasing integration of a new generation of genetic technology, biotechnology, nanotechnology, laser technology, satellite technology, sensor technology, and information technology by criminal justice has made some unprecedented changes in the nature of law enforcement and policing in America. The convergence of these various technologies, particularly the convergence of computer and information technology with other areas, has been quite significant for law enforcement and criminal justice. The role of high-tech policing is particularly evidenced in four areas: collection and sharing of crime data, crime mapping and crime analysis, use of criminal DNA, and crime control and surveillance through GPS (global positioning system) tracking.

Policing and Information Technology

The integration of computer and information technology in criminal justice has radically altered the way crime data and information are gathered, stored, organized, and shared by law enforcement personnel locally, nationally, and globally (National Institute of Justice, 2010). Every 3–4 years, the Bureau of Justice Statistics of the U.S. Department of Justice conducts its Law Enforcement Management and Administrative Statistics (LEMAS) survey. The 2007 LEMAS survey shows that local enforcement agencies across the United States use computers for a variety of law enforcement functions "including record management (79 percent), crime investigation (60 percent), information sharing (50 percent), and dispatch (49 percent)" (Roberts, 2011, p. 72). "Police patrol cars in the United States," as one of the studies from the International Association of the Chiefs of Police Technology Center observed, "are among the most technologically sophisticated and well-equipped vehicles on the road today" (Roberts, 2011, p. 73; see **Figure 5-1**). The study further explained, "Configured with laptop computers or mobile digital terminals . . . automated vehicle location, emergency lights, sirens, and much more, the cockpit of the typical police car might appear . . . as that of a jet airplane" (Roberts, 2011, p. 73).

Figure 5-1 Ford Motor Company's New Police Interceptor, Due to Replace the Crown Victoria Currently Used by Most North American Police Forces

Source: © Boykov/ShutterStock, Inc.

The use of mobile computer technology is particularly central to the present information revolution in law enforcement. The 2007 LEMAS survey shows that more than 90% of law enforcement agencies that serve populations of 25,000 or more use in-car mobile computer terminals and laptops. With these computers, police have instant access to statewide and nationwide central data banks such as the Automated Finger Identification System (AFIS), Integrated Biometric Identification System, and Interstate Identification Index. The 2007 LEMAS survey observed that with in-car mobile terminals, police had access "to an expanding array of information including vehicle records (88 percent); driving records (81 percent); warrants (81 percent); protection orders (66 percent); inter-agency information sharing (60 percent); calls-for-service history (60 percent); and criminal history records (50 percent)" (Roberts, 2011, p. 72). Another area of law enforcement that is rapidly changing through the use of mobile computer terminals is the reporting of field data. Through the in-car mobile computer terminals and laptops, police now can send voiceless dispatches and messages to other police cars or central locations, send traffic tickets directly to the court, write reports without returning to the police station, and respond to calls for service with much more efficiency. The 2007 LEMAS survey found that in doing so, "Police departments of all sizes were much more likely to use electronic methods to transmit criminal incident reports to headquarters, with 60 percent of all agencies in 2007, compared to just 38 percent in 2003" (Roberts, 2011, p. 7).

The increased use of information technology "is increasingly making the system of law enforcement more integrated, connected, and knowledgeable" (Shahidullah, 2008, p. 255). A nationally integrated criminal justice information system has currently emerged "through such programs as the National Law Enforcement Telecommunication System (NLETS), the FBI's National Crime Information Center (NCIC) Network, and the FBI's Criminal Justice Information Services Wide Area Network (CJIS WAN)" (Shahidullah, 2008, p. 255).

All 50 states have created "separate statutes for interstate sharing of criminal records and information, and many states have established separate Criminal Justice Information Centers or Integrated Criminal Justice Information Systems (ICJIS) within their criminal justice departments and agencies" (Shahidullah, 2008, p. 255). Some of these include the Alabama Criminal Justice Information Center, the Connecticut Justice Information System, the Iowa Criminal Justice Information System, the Colorado Integrated Criminal Justice Information System, the Illinois Integrated Justice Information System, the Justice Network of Pennsylvania, the Unified Criminal Justice Information System of Kentucky, the Integrated Criminal Justice Information System of Massachusetts, and the Integrated Criminal History System of Florida (Shahidullah, 2008). The use of mobile computer terminals for information retrieval and data reporting by law enforcement and the creation of different federal and state criminal justice information systems has brought a new era of high-tech policing in America in the 21st century.

Crime Mapping and Predictive Crime Analysis

The second most important dimension of high-tech policing in the United States is the increasing use of crime mapping and predictive crime analysis by law enforcement. Until recently, law enforcement was not directly engaged in crime analysis and crime studies. They were engaged mostly in crime control and prevention. The understanding of crime causation and crime patterns was left mostly for criminologists to explore. The birth of the technology of geographic information systems (GIS) brought a new era of crime analysis by law enforcement (Boba, 2005). The environmental criminologists, particularly since the institution of the Chicago School of Sociology or the Ecological School of Sociology in the 1930s, have been arguing that crime and criminality are intimately connected to the physical space where the offenders live, move, and commit crimes. Crime and criminal activities follow certain patterns, and they can be understood by studying the changes and dynamics of the physical space within which they are committed. Crime is a social phenomenon, as well as a spatial and space-bound phenomenon. Urban and rural areas and slums and suburbs do not have the same rates and patterns of crime. Different physical spaces are used by rational offenders to capture different structures of opportunities. While committing crimes, the offenders leave behind many leads and trails that present a pattern of their criminality. In other words, each and every physical space—a city, town, slum, suburb, school, neighborhood, street, and shopping center—presents a map of its crime rates and patterns that can be studied, understood, and used for crime control and prevention (Harries, 1999).

Before the emergence of GIS technology, crime mapping was mostly done by academic criminologists visiting and surveying different cities, towns, and localities. With the integration of GIS technology into criminal justice beginning in the 1990s, crime mapping has become a new law enforcement task and responsibility for crime control and prevention. Crime mapping is now done by police sitting in their stations, their patrol cars, or at their computers at home. Although they remain invisible, with the aid of GIS technology, the police can create a highly visible topography of the hot spots of crime and the routes through which the offenders make their journeys to the underworld of drugs, gangs, guns, sex, and violence. The invention of a new generation of GIS-based computer software, such as the CrimeStat, GST Crime Map, Analyst's Notebook, Analyst's Workstation, Automated Tactical Analysis of Crime, Graffiti Tracking System, CiteLink, and WebCat, has allowed law enforcement to connect many dots and doubts and fill in many gaps to understand crime density and intensity in a spatial location. These new software technologies of geocoding have brought a new era of spatial modeling and data mining for understanding the patterns of crime from the perspective of the changes and dynamics of time and space (Harries, 1999). Crime mapping improves public safety by revealing crime trends and patterns in a locality by uncovering differences between rural and urban areas or slums and suburbs, by increasing police knowledge about crime density and intensity in a locality, and by increasing community awareness about crime and community involvement in crime control and prevention (National Institute of Justice, 2011).

One of the recent studies (Weisburd & Lum, 2005), using data from the 1997–1999 LEMAS survey of 615 police departments on the use of crime mapping by law enforcement, found that "computerized crime mapping [had] become widely diffused in the police world by 1999 . . . . Even in 1997, about half of the departments (49%) with more than 100 police officers claimed to have computerized crime mapping capabilities" (p. 421). Almost half of the departments (43%) responded that they introduced crime mapping for "hot-spot policing" (Weisburd & Lum, 2005, p. 428). By 2010, almost all law enforcement agencies with more than 100 police officers had began to adopt the technology of crime mapping. The National Institute of Justice's Mapping and Analysis for Public Safety (MAPS) Program created in 2002 (formerly the Crime Mapping Research Center, established in 1997) is the leader in advancing research on crime mapping and the use of GIS technology in law enforcement in America.

As an extension of GIS technology and crime mapping, there is also emerging a new kind of high-tech law enforcement strategy in the United States, known as predictive policing. Since AT&T's designation of 911 for emergency use in 1968, policing has remained mostly reactive in nature. The advent of GIS technology and crime mapping brought a new age of predictive policing (see **Box 5-1**). Predictive policing is a strategy of proactive policing or preventive policing—that is, policing for reading the emerging trends in crime and criminality, growth in criminal hot spots, scenarios of growing gangs and violence, opportunities for new crimes, and changes and transformations in time and space. Predictive policing is based on geographical profiling and spatial analysis of the possible future density

BOX 5-1

The Globalization of the Technique of Crime Mapping: The Case of the United Kingdom

The innovation of crime mapping developed in the United States is now increasingly becoming a global strategy for crime control and prevention. Outside the United States, the United Kingdom has taken major strides to use the technique of crime mapping based on the science of geographic information systems (GIS). The website Police.UK has the capability of providing street-by-street maps and information on hotspots of crime and criminal activities. Recently, British Home Secretary Theresa May said that through the Police.UK website, "people will be able to track what crimes have been committed near public spaces like nightclubs, parks and shopping malls," and that "a crime-mapping website for England and Wales that lets users track what crimes have been committed on a street-by-street basis will now cover places like clubs and rail stations where large groups of people gather." Crime mapping is spreading not only in the countries of the West, but also in many countries of the developing world. South Africa, for example, is using GIS to track cell phone conversations related to criminal activities. The Philippines is using GIS technology to track maritime crime and criminality. Crime mapping is being intensively used in many cities in India, such as Bangalore, Chennai, Delhi, Hyderabad, Kolkata, and Mumbi.

Source: European Security News. (2012, May 30). *U.K.: Crime-mapping website track crimes street by street.* Retrieved from www .europesecuritynews.com/5810/u-k-crime-mapping-website-track-crimes-street-by-street/.

and intensity of criminal activities in a given space. Predictive policing has five major components: "integration of information technology and geospatial analysis to police operations, ability to see the big picture, using cutting-edge data mining and data analysis software, linking to performance of organization, and adapting to changing position" (Uchida, 2009, p. 2). Predictive policing is done mostly with the aid of IBM's Predictive Analysis software. Many police departments, including those in Boston, Chicago, Los Angeles, New York City, Baltimore, and Washington, DC, are currently experimenting with high-tech predictive policing with the help of funds from the National Institute of Justice. The Chicago Police Department was one of the first police departments in the nation to experiment with predictive policing. Although crime mapping has by now become a common law enforcement technology, predictive policing is emerging as a new phase of high-tech policing in the 21st century (see **Box 5-2**).

BOX 5-2

Predictive Policing Could Come (From the United States) to the United Kingdom

The American innovation of predictive policing is presently becoming a new strategy for police modernization in many countries of Europe. Predictive policing is a strategy of predicting or forecasting criminal activities in the same way that meteorologists forecast weather, or seismologists predict earthquake activities, on the basis of information and communication technology. Crime can be significantly controlled through innovative police tactics and police deployment based on predictive policing. In 2011, a police department in Santa Cruz, California reported a 27% drop in reporting of burglaries because of the technique of predictive policing—a higher form of what is also called "intelligence-led policing." On April 18, 2012, about 120 experts from both sides of the Atlantic, members of the International Association of Crime Analysts, and representatives from EUROPOL gathered in the Hague in the Netherlands to discuss recent innovation in the techniques of police modernization, and predictive policing was high on the agenda. The United Kingdom's National Policing Improvement Agency is currently seriously considering the use of the technique of predictive policing. In January 2012, "predictive policing was outlined at a criminal justice seminar in London by [a] U.S. police chief, Captain Sean Malinowski, who has introduced it in a Los Angeles suburb. Chief Constable Nick Gargan, the chief executive of the National Policing Improvement Agency, gave a warm welcome to the 'exciting initiative.' He said U.K. officers were monitoring its effectiveness and could deploy it alongside other methods used by the police."

Sources: Lance, E. (2012, January 13). Predictive policing is not "Minority Report"... at least not yet. Retrieved from http://www .policeone.com/communications/articles/4941161-Predictive-policing-is-not-Minority-Report-at-least-not-yet/; Morris, N. (2012, January 26). 'Predictive policing' could come to UK. *The Independent.* http://www.independent.co.uk/news/uk/crime/predictive -policing-could-come-to-uk-6294669.html.

Policing and DNA Technology

Another important dimension of high-tech policing in the United States is the growing involvement of law enforcement in collecting and storing DNA from crime scenes and criminal offenders. The understanding of the biological makeup of humans through the understanding of DNA is one of the most remarkable discoveries in modern science. The Human Genome Project, completed in 2003, estimated that about 30,000 to 40,000 genes comprise the basic biological building blocks of a human being. The billions of human cells that make up a human body are composed of these genes, and these genes are made up of different molecules such as water, sugar, minerals, fat, proteins, and DNA (deoxyribonucleic acid). Of these different molecules, protein plays a central organizing role in shaping the structure and functions of the cells. The protein molecules define the way we look, grow, function, and evolve, and the biological property that provides the codes to make these proteins is the DNA. What is remarkable is the discovery that DNA has identifiable and stable forms and structures. It is comprised of an ordered set of four chemical pairs (bases), including A (adenine), T (thymine), C (cytosine), and G (guanine). These four pairs are organized in thousands of sequences along the DNA strand and reveal our genetic identity. DNA has made possible, for the first time in the evolution of human knowledge, the ability to find the biological identity of an individual by mapping his or her DNA. The science of DNA is still evolving, and its enormous possibilities are still being explored, but it has already have a great effect on criminal justice (Shahidullah, 2006). Because humans have the peculiar ability to lie and to mystify their acts and identities, the search for the right offender beyond a reasonable doubt has always been a central concern for criminal justice. DNA opened up a new horizon in criminal investigation and identification analysis.

In the United States, the federal DNA policy began to grow first through the creation of a central data bank for criminal DNA—the project of the Combined DNA Index System (CODIS)—by the FBI in 1991. The Violent Crime Control and Law Enforcement Act of 1994 was the first federal statute that established provisions "for the improvement of DNA laboratories and DNA analysis technology. It authorized the FBI to expand and improve the CODIS" (Shahidullah, 2008, p. 261). The Violent Crime Control and Law Enforcement Act of 1994, however, did not create a provision for collecting DNA samples from federal offenders. This was done through the "Anti-terrorism and Effective Death Penalty Act of 1996 . . . DNA Backlog Elimination Act of 2000, Advancing Justice Through DNA Technology Act of 2003, and Justice for All Act of 2004" (Shahidullah, 2008, p. 261). The DNA Analysis Backlog Elimination Act of 2000 particularly expanded the federal law "to collect DNA samples from all persons convicted of federal crimes . . . . The Director of the Bureau of Prisons is authorized to collect DNA through using reasonable force and restraint" (Shahidullah, 2008, p. 261). The DNA Analysis Backlog Elimination Act of 2000 also created the statutory basis to "create a structure of a national system of DNA collection, analysis, and use in criminal justice" (Shahidullah, 2008, p. 261).

The Advancing Justice Through DNA Technology Act of 2003 and the Justice for All Act of 2004 made "it mandatory to collect DNA from individuals convicted of any federal felony, and also from those arrested but not yet convicted. The states also were given the authority to follow the same DNA collection policy strategies" (Shahidullah, 2008, p. 261). Presently, all 50 states have laws to collect DNA from all sex offenders and convicted felons. Many states also have legislation to collect DNA from violent and nonviolent juvenile offenders (Shahidullah, 2006). As of 2011, 24 states and the federal government have laws for collecting DNA from arrestees, and 16 states are in the process of passing such legislation.

Another emerging trend in high-tech policing is the collection of familial DNA—DNA from the relatives of suspected individuals (see **Figure 5-2**). "In familial DNA searches, authorities collect crime scene DNA and search for a near—but not perfect—match with existing DNA in the criminal database, presumably from an incarcerated blood relative of the yet unknown suspect" (Health and Medicine News, 2011, p. 1). Virginia, California,

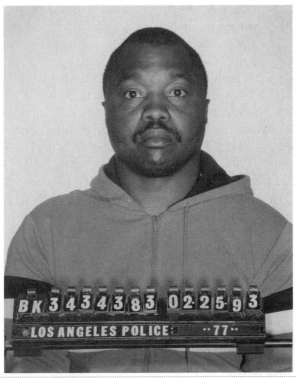

Figure 5-2 A new technique called familial DNA led police to 57-year-old Lonnie David Franklin Jr., who was charged with 10 counts of murder and 1 count of attempted murder in the infamous "Grim Sleeper" slayings (ABC News, 2011).

Source: © Mike Nelson/EPA/Landov.

Colorado, and Pennsylvania have enacted laws for the use of familial DNA. In 2010, Los Angeles police solved a 25-year-old unsolved case of a serial killer, known as "the Grim Sleeper," by linking "an unidentified DNA sample from the crime scene to DNA from the suspect's son. It's the first big forensic case involving what's called familial DNA" (National Public Radio, 2010, p. 1). As of 2011, all 50 states have DNA databases, and they are linked to the National DNA Index System of the FBI. The FBI's CODIS system is now one of the largest DNA databases in the world, and it contains about 5.5 million DNA profiles. "As of January 2010, the National DNA Index System contained over 300,000 forensic profiles and 7.8 million offender profiles" (Suter, 2010, p. 316).

The GPS Tracking System

The use of global positioning system (GPS) technology in criminal justice beginning in the 1990s brought policing and law enforcement and the whole system of sentencing and corrections in America into a new era of crime control and prevention. One of the central challenges in criminal justice has always been the problem of offender sentencing, isolation, separation, and tracking to prevent future offending. The birth of the institution of prison was justified on the ground that for reasons of public safety, violent offenders must be kept separated from the larger society. A new philosophy of community corrections and supervisions currently has been gaining ground in almost all modern criminal justice systems in the context of the use and the proliferation of GPS technology (Hardy, 2010).

GPS technology is a satellite-based navigation system operated by 24 satellites that are orbiting the earth twice a day at a speed of about 7,000 miles per hour. Through the emission of electromagnetic radio waves—the waves that travel at the speed of light—GPS technology, from 12,000 miles above the earth, is able to precisely track the location and the movement of people in any sites and cities and streets on the earth (Garmin Limited, 2011). GPS technology was developed by the U.S. Department of Defense in the late 1970s. By the middle of the 1990s, installation of GPS navigation systems, including the 24 satellites in space, was completed by the Department of Defense. From the beginning of the 1980s, GPS technology was opened up for civilian use, and criminal justice is one of the areas where it began to rapidly expand for offender tracking. During past decade, a number of GPS software technologies came to the market, and they have greatly facilitated the expansion of the use of GPS tracking in criminal justice. Some of the widely used GPS tracking software in criminal justice are Omnilink, Crime Trax, Smart Report, and Smart View. Crime Trax combines crime mapping with GPS technology and is able to review offender compliance to GPS technology and law enforcement performance in GPS tracking by sending a GPS report daily to participating law enforcement agencies. The GPS software Omnilink allows law enforcement "to track sex offenders from the moment they leave prison . . . . Officers are alerted when offenders are not where they should be or if offenders get too close to a forbidden zone" (Omnilink Systems, 2011, p. 2).

Omnilink's domestic violence GPS device—a single-piece ankle bracelet—"gives law enforcement visibility into an offender or defendant's whereabouts in relation to the location of his or her victim" (Omnilink Systems, 2011, p. 2), and through its gang-tracking device, again a single-piece ankle bracelet, law enforcement agencies can "help ensure that gang members stay away from areas where gangs tend to congregate. Location data captured from the device can be correlated with schedules, zones and other parameters to help ensure compliance with court ordered sentences" (Omnilink Systems, 2011, p. 2). Omnilink's gang device can also "create mobile exclusion zones around gang members wearing the Omnilink device. If the gang member enters a specific zone or approaches an area frequented by known gang members, the system automatically alerts the appropriate monitoring officers to respond" (Ominilink Systems, 2011, p. 2).

At the end of 2009, there were about 7.2 million offenders under correctional supervision in the United States. Out of 7.2 million, about 2.1 million remained incarcerated and about 5.1 million remained under community supervision including parole and probation. A significant number of these offenders who are under community supervision are being supervised through the GPS technology, particularly those who are sex offenders, domestic violence offenders, pretrial defendants, house arrest participants, gang members, and truant students (Brown, McCabe, & Wellford, 2007; Omnilink Systems, 2011). Currently, more than 25 states have laws for GPS monitoring of offenders under community corrections, particularly sex offenders and violent criminal offenders released from prison. Some states such as Colorado, Florida, Missouri, Ohio, Oklahoma, and Wisconsin have enacted legislation mandating lifetime GPS tracking of sex offenders after they are released from prison. The Adam Walsh Child Protection and Safety Act of 2006 also mandated GPS tracking of those convicted of sex offenses with children. The U.S. Federal Court is also of the opinion that "legislation implementing GPS tracking of convicted sex offenders is consistent with constitutional substantive due process protections because the legislation not only passes the rational-basis review test . . . but also passes the more stringent test of strict scrutiny" (Stop Child Predators, 2007, p. 3). The use of GPS tracking of offenders has brought many new tasks and responsibilities and the need for new knowledge and training for law enforcement. But it is opening a new horizon of high-tech policing for crime control and prevention. The use of GPS tracking is also rapidly growing in the United Kingdom, Canada, and Australia (see **Figure 5-3**). There are laws for GPS tracking, known as electronic tagging, of convicted sex offenders and violent offenders throughout England and Wales. There are also laws in England and Wales for electronic tagging of youths with a background of repeat offenses.

Information and Communication Technology and Transformation in Policing in the European Union

The increasing integration of information technology, also known as information and communication technology (ICT), to criminal justice has brought fundamental changes in policing not just in the United States but also in many other countries. Outside North America, the effect of ICT on policing is growing particularly in the European Union (EU), whose countries are among the global leaders in advancing ICT technology. There are 6 major EU telecom companies among the top 10 ICT companies in the world, which are: Deutsche Telekom (Germany), Vodafone (United Kingdom), France Telecom (France), TelecomItalia

Figure 5-3 California Parole Agents Supervise About 6,500 Sex Offenders with GPS Ankle Bracelets (as of 2010)

Source: © Michael Buholzer/Thomson Reuters.

(Italy), Telefónica (Spain), and BT (United Kingdom). In areas of computer hardware and components, 3 "European companies are ranked among the world's top ten for semiconductor manufacture: STMicro (FR/IT), Infineon (DE) and Philips (NL)" (European Commission, 2006, p. 19). The United States accounts for about 30% of the world supply of ICT, and the EU accounts for about 20%. The EU's position in the world market is comparable to Japan (European Commission, 2006). Europe's leading role in the growth and innovations of ICT is fundamentally changing Europe's institutions of law, justice, and governance, particularly the institution of law enforcement and policing.

A recent study conducted by the European Commission (2011) found that ICT is being rapidly integrated in policing in Europe in general. The study was based on interviews of police leaders working with ICT projects in Belgium, the Czech Republic, France, Germany, Macedonia, the Netherlands, Romania, Spain, and the United Kingdom. The study was also based on interviews of 20 technology vendors in the field of ICT in policing. The study identified five dominant trends in the use of ICT in policing by those countries. The first is the trend of increasing integration of intelligence data systems. The report explains, "This effort ranges from digitizing criminal records that were previously stored in paper form to developing message formats that allow sharing information across European police organizations" (European Commission, 2011, p. 13). In Romania, the border police have developed a national alert system through which the police anywhere in the country can have access to search warrants of both people and goods. In Spain, the police developed an integrated system of crime and offender information through Internet services. The system vertically integrates "databases of open calls and warnings regarding people and antecedents and histories of people. Horizontally, within all units in Catalonia, the system integrates a variety of 31 databases" (European Commission, 2011, p. 14). In Germany, the federal police, through digitalization, developed an integrated information system that stores the behavioral profiles of offenders—profiles that can be used for crime identification in case of reoffending and recidivism. Italy also has developed an integrated information system to store criminal and forensic profiles of offenders for reconstruction of crime scenes.

Another trend that is growing in the EU countries, as in the United States, is the adoption of mobile computing in European policing. France "introduced a bus that becomes a command post and a laboratory . . . . The command post includes radio technology, a satellite telephone link and an antenna switch with a capacity of 100 telephone lines" (European Commission, 2011, p. 19). In Germany, "a mobile border control office can be folded into a suitcase. It includes a PC with a fingerprint scanner, a reader for digital documents and a printer" (European Commission, 2011, p. 20).

Also growing is the use of surveillance technology by European police in areas of crime observation, border control, image processing, automatic recognition, and lawful interception. In France, "the Police Nationale at the Mayotte island, a French territory in the Indian Ocean, developed an infrared-based video analysis system to automate border surveillance" (European Commission, 2011, p. 26). In the Netherlands and Italy, border police use automated number plate recognition to control the flow of illegal human trafficking. Another effect of ICT on policing in Europe is the increasing use of digital biometrics. In Germany, the federal police use handheld devices that "allow police officers to take digital fingerprints while they are patrolling in trains and airports and verify digital identification documents." (European Commission, 2011, p. 29). In the United Kingdom, police use "mobile scanners to identify people by digital fingerprint technology. The system is especially used to check drivers who were previously identified by the number plate recognition system" (European Commission, 2011, p. 29). Also expanding is the use of social media—including Twitter, Facebook, and Skype—in policing in Europe. The 2011 European Commission study found that in the Netherlands, "the adoption rate for social media is particularly high, where police forces increasingly integrate services such as Twitter, Facebook, Blogs or SMS into their daily operational practices" (European Commission, 2011, p. 35).

Decentralization and Neighborhood Policing in the United Kingdom

The United Kingdom, in contrast to the United States, has a unitary form of government. In a unitary form of government, policing is always a responsibility of the central government, and there is only one system of national policing. Different subnational regions of a unitary government may have some authority in police organization and police management, but their authority is legitimate to the extent that they are recognized by the central government, which in case of the United Kingdom is primarily Parliament. The Police Act of 1996 enacted by the British Parliament—an act that amended the Police and Magistrate Courts Act of 1994 and the Police Act of 1964—provides the present organizational framework of policing in the United Kingdom. There are three major components of the national system of policing in the United Kingdom: metropolitan policing in London, known as Scotland Yard; territorial police forces; and special police forces. Scotland Yard, like the FBI of the United States, has earned a global reputation as one of the most professional and technologically developed police forces in the world. The metropolitan policing agency in London is one of the earliest examples of the rise of modern policing in the 19th century. It was the brainchild of then–British

Secretary Sir Robert Peel, and it was formally established by the British Parliament through the Metropolitan Police Act of 1829. In 1829, it was an organization manned by 1,000 police officers. "Today, the Metropolitan Police Service employs more than 32,500 officers together with about 14,200 police staff, 230 traffic wardens and 4,300 Police Community Support Officers (PCSOs)" (Metropolitan Police, 2011, p. 1).

The territorial police forces that represent different police areas constitute the bulk of policing in the United Kingdom. There are four subregions in the United Kingdom: England, Wales, Scotland, and Northern Ireland. Each of these subregions is divided into a number of police areas, and each police area is controlled by a group of territorial police forces. The territorial police forces of a police area are locally governed by a corporate body that is formed and whose authority is recognized by the British Home Office and Parliament. The territorial police forces of the major cities are also known as Metropolitan Police, which is not to be confused with Scotland Yard. In London, in addition to Scotland Yard, there is also the Metropolitan Police of the City of London and other cities such as Lincolnshire, Northamptonshire, Cleveland, Essex, Manchester, Kent, and Nottinghamshire. The Metropolitan Police are also governed by a corporate body formed under the guidelines of the Police Act of 1996. Each territorial police force is headed by a chief of police or a police commissioner appointed by the local police authority—the corporate body—in consultation with the British Home Office.

The third major component of policing in the United Kingdom is comprised of special police forces created by the central government for law enforcement in specific areas, such as the British Transport Police, the Royalty Protection Branch (armed body guards for the royal family), the Special Branch, the Anti-Terrorist Branch, the Criminal Investigation Department (CID), the Counterterrorism Command, Aviation Security, the National Identification Bureau, the Ministry of Defense Police (for guarding military installations and weapon factories), the Civil Nuclear Constabulary (for guarding nuclear power plants and civilian nuclear sites), the National Criminal Intelligence Service, the National Crime Squad, and the United Kingdom Border Agency. The special police forces, according to the Police Act of 1996, are required to work with the territorial police forces in times of need and urgency. The Serious Organised Crime and Police Act of 2006 gave special power of arrest without a warrant to some groups of special police forces, particularly to those who are working with counterterrorism and border control.

One of the emerging concerns for reforms in policing in most modern systems of criminal justice is the notion of democratization in policing. The rise of modern professional policing characterized by centralization and bureaucratization has vastly improved police capability for law enforcement and crime control and prevention. But professional policing has also greatly weakened police and community connections. With the rise and expansion of professional policing, the traditional informal institutions of policing and crime control became largely isolated. Consequently, since the early 1990s, debate began to address the issues of community involvement and citizen participation in the governance of policing. The idea of a new model of community policing then began to emerge and be studied. At the core of community policing is the notion of the devolution of power in the management and organization of policing.

This movement toward community policing, or what can be broadly defined as democratization in policing, is presently at the center of police reforms in all modern systems of criminal justice. This is not a movement against professionalization in policing or against the use of science and high technology for crime control and prevention. It is, rather, a movement for integrating community knowledge, leadership, philosophy, and resources into professional policing for a more holistic strategy for crime control and prevention. Among all the countries with modern systems of criminal justice, reforms in democratization in policing in recent years have considerably progressed in the United Kingdom. The vision for a new model of democratic policing was first articulated by a report, *Policing in the 21st Century*, prepared by the British Home Office (2010) under the leadership of Theresa May—the British Home Secretary. The report, in the words of Theresa May, "signals the most radical change to policing in 50 years. We will transfer power to policing—replacing bureaucratic accountability with democratic accountability" (British Home Office, 2010, p. 3). The report was presented to the British Parliament in the form of the Police Reform and Social Responsibility Bill in July 2010. The new initiative for democratizing policing came on the basis of the recognition that growing centralization of police management in the United Kingdom in the wake of growing professionalization in policing that started in the 1960s made "the service disconnected from the communities they are there to serve . . . . The approach of the last decade has been for central government to intervene more and more in local policing in an attempt to make it more accountable" (British Home Office, 2010, p. 5). The gap that it is necessary to "fill today is one of accountability, not technology" (British Home Office, 2010, p. 5).

The Police Reform and Social Responsibility Bill has proposed five areas of fundamental reforms in the management of policing in the United Kingdom. First, the Bill proposed that in each police area in England and Wales, except in areas with Metropolitan Police and City of London Police, the police and the crime commissioner will be locally elected by people every 4 years. This is a fundamental reform in the sense that in no country in the world today are police elected by people, except for sheriffs in the United States. Each police area will be governed by a team of elected police, and it will be autonomously governed by an elected crime commissioner. The crime commissioner, in collaboration with the police team and the public, will set the agenda for the business of policing in the police area they represent. In the existing system, police authorities in 43 police areas are elected and independent members. In the proposed reform, the elected crime commissioner will have the authority of appointing the chief constable—the top police officer in the hierarchy of police ranking in the United Kingdom. With the new strategy, the national government will have a role in setting the national police agenda, "but it will have no role in telling the police how to do their job—that is for the police; or in holding them to account for how well they have done it" (British Home Office, 2010, p. 19). In the proposed system, "The public at the ballot box will be the ultimate judges of the success or failure of each commissioner and how well they are serving the community" (British Home Office, 2010, p. 14).

Secondly, the Bill proposed for each police area of England and Wales a police and crime panel consisting of elected local government members and lay members with skills and interests in the success of policing in their localities. The police and crime panel "in each police area will function as a local advisory body. It will advise the Commissioner on their proposed policing plans and budget and consider progress at the end of each year" (British Home Office, 2010, p. 15). The panel will also have the authority to "hold confirmation hearings for the post of Chief Constable and be able to hold confirmation hearings for other appointments made by the Commissioner to his staff, but without having the power of veto" (British Home Office, 2010, p. 40).

The third innovation proposed by the Bill is the strengthened the role of the National Association of Chief of Police Officers (ACPO). The Bill proposed that the ACPO become a "national organization responsible for providing the professional leadership for the police service, by taking the lead role on setting standards and sharing best practice across the range of police activities" (British Home Office, 2010, p. 40).

Fourth, the Bill proposed the creation of a new national crime agency and the abolition of the existing National Policing Improvement Agency. The proposed national crime agency, led by different national level of operational commands such as the Organized Crime Command and Border Policing Command, will develop plans for effective border policing and effective strategies for combating and controlling organized crime. The fifth is the area of reform for police accountability. The Bill proposed the creation of Her Majesty's Inspectorate of Constabulary and an Independent Police Complaints Commission to ensure continuous improvement in police performance and police accountability.

One of the core missions of the proposed reform in policing in the United Kingdom is the expansion and strengthening of local participation in police governance. One such program that already exists is the Neighborhood Policing Program introduced by the Police Reform Act of 2002. The 2002 Act mandated the creation of a group of police community support officers (PCSOs) in each and every neighborhood of the 43 police areas in England and Wales. A report from the National Policing Improvement Agency (2008) estimated that as of 2008, there were more than 16,000 neighborhood policing programs across England and Wales. The program was launched with the following three key missions: increasing neighborhood police visibility, increasing community involvement in setting the neighborhood police agenda and police priorities, and collaborative problem solving in neighborhood crime and justice. The PCSOs in the neighborhoods, comprised of police, local elected officials, and community members, have the statutory authority to engage in such activities as school safety, youth development, hate crime information gathering, family liaison/management and domestic violence, offender management, liquor and firearms licensing, roads policing, and detention-related duties (National Policing Improvement Agency, 2008). The Police Reform and Social Responsibility Bill of 2010 recognized that "the work of neighborhood policing teams to identify and meet the most local priorities in every community is a fundamental element of local policing" (British Home Office, 2010, p. 12).

Beginning in the mid-1990s, community policing emerged as a major innovation in police reform in the United States and other countries. There are, however, certain fundamental differences between the community policing of the United States and the proposed citizen-centered decentralized policing in the United Kingdom. The philosophy of community policing is to redesign the function of policing for more involvement in community-centered crime and justice issues (Greene, 2000). In community policing, redesigning the structure, organization, and authority of police command is not a part of the core mission. The proposed reform for decentralization in policing in the United Kingdom has gone beyond the philosophy of traditional community policing, opting instead for an ambitious program of developing a cadre of national police and police leadership primarily based on local elections. The proposed decentralized and neighborhood-based policing system is scheduled to be in operation in England and Wales in 2012. The effect of this reform strategy on policing and crime control in the United Kingdom will remain an intriguing issue in comparative criminal justice.

Centralization and Super Policing in Germany

The evolution of modern policing in Germany is closely connected to different turns and turbulences of its 20th century political evolution. The modern state of Germany experienced a series of political upheavals in the 20th century that were unmatched in the modern histories of the United States, Canada, England, and France. The creation of the modern state of the Weimar Republic in 1919 marked the beginning of a modern democratic state in Germany. Under the Weimar Republic, Germany's 19 states came under a central government based on a democratic constitution. However, with the rise of Adolf Hitler and the accession of the Third Reich to power in 1933, the whole apparatus of the modern state in Germany was destroyed. In 1945, after the end of World War II and the destruction of Hitler's Third Reich, Germany was occupied by the United States, the United Kingdom, and France. In 1949, Germany was divided: The allied powers of the United States, the United Kingdom, and France established the Federal Republic of Germany in West Germany, while Soviet Russia established the German Democratic Republic (GDR) in East Germany. In 1961, the Berlin Wall was created by the Russian-backed GDR to signal the permanent division of Germany. Beginning in 1989, after the end of the Cold War, the Berlin Wall was dismantled, and East and West Germany were unified under the state of the Federal Republic of Germany. The nature and philosophy of policing in Germany is intimately connected with this historical predicament of Germany's search for a strong centralized government based on the principles of democracy.

There are three types of policing in the Federal Republic of Germany: the Federal Criminal Police, federal police, and state police. The Federal Criminal Police of Germany (*Bundeskriminalamt,* or BKA) was created under a "Law on the Establishment of a Federal Police" enacted by the British Occupation Force in Germany in 1951. The BKA's main mission is to provide "support to the police forces of the federation and of the states in connection with the prevention and prosecution of crimes that involve more than one German state and that are of international significance or otherwise of considerable significance" (*Bundeskriminalamt*, 2012, p. 1). The BKA is comprised of about 5,500 trained police officers as of 2012. Like the FBI of the United States and the Royal Canadian Mounted Police, the BKA has a mandate to investigate crimes in areas of illegal trafficking of weapons and drugs, human trafficking, money laundering, global terrorism, cyber crime, child pornography, and sex tourism. The BKA is the connecting link between Germany and INTERPOL (International Criminal Police Organization) and EUROPOL (European Police Office). Currently, the BKA has nine specialized divisions: international coordination, state security, serious and organized crime, protection, central CID services, law enforcement studies and training, forensic science, information technology, and central administrative affairs. The BKA's "criminal records include approximately 3,700,000 items of personal data on persons who have committed serious offences or crimes of supraregional significance. Approximately 330,000 of the criminal records are available in digitized form" (*Bundeskriminalamt*, 2009, p. 8).

In addition to the Federal Criminal Police Office, there is also a separate federal police agency. In 1955, Germany created a new federal police force called the Federal Border Force. The Federal Border Force (*Bundesgrenzschutz,* or BGS) was an armed and militarized police force for border control and internal security. It was under the control of the Ministry of Defense. In 1998, the BGS was disbanded, and the Federal Police (*Bundespolizei,* or BPOL) was created under the control of the Federal Ministry of the Interior. As of 2012, the BPOL is comprised of about 41,000 personnel, of whom about 33,000 are highly trained, uniformed police personnel. The major roles of the BPOL are in areas of internal security, border security, protection of critical infrastructures, guarding federal buildings, guarding foreign embassies, transportation security, aviation security, counterterrorism, dealing with violent political movements and protests, and coast guard services. There are four specialized command groups within the BPOL: Aviation Group, Counterterrorism Group, Information and Communication Group, and Coast Guard. The national headquarters of BPOL is in Potsdam, and there are eight regional headquarters throughout Germany (Polis: Policing OnLine Information System, 2011).

The Federal Republic of Germany has 16 states (*Laender*) and 16 state police forces, such as the Berlin Police, the Police of Bavaria, the Police of Hamburg, the Police of Saxony, and the Police of North-Rhine Westphalia. Under the present constitution, or the Basic Law for the Federal Republic of Germany, each and every German state has the constitutional right to establish its own organization of policing. The state police and their leadership are under the control of the state Ministry of the Interior. Although they are organized differently in different states, state police services are divided into six major areas: the state Criminal Police Office, the Traffic Police, the Emergency Police, the Waterways Police, the Air Wings, and the Special Weapons and Tactical Units and Mobile Surveillance Units. The state criminal police serve as the main agency for criminal investigations and prosecutions. The Special Weapons and Tactical Units and Mobile Surveillance Units "are organized and managed differently in each of the individual federal states, but, in general, they are used to deal with cases of very serious crime or for special surveillance" (Polis: Policing OnLine Information System, 2011, p. 3).

There are two competing perspectives in the debate and discourse on reforms in policing in Germany. The first perspective is for more demilitarization, decentralization, and
democratization of policing in Germany. The advocates of this approach are strongly in favor
of strengthening the police systems of the 16 federal states. There is a long tradition of
militarization in German policing, dating from the importation of the Napoleonic structure
of policing from France in the 19th century. In the 19th and early 20th centuries, the Napoleonic structure of military policing "was the most common police structure throughout
continental Europe. It was used by countries as diverse as Portugal, the Netherlands, Poland,
Austria-Hungary, and many German States" (Paun, 2007, p. 17). Militarization and centralization in all facets and forces of policing in Germany were completely achieved under the
domination of the Third Reich by Hitler (1933–1945). One of the first political reforms
undertaken by Hitler was the restructuring of the German judicial and policing systems. For
about 12 years of the Third Reich's rule, the core institutions, functions, and values of German policing were built around the philosophy of militarization, centralization, and Nazification. The Gestapo—the police system of the Third Reich—was one of the central
institutions of repression, torture, and brutality. The Gestapo led the Holocaust by the Third
Reich. Many advocates of police reforms in today's Germany are therefore leery of putting
more power into the hands of German federal police (BPOL) and the Federal Criminal Police
of Germany (BKA).

The second perspective is for a more powerful and centralized police force (i.e., super
policing) for the federal government of Germany. The advocates of "super policing" do not
seek Nazification. Instead, they advocate for more centralization, rationalization, and professionalization in German policing. This group of reformers believes that modern Germany
is experiencing the effect of rapid globalization. The rise of new transnational organized
criminal groups and threats of global terrorism have been posing serious challenges to the
traditional institutions of law and order in Germany. The decentralized police forces of the
German states, in view of this group of advocates, are not professionally and technologically
competent to effectively respond to the emerging challenges of global crimes. It is the second
perspective that is now dominant in police reforms in Germany. In 2010, the German Ministry of Internal Affairs took a major initiative to combine the two federal police forces—BPOL
and BKA—into a single federal police force in Germany. As one report observed, "The German government is re-floating a proposal to unite its two federal police forces, creating what
some have called a 'Super police force'" (Spiegel Online International, 2010, p. 1). It is expected
that the German Parliament will enact the proposed reform as a law in 2012 and the creation
of one federal institution of super policing will be completed by 2013.

New Criminal Laws in Modern Criminal Justice Systems: The Criminalization of Child Sexual Abuse

In comparative analysis of criminal justice among societies, understanding the emerging
landscape of laws related to different types of new crimes and criminality in different

countries is a problem of enormous significance. One of the areas that is being increasingly criminalized in almost all modern systems of criminal justice in the West is child sexual abuse (World Health Organization, 2002). In countries with modern systems of criminal justice, there are a number of areas in the domain of sex and intimacy that have been recently decriminalized, such as cohabitation, fornication, adultery, abortion, homosexuality, contraceptive use by unmarried men and women, same-sex marriage, and cohabitation. At the same time, however, there is an expanding process of criminalization in the domain of sex and intimacy, particularly in the domain of child sexual abuse. The United Nations Organization's 2006 *World Report on Violence Against Children*, conducted using data from 139 countries, noted that "an estimated 150 million girls and 73 million boys under 18 have experienced forced sexual intercourse or other forms of sexual violence involving physical contact" (Pinheiro, 2006, p. 33). The World Health Organization estimates that "that more than 800 million people worldwide may have experienced CSA [child sexual abuse], with more than 500 million having experienced contact or intercourse types of abuse" (Johnson, 2008, p. 24). The United Nations Children's Fund (UNICEF) "estimates that in sub-Saharan Africa, Egypt and Sudan, 3 million girls and women are subjected to FGM [female genital mutilation] every year" (Pinheiro, 2006, p. 33). One report presented to the Secretary General of the United Nations in 2006 indicated that " in 21 countries, most of them industrialized, as many as 36 percent of women and 29 percent of men said they had been the victims of sexual abuse during childhood" (Osborne, 2006, p. 1).

Another study on global incidence of child sexual abuse based on a meta-analysis of 217 research studies published between 1980 and 2008 and 331 independent samples with a total of 9,911,748 participants, found that child sexual abuse "prevalence was 127/1000 in self-report studies and 4/1000 in informant studies . . . and highest rates were found for girls in Australia (215/1000) and for boys in Africa (193/1000) (Stoltenborgh, van Ijzendoorn, Euser, & Bakermans-Kranenburg, 2011, p. 79).

The United States official report, *Child Maltreatment 2010,* states that "approximately 695,000 unique children were determined to be victims of child abuse; the overall child maltreatment rate was 9.2 cases per 1000 children. Of these, about 9.2%, or close to 64,000, represented cases of sexual abuse" (as cited in Giardino, 2012, p. 1). In the report, overall, "695,000 substantiated cases emerged from approximately 3.3 million reports of alleged child abuse and neglect, involving about 5.9 million children. In addition to the 9.2% of substantiated cases of sexual abuse, an additional 17.6% were substantiated for physical abuse" (as cited in Giardino, 2012, p. 1). Recently, the FBI estimated that "cases of child sexual exploitation on the Internet had increased by more than 2,026 percent since 1996" (as cited in Wieland, 2008, p. 3). A U.S. Department of Justice report published in 2006 estimated that "there are between 50,000 and 100,000 pedophiles involved in organized pornography [child pornography] rings around the world, and that one third of these operate from the United States" (as cited in Wortley & Smallbone, 2006, p. 3).

Researchers have found that child sexual abuse is positively associated with a variety of psychosomatic abnormalities. Studies have shown that "Math Scholastic Aptitude Test (SAT) scores were significantly lower in abused subjects when matched against comparison subjects and when compared to their own Verbal SAT scores. Childhood sexual abuse appears to be associated with a constellation of neuropsychological deficiencies (Navalta, Polcari, Webster, Boghossian, & Teicher, 2006, p. 45). Childhood sexual victimization is related to a variety of adult psychopathologies, such as "major depression, borderline personality disorder, somatization disorder, substance abuse disorders, posttraumatic stress disorder (PTSD), dissociative identity disorder, and bulimia nervosa" (Putnam, 2003, p. 271). Numerous research studies have shown that "sexually abused children exhibited more sexualized behaviors than various comparison groups" (Putnam, 2003, p. 272).

Modern scientific research and the call from the United Nations Convention of the Rights of the Child and other related international conventions for the protection of the rights of children have led to the development of a new legal landscape for combating child sexual abuse. All countries in the West with modern systems of criminal justice have enacted laws to criminalize child sexual abuse, child pornography, Internet child sexual exploitation, child sexual tourism, commercial exploitation of children, cyber stalking, cyber grooming, date rape, and indecent exposure to children. Mandatory sentencing, mandatory DNA extraction, registration, community notification, residential restrictions, civil commitment, treatment, lifelong GPS tracking, chemical castration, and a variety of other methods of punishment have been developed to deter child sexual abuse. The following sections will discuss some of the homogenizing trends in the development of sex offender registration and notification laws in three countries: the United States, Canada, and the United Kingdom.

Sex Offender Registration and Notification Laws in the United States

In the United States, Congress responded to the challenges of child sexual abuse and child pornography by enacting a series of new laws and legislation from the beginning of the 1990s (Shahidullah, 2008). Some of the most prominent of these pieces of legislation are the Jacob Wetterling Crimes Against Children and Sexually Violent Offenders Act of 1994; Megan's Law of 1996; the Pam Lychner Sexual Offender Tracking and Identification Act of 1996; the Child Pornography Prevention Act of 1996 (CPPA); the Protection of Children From Sexual Predators Act of 1998; the Children's Internet Protection Act of 2000 (CIPA); the Victims of Trafficking and Violence Protection Act of 2000; Aimee's Law of 2000; the PROTECT Act of 2003; the Children Safety Act of 2005; and the Adam Walsh Child Protection and Safety Act of 2006. All of these legislative acts introduced long-term mandatory sentencing for violent and repeat sex offenders, but one of the most innovative policy strategies that remains common to them—the policy strategy that is now being debated in many countries—is the policy of sex offender registration and community notification (Shahidullah, 2008).

The Jacob Wetterling Act of 1994 introduced the innovative policy of sex offender registration in the United States. The Act created the following four major sets of provisions for the states: (1) mandatory creation of a statewide registration system; (2) mandatory state notification of the operation of sex offender registration to the FBI; (3) mandatory sex offender information verification; and (4) mandatory sharing of sex offender registration information among the states and between the states and the federal government.

The Wetterling Act "made a provision of mandatory registration for at least ten years for all child molesters and violent sex offenders, and a provision of registration for life for highly dangerous sex offenders described as sexual predators" (Shahidullah, 2008, p. 166). The enactment of Megan's Law in 1996 further broadened the sex offender registration provisions introduced by the the Wetterling Act. "The Wetterling Act contained a general provision that sex offender registration information be treated as private data . . . Megan's Law eliminated the privacy provision of the Wetterling Act, and it created the provision of mandatory community notification" (Shahidullah, 2008, p. 167).

Under Megan's Law, "states are required, for the necessity of public safety, to release sex offender registration information to the public" (Shahidullah, 2008, p. 167). The Pam Lychner Act of 1996 "further extended the roles and obligations of federal, state, and local governments with respect to the sex offender registration and notification policy" (Shahidullah, 2008, p. 167). The Lychner Act made a provision for "lifetime registration of aggravated sex offenders, repeat sex offenders, and violent sex predators," and "created mandatory penalties for offenders who knowingly fail to register. For repeat sex offenders who knowingly fail to register, the Act made a provision for imprisonment for up to 10 years" (Shahidullah, 2008, p. 168).

More stringent laws for sex offender registration and notification systems in the United States, however, came after the enactment of the Children Safety Act of 2005 and the Adam Walsh Child Protection and Safety Act of 2006. "One of the major purposes of the new law was to establish a comprehensive national system of sex offender registration by developing a national website titled as the Dru Sjodin National Sex Offender Public Website" (Shahidullah, 2008, p. 168).

The Children Safety Act of 2005 introduced a new sex offender notification program—the Megan Nicole Kanka and Alexandra Nicole Zapp Community Program. This program made it mandatory "to electronically notify the FBI, school authorities, housing authorities, employment agencies, social service entities, child welfare agencies, and voluntary organizations dealing with children, within five days of changes in a sex offender's registration information. (Shahidullah, 2008, p. 169). The Children Safety Act "authorized the development of a National Sex Offender Registry (NSOR) that can be electronically accessed by the public and all law enforcement and concerned agencies from anywhere in the country" (Shahidullah, 2008, p. 168). The Act also introduced the provision for mandatory lifetime registration for persons convicted of felony sex offenses and 20 years for non-felony sex offenses" (Shahidullah, 2008, p. 169).

The Adam Walsh Child Protection and Safety Act of 2006, in comparison to the Children Safety Act of 2005, brought more stringent provisions for sex offender registration and notification. Some of the new amendments include a mandatory 15 years registration period for Tier I sex offenders, 25 years registration for Tier II sex offenders, and lifetime registration for Tier III sex offenders. Some of the other amendments include mandatory registration before the completion of a prison term for sex offenders; mandatory extraction of DNA samples from sex offenders; mandatory registration for juvenile sex offenders; mandatory registration of sex offenders in all jurisdictions including schools and places of work; mandatory inclusion of the sex offenders' vehicle descriptions and driver's license numbers in the registration information package; mandatory public access to sex offender information through the Internet; mandatory development by the Department of Justice of a website for nationwide instant and real-time access to sex offender information (Dru Sjodin National Sex Offender Public Website); and the development of a nationwide, federally controlled community notification program (Megan Nicole Kanka and Alexandra Nicole Zapp Community Notification Program).

Sex Offender Flagging and Registration System in Canada

Since the late 1940s, Canada has been trying to develop a tracking system for dangerous sex offenders. In 1947, Canada enacted the Habitual Offender Act and added a Criminal Sexual Psychopath provision in the Criminal Code of Canada. Because of some ambiguity in the Criminal Sexual Psychopath provision, the Canadian Parliament enacted new legislation in 1997. It is this new legislation, the Criminal Law Amendment Act of 1997, that added a dangerous offenders provision in the criminal code and mandated the development of a national flagging system for both dangerous sexual and nonsexual offenders. Studies have shown, however, that the law is applied mostly to track dangerous sexual offenders. The Criminal Law Amendment Act of 1997 also added a new category of long-term offenders. The National Flagging System was introduced in 1995 to track dangerous and long-term offenders, particularly sexual offenders. One 2009 Canadian victimization survey shows that, the rate of sexual assault victimization was 24 per 1,000 population from age 15 years and older.

The National Flagging System (NFS) is designed to collect information on dangerous and long-term sexual offenders by NFS coordinators from law enforcement and correctional agencies in all provinces of Canada. "*Dangerous Offender* application consist of offenders convicted of a serious personal injury offense . . . who exhibited a repetitive and persistent pattern of aggressive behaviors manifested by the failure to restrain those behaviors and/or to control sexual impulses (Bonta & Yessine, 2008, p. 1). The decision to flag an offender as a dangerous/long-term offender is made by NFS coordinators based on relevant information supplied by law enforcement and correctional agencies. "When the decision to flag an offender is made, the Provincial/Territorial coordinator has the added responsibility to communicate the decision to, and exchange information with, police, corrections, Crown prosecutors, and other Provincial/Territorial coordinators" (Bonta & Yessine, 2008, p. 2). The NFS coordinators are responsible, in their own jurisdictions, for creating a data bank on dangerous and long-term offenders in terms of their criminal records, psychiatric evaluations, probation information, correctional documents, court records, and victimization information. One study reports that "between 1978 and April 2005, a total of 384 criminals were designated dangerous. As of July 2006, 333 individuals with a dangerous offender designation were incarcerated" (Victims of Violence, 2008, p. 6).

As an extension of the 1995 National Flagging System, Canada introduced a national sex offender registration system in 2004. In 2000, Ontario was the first province in Canada to introduce the idea of a sex offender registration system through the enactment of Christopher's Law. In 1988, Christopher, 11 years old, was abducted, sexually assaulted, and murdered by a repeat sex offender in Ontario. Christopher's Law made it mandatory for a sex offender in the province of Ontario to report in person to local police and law enforcement agencies within 15 days of his or her conviction for a sex offense, within 15 days of his or her release from prison, within 15 days of his or her change of address and/or name change, and within 15 days after taking residency in Ontario. British Columbia in 2001 and Ottawa in 2002 introduced similar sex offender registration laws. In 2004, with the enactment of the Sex Offender Information Registration Act, the government of Canada introduced a national sex offender registration system.

The national registration system is managed through a central computerized data bank established by the Royal Canadian Mounted Police of the Ministry of Public Safety. The registration process is initiated when law enforcement agents secure a court order. After a court order is approved, the sex offender is notified for registration. A sex offender is legally obligated to register with a law enforcement agency within 15 days after receiving the notification. Registration verification is required once every year and within 15 days of a change in name and address. According to the Sex Offender Information Registration Act, registration is mandatory for 10 years for offenses carrying 2–5 years in prison, 20 years for offenses carrying 10–14 years in prison, and for life for repeat offenders (Ministry of Public Safety, 2011).

Sex Offender Registration and Sarah's Law in the United Kingdom

The sex offender registration and notification system in the United Kingdom is a result of the creation of three major statutory provisions: the Sexual Offender Registration Act of 1997, the Sex Offences Act of 2003, and Sarah's Law of 2008. There are currently about 33,000 registered sex offenders in England and Wales, and they are part of a national computerized data bank called the Violent and Sex Offender Register (VISOR), comparable to the National Sex Offender Registry (NSOR) of the United States. VISOR information is accessible to a number of agencies, including law enforcement in England, Wales, and Northern Ireland; British Transportation Police; British Border Patrol Services; Probation Services; child care agencies; and private and public sector prisons in England and Wales. Some of the key characteristics of VISOR include: United Kingdom–wide coverage, multiagency collaboration and information sharing, and instant transfer of United Kingdom–wide records (National Policing Improvement Agency, 2011). The sex offender registration system in the United Kingdom was first introduced by the Sex Offender Registration Act of 1997. Part I of the Act required certain categories of sex offenders "to notify the police of their name(s) and address and any changes to these details in order to ensure that the information on sex offenders contained within the police national computer is kept fully up to date" (Davidson, 2009, p. 4). Part II of the Act gave "United Kingdom courts jurisdiction to deal with those who commit certain sexual acts against children abroad" (Davidson, 2009, p. 4).

The Act mandated the registration of the following three categories of sex offenders: (1) those who were convicted or cautioned by law enforcement for relevant sex offenses;

(2) those who previously served (before the enactment of the 1997 Act) a prison term or were confined in a mental hospital for committing relevant sexual offenses; and (3) those who are serving community services for committing relevant sexual offenses. The 1997 Act defined relevant offenses to include rape, intercourse with a girl under 13 years; intercourse with a girl between 13 and 16 years; incest by a man (victim under 18 years); buggery (offender 20 years or over and victim under 18 years); indecency with men (offender 20 years or over and victim under 18 years); indecent assault (sentence 30 months or over and victim under 18 years); causing or encouraging prostitution of, intercourse with, or indecent assault on a girl under 16 years; indecent conduct toward a young child; inciting a girl under 16 years to have incestuous sexual intercourse; and indecent photographs of children (possession, taking, showing, or possessing with a view to distributing). The Act also mandated that registration must occur within 14 days of conviction or caution by law enforcement, notification as subject to registration, release from prison or mental hospital, or change of name or address (Devon County Council, 2011).

The Sexual Offences Act of 2003 created a much more expansive list of sex offenses and stringent criteria for sex offender registration and notification. The British Home Office (2004) identified the Sexual Offences Act of 2003 as "the first major overhaul of sexual offences legislation for more than a century" (p. 1). The Act identified more than 60 different kinds of sex crimes and presented them under 14 major categories, including causing sexual activity without consent, rape and other offenses against children under 13, child sex offenses, abuse of a position of trust, familial child sex offenses, offenses against persons with a mental disorder impeding choice, inducements to persons with a mental disorder, indecent photographs of children, abuse of children through prostitution and pornography, exploitation of prostitution, and sex trafficking. The Act is based on the recognition that a child under the age of 13 has no capacity to consent to sexual activity; a child between 14 and 16 years of age has some capacity to consent; and a child between 16 and 18 years of age has a capacity to consent but he or she can be victimized by prostitution, sex trafficking, and pornography. The Act made a clear provision that "all penetrating sex (including penetration of the mouth) of a child under 13 will be automatically classified as rape, with a maximum penalty of life in prison" (British Home Office, 2004, p. 4). The Act also criminalized engaging in sexual activity in the presence of a child, causing a child to watch a sexual act, and meeting a child following sexual grooming including communication by phone or Internet (National Policing Improvement Agency, 2011).

Under the Sexual Offences Act of 2003, as under the National Sex Offender Act of 1997, all sex offenders who were convicted for relevant sex offenses or who committed the relevant sex offenses but were found not guilty by reason of insanity and who were cautioned by law enforcement with respect to such offenses are required to register. The 2003 Act made an indefinite period of registration mandatory for those who are sentenced to imprisonment for life; 10 years of registration for those who received imprisonment of more than 6 months but less than 30 months; and 7 years of registration for those who received imprisonment of 6 months or less. The 2003 Act also made a provision of dual criminality. It made registration and notification mandatory for those who were convicted of the relevant offenses both at home and abroad. Under the Sex Offender Registration Act of 1997, registered sex offenders were required to report name and/or address changes within 14 days. Under the Sexual Offences Act of 2003, they are required to report name and/or address changes in 3 days and changes in residence in 7 days. Under the 2003 Act, all registered sex offenders must notify law enforcement if they plan to stay overseas more than 3 days. The Act also introduced three different kinds of notification orders: prevention orders, harm orders, and foreign travel orders. The prevention orders "allow the courts to impose prohibitions on sexual and violent offenders who pose a risk of serious sexual harm" (British Home Office, 2004, p. 9), whereas the harm orders are introduced to "prevent anyone from sexual conduct or communication" (British Home Office, 2004, p. 9). The foreign travel orders ban travel by putting a ban on "people who have committed an offense against a child from traveling abroad where there is a risk of serious harm to children overseas" (British Home Office, 2004, p. 9). The failure to comply with the above registration and notification provisions is also defined as a crime under the 2003 Act and is punishable with a maximum penalty of 5-year incarceration.

The Violent Crime Reduction Act of 2006 gave "new powers for the police to enter and search the house of a person on the sex offender 'register' in order to assess the risk they might pose by way of reoffending" (Davidson, 2009, p. 4). The Sex Offender Registration Act of 1997 and the Sexual Offences Act of 2003 created a system of registration for sex offenders in the United Kingdom. They did not, however, develop a system of community notification of sex offenders like that of Megan's Law in the United States. This was first introduced in the United Kingdom with the enactment of Sarah's Law in 2008. Eight-year-old Sarah Payne of Sussex was kidnapped, sexually assaulted, and murdered in 2000 by a convicted sex offender named Roy Whiting. Sarah's Law established a community notification system of sex offenders for parents, neighbors, and related law enforcement agencies. Under Sarah's Law, "parents can ask the police about anyone with access to their children. After investigating their concerns, officers will reveal details confidentially only if they think it is in the child's interest" (Hughes, 2010, p. 2).

In 2008, Sarah's Law was introduced in four pilot areas in England and Wales: Cambridgeshire, Cleveland, Hampshire, and Warwickshire. In 2010, the plan was extended to 18 more areas. In 2011, Sarah's Law became a national plan of community notification of sex offenders in the United Kingdom (see **Box 5-3**). One of the policy strategies that is becoming increasingly popular is the development of a national sex offender registration system for long-term tracking of sex offenders.

In addition to the United States, Canada, and the United Kingdom, Australia introduced a national system of sex offender registration system, the Australian National Child Offender Register, in 2005. The National Police Agency of Japan has also established a program on developing a national watch list of child sex offenders, and New Zealand established a national sex offender registration system in 2003. A survey shows that about 97% of the members of the European Parliament are in favor of a European Union–wide sex offender registration and tracking system (BBC News, 2011). Sex offender registration and notification strategies, however, are not the same in all countries. In the United States, the system

BOX 5-3

David Cameron Condemns Supreme Court Ruling on Sex Offenders

In April 2010, the Supreme Court of the United Kingdom ruled that the United Kingdom's policy of life-long registration of some categories of sex offenders without any possibility of review is a violation of the European Convention on Human Rights, particularly the right of respect for private and family life. The present legislation related to sex offender registration in the United Kingdom includes a provision that sex offenders who receive a prison term of more than 30 months will have to remain registered for life and inform the police of their changes of address and when they travel abroad. "The supreme court ruling said the 24,000 people on the sex offender register in England and Wales had a right to a review of whether they should continue to be 'labeled for life' by being kept on the register indefinitely. The judges based their decision on Home Office evidence that 75% of sex offenders who were monitored for 21 years were not reconvicted of any further offence." David Cameron, the present Prime Minister of England, condemns the Supreme Court ruling and said that the parliament and the courts should make laws, and the rights of people should get prominence over the rights of criminals. In order to comply with the Supreme Court decision, the British Home Office decided that sex offenders could apply for review 15 years after serving their time in prison.

Source: Travis, A. (2011, February 16). David Cameron condemns supreme court ruling on sex offenders. *The Guardian.* Retrieved from http://www.guardian.co.uk/society/2011/feb/16/david-cameron-condemns-court-sex-offenders.

is more expansive and pervasive than in Canada and in the United Kingdom (see **Table 5-3**). It is only in the United States that the public has free access to sex offender information. In Canada, the sex offender database is only for law enforcement and related agencies. In the United Kingdom, according to Sarah's Law, if one wants access to the sex offender database, he or she will have to make an application to relevant law enforcement agencies. In Australia, the sex offender database is for the use of law enforcement agencies alone. In addition to the United States, Canada, the United Kingdom, and Australia, sex offender registration laws are also developing in many other countries, particularly in the European Union. A recent survey "found 84% of MPs [of the European Union] agreed that sex offenders should be tracked across Europe and forced to register with local police" (Davidson, 2009, p. 8). Criminalization of child abuse in general and child sexual abuse in particular is thus increasingly becoming a global trend (BBC News, 2011).

■ Summary

There are four different systems of criminal justice among the world's societies: modern, modernizing, traditional, and dual. The modern system of criminal justice has evolved

TABLE 5-3 Sex Offender Registration and Notification Systems in the United States, Canada, and the United Kingdom: A Comparative Look

Policy Strategies	United States	Canada	United Kingdom
Registration requirement	All sex offenders: violent and nonviolent/adult and juvenile; sex offenders who committed sex offenses overseas; persons convicted of production, possession, and distribution of child pornography.	Only for convicted dangerous or designated adult sex offenders; sex offenders who are certified by the court to comply with the Sex Offender Information Registration Act.	Violent and nonviolent adult and juvenile convicted sex offenders; offenders found not guilty by reason of insanity; offenders who are cautioned; and offenders who committed sex offenses overseas.
Reporting for registration	Mandatory registration before the completion of prison term; and reporting no later than 5 days after a sentencing of life imprisonment.	Bill C-16 requires the court to make an order for registration (notification) on application of the prosecutor. Registration is mandatory within 15 days after receiving the notification.	Registration is initiated by law enforcement agencies by receiving a court order (notification); and reporting is mandatory for a sex offender within 3 days after receiving notification (Sexual Offences Act of 2003).
Registration period	Life-term registration for Tier III sex offenders (dangerous and sexual predators); 25 years for Tier II sex offenders; and 15 years for Tier I sex offenders (nonfelony; Adam Walsh Act of 2006).	Lifetime registration for repeat offenders; 20 years for offenses carrying 10–14 years in prison; and 10 years for offenses carrying 2–5 years in prison (National Sex Offender Registry Act of 2004).	Indefinite period for sex offenders who received life imprisonment and sex offenders found guilty by reason of insanity; 10 years for offenses carrying 6–30 months in prison; and 7 years for offenses carrying less than 6 months in prison.
Registration information for sex offender database	DNA; fingerprints; photographs; date of birth; name and home address; Social Security number; vehicle registration number; driver's license number; employment information; and school information.	Name and date of birth; permanent and temporary home addresses; photographs; fingerprints; employment information; and school information.	Photograph, fingerprints, date of birth, name and permanent home address; address of temporary residence (lived at least 7 days); national insurance number; passport information; and foreign travel information.
Community notification and public access to sex offender database	Accessible to all through state web-based community notification systems and a centralized web-based notification system; and the National Sex Offender Registry is managed by the FBI (Megan's Law of 1996 and the Adam Walsh Act [2006]).	Accessible only by accredited law enforcement agencies; the Act of 2004 stated that while rehabilitating the sex offenders and reintegrating them into the community, their privacy interests must be respected and protected.	Accessible by multiple agencies including law enforcement, childcare agencies, transportation department, and border patrol; and public access on the basis of application to law enforcement justifying the need for access to information (Sarah's Law).

within the framework of the modern state and democracy in the West. Its basic philosophy is based on principles of the rule of law, due process of law, and respect for universal human rights. In societies with modern criminal justice systems, there are constitutional protections against unreasonable search and seizure, self-incrimination, and cruel and unusual punishment. The separation of powers and the independence of the judiciary in modern systems of criminal justice limit the power of the executive to deny individual rights, freedom, privacy, and demand for equal justice and equal treatment under the law. The modern systems of criminal justice are based on secular laws, some that historically came from English common law and Napoleonic or Germanic civil law traditions. In most of the modern criminal justice systems, however, legislative or statutory criminal laws are increasingly replacing the traditional criminal codes that came from the English common law and the civil law traditions.

The second type of criminal justice system can be called modernizing systems—systems that are in process of change and reforms for modernity in criminal justice. Most of the societies of Asia, Africa, and Latin America have modernizing systems of criminal justice. One of the defining characteristics of the countries with modernizing systems is that they do not have any strong indigenous legal traditions or religious traditions of law and justice that are sharply in conflict with the fundamental values and institutions of modern criminal justice. Most of the modernizing systems are in those countries that were under Western colonial rule for centuries, and where some of the basic institutions of modern criminal justice such as a modern secular legal tradition, structure of policing and law enforcement, structure of judiciary, prisons, and legal education were created by the colonial governments. In the countries with modernizing systems, the strategic societal elites and political leadership are open to the West and seek to pursue modern reforms in criminal justice.

The third type—a traditional system of criminal justice—is found in those societies that are deliberately opposed to the values and institutions of modern criminal justice. Traditional systems are dominant mostly in the Islamic monarchies and theocracies of the Middle East that are opposed to the values of democracy, secularization, separation of power, and due process of law. In traditional systems, criminal law is predominantly based on religious texts and scriptures. The process of criminalization and decriminalization is defined by the boundaries of religious law and morality. In traditional systems, the crime rate is generally low because of a culture of fear about police torture and unusual punishment such as public execution, banishment, and decapitation. The dominant perspective of understanding of crime in those systems is still the medieval perspective of demonology and the inviolable connection between crime and sin. Saudi Arabia and Iran are two of the classic examples of countries that have deliberately protected a system of traditional criminal justice.

The fourth type—a dualistic system of criminal justice—is found in those countries where there are deliberate political and governmental efforts to combine modern institutions of criminal justice with those of religious or indigenous traditions of law and justice. Some of the countries that have dualistic systems of criminal justice include Pakistan (modern law and Islamic Shari'a law), Malaysia (modern law and Islamic Shari'a law), Nigeria (modern law and Islamic Shari'a law), China (modern law, socialist law, and Confucian social and political traditions), and Russia (socialist law and modern law). Most of the dualistic systems of criminal justice are characterized by political conflicts and tensions with respect to adherence to the values and principles of modern democratic polity and governance.

The countries of the West with modern systems of criminal justice have varied systems of legal traditions (English common law and civil law traditions); different forms of constitutions (written in the United States and unwritten in the United Kingdom); different types of governments (presidential versus parliamentary forms); different types of courts and judicial systems (adversarial versus inquisitorial systems); and different ways of organizing policing and law enforcement (FBI in the United States versus the Royal Canadian Mounted Police versus Scotland Yard in the United Kingdom). They are, however, largely similar in terms of the basic foundations of modern criminal justice—the centrality of the rule of law, dominance of the due process of law, and constitutional guarantee of the right to life, liberty, and property. There are also some homogenizing trends in policy making for crime control in countries with modern systems of criminal justice. Policing, for example, is becoming increasingly formalized and professionalized, and it is being increasingly integrated with modern information technology, biotechnology, and the technology of global positioning systems. This is evidenced in the development of high-tech policing in the United States and the increasing integration of policing and information and communication technology in the countries of the European Union. There are also efforts to strike a balance between formal and informal strategies of policing. This is evidenced from reforms for decentralized and neighborhood policing in the United Kingdom and centralized and super policing in Germany.

Similarly, there are many homogenizing trends in the way criminal laws are evolving in the countries with modern systems of criminal justice. One of the areas is the criminalization of child sexual abuse. During the last 3 decades, new laws and policy strategies have evolved in all modern systems of criminal justice to control and criminalize child sexual abuse. In addition to developing laws for mandatory sentencing and enhanced penalties for child sexual abuse, many countries have developed laws for mandatory sex offender registration and notification. In the United States, this is evidenced by the Jacob Wetterling Crimes Against Children and Sexually Violent Offenders Act of 1994; Megan's Law of 1996; the Pam Lychner Sexual Offender Tracking and Identification Act of 1996; the Child Pornography Prevention Act of 1996 (CPPA); the Protection of Children From Sexual Predators Act of 1998; the Children's Internet Protection Act of 2000 (CIPA); the Victims of Trafficking and Violence Protection Act of 2000; Aimee's Law of 2000; the PROTECT Act of 2003; the Children Safety Act of 2005; and the Adam Walsh Child Protection and Safety Act of 2006. In Canada, this trend of criminalizing child sexual abuse is evidenced by the Criminal Law Amendment Act of 1997, the Sex Offender Information Registration Act of 2004, and the enactment of Christopher's Law in Ontario in 2000. Outside the United States, one of the most wide-ranging sex offender registration and notification systems is found in the United

Kingdom. The United Kingdom's sex offender registration and notification system is based on three statutory provisions: the Sex Offender Registration Act of 1997, the Sexual Offences Act of 2003, and Sarah's Law of 2008. Sex offender registration and notification strategies, however, are not the same in all countries. In the United States, the system is more expansive and pervasive than in Canada and the United Kingdom. It is only in the United States, that the public has free access to sex offender information through the Internet. In Canada, the sex offender database is only for law enforcement and related agencies. In the United Kingdom, according to Sarah's Law, if one wants to have access to the sex offender database, he or she will have to make an application to relevant law enforcement agencies.

■ Discussion Questions

1. What are the different types of criminal justice systems? Why is such a typology significant for comparative criminal justice? Give examples.

2. How is a modernizing system of criminal justice different from a traditional system of criminal justice? What are the defining characteristics of these two competing systems of criminal justice? Identify some of the countries that are pursuing modernization in criminal justice and some that are deliberately opposed to modernization.

3. How is a dualistic system of criminal justice different from a modern system of criminal justice? Name some of the countries that are deliberately attempting to combine modernity and tradition in reforming criminal justice. What are the larger political, social, and ideological contexts that drive the reforms for a dualistic system of criminal justice? Give examples.

4. How are some of the core institutions of criminal justice such as law, policing, and courts organized in a modern system of criminal justice, and how are they different from those of a traditional system of criminal justice? Comment on the evolution and the sources of secular law in modern criminal justice in the West.

5. What is the status of the rise of high-tech policing in the United States? How is high-tech policing fundamentally changing the nature of and the perception about policing in modern societies? Make a comment in this context on the rise and nature of predictive policing in America.

6. Describe the recent laws and legislation adopted for the development of decentralized and neighborhood policing in the United Kingdom. How is the United Kingdom's approach to decentralized policing different from the strategy of community policing in the United States and the emerging notion of super policing in Germany?

7. In many countries in the West, there are some similar trends in the development of criminal laws related to a variety of criminal justice areas such as sex crimes, juvenile justice, DNA laws, drug laws, and cyber crime. Describe in this context the rise of a new generation of sex offender registration laws in the United States, Canada, and the United Kingdom. How is Megan's Law of the United States similar to or different from Sarah's Law of the United Kingdom?

References

BBC News. (2011). *MEPs 'want EU sex offender list.'* Retrieved from http://news.bbc.co.uk/2/hi /uk_news/6958807.stm.

Boba, R. (2005). *Crime analysis and crime mapping.* Thousand Oaks, CA: Sage Publications.

Bonta J., & Yessine, A. K. (2008). *The national flagging system: Identifying and responding to high-risk, violent offenders, 2004-2005.* Ottawa , Ontario: Public Safety Canada.

British Home Office. (2004). *Children and families: Safer from sexual crime—The Sexual Offence Act of 2003.* London, England: Author.

British Home Office. (2010). *Policing in the 21st century: Reconnecting police and people.* London, England: Author.

Brown, T. M. L., McCabe, S. A., & Wellford, C. (2007). *Global technology system (GPS) for community supervision: Lessons learned.* Washington, DC: Department of Justice, National Institute of Justice.

Bundeskriminalamt. (2009). *The* Bundeskriminalamt: *Facts and figures 2009.* Retrieved from www .bka.de/nn_194538/EN/TheBKA/FactsAndFigures/factsFigures__node.html?__nnn=true.

Bundeskriminalamt. (2012). *The* Bundeskriminalamt: *Our mandate.* Retrieved from www.bka.de /nn_194538/EN/TheBKA/OurMandate/ourMandate__node.html?__nnn=true.

Bureau of Justice Statistics. (2007). *Census of state and local law enforcement agencies, 2004.* Washington, DC: Department of Justice, BJS.

CBC News. (2007). *Anti-terrorism Act.* Retrieved from www.cbc.ca/news/background/cdnsecurity

Charkaoui v. Canada (Citizenship and Immigration), 2007 SCC 9, [2007] 1 S.C.R. 350.

Davidson, J. (2009). *Sex offender registration: A review of practice in the United Kingdom, Europe and North America* (Hallman Center for Community Justice Briefing Paper). Retrieved from www .shu.ac.uk/_assets/pdf/hccj-SexOffenderRegBriefPaper.pdf.

Devon County Council. (2011). *Sex Offender Act of 1997.* Retrieved from www.devon.gov.uk/cp -sec-6-10.htm.

European Commission. (2006). *Shaping Europe's future through ICT* (report from the Information Society Technologies Advisory Group). Brussels, Belgium: Author.

European Commission. (2011). *ICT trends in European policing.* Brussels, Belgium: Author.

Garmin Limited. (2011). *What is GPS?* Olathe, Kansas: Garmin Ltd.

Giardino, A. P. (2012). Child sexual abuse. *Medscape Reference.* Retrieved from http://emedicine .medscape.com/article/915841-overview.

Greene, J. R. (2000). Community policing in America: Changing nature, structure, and function of police. In J. Horney (Ed.), *Criminal justice: Policies, processes, and decisions of the criminal justice system* (Vol. 3, pp. 299–370). Washington, DC: Department of Justice.

Halpern v. Canada (Attorney general), 2003 CanLII 26403 (ON CA).

Hardy, E. (2010). Data-driven policing: How geographic analysis can reduce social harm. *Geography Public Safety, 2*(3), 1–5.

Harries, K., for the National Institute of Justice. (1999). *Mapping crime: Principle and practice.* Washington, DC: Department of Justice.

Hughes, M. (2010, March 3). Sarah's Law to be rolled out nationally. *The Independent.* Retrieved from www.independent.co.uk/news/uk/crime/sarahs-law-to-be-rolled-out-nationally-1914989.html.

Johnson, R. J. (2008). Advances in understanding and treating childhood sexual abuse: Implications for research and policy. *Family and Community Health, 31*(1), 24–31.

Keiper, L. (2011). *More states use familial DNA as powerful forensic search tool.* Retrieved from www .reuters.com/article/2011/03/30/us-crime-dna-familial-idUSTRE72T2QS20110330.

McLachlin, B. (2009). The challenge of fighting terrorism while maintaining our civil liberties. Retrieved from www.biicl.org/files/4778_ottawa_wcc.pdf.

Metropolitan Police. (2011). *About the Metropolitan Police Service.* Retrieved from www.met.police.uk/about/.

Ministry of Public Safety. (2011). *National sex offender registry.* Ottawa, Canada: Author.

Mueller, R., Jr. (2009). *Federal Bureau of Investigation: Statement before the Senate Committee on Appropriations, Subcommittee on Commerce, Justice, Science, and related agencies.* Washington, DC: United States Senate.

National Institute of Justice. (1998). *The evolution and development of police technology (A technical report prepared by SEASKATE Inc.).* Washington, DC: Department of Justice.

National Institute of Justice. (2010). *High-priority technology needs 2010.* Washington, DC: Department of Justice.

National Institute of Justice. (2011). *MAPS: How mapping helps reduce crime and improve public safety.* Retrieved from www.nij.gov/maps.

National Policing Improvement Agency. (2008). *Neighborhood policing: The impact of piloting and early national implementation.* London, England: The British Home office.

National Policing Improvement Agency. (2011). *Dangerous persons database—VISOR.* Retrieved from www.npia.police.uk/en/10510.htm

National Public Radio. (2010). *'Grim Sleeper' case brings familial DNA to fore.* Retrieved from http://minnesota.publicradio.org/features/npr.php?id=128495083.

Navalta, C. P., Polcari, N., Webster, D. M., Boghossian, A., & Teicher, M. H. (2006). Effects of childhood sexual abuse on neuropsychological and cognitive function in college women. *The Journal of Neuropsychiatry and Clinical Neurosciences, 18*, 45–53.

Omnilink Systems. (2011). *GPS for criminal justice: Offender monitoring.* Retrieved from www.omnilink.com/Omnilink_Solutions/CriminalJustice/CriminalJustice.html.

Osborne, D. (2006). UN report uncovers global child sexual abuse. *The Independent* (October 12). Retrieved from www.independent.cp.uk.

Parliament of Canada. (2012). *A criminal code definition of "terrorist."* Retrieved from www.parl.gc.ca/HousePublications/Redirector.aspx?File=15.

Paun, C. (2007). *Democratization and police reform* (Master's thesis). Berlin, Germany: Free University of Berlin.

Pinheiro, P. S. (2006). *World report on violence against children.* Geneva, Switzerland: United Nations Organization.

Polis: Policing OnLine Information System. (2011). *Policing profiles of participating and partner states: Germany.* Retrieved from www.polis.osce.org/countries/details.

Putnam, F. W. (2003). Ten-year research update review: Childhood sexual abuse. *Journal of the American Academy of Child and Adolescent Psychiatry, 42*(3), 269–278.

R. v. Morgentaler, [1988] 1 S.C.R. 30.

Roberts, D. J. (2011). Technology is playing an expanding role in policing. *The Police Chief, 78,* 72–73.

Roe v. Wade, 410 U.S. 113 (1973).

Shahidullah, S. M. (2006, February–March). *DNA, juvenile offenders and the changing contours of juvenile justice.* Paper presented at the annual meeting of the Academy of Criminal Justice Sciences, Baltimore, MD.

Shahidullah, S. M. (2008). *Crime policy in America: Laws, institutions, programs.* Lanham, MD: University Press of America.

Shaw, M., Van Dijk, J., & Rhomberg, W. (2003). Determining trends in global crime and justice: An overview of results from the United Nations Survey of Crime Trends and Operations of Criminal Justice Systems. *Forum on Crime and Society, 3*(1), 35–63.

Spiegel Online International. (2010, December 10). *The worlds from Berlin: Streamlined federal police would be no "German FBI."* Retrieved from www.spiegel.de/international/germany /0,1518,733962,00.html.

Stoltenborgh M., van Ijzendoorn M. H., Euser, E. M., & Bakermans-Kranenburg, M. J. (2011). A global perspective on child sexual abuse: Meta-analysis of prevalence around the world. *Child Maltreatment, 16*(2), 79–101.

Stone, C., & Travis J. (2011, March). *Toward a new professionalism in policing* (NCJ 232359). Washington, DC: National Institute of Justice and the Harvard Kennedy School.

Stop Child Predators. (2007). *Constitutionality of GPS tracking of convicted sex offenders.* Retrieved from www.stopchildpredators.org/pdf/SCP_PR041707.pdf.

Suter, S. M. (2010). All in the family: Privacy and DNA familial searching. *Harvard Journal of Law and Technology, 23*(2), 310–398.

Uchida, C. D. (2009). *A national discussion on predictive policing: Defining our terms and mapping successful implementation strategies* (discussion paper). Washington, DC: National Institute of Justice.

United States Government Accountability Office. (2010). *Federal law enforcement retirement.* Washington, DC: Government Printing Office.

Victims of Violence. (2008). *Research: Dangerous offenders.* Ottawa, Canada: Author.

Weisburd, D., & Lum, C. (2005). The diffusion of computerized crime mapping in policing: Linking research and practice. *Police Practice and Research, 6*(5), 419–434.

Weisburd, D., & Neyroud, P. (2011). *Police science: Towards a new paradigm* (NCJ 228922). Washington, DC: National Institute of Justice and Harvard Kennedy School.

Wieland, S. (2008). *The United States: Prostitution and trafficking.* Jsassn International. Retrieved from www.jsassn.wordpress.com/report-prostitution-and-trafficking-in-the-us/.

World Health Organization. (2002). *The world health report 2002: Reducing risks, promoting healthy life.* Geneva, Switzerland: Author.

Wortley, R., & Smallbone, S. (2006). *The problem of internet child pornography.* Center for Problem-Oriented Policing. Retrieved from www.popcenter.org/problems/child_pornography/.

Emerging Trends in Law and Sentencing: The United States, the United Kingdom, Canada, and Australia

CHAPTER

6

▶ CHAPTER OUTLINE

Introduction

New Penology and New Sentencing Laws and Trends in the United States
The Politics of Crime Control in the United States
New Penology and New Sentencing Laws in the United States

New Penology and New Sentencing Laws and Trends in Canada
The Politics of Crime Control in Canada
New Penology and New Sentencing Laws in Canada

New Penology and New Sentencing Laws and Trends in the United Kingdom
The Politics of Crime Control in the United Kingdom
New Penology and New Sentencing Laws in the United Kingdom

New Penology and New Sentencing Laws and Trends in Australia
The Politics of Crime Control in Australia
New Penology and New Sentencing Laws in Australia

Summary

Discussion Questions

References

■ Introduction

The profile of modern criminal justice in the countries of the West is characterized by a series of institutions developed for the humanization of crime control and punishment. The due process of law and constitutional right of protections against unreasonable search and seizure, self-incrimination, and cruel and unusual punishment brought the spirit of modernity to the core of criminal justice. The secularization of law and justice brought about a permanent divide between modern and

221

medieval systems of crime control and punishment. The growth of modern prisons, innovation of alternative sentencing through probation and parole, development of prison-based education and treatment, reentry initiatives, and changes in a number of other areas have vastly modernized criminal justice in the West over the last 200 years. In all countries of the West, criminology has rapidly advanced and brought many new theories and approaches related to crime and criminality.

Since the beginning of the 1970s, a new perspective on crime control and punishment, however, began to dominate criminal justice in the West. Many describe the emerging trend as one that is fundamentally different from that of the 19th and early 20th centuries. The shift has been occurring neither in the domain of the due process of law, nor in the domain of the secularization of law and justice. It is rather more in the areas of crime control and punishment. During the last 4 decades, this new perspective and the new movement in criminal justice has generated an enormous amount of literature and has been described in many terms, such as the rise of the *new penology* (Simon & Feeley, 1995), the rise of a *culture of control* (Garland, 2001), the growth of *harsh justice* (Whitman, 2003), the emergence of a *new punitiveness* (Pratt, Brown, Brown, Hallsworth, & Morrison, 2005), the *race to incarcerate* (Mauer, 2006), and *governing through crime* (Simon, 2007). These are commonly known as the get-tough strategies of crime control and punishment (Shahidullah, 2002). The ideas and strategies of crime control and punishment and the new penology are fundamentally different from those of the old or the progressive penology of the 19th century. The rise of the new penology is commonly associated with the rise and dominance of conservative politics in Western democracies since the 1970s, particularly in the United States. The new penology movement evolved and its theories matured in America during the 1970s and 1980s, and then it began to engulf criminal justice in the rest of the West. In cross-national analyses of criminal justice in the countries of the West, and between the countries of the West and East, understanding how this new penology movement has been shaping the nature and strategies of crime control and punishment is tremendously important.

The spread of the new penology's philosophy has brought some fundamental changes to the understanding of crime and criminality, the extension of control and punishment, and governing of crime and justice in modern societies. Progressive penology was based on the social and individual roots of crime. New penology looks at crime as a systemic problem related to the failure of the criminal justice system. "The language of the new penology is anchored in the discourse of systemic analysis and operation research. It conceives of crime as a systemic phenomenon and crime policy as a problem of actuarial risk management" (Simon & Feeley, 1995, p. 148). Progressive penology's central goal was the transformation of individuals. "New Penology reveals a shift away from the objective of transforming individuals. It embraces a new objective: risk management and the management of the system itself" (Simon & Feeley, 1995, p. 148). One of the central notions in the new penology is that a highly organized, professionalized, and science- and technology-driven system of criminal justice is a precondition for the maintenance of law and order under modernity. The societies under modernity are characterized by organized complexity, diversity, and anonymity, and by unbounded growth of risk and uncertainty. The advocates of new penology therefore argue that in governing crime and justice in modern societies, more attention should be given not to offender rehabilitation, but to development and growth of an efficient system of criminal justice. The modern system of governance of crime and justice must be innovative, knowledge-driven, and proactive, but it must not be in violation of the due process of law and the spirit of modernity in law and justice. Many criminologists have argued that a bureaucratized and specialized system of criminal justice has been growing from the beginning of the rise of modernity and modern states. The idea that the new penology is more concerned with systematic rationality is not something fundamentally new (Dumm, 1987; Foucault, 1977; Garland, 1995). Since the beginning of modernization in the 19th century, the control and regulation of crime and punishment have become a formally differentiated sector of bureaucratic activity. "Historical work makes it clear that these modern arrangements were put in place comparatively recently, and in fact the movement toward systemic differentiation and professionalization continues today" (Garland, 1995, p. 185).

The progressive penology was based on an explanation of the social and economic roots of crime. The new penology does not actively participate in this discourse on the origin of crime. "It is agnostic about the causes of crime," according to Simon and Feeley (1995, p. 164). Two of the most provocative theories supporting the idea of agnosticism about the causes of crime and criminal behavior came from James Q. Wilson and Richard J. Herrnstein's (1985) *Crime and Human Nature: The Definitive Study of the Causes of Crime* and Jack Katz's (1988) *Seductions of Crime: Moral and Sensual Attractions In Doing Evil*. Wilson and Herrnstein claimed that crime cannot be explained by social factors alone, arguing that "the consequences of committing the crime consist of rewards and punishments; the consequences of not committing the crime also entail gains and losses" (1985, p. 44). Thus, crime is a function of choice. Katz presented a similar thesis about crime and criminality. "I propose," he said, "that empirical research turn the direction of inquiry around to focus initially on the foreground, rather than the background of crime" (1988, p. 4). In his view, we can understand, and perhaps control, crime more if we seek to advance our knowledge of how crime is constructed by criminals—what attractions, interests, ideas, fantasies, beauty, and sensibilities entice individuals into the domain of crime and criminality. Some advocates of the new penology, particularly those who come from a conservative political ideology, believe that it is not economic poverty but moral poverty that is at the root of escalating crime and violence in modern societies (Bennett, DiIulio, & Walter, 1996; Bork, 1996). Moral poverty is the "poverty of being without loving, capable, responsible adults who teach the young right from wrong. It is the poverty of growing up in the virtual absence of people who teach the lessons by their own everyday example" (Bennett et al., 1996, pp. 13–14). Furthermore, "it is the poverty of growing up surrounded by deviant, delinquent, and criminal adults in a practically criminogenic environment" (Bennett et al., 1996, pp. 13–14).

The advocates of new penology discovered the centrality of the concept of career criminals for crime control and prevention. "The idea of the career criminal is one of the most appealing representations preferred by the new penology. It offers a picture of the crime problem as rooted in the conduct of a small and specifiable subpopulation" (Simon & Feeley, 1995, p. 164). Crime can be significantly controlled, the advocates of new penology believe, if the career criminals of a society are incapacitated through long-term imprisonment and lifelong surveillance. One of the critical features of progressive penology was its reliance on discretion and individualized justice. The new penology advocates the notion of systemic rationality on the basis of determinate sentencing, institutionalization, and judicial control. During the last 4 decades of the expansion of new penology in policy making for crime and justice in the United States, a number of sentencing and correctional innovations have been made that have vastly transformed the country's criminal justice system. Some of these innovations include the enactment of mandatory minimum sentencing laws, truth-in-sentencing laws; juvenile transfer laws; laws for mandatory extraction of DNA from violent sexual offenders and violent criminals; Rockefeller drug laws (15 years to life in prison for selling 2 ounces of heroin or morphine); Jessica's Law (mandatory prison term of 25 years plus lifelong GPS tracking for sex crimes with children below the age of 12 in Florida); Megan's Law (mandatory sex offender community notification); Project Exile (treating gun crimes as federal crimes); three strikes laws; felony disenfranchisement (denial of voting rights for convicted offenders); and expansion of supermax prisons (Shahidullah, 2008). The expansion of new penology brought similar innovations in Canada, the United Kingdom and other countries of the European Union, Australia, and New Zealand. To provide a comparative understanding of the effect of new penology across the modern criminal justice systems of the West, the following sections will examine the mandatory minimum sentencing laws in the United States, Canada, the United Kingdom, and Australia.

■ New Penology and New Sentencing Laws and Trends in the United States

In the United States, the new penology came to dominate the agenda for policy making in crime control after President Nixon's inauguration in 1969. Nixon took office in the context both the escalation of the Cold War abroad and turmoil at home. "The rise of the civil rights movement, women's movement, sexual revolution, and counterculture in the 1960s created an enormous sense of complexity, uncertainty, and confusion in America's domestic politics" (Shahidullah, 2008, p. 12). In the 1960s, crime and violence rapidly spread across the nation. The 1960s saw four major assassinations in America: John F. Kennedy in 1963, Malcolm X in 1965, Martin Luther King Jr. in 1968, and Robert Kennedy in 1968. The urban murder rate in the early 1960s was 4.7 per 100,000 population (Shahidullah, 2008). By 1970, the rate had increased to 8.3 per 100,000 population. The rate of forcible rape per 100,000 population in 1960 was 17, but it had increased to 38 by 1970. Between 1962 and 1963, the national crime rate increased 9%. Between 1958 and 1963, the crime rate increased five times faster than the population growth. During the same period, street robbery increased 22%. In 1963, 400,000 cars worth about $369 million were stolen, and more than 2 million crimes were reported to law enforcement (Uniform Crime Reports, 1963). From the middle of the 1960s to the end of the 1970s, the homicide rate in America doubled (Uniform Crime Reports, 2003).

The Politics of Crime Control in the United States

In his acceptance speech delivered before the Republican National Convention on August 8, 1968, Nixon said, "The American Revolution was and is dedicated to progress. But our founders recognized that the first requisite of progress is order" (Nixon, 1968, p. 1). In that speech, Nixon declared " a war against organized crime." He said, "The wave of crime is not going to be the wave of the future in the United States of America" (Nixon, 1968, p. 1). Immediately after taking office, "Nixon created an inner circle crime policy team at the White House" (Shahidullah, 2008, p. 13). Nixon's crime policy team developed a new vision for the whole system of law enforcement, courts, prisons, and punishment. "The metaphor of the 'war on poverty' of the previous administration was replaced by a new metaphor of the 'war on crime' or more specifically the 'war on drugs' under the Nixon presidency" (Shahidullah, 2008, p. 13). Nixon's key crime policy initiatives included drugs and organized crime. He signed "three major crime bills: the Organized Crime Control Act of 1969, the Omnibus Crime Control Act of 1970, and the Comprehensive Drug Abuse Prevention and Control Act of 1970" (Shahidullah, 2008, p. 13).

In the two presidencies after Nixon—those of Gerald Ford (1974–1977) and Jimmy Carter (1977–1981)—"crime was not high on the agenda for policy-making. President Ford and President Carter had neither the commitment for reform in criminal justice nor strong ideological support for Nixon's war on drugs" (Shahidullah, 2008, p. 13). Nixon's vision and commitment to a get-tough activist policy on crime and justice returned after President Reagan was inaugurated in 1981. During his presidency, Reagan "signed five major crime Bills passed by Congress: the Comprehensive Crime Control Act of 1984, Sentencing Reform Act of 1984, National Narcotics Leadership Act of 1984, Anti-Drug Abuse Act of 1986, and Anti-Drug Abuse Act of 1988" (Shahidullah, 2008, p. 14). Reagan, like Nixon, "deeply believed and theorized that the war on crime and the war on drugs are essentially a culture war. Crime is essentially a moral problem . . . morality must be judicially enforced and strengthened" (Shahidullah, 2008, p. 14).

America's new penology movement in crime and justice further expanded during the subsequent presidencies of George H. W. Bush (1989–1993), William J. Clinton (1993–2001), and George W. Bush (2001–2009). George H. W. Bush continued to pursue the Reagan legacy in crime policy—the war on drugs, mandatory sentencing, more incarceration, more conservative judges in federal courts, and a moral crusade for the revitalization of family values. During his presidency, George H. W. Bush signed two major executive orders related to crime policy; one of them was related to the President's Drug Advisory Council. The major crime bill he signed was the Comprehensive Crime Control Act of 1990 (Shahidullah, 2008).

When President Clinton took office, there was a shift in American politics, after about 2 decades, from a conservative to a liberal ideology. However, America's crime policy continued to expand under the philosophy of the new penology. Clinton "subscribed to the view that violent crime is the function of a small group of career criminals, and the policy of incapacitation through punishment and imprisonment is the best way to deal with them" (Shahidullah, 2008, p. 17). The Violent Crime Control and Law Enforcement Act of 1994 signed by President Clinton "tightened the truth-in-sentencing requirements, mandated life imprisonment for repeat violent offenders (three-strikes law), banned 19 types of semiautomatic assault weapons, banned the ownership of handguns by juveniles, [and] mandated Megan's Law for state and local law enforcement agencies" (Shahidullah, 2008, p. 17). The act also "approved additional penalties for hate crimes and extended the death penalty to about sixty different types of federal crimes" (Shahidullah, 2008, p. 17). Clinton, through his Violent Crime Control and Law Enforcement Act of 1994 and other legislation, "wanted to create a new blended approach to crime control by combining the conservative and liberal approaches to crime and justice. He was passionately involved in expanding the Reagan legacy of a get tough approach to crime and justice" (Shahidullah, 2008, p. 18); but he also "deeply believed that crime control policies must be ultimately based on economic growth and the expansion of economic benefits and opportunities to all groups and classes of people (Shahidullah, 2008, p. 18). As he once said, "we simply cannot jail our way out of America's crime problem. We are going to have to invest some more money in prevention" (Clinton, 1996, p. 3). Clinton "took a part of the philosophy of new penology—the punishment approach—but left the question of crime and morality largely untouched" (Shahidullah, 2008, p. 18).

George W. Bush, after assuming the presidency in 2001, "brought the issues of both punishment and morality again to the center of policy-making and policy discourses in crime and justice" (Shahidullah, 2008, p. 19). Some of the major crime legislation signed by President George W. Bush included the USA Patriot Act (Uniting and Strengthening America by Providing Appropriate Tools Required to Intercept and Obstruct Terrorism Act) of 2001, the Cyber Crime Security Enhancement Act of 2002, the Illegal Drug Proliferation Act of 2003, the PROTECT Act (Prosecutorial Remedies and Other Tools to End the Exploitation of Children Today Act) of 2003, the Unborn Victims of Violence Act of 2004, the Violence Against Women Act of 2005, and the Adam Walsh Child Protection Act of 2006. These acts created a new category of federal crimes, increased penalties for federal crimes, and vastly expanded the federal mandatory sentencing guidelines.

New Penology and New Sentencing Laws in the United States

The American history of penology since the 1970s has been essentially the history of the growth of get-tough sentencing laws and statutes, which began in earnest with the enactment of the Sentencing Reform Act of 1984 that was passed by Congress with bipartisan support. In the United States Senate, 99 senators voted for the Sentencing Reform Act of 1984 that was signed into law by President Reagan. The Act created the United States Sentencing Commission, whose 7 bipartisan members were appointed by Reagan. Before the Sentencing Reform Act, "federal judges had virtually unlimited discretion to impose any sentence that they felt was appropriate in a given case. There were few constraints on what judges could or should consider when sentencing" (United States Sentencing Commission, 1991, p. 15). Moreover, "while judges wielded tremendous sentencing discretion, the potency of their sanction was often severely diluted by a parole commission that later resentenced the defendant according to its own set of rules" (United States Sentencing Commission, 1991, p. 15).

The Sentencing Reform Act of 1984 had three major objectives: (1) to abolish the system of parole and indeterminate sentencing structures—a system of common practice in federal sentencing since the birth of the republic; (2) to bring uniformity in federal sentencing "so that similar defendants convicted of similar offenses would receive similar sentences" (United States Sentencing Commission, 1991, p. 16); and (3) to introduce proportionality of just punishment in federal sentencing. The Act mandated the United States Sentencing Commission to develop a new set of mandatory minimum sentencing guidelines that would foster the deterrence, incapacitation, and cooperation of federal offenders with the authority (substantial assistance motions) in federal prosecutions (United States Sentencing Commission, 1991).

There are two types of federal sentencing guidelines: federal mandatory minimum sentencing guidelines and federal sentencing guidelines. The mandatory minimum sentencing guidelines are made into law by Congress—they are the statutory guidelines. If a particular offense carries a mandatory minimum prison term, federal judges will have to impose that penalty irrespective of any mitigating factors. If a federal judge does impose a penalty less than or more than the one required by a mandatory minimum statute, he or she will have to justify in writing the reasons for downward or upward departures. Mandatory minimum sentencing guidelines (see **Table 6-1**) that are "widely recognized are those that demand that offenders be sentenced to imprisonment for 'not less than' a designated term of imprisonment. Some are triggered by the nature of the offense, others by the criminal record of the offender" (Congressional Research Service, 1999, p. 2). Another important category of mandatory minimum sentencing is the one that "consists of the flat or single sentence statutes, the vast majority of which call for life imprisonment. There are also capital punishment statutes that require the imposition of either the death penalty or imprisonment for life" (Congressional Research Service, 1999, p. 3).

Federal sentencing guidelines are developed by the United States Sentencing Commission and are approved by Congress. Although they are developed for maintaining general uniformity in federal sentencing, federal judges have some judicial discretion in complying with them. It is the federal mandatory minimum sentencing guidelines that have vastly affected the nature of federal sentencing during the last 3 decades. The federal mandatory sentencing guidelines were first developed for offenses related to illegal drugs and primarily in the context of the war on drugs (see **Table 6-2**). Subsequently, they were expanded to cover a vast number of other federal crimes. In the course of the last 4 decades, Congress has enacted hundreds of crime and justice-related legislation that criminalized thousands of acts and activities (Baker & Bennett, 2004; see **Table 6-3**). For the development of mandatory minimum sentencing guidelines, new federal offenses are grouped into separate offense categories "according to severity" (United States Sentencing Commission, 1991, p. 20).

During the last 4 decades, mandatory sentencing guidelines, related particularly to drug crimes, sex crimes, and violent crimes, have also been developed by all 50 states. Some of the mandatory sentencing strategies developed by the states, such as the three-strikes laws of Washington and California, Rockefeller drug laws of New York, Jessica's Law of Florida, and Project Exile of Virginia have had major effects on criminal justice in the United States

TABLE 6-1 Selected List of Federal Mandatory Minimum Sentencing Statutes

U.S. Code	Offense	Mandatory Minimum Imprisonment
18 U.S.C. 225	Continuing financial crime enterprise	Not less than 10 years and may be life
18 U.S.C. 844(h)	Use of fire or explosives to commit a federal felony	Not less than 10 years for first offense, 20 for the second
18 U.S.C. 844(f)	Burning or bombing federal property	Not less than 5 years nor more than 20 years
18 U.S.C. 924(c)(1)	Use of or possession of a firearm during the commission of a crime of violence or drug trafficking	Not less than 5 years; 25 years for second offense; imprisonment for not less than 30 years for a machine gun or silencer; life imprisonment for second or subsequent machine gun offenses
18 U.S.C. 924(e)(1)	Possession of firearm by three-time violent felons or drug dealers	Not less than 15 years
18 U.S.C. 2113(e)	Killing or hostage taking during the course of robbing	Not less than 10 years; death or life imprisonment if death results
18 U.S.C. 2251	Sexual exploitation of children	Not less than 10 years nor more than 20 years; upon a second conviction, not less than 15 years nor more than 30 years; upon a third conviction, not less than 30 years nor more than life; where death results, death or imprisonment for any term of years or life
18 U.S.C. 2251(a)	Buying or selling children for purposes of sexual exploitation	Not less than 20 years or life
18 U.S.C. 2252(b)	Second and subsequent offense of trafficking in material related to sexual exploitation of children	Not less than 5 years nor more than 30 years
18 U.S.C. 3559(c)	Three strikes	Must be sentenced to life imprisonment
18 U.S.C. 33	Destruction of commercial motor vehicles or their facilities involving high-level radioactive waste	Not less than 30 years

Source: Data from Congressional Research Service. (1999). *Federal mandatory minimum sentencing statutes: A list of citations with captions, introductory comments, and bibliography.* Washington, DC: The Library of Congress.

TABLE 6-2 Selected List of Federal Mandatory Life in Prison and Capital Punishment Statutes

U.S. Code	Federal Offense	Mandatory Minimum Sentencing
18 U.S.C. 34	Destruction of aircraft, commercial motor vehicles, or their facilities where death results	Death or imprisonment for life
18 U.S.C. 115	Kidnapping with death resulting of the member of the family of a federal official	Death or imprisonment for life
18 U.S.C. 351	First-degree murder of a member of Congress	Death or imprisonment for life
18 U.S.C. 930(c)	First-degree murder while in possession of a firearm in a federal building	Death or imprisonment for life
18 U.S.C. 1114	First-degree murder of a federal officer or employee	Death or imprisonment for life
18 U.S.C. 1116	First-degree murder of a foreign dignitary	Death or imprisonment for life
18 U.S.C. 1201	Kidnapping where death results	Death or imprisonment for life
18 U.S.C. 1203	Hostage taking where death results	Death or imprisonment for life
18 U.S.C. 1716	Mailing injurious articles with intent to injure or damage property where death results	Death or imprisonment for life
18 U.S.C. 1751	First-degree murder of the president	Death or imprisonment for life
18 U.S.C. 1959	Murder in aid of racketeering activity	Death or imprisonment for life
18 U.S.C. 2422	Coercing or enticing interstate travel for sexual purposes	Death or imprisonment for life
18 U.S.C. 2423	Transporting minors for sexual purposes	Death or imprisonment for life
18 U.S.C. 2251	Sexual exploitation of children resulting in the death of a child under 14 years of age	Death or imprisonment for life

Source: Data from Congressional Research Service. (1999). *Federal mandatory minimum sentencing statutes: A list of citations with captions, introductory comments, and bibliography.* Washington, DC: The Library of Congress.

as a whole. Under the Three Strikes and You're Out Law in California, if a person has two convictions before committing another crime, he or she will be sentenced to a minimum term of 25 years to life in prison irrespective of the nature of the third offense. Following the examples of Washington and California, a three strikes law was passed by the federal government (18 U.S.C. 3559c) and 28 other states (as of 2009).

The Rockefeller drug laws of New York, enacted in 1973 by then–New York Governor Nelson Rockefeller, made headlines as some of the toughest drug laws in America (see **Table 6-4**). The laws mandated a minimum 15 years to life in prison for selling 2 ounces, or possessing 4 ounces, of cocaine and heroin. Jessica's Law of Florida, enacted in 2006, mandated 25 years to life in prison and lifelong electronic monitoring for first-time sexual molestation of a child and other sexual crimes with children. As of 2011, 32 states have adopted similar legislation for mandatory minimum prison terms for sexual crimes with children. Project Exile, a federal law (Gun Control Act of 1968) adopted by the Commonwealth

TABLE 6-3 Major Crime Legislation Passed by United States Congress, 1970–2010

The Crime Control Substance Act of 1970	The Victims of Trafficking Act of 2000
The Comprehensive Crime Control Act of 1984	The DNA Analysis Backlog Elimination Act of 2000
The Anti-Drug Abuse Act of 1986	The USA Patriot Act of 2001
The Violent Crime Control Act of 1994	The Cyber Security Enhancement Act of 2002
The Jacob Wetterling Act of 1994	The PROTECT Act of 2003
The Sex Crimes Against Children Act of 1995	The Unborn Victims of Violence Act of 2004
Megan's Law of 1996	The Justice for All Act of 2004
The Pam Lychner Act of 1996	The Children's Safety Act of 2005
The Drug-Induced Rape Prevention Act of 1996	The Adam Walsh Child Protection and Safety Act of 2006
The Anti-Terrorism and Death Penalty Act of 1996	The Matthew Shepard and James Byrd, Jr. Hate Crime Prevention Act of 2009

of Virginia and many other states, mandated a minimum term of 5 years in federal prison for the possession of illegal guns.

Since the early 1990s, crime rates in almost all categories have been dropping in the United States (Federal Bureau of Investigation, 2010). Between the 1960s and 1970s, the homicide rate almost doubled. But starting in the 1990s, the homicide rate began to decline: "From 1992 to 2000, the rate declined sharply. Since then, the rate has been stable" (Bureau of Justice Statistics, 2011, p. 1). According to the Uniform Crime Reports, the declining trends in all categories of crimes have continued throughout the first decade of the 21st century. In 2010, violent crime declined 6.2%, murder 7.1%, forcible rape 6.2%, robbery 10.7%, property crimes 2.8%, larceny theft 2.3%, and motor vehicle theft 9.7%.

There is a debate about whether the emerging trend of crime drop in America is related to the mandatory minimum sentencing guidelines, or to other reasons such as shifts in demography, employment growth, education expansion, and larger economic changes and transformations that occurred in the 1990s (Blumstein & Wallman, 2000; Marowitz, 2000). Although economic change, educational growth, and demographic change played a role, the most important factor was modernization in criminal justice, particularly the modernization of law enforcement, expansion of the boundaries of criminalization, and growth of prosecution through the mandatory minimum sentencing guidelines, truth-in-sentencing laws, and other get-tough sentencing strategies. The declining trends in crime have, however, brought an increase in the prison population. In 1980, the U.S. rate of incarceration was 139 per 100,000 population. In 1990, the rate increased to 297 per 100,000 population. In about 2 decades (1990–2009), the incarceration rate increased to 753 per 100,000 population.

During the last 3 decades, concerns have been raised and debates and disputes have been pursued about the constitutionality of some of the measures of the new penology, especially the mandatory minimum sentencing statutes. Until the beginning of the 21st century, the U.S. Supreme Court, particularly the Rehnquist Court (1986–2005), was largely in favor of

TABLE 6-4 Selected List of Federal Mandatory Minimum Sentencing for Drug Offenses

U.S. Code	Federal Offenses	Mandatory Minimum Imprisonment
21 U.S.C. 841(b) (1)(A)	Drug trafficker where the offender has two or more prior convictions for violation of 21 U.S.C. 849 (drug dealing at a truck stop), 859 (dealing to minors), 860 (dealing near a school), 861 (using minors to deal)	Mandatory life imprisonment
21 U.S.C. 841(b) (1)(A)	Drug trafficking in very substantial amounts of controlled substances (e.g., a kilogram or more of heroin)	Not less than 10 years nor more than life imprisonment
21 U.S.C. 841(b) (1)(B)	Drug trafficking in substantial amounts of controlled substances (e.g., 100 grams of heroin)	Not less than 5 nor more than 40 years
21 U.S.C. 841(b) (1)(C)	Drug trafficking in Schedule I or II controlled substances	Not less than 20 years nor more than life if death or serious bodily injury results; not less than 10 years nor more than life if the offender has a prior drug felony conviction; imprisonment for life if the offender has a prior drug felony conviction and death or serious bodily injury results
21 U.S.C. 844	Simple possession of a controlled substance	Not less than 5 nor more than 20 years for possession of cocaine base (crack)
21 U.S.C. 848(a)	Drug kingpin—continuing criminal enterprise violations	Imprisonment for not less than 30 years; and more than life for previous offenders
21 U.S.C. 960(b)(1)	Illicit drug importing/exporting of very substantial amounts of controlled substances (e.g., a kilogram or more of heroin)	Imprisonment for not less than 10 years nor more than life; imprisonment for not less than 20 years nor more than life if the offender has a prior felony drug conviction or if death or serious bodily injury results
21 U.S.C. 960(b)(3)	Illicit drug importing/exporting of Schedule I or II controlled substances	Not more than 20 years, but not less than 20 years nor more than life if death or serious bodily injury results; imprisonment for not more than 30 years if the offender has a prior drug felony conviction; imprisonment for life if the offender has a prior drug felony conviction and death or serious bodily injury results
21 U.S.C. 860	Distribution of controlled substances near schools and colleges	Imprisonment for not more than twice the otherwise applicable maximum term
21 U.S.C. 861	Distribution to a pregnant person or use of those under 21 years of age to distribute controlled substances	Imprisonment for not more than twice the otherwise applicable maximum term

Source: Data from Congressional Research Service. (1999). *Federal mandatory minimum sentencing statutes: A list of citations with captions, introductory comments, and bibliography.* Washington, DC: The Library of Congress.

the war on drugs, and the larger war on crime started in the early of the 1980s. A large number of the U.S. Supreme Court's decisions during the 1980s and 1990s "in areas of police search and seizures, drug law enforcement, juvenile justice, sex offender registration and notification, and sentencing laws and guidelines upheld the get-tough policy strategies" (Shahidullah, 2008, p. 281). The decisions made by the Rehnquist Court in *"Michigan v. Sitz* in 1990, *Illinois v. Wardlow* in 2000, *Illinois v. McArthur* in 2001, *Maryland v. Pringle* in 2003, . . . and *Illinois v. Caballes* in 2005 have redefined the nature and vastly expanded the authority of police search" (Shahidullah, 2008, p. 282).

In 2003, the U.S. Supreme Court ruled in two mandatory sex offender registration and notification cases: *Smith et al. v. John Doe* of Alaska and *Connecticut Department of Public Safety et al. v. John Doe* (Legal Information Institute, 2003). In both cases, the Supreme Court upheld the view that sex offender registration and notification laws are "not in violation either of the liberty clause or the due process clause of the Fourteenth Amendment" (Shahidullah, 2008, p. 283). In the 1990s, many states enacted civil commitment statutes for violent and mentally abnormal sex offenders. The statutes mandated that violent and mentally abnormal sex offenders be confined in state-managed and state-funded mental institutions as long as they are judicially and professionally determined to be of high risk for public safety. In 1979, the Supreme Court made a ruling in *Kansas v. Hendricks* that the Kansas civil commitment statute "does not violate the Constitution's double jeopardy prohibition or its ban on *ex post facto* lawmaking. The Act does not establish criminal proceedings, and involuntary confinement is not punishment" (Legal Information Institute, 1997, pp. 1–2). In 2006, the U.S. Supreme Court refused "to hear an appeal of a 55-year mandatory minimum sentence for a Salt Lake City marijuana dealer who carried a pistol in his boot during his transactions" (Smith, 2006, p. 1).

The U.S. Supreme Court, however, took a different stand about the constitutionality of mandatory sentencing in two recent cases: *Blakely v. Washington* in 2004 and *United States v. Booker* in 2005. In *Blakely v. Washington*, the Court ruled that in following state mandatory sentencing guidelines, a sentence greater than the maximum can only be given within the limits of the Sixth Amendment of the Constitution, by a jury and not by judges. The *Blakely* decision brought a new turning point in the state sentencing system with a ruling that sentences given by judges higher than those recommend by state mandatory sentencing statutes are in violation of the Sixth Amendment's right of jury trial. In *United States v. Booker* in 2005, the U.S. Supreme Court applied the same argument to federal mandatory sentencing guidelines. The *Booker* decision brought into question a more fundamental issue about the nature of the enforcement of federal mandatory sentencing guidelines (see **Box 6-1**). Justice Breyer, in delivering the majority opinion, said that the system of federal mandatory sentencing guidelines "is incompatible with today's Sixth Amendment 'jury trial' holding and therefore must be severed and excised from the Sentencing Reform Act of 1984" (Legal Information Institute, 2005, pp. 2–3). He further added that federal sentencing guidelines should be seen as advisory and not mandatory. If they are mandatory, they are in violation of the Sixth Amendment right to a jury trial.

BOX 6-1

The Perils of Mandatory Sentencing Guidelines: The Case of Crack Cocaine Sentencing

One of the issues that remained as a bone of contention in the U.S. criminal justice community since the introduction of mandatory minimum sentencing guidelines in the mid-1980s is the law of disproportionate sentencing for crack cocaine offenses. The law was created by the Anti-Drug Abuse Act of 1986. The Act made a provision for 5 years of mandatory minimum sentencing and 20 years of mandatory maximum sentencing for the possession of 5 grams of crack cocaine, and 10 years of mandatory minimum sentencing for the possession of 10 grams of crack cocaine. The law made a different provision of sentencing for powder cocaine offenses. To receive 10 years of imprisonment, according to the same law, one needed to commit an offense of possessing 1,000 grams of powder cocaine—a ratio of 100 to 1. The law was based on the assumption that crack cocaine is related to violent crimes, street crimes, and gang crimes. As a result of this law of disproportionate sentencing for crack cocaine, a disproportionate number of blacks were incarcerated during the last 2 decades. A report published by the U.S. Sentencing Project (2004) on federal prison population observed that between 1994 and 2002, "the average time served by African Americans for a drug offense increased by 73%, compared to an increase of 28% for white drug offenders . . . 81.4% of crack cocaine defendants in 2002 were African American, while about two-thirds of crack cocaine users . . . [were] white or Hispanic. The average sentence for a crack cocaine offense in 2002 (119 months) was more than three years greater than for powder cocaine (78 months)." During the last two decades, many criminal justice experts, representatives of judicial communities, criminal justice think-tank organizations, and the United States Sentencing Commission have been pleading to Congress to repeal this law of crack cocaine sentencing. In 2010—after 24 years—Congress passed the Fair Sentencing Act and repealed the law of disproportionate sentencing for crack cocaine. The Fair Sentencing Act eliminated the mandatory minimum sentencing of 5 years for the simple possession of 5 grams of crack cocaine, and made provisions for the consideration of other aggravating factors in cases of crack cocaine sentencing. Before the enactment of the Fair Sentencing Act, the U.S. Supreme Court, through its rulings in *Kimbrough v. United States* in 2007 and *Spears v. United States* in 2009, provided some discretionary powers to lower courts in the determination of sentencing for crack cocaine offenses. The whole regime of mandatory sentencing guidelines that developed in the United States in the wake of the rise of "new penology," however, received a serious blow after *Blakely v. Washington* in 2004 and *United States v. Booker* in 2005. The *Blakely* and *Booker* decisions established that the mandatory sentencing guidelines could not be mandatory, but only "advisory" in nature.

Source: The Sentencing Project. (2004). *The federal prison population: A statistical analysis.* Washington, DC: Author.

■ New Penology and New Sentencing Laws and Trends in Canada

The 1980s saw the beginning of a new era in criminal justice in Canada. Two significant events occurred in that decade that vastly affected Canadian criminal justice. The first is the promulgation of the new constitution and the *Canadian Charter of Rights and Freedoms* in 1982. The new *Charter* firmly established the due process of law as the basic foundation of criminal justice in Canada. The second significant event was the beginning of the new debate and discourse for reforms in the *Criminal Code* of Canada. Before the 1980s, the dominant philosophy of sentencing in particular and criminal justice in general in Canada was based on the ideas of the old penology or the rehabilitative paradigm. From the 1920s and 1930s, under the effect of what is described as new criminology, a perspective began to dominate in Canada, as it did in the United States during the progressive movement of the early 20th century, that the problem of crime and deviance is solvable through the use of science— through the development of science-based treatment. The new criminology "maintained that criminal behavior and ingrained habits caused actual physical changes in the brain; changes that could be reversed by reformative treatment. It was a time of relative confidence in the power of science to solve all social problems" (Parole Board of Canada, 2010, p. 5). Under the philosophy of rehabilitative or progressive penology, the use of probation and parole, indeterminate sentencing, and judicial discretion in sentencing was widespread. The Parole Board of Canada (2010) estimated that "Between 1959 and 1967, the Parole Board granted more than 9,000 paroles from federal penitentiaries, a grant rate of 36 percent of the more than 25,000 applications received" (p. 15). In the 1960s, the Canadian penal system was so lenient that inmates lost interest in applying for parole. The Parole of Board of Canada (2010) observed, "In the 1960s, the prospect of getting a substantial chunk of 'good time' tended to erode many inmates' interest in applying for parole . . . even if an inmate was denied parole, he could still expect to get out early" (p. 15).

The Parole Act of 1969 made a provision for mandatory supervision that "an inmate who had accumulated more than 60 days of remission, and was therefore eligible for release, had to be released to serve his remitted time under supervision in the community" (Parole Board of Canada, 2010, p. 16). The Parole Board of Canada (2010) described the public attitudes toward sentencing and criminal justice in Canada before the 1980s in the following way: "In the climate of the times, people were easily persuaded that there was something terribly wrong with all parts of the criminal justice system—from law enforcement to the courts, to the correctional systems" (p. 23). In the mid-1980s, therefore, get-tough strategies began to spread to Canada and the rehabilitative paradigm began to be challenged. These changes started particularly with the ascendency of the conservative regime of Brian Mulroney (1984–1993) in the political landscape of Canada.

The Politics of Crime Control in Canada

The Progressive Conservative Party, under the leadership of Brian Mulroney, came to political power in Canada in 1984 after more than 2 decades under the rule of the Liberal Party (1963–1984). From the time of Mulroney, described as a leader in bringing the neoconservative perspective to Canadian politics, the ideas of the new penology began to take root in the Canadian criminal justice system. In the late 1970s, a consensus began to grow among the criminal justice policy makers in Canada that serious efforts were needed to reform the Canadian *Criminal Code* because of the lack of any uniformity in the structure of sentencing. To address these issues, Mulroney established the Canadian Sentencing Commission in 1984, the same year he came to power, and the same year the U.S. Congress passed the U.S. Sentencing Reform Act. In 1987, the Canadian Sentencing Commission presented a report on sentencing reforms. The report recommended legislative declaration of purpose and principles for sentencing; a new structure of maximum penalties; abolition of full parole; and a provision for truth-in-sentencing laws (75% of the sentences must be served). To further examine the recommendations of the Canadian Sentencing Commission, the Canadian Parliament established the Standing Committee on Justice and Solicitor General. The Standing Committee published a report, *Taking Responsibility* (Daubney, 1988), and made several recommendations for reforms in Canadian criminal law and criminal justice. In 1990, the Mulroney government made its first national report for reforms in criminal justice on the basis of the recommendations of the Standing Committee on Justice and Solicitor General. The title of the new report was *Directions for Reforms: A Framework for Sentencing* (Solicitor General of Canada, 1990). It was from that time that the Canadian criminal justice system began to move toward the perspective of new penology. The Canadian Parole Board noted that the remarkable event "of the 1990s was the enactment of the Corrections and Conditional Release Act (CCRA) . . . . The CCRA replaced the old Penitentiary Act of 1961 and the Parole Act of 1959 with a new comprehensive legislative framework for federal corrections" (2010, p. 29).

It is through the CCRA that some of the new penology's core ideas such as risk assessment, risk management, and system management began to enter Canada's criminal laws and the organization of its criminal justice. The Parole Board of Canada (2010) further noted that the CCRA "reflected many diverse perspectives and presented many challenges and opportunities. New expressions, born out of research, had found their way into the lexicon of corrections and were formally acknowledged in the new legislation—risk assessment and risk management" (p. 29). The maintenance of public safety—a core concept of the new penology—became the dominant goal for reforming criminal justice through the CCRA and the other enactments.

The Progressive Conservative Party lost political power in Canada in 1993. For the next 13 years, from 1993 to 2006, Canada was ruled by the Liberal Party under the leadership of Kim Campbell, Jean Chretien, and Paul Martin. During the leadership of the Liberal Party, a large number of enactments strengthened the get-tough approach to criminal justice in Canada. Bill C-55 passed by the Canadian Parliament in 1997 broadened the Canadian Dangerous Offender Laws by bringing a series of amendments to the Corrections and Conditional Release Act, the Criminal Records Act, the Prisons and Reformatories Act, and the Department of the Solicitor General Act. It was also under the Liberal Party that Canada introduced the Anti-Terrorism Act of 2001, the Youth Criminal Justice Act of 2003, and the Sex Offender Information Registration Act of 2004.

In 2006, the Liberal Party was voted out of office, and the Conservative Party again came to power in Canada under the leadership of Prime Minister Stephen Harper. Harper took office with a bold promise to be tough on crime and to introduce a major overhaul in the Canadian criminal justice system. One report shows that one third of the bills introduced by the Harper government in 2009 were "tough-on-crime measures, including mandatory minimum sentencing, further criminalizing drugs and eliminating structures that would decrease time between arrest and trial" (Meiners, 2010, p. 1). The Harper government has enacted new laws and introduced new provisions for mandatory sentencing of serious gun crimes; mandatory sentencing and monitoring of violent and dangerous criminals; ending the sentencing discount for repeat murder offenders; abolishing the faint-hope clause used for early parole of murderers; strengthening the national sex offender registry and the national DNA data bank; surveillance of the Internet; and protecting children from Internet sexual exploitation. Three of the major laws passed by the Parliament under the control of Harper are the Tackling Violent Criminal Act of 2008, the Protecting Victims From Sex Offenders Act of 2010, and the Eliminating Pardons for Serious Crimes Act of 2010.

New Penology and New Sentencing Laws in Canada

A new generation of mandatory minimum sentencing guidelines began to evolve in Canada through the amendment of the *Criminal Code* of Canada in 1995. Section 718 of the new legislation stated that "The fundamental purpose of sentencing is to contribute, along with crime prevention initiatives, to respect for the law and the maintenance of a just, peaceful and safe society by imposing just sanctions" (Roberts, 2005, p. 1). The language of the new law and the amendment expressed the philosophy of new penology. The amendment said that the new law must be able to control the escalation of crime and unlawful conduct, strengthen the strategies of deterrence, and separate offenders from society by expanding the scope of incarceration and incapacitation. The new law further stated that "sentences should be proportionate to the offence and reflect the degree of responsibility of the offender" (Section 718.1). Section 718.2 of the *Criminal Code* explained that the aggravating factors must be taken into consideration by sentencing courts. Some of these factors include crimes motivated by hate or prejudice, crimes committed from a position of authority, victimization of a spouse or a child, crime committed for the benefit of organized crime, and crime related to global terrorism (Roberts, 2005).

Mandatory minimum sentencing guidelines in Canada are grouped into four categories: (1) mandatory life sentencing, (2) mandatory sentencing for firearm offenses, (3) mandatory sentencing for repeat offenders, and (4) mandatory sentencing for hybrid offenses (summary offenses and indictable offenses). The new law required that a mandatory sentencing of life in prison be given to those who are convicted of treason, first-degree murder, and second-degree murder. Apart from these offenses carrying mandatory minimum sentencing of life in prison, there are 40 offenses in the three other categories for which mandatory minimum prison terms must be imposed (see **Table 6-5**).

In 2006, Canada enacted a new law called the Tracking Violent Crime Act (Bill C-2). The new law increased the number of mandatory minimum sentencing statutes related to a

TABLE 6-5 Selected Mandatory Minimum Sentencing Guidelines, Canada

Mandatory Life Sentences

Section	Offense	Mandatory Minimum Sentences (MMS)	Enacted
s. 47(1)	High treason	Life (or 25 years)	1976
s. 231(1)–(6.1)	First-degree murder	Life (or 25 years)	1976
s. 231(7)	Second-degree murder	Life (or 25 years)	1976

Selected Mandatory Minimum: Firearm Offense

Section	Offense	Mandatory Minimum Sentences (MMS)	Enacted
s. 236(a)	Manslaughter with firearm	4 years	1995
s. 239(a)	Attempted murder with firearm	4 years	1995
s. 244	Causing bodily with intent with firearm	4 years	1995
s. 272(2)(a)	Sexual assault with firearm	4 years	1995
s. 273(2)(a)	Aggravated sexual assault with firearm	4 years	1995
s. 279(1.1)(a)	Aggravated sexual assault with firearm	4 years	1995
s. 279.1(1)(a)	Hostage taking with firearm	4 years	1995
s. 344(a)	Robbery with firearm	4 years	1995
s. 346(1.1)(a)	Extortion with firearm	4 years	1995
s. 220(a)	Criminal negligence causing death with firearm	4 years	1995

Source: Data from Roberts, J. V., for the Department of Justice, Canada. (2005). *Mandatory sentences of imprisonment in common law jurisdictions: Some representative models—Canada.* Ottawa, Ontario: The Government of Canada.

number of offenses, including firearms violations, gun crimes, and child sexual exploitation. For example, under the previous firearms law, there was a provision of imposing only 1 year of imprisonment for unauthorized possession of a prohibited or restricted firearm that is loaded or near-readily accessible ammunition. Under Bill C-2, the mandatory minimum sentencing for such unauthorized possession was increased to 3 years for first-time offenses, and 5 years for second-time or subsequent offenses. Under the previous law, the offense of trafficking in, or possession for the purpose of trafficking in, a firearm, prohibited weapon, restricted weapon, prohibited device, or any ammunition or prohibited ammunition carried a penalty of 1 year in prison. Under Bill C-2, the penalty increased to 3 years for the first offense and 5 years for second and subsequent offenses. Under the previous law, the offense of importing or exporting a firearm, prohibited weapon, restricted weapon, prohibited device, or prohibited ammunition or component carried a penalty of 1 year in prison. Under Bill C-2, the penalty increased to 3 years for the first offense and 5 years for second and subsequent offenses (Parliament of Canada, 2011).

Canada passed another law, the Truth-in-Sentencing Act (Bill C-25), in 2009. Like Bill C-2, Bill C-25 suggests a similar trend toward more mandatory sentencing statutes and get-tough strategies for crime control and prevention. Bill C-25 "amends the *Criminal Code* (the Code to limit the credit a judge many allow for any time spent in pre-sentencing custody in order to reduce the punishment to be imposed at sentencing, commonly called credit for time served" (Parliamentary Information and Research Service, 2010, p. 1). The Act "changes the two days for one currently credited to one day for one, that is, it limits the credit for pre-sentencing custody to a maximum of one day for one day spent in pre-sentencing custody" (Parliamentary Information and Research Service, 2010, p. 5).

The Canadian Parliament enacted another tough new law in 2010: Eliminating Pardons for Serious Crimes Act (Bill C-23 B). The new law limits the opportunities for violent criminal offenders to apply for pardon. It also limits the power of the Parole Board of Canada to grant a pardon. Before the enactment of this law, an offender, convicted for an indictable offense could apply for pardon after completion of 5 years of his or her term of imprisonment under the Criminal Records Act of 1985. Bill C-23B made a provision that an offender convicted of an indictable offense cannot apply for pardon before serving at least 10 years of imprisonment. The bill also made a provision that an offender convicted of a summary offense cannot apply for pardon before serving at least 5 years of imprisonment. The bill made offenders who are convicted of an indictable offense related to sexual exploitation of minors, who are repeat offenders, and who are serving a term of life imprisonment, ineligible to apply for pardon or record suspension (Mackay, 2010). Under these and other recent get-tough laws, the prison population in Canada, as in the United States, has also significantly increased. But the increase in prison population in Canada, similar to the United States, is also related to a trend of consistent decline in the rates in all categories of crimes. A report from Statistics Canada (2008) noted: "Police-reported crime in Canada continued to decline in 2008. Both the traditional crime rate and the new Crime Severity Index fell 5%, meaning that both the volume of police-reported crime and its severity decreased. Violent crime also dropped" (p. 1).

■ New Penology and New Sentencing Laws and Trends in the United Kingdom

The philosophy of new penology and get-tough strategies of crime control began to expand to Europe in general and to the United Kingdom in particular around the same time it began to dominate in crime and justice policy making in the United States in the 1970s. Three factors contributed to the rise of new penology in the United Kingdom in the 1970s: the rising rate of crime; the escalation of social unrest, particularly the escalation of violence in Northern Ireland; and the accession to power of the conservative political regime of Margaret Thatcher in 1979. It was during the rise of Thatcherism in the 1980s that get-tough-on-crime-control rhetoric and strategies came to dominance in the agenda for crime and justice policy making in the United Kingdom. In its *Criminal Justice Statistics in England and Wales,* the British Ministry of Justice (2010a) reported that about 11 million crimes were reported to law enforcement in 1981. In 1991, the number of reported crimes had increased to about 15 million. By the middle of the 1990s, the crime rate reached a peak. In 1995, the total number of crimes reported to law enforcement climbed to about 18 million. The total number of violent crimes reported in 1981 was about 2 million. Within a decade, the number of violent crimes reported increased to about 2.5 million. In 1995, the number of violent crimes reached a peak of about 4.2 million.

The Politics of Crime Control in the United Kingdom

Margaret Thatcher, who took office at the beginning of this crime boom in the United Kingdom, held the same philosophy as Nixon and Reagan in the United States: that crime is a deeply moral issue. It is the lack of morality and responsibility, mostly on the part of socially disenfranchised groups of people. Crime control must be pursued not by expanding the welfare system but by overhauling the whole system of law enforcement, courts, sentencing, and corrections—the system of criminal justice. "Under the Thatcher government," as one author remarked, "the control of crime became integrated into political and ideological projects" (Lea, 1997, p. 3). The major crime legislation enacted by the British Parliament under Margaret Thatcher and that enlarged the boundaries of criminalization, punishment, and sentencing include the Police and Criminal Evidence Act of 1984, the Criminal Justice Act of 1991, the Criminal Justice Act of 1993, the Sexual Offences Act of 1993, the Criminal Justice and Public Order Act of 1994, the Police Act of 1996, the Crime Sentencing Act of 1997, the Police Act of 1997, and the Sexual Offences Act of 1997. Through such legislations, the ideas and concepts of the new penology—incarceration, incapacitation, mandatory sentencing, more power to law enforcement, and system management—became deeply entrenched in the British criminal justice system in the 1980s and 1990s.

The Labour Party government of Tony Blair starting in the late 1990s continued to expand the sentencing laws and guidelines under the same philosophy of the new penology, using the same rhetoric of the get-tough strategies. In 2004, Blair said, "It is time to mark the end of the '1960s liberal consensus' on law and order" (BBC News, 2004, p. 1). Trailing his party's 5-year plans on fighting crime, Blair argued that "people now want a society with respect and responsibility" (BBC News, 2004, p. 1). During the past 2 decades of the Labour Party's rule, the British Parliament enacted a number of anticrime laws that significantly broadened the boundaries of get-tough strategies in the United Kingdom (see **Table 6-6**). One report observed that the Labour Party under Tony Blair "created more than 3,500 crimes since it gained power in 1997, more than 1,200 through full scale parliamentary legislation" (Doughty, 2009, p. 2).

The Labour Party was voted out of power in 2010. The new prime minister and the leader of the Conservative Party, David Cameron, who took office in 2010, came with a renewed promise to continue "a zero tolerance approach to all crime along with a major prison building programme" (London Evening Standard, 2007, p. 1). In his election campaign, "Mr. Cameron [promised] that if put in power he would end the 'mockery' of criminals being released early" (London Evening Standard, 2007, p. 1). Thus the philosophy of new penology that evolved in the United States in the 1970s and that began to spread in the United Kingdom in the early 1980s has continued to shape and influence the British criminal justice system for the past 3 decades. One of the most significant effects was on the nature of sentencing laws and statutes.

TABLE 6-6 Major Anti-Crime Legislation Enacted by the British Parliament, 1998–2010

Young Offenders: Crime and Disorder Act of 1998	The Sexual Offences Act of 2003
Youth Justice and Criminal Evidence Act of 1999	The Domestic Violence, Crime, and Victims Act of 2003
The Powers of Criminal Court (Sentencing) Act of 2000	The Prevention of Terrorism Act of 2005
The Anti-Terrorism, Crime, and Security Act of 2001	The Serious Organised Crime and Police Act of 2006
The Police Reform Act of 2002	The Police and Justice Act of 2006
The Anti-Social Behaviour Act of 2003	The Serious Crime Act of 2007
The Criminal Justice Act of 2003	The Counterterrorism Act of 2008

New Penology and New Sentencing Laws in the United Kingdom

Criminal sentencing in the United Kingdom is primarily given by two types of courts: magistrate courts and crown courts. The magistrate courts deal with minor offenses described as summary offenses. The magistrate courts also deal with family proceedings and matters of youth justice. They are comparable to American state trial courts and juvenile courts. The crown courts, created by the Courts Act of 1971, deal with serious or indictable offenses. They also hear appeals from the magistrate courts. There are 78 crown courts in England and Wales. In matters of serious crimes and indictable offenses, the judgments of the crown courts are mostly final. Only under special circumstances can they be appealed to the Criminal Division of the Court of Appeal—the highest tier of the British judicial system. Under the Criminal Justice Act of 1991, offenders in magistrate and crown courts are sentenced primarily on the basis of the seriousness of the offense. Typically, there are four types of sentences: discharge, fine, community sentence, and custody or imprisonment (British Ministry of Justice, 2010b). The British Ministry of Justice annually publishes a report called *Criminal Justice Statistics in England and Wales* and a report called *Sentencing Statistics: England and Wales*. An analysis of some of these reports shows that since the middle of the 1990s, more serious offenses are being processed at higher rate; more serious crime offenders are being convicted by the crown courts; more serious crime offenders are being sentenced to prison; and more offenders are being sentenced to prison for longer terms.

Some of the significant changes in the British criminal justice system in recent years have come through the enactment of the Criminal Justice Act of 2003. The Act increased police power for warrantless search and seizure, increased the number of arrestable offenses, and introduced a provision of retrial of offenders found not guilty in the first trial. What is more significant is that the Criminal Justice Act of 2003 created a new generation of mandatory minimum and maximum sentencing guidelines. Like the U.S. Sentencing Reform Act of 1984 that created the United States Sentencing Commission, the Criminal Justice Act of 2003 established the Sentencing Guidelines Council to develop a uniform set of sentencing guidelines. The Criminal Justice Act of 2008 changed the name of the agency from Sentencing Guidelines Council to Sentencing Council. "The Sentencing Council is responsible for preparing and monitoring sentencing guidelines with the aim of ensuring greater consistency in sentencing. Guidelines are also issued by the Court of Appeal in the form of guideline judgments" (Sentencing Council, 2011, p. 1). The Sentencing Council is composed of 13 members and headed by a chairman, who is usually a judge from the Court of Appeal. The chairman and the members of the Sentencing Council are appointed by the Lord Chancellor and Lord Chief Justice. The Coroners and Justice Act of 2009 mandated that the British criminal courts must follow the sentencing guidelines prepared by the Sentencing Council for sentencing of adult offenses committed after April 2010. It is through the research and analysis conducted by the Sentencing Council that a more comprehensive understanding can be reached about the evolving nature of the sentencing guidelines and sentencing trends in the United Kingdom.

The Sentencing Council follows five statutory purposes of sentencing as contained in the Criminal Justice Act of 2003: punishment of offenders, reduction of crime by deterrence, reform and rehabilitation of offenders, protection of the public, and making of reparation by offenders to persons affected by their offenses. The Criminal Justice Act of 2003 mandated that in developing sentencing guidelines, the Sentencing Council must take the issue of the "seriousness of the offence" as an overarching principle (Section 143[1]). The Criminal Justice Act of 2003 states, "In considering seriousness of any offence, the court must consider the offender's culpability in committing the offence and any harm which the offence caused, was intended to cause or might foreseeably have caused" (Section 143[1]). For sentencing decisions, the courts are asked to judge four levels of culpability: intention, recklessness, knowledge of the crime act, and negligence. The courts are asked to consider harm in terms of harm to individual victims, harm to the community, and harm to the public sense of morality. The Criminal Justice Act of 2003 requires that a higher level of culpability be determined by the court if an offense is racially or religiously aggravated; offense is motivated by hostility toward a minority group, or a member or members of a minority group; offense is an abuse of a position of power and trust; offense is committed under the influence of alcohol or drugs; offense is committed with a weapon to frighten or injure a victim; offense is motivated by hate based on sexual orientation or victim's disability; and offense is based on deliberate targeting of vulnerable victims (Sentencing Guidelines Council, 2004).

A new generation of minimum and maximum mandatory sentencing guidelines has evolved recently in the British criminal justice system (see **Table 6-7**) as a result of a number of new enactments such as the Crime and Disorder Act of 1998, the Powers of Criminal Courts (Sentencing) Act of 2000, the Criminal Justice Act of 2003, the Criminal Justice Act of 2008, and the Coroners and Justice Act of 2009. The Crime and Disorder Act of 1998 increased the sentencing for racially, sexually, or religiously aggravated assault from 5 to 7

TABLE 6-7 Some Selected Serious Violent Offenses and Mandatory Maximum Penalty: England and Wales

Offense	Maximum penalty
Manslaughter	Life in prison
Kidnapping	Life in prison
Soliciting murder	Life in prison
Wounding with intent to cause grievous bodily harm	Life in prison
To choke, suffocate, or strangle in order to commit an indictable offense	Life in prison
Using chloroform, etc., to commit any indictable offense	Life in prison
Maliciously administering poison so as to endanger life or inflict bodily harm	Life in prison
Causing bodily injury by explosives	Life in prison
Using explosives, etc., with intent to do grievous bodily harm	Life in prison
Causing explosion likely to endanger life or property	Life in prison
Child destruction	Life in prison
Possession of firearm with intent to endanger life	Life in prison
Use of firearm to resist arrest	Life in prison
Carrying a firearm with criminal intent	Life in prison
Robbery or assault with intent to rob	Life in prison
Aggravated burglary	Life in prison
Hostage taking	Life in prison
Hijacking	Life in prison
Causing death by careless driving when under influence of drink or drugs	Life in prison
Hijacking of ships	Life in prison
Female genital mutilation	14 years
Assisting a girl to mutilate her own genitalia	14 years
Attempting to commit murder or conspiracy to commit murder	Life in prison

Source: Data from Sentencing Guidelines Council. (2008). *Assault and other offenses against the person.* London, England: The Sentencing Council.

years. The Powers of Criminal Courts (Sentencing) Act of 2000 imposed an automatic life sentence for repeat dangerous offenders (Sentencing Guidelines Council, 2008). The Criminal Justice Act of 2003 made a more elaborate provision for defining and sentencing a dangerous offender by creating a separate dangerous offender provision. The Act requires that a term of imprisonment for life is given if an offender (over the age of 18) is convicted of a serious offense; if the court is of the opinion that he or she is a dangerous offender; and if the maximum penalty for the offense is imprisonment for life. The act also made a provision that if an offender committed a serious offense but a sentencing of life imprisonment is not available for it, the sentencing court can impose a sentencing for life or impose an extended sentencing for that offender considering the need for public safety. If a dangerous offender is under the age of 18, according to the Powers of Criminal Courts (Sentencing)

Act of 2000 (Section 91), he or she can be in detention for life for the sake of public safety. The Crime and Disorder Act of 1998 made a provision that if a child commits a serious offense and he or she is a dangerous offender, the magistrate court "shall send him forthwith to the Crown Court for trial for the offence"—a statute that is described in the United States as juvenile transfer.

The Sentencing Council, following the statutory provisions of the Crime and Disorder Act of 1998, the Criminal Justice Act of 2003, the Sexual Offences Act of 2003, the Criminal Justice Act of 2008, the Coroners and Justice Act of 2009, and other criminal statutes, developed a set of definitive guidelines related to a number of offense categories such as offenses against the person, assault, attempted murder, breach of protective order, breach of antisocial behavior order, causing death by driving, assault on children and cruelty to a child, domestic violence, robbery, and sexual violence (see **Table 6-8**). The criminal courts are required to comply with the sentencing methods and structures developed by these definitive

TABLE 6-8 Some Selected Serious Sexual Offenses and Their Mandatory Maximum Penalty: England and Wales

Offense	Maximum Penalty
Rape (Section 1 of the Sexual Offences Act of 2003)	Life in prison
Rape of a child under 13 (Section 5 of the Sexual Offences Act of 2003)	Life in prison
Intercourse with a girl under 16	2 years
Incest by a man	Life in prison
Indecent assault on a woman	10 years
Indecent assault on a man	10 years
Assault with intent to commit buggery	10 years
Abduction of a woman by force or for the sake of her property	14 years
Permitting a girl under 13 to use premises for intercourse	Life in prison
Indecent conduct toward young child	10 years
Burglary with intent to commit rape	14 years
Assault by penetration (Section 2 of the Sexual Offences Act of 2003)	Life in prison
Assault of a child under 13 by penetration	Life in prison
Sexual assault of a child under 13	14 years
Causing or inciting a child under 13 to engage in sexual activity	14 years
Sexual activity with a child	14 years
Engaging in sexual activity in the presence of a child	10 years
Causing a child to watch a sexual act	10 years
Causing a person with a mental disorder to engage in sexual activity	14 years
Causing a person with a mental disorder to watch a sexual act	10 years
Care workers: causing or inciting sexual activity	10 years

Source: Data from Sentencing Guidelines Council. (2008). *Assault and other offenses against the person.* London, England: The Sentencing Council.

guidelines of the Sentencing Council. The Sentencing Council's definitive guidelines describe the statutory provisions, sentencing methods, and sentencing structures. The guidelines contain both mandatory minimum and mandatory maximum sentencing provisions (see **Box 6**-2) . For the offense of an attempted murder, for example, the minimum sentence to be given by the crown court is imprisonment for life. For the offense of causing grievous bodily harm, the minimum mandatory sentence is also imprisonment for life (Sentencing Guidelines Council, 2008).

BOX 6-2

New Penology and "Governance" of Sex Crimes

The spread of the perspective of "new penology" in the countries of the West in the mid-1970s brought some fundamental changes in their policymaking for crime control and prevention in almost all domains of crime and criminality. The deepest effect of the perspective of new penology, however, has been on the domain of sex crimes. During the last 3 decades, there has been a huge growth of legislation in almost all countries of the West related particularly to the governance of sex crimes. In the United States, some of that legislation includes the Jacob Wetterling Crimes Against Children and Sexually Violent Offender Registration Act of 1994, the Violence Against Women Act of 1994, Megan's Law of 1996, the Pam Lychner Act of 1996, the Communication Decency Act of 1996, the Protection of Children From Sexual Predators Act of 1998, the Victims of Trafficking and Violence Protection Act of 2000, Aimee's Law of 2000, Federal Campus Sex Crimes Act of 2000, PROTECT Act of 2003, and the Broadcast Decency Enforcement Act of 2005. Outside the United States, a more expansive regime of sex crimes legislation is found to have grown in the United Kingdom. Some of those include the Sex Offenders Act of 1997, the Protection From Harassment Act of 1997, the Youth Justice and Criminal Evidence Act of 1999, the Protection of Children Act of 1999, the Sexual Offences Act of 2003, and the Criminal Justice and Immigration Act of 2008 (criminalization of the possession of pornography). In almost all countries of the West today, the policy makers in crime and justice are in consensus that sex crimes must be controlled and governed effectively. This consensus has been emerging not only because of the issues of morality, equality, and the need for protection of the rights of women and children, but also because of some fundamental changes in the nature of sex crimes in the context of globalization. The growth of global trafficking of women and children, globalization of sex tourism, the explosion of Internet child pornography, and the rise of transnational gangs of pedophiles have created problems that are fundamentally different from traditional sex crimes such as rape, incest, spousal violence, and child sexual abuse. The rise of the perspective of new penology in the governing of sex crimes in modern societies, therefore, needs to be examined both in local and global contexts of sex crimes.

Source: Easton, S., & Piper, C. (2008, August). New penology and new policies. In *Sentencing and punishment: The quest for justice* (2nd ed.). Oxford, England: Oxford University Press. Retrieved from www.oup.com/uk/orc/bin/9780199218103/easton_ch01.pdf.

The Criminal Justice Act of 2003 also made new provisions for mandatory extraction of DNA samples without consent not just from convicted offenders, but also from those who are arrested for indictable offenses. The United Kingdom's National DNA Database (NDNAD), created in 1995, has rapidly grown under the Criminal Justice Act of 2003 and the Criminal Evidence Act of 1997, which is retrospectively applied. The NDNAD had 1.1 million individual samples in 2000–2001 and about 3.5 million samples in 2005–2006. The number of DNA samples from crime scenes was 103,000 in 2000–2001 and 264,000 in 2005–2006. It is also reported that about 686,000 DNA samples "on the database belong to children between the age of 10 and 17" (Privacy International, 2006, p. 1).

The last 3 decades of growth and expansion of criminal justice in the United Kingdom, particularly the growth of new crime legislation and the creation of a new generation of mandatory sentencing guidelines, has contributed to a significant drop in the crime rate. The 2010 report of the British Crime Survey, based on a survey of 45,000 households, showed that the total number of crimes dropped below 10 million in 2009. In 1995, the total number of crimes reported by the British Crime Survey was about 19 million, and in 1997, it was about 16 million. Since 1997, the number of total crimes fell about 47% (Travis, 2010). The crime drop in the United Kingdom, as in the United States and Canada, however, is associated with a rise in the prison population. In 1970, the total prison population in England and Wales was about 30,000. In 2005, the total prison population increased to about 85,000, and in 2011, that number increased to about 88,000. The British Ministry of Justice's report on the expected prison population (2011–2016) projects that in England and Wales, it will reach about 94,000 by 2016 (British Ministry of Justice, 2010c).

■ New Penology and New Sentencing Laws and Trends in Australia

Australia, a country with about 22 million people (2011 estimate), has a system of criminal justice that closely resembles the criminal justice system of the United States. Like the United States, Australia has a federal system of government. There is one federal constitution. There are also eight state and territorial constitutions (New South Wales, Queensland, South Australia, Western Australia, Victoria, Tasmania, Northern Territory, and Norfolk Island). There are federal criminal laws, crimes, police, courts, and correctional institutions. There are also state criminal laws, crimes, police, courts, and correctional institutions. Like the United States, Australia also abides by the English common law tradition. Most of the modern criminal laws in Australia, like those in United States, include primarily the legislative acts and the judicial decisions of the High Court of Australia (akin to the U.S. Supreme Court).

The nature and magnitude of Australia's crime and criminality, however, show a somewhat different pattern than that of the United States. Crime statistics in Australia are reported by the Australian Bureau of Statistics in two ways. One report is like the Uniform Crime Reporting (UCR) of the United States and Canada and the *Police Crime Statistics* of the United Kingdom—It is based on crimes reported to police and police-recorded crimes. The second report is the Crime and Safety Survey in Australia based on a household victimization survey, which is like the National Crime Victimization Survey (NCVS) of the United States and the British Crime Survey (BCS). In the United States and the United Kingdom, the crime rate began to grow in the mid-1990s, but began to significantly drop in the late 1990s and the early 2000s. Data on crime trends in Australia between 1996 and 2006, analyzed by the Australian Institute of Criminology (2010), show that except for homicide, all other kinds of crimes consistently increased between 1996 and 2008. In 1996, there were about 354 homicides in Australia. In 2006, the number decreased to 290. But during the same period, assault increased more than 30% (623 assaults per 100,000 population in 1996 to 796 per 100,000 population in 2008). During the same period, the total number of sexual assaults increased from 14,542 to 19,733 (80 per 100,000 population in 1996 to 92 per 100,000 population in 2008). The number of robberies, during the same period, remained almost the same, but kidnapping increased from 478 in 1996 to 782 in 2008 (Australian Institute of Criminology, 2010, p. 2). Between 1996 and 2001, motor vehicle theft increased 14%.

The Crime and Safety Surveys conducted by the Australian Bureau of Statistics show a similar pattern of growth in victimization between 1998 and 2005. The 1998 Crime and Safety Survey noted that about 534,100 households were victims of either a break-in or attempted break-in during the 12 months before the survey (Australian Bureau of Statistics, 1999). The 2005 Crime and Safety Survey noted that the number of victims from the same crimes increased to about 7.8 million (Australian Bureau of Statistics, 2006). Between 2001 and 2008, property crimes of all kinds (burglary, motor vehicle theft, break-in, shoplifting, pickpocketing, and bicycle theft), however, began to show a declining trend (Australian Institute of Criminology, 2010). Beginning in 2001, a declining trend in victimization has also been observed in unlawful entry, motor vehicle theft, and other theft.

Although some kinds of traditional crimes are currently in declining trends in Australia, the Australian criminal justice system, at the same time, like that of the United States, the United Kingdom, Canada, and other EU countries, is facing enormous challenges from different kinds of global crimes. Australia is the destination country for illegal human trafficking, illegal trafficking of women and children, and drug trafficking from China, Korea, Thailand, India, Pakistan, and many countries of Eastern Europe. The *Criminal Code* of the Commonwealth of Australia (Sections 270–271) criminalizes "human trafficking in Australia. The penalty for sexual servitude is up to 15 years of imprisonment; the penalty for slavery is up to 25 years of imprisonment; the penalty for deceptive recruitment is up to seven years of imprisonment" (Humantrafficking.org, p. 1). A report published by the Australian Institute of Criminology estimated that in 2003, "crime costs Australia $19 billion while the costs in dealing with crime costs close to another $13 billion . . . It is also twice the nation's annual defense budget" (as quoted in Grabosky & McFarlane, 2007, p. 142).

The Politics of Crime Control in Australia

Australia's policymakers in crime and justice began to use the language of the new penology—systemic reforms, systemic controls, systemic modernization, border control, mandatory sentencing, determinate sentencing, more police and police power, and zero tolerance of policing—starting around the same time in the 1980s as when they began to dominate in crime policy discourses in the United States and the United Kingdom (Weatherburn, 2004). The issue of law and order has remained at the core of political mobilization by both major political parties in Australia—the Labor Party and the Liberal Party—since the middle of the 1990s. One of the studies on recent Australian politics observed that the get-tough crime policy is "a 'big ticket item' that has a significant impact on the likelihood of electoral success. The major political parties in Australia sought to be the 'toughest,' exemplified . . . by the use of imprisonment, the length of sentences and police numbers" (Brenton & Hanley, 2010, p. 1).

In the Australian federal election campaign in 2010, the Labor Party promised to be tough on crime, national security, and border control. In its election manifesto, *Restoring Sovereignty and Control to Our Borders,* the Labor Party "pledged to turn back boats carrying asylum seekers, restore offshore processing of asylum seekers claims, and restore temporary protection visa and mutual obligation. Deterring 'people smuggling' and 'unauthorized arrivals' were the focus" (Brenton & Hanley, 2010, p. 4). In the Queensland state election in 2009, the Labor Party "advocated curfews, minimum mandatory sentencing, detention, naming and shaming and stronger police powers" (Brenton & Hanley, 2010, p. 5), whereas the Liberal Party promised to overhaul Queensland's youth justice system. In the state election in Western Australia in 2008, the Labor Party promised extra police officers and explicitly linked increased policing to public safety and decreased crime activity. They promised "tough anti-hoon legislation, tough new drug laws, [and] tough new domestic violence legislation" (Brenton & Hanley, 2010, p. 5).

The Liberal Party's manifesto, *Protecting Our Police,* called for mandatory sentences for assaults on police and public safety officers, as well as "tougher sentences for grievous bodily harm and serious assaults. They identified 'hoons' and 'young drivers' as concerns and advocated 'harsher' penalties" (Brenton & Hanley, 2010, p. 5). The Liberal Party promised to enact new legislation on truth-in-sentencing laws. It "called for eliminating the automatic one-third discount in sentencing, giving judges the discretion not to make offenders eligible for parole" (Brenton & Hanley, 2010, p. 5). In the 2007 state election in New South Wales, the same language of get-tough strategies in law and order were prominent. The Labor Party promised more police powers, and "focused on creating new offences and aggravating factors, and increasing non-parole periods and minimum jail terms. Other policies included the control of juvenile crimes, gang crimes, drug crimes, and domestic violence" (Brenton & Hanley, 2010, p. 6). The Liberal Party, on the other hand, advocated for reforms in juvenile justice in New South Wales. It "proposed lowering the age of criminal responsibility from 14 to 10–12, changing the definition of juvenile from under 18 to under 17" (Brenton & Hanley, 2010, p. 6).

The philosophy of new penology came to the center of criminal justice policymaking in Australia in the mid-1990s, particularly under the rule of Prime Minister John Howard (1996–2007) of the Liberal Party. Howard, like President Reagan in the United States and Prime Minister Thatcher in the United Kingdom, was his nation's architect of the war on crime, the war on drugs, and the get-tough crime control strategies in Australia. Like Reagan and Thatcher, Howard espoused the philosophy of social conservatism. He believed that crime is a deeply moral problem—a problem of the lack of responsibility and family values, particularly on the part of the marginalized underclass (Mendes, 2001). His "principal social policy concern is to reintegrate the poor and the marginal with what he considers to be mainstream social values and morality such as a commitment to personal responsibility, the work ethic, and the traditional family" (Mendes, 2001, p. 2). Immediately after taking office in 1996, Howard signed the toughest gun control legislative measures ever enacted in Australia. The new gun control laws, enacted in the wake of the Port Arthur gun massacre in Tasmania that killed 35 people, banned private ownership of guns in Australia. As a result of this new law, the Australian government bought back about 650,000 private guns that were later destroyed.

Howard started a new war on drugs in Australia by launching the national illicit drug strategy, "Tough on Drugs" in 1997, the National Drug Strategic Framework in 1998–2003, and the National Drug Strategy—Australia's Integrated Framework in 2004–2009. The core of his new get-tough drug control strategy was reduction of the drug supply and control of the drug trade and trafficking. The new policies enhanced federal police power for drug arrests and drug investigations. A report from the United Nations Office on Drugs and Crime (2008) noted that "one aspect of Australian drug policy, which is not widely known outside the country, are the far reaching powers for the police to detect and investigate drug offences, which go further than in several other industrialized countries" (p. 39). The report further added: "There can be no doubt that larger powers of law enforcement institutions facilitate the detection of criminal organizations, including drug trafficking syndicates, and Australia has clearly had major successes in this regard in recent years" (p. 39). The Tough on Drugs strategy created a new drug policy organization—Australian National Council on Drugs. The council, like the Drug Enforcement Administration of the United States, was entrusted with the task of developing national drug control strategies and coordinating "the knowledge and work of the broad community of experts working in the various fields of drug control at the national and state levels" (United Nations Office on Drugs and Crime, 2008, p. 9).

Howard was also the architect of Australia's war on terror policy strategies. Australia was facing enormous challenges from illegal immigration and illegal human trafficking long before the events of September 11, 2001 in New York. The American declaration of war on terror in 2001 brought a new sense of urgency for homeland security in Australia, and Howard became a strong and a passionate ally of the global war on terror. Howard signed two major antiterrorism pieces of legislation: the Australian Security Intelligence Organization Act of 2003 and the Anti-Terrorism Act of 2005. Both these laws enhanced federal police power to track, investigate, and prosecute terrorism cases. The Anti-Terrorism Act of 2005 amended the *Criminal Code* and explained that "A person commits an offence under this section even if: (a) a terrorist act does not occur; or (b) the training is not connected with preparation for . . . a specific terrorist act."

The act broadened police power for preventive detention, warrantless search and seizure, and electronic surveillance—the provisions that closely resemble some of those of the USA Patriot Act of 2001. Another Howard achievement was the establishment of the Australian Crime Commission (ACC) through the Australian Crime Commission Act of 2002. The primary responsibility of the ACC is to conduct criminal investigations and collect and share criminal intelligence with respect particularly to organized crimes, border crimes, violent crimes, human trafficking, cyber crimes, and global terrorism. The ACC is governed by the Australian Ministry of Home Affairs, a parliamentary joint committee, and an intergovernmental committee composed of ministers from the states and territories. Having replaced the National Crime Authority, the Australian Bureau of Criminal Intelligence, and the Office of Strategic Crime Assessments, the ACC has become Australia's lead criminal investigation and criminal intelligence agency like that of the FBI in the United States.

New Penology and New Sentencing Laws in Australia

The evolution of criminal justice in Australia for the last 4 decades has been characterized by some of the same trends observed in most of the countries of the West: high crime trends in the beginning of the 1970s; growth of get-tough policy reforms in the 1980s and 1990s; declining trends in traditional crimes in the late 1990s; rise of global crimes in the middle of the 1990s; and more reforms for systemic modernization and integration of technology in criminal justice in the beginning of the 21st century. The spread of the new penology philosophy across the criminal justice systems of the West is particularly evidenced by the development of legislation on sentencing reforms and innovations (Law Council of Australia, 2001). In Australia, modern reforms for get-tough sentencing of federal offenders began in the late 1970s. In 1978, the Australian Law Reform Commission (ALRC) was given the task by the government of the Commonwealth of Australia to develop a uniform set of national sentencing guidelines in the wake of the escalating challenges of high crime trends, as well as popular demands for get-tough sentencing laws. Between 1979 and 1989, the ALRC produced a series of reports on federal sentencing reforms (ALRC Report 10, ALRC Report 15, ALRC Report 43, and ALRC Report 44). On the basis of these reports, the Crime Legislation Amendment Act (No. 2) was passed by the parliament in 1989. For about 15 years, the Crime Legislation Amendment Act of 1989 remained as the foundation of federal sentencing guidelines in Australia. In 2004, during the get-tough regime of John Howard, the government of the Commonwealth of Australia asked the ALRC to conduct a new review of the Crime Legislation Amendment Act of 1989, particularly Part IB of the Crimes Act of 1914 inserted into the Crimes Legislation Act of 1989. On the basis of further research, the ALRC (2006) produced a new report on federal sentencing: *Same Crime, Same Time: Sentencing of Federal Offenders* (Report 103). This new ALRC report (No. 103) is presently the key source for federal sentencing laws and guidelines.

One of the peculiarities of the criminal justice system of Australia is that federal sentencing guidelines are borrowed from state sentencing guidelines and "most federal criminal matters are heard in state and territory courts; and the states and territories have almost exclusive responsibility for administering the sentences imposed on federal offenders" (Australian Law Reform Commission, 2006, p. 14). For the establishment of greater uniformity and consistency in federal sentencing, the ALRC report recommended that in federal laws on sentencing, the legitimate purposes of sentencing should be clearly spelled out and they are, according to the ALRC, "retribution, deterrence, rehabilitation, incapacitation of the offender, denunciation and restoration" (Australian Law Reform Commission, 2006, p. 16). ALRC report No. 44, which was one of the major sources of the Crime Legislation Act of 1989, recommended a truth-in-sentencing provision. The report recommended that legislation should require that 70% of imprisonment time is served before an offender is released or entitled to apply for parole. The Australian Parliament passed the Truth in Sentencing Act, and it became a law with royal assent in 2009. ALRC report No. 44 also suggested that imprisonment "should be the punishment of the last resort" but at the same time, it said that imprisonment should be an important part of the federal criminal justice system and that "offenders who commit more serious offences should be punished more severely than those who commit less serious offences" (Australian Law Reform Commission, 1988, p. xviii). For a more rational system of sentencing, the report recommended a set of seven different maximum prison terms for federal and Australian federal territory offenders: life imprisonment, 15 years imprisonment, 12 years imprisonment, 9 years of imprisonment, 7 years of imprisonment, 5 years of imprisonment, 2 years of imprisonment, and 6 months imprisonment.

Report 103 of the ALRC's *Same Crime, Same Time: Sentencing of Federal Offenders* recommended that the following six major factors be considered by the courts before the determination of sentencing: (1) factors relating to the offense, (2) factors relating to the conduct of the offense, (3) factors relating to the conduct of the offender, (4) factors relating to the background and circumstances of the offender, (5) factors relating to the effect of the offense, and (6) factors relating to the effect of conviction or sentence on the offender or the offender's family or dependents (Australian Law Reform Commission, 2006, pp. 168–169). These factors established a more systematic, rational, determinate, and mandatory approach to federal sentencing equal to that of mandatory sentencing guidelines in the United States and the United Kingdom. One factor that is strikingly different in the Australian case is that courts are asked to consider the effect of the sentence on the offender and his or her family (Australian Bureau of Statistics, 2011).

In all Australian states and territories, there are provisions for mandatory sentencing (Law Council of Australia, 2001). The ALRC noted that "Sentencing legislation in most states and territories sets out a list of mandatory factors, which the court must either take into account or to which it must have regard" (Australian Law Reform Commission, 2006, p. 164). Some of the Australian state sentencing trends in areas of violent crimes during the last 3 decades suggest that the proportion of violent prisoners in the sentenced prison population has increased, more custodial sentences are being imposed, sentencing length has grown, and sentencing of violent offenders is becoming tougher. One of the studies on the sentencing of violent offenders in Australia found: "There has been an increase in the median actual estimated sentence lengths for violent offenders. Taken across the four violent offences there was a trend in each jurisdiction towards longer median actual estimated sentence lengths" (Morgan, 2002, p. 9). The same study also observed that "contrary to general media and public perceptions, sentencing of violent offenders is becoming tougher" (Morgan, 2002, p. 9). This finding is based on "the growth in the overall imprisonment rate . . . with the concomitant increase in the proportion of violent prisoners in the prison populations . . . and . . . the overall increase in the median actual expected sentence lengths for violent offences as a group" (Morgan, 2002, p. 57).

A report from the Australian Bureau of Statistics (2011) noted that in the higher criminal courts in Australia, "The majority (85%) or 11,184 of defendants proven guilty in 2009–2010 received a custodial order. This proportion has increased since 2001–2002 when it was 72%" (p. 1). Because of the growth in custodial sentencing, the development of truth-in-sentencing statutes, and the increase in sentencing length, Australia, like the United States, the United Kingdom, and Canada, has also been experiencing a rapid growth in its prison population since the mid-1990s. Between 1982 and 1998, Australia's prison population increased 102% (Australian Institute of Criminology, 1999). In 1997, the Australian imprisonment rate was about 137 per 100,000 population. In 2007, the rate increased to about 170 per 100,000 population. In some states, such as Western Australia, Queensland, and the Northern Territories, the imprisonment rate is higher than the national average. In the Northern Territories, the imprisonment rate is 552 per 100,000 population. The indigenous people, like blacks in the United States and the United Kingdom, have a much higher rate of incarceration in Australia. The indigenous population comprises about 3% of the Australian population, but they constitute about 25% of the prison population.

■ Summary

One of the homogenizing trends that has been expanding during the last 3 decades in all modern systems of criminal justice is what is described as the growth of new penology—the growth of get-tough crime control strategies. In the early 1970s, crime began to increase in all countries of the West. In the wake of increased crime, a get-tough crime control perspective began to dominate in policy making for crime and justice. The rise of the new challenges of global crimes in the mid-1990s further strengthened the policy commitment for get-tough strategies. However, the get-tough strategies are not simply a bundle of new punishment strategies. They also represent a new philosophy of governance in crime and justice that is based on the assumption that crime control in modern societies is not simply a matter of offender treatment and rehabilitation. Crime control is, rather, a matter of restructuring and revamping the whole system of criminal justice. The perspective of new penology particularly suggests getting tougher in sentencing, incarceration, and incapacitation of the offenders, most of whom, according to the advocates of the new penology, come from an underclass, are career criminals, and are devoid of responsibility and morality. It is not social investment in economics and welfare, but rather incarceration and incapacitation, they believe, that are vital in crime control in modern societies.

In the early 1980s, new laws and legislation began to grow in all modern systems of criminal justice to reform the traditional sentencing structures and guidelines. There also began to grow separate agencies in those countries for policy making in sentencing laws such as the creation of the United States Sentencing Commission in 1984, the Canadian Sentencing Commission in 1984, and the United Kingdom's Sentencing Guidelines Council in 2004. A number of new sentencing strategies have evolved during the last 3 decades in the context of the dominance of the new penology perspective. This is evidenced by the growth of new mandatory minimum and maximum sentencing guidelines, the increase in the length of sentencing, the truth-in-sentencing laws, and the limits imposed on judicial discretions in sentencing in the United States, Canada, the United Kingdom, and Australia. The ideas and philosophy of the new penology are closer to the ideas of political conservatism. The new penology during the last 3 decades rapidly advanced in the United States, Canada, the United Kingdom, and Australia, particularly at the time when political power was in the hands of the conservatives. Liberals like President Clinton in the United States and Tony Blair in the United Kingdom, however, were equally attracted to get-tough strategies. This poses a significant question for comparative criminal justice about the specific nature of the governance of crime and justice in the period of late modernity in the 21st century.

■ Discussion Questions

1. What is the meaning and nature of the new penology perspective that has remained a dominant approach to crime control in most countries of the West from the beginning of the 1980s? What are the social and political contexts of the rise of new penology in advanced democracies of the West? How and/or to what extent has the rise of new penology compromised the principle of the due process of law that is central to modernity in criminal justice?

2. Because of the dominance of the new penology perspective in most advanced countries of the West during the last 3 decades, their criminal justice systems are experiencing some homogenizing trends in many areas of criminal law, particularly in laws related to sentencing. Describe in this context the nature of the development of a new regime of mandatory minimum sentencing guidelines in the United States and Canada. Give examples.

3. The rise of new penology in the United Kingdom and Australia brought some substantial changes in their sentencing laws and guidelines in recent decades. How are the reforms in sentencing laws in the United Kingdom similar to or different from those of Australia? Give examples from the development of sentencing lengths and truth-in-sentencing laws in those countries.

4. The new penology movement has been closely associated with the rise of political conservatism in most advanced countries of the West since the early 1980s. Examine this statement in the context of the expansion of the new penology movement in the United States, the United Kingdom, and Australia. Give examples.

5. In the context of the new penology movement, get-tough policy strategies are more visible in the area of sex crimes. Examine this statement and elaborate on some of the new laws and sentencing guidelines related to sex crime offenses in the United States and the United Kingdom. (Hint: the United Kingdom's Sexual Offences Act of 2003, and United States' Megan's Law of 1996 and the Adam Walsh Child Protection and Safety Act of 2006.)

6. In all countries that have adopted get-tough crime control strategies, the rate of all categories of crimes has significantly dropped. Critically examine this statement in the context of contemporary debates on declining crime in the United States, the United Kingdom, and Australia.

7. A group of criminologists and criminal justice experts has been arguing that the rise of the new penology is associated not just with the rise of new conservatism in politics in advanced countries, but also with some of the fundamental transformations in the structure of modern society. Examine this statement by elaborating some of the new structural features of modern society that in fact necessitate and justify a get-tough approach to crime control in particular and law and order in general. (Hint: Read both Foucault's *Discipline and Punish* and Garland's *Culture of Control*.)

■ References

Australian Bureau of Statistics. (1999). *Crime and safety: Australia, 1998*. Canberra, Australia: Author.

Australian Bureau of Statistics. (2006). *Crime and safety: Australia, 2005*. Canberra, Australia: Author.

Australian Bureau of Statistics. (2011). *Criminal courts, Australia, 2009–2010*. Canberra, Australia: Author.

Australian Institute of Criminology. (1999). *Imprisonment in Australia: Trends in prison populations & imprisonment rates 1982–1998*. Canberra, Australia: Author.

Australian Institute of Criminology. (2010). *Australian crime: Facts and figures, 2009*. Canberra, Australia: Author.

Australian Law Reform Commission. (1988). *Sentencing* (Report No. 44). Canberra: Australian Government Publishing Service.

Australian Law Reform Commission. (2006). *Same crime, same time: Sentencing of federal offenders*. Canberra: Australian Government Publishing Service.

Baker, J. S., & Bennett, D. E. (2004). *Measuring the explosive growth of federal crime legislation*. Washington, DC: The Federalist Society for law and Public Policy Studies.

BBC News. (2004, July 19). *Blair urges new era in crime fight*. Retrieved from http://news.bbc.co.uk /2/hi/uk_news/3905547.stm

Bennett, W. J., DiIulio, J. J., & Walter, J. P. (1996). *Body count: Moral poverty and how to win America's war against crime and drugs*. New York, NY: Simon & Schuster.

Blakely v. Washington, 542 U.S. 296 (2004).

Blumstein, A., & Wallman, J. (2000). *Crime drop in America*. Cambridge, England: Oxford University Press.

Bork, R. H. (1996). *Slouching towards Gomorrah: Modern liberalism and American decline*. New York, NY: Harper-Collins.

Brenton, A., & Hanley, N. (2010). *Using fear to win votes: Representations of law and order in contemporary political campaigns in Australia and Britain.* Retrieved from www.apsa2010.com.au/full-papers/pdf/APSA2010_0152.pdf.

British Ministry of Justice. (2001). *Criminal justice statistics in England and Wales.* London, England: British Home Office.

British Ministry of Justice. (2010a). *Criminal justice statistics in England and Wales.* London, England: British Home Office.

British Ministry of Justice. (2010b). *Sentencing statistics: England and Wales.* London, England: British Home Office.

British Ministry of Justice. (2010c). *Prison population projection, 2010-2016: England and Wales.* London, England: British Home Office.

Bureau of Justice Statistics. (2011). *Homicide trends in the U.S: Long term trends and patterns.* Retrieved from http://bjs.ojp.usdoj.gov/content/homicide/hmrt.cfm.

Clinton, W. J. (1996, June 9). *Remarks in roundtable discussion on juvenile crime in Las Vegas* (public policy paper of the president). Washington, DC: Government Printing Office.

Congressional Research Service. (1999). *Federal mandatory minimum sentencing statutes: A list of citations with captions, introductory comments, and bibliography.* Washington, DC: Library of Congress.

Connecticut Department of Public Safety et al. v. John Doe, 538 U.S. 1 (2003).

Daubney, D. (Chair). (1988). *Taking responsibility: Report of the Standing Committee on Justice and Solicitor General.* Ottawa, Canada: House of Commons.

Doughty, S. (2009, July). *Stop giving us all these new laws, says Chief Justice.* London, England: Mail Online.

Dumm, T. L. (1987). *Democracy and punishment: Disciplinary origins of the United States.* Madison: The University of Wisconsin Press.

Federal Bureau of Investigation. (2010, December 20). *Crime rates down across the board.* Washington, DC: Department of Justice.

Foucault, M. (1977). *Discipline and punish: The birth of the prison.* London, England: Allen Unwin.

Garland, D. (1995). *Punishment and modern society: A study in social theory.* Chicago, IL: University of Chicago Press.

Garland, D. (2001). *The culture of control: Crime and social order in contemporary society.* Chicago, IL: University of Chicago Press.

Grabosky, P., & McFarlane, J. (2007). The potential crime to undermine Australia's national security. *Security Challenges, 3*(4), 131–149.

Humantrafficking.org. (2011). *Human trafficking in Australia.* Retrieved from www.humantrafficking.org/countries/australia

Illinois v. McArthur, 531 U.S. 326 (2001).

Illinois v. Caballes, 543 U.S. 405 (2005).

Illinois v. Wardlow, 528 U.S. 119 (2000).

Kansas v. Hendricks, 521 U.S. 346 (1997).

Kimbrough v. United States, 552 U.S. 85 (2007).

Katz, J. (1988). *Seductions of crime: Moral and sensual attractions in doing evil.* New York, NY: Basic Books.

Law Council of Australia. (2001). *The mandatory sentencing debate.* Canberra, Australia: Author.

Lea, J. (1997). *From integration to exclusion: The development of crime prevention policy in the United Kingdom.* Retrieved from http://www.bunker8.pwp.blueyonder.co.uk/misc/polis.htm.

London Evening Standard. (2007, August 8). *Tories finally get tough: Cameron pledges zero tolerance on crime;* p. 1.

Mackay, R., for the Library of Parliament. (2010). *Bill C-23B: Eliminating Pardons for Serious Crimes Act.* Ottawa, Ontario: Parliamentary Information and Research Service.

Marowitz, L. A. (2000). *Why did the crime rate decrease through the 1999? A literature review and critical analysis.* Sacramento, CA: California Department of Justice.

Maryland v. Pringle, 540 U.S. 366 (2003).

Mauer, M. (2006). *Race to incarcerate.* New York, NY: Free Press.

Meiners, E. (2010). *O Canada: Pay heed to tough-on-crime policies, not the national anthem.* Retrieved from http://msmagazine.com/blog/blog/2010/08/20/o-canada-pay-heed-to-tough-on-crime-policies-not-the-national-anthem/.

Mendes, P. (2001). Social conservatism vs harm minimisation: John Howard on illicit drugs. *Journal of Economic and Social Policy, 6*(1), 1–17.

Michigan v. Sitz, 496 U.S. 444 (1990).

Morgan, N. (2002). *Sentencing trends for violent offenders in Australia* (Criminology Research Council Commission report). Canberra, Australia: Criminology Research Council.

Nixon, R. (1968, August 8). *Acceptance speech* (Republican National Convention). Retrieved from www.4president.org/speeches/nixon1968acceptance.htm.

Parliament of Canada. (2011). *Bill C-2: An Act to Amend the Criminal Code and to Make Consequential Amendments to Other Acts.* Ottawa, Ontario: The Canadian Parliament.

Parliamentary Information and Research Service. (2010). *Bill C-25: Truth-in-Sentencing Act.* Ottawa, Ontario: Library of Parliament.

Parole Board of Canada. (2010). *History of parole in Canada.* Ottawa, Ontario: Parole Board of Canada. Retrieved from www.pbc-clcc.gc.ca.

Pratt, J., Brown D., Brown M., Hallsworth, S., & Morrison, W. (2005). *New punitiveness: Trends, theories, perspectives.* Cullompton, England: Willan Publishing.

Privacy International. (2006). *UK DNA database to grow dramatically under the Criminal Justice Act of 2003.* Retrieved from https://www.privacyinternational.org.

Roberts, J. V., for the Department of Justice, Canada. (2005). *Mandatory sentences of imprisonment in common law jurisdictions: Some representative models—Canada.* Ottawa, Ontario: The Government of Canada.

Sentencing Council. (2011). *Sentencing guidelines.* Retrieved from http://sentencingcouncil.judiciary.gov.uk/sentencing-guidelines.htm.

Sentencing Guidelines Council. (2004). *Overarching principles: Seriousness.* London, England: Author.

Sentencing Guidelines Council. (2008). *Assault and other offences against the person.* London, England: Author.

The Sentencing project. (2004). *The federal prison population: A statistical analysis.* Washington, DC: Author.

Shahidullah, S. M. (2002, November). Crime policy in America: The changing paradigms. *Paper presented at the Annual Meeting of the American Society of Criminology.* Chicago, IL.

Shahidullah, S. M. (2008*). Crime policy in America: Laws, institutions and programs*. Lanham, MD: University Press of America.

Simon, J. (2007). *Governing through crime: How the war on crime transformed American democracy and created a culture of fear*. Oxford, England: Oxford University Press.

Simon, J., & Feeley, M. M. (1995). True crime: The new penology and public discourse on crime. In T. G. Blomberg & S. Cohen (Eds.), *Punishment and social control* (pp. 147– 181). New York, NY: Aldine de Gruyter.

Smith et al. v. John Doe, 538 U.S. 84 (2003).

Smith, P. (2006, December 6). *Sentencing: US Supreme Court lets stand pot dealer's 55-year mandatory minimum sentence*. Ottawa, Ontario: Author.

Solicitor General of Canada. (1990). *Directions for reform: A framework for sentencing, corrections and conditional release*. Ottawa, Canada: Author.

Spears v. United States, 553 U.S. (2009).

Statistics Canada. (2008). *Police-reported crime statistics*. Ottawa, Ontario: Author.

Travis, A. (2010, July). *Crime in England and Wales at its lowest since 1981, says survey*. London, England: The Guardian.

Uniform Crime Reports. (1963). *Crime in the United States*. Washington, DC: The Department of Justice, Federal Bureau of Investigation.

Uniform Crime Reports. (2003). *Crime in the United States*. Washington, DC: The Department of Justice, Federal Bureau of Investigation.

United Nations Office on Drugs and Crime. (2008). *Drug policy and results in Australia*. Vienna, Austria: United Nations.

United States Sentencing Commission. (1991). *Mandatory minimum penalties in the federal criminal justice system* (a special report to the Congress). Washington, DC: Author.

United States v. Booker, 543 U.S. 220 (2005).

Weatherburn, D. (2004). *Law and order in Australia: Rhetoric and reality*. Annandale, New South Wales, Australia: Federation Press.

Whitman, J. Q. (2003). *Harsh justice: Criminal punishment and the widening divide between America and Europe*. New York, NY: Oxford University Press.

Wilson, J. Q., & Herrnstein, R. J. (1985). *Crime and human nature: The definitive study of the causes of crime*. New York, NY: Simon & Schuster.

Modernizing Systems of Criminal Justice in Asia, Africa, and Latin America: The First Wave of Modernization

---

▸ CHAPTER OUTLINE

■ Introduction

A vast number of countries in Asia, Africa, and Latin America, commonly called developing countries or the countries of the Third World, are characterized by modernizing systems of criminal justice. These countries have been in the path of modernization in criminal justice for a long time. They have been moving from a traditional to a modern system of criminal justice for about 200 years, from the time of their encounters with European colonial powers. As of 2011, there are 195 independent states in the world containing about 7 billion people. Most of these states and most of these people belong to the developing world of Asia, Africa, and Latin America. Except for the United States, Russia, Japan, and Germany, the top 20 most populated countries are in the developing world. In 2011, China (1.4 billion people) and India (1.2 billion people) contained more than one third of the world's population (7 billion). Asia alone contains more than half (3.9 billion) of the world's people, who live in 44 countries of Asia—Middle East, Southern Asia, Southeast Asia, and Northern Asia. Africa is the world's second largest continent, and it includes 53 independent countries. In Latin America, which includes the regions of South America, Central America, and the Caribbean, there are 32 independent countries. Out of world's 195 independent states, 129 are in the developing world of Asia, Africa, and Latin America, and each of them has a unique system of criminal justice.

This vast number of states in the developing world belong to dozens of cultures and civilizations. They also have traveled through the path of history with different social and political predicaments. They not only have competing systems of law and legal traditions, but also competing perceptions about crime, law, and justice. The civilizations of India, China, and Japan are some of the oldest in the world, and each of these civilizations has now emerged as a separate nation-state in the modern world. The Islamic civilization of the Middle East was dominated by the Ottoman Empire for more than 600 years (1289–1923). Turkey, Iraq, Syria, Jordan, Lebanon, Egypt, Tunisia, Algeria, and many other regions of the Middle East became independent states after the collapse of the Ottoman Empire in the early 1920s. Before the countries of Latin America were colonized by the Spaniards, they were dominated by the highly organized civilizations of the Aztecs, Incas, and Mayans. Before the Portuguese sailed around the Cape of Good Hope in 1488, Africa was dominated by the kingdoms of Mali, Songhai, Benin, and Nigeria. Each of these civilizations and empires and kingdoms—the regions of which now comprise modern states of the developing world—left some enduring legacies in law and justice. The states that belonged to the Ottoman Empire were dominated by Islamic Shari'a Law. In Latin America, the Aztec, Inca, Zapotec, and Mayan civilizations "had formalized legal systems, with established procedures for trials and especially in the case of Aztecs, a professional legal class, the tepantlatoanis. The Aztec empire also possessed a variety of courts of specialized jurisdictions" (Schwabach, 2006, p. 5). In the Aztec courts, "trials were formally conducted; while most proceedings were conducted orally, written evidence was used and written records were at least sometimes created" (Schwabach, 2006, p. 5).

■ Colonial Legacies in Law and Justice: Asia, Africa, and Latin America

In the midst of enormous cultural and civilizational diversities in the developing countries, there is one historical predicament that is common to almost all of them. All (except China, Japan, Korea, and Thailand) came into contact with the West through colonialism. From the days of colonialism, a modernization process started in most of these countries in all spheres of the economy, politics, governance, education, and law and justice. For a comparative analysis of criminal justice in the diverse trajectories of lands and peoples in the developing world, one needs to examine how criminal justice in particular and law and order in general evolved in the context of their encounters with European colonial powers. The European colonial powers set in motion a new process of social change and transformation in the colonies. This was the first wave of modernization in Asia, Africa, and Latin America. This wave continued until the end of colonialism in the early 19th century for Latin America and the middle of the 20th century for Asia and Africa. The purpose of this chapter is to provide an understanding of the historical context of modern criminal justice in Asia, Africa, and Latin America, as well as the nature of its growth and continuity during the creation of the modern states. The chapter will focus on colonial legacies in criminal justice and examine the nature of the rule of law, democracy, and criminal justice in the process of state building during the postcolonial period.

Globalization of European Legal Traditions: Common Law and Civil Law

The history of modernization in criminal justice in the developing countries began with the rise and expansion of European colonialism. With the expansion of colonialism came the expansion of modern law and legal traditions: legal education; the institution of professional policing; the formal structures of the judiciary; and the system of prisons and corrections. Except in some of the British colonies in Africa, precolonial and medieval systems of law and justice largely disintegrated under the effect of colonialism. The process of disintegration, however, took a long time. In the Spanish colonies of Latin America, the disintegration of the indigenous system of law and justice began from the beginning of colonialism in the 15th and 16th centuries. In the British colonies of Asia, particularly in South Asia, the disintegration began with the establishment of direct rule by the British Crown in the middle of the 19th century. Expansion of modernization in criminal justice in the colonies during the mid-19th century is particularly noteworthy because it was also during that time that modern states and modern institutions of criminal justice began to expand in the West.

Colonialism as a system of occupation and governance of foreign lands and as a system of subjugation and domination of foreign peoples for centuries was antithetical to the ideas of the Enlightenment. Many Enlightenment philosophers were opposed to the philosophy of colonialism. When colonialism began in the 15th century, it was primarily a system for the economic plundering of the wealth and resources of the colonies. It obstructed the natural evolutionary process of the colonies from feudalism to capitalism, and from monarchy to democracy. In the mid-19th century, colonialism began to be justified in terms of its mission: globalization of modernity. Even Karl Marx, in his writings on British India, said that India could not have entered into the modern age without the reach of British colonialism. The question of whether colonialism has been a catalyst of change and modernity in the colonies or has permanently destroyed their transformative capacities to evolve to modernity from within is central to the literature of colonial history and postcolonial development. What is historically and empirically true is that colonialism brought to the colonies a whole set of instrumentalities for the growth of modern states, including modern education, modern science and technology, and modern law and justice. In comparative criminal justice, one needs to examine how the institutions of law and justice implanted by colonialism have been evolving since the end of colonialism and in the context of postcolonial development and modernization.

Throughout the developing world of Asia, Africa, and Latin America, colonialism began around the same time as in the Americas, after the arrival of Christopher Columbus in 1492. From 1492 to 1898, for more than 400 years, South America, Central America, and the Caribbean islands were under the colonial rule of Spain. Except for Brazil, which was colonized by the Portuguese in 1500, the whole of Latin America was a Spanish colony for 400 years. Around the same time, in the late 15th century, colonization in Africa began when the Portuguese occupied the coastal areas of Angola and Mozambique in order to participate in the region's expanding slave and gold trade. The more planned and deliberate colonization of the whole continent of Africa by the British, French, Germans, Belgians, and Italians—a process that historians have called the "scramble of Africa"—began in the late 19th century and continued up to the beginning of World War I in 1914. Most of the major African countries were colonized by the British, French, and Germans. The British colonies in Africa included Egypt, Kenya, Tanzania, Zanzibar, Botswana, Zimbabwe, South Africa, Zambia, Namibia, Malawi, Swaziland, and Ghana. The major French colonies included Senegal, Gambia, Mali, Guinea, Ivory Coast, Niger, Burkina Faso, Benin, Togo, Gabon, Algeria, Tunisia, and Morocco. The major German colonies were Cameroon, Rwanda, and Burundi. The Italians colonized the state of Libya in 1911. Asia became open to European colonialism after the discovery of the Cape of Good Hope by the Portuguese in 1488 and after Vasco da Gama sailed to India from Europe in 1498. India was Asia's largest country that remained a British colony for almost 200 years. The political power of India was captured in 1757 by the British East India Company which ruled until 1858 and had received a Charter from the British Crown. In 1858, the British formally established a colonial state in India under the direct control of the British Crown. From 1858 to 1947, for about 100 years, India was ruled as the British colonial state.

After the formal establishment of political power in the colonies, the transformation of the existing institutions of law and justice was one of the first and foremost tasks of the colonial states. A new process of transforming of the law and legal traditions, structure of law enforcement and policing, and constitution of the courts and the judiciary began from colonialism's early days. There also began a new process of criminalization and decriminalization. The transformations in criminal justice in the colonies came much before changes in other areas such as land reforms, education, and science and technology because the development of a framework of law and justice was imperative to establish the basic infrastructure of the colonial state, define its authority, expand its legitimacy, and exercise its control on social and political violence.

The restructuring of the precolonial system of criminal justice first began with the introduction of the European legal systems in the colonies—English common law and Continental civil law. English common law was introduced in the British colonies in Asia and Africa, and in the Caribbean. Continental civil law was introduced in the Spanish, French, and German colonies of Africa, South America, Central America, and the Caribbean (see **Table 7-1**).

TABLE 7-1 European Legal Traditions in Asia, Africa, and Latin America: Colonial Legacies in Criminal Justice in Selected Countries

Dominance of Common Law Tradition	Dominance of Civil Law Tradition	Pluralistic Legal Traditions: Civil Law/Common Law/Customary Laws
Bahamas	Angola	Burkina Faso
Bangladesh	Argentina	Burundi
Barbados	Benin	Cameroon
Belize	Brazil	Chad
Botswana	Cambodia	China
Ghana	Chile	Ethiopia
India	Colombia	Guyana
Jamaica	Costa Rica	Japan
Kenya	Ecuador	Madagascar
Malawi	Honduras	Mali
Namibia	Mexico	Malta
Nigeria	Paraguay	Mauritius Islands
South Africa	Peru	Myanmar
Swaziland	Thailand	Namibia
Tanzania	Turkey	Nepal
Tonga	Ukraine	Papua-New Guinea
Trinidad and Tobago	Uruguay	Philippines
Zambia	Venezuela	Sri Lanka
Zimbabwe	Vietnam	Uganda

Source: Data from JuriGlobe-World Legal Systems, *www.juriglobe.ca/eng/index.php.*

English common law was formally brought to India after the British Parliament passed the Government of India Act in 1858. In 1900, Nigeria began to formally adopt English common law after the British seized political power from the Royal Nigerian Company. In Kenya, English common law was formally adopted in 1920 after the British took political control from the Imperial British East India Company (Deflem, 1994). In the Spanish colonies of South America and Central America, the Spanish Civil Code remained a basis for legal development from the beginning of colonial expansion in the 16th century. From the beginning of decolonization in South America and Central America in the 19th century, however, most of the newly independent countries there began to adopt the French Napoleonic Civil Code. As one legal historian observed, "The model that most appealed to the jurists to draft Latin American codes during the middle of the nineteenth century was the French Civil Code (Code of Napoleon) enacted in 1804" (Karst & Rosenn, 1975, p. 45).

There are three models of codification of Latin American laws: Chilean Code (1846–1858), Argentinean Code (1863–1869), and Brazilian Code (1856–1865). These three codes "served as models for civil codes of most Latin American countries" (Karst & Rosenn, 1975, p. 47). During colonial time, Latin American penal law "was barbaric, and outdated, with cruel and harsh penalties, obsolete offenses and superstitions, and different treatment according to social class" (Karst & Rosenn, 1975, p. 55). After independence, most Latin American countries therefore borrowed the Napoleonic version of the French Civil Code.

As a result of the globalization of the common law and civil law traditions through the process of colonialism, there began a process of secularization in law and legal development in general and criminal law in particular in the colonies. In many of the colonies, such as Nigeria, Egypt, and Kenya, the preexisting religious and customary laws coexisted with the secular tradition of English common law. But both English common law and Continental civil law certainly started a process of secularization in criminal justice in the colonies. They also introduced into the colonial judicial systems the principle of the due process of law, the notion of presumption of innocence, the rule of the burden of proof beyond a reasonable doubt, and the ideas of judicial independence. Many of these principles were violated by their creators in the colonies and by the unequal systems of justice established by the colonial states, but it is also certain that many of these principles were formally integrated into the traditional systems of law and justice in the colonies.

Globalization of European Penal Codes, Policing, and the Judicial System: The Case of British India

Among all the British colonies in Asia, Africa, and the Caribbean, the most expansive system of criminal justice was created in British India. The criminal justice system that was built in India by the successive ruling dynasties of the Mughal Empire—which ruled India for over 200 years (1526–1757)—was based on Islamic law for both Muslims and non-Muslims. The Mughal criminal justice system collapsed after the decline of the Mughal Empire and the capture of India's political power by the British East India Company in 1757. From the beginning of its accession to power, the British East India Company initiated a process of building a centralized criminal justice system in India. Warren Hastings, the first Governor-General of British India (1773–1785) proposed overhauling India's criminal justice by replacing Islamic law with English common law; establishing a centralized chain of command for a criminal justice administration; and creating criminal courts in each district of the Bengal, Bombay, and Madras presidencies. Lord Cornwallis, the next Governor-General of British India (1786–1793), had a far more comprehensive plan for modernization in criminal justice. He introduced a separate office of magistrates, under the control of British covenant civil servants, for the conduct of police and judicial functions. He created four circuit courts, and the British covenant civil servants were appointed as judges of those courts. For reforms in law enforcement and policing, Lord Cornwallis introduced a system that is still in force in India—a system of local police administration under the control of a police officer called a *daroga* in each district of the provinces. Under these new reforms, the traditional local police administrations that were led by local landlords (*zamindars*) were completely divested of their political authority for justice and law enforcement.

More systematic policy developments for reforms in criminal justice in colonial India began in the early 19th century, and the process formally started when the Indian Law Commission was established in 1833 under the chairmanship of Lord Thomas Macaulay. The Commission was given responsibility for codifying criminal law and overhauling the whole system of criminal justice in India. The Commission produced the following five major legal documents: the Indian Police Act of 1861, the Indian Penal Code of 1862, the Indian Evidence Act of 1872, the Indian Code of Criminal Procedure of 1882, and the Indian Code of Criminal Procedure of 1898. Modern criminal justice in India, Bangladesh, Pakistan, Sri Lanka, and many other British colonies in Asia, Africa, and the Caribbean are built on the foundation of these five legal documents. No comparative studies of criminal justice in these countries would be complete without examining the nature and the framework of law and justice introduced by these acts and their evolution during the last century and a half of changes and reforms.

The Indian Penal Code (IPC) of 1862 created a new body of substantive criminal law (Cranenburgh, 1894). It brought India's criminal justice system to a new era of modernization by producing a more rational and uniform system of criminal law (Wright, 2010). Codification of the IPC was not based only on English common law. It also borrowed laws and ideas from the French Criminal Code of 1804, Edward Livingstone's Louisiana Criminal Code enacted in 1822, and Indian customary laws and regulations. The core mission of developing the IPC, as one criminologist summarized, "was to replace the Muslim and Hindu laws overlaid with a mixture of transplanted English laws and East India Company regulations to ensure, as much as possible, a singular standard of justice" (Wright, 2010, p. 6). The IPC "represented progress from what then existed in India . . . and throughout the British Empire . . . . [The] implementation of the rule of law by way of clear and consistent expression of legal powers, the minimizing of discretionary authority and status differences, were significant advances" (Wright, 2010, p. 43).

The IPC was divided into different chapters and sections that identified the nature and types of offenses and related punishments. Crimes were divided into two major types: cognizable (felonies) and noncognizable (misdemeanor). For cognizable offenses, police were given the power to arrest without a warrant. Different offenses were identified in terms of offenses against the state and the armed forces, offenses against public order, violent offenses, property offenses, and offenses related to marriage, family, sex, and morality. Chapter XVI on violent offenses affecting a human body defined the nature of culpable homicide: "Whoever causes death by doing an act with the intention of causing death, or with the intention of causing such bodily injury . . . commits the offence of culpable homicide." Culpable homicide is murder, and IPC stated, "Whoever commits murder shall be punished with death, or imprisonment for life, and shall also be liable to fine."

Section 375 of the IPC defined the nature of sexual offenses. It is interesting to note that the IPC criminalized polygamy and adultery. About polygamy, the IPC says, "Whoever, having a husband or wife living, marries in any case in which such marriage is void by reason of its taking place during the life of such husband or wife, shall be punished with imprisonment" (IPC, 1862, §494). About adultery, the IPC says, "Whoever has sexual intercourse with a person who is and whom he knows or has reason to believe to be the wife of another man . . . is guilty of the offence of adultery, and shall be punished with imprisonment" (IPC, 1862, §497). It also criminalized the sexual harassment of a married woman: "Whoever takes or entices away any woman who is and whom he knows or has reason to believe to be the wife of any other man . . . shall be punished with imprisonment" (IPC, 1862, §498).

The IPC created a new body of offenses such as kidnapping and abduction for murder (§364); kidnapping and abduction for ransom (§364A); kidnapping and abduction for confinement (§365); kidnapping and abduction of a woman to compel her to marriage (§366); kidnapping, abduction, and having sexual intercourse with a girl below the age of 18 (§366A); importation of girl from a foreign country (§366B); selling and buying of minors for purposes of prostitution (§372–373); and selling and buying of any person as a slave (§371). The IPC criminalized many forms of gang behavior such as belonging to a gang of dacoits (§400), belonging to gang of thieves (§401), and even assembling for the purpose of committing dacoity (§402).

The IPC also criminalized insulting the religion of any particular class or group: "Whoever destroys, damages or defiles any place of worship . . . with the intention of thereby insulting the religion of any class of persons . . . shall be punished with imprisonment" (IPC, 1862, §295). Section 295A stated: "Whoever, with deliberate and malicious intention of outraging the religious feelings of any class . . . insults or attempts to insult the religion or the religious beliefs of that class, shall be punished with imprisonment" (IPC, 1862, §295A).

The IPC also criminalized spousal violence: "Whoever, being the husband or the relative of the husband of a woman, subjects such woman to cruelty shall be punished with imprisonment for a term which may extend to three years and shall also be liable to fine" (IPC, 1862, §498A). The IPC criminalized cruelty to women, and Section 498A stated that it means: "harassment of the woman where such harassment is with a view to coercing her . . . to meet any unlawful demand for any property or valuable security" (IPC, 1862, §498A). Criminalization of cruelty to women in India, however, began about 3 decades before the enactment of the IPC with the abolition of the ritual murder of a woman known as *Sati* in 1829 by then–Governor General of India, Lord William Bentinck.

The Indian Police Act, created in 1861, was aimed at creating a new structure of modern policing in India modeled after the Metropolitan Police in London, Royal Irish Constabulary, and Royal Ulster Constabulary (India, Legislative Department, 2010). The Indian Police Act created a centralized police force for each of the provinces of British India. The Act stated in its preamble that "the entire police-establishment under a State Government shall . . . be deemed to be one police-force and shall be formally enrolled; and shall consist of such number of officers and men, and shall be constituted in such manner." The Act outlined the constitution of the police force, magisterial powers of police officers, police roles and responsibilities, local administration, police rules and ethics, and police sanctions and disciplines. About the duties of police officers, the Act stated that "it shall be the duty of every police-officer . . . [to] execute all orders and warrants lawfully issued to him by any competent authority; to collect and communicate intelligence affecting the public peace; to prevent the commission of offences and public nuisances" (Act V, 1861). The Indian Police Act also introduced a system of criminal record keeping by police officers. The act mandated, "It shall be the duty of every officer . . . of a police-station to keep a general diary . . . to record therein, all complaints . . . the names of all persons arrested, . . . [and] the offences charged against them" (Act V, 1861).

In 1861, the British government also introduced the Indian Councils Act of 1861. The Act created the foundation of a modern and professionalized police bureaucracy in India. It introduced a new cadre of police, called Superior Police Services, "later known as the Indian (Imperial) Police, [that] consisted of an Inspector General, Deputy Inspectors General, District Superintendents and Assistant District Superintendents. The Subordinate Police Service in each province consisted of Inspectors, Sub-Inspectors, Head Constables and Constables" (British Library, 2011, p. 1). The members of the Superior Police Services, particularly beginning in 1893, "were appointed by examination or selection in the U.K. In the lower branch, the Subordinate Services were mainly constituted of Indians with some Europeans and Eurasians in the higher ranks" (British Library, 2011, p. 1).

The British colonial government brought many similar changes in law and policing to other colonies in Asia, Africa, and the Caribbean. In 1844, the British colonial government created a royal police force for Hong Kong. One study on policing in Hong Kong found that "a police force was established in Hong Kong as early as 1844 with the primary function of securing law and order and suppressing protest against British rule . . . personnel were largely recruited from other British overseas territories" (Deflem, Featherstone, Li, & Sutphin, 2008, p. 349). The Hong Kong Police Force was "reformed after the model of the Royal Irish Constabulary and recruits from India were enlisted" (Deflem et al., 2008, p. 349). In the African colony of Kenya, the British East Africa Police was established in 1902, and the "inspectors were all European, the assistant inspectors largely Asian, and the rank and file was entirely comprised of Africans" (Deflem, 1994, p. 52). The "Penal Code, the Criminal Procedure Act, and the Police Act which were introduced in colonial Kenya, were all imported from British India" (Deflem, 1994, p. 52). Similar institutions of imperial policing were established in the plantation colonies of the British Caribbean (Anderson & Killingray, 1991b). In all the colonies of Asia, Africa, and Latin America, as one study on colonial policing observed, "Policing played a vital role in the construction of the colonial social order. In Australia, as in India, the police were the first institutions established by the colonial state, and quickly became one of the state's major bureaucracies" (Anderson & Killingray, 1991a, p. 9).

The colonial states in Asia, Africa, and Latin America created the foundation not only of modern law and policing, but also of modern judiciaries in the colonies. During the Mughal administration, criminal justice in India was controlled by a court system characterized by four tiers: courts at capital (emperor's court—court of chief justice); provincial courts (governor's court—provincial court of appeals); district courts (district *Quazi* court, *Faujdari Adalat*, and *Kotwali* court); and *pargana* courts and village courts. Within the Mughul judiciary, there was no separation between the executive and the judiciary, and Muslim law was the basis of criminal law. Modern reforms in the system of the judiciary in colonial India, with the aim of creating a judiciary independent of the executive and a system of judiciary based on secular laws and legal procedures, began in the late 18th century under the rule of the British East India Company, which created a Supreme Court of Judicature and a separate court for the administration of criminal justice called the *nizamat adalat* in 1774. More systematic efforts for judicial reforms began after the enactment of the Indian High Courts Act of 1861, the Indian Penal Code of 1862, the Indian Evidence Act of 1872, the Code of Criminal Procedure of 1882, and the Code of Criminal Procedure of 1898. After the High Courts Act of 1861, separate high courts were established in the presidencies of Calcutta, Madras, and Bombay. A high court, the highest court of criminal appeal, was comprised of a Chief Justice and 15 judges. They were appointed from the covenant civil service and among those who were educated and trained as barristers. The Chief Justice and the judges of the high court were appointed by Her Majesty, the Queen of England. After the enactment of the Government of India Act of 1935, India changed from a unitary form to a federal form of government. The Government of India Act of 1935 established one federal court at the top—the Supreme Court of India—and more high courts for the new provinces.

In the area of the administration of criminal justice, the Code of Criminal Procedure of 1882 established a new hierarchical system of criminal courts with five tiers: courts of session, presidency magistrates, magistrate of the first class, magistrate of the second class, and magistrate of the third class. The Code explained the constitution and power of the criminal courts, terms of judicial appointments, nature of judicial duties and accountability, nature of judicial hierarchy, nature of police power, procedures of police investigation, search and seizure procedures, warrant procedures, procedures of crime reporting, pretrial and trial procedures, and nature of convictions and sentencing (Agnew & Henderson, 1882). One of the remarkable features introduced by the Code of Criminal Procedure of 1882 was the decentralization of the judicial system. The Code declared, "Local government shall establish a court of sessions . . . and appoint a Judge of such Court. It may also appoint Sessions Judges, Joint Sessions Judges and Assistant Sessions Judges to exercise jurisdiction in one or more such courts" (Code of Criminal Procedure, 1882, Chapter II). The Code made provisions for the establishment of criminal courts in each district and in each subdivision of a district. The Code said, "The Local Government may divide any District outside the Presidency—towns into Subdivisions, or make portion of any such District or Subdivision, and may alter the limits of any Subdivision" (Code of Criminal Procedure, 1882, Chapter II). The Code also set forth the power of the different criminal courts to impose punishment. The court of a district magistrate was authorized to impose imprisonment not exceeding 7 years. The courts of the presidency magistrates and the magistrate of the first class were authorized to impose imprisonment not exceeding 2 years and fines not exceeding 1,000 rupees. The courts of the magistrate of the second class were authorized to impose imprisonment not exceeding 6 months, and the court of the magistrate of the third class, not exceeding 1 month (Code of Criminal Procedure, 1882, Chapter II). The Code of Criminal Procedure of 1882 was amended and a new Code of Criminal Procedure was introduced in 1898. The Code of Criminal Procedure of 1898 introduced many more modern provisions of criminal justice, such as the right of indignant defendants to have an attorney.

The British colonial government thus introduced in India a new legal tradition (English common law), criminal laws and legislation (Indian Penal Code of 1862), a structure of policing (Indian Police Act of 1861), a judicial system (High Courts Act of 1861), criminal procedural laws (Codes of Criminal Procedure of 1882 and 1898), evidentiary rules (Indian Evidence Act of 1872), and a system of prisons and corrections (Prison Act of 1894). The colonial government also introduced a modern tradition of legal education in India (Legal Practitioners Act of 1846). It formally began with the opening a professor of law position in the Government Ephistone College in Bombay and Madras and at Hindu College in Calcutta in 1855. In 1857, modern legal education was introduced in the universities of Calcutta, Bombay, and Madras.

Even though they were much more intensive and comprehensive in the British colony of India, similar changes in criminal justice also occurred in other colonies ruled by the British and other European colonial powers in Asia, Africa, and Latin America—the Portuguese, the Spaniards, the French, the Dutch, and the Germans. Indonesia was a Dutch colony for about 350 years and its modern criminal justice system was created mainly by the Dutch. The Dutch colonial state introduced the First Code of Criminal Procedure in Indonesia in 1847. One legal scholar of Indonesia observed that "there are still many legacies of Dutch law remaining valid in Indonesia, including the Civil Law Code, the Commercial Law Code, the Civil Procedure Code, and the Penal Code" (Sujata, 2011, p. 1). Article II of the Interim Regulations of the 1945 Constitution of Indonesia "stated that all existing provisions of law shall remain applicable unless superseded by new laws" (Sujata, 2011, p. 1). The need for understanding the colonial legacies in law and justice in the developing countries of Asia, Africa, and Latin America, therefore, is tremendously significant in comparative criminal justice.

■ Rule of Law, Democracy, and Criminal Justice in Postcolonial Societies

It is equally intriguing for students of comparative criminal justice to examine how it has been evolving in the postcolonial societies of Asia, Africa, and Latin America. The countries of Latin America became independent from the colonial rule more than 150 years ago. Argentina, Chile, Uruguay, Paraguay, Ecuador, and many South and Central American countries got their independence in the 1st and 2nd decades of the 19th century. Venezuela received independence in 1821, Brazil became independent from the Portuguese in 1822, and Mexico became independent in 1821. In Asia and Africa, most of the countries became independent in the 1950s and 1960s. Criminal justice systems in almost all of these countries have some infrastructures of modern criminal justice, but they are still far from modernity. In the postcolonial societies, there are laws in the criminal code that are not applied, and many criminal laws that are applied are not in the criminal code. Structures of modern policing and law enforcement are in place, but police brutality is rampant and police accountability is hardly enforced. These are codes of criminal procedure, but the issues of the due process of law are regularly violated. Structures of a modern judicial system are in place, but judicial corruption is endemic, judicial independence is continuously compromised, and judicial accountability is regularly violated. Crime is growing, but crime reporting is still archaic. Prisons are full, but many of the prisoners are detainees who were not formally convicted and sentenced.

The era of postcolonial development was an era of new hopes and dreams by billions of people who did not see glimpses of modernity and did not share the Enlightenment's achievements. It has also been an era of political crisis and turbulence. In most countries, the military came to power, ruled for decades, and left when the countries were politically and economically in shambles. In most Latin American countries, military-authoritarian regimes ruled for decades and destroyed the core institutions of the rule of law and democracy. With vast economic poverty and enormous problems in the rule of law and democracy, the postcolonial countries of Asia, Africa, and Latin America entered into the 21st century—a century born with unprecedented promises in modern technology, globalization, and democracy. The 21st century was born with new challenges for law and justice as well. The following sections will examine the status of the rule of law and democracy in postcolonial societies. Within the scope of this study, it is not possible to examine the status of the rule of law and democracy in all the countries of the developing world. However, a number of global surveys exist from which some general understanding can be reached. Some of these surveys include the World Bank's Governance Indicators Study, the World Justice Project, the Freedom in the World Survey, the Center for Systemic Peace's State Fragility Index and Matrix, the Global Peace Index, and the World Democracy Index.

The World Bank's Governance Indicators Study

The World Bank has been studying the status of the rule of law and governance in the world's societies since 1996. The status of governance is measured in the performance of these countries in the following six areas: voice and accountability, political stability and absence of violence, government effectiveness, regulatory quality, rule of law, and control of corruption. Three of these indicators are directly related to the nature of criminal justice: the rule of law, political stability and absence of violence, and voice and accountability. The World Bank survey defines the rule of law in terms of "the perceptions of the extent to which the agents . . . have confidence in and abide by the rules of society, and in particular the quality of contract enforcement, property rights, the police, and the courts" (Kaufmann, Kraay, & Mastruzzi, 2010, p. 4).

Within the rule of law, the survey measures a number of concepts such as losses and costs for crime, the nature of violent crime, the extent of criminal victimization, the extent of organized crime, confidence in the police force, confidence in the judicial system, independence of the judiciary, speediness of the judicial process, and law and order. The nature of political stability and the absence of violence is defined as the "likelihood that the government will be destabilized or overthrown by unconstitutional or violent means, including domestic violence and terrorism" (Kaufmann et al., 2010, p. 4). Some of the concepts that are examined in order to measure political stability include the risk of military takeover of political power, risk of civil war, risk of urban riots, extent of political insurgency, political terrorism, political killings, armed conflict, social unrest, violent demonstrations, and possibility of ethnic and religious conflicts. The indicator of voice and accountability is defined by the survey as "the extent to which a country's citizens are able to participate in selecting their government, as well as freedom of expression, freedom of association, and a free media" (Kaufmann et al., 2010, p. 4). Voice and accountability is examined by the nature of democracy index, performance in human rights, accountability of public officials, political rights, civil liberties, and respect for ethnic and religious minorities.

The World Bank survey gathers data on these indicators and concepts from a number of international surveys, international organizations, think tanks, and surveys of expert groups and citizens. Some of these sources include the African Development Bank, Afrobarometer, Asian Development Bank, Transparency International, Global Competitiveness Report, Global Integrity Index, Gallup World Poll, Latinobarometer, World Bank Country Reports, and the U.S. Department of State's Trafficking in Persons Report. The findings of the World Bank's annual survey are presented by ranking (percentile) of 213 countries (in 2010) across the six core dimensions.

The World Bank's (2010b) survey shows that in the rule of law, most countries of the advanced industrialized West, including Australia and New Zealand, have been performing remarkably well. Some of these countries scored at or above the 90th percentile. These included Finland (100), Sweden (99.5), New Zealand (99.1), Denmark (98.1), Norway (98.6), the Netherlands (97.2), Canada (96.7), Australia (95.5), the United Kingdom (93.9), Germany (92.9), and the United States (91.5). These countries are also in the highest percentile in political stability and voice and accountability (see **Table 7-2**), and they have modern systems of criminal justice.

In the rule of law, the World Bank's (2010b) survey shows that most countries of Asia, Africa, and Latin America performed poorly. Most countries are in the 25th–50th percentile. Some developing countries are in the lowest 10th percentile, and they belong mostly to sub-Saharan Africa. In South Asia, a region that contains about 1.6 billion people, four countries are slightly above the 50th percentile in their status in the rule of law. These are Bhutan (59.4), Sri Lanka (53.3), India (55.7), and Maldives (52.8). Four other countries of South Asia are below the 30th percentile. These countries include Bangladesh (27.8), Pakistan (19.3), Nepal (17.9), and Afghanistan (0.5). All of these countries, except Bhutan, scored below the 40th percentile in political stability (see **Table 7-3**). According to the survey, political stability in three major South Asian countries (India, Pakistan, and Bangladesh) is extremely poor, below

TABLE 7-2 Rule of Law: Comparison Across Selected Advanced Countries, 2009

Country	Percentile Rank	Country	Percentile Rank
Australia	95.5	Netherlands	97.2
Canada	96.7	New Zealand	99.1
Denmark	98.1	Norway	98.6
Finland	100.0	Sweden	99.5
France	89.5	Switzerland	96.2
Germany	92.9	United Kingdom	93.9
Japan	88.2	United States	91.5

Source: Data from Kaufmann, D., Kraay, A., & Mastruzzi, M., for the World Bank. (2010). *The worldwide governance indicators: Methodology and analytical issues.* Washington, DC: World Bank Development Research Group.

the 15th percentile. Pakistan is seen as the most politically unstable and volatile country in South Asia, with a score in the 0.5 percentile. These three countries, which contain about 1.5 billion people, are characterized by political instability and serious problems with the rule of law. It is in these three countries, as discussed in the previous section, that the British colonial state created the modern infrastructures of criminal justice through the Indian Police Act of 1861, the High Courts Act of 1861, the Indian Penal Code of 1862, the Code of Criminal Procedure of 1882, and the Code of Criminal Procedure of 1898.

In Latin America, the records of rule of law, political stability and violence, and voice and accountability issues, according to the World Bank's study, are equally dismal. In the rule of law, the major countries of Latin America, except Chile and Brazil, are below the 60th percentile. In political stability, most major countries of Latin America, except Chile, Brazil, and Uruguay, scored below the 50th percentile. The issues of political instability are much more serious in Colombia, Ecuador, Guatemala, Mexico, Peru, and Venezuela.

TABLE 7-3 Rule of Law, Political Stability, and Accountability: Comparison Across South Asian Countries, 2009

Country	Percentile Rank Rule of Law	Percentile Rank Political Stability	Percentile Rank Voice and Accountability
Afghanistan	0.5	0.9	10.0
Bangladesh	27.8	7.5	35.1
Bhutan	59.4	71.2	29.4
India	55.7	13.2	60.2
Maldives	52.8	39.2	44.1
Nepal	17.9	5.2	30.8
Pakistan	19.3	0.5	20.9
Sri Lanka	53.3	11.8	32.2

Source: Data from Kaufmann, D., Kraay, A., & Mastruzzi, M., for the World Bank. (2010). *The worldwide governance indicators: Methodology and analytical issues.* Washington, DC: World Bank Development Research Group.

Most South and Central American countries became independent in the first half of the 19th century. In more than 170 years since then, none of the Latin American countries has been able to join the rank of the world's leading democracies. During the last 4 decades, most countries of Latin America were ruled by military-authoritarian regimes of different kinds.

In the rule of law, political stability, and voice and accountability, the performance of most of the African countries is also very poor (see **Table 7-4**). In performance in the area of the rule of law, the major countries of sub-Saharan Africa are below the 25th percentile, except South Africa and Ghana, which are below the 60th percentile. In the area of political stability, the sub-Saharan countries, except Benin, Ghana, South Africa, Zambia, and Mozambique, are below the 40th percentile. The World Bank's (2010b) survey shows that political stability is a serious problem in Sudan (1.4), Ethiopia (6.1), Nigeria (4.2), Kenya (12.3), Uganda (15.1), and Zimbabwe (9.9). Among the countries of North Africa, the rule of law is poor in Algeria (26.9), Libya (24.5), and Yemen (13.2). In the area of political stability, Egypt, Algeria, and Yemen are below the 25th percentile. In the indicator of voice and accountability, Somalia, Angola, Ethiopia, Gabon, Sudan, and Zimbabwe are below the 15th percentile.

The rule of law and political stability, according to the World Bank (2010b) survey, are also serious problems in Russia and the newly independent countries of the former Soviet Union. The 10 countries of the former Soviet Union, including Armenia, Azerbaijan, Belarus, Georgia, Kazakhstan, Kyrgyzstan, Russia, Tajikistan, Ukraine, and Uzbekistan, scored below the 50th percentile in their performance in the rule of law. The performance of Russia in the categories of the rule of law and political stability is below the 25th percentile. This partly explains the explosion of organized crime in Russia after the collapse of the Soviet Union in the mid-1980s. The performance of the countries of Eastern Europe in the rule of law, political stability, and voice and accountability is better than the performance of the countries

TABLE 7-4 Rule of Law and Political Stability: Comparison Across Selected African Countries

Country	Percentile Rank Rule of Law	Percentile Rank Political Stability	Country	Percentile Rank Rule of Law	Percentile Rank Political Stability
Benin	28.8	61.8	Niger	31.6	14.2
Cameroon	15.6	31.1	Nigeria	10.4	4.2
Ethiopia	23.1	6.1	South Africa	56.1	44.3
Ghana	51.9	50.0	Sudan	5.2	1.4
Kenya	15.1	12.3	Tanzania	40.1	47.6
Malawi	48.6	43.5	Uganda	40.6	15.1
Mali	42.0	34.9	Zambia	37.7	64.2
Mozambique	33.5	63.7	Zimbabwe	0.9	9.9

Source: Data from Kaufmann, D., Kraay, A., & Mastruzzi, M., for the World Bank. (2010). *The worldwide governance indicators: Methodology and analytical issues.* Washington, DC: World Bank Development Research Group.

BOX 7-1

Rule of Law Reform in Post-Conflict Countries

In the early 1990s, development experts and international development assistance organizations have been arguing that economic development is intimately connected to law and justice institutions, and that through law and justice institutions, development is intimately connected to reforms in criminal justice. The argument is that the rule of law is imperative for advancing toward development and modernization for the countries of the developing world, particularly for post-conflict countries and the countries with failed and fragile states. The development of the rule of law does not merely mean the creation of a new judiciary or expanding the scope of legal education. The development experts and international organizations present four justifications for the centrality of the rule of law in the process of development. The first is the rule law for economic development—the expansion of a market economy through the creation of an attractive and predictable investment climate. The second is the rule of law for democracy—to establish a political system that is bound by the rule of law and is dedicated to protect human rights: "The protection of human rights and mechanisms holding government accountable are . . . inherent in rule of law." The third is the rule of law for poverty alleviation. The rule of law is "essential to poverty reduction as the poor suffer more from crime, the impact of crime on their livelihood is greater, and they are less able to access the justice systems." The fourth is the rule of law for peace building—establishing a culture of constitutionalism and an efficient and transparent system of judiciary to resolve conflicts and improve access to justice for all. The contemporary nation of the rule of law "is a more global phenomenon . . . rationalized on the basis of economic development, democracy, and peace." In pursuing comparative criminal justice in post-conflict countries and countries with failed and fragile states, it is, therefore, crucial to examine the extent to which those countries are engaged in pursuing the rule of law as a development paradigm.

Source: Samuels, K. (2006). *Rule of law reform in post-conflict countries: Operational initiatives and lessons learnt.* Washington, DC: The World Bank, Social Development Department.

of South Asia, Africa, and Latin America. In performance in the area of the rule of law, the Czech Republic, Hungary, Latvia, and Slovenia scored above the 70th percentile, and Croatia, Poland, Romania, and Slovakia scored above the 50th percentile (Kaufmann et al., 2010). The East Asian countries also, except South Korea and Malaysia, scored below the 50th percentile in the area of the rule of law. China scored 45.3 in the area of the rule of law and 29.7 in political stability. This shows that more than 3 billion of the world's people (about 7 billion) live in countries that are characterized by very poor performance in the rule of law and political stability (see **Box 7-1**).

The World Justice Project: Rule of Law Index

The World Justice Project (WJP), created by the American Bar Association in 2006, is one of the world's leading think tank organizations that conducts global surveys on the nature of the rule of law among the world's societies. The core mission of the organization is advancing the rule of law around the world. To this end, the organization mobilizes the world's leading experts on the rule of law, government leaders, legal experts, and various law and justice advocacy groups. Since its creation, the WJP has organized international meetings on rule of law issues in the United States, Czech Republic, Singapore, Argentina, Ghana, South Africa, Morocco, Peru, and Malaysia. The WJP is sponsored by some of the world's leading organizations, such as the U.S. Chamber of Commerce, Transparency International, the Inter-American Bar Association, the International Bar Association, Human Rights Watch, Club of Madrid, the Canadian Bar Association, and the Arab Center for the Development of the Rule of Law and Integrity. The WJP's global surveys and activities are funded by the Bill and Melinda Gates Foundation, the National Endowment for Democracy, the Neukom Family Foundation, the Ford Foundation, the Carnegie Foundation of New York, Microsoft Corporation, Intel Corporation, Boeing Company, Walmart Stores, Johnson & Johnson, Hewlett-Packard, Texas Instruments, General Electric Company, and many other philanthropic and corporate organizations.

In 2010, the WJP published its global survey on the status of the rule of law in 35 countries including 20 countries from Asia, Africa, and Latin America. The study, based on both face-to-face and online interviews, surveyed 900 local experts and 35,000 people from three major cities in each of the 35 countries. The survey was based on the WJP's core concept, the Rule of Law Index. The Rule of Law Index is defined by the following 10 core dimensions: (1) limited government powers, (2) absence of corruption, (3) clear and publicized stable laws, (4) order and security, (5) fundamental rights, (6) open government, (7) effective regulation and administration, (8) access to civil justice, (9) effective criminal justice, and (10) informal justice. Three of these dimensions—limited government, fundamental rights, and effective criminal justice—are directly related to issues of comparative criminal justice. The WJP survey measured the dimension of limited government in terms of the extent to which government power is limited by adherence to fundamental laws. The survey measured adherence to fundamental rights in terms of the exercise of the right to life and security of the person, due process of law, freedom of faith and religion, protection of privacy rights, and equal justice. The effectiveness of criminal justice was measured in terms of the due process of law, rights of the accused, impartial system of criminal justice, timely and effective criminal adjudication system, effective criminal investigation system, and opportunities for access to counsel. The 35 countries were ranked by their performance in all dimensions (except informal justice) of the Rule of Law Index. The WJP project noted that the survey questions were "administered to a representative sample of the general public, and to local experts, and then analyzed . . . pursuant to a rigorous triangulation methodology . . . This exercise is one of the world's most comprehensive data sets regarding adherence to rule of law" (2010, p. 12). The Rule of Index used in the survey "comprises more than 700 variables organized into 10 factors and 49 subfactors. These variables are aggregated into numerical scores" (World Justice Project, 2010, p. 12).

The survey results show that in all dimensions of the Rule of Law Index (except informal justice), the countries of North America and Western Europe are at the top, and the countries of Latin America and the Caribbean, South Asia, Central Asia, sub-Saharan Africa, and Eastern Europe are at the bottom of performance (see **Table 7-5**). In the indicator of effective criminal justice, the countries of North America and Western Europe ranked 6th, Latin America and the Caribbean ranked 30th, sub-Saharan Africa ranked 24th, and South Asia ranked 28th out of 35 countries surveyed in the study. The study observed that the "countries in Western Europe and North America tend to outperform most other countries in all dimensions. These countries are characterized by low levels of corruption, with open and accountable governments, and effective criminal justice systems" (World Justice Project, 2010, p. 18). The regions and countries that performed poorly in criminal justice are also the regions and countries that performed poorly in limited government, order and security, and fundamental rights.

Seven countries—Argentina, Bolivia, Colombia, Dominican Republic, El Salvador, Mexico, and Peru—are surveyed from Latin America and the Caribbean region by the WJP. Of these countries, Mexico has one of the poorest systems of criminal justice. Mexico's criminal justice system scored 34 in global ranking of 35 countries followed by Colombia (31), El Salvador (30), and Dominican Republic (24). The WJP survey stated that "most Latin American countries have the highest crime rates in the world [69 per 100,000 population] . . .

TABLE 7-5 The World Justice Project: Rule of Law Index, 2010; Average Ranking by Selected Region

Dimensions: Rule of Law	Sub-Saharan Africa	East Asia and Pacific	Eastern Europe and Central Asia	Western Europe and North America	Latin America and the Caribbean	South Asia
Limited government	23	12	25	5	25	24
Absence of corruption	25	14	22	5	24	28
Clear and stable laws	25	14	24	6	22	24
Order and security	31	11	13	7	28	24
Fundamental rights	25	14	20	5	24	28
Open government	21	14	25	6	22	20
Administration	26	12	25	5	22	29
Access to civil justice	24	14	21	6	23	31
Effective criminal justice	24	11	19	6	30	28

Source: Data from the World Justice Project. (2010). *Rule of Law Index, 2010.* Washington, DC: Author.

much higher than the average figure for Western Europe and North America (9), South Asia (20), and the Middle East . . . (3)" (World Justice Project, 2010, p. 19). The study further noticed that "the high crime rates in the region may be related to the generally poor performance of the criminal investigation and adjudication systems (police investigators, prosecutors, and judges)" (World Justice Project, 2010, p. 19).

In the South Asian region, the study surveyed two countries—India and Pakistan. India performed moderately in government accountability, open government, and clear and stable laws. "Yet India still needs," the survey noted, "to eliminate deficiencies in terms of access to justice, particularly in the area of court congestion and delays in processing cases, where the country ranks at the very bottom" (World Justice Project, 2010, p. 19). Pakistan performed poorly in all dimensions of the Rule of Law Index, "where low levels of government accountability are compounded by the prevalence of corruption, a weak justice system, and high levels of crime and violence" (World Justice Project, 2010, p. 19). From the region of sub-Saharan Africa, the study surveyed five countries: Ghana, Kenya, Nigeria, South Africa, and Liberia. Ghana and South Africa performed moderately in global ranking. Among the 35 countries surveyed, Ghana ranked 16th in its effectiveness in criminal justice, 14th in its adherence to fundamental rights, and 12th in limited government. South Africa ranked 18th in criminal justice, 13th in limited government, and 18th in fundamental rights. The other three countries surveyed—Kenya, Nigeria, and Liberia—are "positioned at the bottom of global ranking" (World Justice Project, 2010, p. 19).

The Economist Intelligence Unit's Index of Democracy

The various dimensions of the rule of law—limited government powers, clear and publicized stable laws, due process of law, order and security, fundamental rights, open government, good governance, access to civil justice, and effective criminal justice—identified by the World Justice Project are the core of democracy. The countries of Western Europe and North America that scored at the top of global ranking in rule of law are also the countries identified as advanced democracies in the world. The countries that performed moderately are the countries of transitional democracies. The countries that performed poorly are the countries with failed democracies; these are the countries sometimes called failed states or fragile states. The *Democracy Index 2010* published by the Economist Intelligence Unit (2010) in the United Kingdom is one of the major surveys on the status of democracy in the world's societies. It provides an important understanding of the nature and functioning of criminal justice among the world's societies. The Intelligence Unit's *Democracy Index* is based on the following five dimensions: (1) electoral process and pluralism, (2) civil liberties, (3) the functioning of government, (4) political participation, and (5) political culture. One of the core ideas used by the Economist Intelligence Unit (EIU) in measuring democracy is the notion of human rights including the principles of the due process of law, independent judiciary, judicial accountability, and civil liberties.

The 2010 report on the status of world democracy by the EIU is based on a survey of 167 independent states. The survey questionnaires included 60 indicators grouped into five categories. Data were gathered from country surveys, public opinion polls, the World Values Survey, Gallup Polls, the Eurobarometer Survey, the Asian Barometer Survey, the Latinobarometer Survey, and the Afrobarometer Survey. The report's findings are presented in terms of the following four types of political regimes: full democracies, flawed democracies, dual regimes, and authoritarian regimes. According to the survey findings, 26 countries can be called full democracies in the world. The first 19 full democracies in the world, except Malta and Czech Republic, are from the regions of Western Europe and North America. The remaining 7 full democracies include Japan, South Korea, Uruguay, Belgium, Mauritius, Costa Rica, and Portugal. There are only 5 countries from Asia, Africa, and Latin America that are, according to the survey, full democracies. The world's full democracies represent only 12.3% of the world's population (see **Table 7-6**).

Out of 167 countries surveyed by the EIU in 2010, 55 countries were identified as completely authoritarian in nature. The study observed, "Many countries in this category are outright dictatorships. Some formal institutions of democracy exist, but they have little substance. There is no independent judiciary" (Economist Intelligence Unit, 2010, p. 32). Out of 55 countries with authoritarian regimes, 26 are located in Africa (including such major countries as Nigeria, Niger, Gambia, Ethiopia, Madagascar, Togo, Cameroon, Angola, Gabon, Rwanda, Egypt, Swaziland, Yemen, Sudan, and Libya); 5 are in Asia (China, North Korea, Vietnam, Laos, and Afghanistan); and the rest are from the Middle East and Central Asia (including such countries as Algeria, Saudi Arabia, Iran, Syria, United Arab Republic, Tunisia, Oman, Qatar, Jordan, Kuwait, Morocco, Bahrain, Kazakhstan, Azerbaijan, and Tajikistan). The world's authoritarian regimes represent about 36.5% of the world's population. If the flawed democracies, hybrid regimes, and authoritarian regimes are combined, 87.7% of the world's population (about 5.5 billion people) live in countries without a stable and meaningful democracy, and the countries with a stable and meaningful democracy are less likely to progress in the modernization of criminal justice.

TABLE 7-6 Democracy Index, 2010 by Regime Type

Regime Type	Number of Countries	Percentage of Countries	Percentage of World's Population
Full democracies	26	15.6%	12.3%
Flawed democracies	53	31.7%	37.2%
Hybrid regimes	33	19.8%	14.0%
Authoritarian regimes	55	32.9%	36.5%

Source: Data from Economist Intelligence Unit. (2010). *Democracy Index 2010: Democracy in retreat (A report from the Economist Intelligence Unit).* London, England: The Economist.

■ Crime and Criminal Justice in the Failed and Fragile States

A large number of states in Asia, Africa, and Latin America are not just flawed democracies or characterized by extreme authoritarianism. They are known as failed or fragile states—those characterized primarily by long and enduring internal conflicts and armed violence. These are the states whose powers are being continuously challenged not externally by wars, but internally by competing political, racial, ethnic, and religious groups and gangs. Some failed and fragile states are themselves the perpetrators of armed conflicts and violence. A failed or a fragile state "is one in which the government does not have effective control of its territory, is not perceived as legitimate by a significant portion of its population . . . and lacks a monopoly on the use of force" (Foreign Policy and the Fund for Peace, 2006, p. 1). The failed states are those countries that fail to satisfy four critical governmental responsibilities: creating and fostering an environment for sustainable and equitable economic growth; building and maintaining legitimate and transparent governance institutions; controlling internal political, ethnic, religious, tribal and other conflicts and violence; and providing for the basic human needs of their population (Rice & Patrick, 2008).

One of the core indicators of a failed state is the nature and extent of internal conflicts and violence. Many states with economic poverty and political underdevelopment do not precisely fit into the definition of failed and fragile states. The failed and fragile states are those where conflicts and violence dominate over the rule of law, and where the states are incapable of controlling the rise of alternative power structures and competing political, tribal, religious, and ideological factions within the territorial boundary of the states. These are states that completely lost control of their monopolies on the institutions of power and repression. The failed and fragile states are not those with sudden and temporary eruptions of conflict and violence. These are states with long and enduring cycles of conflict and violence. The World Bank's (2011a) *World Development Report 2011: Conflict, Security, and Development* found that in the failed and fragile states, "conflicts are not one-off events, but are ongoing and repeated: 90 percent of the last decade's civil wars occurred in countries that have already had a civil war in the last thirty years" (p. 1). The same World Bank study estimated that about "one and half billion people live in areas affected by fragility, conflict, or large-scale, organized criminal violence" (World Bank, 2011a, p. 1). A report from the Geneva Declaration Secretariat (2008), *Global Burden of Armed Violence*, estimated that "more than 740,000 people die each year as a result of the violence associated with armed conflicts and large- and small-scale criminality" (p. 1). The report also found that armed violence is the "fourth leading cause of death for persons between the ages of 15 and 44 world-wide . . . . In Latin America and Africa, armed violence is the seventh and ninth leading cause of death, respectively" (Geneva Declaration Secretariat, 2008, p. 1).

During the last decade, writings related to the nature of the failed and fragile states have grown considerably (Collier, 2007, 2009; Kaplan, 2008; Patrick, 2011). They are also being closely studied by the U.S. Department of State, the U.S. Central Intelligence Agency, the World Bank, the United Kingdom's Department of International Development, the Canadian International Development Agency, and a number of the world's leading think tanks, such as the Foreign Policy Magazine, the Fund for Peace, the Brookings Institution, and the Center for Global Policy at George Mason University. In 2008, the Brookings Institution, a Washington, D.C.–based think tank, conducted a study on the nature of fragility and weakness in 141 states in these four indicators: economic status, the nature of governance and the rule of law, the extent and the intensity of conflict and violence, and the nature of social welfare (Rice & Patrick, 2008). The countries are rated from "0" (extremely weak and fragile) to "10" (strong and developed) in their performance in 4 indicators and 20 subindicators. The researchers found that the 30 most fragile and weakest states of the world—except Afghanistan, Iraq, Haiti, North Korea, Myanmar, and Nepal—are from Africa. The researchers observed that most of the "failed and critically week states are geographically located in sub-Saharan Africa, and to a lesser extent, in South Asia and Central Asia. . . . 23 of the 28 critically weak states are in sub-Saharan Africa" (Rice & Patrick, 2008, p. 13). The researchers found Somalia, with an overall score of 0.52 out of 10, to be the weakest and most fragile state in the world. Somalia was followed by the Democratic Republic of Congo (1.67), Burundi (3.21), Sudan (3.29), Central African Republic (3.33), Zimbabwe (3.44), Liberia (3.64), Angola (3.72), Sierra Leone (3.77), Chad (3.90), Ethiopia (4.46), Rwanda (4.58), Uganda (4.86), Nigeria (4.88), Cameroon (5.12), Yemen (5.18), and Zambia (5.23).

A similar finding was recorded in another report, titled *Global Report: Conflict, Governance, and State Fragility* (Marshall & Cole, 2008). According to this report, the 25 most fragile states of the world, except Afghanistan, Myanmar, and Pakistan, are from the region of sub-Saharan Africa. The report studied 162 countries and assigned them scores from "0" (no fragility) to "25" (highly fragile) in effectiveness and legitimacy in these 4 performance dimensions: the security and effectiveness of criminal justice in containing conflict and violence; the nature of politics and the effectiveness of institutions of governance; the nature and effectiveness of economic institutions; and the effectiveness of social and human capital development. The most fragile states of sub-Saharan Africa scored from "25" (Somalia) to "18" (Burundi, Central African Republic, Liberia, Niger, and Rwanda). The report also found that in 2008, there were 20 countries that experienced major armed conflict and violence in their territories. These countries are Mexico, Colombia, Nigeria (Delta), Chad, Central African Republic, Sudan (Darfur and South Sudan), the Democratic Republic of Congo (Northeast), Ethiopia (Ogaden), Somalia, Yemen, Israel (Gaza), Iraq, Turkey (Kurds), Russia, Afghanistan, Pakistan, India (Kashmir, Maoist, and Assam), Myanmar (various non-Burmese groups), Thailand (Malays), and the Philippines (Moro; Marshall & Cole, 2008). The report from the Geneva Declaration Secretariat (2008) made a similar observation, that states in sub-Saharan Africa and South and Central America are the most fragile states of the world because of their failure to control and contain long and enduring cycles of conflict and violence (see **Table 7-7**).

TABLE 7-7 Selected African, Latin American, and Asian Failed and Fragile States

Africa	Dominant Conflict Type	Latin America	Dominant Conflict Type	Asia	Dominant Conflict Type
Burundi	Ethnic/political	Argentina	Political	Afghanistan	Political/tribal
Chad	Ethnic/political	Bolivia	Political	Azerbaijan	Ethnic/political
Congo	Ethnic/political	Colombia	Drugs and gangs	Bangladesh	Political/religious
Eritrea	Ethnic/political	Ecuador	Drugs and gangs	Cambodia	Political
Ethiopia	Ethnic/political	El Salvador	Drugs and gangs	Iran	Religious/political
Liberia	Ethnic/political	Guatemala	Drugs and gangs	Iraq	Religious/tribal
Niger	Ethnic/political	Honduras	Political	Myanmar	Civil/military
Nigeria	Political/religious	Mexico	Drugs and gangs	Pakistan	Political/religious
Rwanda	Ethnic/political	Nicaragua	Drugs and gangs	Sri Lanka	Ethnic/political
Sierra Leone	Ethnic/political	Paraguay	Political	Saudi Arabia	Religious
Somalia	Political	Peru	Political	Tajikistan	Ethnic/political
Sudan	Ethnic/political	Venezuela	Political	Uzbekistan	Ethnic/political

Source: Data from Marshall, M. G., & Cole, B. R. (2008). *Global report: Conflict, governance, and state fragility.* Fairfax, VA: George Mason University-Center for Systemic Peace.

Criminal Justice in the Failed and Fragile States of Africa

The failed and fragile states not only take an enormous toll on the lives and livings of their citizens, but also limit their growth and development. The World Bank's *World Development Report 2011* observed that "while much of the world has made rapid progress in reducing poverty in the past 60 years, areas characterized by repeated cycles of political and criminal violence are being left far behind" (2011a, p. 1). The report also stated that "on average, a country that experienced major violence over the period from 1981 to 2005, has a poverty rate 21 percentage points higher than a country that saw no violence" (World Bank, 2011a, p. 5). One of the crucial effects of intrastate conflicts and violence in the failed and fragile states is on the nature of crime and criminal justice. In almost all failed, fragile, and post-conflict states, the rate of conventional crime, corruption, and transnational organized crime has rapidly increased. Africa contains most of the failed and fragile states. Africa has also the highest rate of violent crimes among all regions of the world.

A study called *Crime and Development in Africa* by the United Nations Office on Drugs and Crime (UNODC; 2005), showed that Africa "suffers from the highest rates of violent crime in the world, with a 1.1% victimization rate .... According to the victim surveys conducted in urban areas under the ICVS, Africa also ranks highest (11.3%), narrowly edging out the Americas (10.8%)" (p. 53). The homicide rate in the failed states of sub-Saharan Africa in particular and Africa in general (see **Table 7-8**) is more than "20 per 100,000 population compared to the global average of 7.6 per 100,000 population" (Geneva Declaration Secretariat, 2008, p. 5). Some of these countries are Angola, Ethiopia, Lesotho, Namibia,

TABLE 7-8 Homicide Rate in Selected States of Africa per 100,000 Population, 2004

Country	Homicide Rate per 100,000 Population	Country	Homicide Rate per 100,000 Population
Angola	35	Malawi	18
Botswana	23	Nigeria	18
Burkina Faso	18	Rwanda	28
Burundi	37	Sierra Leone	37
Chad	19	South Africa	68
Congo (DR)	35	Sudan	28
Cote d'Ivorie	45	Tanzania	26
Gabon	16	Uganda	25
Kenya	20	Zimbabwe	34

Source: Data from United Nations Office on Drugs and Crime. (2010). *International statistics on crime and justice.* Vienna, Austria: Author.

Swaziland, Uganda, and Zimbabwe. The UNODC report stated that "rates of assault in Africa are higher than on other continents. . . . Police in Southern, Western, and Central Africa record more assaults than police elsewhere" (2005, pp. 56–57).

According to the *United Nations Crime Survey of 2002* (as analyzed by the United Nations Office on Drugs and Crime, 2005), the rate of police-recorded assaults in Southern, Western, and Central Africa was 409 per 100,000 population compared to 258 in North America, 45 in Western and Central Europe, and 5 per 100,000 population in South and Southeast Asia. The *United Nations Crime Survey of 2002* also reported that the rate of police-reported rape is highest in Southern, Western, and Central Africa. The rate is 69 per 100,000 population compared to 32 in North America, 11 in Western and Central Europe, and 2 in South Asia (United Nations Office on Drugs and Crime, 2005). Other forms of violent crimes such as robbery and kidnapping are also highest in the failed and fragile states of Africa. In 2001, the rate of kidnapping in Africa was 5.2 per 100,000 population compared to 2.1 in North America, 2.4 in South and Central America, 1.0 in Europe, and 0.2 in Asia. In summary, "Africa suffers from serious levels of criminal violence. It has the highest levels of murder . . . assault . . . sexual assault . . . and kidnapping (police figures), and the second highest levels of robbery (police figures and victim survey data)" (United Nations Office on Drugs and Crime, 2005, p. 62).

One of the most devastating effects of continuing armed conflicts and violence in the failed and fragile states is that they leave their criminal justice systems in absolute shambles. In the failed and fragile states, the differences between policing and the military vanish. The police become highly militarized, and the military is seen as performing the duty of policing. Police brutality becomes a normal part of police patrol, and the lack of police accountability is politically ignored. Law enforcement in the failed and fragile states is most often not in the hands of the formal institution of policing. It is shared by gangs, thugs, pirates, bandits, and other nonstate armed groups (ABC News, 2007). Homicide rates in the failed and fragile states are highest in the world, yet homicide offenders go mostly unpunished, and homicide victimization goes mostly unnoticed and unreported. In the states with endemic conflict and violence, rape and sexual assault of women and children are also endemic, and they are also largely unreported. In the failed and fragile states, people have little confidence in the police and judicial system. The lack of judicial accountability becomes widespread, and judicial corruption is politically overlooked.

Criminal justice systems of the failed and fragile states are severely weakened by politicization and the militarization of policing; extrajudicial killings; arbitrary arrests and detention; torture in custody; rise of alternative groups of armed gangs and thugs; the lack of judicial independence and accountability; widespread judicial corruption; and an escalating culture of fear due to the lack of security. For the containment of internal conflict and violence, most failed states attempt to politicize and militarize their systems of criminal justice. But politicization and militarization further weaken criminal justice. *World Report 2010*, published by Human Rights Watch (2010), has produced a number of cases of such failed systems of criminal justice in the failed and fragile states of Africa. In the failed state of Eritrea, Human Rights Watch observed that "torture and ill-treatment in detention are routine . . . detention almost always included severe beatings, often leading to permanent physical damage" (Human Rights Watch, 2010, p. 114).

In Liberia, "the undisciplined, poorly managed, and ill-equipped Liberian police were challenged to maintain law and order" (Human Rights Watch, 2010, p. 136) and this necessitated the deployment of the United Nations Peacekeeping forces in 2003. In Nigeria, criminal justice has been incapable, since the end of military rule in 1999, of controlling the spread of armed conflict and violence that has claimed the lives of thousands of people. Human Rights Watch's *World Report 2010* further observed that police in Nigeria "were widely implicated in the extortion of money and the arbitrary arrest and torture of criminal suspects and others. They solicited bribes from victims of crimes to initiate investigations, and from suspects to drop investigations" (2010, p. 149).

In Rwanda, the criminal justice system is incapable of prosecuting the "members of the now governing Rwandan Patriotic Front (RPF) who committed crimes during the genocide, despite estimates by the United Nations High Commissioner for Refugees that the RPF killed between 25,000 and 45,000 civilians in 1994" (Human Rights Watch, 2010, p. 149). In the failed state of Sierra Leone, the judicial system is in shambles: "Serious deficiencies in the judicial system persist, including extortion and bribetaking by officials; insufficient numbers of judges, magistrates, and prosecuting attorneys; absenteeism by court personnel; and inadequate remuneration for judiciary personnel" (Human Rights Watch, 2010, p. 154).

Criminal Justice in the Failed and Fragile States of Central America

The previous section on sub-Saharan countries of Africa discusses how the absence of the rule of law and democracy during cycles of conflict and violence in weak and fragile states can contribute to high crime rates and have long-term debilitating effects on crime and criminal justice. This is also evident in some of the countries of Central America (World Bank, 2010a). The region of Central America consists of seven independent states: Belize,

Guatemala, Honduras, El Salvador, Nicaragua, Costa Rica, and Panama. These 7 states have a population of about 42 million. Like Africa, Central America is a region that is characterized by long and enduring cycles of armed conflict. Four of Central America's countries are recognized as weak and fragile states: Guatemala, Honduras, El Salvador, and Nicaragua. According to the Brookings Institution's study, *Index of State Weakness in the Developing World* (Rice & Patrick, 2008), El Salvador's overall score is 7.10 out of 10 (no fragility) followed by Nicaragua (6.37), Honduras (6.33), and Guatemala (6.15). The score for political stability for these countries, except El Salvador, is less than 5 out of 10. According to the *State Fragility Index and Matrix* developed by the Center for Systemic Peace and Center for Global Policy (Marshall & Cole, 2008), El Salvador scored 6 out of 25 (extremely fragile) followed by Nicaragua (9), Honduras (9), and Guatemala (12). The *Democracy Index 2010* from the Economist Intelligence Unit identified El Salvador and Guatemala as flawed democracies, and Honduras and Nicaragua as hybrid regimes. In the study by the World Justice Project (2010) that surveyed the rule of law in 35 countries, El Salvador received a global ranking of 17 in fundamental rights and 30 in effective criminal justice.

The countries of Central America are slightly better than most of the countries of Africa in the rule of law, development, and progress of democracy. But this is also a region that is characterized by high levels of crime and violence and a fragile system of criminal justice. In the 1960s and 1970s, major civil wars erupted in Nicaragua (Nicaraguan Democratic Force versus Sandinista National Liberation Front), Guatemala (authoritarian military governments versus Movimiento Revolucionario 13 de Noviembre), and El Salvador (authoritarian military government versus National Liberation Front). The civil wars in these countries erupted in the context of the Soviet expansion of communism in the 1960s in Latin America in general and the communist victory in the Cuban revolution in 1959 in particular. Almost 4 decades of civil war killed about 200,000 people in Guatemala; 75,000 in El Salvador; and 60,000 in Nicaragua. The vicious cycles of conflict and violence left these countries not only economically devastated and politically fractionalized but also with enormous supplies of guns and gangs. It is estimated that there are 1.5 million guns in Central America, of which more than 1 million are not registered. A report from the UNODC, *Crime and Development in Central America: Caught in the Crossfire,* noted that illegal guns "are remainders from military conflicts in the region in the 1970s and 80s, most notably in El Salvador, Guatemala, and Nicaragua. After these conflicts ceased thousands of military weapons ended up on the illegal markets in those countries" (United Nations Office on Drugs and Crime, 2007, p. 67).

The gangs of Central America are not composed of young men on street corners trying to engage in purse snatching. Central American gangs—offshoots of the civil war—are highly organized, institutionalized, militarized, and internationalized. The civil war left Central America with a seemingly legitimate culture of gangs and gangsters educated in the skills of murder, rape, kidnapping, human smuggling, drug trafficking, and money laundering (World Bank, 2011b). This is obviously a phenomenon not often found in the weak and fragile states of Africa. It is estimated that in 2005, there were about 1,000

TABLE 7-9 Central American Gang Membership Estimates

Country	Number of Gangs	Total Membership
Belize	2	100
Costa Rica	6	2,660
El Salvador	4	10,500
Guatemala	434	14,000
Honduras	112	36,000
Nicaragua	268	4,500
Panama	94	1,385
Total	920	69,145

Source: Data from United Nations Office on Drug and Crime. (2007). *Crime and development in Central America.* Vienna, Austria: Author.

organized gangs with about 70,000 members in the 7 countries of Central America. Of those 1,000 gangs 434 were in Guatemala, 268 in Nicaragua, and 112 in Honduras. Out of an estimated 70,000 gang members about 36,000 were in Honduras, 14,000 in Guatemala, and 4,500 in Nicaragua (see **Table 7-9**).

Closely related to the problem of guns and gangs in Central America is the problem of drug trade and trafficking. During the civil war, the communist movements were financed by developing a huge regional and international network of illegal drug trafficking. After the end of the civil war, drug trafficking became a part of the region's failing and fragile economy. The UNODC study has recognized that "Central America's geographical position has left it literally 'caught in the crossfire' of the drug trade. The civil wars exposed the region to deep penetration by drug trafficking organizations, as drugs were a source of revenue for the conflict" (United Nations Office on Drugs and Crime, 2007, p. 12). These three offshoots of the civil war in Central America—guns, gangs, and drug trades and trafficking—have not only made the Central American states weak and fragile in the rule of law and democracy, but have also increased crime and violence rates in this region and severely constrained its modernization in criminal justice.

The UNODC's 2011 report, *Global Study on Homicide,* noted that since 1995, homicide rates are in decline in most regions of the world, particularly in Asia, Europe, and North America. The homicide rates, however, are increasing in other regions, particularly in "Central America and the Caribbean, where today it can be seen to be nearing crisis point" (United Nations Office on Drugs and Crime, 2011, p. 10). In 2010, homicide rate by firearms (about 42% of homicides in the world are committed by firearms), among all of the world's regions, was highest in South America (about 75 per 100,000 population), and it was closely followed by the countries of the Caribbean region (67) and Central America (65). In Central America, the highest rate was found in Honduras (82.1 per 100,000 population), El Salvador (66.0), and Guatemala (41.4).

In 2005, the homicide rate of El Salvador was 59.9 and Honduras was 59.6 per 100,000 population. These rates sharply increased between 1999 and 2006. The United Nations

Development Programme (UNDP) report noted that 2,655 homicides were reported in Guatemala in 1999. That number jumped to 5,886 in 2006. In 2001, 303 women were murdered in Guatemala; in 2006, the number increased to 603 (as quoted in Benitez, 2007). Guatemala's Human Rights Commission found that in 2010, about 4,000 children were murdered by gangs. According to the same report, "74.9 percent of the crimes are not reported to police. Fifty-nine percent of the respondents said it was useless to report crimes," and 61.5% of the respondents said crime was their biggest worry (as quoted in Benitez, 2007, p. 2). A report from the U.S. Department of State (2011) similarly observed that "Guatemala has one of the highest violent crime rates in Latin America. In 2010, approximately 55 murders a week were reported in Guatemala City alone" (p. 1). In three provinces of Guatemala, the murder rate is more than 100 per 100,000 population. These provinces are Escuinta (118), Peten (116), and Izabal (109) (United Nations Office on Drugs and Crime, 2007, p. 55).

Honduras is also one of the most violent regions in Latin America and in the world as a whole. In 2006, the Observatory of Violence and Crime in Honduras, set up by the United Nations and the National Autonomous University of Honduras, reported that "in this country of 7.4 million, 710 murders were reported in the first quarter of the year, 100 more than in the same period in 2005" (Mejia, 2006, p. 1). In Honduras, on average, "there are around 15 murders a day, in a country with a population of 7.5 million" (British Broadcasting Corporation, 2011, p. 1). The UNODC's 2007 study, *Crime and Development in Central America: Caught in the Crossfire,* concluded that Guatemala and El Salvador are two of the most violent countries in the world. Particularly alarming in these Central American countries, described as the Northern Triangle, is the brutal nature of their violent crimes, and the targeting of members of law enforcement, the judiciary, human rights groups, and the media. The United Nations Human Rights Office in Guatemala, in a press release from the UN News Centre, said in 2011, "We are extremely concerned about an apparent new trend of targeting public prosecutors in Central America, apparently by organized crime groups" (UN News Centre, 2011, p. 1). In May 2011, in Guatemala, "Allan Stwolinsky, the local auxiliary prosecutor in Coban in the Department of Alta Verapaz, was found decapitated in a plastic bag in front of the governor's house" (UN News Centre, 2011, p. 1). Alarming also is the cruel nature of violent crime against women and children in Central America. Guatemala is often cited as one of the most dangerous places in the world for women (see **Box 7-2**). The UNODC (2007) report, *Crime and Development in Central America: Caught in the Crossfire,* found that in Guatemala, "Female homicide victims are often tortured and mutilated, as they were during the counterinsurgency campaign . . . . Strangulations, the of victims of which are usually female, have risen dramatically in the past five years" (p. 66).

The system of criminal justice in Central America, like the Central American states themselves, are also weak and fragile. It is largely dysfunctional and devoid of legitimacy (see **Figure 7-1**). In fact, it has the same characteristics found in the criminal justice systems of Africa's failed and fragile states: high rates of police and judicial corruption, militarization of policing, rise of alternative armed gangs and thugs, vigilante justice, extrajudicial killings,

BOX 7-2

Violence Against Women in Guatemala

One of the peculiar characteristics of crime and violence in the region of Latin America and the Caribbean is the high level of violence and cruelty against women. There is no region in the world that can match the level of violence and cruelty that has been experienced by women in Latin America and the Caribbean. The country that has made the most headlines for unleashing heinous cruelty and violence against women during the last 3 decades is Guatemala. Guatemala's Human Rights Commission recently noted that "since 2000, almost 5,000 women have been murdered in Guatemala, and each year the body count rises. In 2010 alone, 630 women were killed" (Suarez & Jordon, 2007). According to another source (Sanford, 2008), "Between 2002 and 2005, the number of women killed increased by more than 63% and nearly 40% of these murders happened in or near Guatemala City. Most of the women who are killed are between 16 and 30 years old" (p.105). Sanford (2008) further noted that between 2001 and 2006, the female population in Guatemala increased by 8%. During the same time, the female homicide rate increased by 117%. What is particularly alarming is the brutal nature of violence against women—they are raped, gang-raped, tortured, mutilated, strangled, and then killed. "Their body parts are tied up in garbage bags or abandoned in ditches" (Suarez & Jordon, 2007). It was also seen that after pregnant women were raped and killed, "fetuses . . . were cut out of women's bodies and even hung on trees" (Guatemala Human Rights Commission/USA, 2009, p. 3). The murder story of Maria Isabel Franco, a 15-year-old, is just one example of Guatemala's criminal culture of "femicide" that has horrified the world's consciousness. In 2001, just before the Christmas, Maria was kidnapped, raped, strangled, and killed. Her skull was fractured into dozens of pieces, and her fingernails were forcibly removed. Maria's mother, who was deeply engrossed in shock and sadness, said, "I wish a big earthquake would occur and we could just start over" (Dawson, 2007, p. 1). In 2008, Guatemala passed a new law, the Law Against Femicide and Other Forms of Violence Against Women (Decree 22-2008), to curb the escalation of female homicide. Article 6 of the new decree imposed a penalty of 25–50 years in prison without any possibility for parole for "femicide"—violent murder of a woman motivated by gender. The effect of this new law on further escalation of femicide in Guatemala remains to be seen.

Source: Guatemala Human Rights Commission/USA. (2009). *Guatemala's femicide law: Progress against impunity.* Washington, DC: Author; Dawson, J. (2007, July). *Open invitation to kill: Murder and impunity in Guatemala.* Retrieved from http://womenthrive.org/blog/joan-dawson-open-invitation-kill-murder-and-impunity-guatemala; Sanford, V. (2008). From genocide to feminicide: Impunity and human rights in 21st century Guatemala. *Journal of Human Rights, 2, 104–122;* and Suarez, J., & Jordon, M. (2007). *A report on violence against women in Guatemala.* Washington, DC: GHRC.

and low rates of prosecution and conviction (see **Box 7-3**). The UNODC's 2007 report observed that judges in the region are "subject to financial or political influence. Lack of police and prosecutorial capacity results in very low conviction rates in some instances. For

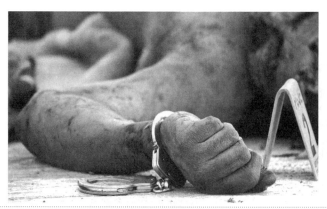

Figure 7-1 Violence, Brutality, and Drug Crimes in Central America

Source: © Reuters/STR/Landov.

example, 2005 figures suggest that murderers in Guatemala had about a 2% chance of being convicted" (United Nations Office on Drugs and Crime, 2007, p. 12). The report further noted that "with regard to corrections, some countries in this region boast large prison populations relative to their capacity to care for them. Large shares of these prison populations have not been convicted of anything—they are incarcerated awaiting trial" (pp. 13–14). Similar observations were made in a 2010 report from Human Rights Watch about the nature of criminal justice in Guatemala. The report said that Guatemala's criminal justice system is incapable of functioning because of the influence of the criminal gangs, mafias, and thugs. "According to official figures, there was 99.75 percent impunity for violent crimes as of 2009. Deficient and corrupt police, prosecutorial, and judicial systems, as well as absence of adequate witness programs, all contribute to Guatemala's alarmingly low prosecution rate" (Human Rights Watch, 2010, p. 244).

In a survey done by Latinobarometer in 2004, 45% of the respondents from Guatemala, 41% from Honduras, and 33% from Nicaragua said that it was possible to bribe a police officer in their countries. In the same study, 38% of respondents from Honduras, 37% from Guatemala, 33% from Nicaragua, and 22% from El Salvador said that it was possible to bribe a judge to get a reduced sentence in their countries. What is particularly noticeable in Guatemala, Honduras, and El Salvador is the widespread corruption and the intimidation of judges and prosecutors by organized criminal gangs. According to Amnesty International, one of the most serious problems "in the administration of justice in Guatemala is the lack of personal security of all those involved in the judicial process" (United Nations Office on Drugs and Crime, 2007, p. 31). The World Bank's 2011 study *Crime and Violence in Central America: A Development Challenge* found that there three main drivers of crime in the region: "drug trafficking, youth violence and gangs, and the availability of firearms" (World Bank, 2011b, p. ii). The report further noted that drug trafficking "is both an important driver of homicide rates in Central America and the main single factor behind rising violence levels in the region. . . . Hotspot . . . areas tend to experience crime at rates more than 100 percent higher than non-hotspot areas" (World bank, 2011b, p. ii).

BOX 7-3

Gangs in Mexico and Central America

A number of research studies have concluded that in the countries of Central America, guns, gangs, and drugs are the major problems for their transitions to democratic political systems, and, hence, to modern systems of criminal justice. The growth of transnational gangs is a particularly formidable challenge for the development of the rule law and democracy in the region. The history of the growth of transnational gangs in Central America is associated with the history of drug trafficking in the region. The United Nations Office on Drugs and Crime estimates that about 90% of illegal trafficking of cocaine in the United States comes from Mexico, and about 42% of that volume is channeled through the countries of Central America known as the Northern Triangle. This drug trafficking is primarily directed and controlled by the transnational gangs of the region. Crimes, violence, corruption, and the growth and escalation of a "gang culture" are intimately connected with the global trafficking of drugs from Mexico and Central America. The transnational gangs of the region have corrupted not only its systems of criminal justice, but also the whole instrumentalities of the state. The rise and dominance of transnational gangs in the management of the economy, politics, and culture have seriously obstructed the economic progress of the countries in the region, as well their prospects for transition to a rule of law and democracy. In recent years, many of the Central American countries have adopted a get-tough approach to gang preventions called *mano dura*. The new policy has criminalized the gangs, increased police power, and made provisions for long-term incarcerations. Research, however, shows that the effects of the new policy "on gangs and crime have been largely disappointing. Most youth arrested under *mano dura* provisions have been subsequently released...Salvadoran police estimated that more than 10,000 of 14,000 suspected gang members arrested in 2005 were later released . . . extrajudicial youth killings by vigilante groups have continued since *mano dura* went into effect, including alleged assassinations of gang suspects and gang deportees from the United States" (Seelke, 2011, p. 11). More recently, many transnational and multilateral policy initiatives are being taken to address this core Central American problem in politics and culture, and most of these initiatives are being organized under the Security Commission of the Central American Integration System (SICA). Some of the key actors are the Inter-American Development Bank, the World Bank, the United Nations Development Program (UNDP), the United Nations Office on Drugs and Crime (UNODC), the United States Congress, and the United States Agency for International Development (USAID).

Source: Seelke, C. R. (2011). *Gangs in Central America*. Washington, DC: Library of Congress, Congressional Research Service.

Like the failed and fragile states of sub-Saharan Africa, the states of the Northern Triangle of Central America suffer from the absence of strong states based on the rule of law and democracy. The power and legitimacy of these states and their systems of criminal justice are being continuously challenged by crime, violence, and corruption. A generalized culture of fear about crime and violence among the common people leads to the further erosion of the legitimacy of those states and their monopoly on the institutions of control and criminal justice. The World Bank's 2011 study noted that "in El Salvador, Honduras and Guatemala, crime victims are 6.5 percent more likely to approve of taking the law into their own hands and are 9 percent less likely to believe that the rule of law should always be respected" (World Bank, 2011b, p. 9).

The rising rates of crime and violence limit the progress of development and democracy, which further worsens the conditions of crime and criminal justice (Gilpin, 2009). The weak and fragile states remain trapped in a vicious cycle of conflict, poverty, crime, and violence. The UNODC's report on *Global Study on Homicide* rightly observed that "the largest shares of homicides occur in countries with low levels of human development, and countries with high levels of income inequality are afflicted by homicide rates almost four times higher than more equal societies" (United Nations Office on Drugs and Crime, 2011, p. 10).

Criminal Justice in the Postauthoritarian States of South America

The continent of South America—the fourth largest continent of the world—consists of the following 12 independent states: Argentina, Bolivia, Brazil, Chile, Colombia, Ecuador, Guyana, Paraguay, Peru, Suriname, Uruguay, and Venezuela. These states are comprised of about 386 million people (2011 estimate). Some of the world's largest cities are in South America, such as Sao Paulo, Brazil (19 million), Buenos Aires, Argentina (13 million), Rio de Janeiro, Brazil (12 million), Bogota, Colombia (8 million), and Santiago, Chile (6 million). Brazil was a Portuguese colony that gained its independence in 1822. What is intriguing about Latin America in general and South America in particular is that the countries of these regions have been struggling to create states based on the rule of law and democracy for more than 150 years. Only two countries—Bolivia and Costa Rica—are identified as full democracies by the Economist Intelligence Unit's *Democracy Index 2010*. The *Democracy Index 2010* named Argentina, Brazil, Suriname, Colombia, Guyana, Paraguay, and Peru as flawed democracies, and Ecuador and Venezuela as dual regimes. The *Index of State Weakness in the Developing World* (Rice & Patrick, 2008) also found that most South American countries have serious problems with the rule of law and democracy. In the areas of governance, rule of law, accountability, and control of corruption, most South American countries, except Argentina, Chile, and Uruguay, scored less than 7 on a scale from 0 (extremely weak) to 10 (very strong). The scores of Venezuela, Paraguay, and Ecuador are less than 5 out of 10 in the area of the rule of law and governance. Chile is the only country in South America, according to the *Index of State Weakness in the Developing World* (Rice & Patrick, 2008), that scored 10 out of 10 in the area of the rule of law and governance. Chile also scored high (9.43) in the area of the absence of conflict and violence within the state. Of all South American countries, Colombia is described as the country with highest intensity of conflict, high rates of crime and violence, and gross violation of human rights. Colombia scored 1.78 out of 10 in the area of conflict and the problem of security (Rice & Patrick, 2008).

The World Justice Project's *Rule of Law Index* of 2010 included in its survey four countries of South America: Argentina, Bolivia, Colombia, and Peru. All four countries received low global ranking in limited government, absence of corruption, fundamental rights, and order and stability. In the protection of fundamental rights, out of 35 countries surveyed and ranked from 1 (highest) to 35 (lowest), Peru received a global ranking of 15, Argentina 21, Bolivia 30, and Colombia 29. In order and stability, Peru received a global ranking of 29, Argentina 25, Colombia 32, and Bolivia 30. According to the World Bank's (2010b) study on the rule of law, political stability, violence, and accountability issues, the records of some South American countries are equally poor. In the rule of law, the major countries of South America, except Chile and Brazil, are below the 60th percentile. In political stability, major countries, except Chile, Brazil, and Uruguay, scored below the 50th percentile (see **Table 7-10**). The issues of political instability, according to this World Bank report, are much more serious in Colombia, Ecuador, Peru, and Venezuela.

The profile of crime and criminal justice in the South American countries is a reflection of their problems with the rule of law and political order and stability. Among all the world's regions, South America has the third highest rate of intentional homicide per 100,000 population at 19. The first is the region of Southern Africa (35) and second is the Caribbean region (28). The countries of South America that have low ratings in the rule of law, protection of fundamental rights, and political order and stability have the highest rates of intentional homicide (see Table 7-10). In the World Bank (2010b) study, Colombia received the lowest ranking in political stability among all the countries of South America. It scored only 7.1 out of 100 in political stability and 39.6 out of 100 in the rule of law. Colombia also has the highest rate of violent crime among all the countries of South America. The region of South

TABLE 7-10 Rule of Law, Political Stability, and Homicide Rate: Selected South American Countries

Country	Percentile Rank Rule of Law	Percentile Rank Political Stability	Homicide Rate (per 100,000 Population), 2004
Argentina	29.7	43.4	5.5
Bolivia	9.9	19.8	5.3
Brazil	49.5	54.2	30.8
Chile	87.7	69.3	5.5
Colombia	39.6	7.1	61.1
Ecuador	7.5	20.8	18.5
Paraguay	16.5	78.83	17.8
Peru	30.2	17.9	12.5
Uruguay	70.8	78.3	6.0
Venezuela	2.8	11.3	48.0 (2010)

Source: Data from The World Bank, 2010b; the United Nations Office on Drugs and Crime, 2004; and the United Nations Office on Drugs and Crime, 2010.

America as a whole has a homicide rate of 19 per 100,000 population. Colombia has a homicide rate of about 61.1 per 100,000 population (United Nations Office on Drugs and Crime, 2004). In the World Bank study, Bolivia received a rating of 9.9 out of 100 in the rule of law and 19.8 in political stability. Bolivia's rate of homicide is also one of the highest in South America (29 per 100,000 population). Ecuador received a rating of 7.5 in the rule of law and 20.8 in political stability, and it has a homicide rate of 19 per 100,000 population.

Among the South American counties, Venezuela, in the World Bank (2010b) study, received the lowest rating in the area of the rule of law and third lowest rating in political stability. Venezuela's murder rate in 2008 was 48 per 100,000 population. According to a study by the National Statistics Institute of Venezuela, a country with 28 million people, there were 19,133 homicides in Venezuela in 2009. This places the homicide rate of Venezuela at 75 per 100,000 population (MercoPress, 2010). According to the Venezuelan Observatory of Violence, an independent think tank organization, "one person is murdered every two hours in Venezuela" (Munzenrieder, 2010, p. 1). A study published in the *New York Times* reported that "Caracas itself is almost unrivaled among large cities in the Americas for its homicide rate, which currently stands at around 200 per 100,000 inhabitant" (Romero, 2010, p. 1) A Venezuelan political leader recently made a comment that "if the 155,000 Venezuelans killed in the last ten years would be lined out, 'we could have a 310.5 kilometres vector of cadavers'" (MercoPress, 2010, p. 1). According to *Foreign Policy Magazine*, "Caracas now ranks as the world's No. 1 murder capital" (Paulin, 2008, p. 1).

Some of the countries of the South America also have the highest rates of robberies among all nations and regions. With 1,275.6 robberies per 100,000 population (2004 data), Chile has highest rate of robberies in the world. Chile is followed by Argentina (905.3 per 100,000 population, 2006 data). Chile and Argentina are followed by Ecuador (398.8), Uruguay (277.5), Peru (156.1), and Venezuela (143.3). One of the World Bank (2010a) studies that analyzed data from Latin American Public Opinion Project surveys shows that the rate of armed robberies (based on the percentage of adult respondents who said they were victimized by armed robberies in the 12 months before the commission of the survey in 2008) among 20 countries of Latin America is highest in Ecuador (15.6%), Venezuela (13.3%), Argentina (12.0%), Chile (8.6%), Colombia (8.0%), Brazil (7.3%), Peru (6.5%), and Bolivia (6.1%). The same survey shows that the 7 of the 8 countries with the highest rate of victimization by burglary (based on the percentage of adult respondents who said they were victimized by burglary in the 12 months before the commission of the survey in 2008) are South American (Haiti being the exception). These countries are Uruguay (9.0%), Peru (8.7%), Bolivia (8.4%), Chile (7.3%), Paraguay (6.5%), Brazil (6.5%), and Ecuador (6.2%).

Among South American countries, the rate of kidnapping is highest in Chile (0.71 per 100,000 population). The World Bank reports that "75 percent of all kidnappings worldwide are committed in Latin America, a region that accounts for just eight percent of the world's population" (Cevallos, 2008, p. 1). In most South American countries and Latin America as a whole, a "particularly used modality is the so-called *express* kidnapping, where a victim is abducted and forced to make as many and as large ATM withdrawals as possible, or the victim's family is asked for payable ransom" (World Bank, 2010a, p. 5). Drug-related crimes are high in Argentina (63 per 100,000 population), Colombia (53 per 100,000 population), Bolivia (46 per 100,000 population), and Peru (35 per 100,000 population; United Nations Office on Drugs and Crime, 2010). The countries of South America also have the highest rates of overall criminal victimization among the 20 countries of Latin America that were surveyed by the Latin American Public Opinion Project in 2008. The survey showed that the 7 countries with the highest rate of overall criminal victimization (based on percentage of the respondents surveyed who said they were victimized by crime in the 12 months before the commission of the survey) are Argentina (28%), Peru (25%), Ecuador (23%), Chile (22%), Uruguay (22%), Venezuela (21%), and Bolivia (19%)(World Bank, 2010b; World Bank, 2011b).

People of Latin America do not have much confidence in criminal justice in their countries. The World Bank (2010a) study, *Crime and Violence in Central America,* observed that "in 2008, across six countries of Central America, 71 percent said that crime is 'very much' a threat to society's well being. This view is fairly constant across countries, irrespective of national crime levels" (p. v). The World Bank study also found that because of escalating crime and violence, there are higher perceptions of insecurity among people in many countries of Latin America, particularly in South America. Data from the 2008 survey by the Latin American Public Opinion Project, analyzed by the World Bank, show the existence of higher perceptions of insecurity in six countries of South America: Argentina (62%), Peru (55%), Chile (49%), Bolivia (47%), Uruguay (43%), and Venezuela (42%). Because of the lack of trust in criminal justice and higher perceptions of insecurity among common people, more than 70% of crimes in the countries across Latin America are not reported to police.

In South America and Central America in general, only 24% of burglaries, 28% of robberies, and 39% of assaults and threats are reported (Gilpin, 2009, p. 8). The World Bank (2010a) study shows that 73% of respondents from El Salvador, 71% from Honduras, 65% from Costa Rica, and 58% each from Nicaragua and Guatemala said they did not report their victimization to police. The survey noted that "people who did not report crime were asked why they did not report. The most common response was that reporting was of no use" (p. 10). According to a study by the Inter-American Commission on Human Rights (2009), "about 63% of people across Latin America do not have confidence in the police, and about 62% of people do not have confidence in the judicial system" (p. 2). The criminal justice systems of the countries of South America in particular and Latin America in general, as in most of the developing countries of Africa and Asia, are characterized by low rates of reporting of crime to police; low confidence in the police; widespread use of torture by police; militarization of policing; corruption in policing; extrajudicial killings; widespread use of impunity; lack of judicial accountability; widespread judicial corruption; low confidence in the judiciary; lack of due process of law; low rates of prosecution and conviction; gross violation of human rights; and imprisonment without trial and conviction.

The UNODC's 2010 report, *International Statistics on Crime and Justice,* which is based on an analysis of the *United Nations Surveys on Crime Trends and the Operations of Criminal Justice Systems* (2002–2006), shows that the median number of prosecutions in the countries of Latin America in 2006 was 191 per 100,000 population compared to 685 in Africa, 376 in Asia, and 973 in Europe. The median number of prosecutions for all countries in 2006 was 657. The median number of convictions in Latin America in 2006 was 75 (per 100,000) compared to 277 in Africa, 264 in Asia, and 698 in Europe. The median number of convictions for all countries in 2006 was 341. The report thus shows that the rates of prosecutions and convictions in the countries of Latin America are lowest among all countries and regions of the world. The rate of attrition of criminal cases and investigations is an important indicator of the effectiveness of a criminal justice system. The median attrition rate in 2006 in the countries of Latin America was 10.9 compared to 6.2 in Africa, 1.8 in Asia, and 1.6 in Europe. The median attrition rate for all countries in 2006 was 2.1. The higher rate of attrition in the countries of Latin America shows the extreme weakness of their criminal justice systems.

The same report also shows that the number of judges and prosecutors in the countries of Latin America and the Caribbean is also much lower than other major regions of the world. In the countries of Latin America and the Caribbean in 2006, there were 5.0 prosecutors per 100,000 population (median) compared to 22.1 in Eastern Europe, 10.2 in the United States and Canada, and 6.9 in Western and Central Europe. The median number of professional judges in Latin America and the Caribbean in 2006 was 5.9 compared to 19.6 in South east Europe, 15.9 in Western and Central Europe, 8.6 in the United States and Canada, and 8.2 in the Middle East. The countries of Latin America and the Caribbean also have one of the lowest numbers of correctional staff in adult prisons, with a median number, in 2006, of 33.0 per 100,000 population, compared to 115 in the United States and Canada, 69.2 in Western and Central Europe, 54.0 in East Africa, and 46.7 in the Middle East (United Nations Office on Drugs and Crime, 2010).

The World Justice Project's *Rule of Law Index 2010* surveyed six Latin American countries out of its sample of 35 countries. One of the indicators that the World Justice Project examined, as mentioned before, was the effectiveness of criminal justice, which was measured by the due process of law and the rights of the accused, equal justice, equal access to justice, independence of the police and the judiciary, fair and speedy trial, and effective pretrial investigation systems. The survey results show that in all these indicators, criminal justice is one of the weakest institutions in the six Latin American countries included in the survey. In a global rating of criminal justice systems from 1 (most effective) to 35 (most ineffective), the Dominican Republic was rated 24, followed by Peru (27), Argentina (28), El Salvador (30), Colombia (31), and Bolivia (35). In view of this survey, some of the world's most ineffective systems of criminal justice are in the countries of South America.

The Inter-American Commission on Human Rights of the Organization of the American States published its *Report on Citizen Security and Human Rights* in Latin America and the Caribbean in 2009. The report detailed some of the major problems and challenges of criminal justice in the region, and notably pointed to lack of compliance with the principles of the due process of law. The report indicated that one of the major obligations of the member states "is linked to the judicial clarification of criminal conduct with the view to eliminating impunity and preventing recurrence of violence. Both the Inter-American Commission and the Court have condemned the impunity of events violating fundamental rights" (Inter-American Commission on Human Rights, 2009, p. 1). With respect to militarization and professionalization of policing in many countries of this region, the Commission clearly stated that criminal justice must be pursued "within the framework of the tools provided for in the international human rights instruments and the enforcement of the rule of law as basic pillars for overcoming poverty and full respect for human rights and dignity" (Inter-American Commission on Human Rights, 2009, p. 2).

■ Summary

A vast number of countries in Asia, Africa, and Latin America are characterized by modernizing systems of criminal justice. Modernization in those countries has been progressing since their colonization by different European powers such as the Spaniards, Portuguese, Dutch, French, German, and British. The understanding of the vicissitudes of this process of modernization in criminal justice in the countries of Asia, Africa, and Latin America is crucial in cross-cultural comparison of criminal justice among the world's societies. It is significant because colonialism brought the European system of law and justice to the colonies. With the advent of modernization in the 19th century, the old structures of criminal justice in the colonies, which had been based on their respective cultures and civilizations, began to crumble. The old colonial systems of law and justice created by the various monarchical and aristocratic regimes of the Middle Ages collapsed with the advent of colonial modernization. This process of modernization in criminal justice has progressed in two phases.

The first phase is one of modernization during the colonial time period. The colonial governments, in the establishment of their colonies, brought their respective legal traditions (e.g., English common law and Continental civil law); created new structures of policing; developed new structures of the court and the judiciary; created many substantive and procedural criminal laws; and introduced new systems of governance in criminal justice in the colonies. It was from that time of colonization that some of the modern ideas about criminal justice (which originated from Montesquieu, Bentham, and Beccaria during the Enlightenment in Europe) began to travel across the world's continents. Some of the principles and philosophies of governing criminal justice enshrined in the English Bill of Rights, American Bill of Rights, and French Declaration of the Rights of Man and of the Citizen began to shape criminal justice in the colonies. One of the major examples of colonial modernization in criminal justice is the process of modernization in British India. The British colonial power created a new structure of criminal justice in India based on English common law. The British introduced the Indian Police Act in 1861, the Indian High Courts Act in 1861, the Indian Penal Code in 1862, the Indian Evidence Act in 1872, the Code of Criminal Procedure in 1882, and the Code of Criminal Procedure in 1898. The British colonial government brought many similar changes in criminal justice to its other colonies, located in Asia, Africa, and the Caribbean. In 1844, the British colonial government created a royal police force for Hong

Kong. The British East Africa Police were established in Kenya in 1902. Similar institutions of imperial policing were established in the plantation colonies of the British Caribbean. Modernization in criminal justice began also in colonies ruled by other European powers. The Dutch colonial state introduced the First Code of Criminal Procedure in Indonesia in 1847, which remains the foundation of criminal justice in Indonesia. In Latin America, the inquisitorial model of law and justice introduced by the Spaniards remained unchanged until the late 20th century. The colonial process of modernization, however, was not an unmixed blessing. The colonial powers wanted to create modern structures of criminal justice based on due process of law, separation of powers, judicial accountability, and modern legal education. But the very nature of colonial power and domination were antithetical to the ideas of the due process of law and judicial modernity.

Most of the institutions of colonial criminal justice did not progress towards further modernization in the postcolonial period. They did not progress because most of the newly independent states themselves were in their infancy, except the states of South America and Central America. From the beginning, the problem of the rule of law and democracy has remained endemic to the newly independent states of Asia, Africa, and Latin America. Because the states did not modernize, intrastate conflicts and violence erupted in many regions, particularly in Africa, and they remained dominant for many decades. In many other regions, particularly in Latin America, the military came to power and ruled for decades. The military-authoritarian regimes of Latin America stunted economic growth, widened social and economic inequalities, militarized the police force, fostered a culture of authoritarianism in civil bureaucracy, destroyed judicial autonomy, expanded a culture of impunity, and buried the principles of the rule of law and democracy. The military-authoritarian regimes of Asia and Africa projected the same characteristics. Throughout these regimes, which began to dominate in the 1960s in Asia, Africa, and Latin America, the world became further polarized economically, and billions of people were thrown into the periphery of modern economic growth, except in some authoritarian countries of Southeast Asia. The decades of military-authoritarian rules and cycles of conflict and violence left more than 100 states in Asia, Africa, and Latin America in shambles and in a state of complete fragility. A comparative analysis of criminal justice in the vast landscape of the developing world must be based on an adequate understanding of these historical, political, and economic contexts and realities.

■ Discussion Questions

1. For comparative criminal justice, what is the significance of studying the effect of colonialism in the developing countries of Asia, Africa, and Latin America? Search the Internet and develop a chart showing the major European colonial powers and their colonies in Asia, Africa, and Latin America in the 19th and 20th centuries.

2. Describe the effect of British colonialism on the creation of a modern structure of criminal justice in the British colonies of Asia and Africa. Discuss in this context the role and nature of the Indian Police Act of 1861, the Indian Penal Code of 1862, and the Indian Code of Criminal Procedure of 1882.

3. The European colonial power established the basic infrastructure of modern criminal justice by exporting the European legal tradition to the colonies. Examine and elaborate this statement in terms of the principles of the secularization of law and justice and the separation of church and state. How did the European legal traditions establish the roots of secularity in law and justice in the colonies?

4. What is the meaning of the rule of law, and why is the rule of law an essential feature of modern criminal justice? Discuss in this context the nature of the rule of law and democracy in the developing countries of Asia, Africa, and Latin America following the World Bank's study on governance indicators.

5. What are key characteristics of the states of Asia, Africa, and Latin America that are considered to be failed or fragile? How is the nature of criminal justice affected by the nature of the states? Discuss this question by drawing data from the World Justice Project's *Rule of Law Index* and the Economist Intelligence Unit's *Democracy Index*.

6. Describe the nature of crime and criminal justice in some of the failed and fragile states of Africa following the United Nations Office on Drugs and Crime's 2005 study, *Crime and Development in Africa*. What are the key issues in crime and criminal justice in Central America's failed and fragile states? Discuss this question following the United Nations Office on Drugs and Crime's subsequent 2007 study, *Crime and Development in Central America: Caught in the Crossfire*.

7. How are the rule of law, political stability, and homicide rates connected? Discuss and explore this question in the context of homicide rates in some of the postauthoritarian states in South America (see UNODC's 2011 report, *Global Study on Homicide: Trends, Contexts, Data*).

■ References

ABC News. (2007). *Kenyan police suspected of executing nearly 500*. Retrieved from http://australianetwork.com/news/stories_to/2082428.htm.

Agnew, F., & Henderson, G. S. (Eds.). (1882). *The code of criminal procedure (the act of 1882)*. Calcutta, India: Thacker, Spink and Co.

Anderson, D. M., & Killingray, D. (1991a). Consent, coercion, and colonial control: Policing the empire, 1830–1940. In D. M. Anderson & D. Killingray (Eds.), *Policing the empire: Government, authority, and control, 1830–1940* (pp. 1–32). Manchester, UK: Manchester University Press.

Anderson, D. M., & Killingray, D. (Eds.). (1991b). *Policing the empire: Government, authority, and control, 1830–1940*. Manchester, UK: Manchester University Press.

Benitez, I. (2007). *Guatemala: Homicide rate—From bad to worse*. Retrieved from www.ipsnews.net/news.asp?idnews=40453.

British Broadcasting Corporation. (2011*). March against violence in Honduras*. Retrieved from www.bbc.co.uk/news/world-latin-america-12593341.

British Library. (2011). *Indian police services*. London, England: Author.

Cevallos, D. (2008). *Latin America: Once again, govts promise to tackle violent crime*. Retrieved from www.ipsnews.net/news.asp?idnews=44186.

Collier, P. (2007). *The bottom billion: Why the poorest countries are failing and what can be done about it.* New York, NY: Oxford University Press.

Collier, P. (2009). *Wars, guns, and votes: Democracy in dangerous places.* New York, NY: Harper Publisher.

Cranenburgh, D. E. (1894). *The Indian penal code.* Calcutta, India: Law Publishing Press (Digitized by Google).

Deflem, M. (1994). Law enforcement in British Colonial Africa: A comparative analysis of imperial policing in Nyasaland, the Gold Coast, and Kenya. *Police Studies, 17*(1), 45–68.

Deflem, M., Featherstone, R., Li, Y., & Sutphin, S. (2008). Policing the pearl: Historical transformations of law enforcement in Hong Kong. *International Journal Police Science and Management, 10*(3), 349–356.

Economist Intelligence Unit. (2010). *Democracy Index 2010: Democracy in retreat* (A report from the Economist Intelligence Unit). London, England: The Economist.

Foreign Policy and the Fund for Peace. (2006). *The failed states index.* Washington, DC: The Fund for Peace and the Carnegie Endowment for International Peace.

Geneva Declaration Secretariat, Krause, K., Muggah, R., and Gilgen, E. (Eds). (2008). *Global burden of armed violence.* Geneva, Switzerland: Geneva Declaration Secretariat.

Gilpin, R., for the United States Institute of Peace. (2009). *Crime, violence, and economic development.* Retrieved from www.securitytransformation.org.

Human Rights Watch. (2010). *World report 2010: Events of 2009.* New York, NY: Author.

India, Legislative Department. (2010). *Act No. V. of 1861 (Regulation of Police): As Modified up to the 1st of August, 1892.* Delhi, India: The Government of India.

Inter-American Commission on Human Rights. (2009). *Report on citizen security and human rights.* Retrieved from www.cidh.org/countryrep/Seguridad.eng/CitizenSecurity.II.htm.

Kaplan, S. D. (2008). *Fixing fragile states: A new paradigm for development.* New York, NY: Praeger Publisher.

Karst, K. L. & Rosenn, K. S. (1975). *Law and development in Latin America: A case book.* Berkeley, CA: University California Press.

Kaufmann, D., Kraay, A., & Mastruzzi, M., for the World Bank. (2010). *The worldwide governance indicators: Methodology and analytical issues.* Washington, DC: World Bank Development Research Group.

Marshall, M. G., & Cole, B. R. (2008). *Global report: Conflict, governance, and state fragility.* Fairfax, VA: George Mason University Center for Systemic Peace.

Mejia, T. (2006). *Central America: Soaring violent crime threatens democracy.* Retrieved from www.ipsnews.net/news.asp?idnews=34743.

MercoPress. (2010, August 24). *Venezuela with one of the world's highest murder rates, according to official data.* Montevideo, Uraguay: Author.

MercoPress. (2011). *Venezuela's homicide rate exposes vulnerable flank of President Chavez.* Retrieved from http://en.mercopress.com/2011/02/10/venezuela-s-homicide-rate-exposes-vulnerable-flank-of-president-chavez.

Munzenrieder, K. (2010). Venezuela murder rate has quadrupled under Hugo Chávez. *Miami New Times.* Retrieved from http://blogs.miaminewtimes.com/riptide/2010/03/venezuela_murder-rate_has_quad.php.

Patrick, S. (2011). *Weak links: Fragile states, global threats, and international security.* New York, NY: Oxford University Press.

Paulin, D. (2008). Caracas: Murder capital of the world. *American Thinker*. Retrieved from www .americanthinker.com/2008/10/caracas_murder_capital_of_the.html.

Rice, S., & Patrick, S. (2008). *The index of state weakness in the developing world*. Washington, DC: The Brookings Institution.

Romero, S. (2010). Venezuela, more deadly than Iraq, wonders why. *The New York Times*. Retrieved from http://www.nytimes.com/2010/08/23/world/americas/23venez.html?_r=1.

Schwabach, A. (2006). Non-western philosophies of law. In A. Schwabach & A. J. Cockfield (Eds.). *Encyclopedia of life support systems*. Oxford, UK: UNESCO.

Sujata, A. (2011). *The development of the prosecutor's jurisdiction in the criminal justice system of Indonesia*. Retrieved from www.unafei.or.jp/english/pdf/RS_No53/No53_12VE_Sujata.pdf.

UN News Centre. (2011, May 31). *UN voices concern at targeting prosecutors and rights defenders in Central America*. New York, NY: United Nations.

United Nations Office on Drugs and Crime. (2004). *International homicide statistics*. Retrieved from Vienna, Austria: Author.

United Nations Office on Drugs and Crime. (2005). *Crime and development in Africa*. Vienna, Austria: Author.

United Nations Office on Drugs and Crime. (2007). *Crime and development in Central America: Caught in the Crossfire*. Vienna, Austria: Author.

United Nations Office on Drugs and Crime. (2010). *International statistics on crime and justice*. Vienna, Austria: Author.

United Nations Office on Drugs and Crime. (2011). *Global study on homicide: Trends, contexts, data*. Vienna, Austria: Author.

U.S. Department of State. (2011). *Guatemala: Country specific information*. Washington, DC: Author.

World Bank. (2010a). *Crime and violence in Central America* (Vol. II). Washington, DC: Author.

World Bank. (2010b). *Worldwide governance indicators*. Washington, DC: Author. Retrieved from http://data.worldbank.org/data-catalog/worldwide-governance-indicators.

World Bank. (2011a). *World development report 2011: Conflict, security, and development*. Washington, DC: Author.

World Bank. (2011b). *Crime and violence in Central America: A development challenge*. Washington, DC: Author.

World Justice Project. (2010). *Rule of law index, 2010*. Washington, DC: Author.

Wright, B. (2010, June). *Bentham's enlightened despotic legislator and colonial rule: Macaulay and the India Penal Code*. Paper presented at the 150th Anniversary of the Indian Penal Code Symposium, Singapore.

Modernizing Systems of Criminal Justice in Asia, Africa, and Latin America: The Second Wave of Modernization

▶ CHAPTER OUTLINE

■ Introduction

In the countries of Asia, Africa, and Latin America, a new movement for state formation on the basis of the rule of law and democracy began in the mid-1980s, as the Cold War was ending. It was also during that time that a second wave of modernization in criminal justice began to engulf the world's developing countries in Asia, Africa, and Latin America. Before the 1980s, development was defined primarily as a process of economic growth—a process of development in industrialization and urbanization. The issues of the rule of law and justice were not prominent in development theories and discourse during the 3 decades of the dominance of military-authoritarianism in the developing world.

The movement for state building in postconflict and postauthoritarian regimes in the late 1980s and the 1990s began with a new perspective about the connectivity between crime and development and between development and criminal justice. Development scholars and international assistance organizations began to assert that crime and development are intimately connected. Crime and violence bring enormous economic costs for developing countries. The Inter-American Development Bank, for example, estimates that "violence costs Latin America as much as 15 percent of its combined annual gross domestic product (GDP)" (Cevallos, 2008, p. 1). The World Bank's 2007 report, *Crime, Violence, and Development: Trends, Costs, and Policy Options in the Caribbean,* noted that economic cost of crime and violence in the region is "close to eight percent of regional GDP if citizen security, law enforcement, and health care are included. Crime and violence also drag down economic growth . . . by polluting the investment climate and diverting scarce government resources" (World Bank, 2007, p. ii). The World Bank study also calculated that "a ten percent reduction in the violence levels of those Central American countries with the highest murder rates could boost annual economic growth per capita by as much as a full one percent" (2007, p. ii).

A new perspective on connectivity between crime and development and relations between development and criminal justice began to emerge in the 1990s, when development began to be defined not only by economic growth, but also by such issues as the rule of law, democracy, access to justice, equal justice, human security, and compliance with international standards of human rights. With the expansion of this new perspective on development, criminal justice reforms came to the core of state building and governance in the developing countries. Transformations of the institutions that provide security, law, and justice came to prominence in the pursuit of development. The World Bank's (2011) *World Development Report 2011: Conflict, Security, and Development* concluded that the key to development in the weak and fragile states today is the building of "legitimate institutions that can provide a sustained level of citizen security, justice, and jobs—offering a stake in society to groups that may otherwise receive more respect and recognition from engaging in armed violence" (p. 8). The challenge in the second wave of modernization in criminal justice is to develop a system that will be based on the rule of law and democracy, on the due process of law, and on the recognition of the centrality of the issues of equal justice, human rights, and citizen security. As a core strategy for pursuing development and state building in developing countries, modernization of criminal justice has indeed emerged as a new movement in recent years. In developing countries, hundreds of international assistance organizations have been working, since the 1990s, for reforms and modernization in many areas of criminal justice (e.g., policing and law enforcement, law and justice, court and prosecutions, judicial accountability, and prison and corrections). Understanding these recent efforts and discourse in the modernization of criminal justice in developing countries is highly significant in comparative criminal justice. The following sections will discuss some of the new initiatives for modernization in policing and judicial systems in selected countries of Asia, Africa, and Latin America.

■ Modernization of Policing in Asia, Africa, and Latin America

The police stand at the front of criminal justice in all countries. They are responsible for receiving and responding to crime reports and information, arresting offenders, performing searches and seizures of criminal evidence, securing criminal property, protecting victims from immediate danger, putting offenders in secure detention, and conducting criminal investigations and interrogations. Police form the first-line defense in outbreaks of violence, riots, and mass protests. They are responsible for protecting state and private properties from destruction by collective violence, organized groups, and gangs. They prepare criminal cases for bail, trials, and adjudications. An offender's fate and destiny largely depend on how police collect evidence and frame the criminal charges. Collection of evidence and framing of charges have remained as some of the core responsibilities of policing since the birth of professional policing in the early 19th century. Police roles and responsibilities in the 21st century have vastly increased in the context of a new global information economy; the rise of new megacities; the birth and expansion of transnational organized crime; and the globalization of a new culture of consciousness about rights, equality, privacy, justice, and fairness. In most of the developing countries of Asia, Africa, and Latin America, the second wave of modernization in criminal justice began with plans and programs for reforms in policing (Pinc, 2010).

The institution of modern policing in the countries of Asia, Africa, and Latin America began, as mentioned earlier, during the days of colonialism. Policing was one of the first institutions to be organized in the colonies. It was one of the first institutions through which European models of organizing criminal justice were implanted in the soils of non-European colonies. It is also one of the colonial institutions that has barely changed and reformed in the postcolonial time period. In most of the failed and fragile states, the police were militarized, politicized, and given impunity to control crime and violence, even if that meant extrajudicial killings and gross violations of human rights. The history of policing in the developing world is a lengthy chronicle of torture, brutality, and violence. For decades, the absence of the rule of law and democracy in the failed and fragile states made policing in most cases dysfunctional. The *World Report 2011* by Human Rights Watch (2011), for example, stated that in Brazil, "police abuse, including extrajudicial execution, is a chronic problem . . . . Police were responsible for 505 killings in the state of Rio de Janeiro alone in the first six months of 2010. This amounts to roughly three police killings per day" (p. 215). The *World Report 2011* said that "police in Sao Paulo state had killed more people over the prior five years than had police in all of South Africa, a country with a higher homicide rate than Sao Paulo" (Human Rights Watch, 2011, p. 215). In Guatemala, extrajudicial killings of gang members by the Guatemalan police force, called "social cleansing," is widespread and rampant. In Venezuela, according to the Venezuelan Office of the Attorney General, "law enforcement agents allegedly killed 7,998 people between January 2000 and the first third of 2009. Impunity for all violent crimes, including those committed by police, remains the norm" (Human Rights Watch, 2011, p. 271).

Stories of police torture and police brutality are also not few and far between in the countries of Asia and Africa. In enforcing the county's new law against human trafficking, Cambodia's police regularly rape, beat up, arrest, and arbitrarily detain "women and girls, including transgender women, involved in sex work" (Human Rights Watch, 2011, p. 299). According to the Human Rights Commission in Uganda, "more than 7,500 complaints of torture and cruel or inhuman treatment have been made" against the Ugandan police between 1997 and 2007, and "many involve claims against a jumble of fierce paramilitary units established by the President, who seized power by force 21 years ago and is still a serving general" (Pflanz, 2007, p. 1).

In Egypt, police brutality was partly responsible for the eruption of the whole nation against the authoritarian regime of Hosni Mubarak. In 2010, Egyptian police beat and killed a 28-year-old man named Khaled Said. Said was "dragged out of an Internet café and beaten in the street by plainclothes police in Alexandria . . . . When images of Said's bloodied face surfaced on the Internet, outraged youth organized on Facebook and called for demonstrations" (*Los Angeles Times,* 2011, p. 1). That demonstration led to the fall of Mubarak's political regime and sent waves of inspiration for democracy movements throughout the Arab world. Police behavior is sometimes the mirror through which people see the image of their political regimes. In many developing countries, serious efforts for reforms in policing began during the second wave of modernization in the context of these and many other stories of a dysfunctional and coercive colonial police culture. There is hardly any country in the developing world today that does not have some laws and programs for reforms in policing. During the last 2 decades, hundreds of national and international studies and commission reports have been made to provide recommendations for police reform in developing countries. The developing countries have enacted hundreds of laws for reforms and modernization in policing.

Reforms and Modernization in Policing: Global Perspectives

There is no debate about the fact that policing in a country must grow within the boundary of its social and cultural milieu. In states with federal political structures, the chain of command for federal police differs from that of state police. In states with unitary political structures, there are national police organizations with a single chain of command. In some countries, police leaders are elected like the county sheriffs in the United States. In some other countries, police leaders are recruited from the rank and file. In many countries of the developing world, police leaders are recruited through civil service examinations. This is a particularly strong tradition in India and other British colonies. Issues related to the nature of police roles and hierarchy, as well as styles of police organization and police management, are primarily local. The police must be knowledgeable about and sensitive to local cultural standards, values, beliefs, mores, and moralities. However, policing must also grow in all countries in terms of some of the universal standards of the rule of law and democracy. There are some international benchmarks—global perspectives—for what constitute modern or democratic policing. These international benchmarks come from a large body of international laws and standards, particularly from the United Nations (UN). Some of these include the Universal Declaration of Human Rights; the UN International Convention on the Elimination of All Forms of Racial Discrimination; the UN Convention on the Elimination of All Forms of Discrimination Against Women; the UN Convention Against Torture and Other Cruel, Inhuman or Degrading Treatment or Punishment; the UN Convention Against Corruption; the UN Standard Minimum Rules for the Administration of Juvenile Justice; the UN Convention on the Rights of the Child; and the UN Code of Conduct for Law Enforcement Officials. There are also many regional standards, such as the UK's Commonwealth of Human Rights Initiative, the Inter-American Commission on Human Rights, the Inter-American Court of Human Rights, the European Charter of Fundamental Rights, the European Court of Justice, the African Charter on Human and Peoples' Rights, the African Court on Human and Peoples' Rights, the Asian Human Rights Commission, and the South Asian Association for Regional Cooperation (SAARC). Regional standards are broadly in consensus with international laws and standards for policing.

International laws and standards are primarily focused on the issues of the rule of law, the due process of law, democracy, and the protection of human rights in different facets of exercising police power and authority. The UN Code of Conduct for Law Enforcement Officials, adopted in 1979, is one of the major international policy frameworks for police reform around the word (see **Table 8-1**). The Code requires police officials in signatory states to recognize the rights set out "in the United Nations Declaration of Universal Human Rights and other international conventions" (Commonwealth Human Rights Initiative, 2011a, p. 1). Article 2 of the UN Code of Conduct states that "in the performance of their duty, law enforcement officials shall respect and protect human dignity and maintain and uphold the human rights of all persons" (United Nations Organization, 1979). Article 5 states that police or the military engaged in law enforcement must not "tolerate any act of torture or other cruel, inhuman or degrading treatment or punishment, nor may any law enforcement official invoke superior orders . . . as a justification of torture" (United Nations Organization, 1979).

The Code clearly states that the police must be responsible for the health and safety of the people who are taken into police custody and detention. Article 6 of the Code states that "law enforcement officials shall ensure the full protection of the health of persons in their custody and, in particular, shall take immediate action to secure medical attention whenever required" (United Nations Organization, 1979). Article 7 of the Code prohibits corruptions for police officials: "Law enforcement officials shall not commit any act of corruption. They shall also rigorously oppose and combat all such acts" (United Nations Organization, 1979).

TABLE 8-1   United Nations Code of Conduct for Law Enforcement Officials: The Global Perspectives for Police Reforms and Police Modernization

Article	Code of Conduct
Article 1	Law enforcement officials shall at all times fulfill the duty imposed upon them by law, by serving the community and by protecting all persons against illegal acts, consistent with the high degree of responsibility required by their profession.
Article 2	In the performance of their duty, law enforcement officials shall respect and protect human dignity and maintain and uphold the human rights of all persons.
Article 3	Law enforcement officials may use force only when strictly necessary and to the extent required for the performance of their duty.
Article 4	Matters of a confidential nature in the possession of law enforcement officials shall be kept confidential, unless the performance of duty strictly requires otherwise.
Article 5	No law enforcement official may inflict, instigate, or tolerate any act of torture or other cruel, inhuman, or degrading treatment or punishment, nor may any law enforcement official invoke superior orders or exceptional circumstances such as a state of war or a threat of war, a threat to national security, internal political instability, or any other public emergency as a justification of torture or other cruel, inhuman, or degrading treatment or punishment.
Article 6	Law enforcement officials shall ensure the full protection of the health of persons in their custody and, in particular, shall take immediate action to secure medical attention whenever required.
Article 7	Law enforcement officials shall not commit any act of corruption. They shall also rigorously oppose and combat all such acts.
Article 8	Law enforcement officials shall respect the law and the present Code. They shall also, to the best of their capability, prevent and rigorously oppose any violations of them.

Source: Data from United Nations Code of Conduct for Law Enforcement Officials, 1979.

The UN Convention Against Torture and Other Cruel, Inhuman or Degrading Treatment or Punishment, adopted in 1984, requires signatory states to ban torture in all areas of law enforcement. It also mandates the criminalization of torture through appropriate legislation. Article 4 of the Convention states: "Each State Party shall ensure that . . . acts of torture are offences under its criminal law. The same shall apply to an attempt to commit torture and to an act by any person which constitutes . . . participation in torture" (United Nations Organization, 1984).

The UN Principles for the Protection of All Persons Under Any Form of Detention or Imprisonment requires signatory states to protect the fundamental rights of people under police detention. Principle III states that "there shall be no restriction upon or derogation from any of the human rights of persons under any form of detention or imprisonment" (United Nations Organization, 1988). Principle XI states that no individuals shall be confined "in detention without being given an effective opportunity to be heard promptly by a judicial or other authority. A detained person shall have the right to defend himself or to be assisted by counsel as prescribed by law" (United Nations Organization, 1988).

The UN Principles on the Effective Prevention and Investigation of Extra-legal, Arbitrary and Summary Executions, adopted in 1989, requires the signatory states to criminalize all police acts of extrajudicial killings. It states that all signatory states: "shall prohibit by law all extra-legal . . . summary executions and shall ensure that any such executions are recognized as offences under their criminal laws, and are punishable by appropriate penalties" (United Nations Office of the High Commissioner for Human Rights, 1989, p. 1). It further states that "exceptional circumstances including a state of war or threat of war, internal political instability or any other public emergency may not be invoked as a justification of such executions" (United Nations Office of the High Commissioner for Human Rights, 1989, p. 1). These and other international laws and standards for police and law enforcement are basically the translations of the English Bill of Rights, the French Declaration of the Rights of Man and of the Citizen, and the Bill of Rights adopted by the United States. These laws and standards are at the core of the formation of a modern state and the advance of modernity in criminal justice. For police reform and modernization in criminal justice in developing countries, the adoption of these international laws and standards are significant challenges. They cannot grow overnight, but a process seems to have started in many developing countries.

Police Reforms and Police Modernization in India

With about 1.2 billion people (2012 estimate), India is the second largest country in the world. India is the only democracy in the developing world. It is also the largest democracy in the world. Since its independence in 1947 from British colonial rule, India, unlike hundreds of other countries in the developing world that were under military authoritarian rule for decades, has been continuously ruled by civilian governments. The Economist Intelligence Unit's (2010) *Democracy Index 2010,* however, identified India as one of the flawed democracies. With an overall score of 7.28 (out of 10), India received a global ranking of 40 out of 167 countries in electoral process and pluralism, functioning of government, political participation, political culture, and civil liberties. India's scores on civil liberties (9.41) and electoral process and pluralism (9.58), however, were higher than some of the countries identified as full democracies by the *Democracy Index 2010* such as the United States, the United Kingdom, Germany, Austria, Spain, and Japan. In the World Justice Project's (2010) *Rule of Law Index* that surveyed 35 countries, India received a global ranking of 9 in open government, 14 in limited government, 20 in fundamental rights, and 23 in order and stability. Of nine indicators used by the World Justice Project, India received a global ranking of 23 out of 35 in the effectiveness of criminal justice. The problems in India's criminal justice are also evidenced in the *World Report 2011* produced by Human Rights Watch. The report stated that "impunity for abusive policing remains a pressing concern in India, with continuing allegations in 2010 of police brutality, extrajudicial killings, and torture. While some policemen were prosecuted for human rights abuses, legal hurdles to prosecution remained in place" (Human Rights Watch, 2011, p. 317). The report further noted that "legislators and officials proposed new laws to prevent torture . . . and prosecute those responsible for sexual violence, but have yet to repeal laws providing effective immunity from prosecution to government officials, including soldiers and police, responsible for human rights violations" (p. 315).

The institution of policing in India is based on the legal framework established by the British colonial government in the middle of the 19th century. The Indian Police Act of 1861, the Indian Penal Code of 1862, the Indian Evidence Act of 1872, the Code of Criminal Procedure of 1882, and the Code of Criminal Procedure of 1898 still define the nature and structure of policing in India. In 1973, India enacted a revised code of criminal procedure. The colonial laws, however, "except for minor amendments, have remained unchanged" (Commonwealth of Human Rights Initiative, 2011b, p. 3). Politically, India has a federal structure. It has a federal government, known as a union government, and it is headed by a prime minister. The Union of India is comprises 28 states and 7 union territories. Article 246 of the Indian constitution gave the states the responsibility of organizing state police forces. India, like the United States, Canada, and Germany, has a dual system of criminal justice—that is, it has both a federal system and a state system of criminal justice. It also has dual system of policing—a federal system of policing and a state system of policing. Article 355 of the Indian constitution gave power to the Parliament of the union government to organize a policing system to oversee maintenance of India's overall law and order and to ensure that the state governments and state policing systems work in compliance with the provisions of the constitution.

The federal police system, which is under the Indian Ministry of Home Affairs, has a number of central police organizations (CPOs), which can be divided into two groups. One group is composed of central paramilitary forces (CPMs) such as the Assam Rifles, Border Security Forces (BSF), and Central Reserve Police Force. The Central Reserve Police Force, led by the officer of the Indian Police Service (IPS), is the core of federal policing in India; it is somewhat comparable to the FBI of the United States, the Royal Canadian Mounted Police, the Special Police Forces of the United Kingdom, and the Federal Criminal Police (BKA) of Germany. The other group involved in India's federal policing is comprised mainly of police research and police development organizations. Some of these include the Bureau of Police Research and Development, the Central Bureau of Investigation (CBI), the National Crime Records Bureau, the National Police Academy, the Intelligence Bureau, and the National Institute of Criminology and Forensic Science. India is one of the few countries in the developing world that has a government-funded institute of criminology for the advancement of criminological research; the institute is like that of the National Institute of Justice in the United States, the Australian Institute of Criminology of the government of Australia, and the Korean Institute of Criminology located in the prime minister's office in South Korea.

The 28 states and 7 union territories of India have their respective systems of policing. There are two main categories of state police: civil police and armed police. The primary responsibility of the civil police is to control and prevent crime, whereas that of the armed police is the maintenance of general law and order including the control of political protests, mass uprisings, riots, and other emergencies. The state police are organized into various administrative units and divisions within the state. The states are divided into different zones, ranges, districts, subdivisions, circles, and police stations. The chief of the state police is called the Director General of Police. The highly centralized state system of policing operates with a single chain of command from the Director General of Police to the Assistant Sub-Inspector of Police in charge of police stations. One of the unique features of the Indian police system is that its leadership is in the hands of officers of the Indian Police Service who are recruited by the central government on the basis of competitive examination. They are specially trained in a national police academy. The officers of the Indian Police Service who work for the states are under the authority of the state governments, and those who work for the central government are under the authority of the central Ministry of Home Affairs (Commonwealth Human Rights Initiative, 2011c).

Police reform and modernization began in India in the 1950s, primarily under the initiatives of the state governments. Since the 1950s, a number of state laws have been enacted for police reforms, such as the Bombay Police Act of 1951, Kerala Police Act of 1963, Karnataka Police Act of 1963, Delhi Police Act of 1978, and Bihar Police Act of 2007. Many state governments also established separate police commissions to study the problems of policing and suggest recommendations for police improvement. A police commission was established in Bihar in 1958, Uttar Pradesh in 1960, West Bengal in 1960, Punjab in 1961, Delhi in 1966, and Assam in 1969. The recommendations of these commissions and the various laws enacted between the 1950s and the 1970s, however, did not bring any significant changes in policing in India. A study conducted by the Commonwealth Human Rights Initiative (2011d) found that commission recommendations were "presented almost exactly on the model of the 1861 Act, resulting in no significant improvement in the performance of behavior of the police . . . Some of these state Acts tightened political control even further over the police force" (p. 3).

In the early 1970s, India's central government began to initiate efforts for reforms in policing. During the past 4 decades, there were four major initiatives that were taken by the central government. These were the Gore Committee on Police Training, created in 1971; the National Police Commission (NPC), created in 1977; the Ribeiro Committee on Police Reforms, created in 1998; and the Padmanabhaiah Committee on Police Reforms, created in 2000. The Gore Committee recommended changes in police training to emphasize the development of modern knowledge and skills for policing, and people-oriented police behavior and attitudes. The NPC produced eight reports between 1979 and 1981. These reports made many recommendations in light of the international law and legal standards for reforms in policing. They recommended legislation and procedures for improving police accountability; reducing political control on the police; making mandatory judicial interventions to address cases of police abuse, particularly rape and abuse of women and torture and death in police custody; developing proper mechanisms for dealing with public complaints about abusive police behavior; protecting the civil rights of the people; protecting the rights of the victims; and recruiting more women in the Indian police. "The major recommendations of the NPC," observed by the Commonwealth Human Rights Initiative (2011d), "have remained unimplemented" (p. 12).

The Ribeiro Committee published two reports: one in 1998 and the other in 1999. One of the major recommendations of the Ribeiro Committee was to set up a security commission or police performance and accountability commission, with advisory powers, in each of the 28 states to deal with issues of policing and police development (Commonwealth Human Rights Initiative, 2011e). The committee also recommended the formation of a district police complaints authority and police establishment board. The committee strongly endorsed the Indian Law Commission recommendation for the separation of the investigative functions of policing from the functions of maintaining law and order. At the federal level, the Ribeiro Committee endorsed the NPC recommendation for the establishment of a central police committee as the apex organization for reform and modernization in policing in India.

The Padmanabhaiah Committee presented a report in 2000. Some of its major recommendations included issues related to police accountability, redressing public grievances, and "insulating the police from politicization and criminalization" (Commonwealth Human Rights Initiative, 2011f, p. 2). The committee recommended the introduction of community policing, mandatory judicial inquiry of police abuse of women in police custody, setting up proper mechanisms to reduce police corruption, and creating a permanent National Commission for Police Standards. The committee also recommended police training in the area of combating new global crimes such as cyber crime and global terrorism. The committee stated, "There is a need for comprehensive reforms in criminal justice administration. Public would soon lose faith in the criminal justice system unless the other components of the system are also not thoroughly overhauled" (Commonwealth Human Rights Initiative, 2011f). Most of the recommendations of both the Ribeiro Committee and the Padmanabhaiah Committee remained unimplemented.

In 2006, the history of police reform in India came to a turning point with the involvement of the Supreme Court of India—an event unique in the history of police reform in developing countries. In 1996, a high-ranking retired Indian police officer named Prakash Singh, who was a Director General of Police in Assam, filed a public interest lawsuit with the Supreme Court of India complaining about the failure of the government of India to implement the various recommendations of the police reform committees and commissions, particularly the NPC's eight volumes of recommendations for police reforms in India. The petitioner argued that because of the lack of any fundamental change in its philosophy and modes of organization and operation since the creation of the Police Act of 1861 by the British colonial state, the institution of policing in India was on the verge of collapse. An overwhelming political and executive control of the police and police organizations, the petitioner argued, had completely crippled the core of the institution. Political control of the police and their investigating agencies, unauthorized detentions, torture in detentions, fabrication of evidence, and malicious prosecutions have led, the petitioner claimed, to serious erosion of the rule of law in the institution of policing in India.

In 2006, the Supreme Court of India presented a judgment in the case of *Prakash Singh and Others vs. Union of India and Others* (see **Table 8-2**). In delivering the judgment, Chief

TABLE 8-2 Supreme Court Directives for the Implementation of Police Reforms in India

Directives	Implementation Goals and Objectives
Directive 1	State Security Commission: The State Governments are directed to constitute a State Security Commission to (i) ensure that the State Government does not exercise unwarranted influence or pressure on the police; (ii) lay down broad policy guidelines; and (iii) evaluate the performance of the State police.
Directive 2	Director General of Police: The State Government is to ensure that the Director General of Police is appointed through a merit-based, transparent process and enjoys a minimum tenure of 2 years.
Directive 3	Minimum tenure for other police officers: The State Government is to ensure that other police officers on operational duties (including Superintendents of Police in charge of a district and Station House Officers in charge of a police station) also have a minimum tenure of 2 years.
Directive 4	Police Establishment Board: The State Government is to set up a Police Establishment Board, which will decide all transfers, postings, promotions, and other service-related matters of police officers of and below the rank of Deputy Superintendent of Police and make recommendations on postings and transfers of officers above the rank of Deputy Superintendent of Police.
Directive 5	National Security Commission: The State Government is to set up a National Security Commission at the union level to prepare a panel for selection and placement of Chiefs of the Central Police Organizations (CPOs), who should also be given a minimum tenure of 2 years.
Directive 6	Accountability—Police Complaints Authority: The State Government is to set up independent Police Complaints Authorities at the state and district levels to look into public complaints against police officers in cases of serious misconduct, including custodial death, grievous hurt, or rape in police custody.
Directive 7	Separation of investigation and law and order police: The State Government is to separate the investigation and law and order functions of the police.

Source: Data from Commonwealth Human Rights Initiative. (2012). *Seven steps to police reform.* Delhi, India: Author.

Justice of the Supreme Court Y. K. Sabharwal said that considering "i) the gravity of the problem; [and] ii) the urgent need for preservation and strengthening of Rule of Law . . . we think that . . . the stage has come for issue of appropriate directions for immediate compliance" (Supreme Court of India, 2006, p. 7). The Supreme Court presented seven directives and asked for immediate compliance by the central government, 28 state governments, and 7 union territories. These directives can be broadly divided into two categories: directives related to the functioning autonomy of the police, and directives related to enhancing police accountability.

Three major issues have been addressed by the seven directives of the Supreme Court. The first is about the politicization of policing in India. This is one of the major problems of police development in India and, indeed, in the whole of the developing world. The Commonwealth Human Rights Initiative rightly recognized that the Police Act of 1861 created by the British colonial government established a system of policing "designed to be absolutely subservient to the executive . . . . The police system in India can be characterized as a regime force which places the needs of politicians . . . over the demands of the rule of law" (2011c, p. 3). The first directive of the Supreme Court is for the establishment of an independent state security commission in each state to deal with the issues of the politicization of policing. The Supreme Court also gave a directive for the establishment of a national security commission for the same purpose. The second issue addressed by the Supreme Court directives is about police accountability. The Supreme Court directed each state to establish a separate police complaints authority both at the state level and in each district to deal with the issue of police accountability. One of the important aspects of this directive is the role assigned to state high courts and state human rights commissions in choosing the leadership of the state police complaints authorities.

Directive 7 of the Supreme Court addresses the third issue—the separation of the investigative functions of police from the functions of maintaining law and order. This separation was strongly recommended by almost all reform commissions and committees. It was particularly emphasized by the Indian Law Commission, the National Police Commission, and the Ribeiro Committee on Police Reforms. The Ribeiro Committee recommended that the investigating police officers should be trained in the scientific method of police investigation. The judgment of the Supreme Court to immediately implement the seven directives is definitely a great step forward for police reforms in India. However, some of the critical issues contained in international law and standards related to the criminalization of police torture, police abuse in detention, and police corruption, as well as protection human rights and the due process of law in policing did not appear prominently in the Supreme Court directives. The issues of community policing, problem–oriented policing, service-oriented policing, police–community relations, and citizen participation in crime control and prevention also did not surface very strongly in commission reports, debates, and discourses on police reforms and modernization in India. However, the case of judicial interventions for police reforms in India is unique.

Police Reforms and Police Modernization in Bangladesh

Bangladesh, with about 152 million people (2012 estimate), is the 8th largest country in the world. It was a part of Pakistan—East Pakistan—from 1947 to 1971. Before 1947, the region that now constitutes Bangladesh was part of the Bengal Province in British India. Like other regions of India, Bengal was ruled by the British for more than 200 years. The criminal justice system of Bangladesh carries the legacy of British colonial rule. The Indian Police Act of 1861, the Indian Penal Code of 1862, the Indian Evidence Act of 1872, the Indian Code of Criminal Procedure of 1882, and the Code of Criminal Procedure of 1898 enacted by the British colonial government also form the foundation of criminal justice in Bangladesh. The criminal justice system of Bangladesh has some of the same characteristics that are found in weak and fragile states of the developing world. Politically, Bangladesh is one of the most fragile states in the world.

The Economist Intelligence Unit's (2010) *Democracy Index 2010* identified Bangladesh as one of the hybrid regimes with a global ranking of 83 out of 167 countries ranked by the study. The hybrid regimes are defined by the study as those that have problems with the functioning of government and political participation. In hybrid regimes, the rule of law is weak, the judiciary is lacking in independence, and corruption is widespread. In the functioning of government indicator used by *Democracy Index 2010,* Bangladesh received a score of 5.43 out of 10 (Economist Intelligence Unit, 2010). About the rule of law and democracy in Bangladesh, a similar profile was set forth by the State Fragility Index and Matrix developed by the *Global Report: Conflict, Governance, and State Fragility* (Marshall & Cole, 2008). In the State Fragility Index and Matrix, Bangladesh received a rating of 12 on a scale of 1 (no fragility) to 25 (highly fragile). In security effectiveness, political effectiveness, economic effectiveness, and social effectiveness, Bangladesh received a rating of 7 out of 13. In security legitimacy, political legitimacy, economic legitimacy, and social legitimacy, Bangladesh received a rating of 5 out of 12 (Marshall & Cole, 2008). In the World Bank's study of governance indicators, the profile of Bangladesh as one of the world's most fragile states remained the same. In the World Bank's study, Bangladesh received a score of 35.1 (percentile scale 0–100) in voice and accountability, 7.5 in political stability, 16.7 in government effectiveness, 27.8 in the rule of law, and 16.7 in corruption (Kaufmann, Kraay, & Mastruzzi, 2010).

There are serious problems in the rule of law, democracy, and political stability in Bangladesh. Any comparative study of criminal justice in Bangladesh must be explored in the context of its enduring problems in political stability and the rule of law. Out of its 40 years of independence, Bangladesh was ruled by the military for about 14 years (from 1976 to 1990). Politics in Bangladesh remained volatile because there were still large sections of the middle class and the elite who were philosophically opposed to the breakup of Pakistan and the creation of Bangladesh. The Father of the Nation of Bangladesh, Sheikh Mujibur Rahman, was assassinated, and most of his family members were brutally killed by an army coup in 1975. After the assassination of Rahman, a new political party was created when the military mobilized some sectors of the middle class and elites who were opposed to the breakup of Pakistan. The creation of this new political party, which was opposed to the very foundation of the sovereign state, caused a seemingly permanent division or permanent grounds for political conflict and violence in Bangladesh. In the 1980s, most of the fundamentalist Islamic forces aligned themselves with the new political party, and that alliance further deepened the political conflict and violence. The criminal justice system of Bangladesh is caught up in the crossfire between competing political parties who believe in conflicting ideologies of state building.

Bangladesh has a unitary form of government. It has one system of national policing under a single chain of command from the Bangladesh Ministry of Home Affairs. As in India, however, there is a dual system of control of the police in Bangladesh. One part of the police administration is headed by an Inspector General of Police (IGP), and the other part of the police administration is in the hands of the Executive Magistrates—the representatives of the executive branch of government. The Bangladesh national police organization comprises the following eight major types of policing: metropolitan policing, a rapid action battalion (RAB), range police, an armed police battalion, special branch police (SB), a criminal investigation department (CID), traffic and highway patrol police, and railway police. The country is administratively divided into 64 districts, each of which is divided into 7 ranges for general police administration (except highway police and railway police). There are 6 metropolitan police forces in 6 major cities: Dhaka, Chittagong, Rajshahi, Khulna, Barisal, and Sylhet. Each metropolitan police force is headed by a metropolitan police commissioner. Rapid action battalion (RAB), created by the Armed Police Battalion Amendment Act of 2003, is a militarized police force comprised mostly of individuals trained in the military. The RAB is headed by a Director-General who is usually a Brigadier General from the military. Representatives of the military occupy almost all of the upper hierarchies of RAB administration. There are 12 RAB battalions in 8 major cities of the country.

Bangladesh became independent in 1971. From 1971 to 2005, for 34 years, there were no major initiatives taken by the government for reforms in policing, primarily because of escalating political conflicts that kept the state in complete fragility. The Indian Police Act of 1861 is still the major framework of law that guides policing in Bangladesh. In 1976, the military government promulgated the Police Officers (Special Provisions) Ordinance of 1976, which brought the police completely under the control of the executive branch and barred judicial interventions on police matters. Between 2005 and 2007, three systematic efforts were undertaken for reforms in policing in Bangladesh (Shahjahan, 2006). The first was the Police Reform Programme (PRP), organized in 2005 by the United Nations Development Programme (UNDP) in collaboration with the government of Bangladesh, the European Commission, the United Kingdom's Department of International Development, and local police and civil society leaders. The PRP is one of the most comprehensive programs for reforms in policing in South Asia. The PRP, located in Bangladesh Police Headquarters in Dhaka, "aims at improving the efficiency and effectiveness of the Bangladesh Police by supporting key areas of access to justice; including crime prevention, investigations, police operations and prosecutions; human resource management and training; and future directions, strategic capacity and oversight" (Bangladesh Police, 2011, p. 1).

There are seven key components of PRP: crime prevention; human resource management; program management; improvement in police investigations, operations, and prosecutions; development of the police code of ethics and oversight strategies; capacity enhancement in combating illegal human trafficking; and development of a modern police information management system. The PRP has brought many state-of-the-art programs for police reforms such as proactive crime prevention strategies, community policing, a victims' support center, integration of women into the police force, formation of a national police training board, introduction of a public attitudes survey on crime and justice, development of forensic investigation skills and technology, development of a computerized national crime data bank, development of a cyber crime investigation unit, and increased integration of information and communication technology (ICT) into policing. Some of these programs have already been implemented, including the establishment of 11 model police stations' ICT facilities; creation of 40,000 neighborhood community policing forums; the opening of a crime prevention center in the Bangladesh police headquarters; the founding of Bangladesh police women's networks; establishment of two forensic laboratories; formation of a national police training board; and initiation of a public perception survey in 2008. Since the inception of the PRP, more than 3,000 police personnel have received training in various areas of police reforms and modernization in Bangladesh (Bangladesh Police, 2011; Commonwealth Human Rights Initiative, 2010).

The second major initiative for reforms in policing was taken in 2007 with the drafting of a new police bill—the Bangladesh Police Ordinance of 2007. It was drafted under the directive of the interim government (i.e., caretaker government) that came to power in 2007, and proposed replacing the Indian Police Act of 1861. The Commonwealth Human Rights Initiative, in one report on police reform in South Asia, stated that the Bangladesh Police Ordinance of 2007 "is an exceptional document . . . It would serve as a template for regional neighbors to emulate. Although it has few weakneses, it is largely a forward-looking approach to policing. Generally, it seeks to establish a democratic form of policing in Bangladesh" (2010, p. 31). The report further stated that the new bill included in its preamble the notion of "human rights," which sets the tone for the draft ordinance: "This document is determined that the police protect human dignity rather than undermine it. If operationalized. . . it will be a drastic change from the manner in which the policing in Bangladesh is typically carried" (2010, p. 31).

The major goal of the ordinance is to make the police "publicly accountable, operationally neutral, functionally specialized, professionally efficient, democratically controlled and responsive to the need of the community" (International Crisis Group, 2009, p. 4). The ordinance proposed the criminalization of political influence on policing. Section 10(2) of the ordinance stated that "direct or indirect influence or interference into police investigation, law enforcement operation, recruitment, promotion, transfer, posting, or any other police functions in an unlawful manner shall be a criminal offence" (Police Ordinance of 2007, as quoted in International Crisis Group, 2009, p. 4). Some of the key provisions of the ordinance include the creation of a national police commission, a national police complaints commission, and a national public safety fund. The Police Ordinance of 2007 has yet to be ratified by the Bangladesh Parliament. There is also a police reform bill pending in the Parliament, called the Torture and Custodial Death Prohibition Bill of 2009.

The third important initiative for police reforms in Bangladesh came from the high court division of the Bangladesh Supreme Court. The high court made an important ruling in 2003 on police actions related to arrest without a warrant, taking people into police custody and police remand, torture and death in police custody, and extrajudicial killings by the police. In 1988, a writ petition was filed by the Bangladesh Legal Aid Services Trust (BLAST) to complain about the abuse of police power. It was alleged that the police "by abusing the power given under section 54 of the Code of Criminal Procedure [1898], has been curtailing the liberty of the citizens" (Supreme Court of Bangladesh, 2003, p. 2). It was also alleged in the writ petition that by taking people into custody through the power given in section 167 of the Code of Criminal Procedure of 1898, the police are violating "the fundamental rights guaranteed under the different Articles of the constitution" (Supreme Court of Bangladesh, 2003, p. 2). The high court heard the case, *Bangladesh Legal Aid and Services Trust (BLAST) v. People's Republic of Bangladesh*, in 2003. The court thoroughly examined Section 54-1 (related to arrest without a warrant), Section 167-1 (related to taking an individual into remand and custody), and Section 176-1 (related to torture and death in police custody) of the Code of Criminal Procedure of 1898. The court further scrutinized Sections 330, 302, and 348 of the Indian Penal Code of 1862, which are still the basis of penal law in Bangladesh. The court found that some of the provisions of the aforementioned sections of the Code of Criminal Procedure of 1898 and the Penal Code of 1862 are in violation of the Bangladesh constitution. The court said that "we have scrutinized two sections of the Code and have found that the provisions of these sections are to an extent inconsistent with the provisions of the constitution and require some amendments." The court further said that clause (5) of Article 35 of the Bangladesh constitution "provides that no person shall be subject to torture or to cruel, inhuman, or degrading punishment or treatment." The court elaborated that taking of an accused in remand for interrogation and extortion of information by force "is totally against the sprit [sic] and explicit provisions of the constitution." On the basis of its analysis and judgments, the high court presented 15 directives to the government and asked the government to implement the directives within 6 months. Some of the major directives related to police abuse are: (1) "No police officer shall arrest a person under section 54 of the Code for the purpose of detaining him under section 3 of the Special Powers Act of 1974," (2) "A police officer shall disclose his identity and if demanded shall show his identity card to the person arrested and to the person present at the time of arrest," (3) "He shall record the reasons for the arrest and other particulars in a separate register till a special diary is prescribed," (4) "He shall furnish the reason for arrest to the person arrested within three hours of bringing him in the police station," and (5) "He shall allow the person to consult a lawyer of his choice if [that person] so desires or meet any of his nearest relation" (Supreme Court of Bangladesh, 2003, p. 21). These directives of the high court have remained largely unimplemented.

Police Reforms and Police Modernization in Kenya

Kenya is one of the weakest and most fragile states in Africa. With about 40 million people (2011 estimate), Kenya is also one of the largest countries in Africa. Ethnically and religiously, Kenya is a diverse country. Seven major ethnic groups (22% Kikuyu, 14% Luhya, 13% Luo, 12% Kalenjin, 11% Kamba, 6% Kisii, and 6% Meru, in addition to 15% other Africans, and 1% non-Africans [Asian, European, and Arab]), make up the Kenyan population. Three major religious groups—Protestant (45%), Roman Catholic (33%), and Muslim (10%)—in addition to those of indigenous beliefs (10%) and other (2%) comprise the population of Kenya (Central Intelligence Agency, 2011). In *Global Report: Conflict, Governance, and State Fragility* (Marshall & Cole, 2008), Kenya received a rating of 15 out 25 (very fragile) in state fragility. In political effectiveness, security effectiveness, economic effectiveness, and social effectiveness, Kenya was rated 7 out of 13 (very effective). In terms of political legitimacy, security legitimacy, economic legitimacy, and social legitimacy, Kenya was rated 8 out of 12 (highly legitimate). The Economist Intelligence Unit's *Democracy Index* (2010) identified Kenya as one of the hybrid regimes with serious weakness in governance, political participation, political culture, and corruptions The World Bank's study of governance indicators (Kaufmann et al., 2010) similarly shows that Kenya has serious weakness in political stability (percentile ranking 12.3), rule of law (15.1), and control of corruption (11.9). In the World Justice Project's (2010) Rule of Law Index, Kenya is identified as one of the weakest of the 35 countries surveyed in terms of limited government powers (35/35), absence of corruption (34/35), order and stability (29/35), and fundamental rights (34/35). Kenya is also one of the weakest countries in the effectiveness of criminal justice (24/35).

The present system of law and justice in Kenya, as mentioned in the beginning of this chapter, is based mostly on the Indian Police Act of 1861, the Indian Penal Code of 1862, the Code of Criminal Procedure of 1882, and the Code of Criminal Procedure of 1898 introduced by the British colonial state. Kenya was a British Crown colony from 1920 to 1963. From 1963 to 2002, Kenya went through a process of turbulent and authoritarian political development. A process of democratization and a discourse on reforming governance in general and criminal justice in particular began after a new regime, under the leadership of Emilio Mwai Kibaki, came to power in 2002. Kenya began to search for a democratic constitution beginning in the 1960s, when Thurgood Marshall was "invited to serve as an advisor in constitutional negotiations. He traveled to Africa for the first time, and then participated in the landmark 1960 Conference on the Kenya Constitution" (Dudziak, 2008, p. 309). In 2010, the Kenyan Parliament approved a new constitution, thereby ending an almost 50-year-long process of searching for a democratic constitution. Chapter 4 of the new constitution explained the Kenyan Bill of Rights. Chapter 4 includes "forty-one Articles and includes a Bill of Rights that guarantees enjoyment of the rights and fundamental freedoms for every person . . . provides for implementation of rights and fundamental freedoms, and for the enforcement of those rights and freedoms" (Ram, 2010, p. 1).

From the beginning of 2000, the international development community and human rights forums in Africa began to be very concerned about the problem of massive police atrocities and police brutalities in Kenya. In 2007, the Kenyan police were implicated "in the execution of nearly 500 men in the country during a . . . crackdown on the ultra-violent Mungiki gang . . . . Victims were executed by a single bullet . . . and their bodies dumped in mortuaries and settlements outside Nairobi" (ABC News, 2007, p. 1).

The *World Report 2011* from Human Rights Watch (2011) found that "impunity remains a pervasive problem in Kenya" (p. 134). Discussions for police reforms in Kenya began after President Kibaki came to power in 2002. In 2003, President Kibaki set up the National Task Force on Police Reform, and in 2004, he announced the launching of community policing in Nairobi (Furuzawa, 2011). But more systematic and comprehensive efforts for reforms in Kenyan police began in the context of the postelection violence of 2007. During this violence, "at least 1,133 people died, 117,216 private properties were destroyed, and more than 600,000 people were displaced" (Gastrow, 2010, p. 1). A report from the International Peace Institute (Gastrow, 2010) observed that after the postelection violence, "there was a realization that the fractured nature of Kenyan society, and its real potential to descend into conflict and violence, demanded a fundamental re-look at the nature and role of the police in Kenya" (p. 1).

In 2009, a vigorous push for police reform in Kenya also came from the United Nations. A United Nations Organization (2009) report on police brutality and extrajudicial killings in Kenya found that Kenyan police "frequently execute individuals and that a climate of impunity prevails. Most troubling is the existence of police death squads operating on the order of senior police officers and charged with eliminating suspected leaders and members of criminal organizations (p. 2). The report further added that "failure in the criminal justice system . . . encourage[s] the commission of unlawful killing by police. The criminal justice system as whole was described as 'terrible.' Investigation, prosecution, and judicial processes are slow and corrupt" (p. 13).

The urgency of police reform in Kenya was also recommended by the Waki Commission report on postelection violence presented to the government in 2008 (Kenyan National Commission on Human Rights, 2008). In May 2009, President Kibaki set up a new 17-member national task force on police reforms, under the chairmanship of Justice Philip Ransely, and gave it a mandate to present a report on comprehensive police reforms in Kenya. The new task force conducted a series of meetings with police officers and police leaders, government officials, and civil society leaders of all eight provinces of Kenya. The members of the task force also visited Botswana, Sweden, and the United Kingdom to gather the best-practice experience of police reforms in other countries (Gastrow, 2010). In November 2009, the task force presented a report containing 200 recommendations. This is the first comprehensive report on police reform in Kenya in its 46 years of independence (Republic of Kenya, 2009). It is expected to be implemented with a cost of 78 billion Kenyan shillings. Some of the major donors include Sweden, the United Kingdom, the Netherlands, Japan, and the United Nations Office on Drugs and Crime (UNODC).

The Ransely task force recommended the establishment of four major organizations centering on the themes of enhancing police accountability and transparency, developing decentralized policing and functional structures, achieving operational neutrality, improving professionalization, developing a police code of ethics, and strengthening police–community relations. The proposed organizations are: (1) the National Planning Council, (2) the Independent Police Oversight Authority, (3) the Police Service Commission, and (4) the Police Reforms Implementation Committee (see **Table 8-3**). In addition, the report recommended an immediate change in the leadership of the police that were in charge during the postelection violence. A month after the publication of the task force report, a new police commissioner was appointed in Kenya. One of the most innovative recommendations was the creation of a permanent police reform implementation commission, which was subsequently established in 2010 by a presidential directive. In its first report in 2010, the Police Reforms Implementation Committee (Republic of Kenya, 2010) stated that it completed the development of four police reform bills: the National Police Service Bill of 2010, the National Police Service Commission Bill of 2010, the Independent Police Oversight Authority Bill of 2010,

TABLE 8-3 Proposed Organizations/Changes for Police Reforms in Kenya:
The Task Force Recommendations

Proposed Organizations/ Changes	Goals and Objectives
The National Planning Council	The task force recommended the creation of a national policing council to harmonize the activities of the two police services of Kenya: Kenyan Police and Administration Police. Among its other functions will be formulating and determining policing policy; setting and enforcing unified policing standards across the country; and ensuring policing accountability at all levels.
Independent Police Oversight Authority	The task force recommended the establishment of a new institution, composed of civilians who will focus on monitoring and investigating police conduct, namely, an independent policing oversight authority. It will be established under the Constitution and will provide clear legislative powers to enable the body to execute its mandate.
Police Service Commission	The task force recommended that matters of police recruitment, promotion, discipline, welfare, and dismissal be removed from the Public Service Commission and vested in an independent institution, namely, the Police Service Commission. This commission will be established under the Constitution and through legislation (Police Service Commission Act).
Police Reforms Implementation Committee	The task force recommended the creation of a police reforms implementation committee to coordinate, monitor, and supervise the implementation of the reforms. It will be composed of local and international policing experts, senior government officials, and police officers, with a civilian chairing the commission.
Decentralizing police services	The task force recommended moving away from an overly centralized command structure of policing by devolving powers and responsibilities to lower levels and by providing greater operational and financial autonomy to commanders at provincial, district, and station levels.
Corruption, code of ethics, and conflicts of interest	The task force recommended the development of a new police code of ethics to address conflicts of interest that police face. The report recommends that, for example, direct or indirect involvement by police officers in certain business activities, such as operating *matatus* (minibuses) and other public transport enterprises, should be prohibited.
Police–community relations	The task force recommended that the completion of the National Policy on Community Policing be fast tracked and that the National Policy should ensure full community involvement in the development and implementation of the policy.

Source: Data from Republic of Kenya. (2009). *Report of the National Task Force on Police Reforms.* Nairobi, Kenya: Author.

and the Private Security Regulation Bill of 2010. The Police Reforms Implementation Committee reported also the completion of the development of a police code of ethics, the decentralization of the Directorate of Complaints, the development of a comprehensive police training curriculum, and the completion of a policy framework for community policing. In

2011, the Police Reforms Implementation Committee unveiled a new strategic plan to implement most of the task force recommendations by 2013 with a cost of about 78 billion (Kenyan shillings). The implementation of most of the 200 recommendations made by the task force, however, depends on the enactment of the four core legislations developed by the Police Reforms Implementation Committee (Republic of Kenya, 2010).

Police Reforms and Police Modernization in Brazil

Brazil, with a population of about 203 million (2011 estimate) is the 5th largest country in the world. Economically and technologically, Brazil is one of the most developed countries in Latin America and in the developing world as a whole. About 66% of Brazilians work in service sectors, 14% in industries, and 20% in agriculture. About 88% of Brazilians are literate, and about 86% of Brazilians live in urban areas. Brazil, however, is a country highly paradoxical in nature. It is also one of Latin America's most violent countries. Police brutalities and police atrocities in Brazil surpass those of the countries of sub-Saharan Africa. Brazil, in fact, is a unique country that has no civilian police force for law enforcement. Law enforcement in Brazil is in the hands of the military police. Legally, the military police are not a part of the Brazilian military. In reality, however, the military police responsible for law enforcement in the civilian domain are an extension of the military. The whole discourse on police reforms and police modernization in Brazil that started with the beginning of democratization in the late 1980s is about how to control and contain the abusive power of this militarized police force. For a comparative analysis of policing in Brazil, the understanding of the growth, power, and abusive nature of this militarized police force is critical (Lilley, 2009).

The Economist Intelligence Unit's (2010) *Democracy Index 2010* identified Brazil as one of the flawed democracies. Brazil received a score of 5.0 out of 10 in political participation and 4.38 out of 10 in political culture. In the area of the rule of law, Brazil received a low rating of 49.5 out of 100 from the World Bank's study of governance indicators (Kaufmann et al., 2010). The system of criminal justice as a whole is one of the weakest branches of the Brazilian government. In the World Justice Project's (2010) *Rule of Law Index*, Brazil received a global rating of .48 out of 1 (highly effective) in the effectiveness of criminal justice. Brazil's rating in the effectiveness of criminal justice is lower than that of Chile (0.59), Peru (0.50), Ghana (0.55), Jamaica (0.52), Bangladesh (0.49), India (0.51), and many other developing countries.

Like the United States, Canada, Germany, and India, Brazil has a federal political structure. There is a dual system of policing in Brazil—a federal system of policing and a state system of policing. The federal system of policing is known as the Federal Police Department (DPF), and it is headquartered in Brasilia. There are federal police units in all 26 states and in the federal district. The federal police are mainly concerned with law enforcement problems of an interstate and international nature related particularly to illegal drugs and narcotic trafficking, human trafficking, cyber crime, money laundering, and other transnational organized crimes. The federal police also perform the functions of air police, highway police, immigration police, coast guard, and border patrol. Brazil's National Police Academy, National Institute of Criminology, and National Institute of Identification are under the control of the DPF. The federal police are under the authority of the Ministry of Justice and are headed by a director appointed by the president.

The state system of policing in Brazil comprises two types of policing—military policing and civil policing. The military police of the states is the core of policing and law enforcement in the states. Most members of the military police either come from the military or are trained by the military. The military police is also organized following military ranks and hierarchies, and its members are trained to use state-of-the-art military weapons, combat strategies, and rules of engagements. In 2004, the government of Brazil created a new organization called the National Force of Public Safety under the command of the police commissioner of the Brazilian Federal Police. This new organization is composed of some of the most highly trained state military police forces. It is Brazil's Army Reserve Corps. Within the National Force of Public Safety, there is also a quick-deployment special battalion (BEPE)—an elite force—composed of some of the more militarily trained police officers who are deployed for special combat and crime-fighting missions (see **Figure 8-1**). The civilian police force of each of the states is primarily a service organization. It is not directly engaged in crime fighting and law enforcement. It is more involved in criminal investigations, prosecutions, and other judicial functions. The civilian police forces of the states are also known as judicial police because they perform many quasijudicial functions.

Figure 8-1 Brazil: BOPE Elite Squad Officers Provide "Cover" for One Another as They Climb into the Back of a Tank

Source: © Buda Mendes/LatinContent/Getty Images.

According to Brazil's Ministry of Justice, there were 600,000 police officers in Brazil in 2007. Out of 600,000, 68% were military police, 21% were civilian judicial police, and 11% were firefighters (Pinc, 2010). The military police of Brazil are more organized, more trained, and more visible with their state-of-the-art of military weapons than the civilian police. One World Bank study (2006), *Crime, Violence, and Economic Development in Brazil,* noted that the military police are less educated than the civilian police: "almost all the civilian police (delegados) have university-level education, as opposed to only 78 percent of commissioned officers in military police force" (p. 46). Brazil's military police are a focal point of national and international experts on police reforms and human rights organizations. The military police are responsible for most of the atrocities, tortures, brutalities, extrajudicial killings, and gross violations of human rights in Brazil. Most of the extrajudicial killings are claimed by the authorities to be the result of acts of resistance. Amnesty International's 2010 report on Brazil found that in Rio de Janeiro, "between January 1998 and September 2009, 10,216 people were killed in the state in incidents registered as 'acts of resistance'" (Amnesty International, 2010, p. 3).

Brazil's military police and Brazilian authorities have been militarizing crime control since crime began to escalate in the early 1990s. Crime began to rapidly escalate in Brazil in the 1990s in response to a host of factors such as increasing poverty, widening racial inequalities, and the arrival of many transnational crimes and criminal gangs. Brazil's militarization of crime control is not only violating the Universal Declaration of Human Rights; United Nations Convention Against Torture and Other Cruel, Inhuman or Degrading Treatment or Punishment; and The United Nations Code of Conduct for Law Enforcement Officials, but is also corrupting the Brazilian military police and the Brazilian security institutions. Allegations are plentiful that some members of the Brazilian military police are not only a part of the Brazilian security, but also a part of the Brazilian criminal gangs.

The militarization of policing in Brazil did not begin during the 1990s. It is one of Brazil's most enduring traditions in law enforcement. The first military police department was created in Brazil through the creation of the Military Division of the Royal Guard Police of Rio de Janeiro in 1809. The military police became a part of Brazil's provincial law enforcement after the overthrowing of the monarchy and the declaration of the Federal Republic of Brazil in 1889. The new Federal Republic of Brazil was created following the American system of federal political structure with a group of autonomous states. The state administration in the new republic of Brazil began centering itself around the institution of military policing. During most of the 20th century, Brazil was also ruled by military regimes or regimes where the military played a dominant role. Particularly strong military-authoritarian regimes ruled from 1964 to 1988. The process of democratization in Brazil, therefore, began in the early 1990s. Brazil is facing the same social and political challenges as other postauthoritarian regimes in Central America and South America. Some of these challenges are the dominance of authoritarianism in civil bureaucracy, the dominance of the military in politics, the high rate of violent crimes, the wider social and economic inequalities, the favorable public opinion for militaristic control of crime and violence, and the political culture of authoritarianism

Figure 8-2 A Brazilian SWAT Team Prepares to Storm into an Area of the Favela Vila Cruzeiro. Officer in Foreground Carries a Fusil Automatique Léger (Light Automatic Rifle)

Source: © Bruno Gonzalez/LatinContent/Getty Images.

(see **Figure 8-2**). The case of Brazil is particularly unique because of a historically entrenched tradition of military policing (Bailey & Dammert, 2006; Hinton, 2006) within the Brazilian state law enforcement system (Albrecht, 2011). One expert on Brazilian security observed that under the military-bureaucratic model, the Brazilian military police "have become a law unto themselves, unaccountable to democratic authorities, and autonomous of both state and society" (Muniz, 2002, p. 1).

Since the beginning of democratization in Brazil in the 1990s, calls for reforms in policing began to grow. Simultaneously, violent crime began to escalate. Between 1980 and 2002, Brazil's homicide rate more than doubled (World Bank, 2006). The homicide rate (homicides per 100,000 population) in Brazil (30.8) is highest among all South American countries after Colombia (61.1). The homicide rate of females aged 10–29 is one of the highest in the world (5.2). Since the beginning of 2000, however, Brazil's homicide rate began to decline in response to a number of poverty reduction and urban renewal and urban safety programs undertaken by the Lula administration. Brazil adopted a number of micro-policy strategies for police reforms in the 1980s and 1990s, but no comprehensive national plan was on the agenda for policy making in crime and justice. The new constitution of 1988 has changed many of the country's institutions, but the institution of policing has remained largely untouched (Leeds, 2007) and "there was still no adequate global analysis of the challenges of crime and human rights" in Brazil (Cardia, 2002, p. 4).

In the 1990s, police reform in Brazil began with the introduction of human rights training for military police officers. The International Committee of the Red Cross Society, under the leadership of a police officer from the United Kingdom, was invited to provide training on human rights to military police officers. Many military officers received training, and human rights issues and principles were integrated into the training curriculum for the military police. The program continued for 2 years (1998–2000) in collaboration with the Brazilian Ministry of Justice and the military police. An independent evaluation panel from the University of Sao Paulo observed that human rights training educated the "trainees to reject torture as a tool to obtain information, accept that prisoners whilst losing some rights, retain others, accept that young offenders should have different treatment; and that human rights also apply to police officers" (Dossett, 2002, p. 5). At the end of the 1990s, Brazil invited Scotland Yard from the United Kingdom to train the Brazilian civil police in the areas of conflict management, interrogation techniques, and crime scene management (Lloyd & Mullender, 2002).

Since the early 1990s, the United Nations Office on Drugs and Crime (UNODC) has also been working with the Brazilian Federal Police for strengthening its capacity for combating organized crime and modernizing its professional training curriculum. As a report from the UNODC noted, "From 1998 to 2005, UNODC supported the execution of two projects coordinated by the Federal Police, with the purpose of improving police training, through the modernization of training structures and methods at the National Police Academy" (United Nations Office on Drugs and Crime, 2011a, p. 1). The report added that one of the strong components of the partnership "relates to joint activities between UNODC and the DPF's National Police Academy, which includes . . . interchange with officers from other countries. Since 2008, 158 policemen from neighboring countries (Argentina, Uruguay, Paraguay, Bolivia and Colombia) . . . have been trained" (2011, p. 1).

In the mid-1980s, the philosophy of community policing began to have an effect on policing in Brazil. Many states began to create an institution known as police–community liaison committees as forums for open-ended discussions on crime and security issues. It is estimated that by 2000, about 800 such police–community liaison committees were created in about 520 municipalities (Macaulay, 2005). In Rio de Janeiro in the mid-1980s, a community policing model entered an experimental phase that was initiated by a commander of the military police and backed by some human rights advocates. Community policing was first formally launched in Sao Paulo in 1985 with the creation of a community policing act by the governor of Sao Paulo (Carlos, 2010). By the mid-1990s, about half of the states of Brazil "implemented state-led community policing experiments" (Brito, 2010, p. 8). The idea of community policing became popular in Brazil, particularly in the context of the Canada–Brazil Technical Cooperation Project on Institutional Violence (1996–1999). In 2000, Brazil's Ministry of Justice made community policing a national model through the development of the National Plan for Public Safety. In 2000, the federal Ministry of Justice began to provide grants to state agencies for the development of community policing (Brito, 2010). The federal initiatives "led to a dramatic rise in the percentage of police agencies that created specific community policing divisions and employed community policing officers" (Brito, 2010, p. 10).

The first decade of the 21st century was a time of unprecedented economic prosperity and social transformations in Brazil under the administration of President Lula, a former trade union leader (2002–2010). Under the Lula administration, two major initiatives were undertaken to reform policing as part of an overall reform strategy in public safety and criminal justice in Brazil. The first is the National Plan for Public Safety (NPPS), introduced in 2004. The main objectives of the NPPS were to "1) modernize and restructure Brazil's various police forces throughout the country and 2) provide state and municipalities with sufficient financial resources to combat crime" (Rosa, 2007, p. 7). Some of the plans for action of the NPPS included regulating gun ownership, improving the witness protection program, improving the National Program for Human Rights, reforming the penal code, modernizing police technology, modernizing police training, combating gangs and social disorder, and developing a national public security information system. The NPPS created a National Secretariat of Public Security (SENASP) for the implementation of these programs.

The second initiative—the National Programme for Public Security with Citizenship (PRONASCI)—was launched in 2007 by the Brazilian Ministry of Justice. The PRONASCI initiated "94 structural actions designed to modernize the police forces and the penitentiary system . . . . To stimulate action at the local level and target resources to areas of greatest need, 11 high-priority metropolitan areas have been identified" (United Nations Congress on Crime Prevention and Criminal Justice, 2010, p. 12). Some of the projects undertaken by the PRONASCI are human rights training for judges, prosecutors, and public defenders; cultural projects for youth at risk; creation of centers for access to justice and conflict resolution; family and youth integration projects for citizenship, leadership, and conflict resolution; cultural projects in libraries, museums, and meeting places for youth in targeted areas of deprivation; centers for women victims of violence; and economic and cultural revitalization of the deprived communities (United Nations Congress on Crime Prevention and Criminal Justice, 2010).

■ Reforms and Modernization in Substantive Criminal Law in Asia, Africa, and Latin America

What is evidenced from the reviews of police reforms in India, Bangladesh, Kenya, and Brazil is that criminal justice in the developing countries of Asia, Africa, and Latin America is an institution that is experiencing many significant changes. The process of evolution in some countries is rapid and radical. In others, it is slow and cautious. But it is certain that the winds of change in criminal justice in the second wave of modernization are swiftly spreading across the developing countries. Reforms and modernization are coming not just in the institution of policing but also in all domains of law and justice. In the context of modernization and globalization, all developing countries are now being challenged to criminalize many areas of acts and deviance that were socially accepted and culturally tolerated for centuries. They are being challenged to criminalize many new forms of acts and behaviors that have been emerging with the advent of the Internet and social media. At the same time, the developing countries are also being challenged to decriminalize many acts and behaviors that violate the basic notions of human rights, privacy, equality, justice, and fairness. The study of how the dynamics of criminalization and decriminalization are unfolding in the countries of Asia, Africa, and Latin America and the cultural and moral conflicts and disputes they generate is of enormous significance in comparative criminal justice. One of the goals in comparative criminal justice is understanding the extent to which a country's criminal laws are socially and culturally specific and the extent to which they are changing and homogenizing under the effect of modernization and globalization. It is mainly through the study of changes and reforms in criminal law in a country that that one can significantly measure the extent to which that country is progressing toward a modern system of criminal justice. In the following sections, changes in the following four areas of substantive criminal law will be examined: the criminalization of sexual harassment, the criminalization of spousal violence, the criminalization of child abuse and violence against children, and the decriminalization of homosexuality. These areas of criminal law have been chosen because they are intimately connected to the issues of rights, privacy, equality, justice, and fairness. Examples have been drawn from different countries of Asia, Africa, and Latin America.

Criminalization of Sexual Harassment

The notion of sexual harassment as a crime punishable by law did not emerge until the middle of the 1980s. For the first time in the history of modern criminal jurisprudence, the U.S. Supreme Court identified sexual harassment as a crime through a landmark decision in *Meritor Savings Banks v. Vinson* in 1986. The Court made a decision that the creation of a "hostile environment" through sexual harassment is a violation of Title II of the Civil Rights Act of 1964. The Court stated that "sexual harassment which creates a hostile or offensive environment for members of one sex is every bit the arbitrary barrier to sexual equality at the workplace that racial harassment is to racial equality" (*Meritor Savings Bank v. Vinson*, 1986).

In 1993, the U.S. Supreme Court made another landmark decision on sexual harassment in *Harris v. Forklift Systems*. The Court said that sexual harassment must not be judged in terms of the notion of psychological harm alone. It must be judged and established in terms of a host of circumstances "which may include the frequency of the discriminatory conduct; its severity; whether it is physically threatening or humiliating, or a mere offensive utterance; and whether it unreasonably interferes with an employee's work performance" (*Harris v. Forklift Systems*, 1993). These two landmark decisions of the U.S. Supreme Court significantly affected the global movement for criminalization of sexual harassment in the 1990s.

Two distinct notions of sexual harassment emerged from the U.S. Supreme Court decisions. The first is the notion of *quid pro quo,* when sexual favors are asked for employment, promotion, tenure, and other work-related benefits. It is the use of professional power for seeking sexual favors and advantage. The second is the idea of sexual harassment as the creation of a hostile work environment through different acts and activities such as sexual bullying, telling of sexual jokes, sexually meaningful touching and conduct, indecent gestures, displaying sexually explicit pictures, discussion of sexual activities and pornography, and using sexually offensive language. Sexual harassment in both forms is widespread around the world. A report from the United Nations Development Fund for Women (UNIFEM), *Violence Against Women Worldwide,* noted that between 40% and 50% percent of women in the European Union countries experience sexual harassment in the workplace. In the United States, "83 percent of girls aged 12–16 experienced some form of sexual harassment in public schools" (United Nations Development Fund for Women, 2011, p. 2). A report from the International Trade Union Confederation (2008) observed that between 30% and 40% of women in the Asia and Pacific region countries experience sexual harassment in the workplace. One of the reports from the International Labor Organization (ILO) observed that between 30% and 50% of women in the countries of Latin America are subjected to sexual harassment in the workplace (International Trade Union Confederation, 2008). A survey by the Center for Transforming India, a nonprofit organization, reported that "nearly 88% of the female workforce in Indian Information Technology . . . companies reported having suffered some form of workplace sexual harassment during the course of their work. Close to 50% of women had been subjected to abusive language and physical contact" (Dhar, 2010, p. 1).

A survey on sexual harassment in China found that about "84 percent of single females below the age of thirty have suffered from sexual harassment, and 77% of those who were sexually harassed were single women between twenty-two and twenty-five years old" (Srivastava & Gu, 2009, p. 46). A survey conducted by the Chinese Academy of Social Sciences found that "48% of women participating in the survey had experienced harassment in the form of obscene jokes or insinuations from their male colleagues, [and that] 13% of women surveyed said they were expected to grant sexual favours in exchange for employment . . . [and] promotion" (Srivastava & Gu, 2009, p. 47).

Sexual harassment is widespread also in many conservative cultures of the Muslim societies. A survey conducted by Egypt's Center for Women's Rights in 2008 described sexual harassment as a social cancer in Egypt. The survey noted that about 83% of Egyptian women and 98% of foreign women visitors in Egypt experience sexual harassment irrespective of the way they dress (Abdelhadi, 2008). Sexual harassment is equally wide-spread in the Arab region from Algeria to Qatar. In a survey on sexual harassment in the Arab region, 27% of Algerian female university students and 21% of females in Qatar said that they were subjected to sexual harassment. The survey also noted that "30 percent of Qatari working females were sexually abused by their bosses in their work premises" (Davies, 2011, p. 2).

Because of its pervasive presence in all countries, the movement for the criminalization of sexual harassment has recently become a worldwide phenomenon. There is hardly any country in the world today that does not have advocacy groups pressing for new laws to criminalize sexual harassment. This movement for the development of national laws against sexual harassment is becoming increasingly global, particularly in the context of a number of international laws, treaties, and organizations on sexual harassment such as the United Nations Convention on the Elimination of All Forms of Discrimination Against Women (CEDAW) in 1979; the Vienna Declaration and Programme of Action adopted by the World Conference on Human Rights in 1993; the Beijing Declaration and Programme of Action adopted by the Fourth World Conference on Women: Action for Equality, Development and Peace in 1995; and the International Labor Organization Declaration on Fundamental Principles and Rights at Work in 1998. In recent years, many countries in Asia, Africa, and Latin America have enacted specific legislation against sexual harassment (Hilton, 2005;

Ore-Aguilar, 1997). Chile enacted a law against sexual harassment in 2005. China enacted a specific national law against sexual harassment in 2007. Pakistan enacted legislation against sexual harassment in 2009.

In some countries, like the United States, sexual harassment laws are being defined through judicial interventions. The Supreme Court of India, in *Vishaka v. State of Rajasthan* in 1997, made a judgment that sexual harassment is a violation of the constitutional protection of the right to life and gender equality. The Supreme Court of India, like the U.S. Supreme Court, defined sexual harassment broadly "to include any unwelcome physical contact, or advances, demands or requests for sexual favours, sexually coloured remarks, displaying of pornography, and other unwelcome physical, verbal or non-verbal conduct of a sexual nature" (as quoted in Srivastava, 2010, pp. 174–175). The Court also made it mandatory for "all workplaces, educational institutions and organized service sectors, private or public with more than 50 employees to introduce sexual harassment prevention policy and set up a complaints committee to investigate into sexual harassment complaints" (as quoted in Srivastava, 2010, p. 175).

In Bangladesh in 2008, the high court division of the Supreme Court in *Bangladesh National Women Lawyers Association v. Government of Bangladesh* made a landmark decision on sexual harassment. The Court developed a set of guidelines against sexual harassment and declared that they be treated as laws against sexual harassment until an act against sexual harassment is passed by the Parliament. The Court said, "we direct that the above guidelines and norms would be strictly observed in . . . work places for the preservation and enforcement of the right to gender equality . . . . These directions would be binding and enforceable in law." (*Bangladesh National Lawyers Association v. Government of Bangladesh*, 2008). The Court also noted that "protection from sexual harassment and right to education and work with dignity is universally recognized as basic human rights. The common minimum requirement of these rights has received global acceptance" (*Bangladesh National Women Lawyers Association v. Government of Bangladesh*, 2008). Similar legislative and judicial interventions for the criminalization of sexual harassment are also seen in many other countries of Asia, Africa, and Latin America (see **Table 8-4**).

Criminalization of Domestic and Sexual Violence Against Women

Along with sexual harassment, domestic violence and sexual violence against women have also emerged in recent years as a new domain of criminality among the world's societies. A number of international surveys have documented that violence against women is pervasive in all societies. The World Health Organization's 2005 report, *Multi-Country Study on Women's Health and Domestic Violence Against Women,* found widespread prevalence of domestic and intimate partner violence in all regions of the world (Shahidullah & Derby, 2010). The study, based on interviews of 24,000 women in 10 countries (Bangladesh, Brazil, Ethiopia, Japan, Peru, Namibia, Samoa, Serbia-Montenegro, Thailand, and Tanzania), observed that the "proportion of women reporting either sexual or physical violence, or both, by a partner ranged from 15% (Japanese cities) to 71% (Ethiopian provinces), with most sites falling between 29% and 62%" (World Health Organization, 2005,

TABLE 8-4 Sexual Harassment Laws and Statutes in Selected Countries of Asia, Africa, and Latin America

Country	Laws and Statutes: Proposed and Enacted
Algeria	Law No. 04-15 (Article 341 criminal code)
Azerbaijan	Law on the Enforcement of Gender Equality, 2006
Bangladesh	Landmark high court decision on sexual harassment, 2009
Bolivia	Act Against Sexual Harassment in the Work and School Environment, 2007
Botswana	Public Service Act of 1999
Chile	Law 20.005 of 2005 on sexual harassment in the workplace
China	Protection of Women's Rights Law, 2007
Costa Rica	Law No. 7476 on sexual harassment in employment and teaching, 1995
Ethiopia	Proclamation no. 414/2004—Criminal Code of Ethiopia
Ghana	Domestic Violence Act 2007 (Act 732)
India	*Vishaka v. State of Rajasthan,* 1997; the Protection of Women Against Sexual Harassment at Workplace Bill, 2010
Jamaica	Anti-Sexual Harassment Bill, 2007
Kenya	Employment Act of 2008
Malaysia	Code of Practice on the Prevention of Sexual Harassment in the Workplace
Morocco	Article 503-1 of the penal code as revised, 2003
Nepal	Act for Gender Equality, 2006
Pakistan	Protection Against Harassment of Women at the Workplace Act of 2010
Paraguay	Law 496/95 amending the labor code law 213/93
Philippines	Anti-Sexual Harassment Act of 1995 (RA 7877)
Tanzania	Sexual Offences (Special Provisions) Act of 1998
Turkey	Turkish Penal Code No. 5237 as amended, 2005
Uzbekistan	DRAFT: Law on guarantees for the rights and opportunities of women and men

Source: Data from UN Secretary-General's Database on Violence Against Women, 2011.

p. 28). Ethiopia, Peru, and Tanzania, the study found, had the highest prevalence of intimate partner violence.

The 2010 report of the United Nations Secretary-General's Campaign to End Violence Against Women (2010) found that "half of all women who die from homicide are killed by their current or former husbands or partners. In Australia, Canada, and Israel 40 to 70 per cent of female murder victims were killed by their partners" (United Nations Secretary-General's Campaign, 2010, p. 2). The report also noted that "in the United States, one third of women murdered each year are killed by intimate partners" (p. 2). The United States Bureau of Justice Statistics found that about 17% of all homicides in the United States in 2007 were committed by intimate partners. "Females made up 70% of victims killed by an intimate partner in 2007, a proportion that has changed very little since 1993. Females were killed by intimate partners at twice the rate of males" (Bureau of Justice Statistics, 2012, p. 1).

The United Nations Population Fund (UNFPA) estimates "that the annual worldwide number of so-called 'honour killing' victims may be as high as 5,000 women" (United Nations Secretary-General's Campaign, 2010, p. 7). A 2007 survey by the All China Women Federation found that "domestic violence existed in 30 percent of the 270 million Chinese families, with over 85 percent of the sufferers being women. About 100,000 Chinese families break up each year as a result of domestic violence" (Xinhua, 2010, p. 1). One of the reports produced by the European Parliament (2010) on *Issues of Violence Against Women in the European Union* observed that "in the 27 countries of the European Union with a total of almost 500 million inhabitants, about 100 million women are estimated to become victims of male violence in their lifetime and 1 to 2 million women are victimized every day" (p. 9). The report further stated that in the European Union counties, "if all forms of violence are taken into account, about 45% have experienced violence" (p. 9). The 2011 United Nations Organization's report *Progress of the World's Women: In Pursuit of Justice* found that in the world as a whole, "603 million women live in countries where domestic violence is not considered a crime and more than 2.6 billion live in countries where marital rape is not a criminal offence" (Provost, 2011).

The movement for the criminalization of domestic violence, intimate partner violence, and sexual violence against women first began in the mid-1970s in the advanced countries of the West in the context of the increasing expansion of the boundaries of freedom and equality for women. By the 1990s, most of the countries in North America and Europe had enacted legislation to criminalize spousal violence and all forms of sexual violence against women, including marital rape, date rape, and trafficking of women for sexual purposes. In the United States, some of the major pieces of legislation on violence against women include the Violence Against Women Act (VAWA) of 1994 (Title IV of the Violent Crime Control and Law Enforcement Act of 1994); the Victims of Trafficking and Violence Protection Act of 2000; the Unborn Victims of Violence Act of 2004; and the Violence Against Women and the Department of Justice Reauthorization Act of 2005 (VAWA). In Europe, there is legislation on violence against women in all countries. The countries belonging to the European Union are obligated under the directives of the European Parliament to develop legislation on violence against women. The European Parliament called on member states to "make domestic violence against women, including rape within marriage and sexual mutilation, a criminal offence and to set up services to help women who are victims of this kind of violence" (Stop Violence Against Women, 2011, p. 1). In 2011, a new Council of Europe Convention on Violence Against Women and Domestic Violence was created by the Parliamentary Assembly of the Council of Europe and the United Nations to strengthen and harmonize related laws and statutes in European countries.

The movement for the criminalization of domestic violence and violence against women emerged as a global agenda in the mid-1970s. A number of international organizations and treaties such as the 1979 United Nations Convention on the Elimination of All Forms of Discrimination Against Women (CEDAW); the 1985 United Nations Decade for Women:

Equality, Development and Peace Conference held in Nairobi; the 1993 World Conference on Human Rights in Vienna (Vienna Declaration and Program of Action); and the United Nations World Conference on Women in Beijing in 1995 contributed to domestic violence and violence against women being brought into the agenda for law and policy making in the countries of Asia, Africa, and Latin America (Shahidullah & Derby, 2010). By the late 1980s, affected by the International Women's Movement and various United Nations initiatives, gender discourse began to rapidly enter into development discourses. The central theme of the gender discourse was the global achievement of equal rights for women. By the end of the 1990s, there was hardly a country in the developing world where there were no women's organizations representing the issues of women's rights, including issues of crimes against women (Shahidullah & Derby, 2010). Under the effect of this new discourse and accompanying processes of modernization and globalization, many countries in Asia, Africa, and Latin America have enacted legislation criminalizing domestic violence and violence against women (see **Table 8-5**).

According to the United Nations secretary-general's database on violence against women, there are about 80 countries that have specific legislation on domestic violence, such as India's Protection of Women From Domestic Violence Act of 2006; Bangladesh's Women and Children Repression Prevention Act of 2000 and the Acid Control of Act of 2002; Sri Lanka's Prevention of Domestic Violence Act of 2005; Brazil's Domestic and Family Violence Law of 2006 (Maria da Penha Law); Ghana's Domestic Violence Act of 2007; Mexico's Women's Access to a Life Free of Violence Act of 2007; and Indonesia's Elimination of Domestic Violence Law of 2004. In China, a comprehensive domestic violence bill drafted by the All China Women's Federation (ACWF) is being currently reviewed by the Chinese legislatures (Xinhua, 2010). The United Nations Organization's 2011 report, *Progress of the World's Women: In Pursuit of Justice,* noted that there are about 125 countries in the world that have criminalized domestic violence through the development of specific legislation. In many countries, laws against domestic violence are also developing through judicial interventions (see **Box 8-1**).

Criminalization of Child Abuse and Sexual Abuse of Children

Out of the world's 7 billion people (2012 estimate), about 1.8 billion are children under the age of 15. This constitutes about 26% of the world's population. In most countries of Asia, Africa, and Latin America, between 40% and 45% of the population are under the age of 18. How crimes against children are defined, perceived, and prosecuted in Asia, Africa, and Latin America is a problem of huge significance in comparative criminal justice. Child abuse and violence against children are widespread all over the world, particularly in the developing world. One of the first and most comprehensive studies on violence against children in different regions of the world, based on the methodology of self-reporting by the children and data collected by nine regional consultative groups, was completed by the United Nations Organization in 2006. The report found that violence against children is widespread but mostly hidden, invisible, unreported, and socially and culturally accepted. Children are abused in multiple settings such as in homes and families, in schools and educational

TABLE 8-5 Domestic Violence and Sexual Violence Against Women: Laws and Statutes in Selected Countries of Asia, Africa, and Latin America

Country	Laws and Statutes: Proposed and Enacted
Angola	DRAFT: Domestic Violence Bill of 2007
Azerbaijan	Law on prevention of domestic violence, 2010
Bangladesh	Domestic Violence Act of 2010; Acid Crime Prevention Act of 2002; and Suppression of Violence Against Women and Children Act of 2000
Brazil	Law 11340 (the Maria da Penha Law) of 2006; Law No. 10.886/2004 specifies domestic violence as a crime under Article 129 the penal code; and compulsory notification of cases of violence against women who are treated through healthcare services (Law No. 10.778/2003)
Cambodia	Law on the prevention of domestic violence and the protection of victims, 2005
China	Law on the protection of the rights and interests of women, as amended in 2005
Costa Rica	Violence Against Women Law, 2007; and Domestic Violence Law No. 7586
Egypt	Law No. 6 of 1998 criminalizing intimidation or threat of force against a wife, offspring, or ascendants
El Salvador	Amendment to the Domestic Violence Act of 2004
Ghana	Domestic Violence Act, 2007 (Act 732)
Guatemala	Law against femicide and other forms of violence against women, 2008
Honduras	Amendments to the penal code regarding offenses of sexual violence, 1997
India	Protection of Women From Domestic Violence Act, 2006; and the Commission of Sati (Prevention) Act of 1987
Indonesia	Law No. 23 regarding elimination of household violence, 2004
Japan	The Prevention of Spousal Violence and the Protection of Victims Act of 2007
Kazakhstan	Draft law on domestic violence, 2008
Mexico	General law on the access of women to a life free of violence, 2007
Nigeria	Domestic Violence (Prevention) bill of 2005
Saudi Arabia	Decree No. 366 (3/12/1429 AH), elimination of the problem of domestic violence, 2008
Sri Lanka	Prevention of Domestic Violence Act of 2005
Vietnam	Law on prevention of and control over domestic violence, 2007

Source: Data from UN secretary-general's database on violence against women, 2011.

settings, in caregiving institutions, in criminal justice institutions, in work settings, and in communities and neighborhoods. The U.N. report found that "violence against children in the home is widespread in all regions . . . . In a survey of students aged 11 to 18 in the Kurdistan Province of the Islamic Republic of Iran, 38.5% reported experiences of physical violence at home" (United Nations Organization, 2006, p. 52).

The study found that in the Republic of South Korea, "kicking, biting, choking and beating by parents are alarmingly common, with a high risk of physical injury—and for a small proportion, disability—as a result" (United Nations Organization, 2006, p. 52). The study

BOX 8-1

The Role of Shari'a Injunction in Local Arbitration: Criminalization of Fatwa in Bangladesh to Stop Violence Against Women

The processes of criminalization and decriminalization, particularly in societies based on the rule of law and democracy, advance through legislative actions and judicial interventions. In a democracy, the key actors for reforms in criminal justice are primarily the members of the legislatures, but judicial interventions are also not few and far between. The criminalization of sexual harassment in the United States, for example, came through judicial interventions (e.g., *Meritor Savings Bank v. Vinson,* 1986). The decriminalization of abortion (e.g., *Roe v. Wade*, 1973) and same-sex relations (e.g., *Lawrence v. Texas*, 2003) in the United States came in the same way—through judicial interventions. In the United Kingdom, the Supreme Court declared the provision of lifetime registration as a violation of the European charter on human rights. Examples of judicial interventions in the process of criminalization and decriminalization in developing countries are also not few and far between. In India, the high court of Delhi in 2009 declared the country's sodomy law as unconstitutional. On appeal, the Indian Supreme Court ruled in favor of the Delhi high court. In 2009, the Supreme Court of Argentina decriminalized the possession of drugs for personal consumption (Arriola Ruling) and invalidated Article 14 of the National Narcotics Law. One of most intriguing examples of recent judicial interventions in the area of criminalization is the ruling of the Bangladesh high court with respect to the criminalization of Shari'a injunction (fatwa). In Islam, where there is no hierarchical priesthood, Islamic injunctions and Shari'a Laws are sometimes interpreted by religious scholars and socially reputed knowledgeable ulemas. These interpretations are called fatwa. From the beginning of the 1980s, a new notion of Islam—Wahhabi Islam—began to spread in Bangladesh. In the context of the spread of Wahhabism, news began to grow that many women, particularly in rural areas, were being subjected to extrajudicial punishments, including beating, torture, and violence for falling in love or indulging in extramarital relations, and adultery. When petitions were filed by various human rights organizations, the Bangladesh high court made a ruling to criminalize fatwa. "The court directed the authorities concerned to take punitive action against the people involved in enforcing fatwa against women. Anyone involved, present, or taking part in or assisting any such conviction or execution would come under purview of the offences under the penal code and be subject to punishment, the court observed. It also observed infliction of brutal punishment including caning, whipping and beating . . . constitutes violation of the constitutional rights" (as quoted in Sarkar, 2010, p. 1). This is one of the intriguing examples of how global and local issues in criminal justice in many developing countries are being debated and disputed among the public, and they are being adjudicated in the court of law. The writ petitions made by human rights organizations against fatwa explicitly mentioned the obligation of Bangladesh under the 1979 United Nations Convention on the Elimination of All Forms of Discriminations Against Women, and the 1984 United Nations Convention Against Torture and Other Cruel, Inhuman or Degrading Treatment or Punishment.

Source: Sarkar, A. (2010, July 9). Fatwa illegal: HC rules against all extra-judicial punishments upon writ petitions. *Daily Star*, p. 1. Dhaka, Bangladesh.

also observed that "in some parts of South Asia, high rates of murder of girls within a few days of birth have been reported, with these deaths often disguised and registered as a still birth" (United Nations Organization, 2006, p. 52).

The World Health Organization estimates that about "150 million girls and 73 million boys under 18 have experienced forced sexual intercourse or other forms of sexual violence involving physical contact, though this is certainly an underestimate" (United Nations Organization, 2006, p. 54). In some countries, young girls who are sexually victimized and who lose their virginity because of rape and other forms of sexual assaults are murdered by family members in deference to the cultural practice of honor killing. "In Pakistan, human rights organizations report that there were over 1,200 cases of so-called 'honour killings' in 2003 alone. They also occur in Jordan, India, Libyan Arab Jamahiriya, the Occupied Palestinian Territory, Turkey, Iraq, and Afghanistan" (United Nations Organization, 2006, p. 56). Many research studies have found that in South Asia, sexual abuse and exploitation of boys is common. In Afghanistan, boys are subjected to sexual abuse "on a regular basis, some become 'lovers' of powerful men and some become exploited in prostitution during certain periods of their lives for survival. Some 'kept' boys receive monetary compensation, while others receive only food, clothing and shelter" (Frederick, 2010, p. 33). In Thailand, one study observed that "girls as young as 10–12 years old service men in the sex industry. Many of the girls typically have sex with ten to fifteen men every day and sometimes as many as 20–30" (Pusurinkham, 2011).

In schools and educational settings, corporal punishment is widespread in the developing countries of Asia, Africa, and Latin America. It was found that "in Egypt, 80% of schoolboys and 67% of schoolgirls had experienced corporal punishment in schools; in Barbados, 95% of interviewed boys and 92% of interviewed girls said they had experienced caning or flogging in school" (United Nations Organization, 2006, p. 118). A survey of 3,577 students from 6 provinces of China "found that 17.5% had experienced one or more forms of corporal punishment by teachers before they were 16 years old; 15% had been hit . . . 7% had been beaten with an object; 0.4% had been locked up" (United Nations Organization, 2006, p. 118). In South Korea, there is a long-standing cultural tradition where "parents ceremonially present their sons' and daughters' to teachers with symbolic canes (the stick of love) at the beginning of the school year, signifying a handing-over of responsibility for the students' discipline to the school" (Farrell, 2011, p. 1).

Abuse and violence against children are also extensive in the institutional settings of criminal justice in developing countries. In most developing countries, there are no separate systems of law and justice for juveniles. In the countries that have separate systems of juvenile justice, laws protecting the rights of the juveniles are not properly implemented. The United Nations Organization (2006) report found that in "most countries in Eastern and Southern Africa . . . separate facilities for children in conflict with the law are scarce, and children under 18 are imprisoned with adult offenders, putting them at even greater risk of violence and sexual abuse" (p. 192). In most developing countries, the boundaries between status offenses and juvenile delinquencies are not clearly drawn, and children are put in prison for minor offenses. Children are seriously abused in pretrial detention jails in most developing countries. The United Nations Organization (2006) report further observed that "the majority of children in detention have not been convicted of a crime, but are simply awaiting trial. In Pakistan, as of March 2003, out of around 2,340 children detained in prisons alone . . . 83% were under trial, or waiting for their trial to start" (p. 191).

A more pervasive form of child abuse and violence against children that is rapidly spreading around the world today is Internet child pornography. One study estimated that in 2006 there were about 4.2 million Internet pornography websites accessible from all around the world. They contained about 420 million pornographic pages. The study also found that there were daily circulations of 2.6 billion pornographic e-mails, daily requests for 68 million pornographic search engines, and monthly downloading of 1.5 billion pornographic materials (peer-to-peer). In 2006, about 72 million people worldwide visited Internet child pornographic materials monthly. The total revenues earned from Internet child pornography was about $96.07 billion in 2006. The highest revenues from Internet child pornography were earned by China ($27.40 billion) followed by South Korea ($25.73), Japan ($19.98), and the United States ($13.33; Family Safe Media, 2011). According to the 2008 Annual Report of the Internet Watch Foundation of the United Kingdom, child pornography is one of the fastest growing online businesses worldwide. The report observed that there were about 1,536 Internet child pornography domains in the United Kingdom in 2008. In those domains, about 69% of the children subjected to sexual exploitation were less than 10 years of age and about 26% were below the age of 6. About 58% of those domains had shown sexually penetrative activity involving a child or children. Internet child pornography is rapidly becoming a global enterprise. The report stated that victims of Internet child pornography are "abused in one country, [and then] the images of their sexual abuse [are] uploaded to the Internet in a different country, [and then] that website . . . hosted on networks in yet another and the content accessible from anywhere in the world" (Internet Watch Foundation, 2008, p. 8).

Of all the world's regions, South Asia is one of the major suppliers of child pornography. It is estimated that out of the world's two million children who are sexually exploited through Internet pornography, one million live in South Asia. In Asia as a whole, Japan is the major producer of Internet child pornography. "Despite its production and distribution being outlawed, Japan is seen as a major global source of child pornography in photo and video form" (European Union Times, 2011, p. 1). Internet child pornography is distributed not just through websites but also through web cameras, emails, egroups, chat rooms, newsgroups, bulletin board systems, and peer-to-peer networks. Child abuse, child sexual exploitation, use of children in Internet child pornography, and other forms of violence against children have serious effects on the lives of the children who are victimized. It is estimated that 33% of the female children of the world who are victimized by abuse and violence suffer from posttraumatic stress disorder syndrome (PTSD). About 13% of the female victims suffer from panic disorders and 7–8% from depression, alcohol, and drug abuse. Among the male children who are victimized, 21% suffer from PTSD, 7% from panic disorder, and 4–5% from depression, alcohol, and drug abuse (United Nations Organization, 2006).

In most countries of North America and Europe with modern systems of criminal justice, there has evolved a new generation of laws and statutes criminalizing child abuse and all forms of violence against children—physical, sexual, verbal, and emotional. In the United States, such enactments as the Child Abuse Prevention and Treatment Act of 1974 (most recently amended in 2010); the Juvenile Justice and Delinquency Prevention Act of 1974; the Jacob Wetterling Crimes Against Children and Sexually Violent Offenders Act of 1994; the Sex Crimes Against Children Act of 1995; Megan's Law of 1996; the Children's Internet Protection Act of 2000; the Trafficking Victims Protection Act of 2000; the Child Obscenity and Pornography Prevention Act of 2002; the PROTECT (Prosecutorial Remedies and Other Tools to End the Exploitation of Children Today) Act of 2003; and the Adam Walsh Child Protection and Safety Act of 2006 have defined most acts of child abuse, child sexual exploitation, Internet child pornography, and other forms of violence against children as federal crimes punishable with enhanced federal penalties.

Similar enactments are found in Canada, Australia, and the countries of the European Union. In 1988, Canada substantially amended its criminal code (Sections 152, 153, 155, and 271) to criminalize different forms of child sexual abuse and child sexual exploitation. In the United Kingdom, the Sexual Offences Act of 2003, as mentioned before, created a new generation of criminal offenses related to sexual abuse of children such as inciting a child to engage in sexual activity, engaging in sexual activity in the presence of a child, causing a child to watch a sexual act, meeting a child following sexual grooming, having or inciting a child to engage in sexual activity by someone in a position of trust, having or inciting a child to engage in sexual activity by a caregiver, and engaging in sexual activity with a child with a mental disorder. The countries of the European Union, including the United Kingdom, are bound by the EU Council Framework Decision established in 2004 to develop new legislation for combating child sexual abuse, Internet child pornography, and other forms of violence against children. The Council Framework Decision made it mandatory for member states to criminalize child sexual abuse; child sexual exploitation; coercion of a child to engage in sexual activity; coercion of a child to engage in prostitution; coercion of a child to participate in pornographic performance; coercion of a child to engage in sexual activity by using power from a position of trust; enticement of a child to engage in sexual activity or engage in pornographic performance for monetary rewards; production, distribution, dissemination, or transmission of child pornography; supplying or making available child pornography; and acquisition and possession of child pornography. The Council Framework Decision clearly noted that "each Member State must make provision for criminal penalties which entail imprisonment for at least one to three years. For certain offences committed in aggravating circumstances, the penalty must entail imprisonment for at least five to ten years" (EUROPA, 2008, p. 1).

The United Nations Convention on the Rights of the Child (CRC) of 1989 is the major international framework of law related to child abuse and violence against children. The CRC "is the first legally binding international instrument to incorporate the full range of human rights—civil, cultural, economic, political and social rights. In 1989, world leaders decided that children needed a special convention just for them" (United Nations Children's Fund, 2011a, p. 1). In 54 Articles and 2 Optional Protocols, the CRC "spells out the basic human rights that children everywhere have: the right to survival; to develop to the fullest; to protection from harmful influences, abuse and exploitation; and to participate fully in family, cultural and social life" (United Nations Children's Fund, 2011a, p. 1). Article 34 of the CRC requires the member states to develop measures to prevent (1) the inducement or coercion of a child to engage in any unlawful sexual activity; (2) the exploitative use of children in prostitution or other unlawful sexual practices; and (3) the exploitative use of children in pornographic performances and materials. Almost all the developing countries of Asia, Africa, and Latin America are signatories of the CRC, and they are, therefore, bound by its mandate to develop laws and institutions to control and prevent child abuse and all forms of violence against children. The CRC requires that all member states adopt a human rights–based approach to legislative reform and integrate the core missions and principles of the CRC into domestic constitutions and legislation (United Nations Children's Fund, 2008). The human rights–based approach to legislative reform means that laws that are to be developed must be based on the universal recognition of the rights of children, and the acts that violate the universal rights of children must be criminalized irrespective of the specific connotations given in various traditional legal systems—English common law, civil law, Shari'a Law, and customary law (see **Table 8-6**).

As of 2008, according to a report from the United Nations Children's Fund (2011b), 92 countries had "prohibited violence against children by law" (p. 1) and initiated reforms to strengthen their criminal justice systems to effectively respond to cases related to child abuse and violence against children. For comparative criminal justice, it is intriguing, however, to see how the cultural and legal peculiarities of different countries with respect to the rights of children and perceptions about the criminality of child abuse and violence against children are different from or conflict with many of the CRC's core human rights–based principles. The idea of the best interest of the child is interpreted in different cultures in different ways. One of the studies by UNICEF found that in Libya and many other countries of West Africa and 12 Latin American countries, "a rapist will be exonerated if he marries his victim . . . If the rapist marries her, the law excuses his crime . . . . Under . . . the Convention [CRC] this would be unacceptable as it violates the most fundamental Convention rights" (Nundy, 2004, p. 4). It is observed that criminalization of child abuse and violence against children in the light of the core principles of the CRC has been progressing relatively easily in the countries that are based on the tradition of civil law. In civil law countries, "international treaties, once ratified, automatically become part of the legal system of that country . . . . This is a welcome indication for global national incorporation of Convention rights, since 75 state parties are governed by Civil law" (Nundy, 2004, p. 8).

The countries with a common law tradition do not perceive that international law and legal treaties automatically become domestic law. In common law countries, international treaties must be translated in terms of domestic laws and statutes. The progress in legislative reforms in common law countries with respect to the implementation of the CRC principles

TABLE 8-6 Child Sexual Abuse Laws and Statutes in Selected Countries in Asia, Africa, and Latin America

Country	Child Sexual Abuse Laws and Statutes
Azerbaijan	Criminal code of the Republic of Azerbaijan adopted in 2000: Forcing of juvenile (minor) into sexual intercourse or satisfaction of sexual passion in other form using violence—5 to 8 years of imprisonment (Article 152).
Botswana	Section 147 of the penal code: Any person who attempts to have unlawful carnal knowledge of any person under the age of 16 years is guilty of an offence and is liable to imprisonment for a term not exceeding 14 years, with or without corporal punishment.
Brazil	Section 247 of Brazilian penal code, 1984: The act to seduce a virgin woman under the age of eighteen (18) or above the age of fourteen (14) and have carnal intercourse with her taking advantage of her inexperience or justifiable confidence—imprisonment of 2 to 4 years.
Chile	Chilean penal code—Article 361 and Law No. 19.927 enacted in 2004: The new law raised the age limit for sexual consent from 12 to 14 years, extended the penal types of child pornography, criminalized new forms of child sexual abuse, increased penalties for child sexual abuse, and increased police power to investigate child sexual abuse cases; violations of child sexual legislation—5 to 20 years of imprisonment.
China	Criminal law of China enacted in 1997: Raping a minor—10 years to life in prison; indecent sexual assault against the will of a minor—5 years in prison or forced labor; sodomy against minor under the age of 14—imprisonment for 5 years or forced labor; organizing, compelling, inducing or harboring girls under fourteen (14) to prostitution—5 to 10 years of imprisonment with fine or confiscation of property; serious offenders will be punished by life imprisonment or death penalty with confiscation of property.
Egypt	Egyptian penal code—Article 267 and the Child Law of 1996: Rape and sexual abuse of a child—life in prison or a certain period of time; rape and abuse of a child by a person in power and authority—life in prison.
India	The India penal code—Section 376: Rape of a minor—10 years to life in prison; Section 376 C, sexual abuse by a person of authority—at least 5 years in prison; Section 366A-B, child prostitution—maximum 10 years in prison; Section 292, child pornography—2 to 5 years in prison.
Kenya	The Kenyan penal code and the Immoral Traffic Prevention Act of 1986: Section 145—Any person who unlawfully and carnally knows any girl under the age of fourteen (14) years is guilty of a felony and is liable to imprisonment with hard labor for 14 years together with corporal punishment.
Malaysia	Malaysian penal code and the Child Act of 2001: The offence of rape and other forms of child sex abuse are punishable under Sections 376 and 376 B of the penal code, as well as the Child Act, 2001; Sections 372, 372A, 372B, and 373 of the penal code criminalize offenses related to child prostitution.
Thailand	The penal code of Thailand: Section 277, rape and sexual abuse of a girl under the age of 13—imprisonment for 7 to 20 years, if bodily harm is caused—15 years to life in prison; death to the victim—death penalty; the Prostitution Prevention and Suppression Act of 1996.

Source: Data from Legislation of INTERPOL Member States on Sexual Offences Against Children, 2012.

are thereby relatively slow and disconnected. In common law countries, such as Egypt, India, Bangladesh, and Costa Rica, however judicial interventions, are having significant effects on the creation of laws criminalizing child abuse and violence against children. In Egypt, the higher court ruled that "circumcision of girls is not an individual right under Islamic law because there is nothing in the Koran which authorizes it and nothing in the Sunna . . . . Henceforth, it is illegal for anyone to carry out [a] circumcision operation" (Nundy, 2004, p. 18).

Internet child pornography is a new domain of child sexual abuse and violence against children. In most countries of the developing world, the traditional penal codes do not define or describe the criminality of Internet child pornography. One of the major surveys on global legislative developments related to Internet child pornography was conducted by the International Center for Missing and Exploited Children in 2008. The study was aimed at gathering laws and legislative developments in the member countries of INTERPOL (International Criminal Police Organization) in five areas: enactment of specific national legislation on Internet child pornography; definitions of child Internet pornography; criminalization of computer-assisted offenses; criminalization of the possession of child Internet pornography; and requirement that Internet service providers report suspected child pornography to law enforcement. The study found that out of 187 member countries of INTERPOL, "only 29 countries have legislation sufficient to combat child pornography offenses" (International Center for Missing and Exploited Children, 2008, p. iii). Out of these 29 member countries, only one country is from Africa (South Africa) and five from Latin America (Brazil, Dominican Republic, Honduras, Panama, and Peru). The remaining 23 countries are from North America, Europe, and Oceania. The survey did not find any Asian country with laws sufficient to combat Internet child pornography. The survey found that in 93 member countries of INTERPOL, either there is no legislation or there is inadequate legislation to combat Internet child pornography. Since the completion of the survey in 2006, many countries of the developing world, such as India, Costa Rica, and Egypt, however, began national debates to criminalize Internet child pornography through legislative developments (Mukherjee, 2007). The 142 member countries of the United Nations who are the signatories (as of 2011) of the Optional Protocol on the Sale of Children, Child Prostitution and Child Pornography of the United Nations Convention on the Rights of the Child are legally obligated to criminalize child Internet pornography.

Decriminalization of Homosexuality

Modernity in criminal justice has progressed by expanding the boundaries not only of crime and criminality but also of liberty, freedom, equality, and privacy. In the progress of modernity in the West, criminalization and decriminalization went hand in hand. During recent decades, many new areas of acts and behaviors were defined as crimes (e.g., sexual harassment, domestic violence, intimate partner violence, date rate, marital rape, and child abuse). Relatively speaking, this process of criminalization, as discussed in the previous section, has been quickly progressing in the developing countries of Asia, Africa, and Latin America. Over the past few decades, a considerable number of acts and behaviors have also been decriminalized in the West on the basis of the principles of liberty, freedom, equality, and privacy in such matters as abortion, use of contraceptives by unmarried women, cohabitation, fornication, adultery, and homosexuality. The progress of decriminalization in these areas came because of the secularization of law and the decoupling of law and morality and crime and sin. Homosexuality is one of the oldest practices in human societies. At the time of the dominance of canonical laws in the Middle Ages, homosexuality was a high crime. In England in the 18th century, homosexuals were burned alive and publicly executed.

With the advent of modernity, the practice of homosexuality began to be seen purely from the perspective of individual liberty, freedom, and privacy. It also began to be seen as an issue deeply embedded in the notion of equality. From the middle of the 1970s, societies in the West have been trying to grapple with the issue of homosexuality primarily from the perspectives of privacy and equality. In *Lawrence v. Texas* in 2003, the U.S. Supreme Court ruled that the Texas sodomy law was in violation of liberty interest protected by the substantive due process law under the Fourteenth Amendment. The Court expounded that the petitioners' "right to liberty under the Due Process Clause gives them the full right to engage in private conduct without government intervention" (*Lawrence v. Texas,* 2003). In 2009, the U.S. Congress passed the Matthew Shepard and James Byrd, Jr. Hate Crimes Prevention Act. The Matthew Shepard Act decriminalized homosexuality by criminalizing discrimination on the basis of sexual orientation. In Canada, homosexuality was decriminalized through the enactment of the Criminal Law Amendment Act of 1968–1969 (Bill C-150). In Europe, 47 countries have laws decriminalizing same-sex consensual acts between adults. Some of these countries include Romania, Albania, Moldova, Ireland, the Russian Federation, Portugal, the United Kingdom, Hungary, Bulgaria, Greece, Sweden, Switzerland, Denmark, the Netherlands, Spain, Norway, Austria, Germany, and Belgium (Council of Europe, 2011).

The movement toward decriminalization of homosexuality in the countries of Asia, Africa, and Latin America began to spread in the early 1970s due to the effect of various human rights–based organizations. By the middle of the 1990s, the issue of decriminalizing homosexuality was pressed by international organizations from the perspective of development as an extension of universal human rights and equality. Starting in the late 1990s, it was also supported by a number of international and regional gay and lesbian advocacy groups. Currently, there is hardly any capital in the developing countries of Asia, Africa, and Latin America where this issue is not hotly debated and disputed. In most of these debates and disputes, the issues of morality conflict with those of rights, liberty, equality, and privacy. In March 2011, at the United Nations Human Rights Council in Geneva, Switzerland, Colombia presented a Joint Statement to criminalize human rights violations on the basis of sexual orientation. A report from the UN Human Rights Council said that "the statement was developed on behalf of a large group of 85 countries from all regions of the world . . . [and it] enjoyed the support of the largest group of countries to-date, on the topic of sexual orientation" (United Nations Human Rights Council, 2011, p. 1).

Out of 85 countries that were signatories of the Joint Statement, there were 11 countries from Africa (Gabon, Democratic Republic of Sao Tome and Principe, Mauritius, Central Africa Republic, Cape Verde, Guinea Bissau, Angola, South Africa, Seychelles, Rwanda, and

Sierra Leone); 17 from Latin America (Argentina, Bolivia, Brazil, Chile, Colombia, Costa Rica, Dominican Republic, El Salvador, Guatemala, Honduras, Mexico, Nicaragua, Panama, Paraguay, Uruguay, and Venezuela); and 2 from Asia (Japan and Nepal). Most of the other countries were from Europe, North America, and Oceania (United Nations Human Rights Council, 2011). Surveys have shown that about 52% of Asian countries and more than 50% of African countries have laws criminalizing homosexuality (International Lesbian, Gay, Bisexual, Trans and Intersex Association, 2011). In Iran, Saudi Arabia, Qatar, Sudan, Northern Nigeria, and Yemen, homosexuality is punishable by death.

A closer analysis shows, however, that about 4 billion people live in the countries where there are laws that decriminalize homosexuality (International Lesbian, Gay, Bisexual, Trans and Intersex Association, 2011). These 4 billion people include the population of China, Japan, Thailand, India, Europe, North America, Oceania, and some African and Latin American countries. In China, homosexuality was decriminalized through the abolition of the Hooligan Act in 1997. In Japan, currently there are no laws criminalizing same-sex relations between two consenting adults. It was decriminalized at the time of the adoption of the Napoleonic Code in Japan in 1880. Homosexuality was decriminalized in India in 2009. The Delhi high court of India in 2009 rendered a landmark decision, by striking down Section 377 of the Indian Penal Code of 1862, that treating sexual relations between two consenting adults as a crime is a violation of Sections 14, 15, 19, and 21 of the Indian constitution (see **Figure 8-3**). Section 377 of the Indian Penal Code defined homosexuality as unnatural offenses and said that "whoever voluntarily has carnal intercourse against the order of nature with any man, woman, or animal shall be punished with imprisonment for life." Having examined Article 12 of the Universal Declaration of Human Rights and Article 17 of the International Covenant on Civil and Political Rights, reviewing a number of U.S. Supreme Court cases related to privacy, and considering the context of escalating violence against lesbian, gay, bisexual, and transsexual (LGBT) persons in India in recent years, the

Figure 8-3 India Court Overturns Gay Sex Ban: Gay Rights Activists Celebrated During a Rally in New Delhi After the City's Highest Court Decriminalized Homosexuality

Source: © ADNAN ABIDI/Reuters/Landov.

high court decided to repeal Section 377 of the Indian Penal Code strictly on the grounds of privacy and equality. The Court concluded by saying that the constitution of India "does not permit the statutory criminal law to be held captive by the popular misconception of who the LGBTs are . . . Discrimination is antithesis of equality" (Nelson, 2009, p. 2). In February 2012, the Supreme Court of India "confirmed the decision of the New Delhi High Court and officially ended the nation's ban on homosexuality" (Kincaid, 2012, p. 1).

It is on the grounds of equality, privacy, and human rights that the movement for the decriminalization of homosexuality is currently spreading across the world. How this process will progress in different counties with different contexts of culture, religion, morality, and civilization is a topic of enormous interest in comparative criminal justice. In the countries of Asia, Africa, and Latin America, the decriminalization of homosexuality is probably one of the final tests of reaching modernity in criminal justice.

■ Reforms and Modernization in Procedural Criminal Law in Asia, Africa, and Latin America

The effects of modernization and globalization on criminal justice in the countries of Asia, Africa, and Latin America can be seen in areas not only of substantive law but also of procedural law and the judiciary. Indeed, reforms in procedural criminal law and the judiciary are more significant because they are more connected to the process of modernization in criminal justice. The nature and profile of substantive criminal law in a country mirror its progress toward modernity. The creation of new domains of criminality in a country in areas such as sexual harassment, domestic violence, child abuse, sexual violence against children, Internet child pornography, hate crime, and cyber crime certainly present a sense of its progress toward modernization in criminal justice. Equally important for modernization are changes in procedural criminal law—the processes of how substantive criminal laws are applied. Changes and reforms in many areas of procedural criminal laws in developing countries have started also from the beginning of the second wave of modernization in the 1980s (see **Table 8-7**).

The reforms began not just in the broader historical context of the English Bill of Rights, the American Bill of Rights, the French Declaration of the Rights of Man and of the Citizen, and the Canadian Charter of the Rights and Freedoms, but also in the context of a number of contemporary documents advocating for international standards in criminal procedural law.

The core point in all these documents is that reforms in criminal justice in developing countries must be based on a framework of the due process of law, meaning that rights of the accused must be preserved in each and every phase of criminal proceedings: human rights must not be violated; torture must not be practiced; rights of protection against self-incrimination must be established; fair and speedy trials must be guaranteed; cruel and unusual punishment must not be imposed; and judicial independence and accountability must be established. Reforms in these areas have been progressing in many countries of Asia, Africa, and Latin America either through the enactment of statutes or through judicial

TABLE 8-7 Global Reforms in Criminal Procedural Law: The Major Frameworks of International Law and Conventions

The United Nations International Covenant on Civil and Political Rights	International Bar Association's Minimum Standards of Judicial Independence (The New Delhi Standards)
The United Nations Initiative on the Rule of Law	European Convention on Human Rights
United Nations Standards and Norms in Crime Prevention and Criminal Justice	American Bar Association's International Standards on Sentencing Procedure
United Nations Charter on the Independence of the Judiciary	American Bar Association's International Standards on Judicial Reform and Judicial Independence
United Nations Convention Against Torture and Other Cruel, Inhuman or Degrading Treatment or Punishment	USAID's Guidance for Promoting Judicial Independence and Impartiality
United Nations Standard Minimum Rules for the Administration of Juvenile Justice (The Beijing Rules)	The United Nations Office on Drugs and Crime's Model Codes for Post-Conflict Criminal Justice

interventions. The following section will discuss the nature and progress of criminal procedural reforms in selected countries of Asia, Africa, and Latin America.

Reforms in Criminal Procedural Law in Asia: The Case of Indonesia

Reforms in criminal procedural law began in Asian countries in the mid-1990s both in the context of demands for modernization in criminal justice from within and in the context of demands from the international community for a new human rights–based approach to modernization in law and justice. In the mid-1990s, signatory countries of different U.N. conventions and international treaties and protocols on human rights began to initiate reforms in criminal procedural law in particular and criminal justice in general. Since the 1990s, different international development organizations also began to support reforms in criminal justice in developing countries as a part of improving governance and economic growth.

In 2011, for example, the Supreme Court of India reinforced the rule that a criminal defendant has the right to a counsel (Zeldin, 2011). In the case of *Md.Sukur Ali v. State of Assam* in 2011, the Gauhati high court "upheld the conviction of the appellant-accused in the absence of counsel" (as cited in Zeldin, 2011, p. 1). On appeal, the Supreme Court of India ruled that "even assuming that the counsel for the accused does not appear because of the counsel's negligence or deliberately, even then the Court should not decide a criminal case against the accused in the absence of his counsel" (as cited in Zeldin, 2011, p. 1). The Court further added that "this is because liberty of a person is the most important feature of our Constitution. Article 21 which guarantees protection of life and personal liberty is the most important fundamental right of the fundamental rights guaranteed by the Constitution" (as cited in Zeldin, 2011, p. 1).

In 2011, the Parliament of the Ukraine passed a number of significant amendments in its criminal code and criminal procedural laws. Some of these amendments "provide for better guarantees of the rights of the accused persons, specify the role of jurors in criminal trials, regulate the process of studying case materials by the defendant, and define the duties of investigators" (Roudik, 2011, p. 1). In 2010, the Parliament of Malaysia passed a law and made an amendment in its criminal procedural code to include plea bargaining in criminal cases. The amendment made a provision for "a 50% reduction from the maximum sentence for an offense" (Buchanan, 2010, p. 1). In 2009, the Supreme Court of Nepal ordered the government of Nepal to develop legislation criminalizing torture. Nepal is a signatory of the United Nations Convention Against Torture and Other Cruel, Inhuman or Degrading Treatment or Punishment. In 2009, the Parliament of Taiwan passed a law to ensure that criminal defendants receive a fair and speedy trial (Zeldin, 2009). Among the Asian countries that initiated major reforms in criminal procedural laws in recent years, Indonesia is a case in point.

The criminal justice system of Indonesia is based on the civil law tradition introduced by the Dutch colonial power. The Dutch ruled Indonesia for about 340 years. The Dutch criminal procedural code was introduced in Indonesia in 1847. The country became independent from the Dutch in 1947, but the colonial criminal procedural code remained unchanged until 1981. In 1981, a new national criminal procedural code, known as Kitab Undang-Undang Hukum Acara Pidana (KUHAP), was introduced. The new national code introduced many new provisions such as the doctrine of the presumption of innocence, protection of the rights of the accused to have counsel, compensation for wrongful arrest and conviction, and time limitations on pretrial detention. A close analysis, however, shows that the KUHAP of 1981 failed to establish "a right against self-incrimination or a standard of proof that protects the presumption of innocence. Equally importantly, there is no regular judicial avenue at the pretrial stage to assert that rights have been violated by the police" (Strang, 2008, p. 197).

Many of the provisions of the 1981 procedural code could not even be properly implemented within the legal and political culture of the military-authoritarian government of General Suharto, who ruled the country for more than 30 years (1967–2000). A new debate for more fundamental reforms in criminal procedural law began after Suharto was removed from power, and a process of democratization began in early 2000. In 2000, the Indonesian Ministry of Law and Justice set up a national committee to draft a new code of criminal procedure to replace the KUHAP of 1981. After 8 years of deliberations and consultations and the active involvement of many international assistance organizations, particularly the U.S. Department of Justice's Office for Overseas Prosecutorial Development, Assistance, and Training (OPDAT), a new criminal procedural code was created and approved by the Indonesia Ministry of Law and Human Rights in 2008. Some of the provisions introduced by the new KUHAP include protection of rights against self-incrimination, protection of privacy rights in pretrial detention; protection of the rights against unreasonable search and seizure; more power in the hands of the prosecutors for pretrial investigations and indictment; introduction of plea bargaining; the use of exclusionary rules; admissibility of electronic evidence; and promotion of adversarial trial procedures. About the right to remain silent, the new KUHAP "added an explicit statement of the right against self-incrimination. In addition, they established that the investigator was affirmatively required to provide *Miranda*-like warnings to the suspect to inform him or her of this right" (Strang, 2008, p. 212).

Under the old KUHAP, a defendant could be put in detention for up to 20 days without judicial review. Under the new KUHAP, a defendant cannot be detained more than 5 days without judicial review. Under the new KUHAP, police can conduct a search without a warrant in some extraordinary circumstances and with probable cause, but retroactive judicial approval must be received within 24 hours of such warrantless searches (Strang, 2008, p. 213). About the interception of electronic communications, the new KUHAP requires judicial approval "based on a written application from the prosecutor, requires a showing of investigative necessity, and limits the duration of the interception to thirty days, with one thirty-day extension permitted" (Strang, 2008, p. 214). One of the significant changes brought in by the new KUHAP is the protection of the fundamental rights of the defendants in pretrial investigations. The new KUHAP proposed a system of pretrial investigation with dual responsibilities of the police and the prosecutors. The provision for the participation of prosecutors in pretrial investigations was made for necessary checks and balances. The new KUHAP also established the Office of a Commissioner Judge to preside over the pretrial stage of a case. The commissioner judges are given a list of responsibilities that include "authorization of search warrants, electronic surveillance, detention and bail, and appointment of legal counsel, all traditional judicial functions generally lacking in the current Indonesian system" (Strang, 2008, p. 216). The commissioner judges are given the authority to suppress evidence collected in violation of the search and seizure principles.

One of the most fundamental reforms made by the new KUHAP is the integration of the adversarial system of justice to the traditional inquisitorial system of justice in Indonesia. The new codes particularly emphasized the adversarial nature of the trial. Under the new KUHAP, criminal trials begin with opening statements from both parties. The prosecution and the defense then occupy the stage for bringing and questioning the witnesses. In the new adversarial form of the trial, "it will be the parties, and not the trial judge, who will initially ask questions of their respective witnesses followed by examination by the opposing party.... Finally, the parties will have an opportunity to make brief closing oral arguments" (Strang, 2008, p. 219).

Many legal observers of comparative criminal law and criminal justice believe that the new KUHAP has brought some fundamental changes in criminal justice in Indonesia. The new procedural laws of adopting the doctrine of the presumption of innocence, protecting the right against self-incrimination, and applying the exclusionary rules are fundamental changes toward protecting the due process rights of the defendants. "The decision to firmly establish these rights could be seen as part of larger rejection of confidence in the inquisitorial model of a unified, neutral investigation by the State. This movement makes the Indonesian system decidedly more adversarial" (Strang, 2008, p. 224).

Reforms in Criminal Procedural Law in Latin America: The Case of Chile

Serious reform efforts aimed at modernization of criminal justice in the countries of Latin America began after the end of the military-authoritarian rule and at the beginning of democratization in the 1990s. During the next 2 decades, most countries of Latin America initiated major reforms for a transition to modern criminal justice based on the due process of law and compatible with international standards of justice and human rights (Langer, 2007). The impetus for change came mainly from Latin America's growing community of legal experts and professions, new governmental actors, and civil society leaders. It also came from various international organizations such as the Inter-American Development Bank, the Inter-American Commission on Human Rights, the United Nations Development Programme's (UNDP's) Rule of Law and Access to Justice Initiative, the United Nations Latin American Institute for the Prevention of Crime and the Treatment of Offenders (ILANUD), the United Nations Office on Drugs and Crime (UNODC), the United States Agency for International Development (USAID), the United States Department of Justice's Office of Prosecutorial Development and Training, the German Society for Technical Cooperation (GTZ), and the American Bar Association's Rule of Law Initiative in Latin America and the Caribbean. The broader context for reforms in criminal justice in Latin America was the beginning of the process of democratization and the spread of a new human rights–based approach to development in the early 1990s.

Beginning at that time, when an intellectual search for reforms in criminal justice began to spread across the continent, the inquisitorial model of justice—a model that was dominant in Latin America for almost 500 years, since the beginning of colonization in the 15th century—was seen as the most problematic institution in law and justice in Latin America. The inquisitorial model of justice is structurally and philosophically based on the ideas of the negation of the due process of law. It is based on the dominance of judges, and it does not allow much of a role for the prosecutors and the defense. It believes in securing confessions even by the use of force and torture. In the inquisitorial model, pretrial detention is mandatory; each and every offense, irrespective of seriousness, must be charged; plea bargaining is unknown; pretrial investigation is hidden; rights of protection against self-incrimination are not upheld; and public trial rights are violated. The inquisitorial model is not based on jury trial, and judges are responsible for both pretrial investigations and posttrial adjudications. A judge can come to a verdict on the basis of evidence collected by him in pretrial investigation without any securitization or challenge either from the prosecutor or the defense. There is a wider consensus within the legal community in Latin America that this inquisitorial system of justice has been partly responsible for the gross violation of human rights under the military-authoritarian regimes that prevailed in Latin America for most of the 20th century. In the 1990s, most Latin American countries, therefore, began to initiate reforms in criminal justice primarily by transitioning from the inquisitorial model to the adversarial model of justice (see **Table 8-8**).

During the last 2 decades, about 14 Latin American countries initiated significant reforms in criminal procedural laws (Hafetz, 2002). As one author on criminal justice reforms in Latin America observed: "These reforms are . . . the deepest transformation that Latin American criminal procedure has undergone in nearly two centuries. . . . They [introduced] . . . a move from an inquisitorial to an accusatorial or adversarial system" (Langer, 2007, pp. 617–618). They all share the perspective necessary for building criminal justice on the basis of the due process of law. In most of these countries, new laws and statutes have been passed by legislatures for adopting the doctrine of the presumption of innocence, criminalizing torture and forced confessions, limiting pretrial detention, introducing the scope for plea bargaining, establishing noncustodial detention, widening the participation of prosecutors in pretrial investigations, announcing the principle of prosecutorial discretion, expanding the role of defense attorneys, introducing exclusionary rules, strengthening public and open trials, protecting the victim's rights, modernizing legal education, and expanding the modern science of criminology and criminal justice.

The Chilean reforms in criminal justice in general proceeded through two stages. The first stage was in the early 1990s, when President Patricio Aylwin (1990–1994) took office and initiated reforms. Two of the major achievements of that time were the establishment

TABLE 8-8 Reforms for Adversarial System of Justice in Selected Latin American Countries, 1991–2006

Country	Introduction of New Adversarial Code Since 1997	Year of Adoption of the Adversarial Code
Argentina	Yes	1997
Chile	Yes	2000
Colombia	Yes	2004
Costa Rica	Yes	1995
Dominican Republic	Yes	2002
Ecuador	Yes	2000
El Salvador	Yes	1997
Guatemala	Yes	1992
Honduras	Yes	1999
Nicaragua	Yes	2001
Paraguay	Yes	1998
Peru	Yes	2004
Venezuela	Yes	1998

Source: Data from Langer, M. (2007). Revolution in Latin American criminal procedure: Diffusion of legal ideas from the periphery. *The American Journal of Comparative Law, 55,* 617–676.

of a council of magistrates for judicial recruitment and administration and the creation of a judicial academy for training judges. The second stage of reform covered mainly the decade of 1995–2005, which began with the active engagement of the government of Eduardo Frei Ruiz-Tagle (1994–2000). It was a decade of reforms for a transition to the adversarial system of justice in Chile. Three of the major achievements of this period were the establishment of an autonomous body called the National Prosecution Service (*Ministerio Publico*), the creation of the Office of Public Defenders (*Defensoria Penal Publica*), and the creation of the Office of the Supervisory Judge (*Juez de Garantia*). In 1999, the Chilean Congress passed a law to create the *Ministerio Publico*. The *Ministerio Publico* "began the replacement of Chile's written criminal justice system with a more public and oral based system. It also shifted responsibility for carrying out initial investigation and prosecuting criminal cases from the judges to the Ministerio Publico itself" (Fensom, 2004, p. 88). The Office of Public Defenders was created in 2000 to provide legal services to all defendants irrespective of their economic ability to obtain legal services. The Office of the Supervisory Judge was created to oversee the observance and implementation of the due process of law during pretrial investigations and interrogations.

One of the remarkable features of the introduction of the adversarial system of justice in Chile was the creation of new rules for pretrial detentions. One of the international reports on pretrial detentions observed that in Chile, "broad revisions to the rules governing pretrial detention were a central component of this transformation, which was widely recognized as the most revolutionary change in the country's legal system since the 19th century" (Open Society Justice Initiative, 2008, p. 44). Among the Latin American countries that initiated reforms in criminal procedural laws beginning in the 1990s, Chile has achieved remarkable progress. It has been aptly recognized by the U.S. Department of State's 2011 *Human Rights Report* on Chile. The report found that in Chile, "defendants enjoy a presumption of innocence and have a right of appeal . . . . [The] law provides for the right to a fair trial, and an independent judiciary generally enforces this right" (United States Department of State, 2011, p. 1). The report additionally observed that "national and regional prosecutors investigate crimes, formulate charges, and prosecute cases. Three-judge panels form the court of first instance; the process is oral and adversarial, [and] trials are public" (United States Department of State, 2011, p. 1). The report stated further that the new law "provides for the right to legal counsel and public defender's offices across the country provide professional legal counsel to anyone seeking such assistance. Defendants can confront or question witnesses against them and present witnesses and evidence on their behalf" (United States Department of State, 2011, p. 1).

Reforms in Criminal Procedural Law in Africa: The Case of Nigeria

Reforms for modernization in criminal justice in general and criminal procedural codes in particular are also not few and far between in the countries of Africa. There is hardly any African country where the government is not engaged in reforming criminal justice, where the leaders of the legal community and the civil society are not demanding innovative reforms in criminal justice (Ladan, 2010), and where there are no international assistance organizations working to provide technical assistance for planning and implementation of reforms in criminal justice (Penal Reform International, 2000). The central concern for reforms in criminal justice in Africa is the same as that of Asia and Latin America, which is the modernization of criminal justice on the bases of both the due process of law and the international standards on human rights, fair and speedy trial, access to justice, and judicial accountability.

The East African countries of Burundi, Rwanda, Kenya, Tanzania, and Uganda are currently in the process of creating a new regional bloc—the East African Political Federation. In order to harmonize the laws related to criminal justice systems in these countries, Burundi and Rwanda are moving from their Belgian heritage of a civil law tradition to the English common law tradition of Kenya, Tanzania, and Uganda (Goitom, 2009). In 2009, Burundi adopted a new penal code that criminalized torture. Article 23 of the new penal code of Burundi stated that no one "should be treated in an arbitrary manner by the state and its organs" (as quoted in Johnson, 2009, p. 1). The new law further stated that "the country must compensate any victim of such arbitrary treatment. The purpose of the compensation is to repair damage caused by government agencies" (as quoted in Johnson, 2009, p. 1). In 2011, the Gambian National Assembly amended three laws: the Drug Control Act of 2003, the Criminal Code Act of 1933, and the Trafficking Persons Act of 2007. The Gambian National Assembly also "abolished the death penalty for drug-related offenses while making other penalties for such offenses stiffer. Under the new law, the maximum penalty for the same offense is reduced to life in prison" (Goitom, 2011, p. 1).

South Africa has brought many significant changes to its criminal procedural codes through the Criminal Procedure Second Amendment Act of 1996, the Criminal Procedure Second Amendment Act of 2001, the Criminal Procedure Second Amendment Act of 2003, and the Criminal Procedure Amendment Act of 2008. These amendments have considerably strengthened the due process rights of defendants. The Criminal Procedure Second Amendment Act of 1996 made provisions that no person shall be detained for an indefinite period without giving an opportunity for a preliminary hearing, and a charge must be brought against or the reason for an arrest must be explained to an accused within 48 hours of his or her arrest. The Criminal Procedure Second Amendment Act of 2001 stated that the accused must be given opportunities for plea-bargaining for sentencing reductions and sentencing agreements.

Corporal punishment as a judicial sentence was abolished in South Africa through the enactment of the Abolition of Corporal Punishment Act of 1997. The act said that "any law which authorizes corporal punishment by a court of law, including a court of traditional leaders, is hereby repealed to the extent that it authorizes such punishment" (Republic of South Africa, 1997). The act also criminalized corporal punishment in school settings. In Kenya, the Criminal Law Amendment Act 5 of 2003 criminalized torture and corporal punishment. The act of 2003 repealed Section 28 of the Evidence Act that made confessions to the police while in police custody admissible in court as evidence (United Nations Organization, 2007, p. 7). Section 25A of the act of 2003 stated that "a confession or any admission of a fact tending to the proof of guilt by an accused person is not admissible and shall not be proved against such person unless it is made in the court" (Criminal Law Amendment Act 5, 2003, §25A).

Reforms in criminal justice in Africa are greatly aided by international development, human rights, law and justice, and nongovernmental organizations. The case of Nigeria presents three examples of how criminal justice reforms have been advancing in Africa under the auspices of many international organizations (United Nations Office on Drugs and Crime, 2003, 2011b, 2012). The first is the project called Strengthening Judicial Integrity and Capacity in Nigeria. The project was launched in 2001 and was organized and funded by the United Nations Office on Drugs and Crime, the USAID-funded National Center for State Courts, the German Agency for Development Cooperation, and the United Kingdom's Department of International Development. This project was part of a global justice reform initiative introduced by an International Judicial Group formed by the UNODC in 2000. The International Judicial Group was formed with the participation of the Chief Justices of Uganda, Tanzania, South Africa, Nigeria, Bangladesh, India, Nepal, Sri Lanka, Egypt, and the Philippines. It was formed in consultation with the Chief Justice of Nigeria, Chief Justices of the Nigerian states, the Nigerian Federal Minister of Justice, and representatives from police and prison services.

The project was focused on the following 5 key objectives: (1) improving access to justice; (2) improving the quality and timeliness of the court process; (3) strengthening of public confidence; (4) strengthening the public complaints system; and (5) improving coordination within the criminal justice system. These 5 objectives were implemented and measured based on 57 indicators such as reducing backlog, reducing court delays, increasing public information on bail, developing a strong legal aid system, developing a transparent complaint system, and harmonization of laws and penalties. For effective implementation, several committees were formed with representatives from the Nigerian legal community, the Nigerian Bar Association (2011), and the justice sector. A major partner in the implementation of this project was the Nigerian Corrupt Practices Commission. The project has initiated reforms in a number of judicial and criminal justice areas such as the creation of an Alternative Dispute Resolution System in the Lagos State high court (Lagos Multi-Door Courthouse); strengthening of the electronic court record system in the Lagos State high court; installation of complaint boxes in all 157 Lagos courts; the establishment of a judicial reform center in Abuja (the Strategic Planning Center); and the creation of an administration of justice committee in Benue state (United Nations Office on Drugs and Crime, 2003).

In 2006, the UNODC, in collaboration with the European Union, launched the second project on justice reforms in Nigeria called Support to the Economic and Financial Crime Commission and the Nigerian Judiciary (Zeldin, 2010a). The project goal was to assist "the Nigerian Judiciary and other justice sector stakeholders in the strengthening of integrity and capacity of the justice system at the Federal level and within 10 Nigerian States" (United Nations Office on Drugs and Crime, 2012, p. 1). The project was completed in 2010. A report from the UNODC observed that the effects of this project on the Nigerian justice system in general and the criminal justice system in particular between 2002 and 2007 were impressive. The report said that "the justice system had become significantly more accessible, with the average time prisoners had to spend in remand reducing from 30 months in 2002 to less than 12 months in 2007" (United Nations Office on Drugs and Crime, 2012, p. 2). The UNODC report also observed that "the general awareness of prisoners with regard to bail has improved with 68% of the respondents being aware of their right to apply for their bail in 2007 as opposed to only 43% in 2002" (United Nations Office on Drugs and Crime, 2012, p. 2).

In addition, the UNODC report found that as a result of this project, the prisoners "had better access to legal assistance, with 56% being represented by [a] lawyer as opposed to only 38% in 2002" (United Nations Office on Drugs and Crime, 2012, p. 2). Similar progress has been achieved in the area of the quality and timeliness of justice delivery. The report said that the "administrative systems of the courts have also improved, with 87% of judicial officers finding the record-keeping efficient or very efficient, as opposed to only 44% sharing this opinion in 2002" (United Nations Office on Drugs and Crime, 2012, p. 2). Improvements have also been noticed in areas of judicial independence and public confidence in the judiciary. The report observed that in 2007, "those court users who indicated that they would use the courts again based on their experience increased from 58% in 2002 to 69% in 2007" (United Nations Office on Drugs and Crime, 2012, p. 2).

The third international project is about reforms in pretrial detention in Nigeria. Pretrial detention is one of the major issues in criminal justice in all countries of Asia, Africa, and Latin America (Hafetz, 2002; Open Society Justice Initiative, 2008, 2011). It is during pretrial detentions that most of the due process rights are violated, tortures are inflicted, and forced confessions are made (Zeldin, 2010b). The Eighth United Nations Congress on the Prevention of Crime and Treatment of Offenders stated that "pretrial detention may be [justified] ... if there are reasonable grounds to believe that the persons concerned have been involved in the commission of the alleged offenses and there is a danger of their absconding or committing further serious offences" (United Nations, 1990, p. 158).

The Eighth United Nations Congress established some minimum standard rules for pretrial detention. The rules stated that pretrial detainees must have the right to be immediately assisted by legal counsel; the right to have immediate access to legal aid; the right to challenge the validity of the detention by *habeas corpus*; and the right to be visited by family members. The rules also stated that efforts must be made to avoid pretrial detention by developing effective noncustodial measures.

International rules and standards for pretrial detention are grossly violated in most countries of Asia, Africa, and Latin America. It is estimated that "on any particular day around the world, about three million people are held in pretrial detention. During the course of an average year, 10 million people are admitted into pretrial detention" (Open Society Justice Initiative, 2008, p. 11). A survey done by the International Center for Prison Studies has shown that out of all the world's regions, Asia has the highest percentage of pretrial detainees among its prison population (47.8), followed by Africa (35.2), the Americas (25.2), and Europe (20.5). Among African countries, Nigeria has the highest percentage of pretrial detainees in its prison population. The Nigerian Bar Association (2011) estimated that about 77% of Nigeria's prison population is composed of pretrial detainees. The Open Society Justice

Initiative's (2011) report estimated that "the average length of pretrial detention in Nigeria is 3.7 years" (p. 15).

One of the major concerns for reforms in criminal procedural law and criminal justice in Nigeria, therefore, is the issue of pretrial detention. In 2004, one of the international nongovernmental organizations on justice reforms—the Open Society Justice Initiative—developed a 2-year pilot project called Reform of Pretrial Detention and Legal Aid Service Delivery in Nigeria. The project, developed in collaboration with the Nigerian police and the Nigerian Legal Aid Council, aimed to address the problem of pretrial detention in four Nigerian states (Ondo, Imo, Kaduna, and Sokoto). The project began with concerns that the lack of legal representation, lack of coordination among different sectors of criminal justice, lack of a firm cap on the length of pretrial detention, and the tendency of the Nigerian police to charge suspects for custodial detention in courts that do not have trial jurisdiction are some of the important reasons for the high percentage of pretrial detainees among the Nigerian prison population. The project implemented an effective system of legal representation for arrested suspects by introducing a duty solicitor scheme in which trained lawyers were on 24-hour call at designated police stations. The project also introduced a case file management system for different criminal justice agencies in order to improve management of the pretrial process. In the four states, project leaders worked with leaders of the judiciary to mandate effective judicial monitoring of the pretrial custodial order and limiting pretrial custody to 9 months. In collaboration with the Nigerian Ministry of Justice, the project developed two legislative proposals. These were the Legal Aid Amendment Bill and the Administration of Criminal Justice Bill. The Legal Aid Amendment Bill proposed to increase the number of lawyers in the Nigerian Legal Aid Council from 90 to 1,000. The Administration of Criminal Justice Bill proposed limiting the time of pretrial detention to a maximum duration of 30 days, irrespective of the alleged offense (Open Society Justice Initiative, 2008). Evaluation of the project shows that it had some significant effects. Before the project was launched, there were 3,111 pretrial detainees in the four pilot states. On average, each detainee was serving a time of 20 months. "By December 2005, the project had secured the release of 611 detainees from prison custody, plus an additional 644 persons from police custody" (Open Society Justice Initiative, 2008, p. 98). The project also achieved "a significant reduction in the average duration of pretrial detention in the pilot states of Imo (–88 percent), Ondo (–31 percent), Kaduna (–86 percent) and Sokoto (–61 percent)" (Open Society Justice Initiative, 2008, p. 98). As a result of this project, the average length of detention in the pilot states was reduced from 20 months to 5.7 months.

■ Summary

Most of the colonies of Latin America became independent in the early 19th century. The independent countries of Latin America have therefore been in the process of state building for more than a century and a half. The colonies of Asia and Africa became independent in the 1950s and 1960s. From the 1950s to the 1980s, the postcolonial countries of Asia and Africa were engaged in state building. It was primarily a period of political development and the formation of a modern state. For many countries, however, this period turned into a lengthy period of intense intrastate political conflicts and violence. The rise of political conflicts and violence led to the rise of military-authoritarian regimes in most countries of Asia, Africa, and Latin America. The birth of the Cold War in the 1950s, which created a bipolar world order of capitalism and socialism, was partly responsible for the rise of a new generation of failed and fragile states in the developing countries during the 1970s and 1980s. In the failed and fragile states, the progress of modernization in criminal justice meant mainly the rise of militarized police forces. In the military-authoritarian regimes, the notion of the separation of power was completely violated. The legislatures and the judiciary were completely controlled by the executive. Thus, the system of criminal justice in the failed and fragile states and in the authoritarian regimes was mostly in shambles. In the 1990s, the countries of Asia, Africa, and Latin America also began to be challenged by the growth of new global crimes. Many new global crimes began to expand during the rise of the information economy, the spread of globalization, and the open door policy of the West after the end of the Cold War in the middle of the 1980s. All of these developments led to the beginning of a new era of change and transformation—a second wave of modernization—in criminal justice in developing countries in the 1990s.

In the 1990s, a new perspective on development began to emerge and engulf the countries of the developing world. This is the perspective of a human rights–based approach to development, which brought the notions of human rights, human security, and justice to the center of development. A new perspective of connectivity between crime and development and between development and criminal justice began to emerge in the 1990s. Development began to be defined not by economic growth, but by such issues as the rule of law, democracy, and access to justice, equal justice, human security, and compliance with the international standards of human rights. With expansion of this new perspective on development, reforms in criminal justice came to the core of state building and governance improvement in developing countries. Transformation in the institutions that provide security, law, and justice came to prominence in the pursuit of development.

This chapter has discussed how reforms and modernization in policing are being pursued in India, Bangladesh, Kenya, and Brazil; how new boundaries of criminal law are being created in such areas as sexual harassment, domestic and sexual violence against women, and child abuse and violence against children; how laws decriminalizing homosexuality are growing and are also being challenged in many countries; and how many due process issues and rights are being addressed, reformed, and strengthened. In the area of reforms in policing, the growing trends are for ensuring police accountability, criminalization of police torture, professionalization in policing, and the expansion of democratic policing. The cases of India and Bangladesh suggest a new trend of judicial interventions for police reforms in the developing world. Examples of the growth of laws criminalizing sexual harassment, domestic violence, and child abuse and those decriminalizing homosexuality suggest a trend of homogenization in substantive criminal law among the world's societies.

Examples of change and transformation in procedural criminal laws suggest a trend toward increasing compliance with international standards of law and justice, as well as a trend toward homogenization and harmonization in procedural criminal law among the world's societies. Change from the inquisitorial model of justice to the adversarial system observed among many Latin American countries is particularly significant. In Africa, examples of projects for reforming pretrial detention rules and procedures in Nigeria pursued by the Open Society Justice Initiative and a project for reforming the Nigerian judiciary by the United Nations Office on Drugs and Crime suggest how deeply many international organizations are engaged in efforts for reforming and modernizing criminal justice in the developing countries of Asia, Africa, and Latin America. Within the scope of this chapter, only a few cases for reforms and modernization in criminal justice have been explained, but this movement in the direction of modernization of criminal justice has become a global process of changes and transformations. A comparative analysis of criminal justice must begin with an understanding of some of these changes and transformations in criminal justice that are swiftly spreading around the developing world.

■ Discussion Questions

1. There are some international benchmarks and legal standards for reforms in policing, judicial systems, prisons, and the treatment of offenders. Describe some of the international standards for reforms in criminal justice in developing countries. (Examples: United Nations Convention Against Torture and Other Cruel, Inhuman or Degrading Treatment or Punishment; International Covenant on Civil and Political Rights; and United Nations Convention on the Rights of the Child.)

2. Modernization and globalization are expanding the boundaries of crime and criminality in many developing countries. Examine this statement in the context of the passage of new criminal laws related to sexual harassment. Comment on whether there is a trend toward the homogenization such criminal laws among the world's societies. Cite examples.

3. Modernization and globalization are expanding the boundaries of crime and criminality in many developing countries. Examine this statement in the context of new criminal laws with respect to child abuse and violence against children in developing countries. Comment on whether there is a trend toward the homogenization of such criminal laws among the world's societies. Cite examples.

4. Modernization and globalization are expanding the boundaries of crime and criminality in many developing countries. Examine this statement in the context of new criminal laws in developing countries with respect to spousal violence and violence against women. Cite examples.

5. Modernization and globalization are expanding the boundaries not just of criminalization but also decriminalization. Examine this statement in the context of the movement for decriminalization of homosexuality in the developing countries of Asia, Africa, and Latin America. Review the Indian high court decision on homosexuality.

6. Among the world's societies, there is currently a globalizing trend with regard to the due process of law partly under the effect of the evolving international standards of law and justice and partly under the effect of the expanding role of international governmental and nongovernmental organization. Explain this statement by discussing examples of reforms in procedural criminal laws from some of the selected countries of the Asian region.

7. Among the world's societies, there is currently a globalizing trend with regard to the due process of law partly under the effect of the evolving international standards of law and justice and partly under the effect of the expanding role of international governmental and nongovernmental organizations. Explain this statement by discussing examples of reforms in procedural criminal laws from some of the selected countries of the African region.

8. Partly under the effect of the evolving international standards of law and justice and partly under the effect of the expanding role of international governmental and nongovernmental organizations, there is currently a trend toward the globalization of the due process of law. Explain this statement, giving examples of reforms in procedural criminal laws from some of the selected countries of the Latin American region.

9. Read the reports Socio-Economic Impact of Pretrial Detention (2011) and Reducing the Excessive Use of Pretrial Detention (2008), both published by the Open Society Justice Initiative, an international think tank on crime and justice in the developing world. On the basis of your reading, conduct a comparative study of the nature and extent of the problem of pretrial detention in different regions of the world, including North America and Europe.

10. A number of international organizations such as the UNODC, the UNDP, the World Bank, the UN Rule of Law Initiative, and the American Bar Association's Rule of Law Initiative are currently engaged in the improvement of the judiciary in the developing countries of Asia, Africa, and Latin America. On the basis of your reading of some these international efforts, discuss the major problems of the judiciary in developing countries.

■ References

ABC News. (2007). *Kenyan police suspected of executing nearly 500*. Retrieved from http://www.abc.net.au/news/2007-11-06/kenya-police-suspected-of-executing-nearly-500/716682.

Abdelhadi, M. (2008). *Egypt's sexual harassment 'cancer.'* BBC News, Cairo. Retrieved from http://news.bbc.co.uk/2/hi/7514567.stm.

Albrecht, J. F. (2011). *The police in Brazil: Both formal and informal actors in justice administration*. Retrieved from www.mypolice.ca/research_and_publications/PoliceBrazil.htm.

Amnesty International. (2010). *Brazil—Amnesty International Report 2010*. Retrieved from www.amnesty.org/en/region/brazil/report-2010.

Bailey, J., & Dammert, L. (Eds.). (2006). *Public security and police reform in the Americas*. Pittsburgh, PA: University of Pittsburgh Press.

Bangladesh National Women Lawyers Association v. Government of Bangladesh, Writ Petition No 5916 (2008).

Bangladesh Police. (2011). *Police reform programme.* Dhaka, Bangladesh: Ministry of Home Affairs.

Brito, C. (2010). *Strategic community policing in Brazil.* Retrieved from www.ecprnet.eu/databases /conferences/papers/151.pdf.

Buchanan, K., for the Global Legal Monitor. (2010). *Malaysia: New provisions on plea bargaining to come into force.* Washington, DC: Law Library of Congress.

Bureau of Justice Statistics. (2012). *Intimate partner violence.* Washington, DC: Office of Justice Programs, BJS.

Cardia, N. (2002, May). *What role for federal government?* Paper presented at the workshop on Police Reform in Brazil: Diagnosis and Policy Proposals. Oxford, England: Center for Brazilian Studies.

Carlos, B. (2010, August–September). *Strategic community policing in Brazil.* Paper presented at the European Consortium for Political Research. Dublin, Ireland.

Central Intelligence Agency. (2011). *Kenya—CIA—The world factbook.* Washington, DC: Author.

Cevallos, D. (2008). *Latin America: Once again, govts promise to tackle violent crime.* Inter Press Service. Retrieved from http://ipsnews.net/news.asp?idnews=44186.

Commonwealth Human Rights Initiative. (2010). *Feudal forces: Reform delayed: Moving from force to service in South Asia policing.* Delhi, India: Author.

Commonwealth Human Rights Initiative. (2011a). *International laws and standards that affect policing.* Delhi, India: Author.

Commonwealth Human Rights Initiative. (2011b). *Police organisation in India.* Delhi, India: Author.

Commonwealth Human Rights Initiative. (2011c), *India: Police structure and organisation.* Delhi, India: Author.

Commonwealth Human Rights Initiative. (2011d). *The National Police Commission.* Delhi, India: Author.

Commonwealth Human Rights Initiative. (2011e). *The Ribeiro Committee on Police Reforms.* Delhi, India: Author.

Commonwealth Human Rights Initiative. (2011f). *Padmanabhaiah Committee on Police Reforms.* Delhi, India: Author.

Council of Europe. (2011). *Discrimination on grounds of sexual orientation and gender identity in Europe.* Paris, France: Author.

Davies, C. (2011). *Sexual harassment from Muslim men, common in Egypt* (CNN report). Retrieved from http://eternian.wordpress.com/category/pakistan/.

Dhar, A. (2010). *India: 88% women victims of sexual harassment at workplace.* Retrieved from http://power2women.in/news/women-sexual-harassment-workplace/.

Dossett, G. (2002, May). *Re-training the military police.* Paper presented at the workshop on Police Reform in Brazil: Diagnosis and Policy Proposals. Oxford, England: Center for Brazilian Studies.

Dudziak, M. L. (2008). A Bill of Rights for Kenya: Marshall's Role. In *Justice for All: The Legacy of Thurgood Marshall* (U.S. State Department online publication). Retrieved from http://iipdigital.usembassy .gov/st/english/publication/2008/05/20080501224049myleen0.6964335.html#axzz20RA62Sy7.

Economist Intelligence Unit. (2010). *Democracy index 2010: Democracy in retreat.* London, England: The Economist.

EUROPA: Summaries of EU legislation. (2008). *Combating the sexual exploitation of children and child pornography.* Brussels, Belgium: European Union.

European Parliament. (2010). *The issues of violence against women in the European Union* (by C. Genta). Brussels, Belgium: Author.

European Union Times. (2011). *Japan child porn cases surge to record high.* Retrieved from www.eutimes.net/2011/02/japan-child-porn-cases-surge-to-record-high-child/.

Family Safe Media. (2011). *Internet pornography statistics.* Retrieved from www.familysafemedia.com/pornography_statistics.html

Farrell, C. (2011). *South Korea: Corporal punishment in schools.* Retrieved from www.corpun.com/counkrs.htm.

Fensom, M. (2004). *Judicial reform in the Americas: The case of Chile.* (Doctoral dissertation). Gainesville: University of Florida.

Frederick, J., for the United Nations Children's Fund. (2010). *Sexual abuse and exploitation of boys in South Asia.* New York, NY: United Nations.

Furuzawa, Y. (2011). Two police reforms in Kenya: Their implications for police reform policy. *Journal of International Development and Cooperation, 17*(1), 51–69.

Gastrow, P. (2010). *The complexity of Kenya and its police reforms.* Retrieved from www.ipacademy.org/images/pdfs/gastrow_kenya_fullreport.pdf.

Goitom, H., for the Global Legal Monitor. (2009). *Burundi/Rwanda: Possible switch of legal tradition.* Washington, DC: Law Library of Congress.

Goitom, H., for the Global Legal Monitor. (2011). *Gambia: Death penalty for drug offenses abolished.* Washington, DC: Law Library of Congress.

Hafetz, J. L. (2002). Pretrial detention, human rights, and judicial reform in Latin America. *Fordham International Law Journal, 26*(6), 1754–1777.

Harris v. Forklift Systems, 510 U.S. 17 (1993).

Hilton, R. (2005). *Adopting "U.S. Style" sexual harassment prohibition laws in Asia and the European Union.* Retrieved from www.synergisminternational.com/resources/Adopting%20US%20Sexual%20Harassment%20Laws%20in%20Germany%20and%20Japan.pdf.

Hinton, M. S. (2006). *The state on the streets: Police and politics in Argentina and Brazil.* Boulder, CO: Lynne Rienner Publishers.

Human Rights Watch. (2011). *World Report 2011.* New York, NY: Author.

International Center for Missing and Exploited Children. (2008). *Child pornography: Model legislation & global review.* Alexandria, VA: Author.

International Crisis Group. (2009). *Bangladesh: Getting police reform on track* (Asia report No. 182). New York, NY and Brussels, Belgium: Author.

International Lesbian, Gay, Bisexual, Trans and Intersex Association. (2011). *State-sponsored homophobia: A world survey of laws criminalizing same-sex sexual acts between consenting adults.* Brussels, Belgium: Author.

International Trade Union Confederation. (2008). Stopping sexual harassment at work—A Trade Union Guide. Retrieved from www.ituc-csi.org/IMG/pdf/Harcelement_ENG_12pgs_BR.pdf.

Internet Watch Foundation. (2008). *Annual and charity report.* London, England: Author.

Johnson, C., for the Global Legal Monitor. (2009). *Burundi: Torture criminalized in revised code.* Washington, DC: Law Library of Congress.

Kaufmann, D., Kraay, A., & Mastruzzi, M., for the World Bank. (2010). *The worldwide governance indicators: Methodology and analytical issues.* Washington, DC: World Bank Development Research Group.

Kenya National Commission on Human Rights. (2008). *On the brink of the precipice: A human rights account of Kenya's post-2007 election violence.* Nairobi, Kenya: Author.

Kincaid, T. (2012). *India's Supreme Court affairs decriminalization of homosexuality.* Retrieved from www.boxturtlebulletin.com/2012/02/16/42070.

Ladan, M. T. (2010, January). *Enhancing access to justice in criminal matters: Possible areas for reform in Nigeria.* Paper presented at the National Workshop on Law Development organized by the Nigerian Law Commission. Abuja, Nigeria.

Langer, M. (2007). Revolution in Latin American criminal procedure: Diffusion of legal ideas from the periphery. *The American Journal of Comparative Law, 55,* 617–676.

Lawrence v. Texas, 539 U.S. 558 (2003).

Leeds, E. (2007). Serving states and serving citizens: Having steps towards police reform and implication for donor intervention. *Police and Society, 17*(1), 21–37.

Lilley, S. (2009, December 8). *Brazilian police accused of extrajudicial force.* Retrieved from www .msnbc.msn.com/id/34324717/ns/world_news-americas/t/brazilian-police-accused-extrajudicial -force/#.T_8jhI64Ldk.

Lloyd, T., & Mullender, D. (2002). *Re-training the civil police.* Paper presented at the workshop on Police Reform in Brazil: Diagnosis and policy proposals. Oxford, England: Center for Brazilian Studies.

Los Angeles Times. (2011, June 6). *Egypt: On anniversary of Khaled Said's death, complaints on police brutality and corruption.* Retrieved from www.twylah.com/LATimesworld/tweets/77812565757005824.

Macaulay, F. (2005). Civil society-state partnerships for the promotion of security in Brazil. *Civil Society Observer, 2*(1), 1–20.

Marshall, M. G., & Cole, B. R. (2008). *Global report: Conflict, governance, and state fragility.* Fairfax, VA: George Mason University Center for Systemic Peace.

Md Sukur Ali v. State of Assam. [2011] INSC 195. Supreme Court, 24.

Meritor Savings Bank v. Vinson, 477 U.S. 57 (1986).

Mukherjee, D. (2007). Child pornography: A comparative study of India, USA, and EU. *Calcutta Criminology Law Journal.* Retrieved from http://works.bepress.com/dyutimoy_mukherjee/3/.

Muniz, J. (2002). *Reform of the military police: The military model and its effects.* Paper presented at the workshop on Police Reform in Brazil: Diagnosis and Policy Proposals. Oxford, England: Center for Brazilian Studies.

Nelson, D. (2009, July). *India overturns 148-year-old law banning homosexuality.* London, England: Telegraph Media Group Ltd.

Nigerian Bar Association. (2011). *Concept note for NBA conference on criminal justice reform #17–20 July 2011.* Retrieved from www.nba.org.ng/web/concept-note-for-nba-conference-on-criminal -justice-reform-17-20-july-2011-.html.

Nundy, K. (2004). *The global status of legislative reform related to the Convention on the Rights of the Child.* New York, NY: United Nations.

Open Society Justice Initiative. (2008). *Reducing the excessive use of pretrial detention.* New York, NY: Author.

Open Society Justice Initiative. (2011). *Socioeconomic impact of pretrial detention.* New York, NY: Author.

Ore-Aguilar, G. (1997). Sexual harassment and human rights in Latin America. *Fordham Law Review, 66*(12), 631–645.

Penal Reform International. (2000). *Access to justice in sub-Saharan Africa: The role of traditional and informal justice systems.* London, England: Author.

Pflanz, M. (2007, November 21). *Commonwealth's Uganda accused of torture.* London, England: Telegraph Media Group Ltd.

Pinc, T. M. (2010). *Police reform: A determinant of democracy's development.* Retrieved from http://opensiuc.lib.siu.edu/cgi/viewcontent.cgi?article=1018&context=pnconfs_2010.

Provost, C. (2011, July). UN Women justice report: Get the data. *The guardian.* Retrieved from www.guardian.co.uk/global-development/poverty-matters/2011/jul/06/un-women-legal-rights-data.

Pusurinkham, S. (2011). *Child prostitution in Thailand* (AGW: A Global Witness Magazine). Retrieved from www.thewitness.org/agw/pusurinkham.121901.html.

Ram, C. (2010). *The new constitution of Kenya* (from *Stabroek News*). Retrieved from www.stabroeknews.com/2010/guyana-review/11/30/the-new-constitution-of-kenya-an-analysis-by-christopher-ram/.

Republic of Kenya. (2009). *Report of the National Task Force on Police Reforms.* Nairobi, Kenya: Author.

Republic of Kenya. (2010, July 19). *Report of the police reforms implementation committee for period January–June, 2010.* Nairobi, Kenya: Ministry of Provincial Administration and Internal Security.

Republic of South Africa. (1997, September 5). Abolition of Corporal Punishment Act, 1997. *Government Gazette.* Cape Town, South Africa.

Roe v. Wade, 410 U.S. 113 (1973).

Rosa, L., for the Massachusetts South America Office. (2007). *Brazil security industry.* Retrieved from www.massbrazil.com.br/en/files/Brazil%20Security%20Industry.pdf.

Roudik, P., for the Global Legal Monitor. (2011). *Ukraine: Amendments to criminal legislation.* Washington, DC: Law Library of Congress.

Shahidullah, S. M., & Derby, C. N. (2010). Criminalisation, modernisation, and globalisation: The US and international perspectives on domestic violence. *Global Crime, 3*(10), 196–223.

Shahjahan. A. S. M. (2006). Police reforms in Bangladesh. In Asian Development Bank, *Strengthening the criminal justice system* (pp. 39–61). Dhaka, Bangladesh: Asian Development Bank.

Srivastava, D. K. (2010). Progress of sexual harassment law in India, China, and Hong Kong: Prognosis for further reform. *Harvard International Law Journal* (Online), *51,* 172–180.

Srivastava, D. K., & Gu, M. (2009). Law and policy issues on sexual harassment in China: Comparative perspectives. *Oregon Review of International Law, 11*(43), 43–70.

Stop Violence Against Women. (2011). *Regional law and standards: European Union.* Retrieved from www1.umn.edu/humanrts/svaw/domestic/laws/regional.htm.

Strang, R. R. (2008). More adversarial, but not completely adversarial: Reformasi of the Indonesian criminal procedure code. *Fordham International Law Journal, 32*(1), 188–231.

Supreme Court of Bangladesh. (2003). *Bangladesh Legal Aid and Services Trust (BLAST) v. People's Republic of Bangladesh, 2003.* Dhaka, Bangladesh: High court division (Writ Petition No. 3806 of 1998).

Supreme Court of India. (2006, September 9). *Prakash Singh and Others vs. Union of India and Others.* Retrieved from http://www.humanrightsinitiative.org/programs/aj/police/india/initiatives/compliance_with_supreme_court_directives.pdf.

United Nations Children's Fund. (2008). *Handbook on legislative reform: Realising children's rights* (Vol. 1). New York, NY: United Nations.

United Nations Children's Fund. (2011a). *Convention on the rights of the child.* New York, NY: United Nations.

United Nations Children's Fund. (2011b). *United Nations rule of law.* New York, NY: United Nations.

United Nations Congress on Crime Prevention and Criminal Justice. (2010, April). *Workshop on practical approaches to preventing crime.* Salvador, Brazil. Retrieved from www.un.org/en/conf/crimecongress2010/.

United Nations Development Fund for Women (UNIFEM). (2011). *Factsheet: Violence against women worldwide*. New York, NY: United Nations.

United Nations Human Rights Council. (2011). *UN Human Rights Council: A stunning development against violence*. Retrieved from www.hrw.org/news/2011/03/22/un-human-rights-council -stunning-development-against-violence.

United Nations Office of the High Commissioner for Human Rights. (1989). *Principles on the effective prevention and investigation of extra-legal, arbitrary and summary executions*. New York, NY: Author.

United Nations Office on Drugs and Crime. (2003). *Strengthening judicial integrity and capacity in Nigeria* (Progress Report #2). Vienna, Austria: Author.

United Nations Office on Drugs and Crime. (2011a). *Partnership with the federal department: Brazil and the Southern Cone*. Vienna, Austria: Author.

United Nations Office on Drugs and Crime. (2011b). *Resource guide on strengthening judicial integrity and capacity*. Vienna, Austria: Author.

United Nations Office on Drugs and Crime. (2012). *Support to the Economic and Financial Crimes Commission and the Nigerian judiciary*. Vienna, Austria: Author.

United Nations Organization. (1979). *Code of conduct for law enforcement officials*. New York, NY: Office of the United Nations High Commission for Human Rights.

United Nations Organization. (1984). *Convention against torture and other cruel, inhuman and degrading treatment*. New York, NY: Author.

United Nations Organization. (1988). *Principles for the protection of all persons under any form of detention or imprisonment*. New York, NY: Author.

United Nations Organization. (1990). *Prevention of crime and the treatment of offenders*. New York, NY: Author.

United Nations Organization. (2006). *World report on violence against children*. New York, NY: Author.

United Nations Organization. (2007). *Consideration of report submitted by state parties under Section 19 of the Convention Against Torture and Other Cruel, Inhuman or Degrading Treatment or Punishment: Kenya*. New York, NY: Author.

United Nations Organization. (2009). *Report of the special rapporteur on extrajudicial, summary or arbitrary executions* (Philip Alston report). New York, NY: Human Rights Council, United Nations.

United Nations Organization. (2011). *Progress of the world's women: In pursuit of justice*. New York, NY: UN Women.

United Nations Secretary-General's Campaign to End Violence Against Women. (2010). *Violence against women: The situation*. New York, NY: The United Nations.

United States Department of State. (2011). *Human rights report: Chile*. Washington, DC: Author.

Vishaka v. State of Rajasthan, AIR 1997 Supreme Court 3011.

World Bank. (2006). *Crime, violence, and economic development in Brazil: Elements for effective public policy*. Washington, DC: Author.

World Bank. (2007). *Crime, violence, and development: Trends, costs, and policy options in the Caribbean*. Washington, DC: Author.

World Bank. (2011). *World development report 2011: Conflict, security, and development*. Washington, DC: Author.

World Health Organization. (2005). *Multi-country study on women's health and domestic violence against women*. Geneva, Switzerland: Author.

World Justice Project. (2010). *Rule of law index, 2010*. Washington, DC: Author.

Xinhua. (2010). *Government and policy: China mulls legislation on domestic violence.* Retrieved from www.chinadaily.com.cn/china/2011-04/15/content_12329704.htm.

Zeldin, W., for the Global Legal Monitor. (2009). *Taiwan: Move to better protect right to fair and expeditious criminal trial.* Washington, DC: Law Library of Congress.

Zeldin, W., for the Global Legal Monitor. (2010a). *European Union/Nigeria: Conference held on improving judicial performance evaluation.* Washington, DC: Law Library of Congress.

Zeldin, W., for the Global Legal Monitor. (2010b). *Nepal: Supreme Court orders formulation of law against torture.* Washington, DC: Law Library of Congress.

Zeldin, W., for the Global Legal Monitor. (2011). *India: Supreme Court ruling on right to counsel.* Washington, DC: Law Library of Congress.

The Traditional Systems of Criminal Justice: Islamic Jurisprudence and Shari'a Law

CHAPTER

9

▶ CHAPTER OUTLINE

■ Introduction

The dividing line between modern and traditional systems of criminal justice is the nature of law and the principle of the separation between state and religion. In the modern systems of criminal justice in North America and Europe, and in the modernizing systems of criminal justice in a large number of countries in

Asia, Africa, and Latin America, criminal laws are based on either the tradition of the English common law or the civil law tradition of continental Europe. The English common law and the civil law traditions have many differences in terms of the role of the judges and judiciary, the relationship between the judiciary and the legislature, the law-making powers of the judges and legislatures, the nature of evidentiary rules, and reliance on precedence in criminal trials. There is, however, a fundamental similarity between these two legal traditions. Both are secular in nature, and they make a sharp distinction between the canonical law of the Middle Ages and the secular law of the modern world. Both are based on the core principle of the separation of state and religion and the fundamental values of the Enlightenment with respect to human rights and dignity and a perennial belief in human progress on the basis of science and reason. The struggle for changes and reforms in modern and modernizing systems of criminal justice is primarily a strategy for understanding the reasons for crime and criminality and the development of the strategies of crime control and prevention on the basis of the principles of modernity and the Enlightenment such as the rule of law, democracy, and the due process of law. In secular criminal law, crime and sin and crime and morality must remain separated. In secular criminal law, a crime is a crime if it is defined as a crime by laws made by judges, judiciaries, and legislatures.

In traditional systems of criminal justice, state and religion are inseparable and crime and sin and crime and morality are indivisible. In a traditional system, the state is an instrumentality for the realization of the faith and values of religion in all realms of life, including law and justice. A traditional system of criminal justice can emerge only within the framework of a theocratic state. A country that still preserves and applies its culture and customary laws in criminal justice is not necessarily a theocratic state harboring a traditional system of criminal justice. There are only two countries in the modern world that can be defined as strictly theocratic in nature: the Islamic theocracies of Saudi Arabia and Iran. It is only in Saudi Arabia and Iran that criminal justice is strictly traditional and based on the holy scriptures of the Islamic religion—Shari'a Law. There are no theocracies in the rest of the Muslim world. The Islamic theocracies of Saudi Arabia and Iran are Muslim societies, but all Muslim societies—that is, societies where Muslims form the majority of the population—are not Islamic theocracies (Armstrong, 2002). Some Muslim countries have dual systems of criminal justice that seek to combine secular laws with some of the specific provisions of Shari'a Law. This chapter will discuss the global distribution of the Muslim population, the nature of substantive and procedural criminal law in Islamic jurisprudence, and the profile of criminal justice in the Islamic empires of the Ottomans (1300–1920) and Mughals (1526–1757).

■ Global Distribution of the Muslim Population

Understanding the global distribution of the Muslim population is particularly significant in comparative criminal justice because of the recent rise of a global fundamentalist movement within the religion of Islam and the birth of a new discourse about the adoption of Shari'a Law not just in countries where Muslims form a majority, but also in regions and countries—such as in Europe and North America—where they form a significant minority. In this context, an understanding of the emerging trends in the evolution of law and criminal justice in Muslim societies is hugely important. Muslim population of the world is about 1.57 billion (2009 estimate). Muslims comprise 23% of the world's 7 billion people (2012 estimate). Research has shown that by 2030, the Muslim population is projected to grow "at about twice the rate of the non-Muslim population . . . an average annual growth rate of 1.5% for Muslims, compared with 0.7% for non-Muslims . . . Muslims will make up 26.4% of the world's total projected population of 8.3 billion in 2030" (Pew Research Center, 2011, p. 1).

Muslims live in all countries and regions of the world, but the largest concentrations of Muslims are in Asia, the Middle East, and North Africa (see **Table 9-1**). About 60% of Muslims live in Asia, and 20% live in the countries of the Middle East. About two thirds of Muslims worldwide live in 10 countries. These countries are Indonesia (203 million), Pakistan (174 million), India (161 million), Bangladesh (145 million), Egypt (79 million), Nigeria (78 million), Iran (74 million), Turkey (74 million), Algeria (34 million), and Morocco (31 million). In Indonesia (88.2%), Pakistan (96.3%), Bangladesh (89.6%), Egypt (94.6%), Iran (99.4%), Turkey (98%), Algeria (98%), and Morocco (99%), Muslims form the majority of the population. Out of all Muslim populations in Asia, about 50% live in South Asia (India, Pakistan, and Bangladesh), 26% live in Southeast Asia, and 24% live in Central–Western Asia. Indonesia is the world's largest Muslim country (203 million Muslims) followed by Pakistan (174 million), Bangladesh (145 million), and Egypt (78 million). Although they comprise about 13.4% of India's population, the total number of Muslims in India (160 million) is higher than the combined Muslim populations of Saudi Arabia, Sudan, Yemen, Syria, Tunisia, Libya, Jordan, Kuwait, the United Arab Emirates, Bahrain, and Oman. The total Muslim population of India is also much higher than the combined population of Saudi Arabia (25 million) and Iran (74 million). The Organization of the Islamic Conference, created in 1969, is composed of 57 Muslim countries.

In the Middle East and North Africa, the 11 countries with the highest percentage of Muslims in the population are Egypt (94.6%), Algeria (98%), Morocco (99%), Iraq

TABLE 9-1 Muslim Population by Region

World Regions	Estimated 2009 Muslim Population	Percentage of Population That Is Muslim	Percentage of World's Muslim Population
Asia-Pacific	972,537,000	24.1%	61.9%
Middle East and North Africa	315,322,000	91.2%	20.1%
Sub-Saharan Africa	240,632,000	30.1%	15.3%
Europe	38,112,000	5.2%	2.4%
Americas	4,596,000	0.5%	0.3%
World total	1,571,199,000	22.9%	100%

Source: Data from PEW Research Center. (2009). *Mapping the global Muslim population: A report on the size and distribution of the world's Muslim population.* Washington, DC: The PEW Forum on Religion and Public Life.

(99%), Sudan (71%), Saudi Arabia (97%), Yemen (99.1%), Syria (92.2%), Tunisia (99.5%), Libya (96.6%), and Jordan (98.2%). Except in Saudi Arabia, criminal justice systems in none of these predominantly Muslim countries of the Middle East and North Africa are based exclusively on Shari'a Law. The sub-Saharan region of Africa contains about 15% of the world's Muslim population (241 million), and they are mostly in 10 countries: Nigeria (78 million), Ethiopia (28 million), Niger (15 million), Tanzania (13 million), Mali (12 million), Senegal (12 million), Burkina Faso (9 million), Somalia (9 million), Guinea (8 million), and Ivory Coast (8 million). Except in Northern Nigeria, criminal justice systems in none of these major Muslim-populated sub-Saharan countries are governed by Shari'a Law.

In Europe, there are about 38 million Muslims, and they live mainly in 10 countries: Russia (16 million), Germany (4 million), France (3.5 million), Albania (2.5 million), Kosovo (1.9 million), the United Kingdom (1.6 million), Bosnia-Herzegovina (1.5 million), the Netherlands (946,000), Bulgaria (920,000), and the Republic of Macedonia (680,000). In the Americas, there are 6 countries with the largest Muslim population: the United States (2.5 million), Argentina (784,000), Canada (657,000), Brazil (191,000), Mexico (110,000), and Venezuela (94,000). Among the 27 countries belonging to the European Union, the highest number of Muslims is in Germany (4 million), followed by France (3.5 million), and the United Kingdom (1.6 million; PEW Research Center, 2009).

■ Shari'a Law: The Legal Tradition of Islam

Sources of the Shari'a Law and Islamic Jurisprudence

Shari'a Law or Islamic Law is the body of the core principles of Islam. It is not just a set of criminal laws. It is a body of rules and principles about the Islamic way of life as a whole (see **Figure 9-1**). "Shari'ah literally means a way to the watering-place or path apparently to seek felicity and salvation" (Kamali, 2008, p. 2). The Quran addressed to the Prophet Muhammad: "Thus we put you on the right way [shari'atan] of religion. So follow it and not the whimsical desire (hawa) of those who have no knowledge" (as quoted in Kamali, 2008, p. 2). Shari'a Law is based on two sets of sources: primary sources and secondary sources (Hallaq, 2009). The primary sources include the holy scriptures of the Quran and the Sunna—the life and teachings of the Prophet Muhammad. The Quran contains the divine rules and instructions about what is just and unjust, sacred and profane, right and wrong, moral and immoral, good and bad, and desirable and undesirable for a stable social order. The Quran said that the revelations that were sent to the Prophet Muhammad and those that were sent before him to other prophets are the guiding principles of building a just and good human community. In Surah Al-Baqarah, the Quran stated: "Indeed, those who believed and those who were Jews or Christians or Sabeans [before Prophet Muhammad]—those [among them] who believed in Allah and the Last Day and did righteousness—will have their reward with their Lord" (Chapter 2.62).

The revelations of the Quran are unchangeable, and they are to be believed as valid across time and space. Shari'a rules and laws emanated mostly from the verses of the Quran that

Figure 9-1 Women Pray in a Mosque in Banda Aceh. Recently imposed Shari'a laws require women to wear headscarves, and the province's newly formed Shari'a police have carried out arrests of women who are not properly covered up. Religious conservatism is on the rise in Banda Aceh and some larger towns across the province of Aceh in Indonesia.

Source: © Tarmizy Harva/Reuters/Landov.

were revealed to the Prophet Muhammad in Medina, where he was able to establish the first Islamic state: "The . . . rules of Quran were . . . revealed during the ten years of the Prophet's residence in Madinah and . . . towards the end of that period. . . . Muslims were a minority in Makkah, [and] had no power to enforce a law" (Kamali, 2008, p. 3). The law and legal rulings for governance "did not feature in the Quran during the Makki period. The legal rules of the Quran are of limited scope and are decidedly peripheral to its dogma and moral teachings" (Kamali, 2008, p. 4). Most of the verses of the Quran revealed to the Prophet Muhammad in Mecca were philosophical and spiritual in nature. Muslim scholars estimate that about 350 out of a total of over 6,200 verses and 85 out of 114 *surahs* were revealed in Medina (Kamali, 2008). The specific penal rules included in the verses of the Quran "which later became known as *hudud* were revealed mainly in Surah Al-Maidah during the last two years of the Prophet's life" (Kamali, 2008, p. 3).

Another primary source of Shari'a Law is the Sunna or the Hadith—the rules and principles of the life of the Prophet Muhammad. It is believed that the Prophet Muhammad not only established and propagated the religion of Islam, but also exemplified during his life as a prophet the true nature of a Muslim—the true nature of a righteous, virtuous, and moral human being. The Prophet made a number of rulings about the meanings and the teachings of the Quran to his disciples, and those are also part of Shari'a Law. In Surah Al-Maidah, the

Quran stated that "our Rosool's [Prophet] duty is only to convey my message clearly" (Al-Maidah, 5:90–93). The Quran therefore said that the demeaning of the Prophet Muhammad is equal to the demeaning of Allah—the almighty God. The Quran further said that a Muslim, who believes in Allah and the Quran, must believe in Muhammad as the Prophet. In Surah An-Nisa, the Quran said: "Believe in Allah, His Rasool [Prophet], the Book which He revealed to His Rasool, and every book which He previously revealed. He who denies Allah, His angels, His Books, His Rasool, and the last day has gone far astray" (4:136–141). The Prophet Muhammad "himself consistently referred to the Quran as a source of authority and only in his later years in Madinah did he refer to his own teachings and example (Sunnah) as a guide to conduct" (Kamali, 2008, p. 4).

The secondary source of Shari'a Law is the whole body of the specific rules and interpretations of the divine principles of the Quran and the Hadith provided by the Islamic religious judges and scholars (imams, muftis, *qadis*, and ulemas) at different times in the history and evolution of Islam. Islamic jurisprudence has grown and expanded during the 1,400 years since the birth of Islam, largely on the basis of the interpretations of Islamic scholars. Islamic law, unlike English common law and continental civil law, "is a scholarly discourse consisting of the opinions of religious scholars, who agree, on the basis of the Text of the Koran, the prophetic *hadith* and the consensus of the first generation of Muslim scholars" (Peters, 2005, p. 1).

Many Muslim scholars made a distinction between Shari'a and *fiqh*. In its strict sense, Shari'a is a body of principles about the moral teachings of Islam based on the Quran and the Sunna. *Fiqh*, on the other hand, is the translation of the moral teachings of the Shari'a into law and legal instructions. This translation of the moral teaching of the Shari'a into law and legal codes has happened over a long period of more than 3 centuries after the death of the Prophet Muhammad in 632. As Muslim scholar Kamali (2008) stated:

> The word Shari'ah does not seem to have been used by even the pious Caliphs (*Khulafa al-Rashidun*) following the demise of the Prophet, nor have they used its equivalent *fiqh* in the sense of a legal code. These terminologies emerged much later and consist mainly of juristic designations that found currency when a body of juristic doctrine was developed over a period of time (Kamali, 2008, p. 5).

The development of Islamic jurisprudence, commonly known as Shari'a Law, has occurred primarily on the basis of the methodology of *ijtihad*—the judgments, analogy, logics, reasoning, and consensus of Muslim scholars. Islamic scholars in crime and justice used the methodology of *ijtihad* to translate the teachings and principles of the Quran and the Sunna into both substantive and procedural Islamic criminal laws. As Kamali (2005) explained:

> *Ijtihad* is the most important source of Islamic law next to the Qur'an and the *Sunnah*. The main difference between *ijtihad* and the revealed sources of the *Shari'ah* lies in the fact that *ijtihad* is a continuous process of development whereas divine revelation and prophetic legislation discontinued upon the demise of the Prophet (p. 215).

About the centrality of the notion of *ijtihad*, Kamali further added that:

> The essential unity of the *Shari'ah* lies in the degree of harmony that is achieved between revelation and reason. *Ijtihad* is the principal instrument of maintaining this harmony. The various

sources of Islamic law that feature next to the Qur'an and the *Sunnah* are all manifestations of *ijtihad*, albeit with differences that are largely procedural in character (Kamali, 2005, p. 215).

The methodology of *ijtihad*, however, does not allow the religious scholars and judges to go beyond the framework of the divine law and principles of the Quran and the teachings of the Sunna. "Notwithstanding the fact that human reason always played an important role in the development of the Shari'ah through the medium of ijtihad, the Shari'ah itself is primarily founded in the divine revelations" (Kamali, 2008, p. 4).

Shari'a Law, the Sunnis, and the Shiites

Another significant historical event related to the rise of the Islamic state in general and Islamic jurisprudence in particular that also needs to be understood in pursuing comparative criminal justice in Muslim societies is the historical creation of the two denominations of Islam: the Sunnis and the Shiites. Sunnis and Shiites believe in the same Quran and the same Sunna, but they interpret Islamic law in different ways (Armanios, 2004). It is argued that the Shiite interpretation of Islamic law "allows more space for human reasoning" (Armanios, 2004, p. 2). This historical division came on the basis of competing interpretations of different tribes of Medina about how to select the successors of the Prophet Muhammad to lead the Islamic state. The Prophet died in 632—10 years after the establishment of the Islamic state—and he did not choose a successor before his death because there was no tradition of hereditary rule in pre-Islamic tribal Arab societies. One group of tribal leaders, after the death of the Prophet, decided to designate a caliph by holding elections among the Muslim believers. Another group was of the opinion that a caliph should be selected from among the heirs of the Prophet Muhammad who established the Islamic state (Arnold, 2010). The former group is known as the Sunnis, and the latter group is known as the Shiites. The Shiites believe that Ali bin Abi Talib, who was the fourth caliph (656–661) and the Prophet's first cousin and son-in-law, was the legitimate heir of the Prophet Muhammad.

The most crucial time of divide between these two denominations came about a half century after the death of the Prophet Muhammad and immediately after the death of Ali, the fourth caliph. After the death of Ali, his eldest son, Hassan, was expected to assume the throne. At that time, a major power struggle was begun by Muawyaih—a powerful political leader of Damascus. Ali's eldest son was poisoned to death and his youngest son, Hussein, was killed in battle in Karbala. This ended the political control of the new Islamic state by the family members of Prophet Muhammad, and this was the beginning of the permanent division between the Sunnis and the Shiites. About 85% of the world's Muslims are Sunnis. The major Muslim countries that have the highest number of Shiite Muslims include Iran (93%), Oman (75%), Bahrain (65%), Azerbaijan (61%), Iraq (55%), Lebanon (40%), Yemen (36%), Kuwait (30%), and Pakistan (25%).

The Four Schools of the Islamic Jurisprudence

There is no one universally accepted script of Shari'a penal law in Islamic criminal justice because (1) Islam spread to different cultures and disparate regions and civilizations of the world; (2) Islam does not have a universal system of priesthood or a papal authority;

(3) Islamic penal laws have been established over a long period of time primarily on the basis of the *ijtihad* of Islamic scholars; and (4) Islamic laws are not codified. The historians of Islamic jurisprudence claim that "the first 150 years of Islam were characterized by an almost untrammeled freedom of juristic reasoning in all solutions of problems not specifically regulated by divine revelation" (Coulson, 1969, as quoted in Terrill, 2009, p. 615). This was particularly true during the Umayyad dynasty that ruled the new Islamic empire from Damascus for almost 90 years (661–750). During the Umayyad dynasty, the center of the growth of the Islamic state and its law and justice was moved from the Arabian Peninsula (Medina) to Damascus, Syria. The Umayyad dynasty established the first Islamic empire that covered about 5 million square miles and spread to the regions of North Africa, Central Asia, South Asia, the Middle East, the Iberian Peninsula, and Sicily. This expansion of the Islamic empire needed a decentralized system of governance, and it was during the Umayyad dynasty that the Islamic judiciary was separated from the executive, and separate judicial systems were formed in different parts of the empire under the leadership of Islamic judges and jurists (*qadis*). This process of judicial decentralization led to the growing role of independent opinion and analytical reasoning (*ijtihad*) in the interpretation of Islamic jurisprudence. When Islamic judges and jurists of disparate cultures and civilizations faced new cases for judicial deliberations, they began to depend largely on their reasoned judgment to interpret the Quranic and the Prophetic tradition in Islamic law. This process eventually led to the rise of different schools of Islamic jurisprudence because of "the tension between divine revelation from Islamic scriptural sources and human reason associated with legal questions and practical cases. This tension was central to the debates and emergence of Islamic legal theory" (Terrill, 2009, p. 615). Historically, four major competing schools, representing four perspectives, of Islamic law and jurisprudence have evolved: Hanafites, Malikites, Shafiites, and Hanbalites. All four schools emerged within 250 years after the death of the Prophet Muhammad in 632. One of the major differences among these four schools is the extent to which the *ijtihad*—the methodology of personal and analytical interpretations of the sacred scriptures of the Quran and the Sunna—is acceptable as a basis for Islamic jurisprudence. They also differ about the role of *ijma* (consensus) in the interpretation of the Quran and the Sunna.

The Hanafi school can be traced back to the ideas and writings of Imam Numan Abu Hanifa, who lived in Kufa, Iraq, in the middle of the 8th century (700–768). It is believed that the ideas of the Hanafi school include some of the most liberal interpretations of Islamic law. The Hanafi school made *ijtihad* the central methodology for the development of Islamic jurisprudence. The advocates of the Hanafi school believe that through application of analogical reasoning (*ijtihad)* and consensus (*ijma*) among Islamic scholars and jurists, Islamic law and jurisprudence can be adapted to different times and spaces. Any law or ruling made on the basis of a consensus (*ijma*) at a given point of time, according to Hanafites, is changeable if there arises a valid challenge and there is a new juridical consensus. Islamic jurisprudence thus can evolve from one mode of consensus to another on the basis of analogical reasoning (*ijtihad*). The Hanafi school received a greater legitimacy because of its acceptance by the followers of Caliph Ali in Kufa, Iraq, in the middle of the 8th century.

The ideas and views of the Malikites or the Maliki school of Islamic jurisprudence are close to the Hanafites. The Maliki school is traced back to the preaching of Imam Malik ibn Anas (713–796), who was respected in his time "as Imam of Medina" (Janin & Kahlmeyer, 2007, p. 55). Most of the school's ideas are derived from the legal practices of Medina. Imam Malik's major work, *The Beaten Path* (*Al-Muwatta*), "is the oldest surviving compendium on Islamic law" (Janin & Kahlmeyer, 2007, p. 55). Like Imam Numan Abu Hanifa, he also made *ijtihad* and *ijma* the central methodological tools for the understanding, interpretation, and use of Islamic jurisprudence. Historians of Islamic jurisprudence believe that

> the consensus of local legal opinion was so important to him that, in case of conflict, he held that it should even take precedence over *hadith*. Malik was one of the first to try to bridge the gap between three disparate sources of authority: local doctrines, local scholars, and the reported teachings of the prophet (Janin & Kahlmeyer, 2007, p. 55).

Many scholars on Islamic jurisprudence believe that the early period of Islamic jurisprudence

> was characterized by an uninhibited use of personal reasoning (ra'y) to regulate cases not specifically governed by a text of the Quran or a decision of the prophet, so that Maliki and Hanafi doctrines, naturally enough, diverged in so far as they rested upon and reflected the popular social traditions and environment of two different localities [Kufa and Medina] (Coulson, 2011, p. 1).

The Shafiites and the Hanbalites, on the other hand, form two of the most orthodox schools of Islamic jurisprudence. The Shafii school, developed by Muhammad ibn Idris al-Shafii (767–819) in Cairo, Egypt, places very little significance on the role of analytical reasoning (*ijtihad*) and consensus (*ijma*) in the understanding and interpretation of Islamic jurisprudence. Al-Shafii's major work, *Treatise on the Foundation of Islamic Jurisprudence* (*al-Shafii's Risala*), was written around 815. In his time, Islamic jurists and Islamic legal theorists were trying to understand the role of two competing concepts.

> The first was the common religious practices of the Islamic community. The second was the authority of the traditions (*hadith*) associated with Muhammad himself. Al-Shafii came down firmly on the side of the traditions. He held that they were a source of the divine will and complemented the Quran. It followed, then, they could not be negated by any objective criticism of their contents (Janin & Kahlmeyer, 2007, p. 58).

He believed that Islamic jurisprudence must be based on both the Quran and the Sunna. The teachings of Prophet Muhammad, he claimed, were the expressions of the holy Quran, and hence "*sunna* has a holy quality too" (Janin & Kahlmeyer, 2007, p. 60). The rationalism of the Romans, Al-Shafii believed, would permanently corrupt the doctrines of law based on the divine rules of the Quran and the sacred rulings of the Sunna (Hersi, 2009).

The same is true about the adherents of the Hanbali school that is traced back to the preaching and writings of Ahmad ibn Hanbal (780–855), known as the "Imam of Baghdad" (Janin & Kahlmeyer, 2007, p. 62). The legal theories of the Hanbali school emerged in response to Caliph al-Mamun's endorsement of the movement of Mutazili teachings in Islam in the early 9th century. "This movement and line of thought urged Muslims to adopt the rationalist approaches of the Greek philosophers (which were then available in Arabic translation)" (Janin & Kahlmeyer, 2007, p. 61). The supporter of the Mutazili teachings held the view that the "Quran was a 'created' work" (Janin & Kahlmeyer, 2007, p. 63), and hence, it needs to be rationally understood and interpreted. To enforce the new perspective, Caliph al-Mamun appointed "his chief of police, who set up an inquisitions that would continue for about 20 years" (Janin & Kahlmeyer, 2007, p. 63). Imam Ahmad ibn Hanbal was seriously opposed to the Mutazili interpretation that the Quran was a "created work." He believed that the Quran is an "uncreated" (Janin & Kahlmeyer, 2007, p. 63) eternal word of God. For his belief in the traditionalist interpretation of the Quran, Hanbal was tortured, flogged, and jailed by the government of Caliph al-Mamun. Thus the adherents of the Hanbali school are regarded as the most conservative, and they are more adamant in rejecting the significance of analytical reasoning (*ijtihad)* and consensus (*ijma)* in the understanding and interpretation of Islamic jurisprudence.

By the end of the 9th century, the evolution of competing interpretations about the nature of Islamic jurisprudence came to an end, and the four schools—Hanafites, Malikites, Shafiites, and Hanbalites—remained dominant in different regions of the world. The Hanafi school is dominant in the countries of the Middle East (mainly in Egypt, Syria, Lebanon, Iraq, Jordan, Sudan, and Turkey) and the India subcontinent including India, Pakistan, and Bangladesh. During the 500 years of the Ottoman Empire, the Hanafi school was dominant in the regions controlled by the Ottomans. During the 200 years of Mughal rule in India, the Hanafi school was dominant in the regions now comprising the independent states of India, Pakistan, and Bangladesh. The dominance of the Maliki school remained confined mostly to the regions of northern, western, and central Africa—the regions that comprise the countries of Algeria, Libya, Morocco, Tunisia, Nigeria, Niger, Chad, Gambia, and Gabon. The Shafii school remained dominant in Southeast Asia, East Africa, and the Southern part of the Arabian peninsula. The Hanbali school is the most orthodox and is dominant in the Kingdom of Saudi Arabia. The nature and extent of the effect of Shari'a Law in the governance of crime and justice in the Muslim countries today significantly depends on their historical adherence to one these four different schools of Islamic jurisprudence. One scholar on Islamic law stated that the "division between the schools in matters of substantive law goes deeper," and that "each school represents a cohesive system of law which has its own distinctly individual characteristics in terms of social values and juristic principles" (Coulson, 2011, p. 3).

■ Substantive Criminal Law in Islamic Criminal Jurisprudence

Substantive Criminal Law in Islam: *Hudud* Crimes

There are three broad types of crimes in Islamic criminal law: *hudud* crimes (serious crimes), *qisas* crimes (revenge crimes), and *ta'zir* crimes (less serious crimes). The *hudud* crimes are those acts and activities that violate the divine commands and claims of God. Some of the *hudud* crimes are rape, incest, fornication, premarital sex, adultery, homosexuality, theft of property, banditry, consumption of intoxicating alcohols, gambling, false accusations, and apostasy. Islamic criminal justice is centered on the philosophy of establishing a good society on the basis of some universal principles of human welfare. There are five of these principles: the preservation of life, the preservation of lineage, the preservation of property, the preservation of reason, and the preservation of faith and religion. The *hudud* crimes are violations of these five core principles of human welfare. Murder is a *hudud* crime because it is a violation of the sanctity of life. Adultery, rape, incest, premarital sex (*zina*), and homosexuality are *hudud* crimes because they are violations of the sanctity of marriage and family. Theft is a *hudud* crime because it is transgression against the sanctity of private property. Intoxication through the consumption of alcohol is a *hudud* crime because it is a transgression against reason. Apostasy (*ridda*) destroys the moral foundation of faith and religion and, hence, is a *hudud* crime. The Quran described the *hudud* crimes as sinful, and hence, they are also criminal in Islamic criminal jurisprudence. In terms of *hudud* crimes, Islamic criminal justice or Shari'a Law does not make a difference between crime and sin and crime and evil—a difference that is basic to modern criminal jurisprudence.

The *hudud* crimes are described particularly in the verses of the Quran that were revealed to the Prophet Muhammad in Medina. In Section 1 of Surah An-Nisa, revealed in Medina, the Quran (4:15–16) stated that if any men or women are guilty of fornication, "punish them both. If they repent and mend their ways, leave them alone. Surely, Allah is the Acceptor of Repentance, and Merciful" (The Institute of Islamic Knowledge, 1997, p. 174). In Section 4 of the Surah An-Nisa, the Quran (4:23) commanded:

> Forbidden to you *for marriage* are: your mothers, your daughters, your sisters, your paternal aunts, your maternal aunts, daughters of your brothers, daughters of your sisters, your foster mothers, your foster sisters, the mothers of your wives, your stepdaughters . . . [and] wives of your own real sons (The Institute of Islamic Knowledge, 1997, p. 175).

In Surah Al-Isra, revealed to the Prophet Muhammad in Medina, the Quran warned: "you shall not go near the unlawful sex; surely it is a shameful deed and an evil way (*opening the door to other evils*). You shall not kill anyone whose killing Allah has forbidden" (17:31–40). In Section 27 of Surah Al-Baqarah, the Quran (2:219–220) prohibited the drinking of alcohol: "They ask about drinking and gambling. Tell them. There is greater sin in both, *although they may* have some benefit for men; but their sin is greater than their benefit" (The Institute of Islamic Knowledge, 1997, p. 137). The Islamic jurists interpret that the Quran prohibited not drinking but the act of getting drunk.

Substantive Criminal Law in Islam: *Qisas* Crimes

The second category of crimes—the *qisas* crimes—are known in Islamic jurisprudence as those offenses for which punishments are retaliatory in nature. The *qisas* crimes are based on the old biblical principle of "eye for an eye." The *qisas* crimes, like *hudud* crimes, are also serious crimes and are prohibited by the Quran. The *qisas* crimes include willful and non-negligent murder, aggravated assault, aggravated assault with a deadly weapon, and bodily injury. At the core of a *qisas* crime is the notion of retaliation as a measure of prevention. In Section 7 of Surah Al-Maidah, the Quran stated: "We ordained in *Tawra't* for them: 'A life for a life, an eye for an eye, a nose for a nose, an ear for an ear, a tooth for a tooth, and a wound for a wound an equal retaliation' " (5:44–45). The tradition of retaliation or reciprocal justice, however, is much older than Islamic jurisprudence. The Code of Hammurabi said in 1700 BC:

> If a man put out the eye of another man, his eye shall be put out (An eye for an eye); If he break another man's bone, his bone shall be broken; If a man knock out the teeth of his equal, his teeth shall be knocked out (A tooth for a tooth) (Codes 196; 197; 200).

The Talmud—the oral, or Rabbinic, laws of Judaism—called it the "measure-for-measure" retribution. The Torah—the written laws of Judaism—explained the need for reciprocal justice or retributive justice for the prevention of dangerous crimes. The notion of reciprocal justice was also found in Roman law and its Twelve Tables, codified in 450 BC (*lex talionis*—the law of talion).

Substantive Criminal Law in Islam: *Ta'zir* Crimes

The third category of crimes in Islamic jurisprudence is known as *ta'zir* crimes. *Ta'zir* crimes are man-made offenses that are known as crimes by Islamic judges and jurists. *Ta'zir* crimes are not offenses identified in the Quran. Islamic judges and jurists are given the authority to derive a list of activities to be defined as *ta'zir* crimes through *ijtihad* (logical and independent reasoning). *Ta'zir* crimes are mostly those offenses that endanger public order or state security (Peters, 2005). They are somewhat comparable to statutory laws in modern criminal justice except for the fact that statutory laws are created by legislatures and are codified, whereas *ta'zir* crimes are defined and created mostly by Islamic judges and jurists and are not always codified. The nature and number of *ta'zir* crimes can vary in different Muslim societies depending on social and cultural milieus and the varying modes of *ijtihad* by Islamic judges and jurists. Some examples of *ta'zir* crimes are weapons possession, drug addiction, robbery, organized crime, cyber crime, treason, rebellion, espionage, sedition, perjury, bribery, corruption, embezzlement, intentional abuse of power, obstruction of justice, vagrancy, indecent exposure, sexual harassment, and unlawful assembly. Central to *ta'zir* crime is the notion of judicial autonomy and legislative independence in developing substantive criminal law within the framework of Shari'a and Islamic jurisprudence.

Crime and Punishment in Islamic Criminal Jurisprudence

Shari'a Law and Islamic criminal jurisprudence prescribe three different forms of punishment for the three different categories of crimes, which are devised on the basis of three different philosophies of punishment or three different judicial philosophies (see **Table 9-2**). These philosophies are deterrence (*hudud* crimes), retribution or restitution (*qisas* crimes), and rehabilitation (*ta'zir* crimes). The punishments for *hudud* crimes and *qisas* crimes are in the nature of mandatory and determinate sentencing. The punishments for *ta'zir* crimes are in the nature of indeterminate sentencing. These three different sentencing strategies are also used in modern criminal justice, but one of the crucial differences is that in Islamic criminal jurisprudence, the determinate sentencing laws of *hudud* crimes and *qisas* crimes are divinely imposed—they are mandated by the Quran. In one of his sermons (the Hadith),

TABLE 9-2 Different Types of Crime and Punishment in Islamic Criminal Law

Crime Types	Punishment Philosophy	Proof	Punishment Types	Avoidance of Punishment
Selected *Hudud* Crimes				
Theft	Deterrence	Adultery and	Decapitation	Repentance
Adultery		fornication: 4	Amputation	Forgiveness
Fornication		witnesses or	Public execution	Pardon (by state
Defamation		confession	Flogging	authorities
Apostasy		For all other	Beheading	only)
Intoxication		*Hudud* crimes:		
Highway robbery		2 witnesses and		
Rebellion		confession		
Selected *Qisas* Crimes				
Murder	Deterrence	2 witnesses or	Death by	Repentance
Bodily injury	Retribution	confession	retaliation	Forgiveness
Aggravated assault	Restitution		Blood money	Pardon (by
			Loss of	victims or
			inheritance	victims'
			Compensation	families only)
Selected *Ta'zir* Crimes				
Weapons possession	Deterrence	Sodomy: 4	Fines	Repentance
Drug addiction	Rehabilitation	witnesses or	Warnings	Forgiveness
Bank robbery	Reentry	confession	Ostracism	Pardon (by state
Corruption	Restitution	For all other	Flogging	authorities
Bribery		*Ta'zir* crimes:	Imprisonment	and victims
Embezzlement		2 witnesses or	Exile	or victims'
Obscenity		confession	Public execution	families)
Obstruction of justice				
Statutory crimes				

Source: Data from Lippman, M., McConville, S., & Yerushalmi, M. (1988). *Islamic criminal law and procedure.* Westport, CT: Praeger.

the Prophet Muhammad said that great sins (Al-Kabai'r) are: "(1) to join others as partners in worship with Allah, (2) to murder a human being, (3) to be undutiful to one's parents (4) and to make a false statement, [or] to give a false witness" (Shahih Al-Bukhari, 2011).

In Section 5 of Surah Al-Maidah, the Quran said: "We ordained for the Children of Israel that whoever kills a person, except as a punishment for murder or mischief in the land, it will be *written in his book of deeds* as if he had killed all human beings" (The Institute of Islamic Knowledge, 1997, p. 198). Islamic law also has serious punishments for highway robbery, banditry, and apostasy (rejection or abandonment of Islam after the acceptance of and conversion to Islam). These crimes are defined in the Quran as a waging of war against God and are regarded as injurious to a stable Muslim community and social order. In the same section of Surah Al-Maidah, the Quran (5:33–34) said that

> the punishment for those who wage a war against Allah and His Rasool and strive to create mischief in the land, is death or crucifixion, or the cutting off their hands and feet from opposite sides or exile from the land *based on the gravity of their offense*. This will be their humiliation in this world and in the hereafter they will have grievous punishments (The Institute of Islamic Knowledge, 1997, p. 198).

Muslim jurists believe that because the Quran prescribed different types of punishments for highway robbery and banditry, there remains a scope for reasoned judgments. The adherents of the Maliki school claim that sanctions will depend on the nature of the specific crimes and the specific number of persons involved. The advocates of the Hanfi, Shafii, and Hanbali schools claim that punishment for robbery and banditry should depend on the severity of the offenses. They suggest that

> if a bandit kills he will be subject to execution by sword; if he steals money, his hands and feet will be cut off from opposite sides; if he only threatens the travelers, and frightens without killing or stealing, he will be expelled out of the land (this will include imprisonment); if the bandit kills and steals property at the same time, he will be crucified (Sanad, 1991, as quoted in Terrill, 2009, p. 627).

For apostasy, the Quran did not prescribe any determinate sentencing but said there would be punishment. In Section 27 of Surah Al-Baqarah, the Quran (2:217–218) warned that "if any of you turns back from his religion [Islam] and dies as an unbeliever, his deeds will become void in this life and in the hereafter. He will be the inmate of the hellfire, to live in there forever" (The Institute of Islamic Knowledge, 1997, p. 137). In Section 34 of the same Surah, the Quran (2:256–257) also declared that "there is no compulsion in religion" (The Institute of Islamic Knowledge, 1997, p. 143).

The punishment for *qisas* crimes, like that of *hudud* crimes, is also physical in nature (see **Figure 9-2**). Murder is one of the major *qisas* crimes. Islamic law defines three major types of murder (manslaughter) depending on the notions of *mens rea* (the criminal mind) and *actus reus* (actual commission of the criminal act), as well as weapons used. These three types are willful murder that is defined in the common law as murder with malice and forethought (first-degree murder); voluntary manslaughter (intentional killing but with no prior intent to kill); and involuntary manslaughter (which results from recklessness or criminal negligence; second-degree murder). The Quran prescribed the punishment of retaliation only for first-degree murder. For other types of murders, punishments such as fasting for two months, helping the poor, compensation (blood money), and loss of inheritance are prescribed. The punishment of retaliation is also prescribed in case of deliberate and intentionally caused serious bodily harm or disfigurement. "In the event of a wounding, the offender's punishment is subjected to an identical harm. One who intentionally cuts off the hand of another has his hand severed in retaliation" (Lippman,

Figure 9-2 A version of Islamic law was introduced in the province of Aceh in Indonesia in 2009 as part of negotiations to end the 29-year war between separatist rebels and the military. The law bans gambling and drinking alcohol and makes it compulsory for women to wear headscarves.

Source: © Tarmizy Harva/Thomson Reuters.

McConville, & Yerushalmi, 1988, pp. 51–52). The punishment for *qisas* crime is retaliation, but in Section 7 of Surah Al-Maidah, the Quran (5:44–45) also said that "if any one remits retaliation by charity, it will be an act of atonement for him" (The Institute of Islamic Knowledge, 1997, p. 199).

The punishments for *ta'zir* crimes are not divinely ordained. *Ta'zir* crimes are legislative statutes, and hence, *ta'zir* punishments are also legislative mandates. *Ta'zir* punishments, according to Islamic jurisprudence, must be based on the philosophy of rehabilitation and not retribution. They must also be based on the principle of the proportionality between crime and punishment and the notion of universality and generality. They should apply equally to all persons, groups, and institutions. The *ta'zir* offenders must receive the equal protection of the law—a protection that is at the core of the notion of the due process of law in modern criminal jurisprudence. *Ta'zir* punishments are also based on the notion of utilitarianism (i.e., punishment must be socially and collectively beneficial—it must secure and strengthen the collective good and the public interest). It is an indeterminate and discretionary form of sentencing in which the judges enjoy a wide range of options for the imposition of punishments ranging from a fine to the death penalty. Some of the major forms of *ta'zir* punishments include death penalty, public execution, whipping, short-term imprisonment, long-term imprisonment, imprisonment for life, incapacitation through banishment or exile, and fines. Of these different forms, whipping is the one that is more commonly used in the countries where criminal justice is partly or wholly based on Shari'a law and Islamic criminal jurisprudence. Some Islamic jurists "recognize the right of the ruler, at the request of the victims, to pardon a *Ta'zir* offense" (Lippman et al., 1988, p. 53).

■ Procedural Criminal Law in Islamic Criminal Jurisprudence

The Concept of Justice in the Quran

The concept of justice (*idl*), according to Islamic jurisprudence, is central to the governance of the Islamic state. In Section 4 of Surah Al-Anbiya, revealed to the Prophet Muhammad in Mecca in the early days of the rise of Islam, the Quran (21:42–47) stated:

> On the Day of Judgment we shall set up scales of justice so that no one will be dealt unjustly in any way; even if *someone has an act* as small as a grain of master seed We will bring it to account, and sufficient are We to settle the accounts (The Institute of Islamic Knowledge, 1997, p. 375).

In Section 20 of Surah An-Nisa, revealed to the Prophet Muhammad in Medina, the Quran (4:135) ordained: "O believers stand firm for justice and bear true witness for the sake of Allah, even though it be against yourselves, your parents, or your relatives. *It does not matter* whether the party is rich or poor" (The Institute of Islamic Knowledge, 1997, p. 187). In Section 6 of Surah Al-Maidah, the Quran (5:41–43) ordained again: "If you do act as judge, judge . . . with fairness, for Allah loves those who judge with fairness" (The Institute of Islamic Knowledge, 1997, p. 199). Central to the Quranic concept of justice are the notions of fairness, equality, evidence, proof, repentance, confession, forgiveness, protection of the rights of privacy, and protection of the rights of the women, poor, orphans, sick, and handicapped. It is through these and other related notions of the Quran and the Sunna that a set of procedural criminal laws have evolved in Islamic jurisprudence.

Due Process of Laws in Islamic Criminal Jurisprudence

The Quran mandated that in understanding and applying the divine rules and principles, serious and careful investigations must be conducted. It is a Quranic mandate that an Islamic judge "must search for the truth by allowing both the defendant and the plaintiff to present their side of the case and then carefully examining the evidence before declaring the verdict" (Kusha, 2004, p. 125). In Section 13 of Surah An-Nisa, the Quran (4:94) said: "O believers, when you struggle in the way of Allah, investigate carefully, and do not say to anyone who offers you a salutation: 'You are not a believer' . . . make a thorough investigation *before considering someone an unbeliever*" (The Institute of Islamic Knowledge, 1997, p. 183). Many Islamic jurists interpret this mandate as applying to criminal justice. A considerable number of verses in the Quran also establish strict rules of evidence in Islamic justice. One scholar on Islamic jurisprudence observed that "the rules of evidence . . . elaborated in the Koran and the Sunna and its early applications, have always been a bulwark for the rights of the accused as have the rules governing the qualifications and conduct of judges and witnesses" (Bassiouni, 1998, p. xi). One of the manuals of Hanbalite Islamic law states that "in the context of punishment of adultery and sodomy by death, there is the reminder of the tradition to the effect that it is preferable for an Imam [judge] to forgive rather than err in his judgment" (West & Green, 1997, p. 114).

The right of protection against unusual search and seizure, for instance, is at the core of the Western notion of the due process of law. The Fourth Amendment of the U.S. Constitution guarantees "the right of people to be secure in their persons, houses, papers, and effects, against unreasonable searches and seizures." In Surah An-Nur, the Quran (24:27–29) warned:

> O believers, do not enter houses other than your own until you have sought permission and said greetings of peace to the occupants; this is better for you, so that you may be mindful. If you do not find anybody therein, still, do not enter until permission is given to you (The Institute of Islamic Knowledge, 1997, p. 401).

The Quran also prohibited spying. This Quranic sense of privacy, many Islamic jurists believe, is extended also to law enforcement and Islamic criminal justice. One scholar on Islamic jurisprudence claimed that

> textual support for some search and seizure protections do indeed appear in the Quran and the Traditions (Sunna), the sacred texts that are the primary sources of Islamic law. Muslim jurists of both classical and modern times have also articulated rules or doctrines of search or seizure on the basis of these sacred texts (Sadiq, 2009, p. 1).

Some of the major principles of the due process of law such as fair and public trial, right of the accused to remain silent, not to secure confessions by force, presumption of innocence, and need for the establishment of criminal guilt based on the doctrine of proof beyond reasonable doubt, particularly in cases of *hudud* and *qisas* crimes, are basic to Islamic jurisprudence (Kusha, 2004; Saifee, 2003). Islamic jurisprudence, "in general, recognizes the right of both plaintiff and accused to present evidence and to have access to counsel during pre-trial interrogation, at trial and, if the accused is convicted, at the execution of the sentence" (Lippman et al., 1988, p. 64).

The right of the accused and the plaintiff was recognized by the Sunna. It is stated in one of the hadiths that "the Prophet, when granting Ali the governorship of Yemen, advised, 'If two adversaries come to you for arbitration, do not rule for the one, before you have similarly heard from the other'" (Lippman et al., 1988, p. 64). The role of mitigating and exculpatory circumstances are recognized in cases of *ta'zir* crimes. In Islamic criminal justice, a trial is a primarily judicial process in which the Islamic judges (*qadis*) play the dominant role in criminal investigations, adjudications, and convictions. As in the common law system, there are no significant roles for the prosecutors in an Islamic criminal trial (Haleem, Sherif, & Daniels, 2003). There are also no provisions for pretrial detention in Islamic criminal law. In case of pretrial investigation, the Quran "explicitly prohibits the use of beatings, torture or inhuman treatment to extract a confession. Torture is sin. The Prophet warned that 'God shall torture on the day of Recompense those who inflict torture on people in life'" (Lippman et al., 1988, p. 63). The notion of exclusionary rule also exists in Islamic justice. In Islamic criminal trial, "the majority of jurists would exclude from evidence confessions obtained by force or deceit" (Lippman et al., 1988, p. 63). There is, however, no concept of plea bargaining in *hudud* and *qisas* crimes. But there are the notions of repentance and forgiveness. One of the major differences between the modern notion of the due process of law and the Islamic due process of law is related to the principle of cruel and unusual punishment.

In three different forms of crime in Islamic law, there are three distinct forms of evidentiary rules. In *hudud* and *qisas* crimes, the evidentiary rules are much stricter than *ta'zir* crimes. The rules of evidence in cases of adultery and fornication, for example, are clearly explained in the Quran. In Section 3 of Surah An-Nisa, the Quran (4:15–16) mandated that "if any of your women are guilty of fornication, ask for four *reliable* witnesses among yourselves against them" (The Institute of Islamic Knowledge, 1997, p. 174). In Section 1 of Surah An-Nur, the Quran further mandated the strict requirement of four reliable witnesses for the establishment of the guilt of illegal sex including adultery, rape, incest, and fornication. In Surah An-Nur, the Quran (24:6–10) said:

> Those men who accuse their own wives but have no witness except themselves, each one of them shall be made to swear four times by Allah that his charge is true, and the fifth time calls for curse of Allah upon himself, if he is lying. *As for the wife*, the punishment shall be averted from her if she swears four times by Allah that his (her husband's) charge is false (The Institute of Islamic Knowledge, 1997, p. 399).

The requirement of four witnesses to establish the guilt of adultery and fornication is one of the core procedural laws in Islamic jurisprudence. All *hudud* offenses generally require at least two witnesses of good social reputation, but the Quran mandated the requirement of four witnesses in cases of adultery and fornication (Terrill, 2009). Islamic scholars are in consensus that four male Muslim witnesses must have social reputation in their communities as honest and righteous men. They must have seen the act of physical intercourse, and they must have seen it not by design but by chance. "The physical act of intercourse must have been observed by four reputed man, not deliberately but accidentally" (Terrill, 2009, p. 628). A sexual encounter that does not include sexual intercourse is not a *hudud* crime. Many sexual activities and behaviors that are considered serious sexual offenses in modern criminal justice systems in the West such as indecent exposure, fondling, possession of child pornography, and child sex trafficking will be considered *ta'zir* crimes in Islamic jurisprudence (Terrill, 2009).

As an extension of this evidentiary rule for four witnesses in the case of adultery and fornication, the Quran made the act of giving false witness a *hudud* crime. In Surah An-Nur, the Quran (24:3–5) said, "Those who accuse a chaste woman of *fornication,* and do not produce four witnesses *to support their allegations,* shall be flogged with eighty lashes and their testimony shall not be accepted" (The Institute of Islamic Knowledge, 1997, p. 399). The Quran also made defamation, false accusation, and slandering a *hudud* crime. In Section 16 of Surah An-Nisa, the Quran stated that "if any one commits crime and charges an innocent person with it . . . he indeed shall bear the guilt of slander and a flagrant sin" (4:105–112).

Section 2 of Surah An-Nur (24:11–20) stated that those who love to spread slanders "will have a painful punishment in this life and in the Hereafter" (The Institute of Islamic Knowledge, 1997, p. 400). By making false witness and false accusation as violations of the divine law, the Quran puts serious procedural checks on the litigation of *hudud* crimes as a whole. There is also a provision in Shari'a Law that if enough evidence is not available to define a crime identified by the Quran as a *hudud* crime, it can be treated as a *ta'zir* crime on the basis of judicial consensus (*ijma*) and *ijtihad* (Mohamed, 2011).

Islamic scholars and jurists commonly believe that even though the punishments for *hudud* crimes are harsh and divinely mandated, their crucial objective "is not to punish, but to restrain and deter man from committing crime and offence," and "to achieve this objective, hudud is daunting and intimidating, so that man will be frightened of the crime and will stay away from it" (Abdullah, 2011, p. 2). Those who are insane, mentally retarded, juveniles, old, sick, and/or ignorant of the law are exempted from *hudud* crimes. As one Islamic scholar found: "Umar a'Khatab, the second caliph, did not sentence hudud laws on those who committed adultery or premartital sex, because of the ignorance of the crime" (Abdullah, 2011, p. 3). The *hudud* crimes are punishable if they are committed in public. The Prophet Muhammad said, "Do not come near evil that has been forbidden by Allah, who so ever has, then he should conceal it with Allah's veil and repent to Allah" (as quoted in Abdullah, 2011, p. 3). *Hudud* punishments are based on strict rules of evidence and on the judicial principle that in common law is known as the principle of beyond reasonable doubt, which also brings the judicial obligation in Islamic jurisprudence to apply the notion of the presumption of innocence. Moreover, all *hudud* crimes committed by first-time offenders are pardonable on the basis of confessions, repentance, and forgiveness.

The Quran, however, mandated how some of these divinely determined sentencing laws can be avoided on the basis of confessions, repentance, and forgiveness. In Islamic criminal justice, the notions of confessions, repentance, and forgiveness are more central than the infliction of punishments of the eye-for-an-eye type. In Section 6 of Surah Al-Maidah, the Quran stated that "male or female, whoever is guilty of theft, cut off the hand (*that was used in theft*) of either of them as a punishment for their crime. This is *exemplary punishment* ordained by Allah" (5:38–40). In the same verse, the Quran adds, "But whoever repents after committing the crime and reforms his conduct, Allah will surely turn to him with forgiveness" (The Institute of Islamic Knowledge, 1997, p. 198). In Section 16 of Surah An-Nisa, the Quran (4:105–112) also stated that "if any one does evil or wrongs his own soul and then seeks Allah's forgiveness, he will find Allah Forgiving, Merciful" (The Institute of Islamic Knowledge, 1997, p. 185). But the Quran said also that confessions and repentance from repeat offenders will not be acceptable to Allah. In Section 3 of Surah An-Nisa, the Quran stated that "repentance with Allah (*right to be forgiven by Allah*) is only for those who do something evil in ignorance and repent as soon as they realize it. Allah will pardon them" (4:17–18). However, the Quran said in the same verse that "there is no repentance for those who persist in their evil deeds . . . for them We have prepared a painful punishment" (The Institute of Islamic Knowledge, 1997, p. 174).

In the case of *hudud* crimes, criminal trials must be initiated by the state authorities. In the case of *qisas* crimes, criminal trials must be initiated by the victims or victims' families (Haleem et al., 2003). The philosophy behind *qisas* punishment is retribution and retributive justice. In Section 4 of Surah Al-Isra, the Quran proclaims, "If any one is killed unjustly, We have granted the right of retribution to his heir," but immediately warned, "Let him not carry *his vengeance* too far in killing the culprit as he is supported by *the law* (17:31–40). The right of retribution in *qisas* punishment is not precisely in the hands of the judges. It is the right given to the relatives of the victims. If the relatives of the victims want retribution in case of a homicide, for example, the standard view in the law is that "the way of executing the death penalty for homicide must be similar to the way the victim was killed, and that under supervision of the authorities, the heirs may carry out the death penalty themselves" (Peters, 2005, p. 30). However, modern Islamic law, one Islamic scholar claimed, "requires the government to carry out the qisas punishment. Historically, some grieving family members may have tortured the offender in the process of punishment. Now the government is the independent party that administers the punishment" (Madkoar, 2011, p. 10). If the relatives of the victims forgive the crime, however, the government does not have the right to impose any form of punishment on the offender. The relatives of the victims are also given the right to ask for restitution in the form of monetary compensation known in Shari'a Law as *diya* (blood money). As one historian of Islamic jurisprudence observed: "Blood money (diya) in cases of homicide or wounding is a financial compensation for damages suffered by the heirs of the victim (in case of homicide) and for the victim himself (in case of bodily harm)" (Peters, 2005, p. 7). There are, of course, provisions that if the offender is a juvenile or insane, there will be no retaliation and no compensation. If the victim or the relatives of the victims forgive or pardon, there will be no retaliation, but compensation can still be enforced. There is also a provision that only the male blood relative of the victim (father or grandfather) can claim *diya* in case of death (Terrill, 2009). Some scholars suggest that the notion of blood money or diya "is the predecessor of the modern notion of victimology" (Terrill, 2009, p. 632).

As *ta'zir* crimes are related mostly to the maintenance of collective peace and order and national and state security, litigation in *ta'zir* crimes is also initiated by the state authorities. *Ta'zir* crimes follow all the general rules of criminal procedures applied in cases of *hudud* and *qisas* crimes. One of the major differences between *hudud* and *qisas* crimes, however, is that if the strict rules of evidence needed for *hudud* and *qisas* crimes are not satisfied, they must be treated as *ta'zir* crimes. *Ta'zir* punishments are indeterminate in nature, and they are not divinely prescribed. "The proclamation of Ta'zir in theory is limited by the letter and spirit of the Koran and the *Sunna*, and such offenses may not be punished more severely than *Hudud*" (Lippman et al., 1988, p. 122). One of the Islamic jurists noted that "ta'zir crimes were not codified at the inception of the Islamic state in order to give the ruler as the judge the flexibility to respond to subsequent changes of circumstances through the instrumentality of the criminal law" (as quoted in Lippman et al., 1988, p. 88). Because wide discretionary powers are given to judges in case of *ta'zir* crimes, the right to counsel by *ta'zir* defendants is protected.

■ Islamic Jurisprudence in Practice: Criminal Justice in Two Historical Islamic Empires

The Islamic criminal jurisprudence that was briefly discussed previously is a set of principles based on the divine rules of the Quran and the tradition of the Sunna. In order to understand how Islamic criminal jurisprudence is applied in practice and how Shari'a Laws are implemented within the Islamic criminal justice system, one needs to understand both the rise and expansion of the Islamic state and the development of Islamic criminal justice within those states at different periods of Islam's 1,400-year history (Feldman, 2008; Peters, 2005). To discuss the whole history of state formation in Islam is beyond the scope of this chapter. The following sections, however, will comparatively reflect on the nature of Islamic criminal jurisprudence in two specific historical cases: the early medieval Islamic empire of the Ottomans and the Mughal Empire of India.

The Prophet Muhammad established the first Islamic state in Medina in 622. From this beginning in the early 7th century, the Islamic state continued to grow and expand in different forms and through different caliphs until the end of the Ottoman Empire in the 1920s. After the death of the Prophet Muhammad, there were four successive caliphs who ruled the Islamic state: Abu Bakr (632–634), Umar bin al-Khattab (634–644), Uthman ibn Affan (644–656), and Ali bin Abi Talib (656–661). During the reign of these four caliphs, the Islamic state of Medina turned into a large Islamic empire including the countries of Syria, Egypt, Iraq, Lebanon, Palestine, Algeria, Morocco, Sudan, and Tunisia. After the death of Ali, the expansion of Islam gave birth to different Islamic dynasties. There were three major successive dynasties that ruled the Islamic empire until the 1920s. These dynasties were the Umayyad dynasty (7th–8th century), Abbasid dynasty (8th–13th century), and Ottoman dynasty (13th–20th). During the 1,400 years of rule by these successive dynasties, the religion of Islam and the Islamic empire further expanded in many countries of Africa, Asia, and Europe. The seat and center of Islamic power were moved from Medina to Kufa, Iraq, by Caliph Ali. After the death of Ali in 661, the center of Islamic power moved to Syria under the Umayyad dynasty. Under the Abbasid dynasty, the center of power again moved to Bagdad, Iraq, where it remained for more than 4 centuries before moving to Istanbul, Turkey, under the Ottoman Empire. With the expansion of Islam and the Islamic dynasties and empires, the influence of Islamic jurisprudence on the law and justice of disparate regions and cultures vastly expanded. One of the historical realities is that with the expansion of the Islamic states and empires across a variety of cultures and civilizations, Shari'a Law began to be differently interpreted, and there emerged an increased role of *ijtihad* and *ijma* in adapting Islamic jurisprudence in varying cultural and civilizational contexts. As Islam expanded to alien lands and began to be embraced by people of different races and preexisting religions, Shari'a Law had to accommodate the existing local cultures, creeds, mores, and moralities. With the spread of Islam, the advancing system of Islamic jurisprudence and its Islamic imams, jurists, and Sufis had to compromise with the prevailing systems of law, politics, and justice in the new lands and new civilizations.

Islamic Jurisprudence in the Ottoman Empire, 1300–1920

The Ottoman Empire was one of the largest empires built in the early Middle Ages as a result of the expansion of Islam. It was also one of the last Islamic empires and one of the last citadels of the political order of Islam. The Abbasid dynasty of Islam created by the Shiites in 754 was destroyed by the invasion of the Mongols. The Mongols, under the leadership of Hulagu Khan, invaded, burned, and massacred citizens of the city of Baghdad in 1258. It is estimated that the Mongols killed about a million people during the invasion of Baghdad, and that brought the collapse of the Abbasid dynasty. But the collapse of the Abbasid dynasty did not stop the spread of Islam and the political order of the Islamic state. In 1299, there began the growth of another Islamic empire—the Ottoman Empire. The name Ottoman came from its Turkish founder Osman. Major expansion of the empire began in the middle of the 15th century when the Ottomans captured the city of Constantinople, which led to the collapse of the Byzantine Empire. At the zenith of its political and military power in the 15th and 16th centuries and with its capital moved to Istanbul, the Ottoman Empire occupied a landmass of 2.7 million square miles and was comprised of a vast number of territories from North Africa, Middle East, Asia, and Europe. In the middle of the 19th century, the empire was inhabited by about 35 million people who belonged to more than 20 language groups and all major religions of the world. Today, more than 25 countries of the Middle East, North Africa, Asia, and Europe occupy the territories that were part of the Ottoman Empire. The Ottomans are remembered for their unique ability to build one of the largest and most highly centralized military-bureaucratic states in the Middle Ages.

The historians of Islamic jurisprudence, however, are intrigued by the ability of the Ottomans to establish a highly bureaucratized and centralized Islamic judicial system and use it as one of the major governing institutions of the empire. One historian of the Ottoman Empire wrote that in the whole empire, the Shari'a judicial system "played a major role; in the Ottomans its communal ties not only served to tie together . . . the courtly . . . and more popular urban life, but became the most seminal single inspiration of the higher cultural forms of the courtly life" (Hodgson, 1974, p. 105). "The main characteristics of the Ottoman sharia judiciary," wrote another historian, "was the integration of the kadi offices into the Empire's ruling institutions and its hierarchical organization. This organization was established during the mid-sixteenth century and developed through the following centuries" (Akiba, 2005, p. 44).

From the 16th to the beginning of the 19th century, Shari'a was the dominant form of judicial system in the empire. The system comprised different types of Shari'a courts and *qadi* courts. At the top of the judicial hierarchy was the *qadi* court of Istanbul—the capital of the empire. The second tier was comprised of the *qadi* courts of Mecca and Medina. The third tier included the *qadi* courts of urban provinces such as Damascus, Baghdad, Busra, and Jerusalem. The fourth tier comprised the *qadi* courts of the empire's rural districts and provinces. This hierarchical Islamic judicial system was governed by a hierarchical system of Islamic judges and jurists centrally appointed by the emperor. At the top of the Islamic judicial hierarchy was the chief mufti (known as shaykh-al-Islam).

The chief mufti of Istanbul was the chief legal authority of the Islamic judicial system of the whole empire. He had the authority over what is in modern constitutional language called judicial review—authority to scrutinize the compatibility of the secular laws and ordinances of the emperor with the rules and principles of Shari'a law. In the provinces, the Islamic judicial system was under the control of a separate ulema elite trained in Islamic education from the madrasas (Islamic schools). The ulema elite, as historian Hodgson (1974) wrote, "had great prestige and came to have great authority and even great power . . . . As qadis and muftis they had positions of considerable impunity and were well organized" (p. 108). Like the military and civil bureaucracies, the ulema elites of the empire were also state officials and "they were closely integrated into the state. Their organizations throughout the empire were centered at Istanbul, where their head was dismissible at will by the padishah [emperor]" (Hodgson, 1974, p. 108).

The Islamic judicial system and the whole hierarchy of Islamic judges and jurists in the Ottoman Empire were governed predominantly by the Hanafi school of Shari'a law. In the whole empire, "Hanafi law became the sole law applied in official courts, at the expense of Shafi'i, Shi'i, and Maliki law" (Hodgson, 1974, p. 110). To apply the doctrines and the principles of the Hanafi school of Shari'a law throughout the judicial system was indeed an imperial mandate. "The Ottoman Sultans made use of this principle and directed the *qadis* they appointed to apply the most authoritative Hanafite views" (Peters, 2005, p. 71).

What is most significant about this aspect of the imperial adherence to the Hanafi school of Shari'a law is that throughout the centuries of existence of the Ottoman Empire, the role of *ijtihad* (analytical reasoning) and *ijma* (judicial consensus) were at the core of the application of the principles of Shari'a law within the judicial system. Peters, a historian of Islamic jurisprudence, observed again that "by using their power to delimit the qadis' jurisdiction, the Ottoman Sultans, in cooperation with the jurists, created an Ottoman-Hanafite body of Shari'a law that was unequivocal and more predictable in its application, and therefore offered more legal security" (2005, p. 72). Because of enormous complexities produced by disparate nations and cultures within the empire, Shari'a law became largely codified under the guidance of the imperial authority. Historian Hodgson (1974) observed again that:

> along with the standardization of the imperial qanun law went a standardization of the overarching Shari'ah system into which it was to fit. The result was a comprehensive and up-to-date legal system for all the diverse lands of the empire (p. 110).

Another significant factor that needs to be explored in understanding the nature of Islamic jurisprudence in the Ottoman Empire is that Shari'a Law had to coexist with secular laws and ordinances (*qanun*) promulgated by the imperial authority. The Ottoman law, as Peters (2005) explained, "was the result of the interaction between the Ottoman Hanafite, jurists, and the state officials" (Peters, 2005, p. 79). The Ottoman *qanun* was the "product of the centralized and bureaucratic character of the empire. It provided uniform standards of official conduct that were followed in all parts of the empire" (Peters, 2005, p. 72). The enforcement of criminal law was the responsibility of both religious judges (*qadis*) and the executive officials of the sultans; and in the Ottoman Empire, most of the executive officials were Christians. In the Ottoman criminal justice system, the Ottoman Sultans preserved the role of local customs and communities in criminal trials. There were legal provisions for securing testimonies from local groups and communities with respect to the criminal nature and behavior of the offenders. Thus the classical doctrine of Shari'a law had to adapt to the prevailing systems of law, politics, culture, and the modalities of governance in different lands and regions of the Ottoman Empire.

Significant also is the historical fact that by the beginning of the 19th century, the monolithic structure of the Ottoman Empire's Islamic judicial system began to change, and there began the dominance of a new secular system of justice based on secular legal codes. This began particularly during the period known as the Tanzimat reform (1839–1876). During the period of the Tanzimat reform, a dual system of justice existed in the Ottoman Empire: one was the classical Islamic system of justice based on Shari'a Law, and the other was a two-tiered judicial system based on the *qanun*—the laws and decrees of the imperial authority. The Shari'a system, although it had different types of courts in different provinces and regions, did not a have multitiered courts system based on the right to appeal (Sentop, 2008). After the Tanzimat reform in the early 19th century, "the Ottoman judicial system underwent significant changes. New courts were established, the Western system of assembled judges was introduced, and a two-stage judicial system was adopted" (Sentop, 2008, p. 156). Many historians of the Ottoman Empire claimed that since the middle of the 19th century, the Islamic judicial system was not dominant in Ottoman criminal justice (Rubin, 2009). The role of Shari'a was confined to settling disputes related to family matters. One observer of this transition in Ottoman judicial system wrote that enactment of many secular codes and the introduction of a new secular court system in the Ottoman empire in the 19th century "eventually reduced the scope of the sharia jurisdiction more or less to matters concerning personal jurisdiction and waqf" (Akiba, 2005, p. 43). The birth of modernization and the rise of modern secular states in Europe in the 19th century led to significant transformations in the classical Islamic judicial system in the Ottoman Empire (Krawietz & Reifeld, 2008).

Islamic Jurisprudence in the Mughal Empire, 1526–1757

Until the beginning of the 7th century, India was predominantly a Hindu civilization. The Indian Hindu civilization at that time was more than 2,000 years old. Islam reached India in the beginning of the 7th century during the Umayyad dynasty that ruled from its capital in Damascus, Syria. Many historians claim that the spread of Islam in India in the 7th century was an extension of trade and commercial relations that India had with the Arabs since ancient times. The political power of India, however, was not immediately changed. Until the beginning of the 13th century, power in India was in the hands of the ruling aristocracies of the Hindus. The Hindu aristocracies of India lost their political power in the beginning of the 11th century. From the 11th to the middle of the 18th century, India was ruled by three successive Islamic dynasties that came mainly from Turkey and Persia. These dynasties were the Ghaznavid Empire (1010–1187), the Ghurid Empire (1206–1525), and the Mughal Empire (1526–1757). It was during the rule of these three successive Islamic dynasties that Islamic jurisprudence remained at the center of law and justice in India.

Of all the Islamic dynasties, the Mughals in particular built a highly centralized and bureaucratized system of law and governance. During the reign of Emperor Akbar (1556–1604) especially, all the disparate regions and frontiers of India were ruled by a vastly organized and centralized bureaucracy located in Delhi—the capital of the Mughal Empire. The Mughal Empire was ruled by five major Mughal dynasties. The empire was established by Zaheeruddin Babur in 1526, and then it was successively ruled by Jalaluddin Muhammad Akbar (1556–1604), Nuruddin Muhammad Jahangir (1605–1627), Shahabuddin Muhammad Shah Jahan (1627–1658), and Moinuddin Muhammad Aurangzeb Alamgir (1658–1707).

After the death of Babur, the Mughals temporarily lost power, and India was ruled for 15 years by the Suri dynasty (Sher Shah Suri and Islam Shah Suri), which came from the Pashtun descendents in Afghanistan.

The Mughal Empire that existed for more than 2 centuries in India was an Islamic empire. Islamic Shari'a was the law of the land. But the historians of the Mughal Empire share the view that the Mughals did not come to India with the purpose of spreading Islam. The Mughals established a system of Islamic judiciary, but it was not as dominant as the Islamic judiciary established in the Ottoman Empire. Different successive Mughal rulers had different perspectives on the nature and role of Islamic jurisprudence. The judicial system established by the Mughals was dualistic in nature. The judicial system built for the Muslims of India was governed by Islamic Law, whereas the judicial system built for the non-Muslims (Hindus, Christians, Jews, and others) was governed by their respective religious codes and local customary rules. It was also dualistic in terms of regional control. In terms of the judiciary and the role of Islamic law, the Mughals controlled only the cities and urban provinces. The regions outside the cities and urban provinces were controlled by local religious codes and customary laws. The Mughal judicial system was also dualistic in terms of the organization of civil and criminal courts. The Islamic courts of the *qadis* were based on Islamic law. The imperial courts and the courts controlled by the executive officials of the emperor were governed primarily on the basis of imperial codes and ordinances.

There were four tiers of courts in the Mughal judicial system. The first tier of the courts of the capital was composed of the emperor's court, the court of chief justice, and the chief revenue court. The emperor court was governed and presided over by the emperor himself. It had jurisdiction in both civil and criminal matters. The court of chief justice was the chief Islamic or Shari'a court. It was headed by the chief *qadi* of the empire called the *Quzi-ul-quzat*, appointed by the emperor. The second tier of courts was composed of the provincial courts—the provincial governors courts, the provincial Islamic courts, and the provincial revenue courts. The third tier of courts in the Mughal judiciary was composed of district courts. There were district Islamic courts (*qazi-e-sarkar*), district criminal courts (*faujdar* courts), *kotwali* courts for petty crimes, and district revenue courts. The fourth tier was called *parganah* courts. They were comprised of *parganah* Islamic courts (*qazi-e-parganah*), *parganah kotwali* courts, and *parganah* revenue courts (Halim, 2004). In the Mughal judicial system, there was no independence of the judiciary. The judicial functions were performed, as in the Ottoman Empire, by both the Islamic judges and jurists, and the executive officials of the empire including the emperor himself.

Many historical studies have shown that the role of Islamic jurisprudence in the Mughal Empire was confined only to the capital and to urban and provincial courts. One noted Indian historian, Jadunath Sarkar (1920) noted that "every provincial capital had its qazi [Islamic judge], appointed by the Supreme Qazi of the Empire (the Qazi-ul-quzat); but there were no lower or primary courts under him, and there were no provincial courts of appeal" (p. 13). Sarkar further observed that in rural administration during the reign of the Mughals, "the Indian usage was allowed to prevail, while the foreign mode [Islamic jurisprudence] swayed almost exclusively the court (which was a personal matter of the sovereign) and the higher official circles (who drew their inspiration from Persia and Egypt)" (1920, p. 7). Local laws and customs were respected as long as they did not conflict with the core principles of Islamic jurisprudence.

Another observation made by many historians of the Mughal Empire is that the Islamic judges, jurists, and scholars of the empire were relatively free to use *ijtihad* (logic and analytical reasoning) and *ijma* (judicial consensus) in the deliberation of Shari'a Law. Within the Mughal judicial system based on the Islamic law, as historian Sarkar observed, "there was a wide latitude in the interpretation of the words of the Quran" (1920, p. 14). Sarkar further observed that "Indian judges turned to the known decisions of the pious Muslim kings and eminent Muslim jurists of the past, in the chief centres of Islamic thought and civilization outside India" (1920, p. 14). The Islamic judges carried "a digest of Islamic law and precedent compiled from the accepted Arabic writers ... [However,] their character varied with the sovereign's choice among the four schools of law, viz., the Hanafi, the Maliki, the Shafii, and the Hanbali (Sarkar, 1920, p. 15).

Another historian of criminal justice in the Mughal Empire similarly found that with respect to criminal cases, *qazis* of the empire "had a wide field to his discretion under the king's instruction" (Sangar, 1998, p. 26). The Mughal emperors, except Emperor Aurangzeb (1658–1707) and to some extent Emperor Shah Jahan (1627–1658), were liberal about the application of the Islamic law throughout the empire whose population consisted mostly of Hindus. Aurangzeb tried to expand Shari'a law in the empire by destroying the foundations of other religions. One historian noted that Aurangzeb reversed the policy of conciliation with the Hindus: "In 1659, he forbade drinking, gambling, prostitution, the use of narcotics and other vices .... In 1668, he banned music at court, imposed poll-tax on non-Muslims, ordered the destruction of Hindu temples, and sponsored the codification of Islamic laws" (Lapidus, 2002, p. 379). He employed a special cadre of religious police (*muhtasib*) to enforce Shari'a laws against drinking, blasphemy, and religious and moral crimes. The poll tax, or "*jizaz*," was imposed on the Hindus to perform their religious rituals and observe their religious festivals. Aurangzeb was an orthodox Muslim but belonged to the Hanafi school of Islamic jurisprudence. After he forcefully took over the imperial power, Aurangzeb imprisoned his father, Emperor Shah Jahan, the creator of the Taj Mahal. The orthodox and intolerant religious policy of Emperor Aurangzeb, many historians believe, was the main reason for the rise of many revolts in the empire of his time and its eventual downfall in 1707.

Tolerance of religious diversity was the principal governing philosophy of Emperor Babur—the architect of the Mughal Empire in India. In 1529, 3 years after he assumed the imperial power, Babur wrote his memoirs (*Wasiyyat-namd-i-majchfi*) in Persian. In his memoirs, Babur wrote: "The realm of Hindustan is full of diverse creeds .... It is but proper that thou, with heart cleansed of all religious bigotry, should dispense justice according to the tenets of each community" (Jaffar, 1936, p. 23). Babur further expanded his imperial philosophy stating that the temples of the Hindus should not be damaged, and "Dispense justice so that the sovereign may be happy with the subjects and likewise the subjects with their sovereign. The progress of Islam is better by the sword of kindness, not by the sword of oppression" (Jaffar, 1936, p. 23).

Both Emperor Humayun and Sher Shah were devout Sunni Muslims, but they were deeply tolerant of religious diversity. Of all the Mughal emperors, Akbar, however, was surprisingly modern in terms of his imperial policy and the role of Islamic jurisprudence in the dispensing of justice in a land of competing religious groups and communities. One historian commented that Akbar's reign "was characterized by the freedom of worship and the liberty of consciousness" (Jaffar, 1936, p. 131). Akbar was a devout Sunni Muslim, and he "appointed Qazis and muftis in every part of his kingdom in order to administer justice in accordance with the code of Islam" (Jaffar, 1936, p. 117), but he advised his religious judges and jurists to apply reason and not bigotry in the dispensing of justice. In 1582, Akbar prohibited the imposition of the death penalty by the provincial governors and the *qazis* without his approval (Sangar, 1998). The same imperial policy was upheld in the Ottoman Empire. In 1545, Khoja Chelebi, the chief mufti of the Ottoman Empire (shaykh-al-Islam) presented a fatwa that in applying Shari'a Law, the *qadis* must derive "their authority only from the monarch, and bound to apply the Shari'a according to his directives" (Hodgson, 1974, p. 110). Historian Hodgson commented that "this was a somewhat strongest form of the same principle that Akbar asserted in India a few years later" (1974, p. 110).

Akbar's imperial policy is contained in a remarkable treatise called *Akbarnama*. The third volume of *Akbarnama* was written by Akbar's adviser and court historian, Abul Fazl ibn Mubarak, and it is called the *Ain-i-Akbari*. The *Ain-i-Akbari* is one of the most precious historical documents from the Middle Ages, and it is comparable to the historical significance of the Code of Hammurabi. Most Muslims believe that idolatry and polytheism are great sins. Abul Fazal wrote in the *Ain-i-Akbari* that "the symbols and the images that Hindus carry are not idols, but merely are there to keep their minds from wandering . . . only serving and worshiping God is required" (Blochmann, 1927/1993). This signifies Akbar's imperial policy toward Hindus and the greatness of his ideas on the freedom of religion. Akbar once said to a group of religious judges and scholars that "we ought to bring the different religions of India into one, but in such a fashion that they should be one and all: with greatest advantage of taking what is good in every creed and discarding the remainder" (Jaffar, 1936, p. 127). Akbar was a great follower of Sufism, the mystical philosophy of Islam. He even ventured to create a new religion. The historian called it Din-i-Ilahi. Akbar saw his new religion primarily as a political code and not a religious creed "prepared by a politician and not prophet, in accordance with the conditions of the country, the tendencies of the times, and the sentiments of the subjects" (Jaffar, 1936, p. 130).

In the previous sections, the histories of the empires of the Ottomans and the Mughals were briefly discussed to emphasize the point that an understanding of the nature and role of the state is crucial in understanding the rise and expansion of Islamic law and justice (Feldman, 2008; Janin & Kahlmeyer, 2007; Peters, 2005). In any comparative study of criminal justice in the countries that were ruled for centuries, before the expansion of European colonialism, by the Islamic empires, an understanding of how and to what extent the Islamic jurisprudence and Shari'a Law governed and transformed their local institutions of the state, law, and justice is needed, as is an understanding of the extent the local institutions of the state, law, and justice changed and reformed Islamic jurisprudence and Shari'a Law.

■ Summary

Understanding the nature of criminal justice in the Muslim societies of the world is significant in understanding criminal justice among the world's societies. There are 57 countries where Muslims form the majority of the population. Out of the world's 7 billion people, about 1.57 billion are Muslims. Muslims live in all countries and regions of the world, but the largest concentrations are in Asia, the Middle East, and North Africa. Muslims are projected to make up 26.4% of the world's population in 2030 (Pew Research Center, 2011, p. 1). In Europe, there are about 38 million Muslims. The United States has the largest Muslim population in the Americas at 2.5 million. Among the 27 countries belonging to the European Union, highest number of Muslims is in Germany (4 million; Pew Research Center, 2009).

One of the points made in this chapter is that a traditional system of criminal justice, where the state and religion are seen as inseparable and crime and sin and crime and morality are perceived as indivisible, can emerge only within the context of a theocratic state. There are only two theocratic states in the modern world: Saudi Arabia and Iran. All Muslim societies are not theocratic in nature and Shari'a Law is not the dominant tradition in law and justice in most of the Muslim societies of the world. An assertion has also been pursued in this chapter, on the basis of several citations from the Quran and the Hadith, that Islamic criminal justice is based on a number of principles that are also at the core of modern criminal justice and the due process of law such as justice and fairness, presumption of innocence, strict application of the rules of evidence (particularly in *hudud* and *qisas* crimes), proportionality between crime and punishment, the right of protection against unreasonable searches and seizures, the right to have counsel, the role of mitigating and exculpatory circumstances (*ta'zir* crimes), rehabilitation on the basis of forgiveness and repentance, and the criminalization of torture. The Quran prohibits the use of beatings, torture, and inhuman treatment.

Islamic criminal justice, based on the divine revelations of the Quran and the teachings of the Prophet Muhammad (the Sunna or Hadith), divides criminal offenses into three major categories: *hudud* offenses, *qisas* offenses, and *ta'zir* offenses. Punishments for these different offenses are based on three different philosophies. Punishments for *hudud* crimes, such as adultery, fornication, highway robbery, and theft, are divinely ordained and mandatory. They are based on the philosophy of deterrence. The Quran, however, has explicitly said that physical punishment mandated for *hudud* crimes can be or should be avoided on the basis of forgiveness and repentance. Punishments for *qisas* crimes (murder for murder or an eye for an eye) are also divinely ordained, and they are based on the philosophy of retribution and restitution. The Quran again has explicitly mandated that the state does not have the right to punish an offender who committed *qisas* crimes if he or she is forgiven by the victim or victim's family members. In the case of forgiveness for a *qisas* crime, the Quran has a provision for the victim or his or her family to receive financial compensation (restitution or blood money) from the offender or offender's family and relatives. The punishments for *ta'zir* crimes—the third category of offenses in Islamic criminal justice—such as drug addiction, bank robbery, bribery, corruption, and other statutory offenses are not divinely ordained.

There are four major schools of Islamic jurisprudence, and they have four competing ideas of how Shari'a Law should be understood, interpreted, and implemented within the Islamic system of criminal justice. These schools are the Hanafites, Malikites, Shafiites, and Hanbalites. All four schools emerged within 250 years after the death of the Prophet Muhammad in 632. One of the major differences among these four schools is the extent to which the *ijtihad*—the methodology of logic and analytical reasoning—of the sacred scriptures of the Quran and the Sunna is acceptable as a basis for Islamic jurisprudence. They also differ about the role of *ijma* (judicial consensus) in the interpretation of the Quran and the Sunna. It is believed that the ideas of the Hanafi school include some of the most liberal interpretations of the Islamic law. The Hanafi school made *ijtihad* the central methodology for the development of Islamic jurisprudence. The advocates of the Hanafi school believe that with application of analogical reasoning (*ijtihad*) and consensus (*ijma*) among the Islamic scholars and jurists, Islamic law and jurisprudence can be adapted to different times and spaces. The Shafiites and the Hanbalites, on the other hand, form two of the most orthodox schools of Islamic jurisprudence. The adherents of the Shafii and Hanbali schools reject the significance of analytical reasoning (*ijtihad*) and consensus (*ijma*) in the understanding and interpretation of Islamic jurisprudence and Shari'a Law.

The examination of the nature of criminal justice in the Ottoman and Mughal empires in the late Middle Ages reveal that the implementation of Shari'a Law and Islamic jurisprudence significantly depend on the political nature and ideology of the state. In the medieval state of the Ottoman Empire, criminal justice was based on the ideas of the Hanafi school of Islamic jurisprudence. It was because of the imperial adherence to the Hanafi school of Shari'a Law that throughout the Ottoman Empire, the roles of *ijtihad* and *ijma* were at the core of the application of the principles of Shari'a Law in the Ottoman judicial system. Because of the liberal interpretation of Islamic jurisprudence by the Ottoman ruling elite, Islamic criminal law had to coexist with secular law and ordinances (*qanun*) promulgated by the imperial authority. Beginning in the mid-19th century, Islamic criminal justice in the Ottoman Empire coexisted with a secular system of justice based on secular legal codes.

In medieval India, the Mughals established a system of Islamic judiciary, but it was not as dominant as the Islamic judiciary established in the Ottoman Empire. Different Mughal rulers had different perspectives about the nature and role of Islamic jurisprudence. The judicial system established by the Mughals was dualistic in nature. The judicial system built for the Muslims of India was governed by Islamic law. The judicial system for non-Muslims (Hindus, Christians, Jews, and others) was governed by their respective religious codes and local customary rules. It was also dualistic in terms of regional control. In terms of the judiciary and the role of Islamic law, the Mughals controlled only the cities and urban provinces. The regions outside the cities and urban provinces were controlled by local religious codes and customary laws. The Mughal judicial system was also dualistic in terms of the organization of civil and criminal courts. The Islamic courts of the *qadis* were based on Islamic law. The imperial courts and the courts controlled by the executive officials of the emperor were governed primarily on the basis of secular imperial codes and ordinances.

Because of the liberal political perspective of most of the Mughal emperors, the Islamic judges, jurists, and scholars of the empire were relatively free to use *ijtihad* (logic and analytical reasoning) and *ijma* (judicial consensus) in the deliberation of Shari'a law. Within the Mughal judicial system based on Islamic Law, as historian Sarkar observed, "there was a wide latitude in the interpretation of the words of the Quran" (1920, p. 14).

■ Discussion Questions

1. Discuss the significance of understanding the nature of Islamic criminal justice for a comparative analysis of criminal justice among the world's societies. How are some of the intrasystemic and extrasystemic issues in Islamic criminal justice different from those of modern systems of criminal justice?

2. What are the four major schools of Islamic jurisprudence, and how are they different from one another in terms of their interpretations of the nature of Shari'a Law? Focus particularly on the differences between the Hanafi and Hanbali schools of Islamic jurisprudence.

3. What are the sources of Shari'a Law, and what is the nature of substantive criminal law in Islamic jurisprudence? Explain, citing some sources from the Quran, the differences between *hudud* offenses and *qisas* offenses and *hudud* punishments and *qisas* punishments.

4. Outline the nature of procedural criminal law in Islamic jurisprudence with respect to some of the due process laws in modern criminal justice. Focus particularly on your understanding of the application of strict rules of evidence in Shari'a Law in cases of adultery, sodomy, and fornication. Give examples.

5. Many Islamic scholars have commented that Islamic jurisprudence is highly flexible and compatible with modern criminal justice. Expand this statement in light of your understanding of some of the revelations of the Quran with respect to procedural criminal law in Islamic jurisprudence. Focus particularly on the notions of justice on the basis of forgiveness and repentance.

6. Shari'a Law was the basis of criminal justice in the medieval Islamic empire of the Ottomans for almost 500 years. How was Shari'a Law applied in the dispensing of law and justice in the Ottoman Empire, and to what extent was it influenced by the specific political nature of the Ottoman state? Give examples.

7. What are the similarities and differences in the application of Shari'a Law in the medieval Islamic empires of the Ottomans and the Mughals? What specific lessons do we learn from the criminal justice systems of these two empires about the role of Shari'a Law in disparate lands and regions of the Islamic civilization? Give examples.

■ References

Abdullah, H. F. (2011). *Characteristics of* hudud*: The Islamic criminal law.* Retrieved from http://groups .yahoo.com/group/alFikrah/message/21835.

Akiba, J. (2005). From *Kadi* to *Naib*: Reorganization of the Ottoman Sharia judiciary in the Tanzimat period. In C. Imber, K. Kiyotaki, & R. Murphey (Eds.), *Frontiers of Ottoman studies: State, province, and the West.* New York, NY: St. Martin Press.

Armanios, F. (2004). *Islam: Sunnis and Shiites*. Washington, DC: The Library of Congress, Congressional Research Service.

Armstrong, K. (2002). *Islam: A short history*. New York, NY: Modern Library—A Division of the Random House.

Arnold, T. W. (2010). *The caliphate*. New Delhi, India: Adam Publisher and Distributors.

Bassiouni, M. C. (1998). Foreword. In M. Lippman, S. McConville, & M. Yerushalmi. *Islamic criminal law and procedure: Religious fundamentalism v. modern law*. Westport, CT: Praeger.

Blochmann, H. (tr.). (1993). *Ain-i-Akbari by Abul Fazl Allami*. Calcutta, India: The Asiatic Society of Bengal. (Originally published in 1927.)

Coulson, N. J. (2011). *Conflicts and tensions in Islamic jurisprudence*. Chicago, IL: The University of Chicago Press.

Feldman, N. (2008). *The fall and rise of the Islamic state*. Princeton, NJ: Prince ton University Press.

Haleem, M. A., Sherif, A. O., & Daniels, K. (Eds.). (2003). *Criminal justice in Islam: judicial procedure in the Shari'a*. New York, NY: I. B. Tauris & Co.

Halim, M. A. (2004). *The legal system of Bangladesh: A comparative study of problems and procedure in legal institutions*. Dhaka, Bangladesh: CCB Foundation.

Hallaq, W. B. (2009). *An introduction to Islamic law*. New York, NY: Cambridge University Press.

Hersi, R. (2009). *A value oriented legal theory for Muslim countries in the 21st century: A comparative study of both Islamic law and common law systems*. Cornell Law School Inter-University Graduate Student Conference Papers. Paper 29. Retrieved from http://scholarship.law.cornell.edu/lps_clacp/29.

Hodgson, M. G. S. (1974). *The venture of Islam: Conscience and history in a world civilization* (Vol. 3). Chicago, IL: University of Chicago Press.

Jaffar, S. M. (1936). *The Mughal Empire from Babar to Aurangzeb*. Peshawar, Pakistan:, Ripon Printing Press.

Janin, H., & Kahlmeyer, A. (2007). *Islamic law: The Sharia from Muhammad's time to the present*. Jefferson, NC: McFarland & Company.

Kamali, M. H. (2005). *Principles of Islamic jurisprudence*. Cambridge, England: Islamic Textbook Society.

Kamali, M. H. (2008). *Shari'ah law: An introduction*. Oxford, England: One World Publications.

Krawietz, B., & Reifeld, H. (2008). *Islam and the rule of law: Between Sharia and secularization*. Berlin, Germany: Konrad Adenauer Stiftung.

Kusha, H. R. (2004). *Defendant rights: A reference handbook*. Santa Barbara, CA: ABC-CLIO.

Lapidus, I. M. (2002). *A history of Islamic societies*. New York, NY: Cambridge University Press.

Lippman, M., McConville, S., & Yerushalmi, M. (1988). *Islamic criminal law and procedure*. Westport, CT: Praeger.

Madkoar, M. S. (2011). *Human rights from an Islamic worldview: An outline of* Hudud, Ta'zir, & Qisas. Retrieved from www.muhajabah.com/docstorage/hudud.htm.

Mohamed, M. B. (2011). *The concept of* Ta'zir *in the Islamic criminal law*. Retrieved from www.sunniforum.com/forum/showthread.php?6205-The-Concept-of-Ta%92zir-in-Islamic-Criminal-Law.

Peters, R. (2005). *Crime and punishment in Islamic law: Theory and practice from the sixteenth to the twenty-first century*. Cambridge, England: Cambridge University Press.

Pew Research Center. (2009). *Mapping the global Muslim population: A report on the size and distribution of the world's Muslim population*. Washington, DC: The Pew Forum on Religion and Public Life.

Pew Research Center. (2011). *The future of the global Muslim population: Projections for 2010–2030.* Washington, DC: The Pew Forum on Religion and Public Life.

Rubin, S. (2009). Ottoman judicial change in the age of modernity: A Reappraisal. *History Compass, 7*(1), 119–140.

Sadiq, R. (2009). Islam's Fourth Amendment: Search and seizures and in Islamic doctrine and Muslim practice. *Georgetown Journal of International Law, 40*(3), 703–806.

Sahih Al-Bukhari, S. (2011). *Blood money (Ad-Diyat)* (M. M. Khan, Trans.). Retrieved from www.searchtruth .com/hadith_books.php.

Saifee, S. (2003). Penumbras, privacy, and the death of morals-based legislation: Comparing U.S. constitutional law with the inherent right of privacy in Islamic jurisprudence. *Fordham International Law Journal, 27*(1), 369–454.

Sangar, S. P. (1998). *Crime and punishment in Mughal India.* New Delhi, India: Reliance Publishing House.

Sarkar, J. (1920). *Mughal administration.* Patna University Readership Lectures. Calcutta, India: M. C. Sarkar & Sons.

Sentop, M. (2008). Court of law. In G. Agoston & B. Masters (Eds.), *Encyclopedia of the Ottoman Empire* (p. 156). New York, NY: Facts on File.

Terrill, R. J. (2009). *World criminal justice systems: A survey.* Southington, CT: Anderson Publishing.

The Institute of Islamic Knowledge. (1997). *Al-Qur'an: The guidance for mankind* (Muhammad Farooq-i-Azam Malik, Trans.). Houston, Texas: Author.

West, D. J., & Green, R. (1997). *Sociolegal control of homosexuality: A multi-nation comparison.* New York, NY, and London, England: Plenum Press.

Islamic Jurisprudence, Shari'a Law, and Criminal Justice in Saudi Arabia and Iran

■ Introduction

We examined the nature of Shari'a Law and Islamic jurisprudence and the specific nature of their applications in the traditional systems of criminal justice in the medieval Islamic empires of the Ottomans and the Mughals in India. There are 59 countries in the world where Muslims form the majority of the population, but Shari'a Law is not the foundation of criminal justice in most of these countries. Some of them, such as Iraq, Indonesia, Nigeria, Malaysia, and Pakistan, have been trying to combine Shari'a Law with their existing legal traditions (i.e., common law tradition and civil law tradition), but criminal justice is not exclusively based on Shari'a Law in any of these countries (Otto, 2010). Shari'a Law is the exclusive foundation of criminal justice in only two countries of the Muslim world—Saudi Arabia and Iran. The recent resurgence of interest in the study of Shari'a Law, particularly in Europe and North America, has grown not because of its wide application in the Muslim countries of the world, but because of the increasing globalization of the Wahhabist perspective of Islam—a perspective that believes in the divine legitimacy of "jihad" against those who do not believe in the Wahhabist interpretation of Islam. It is this globalization of Wahhabist ideology, particularly its increasing expansion among the some groups of Muslims in Europe and North America, that has become a major concern for criminal justice in these regions. In the United States, the United Kingdom, France, and Germany, demands among many Muslims are growing for the integration of Shari'a Law to those countries' existing system of legal traditions. France has recently criminalized the observance of a number of Shari'a rites and rituals in public places. In the United Kingdom, many Muslim-majority enclaves are unilaterally imposing Shari'a ban on drugs, drinking, porn, and prostitution. These issues are bringing new stresses and challenges for the criminal justice systems in these countries. For a student of comparative criminal justice today, it is imperative to understand the nature of Shari'a Law and its practice in Muslim countries. It is imperative also to understand the dynamics behind the recent rise and globalization of radical political Islam imbibed with the ideology of Wahhabism. It is in this context that this chapter will examine the specific nature of applications of Shari'a Law and Islamic jurisprudence in Saudi Arabia and Iran.

■ Islamic Jurisprudence, Shari'a Law, and Criminal Justice in Saudi Arabia

The state of Saudi Arabia was established in 1932 when a number of tribal regions of the Arabian Peninsula were combined under the control of a centralized monarchical government. The Saudi monarchy was established by the military conquest of different tribes and tribal regions by the armies of the Al-Saud family under the leadership of Abd Al Aziz ibn Saud. Since then, the hereditary Saudi monarchy has been governing through the kings and princes of the Saud family. Saudi Arabia is not only a monarchical but also a theocratic form of government. The Saudi monarchy does not have a separate constitution. Its law and justice system is based on the holy scriptures of the Quran. Any systemic comparative understanding of criminal justice in Saudi Arabia and its nature of governance on the basis of Shari'a Law needs to begin with understanding the specific nature of the formation of the Saudi state, the nature of the state ideology, and the historical nature of law and justice in the tribes and regions that now constitute the monarchy of Saudi Arabia. One historian of Saudi Arabia noted that "the dominant narrative in the history of Saudi Arabia in the twentieth century is that of state formation, a process that started in the interior of Arabia under the leadership of Al-Sa'ud" (Al-Rasheed, 2002, p. 1).

Social and Historical Context of the Kingdom of Saudi Arabia

One of the most significant features of the Kingdom of Saudi Arabia is that the regions that now comprise the monarchy were historically at the periphery of the power and influence of the major Islamic empires. During the three successive Islamic dynasties that ruled Islamic civilization for more than 1,200 years—the Umayyad dynasty (7th–8th century), the Abbasid dynasty (8th–13th century), and the Ottoman dynasty (13th–20th century)—the regions that now make up the Kingdom of Saudi Arabia were politically and culturally isolated. One historian noted that before the rise of Wahhabism in the eighteenth century, "there was no all-Arabian power, and no peace or stability in the peninsula. For centuries, Arabia had been fragmented, mostly into small or tiny oasis states or their associations, nomadic tribes or their confederations" (Vassiliev, 1998, p. 59).

The remarkable achievements of Islamic civilizations in the transformation of law, science, and justice and the great philosophical ideas of such Islamic scholars as Al-Biruni (973–1048), ibn Sina (980–1037), Al-Ghazali (1058–1111), and ibn Rushd (1126–1198) did not reach Saudi Arabia's tribes and tribal regions—regions that remained vastly separated from one another for centuries. The physical terrain of Saudi Arabia comprises of about 830,000 square miles, of which about 95% is desert lands. Even the Ottoman Empire, which deeply penetrated into each and every major region of the Middle East, left the social and political lives of the small towns of Mecca, Medina, and Jidda untouched. Historians observed that there were small Ottoman military garrisons in Mecca, Medina, and Jidda, "and officials were sent from Istanbul to Mecca and Medina. Nevertheless, Ottoman power in Hijaz was nominal and local rulers generally enjoyed a substantial degree of autonomy in local affairs" (Vassiliev, 1998, p. 59).

The Portuguese, Dutch, French, and British had a presence in the Arabian Peninsula and had trade relations with some of its regions beginning in the mid-17th century. After the decline of the Ottoman Empire in the early 20th century, the major regions that now comprise Saudi Arabia—Najd, Hasa, Hijaz, and Asir—came under the control of the British colonial empire, but they were never formally colonized (Al-Rasheed, 2002), and hence, they never were faced and challenged by the social and historical forces of modernity before the end of the 20th century. The historians observed that before the rise of Wahhabism, "Arabia had largely been left to itself for several decades" (Vassiliev, 1998, p. 60). Understanding this history of the relative isolation of the tribes and tribal regions of the Kingdom of Saudi Arabia from the social and political dynamics of the Islamic civilizations and the civilization of the West for centuries is vital for understanding its unique nature of law and justice in the contemporary period.

Equally significant for a comparative understanding of crime and justice in Saudi Arabia is an understanding of the social and political structures of the tribes and tribal regions that now comprise this unique monarchy. At the advent of this new monarchy in the 1930s, its distant and disparate regions were still under a medieval system of politics and governance. Historians observed that "the slow development of the economy and the stable age-old social structures allow us to assume that life in the nineteenth and twentieth centuries in Arabia had not changed greatly since the medieval times" (Vassiliev, 1998, p. 30). They further observed that "Arabia had no towns in the strict sense, in other words where the greater part of the population subsisted on means other than agriculture. Mecca was an outstanding exception. The notions of 'town' and 'large oasis' mostly coincided Al-Diriya" (Vassiliev,

1998, p. 34). The major economic activity of these regions included irrigated farming and nomadic animal husbandry. Politically, each oasis state and tribal group was led by a sheikh who was "a patriarchal elder and the manager of economic activities. He guided the tribes' migrations, allocated pastures and wells and chose the time and place to pitch the camp. The sheikh might act a judge, or arbiter in disputes" (Vassiliev, 1998, p. 51).

For civilian matters, each sheikh was aided by a tribal council (*majlis*). The tribal councils had major responsibilities in controlling crime and dispensing law and justice. For the conduct and the control of external invasions, each sheikh was aided also by a group of military personnel under the command of a military leader called an *aqid*. Traditionally, the sheikhs received annual tributes from different seminomadic groups and settled peasant communities in return for providing their security and protections. When a number of oasis states formed a larger political community, it was headed by an amir (king or a prince).

The social structure of the tribal regions of Arabia was patriarchal, despotic, militaristic, and hierarchical in nature. At the apex of power and social status was the Bedouin nobility consisting of the families of the amirs, the sheikhs, and their military vassals. The members of the nobility placed themselves above the common Bedouins, peasants, and slaves. The second stratum of the Arab tribal societies was formed by two groups of Bedouins: the camel breeders and sheep or goat breeders. The camel-breeding nomads, however, "were considered genuine bedouin" (as quoted in Vassiliev, 1998, p. 32). The third stratum was composed of the peasants and craftsmen. The craftsmen particularly were "more despised in Arabian society than were the 'lower' tribes. Professional handicrafts, especially weaving, were considered the worst occupation for an Arab" (Vassiliev, 1998, p. 57). At the bottom of the social structure were the slaves and freedmen. "Slavery persisted in Arabia for many centuries. Most slaves were brought to the peninsula from East and Central Africa . . . . The slave trade was concentrated chiefly in Mecca but was conducted in other towns, too, such as Hufaf and Muscat" (Vassiliev, 1998, p. 49). Most of the Arab slaves were a part of the families of their masters. The female slaves worked as "concubines, mainly of the urban nobility" (Vassiliev, 1998, p. 49).

In the 18th century, there were three different systems of justice in the regions that now comprise the Kingdom of Saudi Arabia. The first was the Ottoman system of justice that was based on the Hanafi school of Shari'a Law. In the regions under the control of the Ottoman system of justice, particularly in the province of Hijaz and the city of Mecca, the *qadis* (Islamic judges) appointed by the Ottoman sultans were responsible for dispensing law and justice. Under the Ottoman system, the *qadis* were allowed to use *ijtihad* (logical reasoning) and *ijma* (judicial consensus) in the interpretation and implementation of Shari'a Law. Under the Ottoman system of justice, Shari'a Law was used also in combination with secular laws (decrees and ordinances of the Ottoman sultans) and customary laws. The second system of justice was the system that was found in the region of Najd. "Under this system, an Amir (similar to regional governor), with the assistance of one judge, represented the law. The Amir would try to solve the disputes submitted to him or refer them to the judge for a final ruling" (Al-Farsy, 1991, p. 34). The third was the local tribal system of justice based on customary tribal laws. "Here, the conflicting parties would refer their disputes to the individual tribe's law, and its own lawyers would give decisions according to precedent" (Al-Farsy, 1991,

p. 34). One of the major customary laws among the tribes of Arabia was the law of the blood feud. It was the law of revenge and the law of vengeance. One historian found that "the blood feud among the Bedouins embraced the relatives up to the fifth generation. Whole groups of kinsmen affected by blood feud would leave their tribes and seek refuge with the powerful sheikh of an alien tribe" (Vassiliev, 1998, p. 42). The victims or their families were disgraced forever if they neglected "the duty of revenge . . . . That hatred is inherited by sons from fathers and ceases only with the extinction of one of the kin unless the families agree to sacrifice the guilty or to pay the blood money" (Vassiliev, 1998, p. 42).

Under the customary laws of the Bedouins, raiding (*ghazu*) and plundering of the resources of other tribes were legal and justified. But they were not legal and justified within the tribe. As one historian noted: "Raiding was considered the most noble occupation, and the dream of plunder consistently excited the bedouin's imagination. Participation in *ghazu* was voluntary, but in practice, the bedouin, especially the young men, could not decline invitation" (Vassiliev, 1998, p. 46).

The Ideological Context of the Kingdom: The Rise of Wahhabism

The crime and justice system of Saudi Arabia is based on a strict and a conservative interpretation of the Islamic jurisprudence and Shari'a Law. This system came into being as a result of the monarchy's more than two centuries of political associations with an Islamic reformist movement described as the rise of Wahhabism. Wahhabism is an Islamic reformist movement that was started by an Arab religious scholar named Muhammad ibn Abd al-Wahhab in the middle of the 18th century. Abd al-Wahhab (1703–1792) was born in a religious family and was brought up in the region of Najd. The historians of this Islamic reformist movement claimed that from his childhood, Abd al-Wahhab began to be frustrated about the corruption of the religion of Islam through the infusions of the tribal beliefs and rituals of polytheism. As a young man, he travelled to Mecca, Medina, and other centers of Islamic learning in the region to learn more about the basic teachings of Islam. He traveled to Baghdad, Damascus, and many cities of Iran and India for firsthand knowledge about the nature and practice of Islam in those regions. After returning from these religious trips, he returned to Najd and started preaching his own philosophy of Islam that is now described as Wahhabism. One of his best known books, which was translated into English, is *The Book of Divine Unity* or *Book of Monotheism* (*Kitab-al-Tawhid*).

Wahhabism is not a new religious sect or a religious cult. It is, rather, a call to return to the fundamentalist interpretation of Islamic life and Islamic law and jurisprudence. It is based on the claim that when Islam reached different lands, peoples, cultures, and civilizations, it began to be corrupted under the influence of competing ideas and interpretations of disparate groups of religious scholars and political regimes. Islam began to deviate from the basic principles of the Quran and the Sunna, the advocates of Wahhabism claimed, through the use of *ijtihad*, *ijma*, and *bida* (innovation of ideas without precedent). Abd al-Wahhab believed that the Ottoman sultans destroyed the basic principles of Islam by adhering to the Hanafi school of jurisprudence that allows open interpretations of the Quran and the Sunna by the *qadis*. "Because the Ottoman sultans did not conform to his vision of Islam, Abd-al-Wahhab declared that they were apostates and worthy of death" (Armstrong, 2002, p. 135). The advocates of Wahhabism believed that the Hanbali school of Islamic jurisprudence provided the most accurate interpretation of Islamic jurisprudence and Shari'a Law. Abd-al-Wahhab "was a typical reformer, in the tradition of Ibn Taymiyyah [an *alim* of Damascas, 1263–1328]. He believed that the current crisis was best met by a fundamentalist return to the Quran and *sunnah*" (Armstrong, 2002, p. 135).

There are four distinctive ideas of the reformist movement of Wahhabism. First, it suggested that Islam is purely a monotheist religion. There is no space in Islam for the practice of polytheistic rituals such as idol worship, worship of the cults of the Islamic saints, offering prayers at the graves of the saints or building mosques on their graves. In pure Islam, prayer must be offered only to Allah, whose authority is undividable and not to be shared. Among the Arabian tribes and tribal regions in the 18th century, many historians noted, "The cult of saints was widespread. Pre-Muslim religious beliefs and cults—sorcery, idol worship, sun worship, animism, fetishism, and cult of ancestors—coexisted and became interwoven with Islam" (Vassiliev, 1998, p. 72). The second important message of Wahhabism is that all authorities of mediations between Allah and his believers in Islam must be abandoned. Wahhabism even prohibits the worshipping of the Prophet Muhammad. "Pious people, and the Prophet's Companions and saints should not be revered excessively and mosques should not be erected above their graves. Too much care should not be taken of the graves, and gravestones should not be idolized" (Vassiliev, 1998, p. 74). Third is the idea that the paying of *zakat* is not voluntary but mandatory in Islam. The fourth is the notion that jihad is mandatory and obligatory to protect, preserve, and propagate the true meaning of Islam. Abd al-Wahhab preached the sanctity of monotheism and was against "all forms of mediation between God and believers" (Al-Rasheed, 2002, p. 16). He preached that it was mandatory to pay *zakat* (tax to the leader of the Islamic community) and it was an obligation to declare "jihad" (holy war) "against those who did not follow these principles" (Al-Rasheed, 2002, p. 16).

The rise of the Wahhabi movement in Islam and the rise of the Saudi state under the leadership of the family of Al-Saud are intimately connected. The Wahhabi movement was born and expanded in the same town of Njad where the family of Al-Saud became politically most dominant in the middle of the 18th century. After the Wahhabi movement was born, it needed political support for its expansion across the Arab regions. Abd-al-Wahhab "tried to create an enclave of pure faith, based in his view of the first ummah of the seventh century" (Armstrong, 2002, p. 135). Abd-al-Wahhab's reformist ideas did not immediately grow and expand from within. They had to be forced from above through the idea of jihad—a military expedition for the expansion of true Islam (Al-Rasheed, 2002). The Al-Saud family at the same time was looking for a broader ideology to bring the disparate regions of Arabia under the control of a centralized state. For his radical and puritanical views, Abd al-Wahhab was not very well liked in his native city of al-Uyayna. He was expelled from al-Uyayna in 1744. Abd al-Wahhab then moved to the Najd region—a region dominated by the Saud tribe. "There in the village of Dariyah, he converted the Saud tribe [into Wahhabism], which was led by the chieftain Muhammad ibn-Saud" (Janin & Kahlmeyer, 2007, p. 92).

The marriage between Wahhabism and the political ambition of the Saud family gave birth to the idea of the modern Kingdom of Saudi Arabia in the middle of the 18th century. "Wahhabism provided a novel impetus for political centralisation. Expansion by conquest was the only mechanism . . . to rise above the limited confines of a specific settlement. With the importance of *jihad* in Wahhabi teachings, conquest of new territory became possible" (Al-Rasheed, 2002, p. 19). The new religio-political doctrine of Wahhabism "impregnated the Sa'udi leadership with a new force which proved to be crucial for the consolidation and expansion of Sa'udi rule" (Al-Rasheed, 2002, p. 19). The tribes who willingly accepted Wahhabism "were expected to swear allegiance to its religio-political leadership and demonstrate their loyalty by agreeing to fight for its cause and pay *zakat* to its representatives. Those who resisted were subjected to raids that threatened their livelihood" (Al-Rasheed, 2002, p. 19). The first Saudi state was created in 1744, but it was destroyed by the armies of the Ottoman Empire in 1818. The first Saudi state included the cities of Mecca and Medina. In 1824, the Saud family established the second Saudi state (1824–1891), conquering more regions under the ideological banner of Wahhabism. Finally, after about 180 years of military expeditions and the consolidation of different Arab regions under the central political leadership of the Saud family based on the ideology of Wahhabism, the modern Kingdom of Saudi Arabia was born in 1932. The present system of law and justice in Saudi Arabia, therefore, cannot be properly examined without understanding its ideological roots in the Islamic reformist movement of Wahhabism.

Architecture of the Present System of Criminal Justice in Saudi Arabia

The present system of law and justice on the basis of the Wahhabi perspective or the Hanbali school of Islamic jurisprudence began to evolve in the Saudi monarchy in the 1920s. From that time, however, the history of law and justice in Saudi Arabia can be described as a struggle for the kings and *qadis* to create a balance between Shari'a Law and modernity within the sociopolitical dynamics of the evolving kingdom. The struggle, in other words, is about the proper understanding of the nature of "*ijtihad* freedom" (Vogel, 2000, p. 95) that can be given to Islamic judges and jurists for the interpretation of Shari'a Law—for the application of the Quran and Sunna in criminal justice. It can be noted here that the same struggle or challenges about the proper understanding of the nature of *ijtihad* freedom with respect to Shari'a Law was faced by the sultans of the Ottoman Empire and the emperors of the Mughal dynasties in India in the late Middle Ages.

The present system of Shari'a law and justice in Saudi Arabia has evolved through three stages. The first stage began in 1927 when King Abdul Aziz Al Saud conquered the western region of the Arabian Peninsula that included the cities of Mecca and Medina. Before 1927, the Shari'a judicial system of the Arab tribal regions was relatively simple. The judicial system of each town was in the hands of single ulema appointed by the Saudi sheikhs. The ulema worked with the amir of the town or the region to settle disputes. The criminal procedure was "almost entirely oral, records few, and adjudication expeditions in the extreme. Courts imposed no fees. The only appeal would be through complaint to the ruler who would refer most matters to senior ulemas" (Vogel, 2000, p. 88). In 1927, King Abdul Aziz introduced a new judicial model for Hejaz and the cities of Mecca and Medina. Before it was conquered by King Abdul Aziz in 1927, Hejaz already had a relatively more organized system of courts introduced by the Ottoman Empire. The Ottoman courts in Mecca and Medina were headed by a chief judge who was almost always recruited from the Hanafi school of Islamic jurisprudence. The chief judge was aided by three deputy judges, who were recruited from the other three schools of Islamic jurisprudence (Vogel, 2000). In 1927, King Abdul Aziz, in a written royal decree, extended the Ottoman judicial system as a new model for law and justice in Hejaz. He introduced a multilayered courts system, made provisions for the appointment of judges from all four schools of Islamic jurisprudence, and introduced a new system of appeal for criminal cases and convictions, particularly for those related to the death penalty and decapitation. The new model had a two-tiered system of criminal trial courts. The first tier, known as Summary Courts, was responsible for all criminal matters except the adjudications for *hudud* crimes. The trial and adjudication for *hudud* crimes were the responsibility of the second tier, called Great Shari'a Courts, that existed mostly in large cities. In the Great Shari'a Courts, criminal cases were heard by "panels of three judges" (Vogel, 2000, p. 90). The appeals in criminal cases were heard by a Supreme Judicial Council and a Board of Review. "Theoretically, above the supreme judicial authority is always the king himself" (Vogel, 2000, p. 91). The second stage of the evolution of the Shari'a judicial system started when this Hejaz model of the judiciary was extended to the whole kingdom in 1957. This extension of the judiciary of Hejaz through the entire kingdom became an effort to develop a more centralized system of governance, law, and justice in the kingdom in the 1960s. In 1953, King Abdul Aziz created the Council of Ministers, and in 1970, King Faisal created the Ministry of Justice "to assume the administration of the courts" (Vogel, 2000, p. 91).

The third stage of the evolution of the Shari'a judiciary in Saudi Arabia began with the promulgation of the Law of the Judiciary in 1975 (Royal Embassy of Saudi Arabia, 2012a). Article 1 of the Law of the Judiciary states that "judges are independent and, in the administration of justice, they shall be subject to no authority other than the provisions of Shari'ah and laws in force. No one may interfere with the Judiciary." Article 5 of the Law of the Judiciary prescribed the present (1975–2007) composition of the Shari'a court into four tiers: (1) the Supreme Judicial Council, (2) the appellate court, (3) general courts, and (4) summary courts. The Supreme Judicial Council is headed by a chairman and includes 10 other members (5 full-time and 5 part-time). The chairman and the members of the Supreme Judicial Council are appointed by the king from among the kingdom's best and most experienced Shari'a judges, jurists, and scholars. According to Article 8 of the Law of the Judiciary, the Supreme Judicial Council has four major functions: (1) examine "Shari'ah questions as, in the opinion of the Minister of Justice, require statement of general Shari'ah principles;" (2) examine "issues which in the opinion of the King, require that they be reviewed by the Council;" (3) "provide opinions on issues related to the judiciary at the request of the Minister of Justice;" and (4) "review death, amputation, or stoning sentences." The Supreme Judicial Council has a permanent panel comprised of all 5 full-time. It also has a general panel comprised of all members of the council.

Article 10 of the Law of the Judiciary described the composition and function of the Appellate Court: It said that "The Appellate Court shall be composed of a Chief Judge and a sufficient number of judges from among whom deputy chief judges shall be designated as needed and in the order of absolute seniority in the service." Article 10 empowered the Appellate Court to establish panels to examine criminal cases, cases related to personal status, and other relevant cases. Each panel has to be headed by the Chief Judge or one of his representatives. The Chief Judge of the Appellate Court is appointed by the king, and the deputies of the Chief Judge are appointed by the Ministry of Justice on the basis of the recommendations of the Supreme Judicial Council (Article 11). Article 15 of the Law of the Judiciary states that "Decisions of the Appellate Court shall be rendered by three judges, except in cases involving death, stoning, and amputation sentences, in which case the decisions shall be rendered by five judges." Article 14 mandated that in case of conflicting decisions made by different panels of the Appellate Court, the matters must be referred to the Supreme Judicial Council for a decision related to general Shari'a principles.

Article 22 of the Law of the Judiciary of 1975 explained the functions of the third tier of the Saudi judicial system—the General Courts. The number and composition of the General Courts are determined by the Ministry of Justice on the recommendations of the Supreme Judicial Council. Article 25 made a provision that "judgments of the General Court shall be rendered by a single judge, except in cases involving death, stoning, and amputation as well as other cases specified by law, where judgment shall be rendered by three judges." Article 25 further explains that "in cases where death, stoning, or amputation is inapplicable, the judges handling the case should decide on the appropriate discretionary punishment or otherwise, as required by the Shari'ah." Article 24 explains the nature of the fourth tier of the Saudi judicial system—the Summary Courts. The number and composition of the Summary Courts are determined also by the Ministry of Justice on the recommendations of the Supreme Judicial Council. In summary courts, judgments are rendered by a single judge (Article 25).

The functions of crime control and the criminal justice system of Saudi Arabia are performed and organized not only by different types of Shari'a courts, the Ministry of Justice, and the Supreme Judicial Council, but also by a number of executive, legislative, and independent agencies created by the monarchy. In 1992, for the first time, a new constitution was introduced in Saudi Arabia. It was called the "Basic System of Governance" or "Basic Law" (Royal Embassy of Saudi Arabia, 2012b). The various types of governance reforms introduced by the Basic Law brought some significant effects on the functioning of the Shari'a judicial system and criminal justice. The Basic Law formally established Saudi Arabia as a hereditary Islamic monarchy and the Quran and the Sunna as the constitution (Article 1). The Basic Law made the king the supreme authority of the kingdom responsible for appointing the Prime Minister, the Council of Ministers, the Chief of the Supreme Judicial Council, and the heads of other governmental bodies and agencies (Article 58). The Basic Law also made Shari'a the source of all laws, rules, and regulations of the kingdom. Article 8 explained that "government in the kingdom of Saudi Arabia is based on the premise of justice, consultation, and equality in accordance with the Islamic Shari'ah." Article 48 stated that "the courts will apply the rules of the Islamic Shari'ah in the cases that are brought before them, in accordance with what is indicated in the Book and the Sunnah, and statutes decreed by the Ruler."

The Basic Law made the judiciary independent from the control of the executive. "The Judiciary is an independent authority. The decisions of judges shall not be subject to any authority other than the authority of the Islamic Shari'ah" (Article 46). The constitution made the king solely responsible for implementation of the Shari'a. "The King shall rule the nation according to the Shari'ah. He shall also supervise the implementation of the Shari'ah" (Article 55). The Basic Law also made some provisions that can be called the monarchy's Bill of Rights. Article 36 states that "the state provides security for all its citizens and all residents within its territory and no one shall be arrested, imprisoned, or have their actions restricted except in cases specified by statutes." Article 37 is about unusual searches and seizures: "The home is sacrosanct and shall not be entered without the permission of the owner or be searched except in cases specified by statutes." Article 38 ruled that "there shall be no crime or penalty except in accordance with the Shari'ah or organizational law." It can be noted here that only *hudud* and *qisas* crimes are adjudicated on the basis of the Shari'a law. *Ta'zir* crimes are primarily statutory crimes, and they are adjudicated mainly on the basis of statutory laws. What is most significant in the Basic Law from the perspective of criminal justice is Article 46, which states that the judiciary is independent except "in the case of the Islamic Shari'ah." That means the functioning of Shari'a Law, related particularly to Shari'a crimes and punishments, is subject to checks and balances by bodies external to the Shari'a courts, particularly the institution of the monarchy—the king.

As an extension of developing and formalizing the structure of the government, the Basic Law also created (Article 68) a legislative body known as the Consultative Council or *Majlis as-Shura*. There are currently 150 members of the Consultative Council, and all of them are appointed by the king from among reputed Saudi citizens who are at least 30 years of age. The Consultative Council is primarily an advisory body to the king. It has power to propose new statutory laws, to interpret and analyze existing statutes, to review the performance of various ministries and governmental agencies, and review international treaties and agreements. The Council is headed by a Speaker, who is assisted by a Vice Speaker, Assistant Speaker, and Secretary General. Currently, the Consultative Council is composed of 25 consultative committees or departments. One of them, the Islamic and Judicial Affairs Committee, deals with many issues related to legal opinions and scholarly research on Shari'a Law, and the Committee for the Promotion of Virtue and the Prevention of Vice. The Islamic and Judicial Affairs Committee of the Consultative Council is relevant for understanding criminal justice in Saudi Arabia because it plays a role in developing criminal statutes related particularly to *ta'zir* crimes, and it has the power to review the functions and performance of the Ministry of Justice that is responsible for organizing the kingdom's more than 300 Shari'a courts and the Supreme Judicial Council that is responsible for reviewing decisions made by those Shari'a courts.

In addition to the institutions of the monarchy, the Ministry of Justice, the Islamic and Judicial Affairs Committee of the Consultative Council, the Shari'a criminal courts, and the

Supreme Judicial Council, there are also three other agencies that play important roles in organizing and directing criminal justice in Saudi Arabia. These are the Senior Council of Ulema, the Board of Grievances, and the Committee for the Promotion of Virtue and the Prevention of Vice. All these agencies are created by the government. The Senior Council of Ulema is comprised of about 40 of the kingdom's senior religious scholars who are charged with the responsibility of interpreting Shari'a Law in terms of fatwa or general principles. It is created by Article 45 of the Basic Law: "The sources of the deliverance of fatwa in the Kingdom of Saudi Arabia are God's Book and the Sunnah of His Messenger." The Senior Council of Ulema plays an important role in making the criminal statutes related to *ta'zir* crimes. "In many cases," noted a reputed legal scholar of Saudi Arabia, "its participation has been crucial in gaining public support for . . . statutory laws" (Ansary, 2011, p. 7).

The Board of Grievances, on the other hand, is an independent administrative judicial body created in 1982 (Royal Embassy of Saudi Arabia, 2012c). The Board of Grievances is an organization closely parallel to the Shari'a courts. But it is directly affiliated with the monarchy and is not under the control of the Ministry of Justice. It is an independent administrative judicial commission "responsible directly to His Majesty the King" (Article 1 of the Law of the Board of Grievances). The Board of Grievances is comprised of a president, one or more vice presidents, and a number of assistant vice presidents and members who specialize in "Shari'ah and law" (Article 2). In the area of criminal justice, the Board is authorized to adjudicate crimes of corruption, bribery, forgery, and other forms of commercial and economic crimes (Article 8). The Board is organized in three circuits: Board of Appeal Circuits, Appeal Circuits, and First-Instance Circuits (Article 6). The Board's headquarters are in the city of Riyadh.

The Committee for the Promotion of Virtue and the Prevention of Vice is a separate organization that is entrusted with the task of enforcing Shari'a Law in the nation. The Shari'a, as mentioned before, is not just about *hudud* and *qisas* crimes. It is seen as a complete way of life. It defines the ways in which one should behave, dress, and conduct oneself in public domains. The Shari'a defines the boundaries of what is moral and immoral and what is sin and evil. The Committee for the Promotion of Virtue and the Prevention of Vice, under the Ministry of the Interior and direct command of the king, enforces the Shari'a rules on proper Islamic behavior by deploying a special group of religious police called *mutaween*. The *mutaween* forces are responsible for overseeing whether people are drinking in public, whether they are observing prayers on time, whether shops are closed during prayer times, whether women are properly veiled and covered, whether men and women are socializing in public, whether women are driving without being accompanied by a man, whether women are smoking in public, whether drugs are being sold on the streets, whether anybody is carrying pornographic materials, and whether anybody is practicing witchcraft or participating in many other acts and behaviors that are prohibited under Shari'a Law (Raphael, 2009). Like the police belonging to the public security branch under the control of the Ministry of Interior, the religious police do not have any authority for the enforcement of general law and order.

Criminal Justice in Saudi Arabia: The Nature of Criminal Procedural Laws

Crimes and criminal laws in Saudi Arabia, except *ta'zir* crimes, are defined by the Shari'a. *Ta'zir* crimes are defined and *ta'zir* laws are enacted by the monarchy on the basis of consultations with and recommendations from the Council of Ministers and the Consultative Council. For a comparative understanding of the role of the Shari'a in criminal justice in Saudi Arabia, what is more important to explore, therefore, is not how substantive laws and statutes are made (they are already made by the Quran and the Sunna), but how Shari'a Laws are applied—the procedural guidelines for the interpretation and application of Shari'a law and justice. The search for a comparative understanding of the role of the Shari'a in criminal justice in Saudi Arabia, in other words, is a search for an understanding of the extent to which there is developing a legal space within the Shari'a for the inclusion of some of the modern principles of the due process of law and human rights. The Kingdom of Saudi Arabia has a traditional system of criminal justice because it is based on the tradition of Shari'a Law, but the Kingdom of Saudi Arabia in terms of many of its other domains such as the economy, science, and education is aggressively growing as a modern and global society. For students of comparative criminal justice, it would be highly intriguing to explore the extent to which the traditional system of criminal justice in Saudi Arabia is making, within the framework of Shari'a, a legal and cultural space for modernity. This process of modernizing the Shari'a can be understood from some of the laws of the criminal procedure and the laws of the Shari'a court in the kingdom.

The Law of the Judiciary, promulgated by royal decree in 1975; the Law of the Board of Grievances, promulgated by royal decree in 1982; the Law and Regulations of the Bureau of Investigation and Public Prosecution, promulgated by royal decree in 1989; the Law of Procedure Before Shari'a Courts, promulgated by royal decree in 2000; the Law of Criminal Procedure promulgated by a royal decree in 2001, and the Code of Law Practice, promulgated by royal decree in 2001, set forth some of the major procedural guidelines in the implementation of Shari'a Law in Saudi Arabia. Some of the major due process issues have been addressed and codified, particularly by the Law of Criminal Procedure, promulgated in 2001 (Royal Embassy of Saudi Arabia, 2012d). This compendium of criminal procedural law is divided into eight chapters that contain 225 articles. These various chapters of the Law of Criminal Procedure describe the nature of criminal action (Chapter 2); procedures relating to criminal evidence (Chapter 3); procedures related to criminal investigations (Chapter 4); trial procedures (Chapter 6); and appeal procedures (Chapter 7). Similar to the Fourth Amendment of the Bill of Rights in the U.S. Constitution, Article 41 of Saudi Arabia's Law of Criminal Procedure defines the right of protection against unreasonable searches and seizures. The Article states: "a criminal investigation officer may not . . . search any inhabited place except in the cases provided for in the laws, pursuant to a search warrant specifying the reasons for the search, issued by the Bureau of Investigation and Prosecution." A search, however, can be conducted without a warrant if there is a probable cause. Article 43 of the Law of Criminal Procedure noted that "in the case of flagrante delecto, a criminal investigation officer may search the dwelling of the accused and collect relevant items that may help determine the truth, if there is credible evidence that such items exist there." If a search is conducted without a warrant, it must be immediately reported in writing to the Bureau of Investigation and Prosecution. Article 33 of the Law of Criminal Procedure states that after a person is arrested from the scene of the crime, "the Bureau of Investigation and Prosecution shall be immediately notified. In all cases, the person under arrest shall not be detained for more than twenty-four hours, except pursuant to a written order from the Investigator."

Article 34 of the Law of Criminal Procedure, closely resembling the Fifth Amendment of the U.S. Constitution, states that immediately following an arrest, the investigating officer must hear and record the statement from the accused. If the accused fails to establish his innocence, he or she must be interrogated within 24 hours, and the investigating officer must determine whether he or she should be released or detained. In detention, a person "shall not be subjected to any bodily or moral harm. Similarly, he shall not be subjected to any torture or degrading treatment" (Article 2). Article 39 of the Law of Criminal Procedure said that "whoever has any information that a person is unlawfully or improperly imprisoned or detained, or is imprisoned or detained in a place not intended for imprisonment or detention, shall notify the Bureau of Investigation and Prosecution." The same article further added that if the members of the Bureau of Investigation and Prosecution are notified, they "shall immediately proceed to the place where the . . . detainee is kept and shall conduct the . . . investigation. If it is found that such imprisonment or detention is unlawful, he shall order the release of the prisoner or detainee." The Law of Criminal Procedure of Saudi Arabia, like the Sixth Amendment of the U.S. Constitution, guarantees the rights of the accused to have counsel: "Any accused person shall have the right to seek the assistance of a lawyer or a representative to defend him during the investigation and trial stages" (Article 4 of the Law of Criminal Procedure).

The major responsibility of criminal investigation in Saudi Arabia is entrusted to an organization called the Bureau of Investigation and Prosecution, established in 1989. It is attached to the Saudi Ministry of the Interior, is headquartered in Riyadh, and has branches or circuits in all provinces of the kingdom. Its major functions are some of those that are performed in the United States by the FBI, federal and state grand juries, and federal and state prosecutors. The Bureau of Investigation and Prosecution is headed by a chairman appointed by the king. The Bureau also includes a vice chairman, a number of heads and deputy heads of different investigation and prosecution circuits, and a number of investigators of different ranks and categories. According to Article 3 of the Law and Regulations of the Bureau of Investigation and Public Prosecution (Royal Embassy of Saudi Arabia, 2012e), the Bureau is assigned jurisdiction over criminal investigations, criminal prosecutions before judicial bodies, appeal of judgments, supervision of the execution of criminal sentences, monitoring prison and detention centers, supervising the legality of imprisonment and detentions, releasing those who are imprisoned and detained illegally, and reporting to the Ministry of the Interior every 6 months regarding the condition of the prisons and detention centers of the kingdom. The Bureau's investigative functions are independent from any external encroachment, but it must work within the framework of Shari'a Law. Article 5 of the Law and Regulations of the Bureau states that "members of the Bureau are totally independent, and they shall not be subject in conducting their work except to the provisions of Islamic *Shari'ah* and the relevant laws, and no one shall interfere in their work." The members of the Bureau must also be educated and trained in Shari'a Law. Article 26 of the Saudi Criminal Procedure said that criminal investigations can be conducted by many other persons, such as the directors of police and their assistants, public security officers, secret service officers, intelligent officers, prison directors, border guard officers, special security forces, heads of the Committee for the Promotion of Virtue and the Prevention of Vice, and captains of Saudi ships and airplanes. But all of these different investigating groups and individuals must immediately and properly notify the Bureau of Investigation and Prosecution about their specific criminal investigating actions.

Traditionally, the Shari'a Law was based on closed trials. Article 61 of the Law of Procedure Before Shari'a Courts (Royal Embassy of Saudi Arabia, 2012f) described that Shari'a proceedings "shall be in open court unless the judge on his own or at the request of a litigant closes the hearing in order to maintain order, observe public morality, or for the privacy of the family." The traditional Shari'a court proceedings were mostly oral in nature and were not usually kept in writing. Article 62 of the Law of Procedure Before Shari'a Courts mandated that "argument shall be oral. This, however, shall not preclude the presentation of statements or defenses in the form of written briefs, copies of which shall be exchanged between the litigants." It is further stated that "the court shall grant the litigants sufficient time to review and respond to the documents as circumstances warrant" (Article 62). It is also specified that the court clerks must "enter the minutes of the argument in the record, stating the date and hour each argument began and the hour it ended, the name of the judge and the names of the litigants or their attorneys-in-fact" (Article 68).

Traditionally, particularly in the Islamic empires of the Middle Ages, the functioning of the Shari'a courts was not directly controlled and supervised by any governmental authority or agencies. In Saudi Arabia, the Shari'a courts functioned (before the promulgation of the new Law of the Judiciary in 2007) under the control of the Ministry of Justice (see **Table 10-1**). Article 87 of the Law of the Judiciary stated that it is the responsibility of Ministry of the Justice to supervise the Shari'a courts and "other judicial panels, take actions, and submit to the appropriate authorities such proposals and projects as may secure the proper standard for the justice system in the Kingdom."

Traditionally, the Shari'a judges or ulemas were not formally trained and educated in Islamic law and jurisprudence. The Code of Law Practice in Saudi Arabia, promulgated in 2001, mandated that Shari'a judges and attorneys are registered and licensed by the Ministry of Justice, and that they are trained and educated in Islamic jurisprudence (Royal Embassy of Saudi Arabia, 2012g). Article 3 of the Code of Law Practice stated that a practicing lawyer in Saudi Arabia "must be a holder of a degree from a Shari'ah college or a bachelor of law from one of the Kingdom's universities or an equivalent of any of these degrees obtained

TABLE 10-1 Some of the Major Provisions of Criminal Procedural Law in Saudi Arabia Under the Shari'a Framework

Article	Provisions
Article 1	Courts shall apply Shari'ah principles, as derived from the Qur'an and Sunnah (Traditions of Prophet Muhammad peace be upon him) to cases brought before them. They shall also apply state promulgated laws that do not contradict the provisions of the Qur'an and Sunnah, and shall comply with the procedure set forth in this Law.
Article 2	No person shall be arrested, searched, detained, or imprisoned except in cases specified by the law. Detention or imprisonment shall be carried out only in the places designated for such purposes and shall be for the period prescribed by the competent authority.
Article 3	No penal punishment shall be imposed on any person except in connection with a forbidden and punishable act, whether under Shari'ah principles or under statutory laws, and after the person has been convicted pursuant to a final judgment rendered after a trial conducted in accordance with Shari'ah principles.
Article 4	Any accused person shall have the right to seek the assistance of a lawyer or a representative to defend him during the investigation and trial stages.
Article 9	Sentences shall be appealable by either the convicted person or the Prosecutor.
Article 10	Criminal panels of the Appellate Court shall consist of five judges to review sentences of death, stoning, amputation or qisas (retaliatory punishment) in cases other than death. For other cases, they shall consist of three judges.
Article 11	Sentences of death, stoning, amputation, or qisas in cases other than death that have been affirmed by the Appellate Court shall not be final unless affirmed by the Permanent Panel of the Supreme Judicial Council.
Article 12	If the Supreme Judicial Council does not affirm the relevant sentence in implementation of Article 11 hereof, the said sentence shall be reversed and the case shall be remanded for reconsideration by other judges.
Article 18	No criminal action shall be initiated nor investigation proceedings conducted in crimes involving a private right of action, except through a complaint by the victim or his representative or heirs, filed with the competent authority, unless the Bureau of Investigation and Prosecution considers that the filing of such an action and the investigation into those crimes will serve the public interest.
Article 38	Any prisoner or detainee shall have the right to submit, at any time, a written or verbal complaint to the prison or detention center officer and request that he communicate it to a member of the Bureau of Investigation and Prosecution. The officer shall accept the complaint and promptly communicate it [to the Bureau of Investigation and Prosecution].
Article 41	A criminal investigation officer may not enter or search any inhabited place except in the cases provided for in the laws, pursuant to a search warrant specifying the reasons for the search, issued by the Bureau of Investigation and Prosecution. However, other dwellings may be searched pursuant to a search warrant, specifying the reasons, issued by the Investigator.
Article 55	Mail, cables, telephone conversations, and other means of communication shall be inviolable and, as such, shall not be perused or surveilled except pursuant to an order stating the reasons thereof and for a limited period as herein provided for.
Article 193	The accused, the Prosecutor, and the claimant of the private right of action shall be entitled to appeal any judgment whether it relates to conviction, acquittal, or lack of jurisdiction. The court shall notify these parties of such right upon reading of the judgment.

Source: Data from Law of Criminal Procedure (Royal Decree M/39, 2002), Kingdom of Saudi Arabia.

from abroad." The practicing Shari'a attorneys are also obliged to follow a professional legal code of ethics published by the Ministry of Justice. Article 23 of the Code of Law Practice proclaimed that "a lawyer shall not disclose any confidential information which has been communicated to him or of which he has become aware in the course of practicing his profession even after expiration of his power of attorney."

One of the most controversial aspects of Shari'a Law is the nature of punishment for *hudud* crimes and *qisas* (retaliatory) crimes. These punishments, such as the death penalty or stoning for adultery and fornication, flogging and amputation for stealing, and punishments of retribution, are sanctioned by the Quran, and they are unchangeable. Punishments for *ta'zir* crimes or statutory crimes are fines and incarceration, and they are relatively less controversial. In recent years, a series of laws pertaining to *ta'zir* crimes has been enacted through royal decrees based on recommendations of the Ministry of Justice and the Council of Ministers in such areas as money laundering, computer crimes, terrorism, human trafficking, drug trafficking, and the sale and manufacturing of illegal arms. New minimum mandatory sentencing guidelines have been proposed for the prosecution of these crimes. Article 7 of the Information Technology (IT) Criminal Act, for example, imposed a penalty of not less than 10 years of imprisonment and fines of five million Saudi riyals for "creating or publishing a site for terrorist organizations on the information network or any computer system to facilitate communications with the leaderships of such organizations or any of their members, marketing or financing their ideologies." Article 3 of the Anti-Human Trafficking Act imposed a penalty of not more than 15 years or a fine of not more than one million riyals or both for participation in human trafficking. These kinds of *ta'zir* punishments are similar to mandatory minimum sentencing guideline in the United States, Canada, the United Kingdom, and Germany, and they do not stir any serious controversies in studies on comparative criminal justice.

For an understanding of the most controversial punishments related to *hudud* and *qisas* crimes and how they are devised and imposed, one needs to examine the nature of judicial deliberations in the criminal Shari'a courts and the nature of checks and balances on the implementation of such punishments. All forms of *hudud* and *qisas* punishments imposed by the Shari'a criminal courts, as mandated by Article 11 of the Law of Criminal Procedure, must be reviewed by the Supreme Judicial Council (after the promulgation of the new Law of the Judiciary in 2007, this responsibility was given to the Supreme Court of Saudi Arabia). They must also be reviewed and approved by the king before they are implemented. The adjudication of *hudud* and *qisas* crimes is also based on strict evidentiary rules. These rules in the Middle Ages were probably reluctantly imposed, particularly in rural and remote areas by the ulemas and *qadis*. But within the modern structure of procedural law in Saudi Arabia, these evidentiary rules related to the establishment of *hudud* and *qisas* crimes are seriously applied and examined. Checks are also imposed by the fact that defendants have rights to seek the help of counsel equally educated and trained in the Shari'a law like the *qadis* and judges of the Shari'a courts, and all court proceedings are formally documented and preserved.

Islamic Criminal Justice in Saudi Arabia: The Search for Balance Through Reforms in Criminal Justice

Even though the Saudi system of criminal justice is based on the strict interpretation of the Quran and the Sunna advocated by Wahhabism and the Hanbali school of Islamic jurisprudence, there has grown over the years a significant space for the role of *ijtihad* and *ijma* in the interpretation of Shari'a crimes and punishments. Vogel, a close observer of law and justice in Saudi Arabia, noted that the judges of the Shari'a court in Saudi Arabia follow the legal doctrines of the Hanbali school of Islamic jurisprudence, "but . . . they are free to adopt views from other schools, or even from outside the four schools altogether, as long as they base their view, following proper procedures of the Quran and the Sunna" (2000, p. 10). In case of punishments for *hudud* crimes, the Quran has kept a number options open: punishment (decapitation and flogging), repentance, and forgiveness. Forgiveness is described by the Quran as a noble act. In case of *hudud* crimes, the judicial decisions are entirely in the hands of the *qadis* and Islamic judges to make a choice from the range of various sentencing options given by the Quran. There are instances where the Saudi Arabia Supreme Court and the king did not approve the sentences imposed by the Shari'a courts. In 2007, a Shari'a General Court in Qatif sentenced a 20-year-old woman described as the "Qatif girl," to receive 200 lashes for bringing a complaint that she was abducted and gang-raped by seven men when she was traveling in a car with her boyfriend. According to Shari'a Law, in case of rape and fornication, both victims and offenders are to be punished. The Qatif girl was punished for her alleged immorality for being with a man to whom she was not married. King Abdullah pardoned the woman in 2007. In 2009, a Shari'a court imposed a punishment of 60 lashes and a 2-year travel ban on a female Saudi journalist working for the Lebanese Broadcasting Corporation (LBC). She was charged for broadcasting a report called *Thick Red Line,* in which a Saudi man bragged about his sexual escapades. King Abdullah changed the Shari'a court's ruling and pardoned the journalist, who claimed that she did not participate in the production of the report. In 2009, a Shari'a court in Medina imposed a death penalty on a Lebanese TV presenter for publicly practicing sorcery. On appeal, a Shari'a Appellate Court in Mecca upheld his death penalty and sent the case to the Supreme Court for ratification. (The Supreme Court was established after the promulgation of the new Law of the Judiciary in 2007. The responsibility of reviewing cases from the Appellate Courts before 2007 was in the hands of the Supreme Judicial Council.) In 2010, the Supreme Court of Saudi Arabia declined to ratify the death penalty and sent the case back to the Medina court for retrial. The Supreme Court said that "the death sentence for Ali Hussain Sibat was inappropriate because there was no proof that others were harmed as a result of his actions" (Amnesty International, 2010, p. 1). In April 2011, a Filipino man, who was sentenced to death by a Shari'a court for drug smuggling into the kingdom, was pardoned by King Abdullah. In 2005, King Abdullah pardoned three Libyan men who were convicted of plotting to assassinate then–Crown Prince Abdullah. In 1999, King Fahd granted executive clemency to a Filipino nurse who was sentenced by a Shari'a court to receive 150 lashes and 7 months in prison for drug possession. In 2002, Saudi Arabia had about 30,000 people in prison. King Fahd ordered the release of 13,768 prisoners jailed for minor criminal offenses. This was done as a measure for prison reform by lowering the rate of incarceration in Saudi Arabia. Such instances of royal pardon and executive clemency are not few and far between in the history of criminal justice in Saudi Arabia. The pertinent point is that in punishment for *hudud* crimes and also *ta'zir* crimes, there is a range of options in the Quran. There are religiously justifiable options for clemency and forgiveness through both judicial and executive interventions.

What is more problematic in Shari'a Law is punishment for *qisas* crimes based on the judicial philosophy of retribution. Retribution is sanctioned by the Quran. *Qisas* punishments for murder and other aggravated assaults cannot be pardoned by the king or any state authorities within the framework of Shari'a Law. It can be pardoned only by the victims and their adult male relatives, sometimes in exchange for blood money. In classical times, retributive punishments were carried out by the victims or their male relatives. Today, in Saudi Arabia and other countries that follow Shari'a tradition, the state, on behalf of the victims, carries out the retributive punishments including death penalty and decapitation. If the victims or their relatives waive the right of retribution, the punishment for *qisas* crimes can be changed, and the offenders even can be pardoned through executive clemency.

A Sri Lankan maid named Rizana Nafeek went to Saudi Arabia for work in 2005. She was hired for childcare, and a 4-month old baby died in her arms while she was bottle-feeding. She was convicted by a Shari'a court of strangling the baby and sentenced to death by beheading, and her sentencing was approved by the Supreme Court of Saudi Arabia in 2010. Nafeek is still in prison and is scheduled to be beheaded. The king cannot pardon Nafeek, although many appeals have been made by her family, the government of Sri Lanka, and many international human rights organizations. It has been learned, however, that negotiations are under way with the parent of the victim to waive his or her right of retribution in return for blood money. The fate of Nafeek depends on the outcome of this negotiation.

In 2006, a poor woman from West Java in Indonesia named Darsem Binti Dawud went to Saudi Arabia for better economic opportunities. In 2009, a Shari'a criminal court in Riyadh sentenced her to death by beheading for murdering her Yemeni employer. She confessed her crime, but she said she did it in self-defense when she was going to be raped by her employer. In this case, the family of the victim waived the right of retribution and demanded blood money. The money was paid by the government of Indonesia (about $533,000), and Darsem escaped the punishment of beheading. In 2005, a Shari'a court in the city of Dammam "sentenced Puthan Veettil Abd ul-Latif Noushad, an Indian citizen, to be punished by having his right eye gouged out in retribution for his role in a brawl in April 2003 in which a Saudi citizen was injured" (Human Rights Watch, 2005, p. 1). The Shari'a court said the punishment could be avoided only if the right of retribution is waived by the victim. In 1997, two British nurses, Deborah Parry and Lucille McLauchlan, were convicted of murdering their colleague, an Australian nurse named Miss Gilford, in the King Fahd Military Medical Center in Dharan, Saudi Arabia. Both of them were sentenced to death by beheading by a Shari'a court. In 1999, the victim's family waived the right of retribution and received blood money, and the two British nurses escaped death by beheading. There is an abundance of examples of *qisas* punishments that have been either avoided through the payment of blood money or changed to imprisonment.

Thus in the case of *hudud* crimes and *ta'zir* crimes, the power of alternative sentencing is in the hands of both the judiciary and the executive branches. It depends primarily on the perspective of the Islamic judges. In Saudi Arabia, most Islamic judges of the Shari'a courts represent the conservative and most orthodox interpretation of the Shari'a based on the ideology of Wahhabism and the Hanbali school of Islamic jurisprudence. In the case of *qisas* crimes, the power to forgive or to waive the right of retribution is given by the Quran only to the victims and the adult male members of their families. Pertinent to remember, as mentioned before, is that the Quran said, in Section 4 of Surah Al-Isra, that "We have granted the right of retribution to his heir, but let him not carry *his vengeance* too far in killing the culprit, as he is supported *by the law*." This verse puts serious limits on the imposition and execution of *qisas* punishments, and it seems that securing the waiver of the right of retribution by the victim and their families in Islamic criminal justice should be a responsibility not only of the offender but also of the state. With respect to *qisas* crimes, Islamic criminal justice necessitates the development of judicial institutions for victim–offender relations, negotiations, and restitutions.

Shari'a Law functions within a defined framework based on the Quran and the Hadith, but there remains a great scope for alternative punishments and alternative dispute resolutions. The cruel and unusual punishments such as beheading, decapitation, and flogging are avoidable within the framework of the Shari'a on the basis of *ijtihad*, *ijma*, and the supreme understanding of the core message of the Quran on the issues of justice, fairness, repentance, and forgiveness. The Quran has revealed through its various verses that humans are not infallible and they have temptations to commit acts that are evil and sinful. The Quran at the same time revealed that humans can be changed and rehabilitated. In Section 16 of Surah An-Nisa, the Quran said: "If anyone does evil or wrongs his own soul and then seeks Allah's forgiveness, he will find Allah Forgiving, and Merciful." The issues of alternative sentencing and offender rehabilitation are crucial to Islamic jurisprudence—a perspective that is, of course, not adequately appreciated by many of the ulemas and Islamic jurists in Saudi Arabia who belong to Wahhabism and the Hanbali school of Islamic jurisprudence.

Shari'a Law is not based on codification, and hence, there remain wide discretions in the interpretation of Shari'a crimes and criminal punishments among the *qadis* and Islamic jurists. It is to address these possibilities of wide discretions that different schools of Islamic jurisprudence have emerged, and the issues of *ijtihad* and *ijma* have remained central to deliberations in Islamic jurisprudence since the establishment of the first Islamic state in Medina in 622 by the Prophet Muhammad. It is also for this reason of the centrality of *ijtihad* and *ijma* in the interpretation of Islamic jurisprudence that there were tensions between the Islamic jurists and the state power in all Islamic empires of the past including the Ottoman Empire and the Mughal Empire. This is also true of the modern Kingdom of Saudi Arabia. There are three competing groups in the shaping of criminal justice in Saudi Arabia. The first group is represented by the monarchy, which is highly open to the West and in favor of modernization within the framework of Islam. The second is the group of modernist Islamic ulemas who view that there is scope for modernization in all realms of life, including criminal justice, remaining within the Shari'a framework, and interpreting Shari'a in terms of *ijtihad* and *ijma*. Some of these state-employed ulemas of the Shair'a courts and other related executive agencies are educated and trained in law and jurisprudence from the West. They are open to study alternative legal traditions to enrich Islamic jurisprudence. They are also open to understanding the logic and arguments of the competing schools of Islamic jurisprudence. The third is the most conservative and orthodox group of ulemas who still belong to the classical Islamic tradition and Wahhabism. They are sharply opposed to widening the scope of *ijtihad* and *ijma* in the interpretation of the Shari'a (Hegghammer, 2008; Nolan, 2011; Teitelbaum, 2000). A more radicalized section of this conservative group has given birth to what is known as radical political Islam and a new movement of global jihad—a strategy that was central to the expansion of Wahhabism in early 18th-century Arabia.

Since the reign of King Faisal, great strides toward modernization began in Saudi Arabia. He introduced the Law of the Judiciary and established the Department of Justice. In 1966, the king's nephew was killed while battling police and protesting against the introduction of television broadcasting in Saudi Arabia. The king did not take any actions against the police for killing his nephew. In 1975, the king was assassinated by another nephew (Prince Faisal bin Musaid), apparently for his modernist approach to governance of the kingdom. King Khalid introduced the Law of the Board of Grievances by a royal decree in 1982. King Fahd, during his reign (1982–2005), introduced some of the most significant judicial reforms in the kingdom, such as the Law and Regulations of the Bureau of Investigation and Public Prosecution, the Law of Procedure Before Shari'a Courts, the Law of Criminal Procedure, and the Code of Law Practice. The reign of King Fahd is also characterized by one of the most turbulent times of relations between the monarchy and the Wahhabi ulemas. In 1992, a group of 107 ultraorthodox ulemas presented a memorandum, "Memorandum of Advice," to King Fahd to cut relations with the West and to strictly enforce Shari'a Law in the kingdom. In 1994, some of the Wahhabi ulemas openly revolted against the monarchy for its open approach to modernization. The march of the Saudi monarchy toward modernization, however, did not stop with the revolt of the ulemas. It rather began with new intensity with the accession of King Abdullah to the throne in 2005.

In 2007, King Abdullah introduced a new body of laws (Law of the Judiciary, Royal Decree No. M/78, 2007) to reform the Shari'a judiciary. These new laws "replaced regulations in force for more than 30 years in the case of the judiciary, and about 25 years for the Board of Grievances" (Ansary, 2011, p. 15). About $2 billion were allocated for the implementation of the new laws promulgated through a royal decree in 2007. In the words of a Saudi legal expert, who received his doctoral degree in judicial sciences from the University of Virginia's School of Law in the United States, "The intention of the new law is to shape the Saudi Judicial system so that it can meet a higher judicial standard set by . . . the Law of Criminal Procedures and Procedures before Shari'ah Courts Law in 2001 to 2002" (Ansary, 2011, p. 16). Under the new law, the Supreme Judicial Council was replaced as the highest court of the kingdom. It remained only as the highest administrative body to supervise all the Shari'a courts of the kingdom. The 2007 Law of the Judiciary created a new court structure for the kingdom. The new structure is composed of the High Court, Courts of Appeals, and

First-Degree Courts. The First-Degree Courts are composed of General Courts, Criminal Courts, Personal Status Courts, Commercial Courts, and Labor Courts. The High Court, or the Supreme Court of the Kingdom, was given the task of supervising "the implementation of Islamic law (Shari'ah) and regulations enacted by the King . . . . The High Court will review rulings issued or upheld by the Courts of Appeals, including those which relate to cases punishable by death, and other certain major crimes" (Ansary, 2011, p. 17). A president who is appointed by the king heads the newly constituted Supreme Court. The king appoints the 10 judges of the Supreme Court with recommendations from the Supreme Judicial Council. The new law of 2007 reconstituted the structure of the Courts of Appeal with more power to overturn the decisions of the lower courts. The Courts of Appeal for the Criminal Circuits, composed of a panel of five judges, were given the jurisdiction to hear appealable cases from the lower courts related particularly to death penalty, decapitation, and other serious *hudud* and *qisas* punishments.

In 1982, King Khaled established the Board of Grievances as an independent administrative judicial commission with jurisdiction to hear and review civil and criminal cases. The new Law of the Judiciary of 2007 further widened the scope and functions of the Board of Grievances. The Law of the Judiciary established the Board of Grievances as a hierarchical judicial agency composed of a High Administrative Court, Administrative Court of Appeals, and Administrative Courts. One of the major functions of the Board of Grievances is to supervise the proper implementation of the Shari'a Law by reviewing decisions made by different tiers of the Shari'a court. The reforms of 2007 introduced by King Abdullah not only increased more checks and balances on the role of functioning of the Shari'a courts, but also widened the scope of *ijtihad* and *ijma* in the interpretation of Shari'a and Islamic jurisprudence.

Another major development has been the beginning of the codification of Shari'a Law after the promulgation of the new Law of the Judiciary in 2007. The concept of *codification* implies the development of codes by compiling various forms of statutes, rules, and regulations that define the nature of crime and the boundaries of punishment in consistent and predictable ways. Codification helps those who govern and those who are governed to know the boundaries of law and legality—the boundaries of behavior that are proper and improper, permissible and impermissible, and acceptable and not acceptable. Codification reduces the scope for discrete interpretations of the law. The history of the codification of law is older than the history of Shari'a Law. Some of the major historical developments of legal bodies include the Code of Ur-Nammu (2060 BC); the Code of Hammurabi (1772 BC); the Roman Law of the Twelve Tables (Lex Duodecim Tabularum—439 BC); the Roman (Justinian) Law of Corpus Juris Civilis (Body of Civil Law—434 BC); the Tang Code of China (653 AD); the Great Qing Code of China (1740); and the Napoleonic Code of France (1804). In the United States, the codification of English common law began in the late 18th century (e.g., the Judiciary Act of 1789). The movement for the codification of law is intimately connected to the modernization of criminal justice. There are two perspectives about the codification of Shari'a Law. One group of Islamic religious scholars and jurists adheres to the opinion that Shari'a Law is based on the Quran and Sunna and, hence, it cannot and must not be codified. Codification will remove the basis of the divine legitimacy of Shari'a Law. Another group—a relatively modernist group of Islamic scholars and jurists—believes that Shari'a Law needs to be codified for its just enforcement in the context of varying times and spaces. The recent move for the codification of Shari'a Law in Saudi Arabia came from the modernist monarchy, but the kingdom's Council of Ulema has also supported it. The process of the codification of Shari'a Law in Saudi Arabia is expected to be completed by 2015 (see **Box 10-1**).

What these various legal and judicial reforms that started after the promulgation of the Law of the Judiciary in 1975 suggest is that Saudi Arabia has a traditional system of criminal justice based on Islamic jurisprudence, but it is a system that is not stagnant and static. The Saudi monarchy, since the days of King Faisal in the mid-1960s, has been trying to achieve a balance between tradition and modernity in all realms of the kingdom, including criminal justice. Shari'a law entered into the age of modernity with the creation of the Kingdom of Saudi Arabia. The degree to which the Shari'a tradition will accommodate within its canonical framework some of the modern precepts of criminal justice such as the codification of law, due process of law, fair and equal justice, rejection of cruel and degrading punishments, and adherence to the universal standards of human rights, depends on the future of relations between the radical and ultraorthodox Wahhabi ulemas, and the relatively modernist groups of ulemas and the monarchy.

■ Islamic Jurisprudence, Shari'a Law, and Criminal Justice in Iran

As the understanding of the nature, role, and effect of Wahhabism and the monarchy is critical to the understanding of the nature of law and justice in Saudi Arabia, the understanding of the nature, role, and effect of Shiism and the Shiite clergy is critical to the understanding of law and justice in Iran. Although a traditional system of criminal justice is found both in Saudi Arabia and Iran, there remain some fundamental differences in the way Islamic jurisprudence and Shari'a Law are perceived and practiced in these two countries. These differences are embedded in their respective sects of Islam and their roots in different paths of evolution in power and politics. In Saudi Arabia, there is no separation between religion and the state, but they are not the same. The ruling monarchs of Saudi Arabia are devout Muslims, but they do not belong to the Islamic clergy of Saudi Arabia. In Saudi Arabia, the Islamic clergy that governs law and justice is not in political power. The Islamic clergy is governed by the monarchy. In Iran, religion and the state are not only inseparable but they are also the same. The Islamic clergy that holds the political power in Iran is also intimately connected to the governance of law and justice. The kingdom of Saudi Arabia began in the early 20th century with a traditional system of criminal justice. Through a series of institutional reforms, Saudi Arabia today is trying to develop a modern system of justice within the framework of Shari'a Law. The state of Iran, on the other hand, was born with the philosophy of a modern state and modern system of law and justice in the early 20th century. But the progress of modernity in Iran collapsed within a period of less than half a century.

BOX 10-1

Saudi Arabia Gets Ready to Put Order in Its Courts

Winds of change for modernization in criminal justice have been swiftly engulfing the kingdom of Saudi Arabia since the beginning of 2007. For a number of issues, such as the violation of the rights of women, the imposition of the death penalty for blasphemy, juvenile executions, and the widespread use of cruelty and punishments, the kingdom of Saudi Arabia has been the subject of worldwide condemnation. In 2007, His Majesty King Abdullah responded to global concerns for violations of human rights in Saudi Arabia by developing a massive program for judicial reforms in the kingdom at a cost of about $2 billion. It began with the promulgation of the new Law of the Judiciary by Royal Decree in 2007. After the promulgation of the Law of the Judiciary of 2007, the Supreme Judicial Council, the kingdom's highest tier of the judiciary, usually dominated by ultra-orthodox clergy believing in the Wahhabi perspective, was stripped of its judicial responsibility. The Supreme Judicial Council was given the administrative responsibility of supervising the kingdom's approximately 300 Shari'a courts, and developing programs for a new generation of Islamic jurists educated and trained in Islamic law, international law, and different Western legal traditions. Reforms began for the creation of legal specializations in such areas as criminal law, family law, commercial law, and international law. The Law of the Judiciary of 2007 created a separate high court for the kingdom—the Supreme Court of Saudi Arabia—following the tradition of most of the countries of the world, particularly of the West. The Supreme Court is composed of the 10 most distinguished Islamic jurists of diverse legal backgrounds, and they are appointed by His Majesty the King of Saudi Arabia. Another significant development has been the beginning of the codification of Shari'a law. "The Council of Senior Ulema, the country's top religious panel, endorsed codification of Shari'a in March 2010" (Wagner, 2011, p. 1). Frank E. Vogel, an expert on law and justice in Saudi Arabia, described these efforts for reforms in criminal justice in Saudi Arabia as "seismic events within the world of Saudi Shari'a politics" (Brown, 2012, p. 1). However, how these reforms initiated by a modernist group of royalty in power will change the traditional system of criminal justice in Saudi Arabia—a heartland of believers in the orthodox interpretation of Wahhabi Islam—remains to be seen. "The conservatives think that any change to the way Shari'a is implemented means liberal modernization and modernization is a western influence," said the lawyer who practices in Jeddah (Wagner, 2011, p. 2).

Sources: Wagner, R. L. (2011, February 24). Saudi Arabia gets ready to put order in its courts. *The Jerusalem Post.* Retrieved from www .jpost.com/MiddleEast/Article.aspx?id=209745; Brown, N. J. (2012, June 10). Why won't Saudi Arabia write down its law? *Foreign Policy.* Retrieved from http://mideast.foreignpolicy.com/posts/2012/01/23/why_wont_saudi_arabia_write_down_its_laws.

The structure of the modern state was completely destroyed during the Islamic Revolution in Iran in 1979. A group of Shiite clergy came to power in 1979 and established a theocratic state in Iran. Another critical difference between Saudi Arabia and Iran is that Saudi Arabia as a kingdom was born with the blessings of the West, and the Saudi monarchy has been historically close to the West. The theocratic state of Iran, on the other hand, was born by destroying the modern institutions of the West. The theocratic state of Iran was born with a challenge to the West and with enormous hatred against the values and ideologies of Western modernity. A comparative study of criminal justice in Iran needs to begin with an understanding of the specific nature of political evolution in Iran that led to its transformation from modernity to tradition.

The Political Evolution of Iran and the Rise of the Iranian Theocracy

Saudi Arabia is a part of the great civilization of the Arabs, but the kingdom of Saudi Arabia is relatively new. Iran is part of a civilization that is more than 2,500 years old. Islam began to spread to Iran, historically known as the Persian civilization, in the middle of the 7th century. By the 11th century, a majority of Iranians were converted from Zoroastrianism to Islam. In the Middle Ages, Iran was ruled by two successive Islamic dynasties: the Safavid dynasty (1501–1750) and the Zand dynasty (1750–1794). In the 19th century and the early part of the 20th century, Iran was ruled by the Qajar dynasty (1794–1925) led by the Turkmen tribe of Azerbaijan. In the 16th century, Safavid King Shah Ismail converted Iran from Sunnism to Shiism. Since the days of the Safavid dynasty, there began the gradual development of a special class of Shiite clergy in Iran different from the Sunni clergy of the Ottoman Empire. The doctrine of Shiism is based on two fundamental beliefs. The first is that the Islamic conception of justice can be realized only through the realization of divine knowledge and the role of imams (Islamic scholars and rulers). The second is called the doctrine of the "Twelve Imams." The doctrine of the "Twelve Imams" is based on the belief that after the Prophet Muhammad, Islam survived, progressed, and thrived because of the role of Imams, particularly the role of Ali ibn Abu Talib. The Shiites of Iran believe that in an Islamic country, "temporal justice can be served only if the Shii Imams' heritage, particularly of the First Imam, Ali ibn Abu Talib, is emulated under the Shi'ite clergy's hegemonic control" (Kusha, 2002, p. 132). At the beginning of the 16th century, when the Safavids' rulers declared Shiism as a state religion, the Shiite clergy in Iran began to exert political power and influence, particularly in the domain of law and justice. One scholar on criminal justice in Iran observed that "from the time of the Safavids, to the time of the Qajars, to the time of the Constitutional Revolution and the Pahlavi monarchs, the Shi'ite clergy had demanded that Iran's education and justice systems . . . be left to its control" (Kusha, 2002, p. 132).

During the Safavid dynasty, religious judiciary considerably expanded, and the Shiite clergy was highly dominant in power and politics. "The development of a new religious hierarchy in this period led to the further domination of *mazalem* (grievance) courts in the judicial system" (Floor, 2009, p. 20). The dominance of the doctrine of Imami Shiism during the Safavid period "superseded the Sunnite schools of jurisprudence and the Shi'ite scholars replaced their Sunnite counterparts" (Floor, 2009, p. 20). But after the fall of the Safavid dynasty in 1722, which had ruled Iran for more than 250 years, "The official, state-appointed, religious judiciary declined in significance" (Floor, 2009, p. 9). The Afghans who replaced the Safavids and ruled Iran for 8 years were Sunnites, and "Nader Shah Afsar, who ousted the Afghans, was indifferent to Shi'ism" (Floor, 2009, p. 9). During the Qajar dynasty that ruled Iran for about 130 years, "there continued to be secular (orfi) and religious (sari'a) courts, under secular and religious officials, respectively. Both types of judges were appointed by the shah" (Floor, 2009, p. 9). Historians claim that "from the beginning of Islamic rule in Persia, both a secular and a religious judiciary co-existed: the *orfi* court applying the common law, the tribunal of religious judge (qazi) applying the sacred law (sari'a)" (Floor, 2009, p. 1). During the periods of subsequent political evolutions, however, the *orfi* court applying the common law became dominant (Floor, 2009).

The history of the development of a modern state in Iran began from the first Constitutional Revolution in Iran in 1906 (Arjomand, 1984, 1988). In 1906, Muzaffar-e-Din Shah, the last ruler of the Qajar dynasty, issued a decree for the abolition of the monarchy and creation of a new republic in Iran. He laid the groundwork for the creation of a parliament (*majles*), a constitutional assembly, and a new constitution. He signed the new constitution in 1906, and that marked the end of the 400 years of medieval rule of Iran by different Islamic dynasties. From the beginning of the new republic in Iran, there began the expansion and codification of the secular law by extensively borrowing from the civil law tradition of continental Europe, particularly the French Napoleonic Code. The secularization of Iran's legal system began, as one scholar on Iranian legal development observed, "in 1910 with the establishment of the Central Public Prosecutor's Office, and a year later, when the Ministry of Justice was reorganized to perform its constitutional mandate of centralizing the country's legal system" (Entessar, 1998, p. 93). The process of the codification of secular law based on the civil law tradition, however, began with the expansion of the religious judiciary. Article 1 of the constitution of 1906 stated that "the State religion of Iran is Islam, according to the true Jafariya doctrine, recognizing Twelve Imams." The Shiite clerics were allowed to maintain exclusive control over family law, such as the law of marriage, divorce, succession, and the like. It is believed, however, that at that time, the Shiite clergy began to expand their influence on the judicial system of the new state of Iran because of the lack of a stable centralized system of governance under the control of secular leadership (Entessar, 1998).

From 1925 to 1979, Reza Khan and his son, Muhammad Reza Shah Pahlavi, governed Iran. It was under the Pahlavi dynasty that ruled Iran for more than half a century that modernization and secularization began in all spheres of life including law and justice. After Reza Shah assumed power in 1925, he "embarked upon an ambitious program of overhauling the traditional Iranian legal system and codifying the law away from its Islamic roots and towards the European legal tradition" (Entessar, 1998, p. 93). The process of the secularization of the legal system in Iran further intensified under the rule of Mohammad Reza Shah Pahlavi, who ruled Iran from 1941 to 1979. The rule of Mohammad Reza Shah Pahlavi was indeed an experiment in the possibility of modernization in the heartland of Shiite Islam in Iran. Mohammad Reza Shah introduced a new process of professionalization in legal education and practice in Iran. He introduced a law in 1946 that "required that judges hold a degree from the Faculty of Law at Tehran University (or an equivalent foreign university)" (Entessar, 1998, p. 93). The law further required that "the current judges who were not graduates of Tehran University's Law Faculty or its foreign equivalent must pass an examination in both Iranian and international law in order to remain employed as judges by the Ministry of Justice" (Entessar, 1998, p. 94). Under the 38 years of rule of Mohammad Reza Shah, modernization rapidly progressed in all sectors of Iranian society. But this progress, particularly in law justice, created new tensions between the secular and religious judiciaries. The process of professionalization in legal education and practice removed a large number of the Shiite clergy from the secular judiciary. The net effect of this process "was the disbarment of the overwhelming majority of the *ulema* and their removal from cherished judicial positions" (Entessar, 1998, p. 94).

It is this disgruntled group of the Shiite clergy that began to agitate against modernization and against the political regime of Mohammad Reza Shah in the middle of the 1960s. The discovery of oil in Iran and the growing presence of Western powers on Iranian soil in the beginning of the 1960s further intensified the political tensions between the modernists and the conservative Shiite clergy. Ayatollah Khomeini was arrested and exiled in 1964 for organizing political agitations against the government of Mohammad Reza Shah. It is this conservative Shiite clergy, aligned with a part of the military leadership, that took over the political power of Iran in 1979 under the leadership of Ayatollah Khomeini. After about 70 years of progress toward modernization, the regime of Mohammad Reza formally collapsed in February 1979, and the modern world saw the rise of a new theocratic state in Iran under the leadership of a Shiite clergy that was claiming political power for the first time since their origins more than 400 years earlier under the Safavid dynasty. The understanding of this historical conflict between religious and secular judiciaries and religious and secular political leaderships is vital in understanding Iran's present system of Shari'a Law and justice in the 21st century.

Shiite Islam and the New Criminal Justice System in Iran

The new leadership of the Shiite clergy in Iran, immediately after coming to power, announced the destruction of the modern state and modern system of law and justice. The old constitution of 1906 was quickly replaced, and a new constitution was promulgated for the Islamic Republic of Iran in December 1979. Article 1 of the new constitution (Middle East Constitutional Forum, 2012) states: "The form of government of Iran is that of an Islamic Republic, endorsed by the people of Iran on the basis of their long-standing belief in the sovereignty of truth and Koranic justice." Article 4 of the new constitution states: "All civil, penal, financial, economic, administrative, cultural, military, political, and other laws . . . must be based on Islamic criteria. This principle applies absolutely and generally to all articles of the Constitution as well as to all other laws and regulations." The new constitution also explicitly mentioned that the Republic of Iran will be based on the beliefs and values of Shi'ia Islam. Shi'ia Islam believes in the Quran but interprets it in terms of the views of its Imams (religious scholars). Shi'ia Islam of Iran is particularly based on the teachings of Abu Abdullah Ja'far bin Mohammed al-Sadeq, known as the Ja'fari school of Islamic jurisprudence. Article 12 of the constitution states: "The official religion of Iran is Islam and the . . . Ja'fari school [in usual al-Din and fiqh], and this principle will remain eternally immutable." Article

12 goes on to say that "other Islamic schools, including the Hanafi, Shafi'i, Maliki, Hanbali, and Zaydi, are to be accorded full respect, and their followers are free to act in accordance with their own jurisprudence in performing their religious rites."

The preamble of the constitution described it "as both an ideological and theological document. Ideologically, the Constitution imposes rather severe restrictions on the civil rights" (Arjomand, 1992, p. 1). Individuals are barred from joining any gatherings or demonstrations that are "detrimental to the fundamental principles of Islam" (Article 27). Article 2, Section 1, explicitly expresses the theocratic nature of the constitution. It states that the Islamic Republic of Iran "is a system based on the belief in the single God (as stated in the phrase 'There is no God except Allah'), His exclusive sovereignty and the right to legislate, and the necessity of submission to his commands." Section 2 of Article 2 states that the Islamic Republic of Iran is based on belief in "divine revelation and its fundamental role in setting forth the laws." Section 3 of Article 2 states that the Islamic Republic of Iran is based on the belief in "the justice of God in creation and legislation."

Chapter 11 of the constitution described the nature of the Islamic judiciary in Iran. One of the fundamental changes introduced by the new Islamic regime is a law that required that all judicial posts must be held by high-ranking clerics of *mojtahids*. Through the promulgation of this law, the secular system of justice that coexisted with the religious judiciary in Iran for more than 400 years since the beginning of the rule of the Safavid dynasty in the early 16th century was completely overthrown. In 1980, the newly created Supreme Court of Iran invalidated the old court structure and all the laws of the previous regimes that did not conform to the principles of the Shi'ia Islam. "The traditional duality of the judiciary system in Persia, which had been recognized in the earlier constitution, has thus been replaced by a single theocratic system exclusively under the clerical control" (Arjomand, 1992, p. 11).

The new judicial structure is composed of the following four major categories of courts: Revolutionary Courts, Public Courts, Courts of Peace, and Supreme Court of Cessation. The criminal courts are within the Public Courts, and there are two types of criminal courts: the First-Class Criminal Courts (there are about 86 of these) and the Second-Class Criminal Courts (there are about 156 of these). The first-class criminal courts deal mostly with serious crimes (*hudud* crimes and *qisas* crimes). The second-class criminal courts deal mostly with *ta'zir* crimes and petty crimes. The first-class criminal courts are composed of two judges, a presiding judge and an advisor. The second-class criminal courts are composed of a single judge (Lawyers Committee for Human Rights, 1993). Criminal cases are also tried in the country's 70 branches of revolutionary courts or tribunals. The revolutionary courts and tribunals try "crimes against national security, narcotics smuggling, and acts that undermine the Islamic Republic" (Sial, 2006, p. 3). Criminal trials in the revolutionary courts are mostly secret, and there are very few procedural safeguards. "Decisions rendered in revolutionary courts are final and cannot be appealed" (Sial, 2006, p. 4). There are also Special Military Courts, Special Courts for the Clergy, and the Court of Administrative Justice. The military courts and the special courts for the clergy deal with criminal violations of the rules and principles of the Shiite Islam and the Shari'a by members of the military and the clergy. The decisions rendered by the special courts of the military and the special courts of the clergy are also final and not appealable (Sial, 2006).

The new Islamic judicial system created in 1979 was put under the control of the Supreme Judicial Council composed of the Chief Justice of the Supreme Court, the Prosecutor-General, and three appointed judges. In 1989, through a constitutional amendment (Constitution of Iran as Amended in 1989), the Supreme Judicial Council was abolished, and the post of Head of the Judiciary was created. The Head of the Judiciary is appointed by the Supreme Leader, who in turn appoints the Chief Justice of the Supreme Court and the Chief Public Prosecutor (Sial, 2006). What is significant is that the entire judicial system of Iran after the Islamic Revolution in 1979 was placed almost exclusively under the control and dominance of the Shiite clergy. "The attorney general, like the chief justice, must be a mujtahid and is appointed to office for a five year term by the faqih (Article 162). The judges of all the courts must be knowledgeable in Shari'a jurisprudence" (Sial, 2006, p. 4). In 1982, the Supreme Leader of Iran "expressly ordered that all pre-revolutionary laws should be disregarded and declared that judges who continued to enforce pre-revolutionary secular legislation would be liable to prosecution" (Lawyers Committee for Human Rights, 1993, p. 3).

At the top of the executive, legislative, and judicial branches of the government in Iran is the Office of the Supreme Leader. Presently, Ayatollah Ali Khamenei is the Supreme Leader of Iran. The Supreme Leader of Iran is like the President of the United States and the Prime Minister of the United Kingdom. The Supreme Leader is elected by an assembly of experts. The assembly of experts is a body of 86 "virtuous and learned" Shi'ite clerics who are elected by the public for 8 years (Sial, 2006). The Supreme Leader is responsible for, according to Article 110 of the Constitution: (1) the delineation of the general policies of the Islamic Republic of Iran after consultation with the nation's Exigency Council; (2) the supervision of the proper execution of the general policies of the system; (3) the issuing of decrees for national referenda; (4) assuming supreme command of the armed forces; and (5) the declaration of war and peace and the mobilization of the armed forces. In Iran, the armed forces are directly under the control of the Supreme Leader. It is not under the control of the President and the executive branch of the government. The Supreme Leader also appoints the Council of Guardians, the Head of the Judiciary, the Chief Commander of the Islamic Revolutionary Guard, and the supreme commanders of the armed forces. One of the major responsibilities of the Supreme Leader is to oversee the governance of the republic in terms of the principles of Shi'ia Islam and the Quranic law.

The Supreme Leader is aided by a president, the Council of Guardians, the Expediency Council, and the Islamic Consultative Council. The Islamic Consultative Council is the law-making body (legislature) of 290 members of the Shiite clergy elected for 4 years. But its law-making functions are controlled by the Council of Guardians, composed of 12 Shiite clerics. Six members of the Council of Guardians are appointed by the Supreme Leader, and six are appointed by the Head of the Judiciary. The Council of Guardians is responsible for overseeing that all laws of the land are made within the framework of Shi'ia Islam and the Shari'a Law. Article 91 of the Constitution states that "to safeguard the Islamic ordinances and the Constitution, in order to examine the compatibility of the legislation passed by the

Islamic Consultative Assembly with Islam, a council to be known as the Guardian Council is to be constituted."

In addition to the judicial system, these various governmental bodies—the Office of the Supreme Leader, the Office of the President, and the Council of Guardians—affect criminal justice in Iran in many significant ways. One of the major differences between the criminal justice systems in Saudi Arabia and Iran is that in Saudi Arabia, a number of judicial and executive bodies and institutions for checks and balances on the role and functioning of the Shari'a courts have evolved, such as the Supreme Court of Saudi Arabia, the Department of Justice, the Supreme Judicial Council, the Board of Grievances, and the institution of the Saudi monarchy. In Iran, on the other hand, the judges of the criminal Shari'a courts are relatively independent, and they have wide discretionary powers of interpreting the Shari'a Law and the Shiite Islam. A report from the Lawyers Committee for Human Rights (1993) noted that in Iran, "religious judges holding the status of Mojtahed who occupy the vast majority of judicial positions in penal courts cling to their authority to issue judgments on the basis of their own religious opinions or Fatwa" (p. 9). The report further noted that religious judges in Iran "are free to make their own decision on the basis of their own interpretations of Islamic Law" (p. 9).

Criminal Justice System in Iran: The Nature of Substantive Criminal Law

Criminal law in Iran before the Islamic Revolution and the capturing of the political power of Iran by the Shiite clergy in 1979 was based exclusively on the civil law tradition of continental Europe. During Iran's period of modernization under the rule of Mohammad Reza Shah Pahlavi, the religious judiciary was concerned only with domestic and family-related cases. At that time, "criminal law and criminal procedural law were divorced from Islamic law. Punishments such as stoning and dismemberment were made illegal and religious judges were not permitted to impose penalties in matters which were considered as criminal under Islamic law" (Lawyers Committee for Human Rights, 1993, p. 3). In 1979, the Constitution of the Islamic Republic of Iran made Islamic law—the Shari'a—the basis of both civil and criminal laws in Iran (Article 4). The civil law tradition of continental Europe was completely overthrown. It is estimated that within 4 years of the Islamic Revolution, "about 2,000 laws had been passed" (Lawyers Committee for Human Rights, 1993, p. 3). One of the most significant developments was the promulgation of the Islamic Penal Code on the basis of the partial codification of the Shari'a Law (Mission for Establishment of Human Rights in Iran, 2012). One scholar on Iranian criminal justice observed that "the first Islamic Majles and the Guardian Council promptly codified features of the shari'a by passing two landmark bills: the Qanon-e Ta'zir (Discretionary Punishment Law) and Qanon-e Qesas (Retribution Law)" (Abrahamian, 1999, p. 133). The enactment of the *ta'zir* law provides "judges the authority to execute and imprison those found guilty of 'declaring war on God' and 'plotting with foreign powers' . . . [and] gives them the power to mete out as many as seventy lashes to those who insult government officials" (Abrahamian, 1999, p. 133). The enactment of the *Qanon-e Qesas* mandated death by hanging, stoning, or decapitation "for serious offenses against God—apostasy, fornication, homosexuality, and habitual drinking" (Abrahamian, 1999, p. 133).

The Islamic Penal Code was first passed by the Council of Guardians in 1982 as an experiment in criminal law for a period of 5 years. Since then, it has been extended several times. An amended version of the Islamic Penal Code was passed by Iran's Islamic Consultative Council in July 1991. It was ratified by Iran's Expediency Council in November 1991. Before 1996, there were four major chapters or books in the penal code. In 1996, Book Five on *ta'zir* crimes (*Ta'zirat*) was added. The most recent extension of the penal code was approved by Iran's Islamic Consultative Council in 2010 and was put in action by Iran's president in 2011. The Islamic Penal Code of Iran identified the following four types of crimes and four categories of criminal punishments (Section 7, Chapter 2): *hudud* crimes and punishments; *qisas* crimes and punishments; *diyat* crimes and punishments; and *ta'zir* crimes and punishments. Book Two of the penal code defines eight types of *hudud* crimes: adultery, sodomy, lesbianism, pimping, malicious sexual accusations, intoxication, civil unrest, and theft. In the Quran, civil unrest and pimping have not been explicitly mentioned as *hudud* crimes. *Hudud* crimes in the Quran are explicitly those for which punishments are divinely sanctioned, and there are no divine punishments sanctioned for civil unrest and pimping (Alasti, 2006). Book Three of the penal code names two types of *qisas* crimes: crimes of murder and crimes of aggravated physical assault resulting in bodily harm. Book Four of the penal code explains the nature of monetary compensation (blood money) and the procedures of paying the blood money. Book Five of the penal code outlines 29 *ta'zir* crimes and crimes that are punished for deterrence. Some of these include crimes against national security, usury and bribery, disobedience of state officials, personal insults, offenses against public morality, offenses against family duty, and bankruptcy.

One of the noticeable aspects of the Islamic Penal Code of Iran is its various provisions for capital punishment (Project on Extra-Legal Execution in Iran, 2011). There are 133 capital offenses in the penal code. Of these 133 capital offenses, 31 are for *hudud* crimes (see **Table 10-2**), 4 for *qisas* crimes, and 98 for *ta'zir* crimes (see **Table 10-3**). The *hudud* punishments are for all 8 categories of *hudud* crimes: adultery, sodomy, lesbianism, pimping, malicious sexual accusations, intoxication, civil unrest, and theft. Sections 81–218 in the penal code described the nature of these *hudud* crimes and the conditions under which *hudud* punishments are imposed. Section 81, for example, states that "Zina shall be punishable by Hadd only when the person charged with Zina fulfills the following conditions: puberty, sanity, free will and maturity." Section 123 of the penal code states that "the drinking of an intoxicant, whether in a small or large quantity, whether it has intoxicated the person or not, and whether it is pure or mixed, shall be punishable by Hadd." According to Section 123, drinking beer is punishable by eighty lashes. It states that "beer, even if it is not an intoxicant, falls under the category of liquor, and drinking it shall be punishable by the Hadd." Section 135 says that "whenever a person drinks liquor several times, and every time Hadd is executed on him, if he is convicted for the third time, he shall be punished by death." The *hudud* punishment for sodomy in the Iranian penal code is death. Section 142 asserts that "sodomy shall be punishable by death only when the person committing it and the person with whom it has been committed are both adult, sane and have free will." If sodomy

TABLE 10-2 The Penal Code of the Islamic Republic of Iran: Capital Offenses for *Hudud* Crimes

Hudud Offenses	*Hudud* Punishment	*Hudud* Offenses	*Hudud* Punishment
Zina with relatives with whom marriage is prohibited	Death penalty	Third conviction for intoxication	Death penalty
Zina with step-mother	Death penalty	Fourth conviction for theft	Death penalty
Zina between non-Muslim male and Muslim female	Death penalty	Armed robbery or highway banditry	Death penalty
Male-to-female rape	Death penalty	Carrying a weapon to create terror and fear	Death penalty
Zina by married female with mature male	Death penalty	Taking up arms against the Islamic state	Death penalty
Fourth conviction of an unmarried person for *zina*	Death penalty	Plotting to overthrow the Islamic state	Death penalty
Zina by married male	Death penalty	Participating in a coup d'etat government	Death penalty
Sodomy between mature males	Death penalty	Innate apostasy (a Muslim who abandoned the religion—one parent Muslim)	Death penalty
Male-to-male rape	Death penalty	Parental apostasy (a Muslim who abandoned the religion—both parents non-Muslim)	Death penalty
Sodomy with a minor	Death penalty	Blasphemy/cursing the Prophet	Death penalty
Sodomy between Muslim and non-Muslim	Death penalty	Heresy	Death penalty
Fourth conviction for sodomy and lesbian relations	Death penalty	Witchcraft	Death penalty

Source: Data from Project on Extra-Legal Executions in Iran, 2011.

is with a minor, the person committing the sodomy receives the death penalty and the minor receives a *ta'zir* punishment (Section 143). Section 152 of the penal code prescribes punishment for masturbation. It states that the "Hadd for tafkheedh (or masturbation through rubbing the male organ between the thighs of another) and similar acts between two men done without penetration shall be one hundred lashes to each." Section 152 further explains that "if the person committing the offence happens to be a non-Muslim and the person with whom the act has been done is a Muslim, the Hadd for the former shall be death." For lesbian relations, the penal code imposed "one hundred lashes for each of the women" (Section 159). Irrespective of gender, the *hudud* punishment for malicious sexual accusations is eighty lashes (Section 170). Section 199 of the penal code describes the nature of *hudud* punishment

TABLE 10-3 The Penal Code of the Islamic Republic of Iran: Capital Offenses for *Ta'zir* (Statutory) Crimes

Ta'zir Offenses	*Ta'zir* Punishment	*Ta'zir* Offenses	*Ta'zir* Punishment
Inciting the armed forces to rebel, flee, surrender, or abandon	Death penalty	Promoting, distributing, or trading obscene material via computer or broadcast systems	Death penalty
Setting fire to monuments, buildings, ships, and airplanes	Death penalty	Establishment of corruption and prostitution centers	Death penalty
Destruction, arson, or damage of infrastructural or public service institutions	Death penalty	Establishment of weblogs and websites promoting corruption, prostitution, and heresy	Death penalty
Attempted assassination of the supreme leader	Death penalty	Trafficking of persons under the age of 18	Death penalty
Offending Islam and its sanctities in the press	Death penalty	Human trafficking for sexual exploitation	Death penalty
Cultivation and production of narcotic drugs	Death penalty	Possession, concealment, transportation, and manufacturing of heavy arms	Death penalty
Third conviction for purchase and possession of 5–20 kg of narcotic substances	Death penalty	Armed resistance against government officials	Death penalty
Repeat conviction for more than 20 kg of narcotic drugs	Death penalty	Smuggling radioactive or microbial substances	Death penalty
Armed smuggling of any illegal narcotic drugs	Death penalty	Armed smuggling and hooliganism	Death penalty
Disrupting the monetary system of the country	Death penalty	Commission of a crime against internal or external security	Death penalty
Bribery, embezzlement, and fraud	Death penalty	Distribution of poisonous, microbial, and dangerous substances	Death penalty
Producing obscene works made by means of force	Death penalty	Abduction for the purpose of rape or ransom	Death penalty
Producing obscene works made by means of the sexual abuse of others	Death penalty	Insulting the sanctity of Islam or any of the prophets, infallible imams, or the Prophet Mohammad's daughter	Death penalty

Source: Data from Project on Extra-Legal Executions in Iran, 2011.

for participating in civil unrest. It states that "every individual or group who creates a plan for the overthrow of the Islamic regime . . . shall be termed muharib and one engaged in spreading corruption on earth (mufsid fi al-ard)." Section 200 further explains that "everyone who volunteers for an important post in the coup d'etat government as a part of the plan for overthrowing the Islamic regime . . . shall be deemed muharib and one spreading corruption on earth (musfif fi al-ard)." Section 202 explains that those *hudud* punishments for participating in civil unrest or in activities for overthrowing the Islamic regime of Iran shall be one of the following: beheading, crucifixion, amputation of right hand and left foot, or banishment. For the stealing of protected property by an adult, the penal code has imposed a sentence of cutting off the four fingers of the right hand for the first offense, cutting off the left foot for the second offense, life in prison for the third offense, and death by hanging for the fourth offense (Section 218).

Sections 1–80 of the Penal Code of Iran describe the nature of *qisas* crimes and punishments. The penal code describes two kinds of *qisas* crimes: *qisas* for life and *qisas* for a part of the human body. *Qisas* punishment for life means punishment for a willful murder. Section 1 states that willful murder "is punishable by Qisas (or retaliation) and the heirs to the person murdered (owliya al-dam) may kill the murderer with the permission of a Muslim ruler (wali) or his representative." Before the execution of *qisas* for life, securing the permission of the heir of the victim is mandatory (Section 15). If a father kills his son or grandfather kills his grandson, the *qisas* punishment, however, is not applicable. Section 16 says that "a father or paternal grandfather who kills his son (or grandson) shall be liable only to pay the Diyat for the murder to the heirs as a Ta'zeer." The penal code also states that the killing of an individual sentenced to death is not a *qisas* crime (Section 22). If the murderer is a pregnant woman, the penal code says that *qisas* should be imposed after the delivery of child (Section 48).

With respect to *qisas* for a part of the human body, Section 55 of the penal code rules that the inflicting of physical injury, "if willful, is punishable by Qisas, and the person with whom the offence has been committed (majniyy 'alayh) may, with the permission of the judge subject the offender to Qisas." Section 61 adds that in case of *qisas* punishment for physical injury, "equality of the location is to be observed, so that the part of the body of the right side of the offender shall be subjected to Qisas against a part of the right side of the body." Section 61 further explains that "where the offender has no right hand, his left hand shall be cut, and if he has even no left hand his foot shall be cut."

In 2008, a draft bill was proposed for the enactment of permanent legislation for the Islamic Penal Code of Iran. The draft bill has proposed to eliminate capital punishment for same-sex relations (proposed punishment 100 lashes), lesbianism (proposed punishment 100 lashes), false accusation of fornication or sodomy (proposed punishment 100 lashes), cursing the Prophet (the scope has been reduced to swearing at the Prophet of Islam), and drinking (proposed punishment 80 lashes). The bill, however, has proposed to extend capital punishment for a wide variety of crimes related to corruption on earth (such as arson, disruption of the economy, destruction and terror, distribution of dangerous poisons and microbiological matters, establishment of prostitution, and creation of blogs and websites to propagate corruption). The bill has proposed capital punishment also for apostasy, heresy, witchcraft, and crimes that are moralistic in nature such as armed robbery, gangs, banditry, Internet pornography, trafficking of women and children for sexual exploitation, kidnapping for rape and extortion, and illegal trafficking of conventional weapons (International Federation for Human Rights, 2009).

Criminal Justice System in Iran: The Nature of Procedural Criminal Law

The criminal procedural laws in Iran are of two types. One set of laws describes what is called the due process of law in modern systems of criminal justice. Another set of laws is related to the definition, imposition, and execution of Shari'a punishments. The second set of laws is related primarily to evidentiary rules of different kinds of crimes. Some of the due process laws are described in Chapter III of the Constitution of the Islamic Republic of Iran. Article 32 , for example, defines the rights of the detainees. It states that a person may not be arrested "except according to and in the manner laid down in the law. If someone is detained . . . within at most 24 hours the file on the case and preliminary documentation must be referred to the competent legal authority." Article 35 of the constitution states that the accused has a right to have an attorney. The article says that the accused parties are "entitled to select a lawyer for themselves. If they do not have the capacity to do this, the means of a lawyer being appointed to act for them must be made available to them." Article 37 establishes the notion of the presumption of innocence: "Innocence is the basic principle. No person is considered legally guilty, except in cases where his guilt is established in a competent court." Article 38 prohibits torture for securing confessions: "Any kind of torture . . . to extract an admission of guilt . . . is forbidden. Compelling people to give evidence, or confess or take an oath is not allowed. Such evidence or confession or oath is null and void." Article 578 of Iran's penal code states that if the authorities and employees of the judiciary and law enforcement inflict "corporal harm and torment upon an accused in forcing him to confess, he shall, in addition to being subject to Qisas . . . [be] sentenced to a term of six months to three years in prison." Article 129 of Iran's Penal Procedure Code "provides that the investigating judge shall not resort to compulsion and duress when interrogating a defendant" (Redress Trust, 2003, p. 7).

In three different kinds of crimes—*hudud* crimes, *qisas* crimes, and *ta'zir* crimes—there are different rules of procedure and different rules of evidence (Alasti, 2006). Because all the procedural rules and the rules of evidence cannot be described within the scope of this chapter, some examples are given in the following section. Sections 81–218 of the Islamic Penal Code, as mentioned earlier, discussed some of the substantive issues and the procedural laws related to *hudud* crimes. The crime of *zina* or adultery is established, for example, on the basis of confessions. Section 85 of the penal code states that "whenever a man or a woman confesses in four (separate) meetings of having committed Zina, he or she shall be sentenced to Hadd for Zina." Section 85 further adds that if confessions are made less than four times, "he/she shall be given Ta'zeer punishment." Section 86 says that "a confession shall be legally effective only when the person making confession fulfills the following conditions: puberty, sanity, free will and intention." The evidentiary rule for adultery or *zina* is described in Section 91 of the penal code: "Zina is proved by the evidence of four men of reputed integrity ('adl) or three men and two women all of reputed integrity, whether it is punishable by Hadd of lashes or that of stoning to death." It should be noted here that most Islamic jurists are of the view that the witnesses of *zina* must be four reputed males who have seen the act of intercourse not by choice but by accident. Section 94 of the penal code says that "the testimony cited by the witnesses must be based on personal observation, so that a testimony based on mere conjecture shall have no legal effect." There is also a scope for avoiding *hudud* punishment for *zina* through repentance. Section 98 of the penal code says that "whenever a man or woman committing Zina repents before the evidence is cited, Hadd shall be set aside, but if he/she repents after the evidence has been cited, the Hadd shall not be set aside." Section 114 states that when the Zina of a person "is established by his own confession, at the time of stoning him to death the judge shall pelt the first stone on him and he shall be followed by others." Section 144 goes on to say that "if the Zina is proved by evidence of witnesses, the witnesses shall start pelting stones, and they will be followed by the judge and then by others."

The evidentiary rules for sodomy are the same as for those of *zina* or adultery. Section 145 of the penal code rules that "sodomy shall be established in respect of the person making confession four times of having committed sodomy." Four reputed men must also physically see the act of sodomy. Section 148 states that "sodomy is established by the evidence of four men of reputed integrity who should have personally observed the performance of the act." If there are fewer than four witnesses, "sodomy shall not be established, and the witnesses shall be liable to the Hadd for false accusation of sodomy" (Section 149). In case of sodomy, however, the Shari'a judges are given some discretionary powers. Section 151 says that in case of sodomy, "the (Shari'ah) judge may give his judgment on the basis of his knowledge acquired through the customary sources." The *hudud* punishment for sodomy can also be avoided through repentance before the presentation of evidence by four witnesses (Section 156). The procedures for establishing lesbianism are the same as for *zina* and sodomy: personal observation of the act of lesbianism by four reputed men (Section 158). The *hudud* crimes against national security are described in the penal code as acts of "spreading corruptions on earth." The acts of spreading corruptions on earth are established on the basis of a single confession or "by the evidence of only two men of reputed integrity" (Section 201). The *hudud* punishment for the crime of theft is established on the basis of confessions made twice and "evidence of two men of reputed integrity" (Section 216).

The evidentiary rules for *qisas* (murder and aggravated assault) are different from those of *hudud* crimes. The evidentiary requirements for *hudud* crimes are confessions and witness testimonies. *Qisas* crimes must be established on the basis of four types of evidence: confession, physical evidence, oath taken by the complainant, and intuition of the judge (Section 27 of the penal code). "A willful murder is established by confessions of willful murder, although it is made only once" (Section 28). The confession for willful murder must be made out of free will and voluntarily. The person making the confession must be a mentally sane adult. The establishment of a willful murder must also be based on "the evidence of two men of reputed integrity" (Section 33). If the defendant in the case of a willful murder pleads not guilty, then the burden of proof is on the defendant. There are also strict procedural laws for the execution of *qisas* punishments. Section 43 of the penal code states that "a willful murder is punishable by Qisas, but with the consent of the heirs of the deceased (waliyy-i-dam) and the murderer it may be changed into a full Diyat or less or more than a full Diyat [Blood Money]." Section 47 says that "the heirs to the deceased (owliya-i-dam) who have the option for Qisas are all the heirs to the deceased except the husband or wife who have no option for Qisas as to its pardon or execution." In *qisas* related to a part of the body, the following procedures establish the process of retaliation: (1) equality of the part of the body in matter of soundness; (2) equality of the parts of the body in matter of being real (as against artificial or surplus); (3) equality in the location of the part of the body inflicted; (4) the *qisas* may not likely cause the loss of life to the offender; and (5) the *qisas* must not exceed the quantum of offense (Section 58).

Hudud and *qisas* punishments such as beheading, amputation, cross-amputation, flogging, stoning, and retaliation for bodily harms are considered, as mentioned before, as cruel and unusual in terms of all the constitutions of the modern states and the universal standards of human rights. It is these types of punishments that are seen as problematic in bringing Shari'a Law within the framework of the modern due process of law in particular and the framework of universal human rights in general. Many Islamic jurists, however, claim that within the framework of the Shari'a Law, those punishments are not to be easily taken and commonly imposed. Those punishments were described in the Quran primarily as measures for deterrence and not for their wide applications for crime control. The Quran set extremely strict evidentiary rules for the use of cruel and unusual punishments (*hudud* and *qisas* punishments). One scholar on Islamic justice noted that among all of the prevailing legal systems in the world, Shari'a Law is one of the most rigorous with respect to establishing evidence for illegitimate sex (Kusha, 2004). In Section 7 of Surah Al Maidah, the Quran said, "if any one remits the retaliation by way of charity, it will be an act of atonement for him."

Amputation for theft is prescribed in the Quran, but the Quran immediately said that "this is an *exemplary punishment*" and "whoever repents after committing the crime [theft] and reform his conduct, Allah will surely turn him with forgiveness" (Section 6, Surah Al-Ma'idh). The Prophet Muhammad said that "it is better for a judge to make a mistake in acquitting a culprit rather than to punish an innocent" (Ahmed, 2009, p. 3). The Prophet Muhammad also said, "repeal Hudud to the extent you find a way for it" and "repeal Hudud on the basis of doubts" (Ahmed, 2009, p. 3). Moreover, in Islamic jurisprudence, offenses that are not committed in public are not crimes. Investigation of offenses committed in privacy is not allowed in Islamic jurisprudence. Naqvi, an Islamic jurist, claimed that in Islam, "investigation and gathering information, except in public offenses, are forbidden and prohibited. In circumstances where an offense is of an individual, private nature and has not been committed publicly, its disclosure . . . is disapproved . . . [and] considered . . . a sin"

(Abdorrahman Boroumand Foundation, 2011a, p. 1). The right of protection against self-incrimination seems to be one of the major principles of Islamic jurisprudence. The offenders who committed their offenses in privacy are required not to disclose their offenses in public.

The strict rules of evidence to establish *hudud* and *qisas* crimes, the public nature of criminal offenses, repeated revelations of the Quran to preserve the sanctity of life and search for repentance and forgiveness in dealing with human sin and evil, and the teachings of Prophet Muhammad to "repeal Hudud to the extent you find a way for it" (Ahmed, 2009, p. 3) make Islamic jurisprudence highly flexible and compatible with modern criminal justice that is also based on the same principle of governing crime and punishment on the basis of preserving the sanctity and the dignity of human life known as due process. But this perspective about Islamic jurisprudence is not clearly recognized in the traditional system of criminal justice in the Islamic Republic of Iran based on the Ja'fri school of Islamic jurisprudence and the Shi'ia Islam based on the doctrine of "Twelve Imams."

Islamic Criminal Justice in Iran: Local and Global Challenges

The Islamic Penal Code of Iran has detailed hundreds of procedural laws related to the evidentiary rules and the rules of executing the *hudud* and *qisas* punishments. Some of the major issues that are widely debated about the criminal justice system of Iran, however, are not related to the internal rules of procedures based on Islamic jurisprudence and the Shari'a Law. The major concerns are related to such problems as the organization of the criminal courts, limits on the independence of the judiciary, conduct of secret trials in the revolutionary courts, extension of capital punishment for a wide variety of statutory crimes (*ta'zir* crimes), extension of capital punishment for juveniles, mass executions, expansion of an unequal system of justice, and gross violations of the international standards of human rights. The Iranian judicial system is based on the inquisitorial model of justice (Article 193 of the penal code). In the criminal courts, the revolutionary courts, and the special courts for the military and the clergy, the Islamic judges play the role of both judges and prosecutors. The defendants have the right to have an attorney, but the defense attorneys within the inquisitorial system of justice do not have any significant role. Article 198 of the penal code ruled that trials are public but "courts have discretions to exclude the public in a wide range of cases" (Redress Trust, 2003 p. 13), The Iranian constitution prohibits torture (Article 38), but there are allegations that torture and human rights violations are rampant in the criminal justice system in Iran. Torture is widely practiced by the religious police of Iran and in Iranian jails and detention centers (Human Rights Watch, 2010a). The United Nations Organization's report, *The Situation of Human Rights in the Islamic Republic of Iran*, observed "a pattern of systematic violation of human rights in Iran" (Shaheed, 2009, p. 10).

What is particularly disturbing to the world community of nations about criminal justice in Iran is its extension of mandatory capital punishment for a wide variety of statutory crimes. The United Nations Organization's report (Shaheed, 2011) observed that in 2010, there were about 300 secret executions at Vakilabad prison (see **Box 10-2**) The report said that Vakilabad officials, in violation of Iranian law, allegedly carried out the executions without the knowledge or presence of the inmates' lawyers or families and without prior notification to those executed. It has also been reported that at least 146 secret executions took place in 2011 (Shaheed, 2011, p. 19).

Mass execution in Iran, however, began during the early days of the new Islamic regime. Immediately after capturing political power in 1979, the regime set up a new criminal justice system under the control of Revolutionary Tribunals headed by Shi'ite clerics chosen by the Supreme Leader. Within a period of 2 years, "the Revolutionary Tribunals executed 757 for 'sowing corruption on earth'—a term not heard in Iranian courts since 1909" (Abrahamian, 1999, p. 125). It is estimated that between 1981 and 1985, about 5,542 people were executed in Iran. Out of these 5,500 people, 4,995 were political prisoners (Mojahedins) and 547 were Marxists. Out of all political prisoners executed, 716 were women. Out of all Marxists executed, 42 were women (Abrahamian, 1999). Also, out of 4,995 Mojahedins who were executed,

---

BOX 10-2

United Nations Report on Executions and the System of Criminal Justice in Iran

On October 2011, Ahamed Shaheed, former Foreign Minister of Maldives, presented a report on human rights abuse and executions in Iran to the Human Rights Council of the General Assembly of the United Nations. Shaheed's report, prepared based on interviews of the members of the Iranian Diaspora, members of various international organizations, and members of various non-governmental organizations, and on the analysis of dozens of global reports, is one of the most authoritative accounts of the situation of human rights in Iran (Shaheed was denied entry to Iran, although repeated requests were made on behalf of the United Nations). The report documented that executions in Iran dramatically increased between 2003 and 2011. In 2003, Iran executed about 95 people; in 2007, the number reached around 310; in 2010, the number increased to approximately 540; and in 2011, the number of executions grew to about 670. The report noted that "81 per cent of all cases of capital punishment in 2011 were related to drug trafficking, while 4.3 per cent and 4.1 per cent were related to *Moharebeh* (enmity with God) and rape, respectively." The report documented that in the criminal justice system of Iran, "violations of the due process rights are chronic" (p. 10); people "were not presented with a warrant . . . for arrest during their interrogations" (p. 10); and many "endured unlawful searches and seizures, and had been held for weeks, even months, in solitary confinement." Iran is an Islamic Republic constitutionally based on Shari'a Law. It can be recalled here that in Section 13 of Surah An-Nisa, the Quran says: "O believers, when you struggle in the way of Allah, investigate carefully." The Prophet Muhammad warned that "God shall torture on the day of Recompense those who inflict torture on people in life."

Source: Shaheed, A. (2011). *The situation of human rights in the Islamic Republic of Iran.* New York, NY: United Nations Organization.

"1,362 (27%) were high school pupils; 1,809 (36%) were high school graduates . . . and 1,290 (26%) were college students" (Abrahamian, 1999, p. 130). It is further learned that "of the Mojahedin dead whose age is unknown, more than 76 percent were under twenty-six years old and 20 percent of them were under twenty" (Abrahamian, 1999, p. 132). What is even more disturbing is the increasing number of juvenile executions in Iran (see **Box 10-3**). A report from the International Federation for Human Rights (2009) found that "Iran ranks as the world's top child executioner" (p. 27).

In Section 34 of Surah Al-Baqarah, the Quran commands that through Islam, the "true guidance has been made clearly distinct from error. Therefore, whoever renounces 'Taghoot' (false deities) and believes in Allah has grasped firm hand-hold that will never break" (2:256–257). But the Quran commands again that "There is no compulsion in religion." (Surah Al-Baqarah, Section 34). Most Muslim jurists claim the Quran did not prescribe any mandatory punishment for apostasy (Saeed & Saeed, 2004). According to the revised Iranian Penal Code, approved in 2008, there are two types of apostasy: innate and parental. Article 225-4 of the revised penal code finds that "Innate Apostate is someone whose parent (at least one) was a Muslim at the time of conception, and who declares him/herself a Muslim after the age of maturity, and leaves Islam afterwards." Parental apostasy is described by Article 225-5, which says, "Parental Apostate is one whose parents (both) had been non-Muslims at the time of conception, and who has become a Muslim after the age of maturity, and later leaves Islam and returns to blasphemy." Article 225-7 declares that innate apostasy is a *hudud* crime and, for males, is publishable by death (Article 225-8). The punishment for innate apostasy by a female is life imprisonment (Article 225-10). The criminalization of faith in Iran created a tremendous sense of fear about criminal justice among the religious minorities in Iran, particularly among the followers of Christianity, Judaism, Zoroastrianism, and Baha'ism. A report from the International Federation for Human Rights (2009) indicated that between 1979 and 2003, "more than 200 Baha'is had been executed or otherwise killed" (p. 31). The report also states that "a well known documented case of judicial execution of a Christian is Soodmand, pastor of Assemblies of God in Mashhad in eastern Iran. He was sentenced to death for apostasy and executed in December 1990" (2009, p. 33). Like the believers in alternative faiths, the believers in alternative lifestyles also live in a state of fear and terror in Iran. A recent report from Human Rights Watch (2010b) described the believers in alternative lifestyles in Iran—the sexual minorities—as a buried generation. These are gross violations of Articles 32, 37, and 38 of the constitution of the Islamic Republic of Iran. The sanctity of life is central to the religion of Islam as it is for all other religions. The philosophy behind the *qisas* punishment is the sanctity of life. In Section 22 of Surah Al-Baqarah, the Quran says: "O men of understanding: There is *sanctity of life* for you in the law of retaliation, so that you may become pious" (2:178–179). A close examination of the workings of the Iranian criminal justice system will reveal that that the Islamic state of Iran is grossly violating not just the international standards of human rights but also this divine command of the Holy Quran (see **Table 10-4**).

BOX 10-3

Juvenile Executions in Iran: The Case of Delara Durabi

Iran is one of the modern civilized countries that still executes juveniles for crimes committed before the age of 18. According to Iran's Penal Code, promulgated in 1982, the minimum age to be treated as a juvenile for a male is 14 years and 5 months, and for a female is 8 years and 8 months. Iran's Penal Code also includes a provision that capital punishment for *hudud* and *qisas* crimes is to be carried out irrespective of the considerations of age. Executions of juveniles under the age of 18 are strictly prohibited by United Nations Convention on the Rights of the Child, and Iran is one of the countries that ratified the convention. But Iran is continuing to execute juveniles in violation of its commitment to this United Nations Convention on the Rights of the Child. On September 21, 2011, Iran publicly executed a juvenile named Alireza Molla-Soltani, who was 17 at the time of his execution. A juvenile named Hamid Hashemi was executed in prison for his alleged participation in political protest. Hamid was 16 years old at the time of his execution. In November 2011, two juveniles (Rouhollah Dedashi and Alireza Molla-Soltani) were hanged in public, and both of them were under the age of 18. One such event that shocked the international world is the execution of a female juvenile named Miss Delara Darabi in Iran in May 2009. Durabi was executed for a murder she never committed. When she was 17, she confessed to the murder to save her boyfriend. Her parents and lawyers were not even informed of the

BOX 10-3

(Continued)

time and date of execution. After knowing that her execution was impending, she made a frantic call to her mother, and that call outraged the consciousness of the civilized world. "Miss Darabi made a tearful call early on Friday to her parents to say she could see the gallows and noose, according to media reports from Tehran. 'Mother they are going to execute me, please save me,' she pleaded. But a prison official then grabbed the phone and told her distraught mother: 'We are going to execute your daughter and there's nothing you can do about it.'" Again, we should remember that in Surah Al-Baqarah, the Quran says: "O men of understanding: There is security of life for you in the law of retaliation" (2:178–179).

Source: Sherwell, P. (2009, May 2). Iran executes woman for alleged murder committed as a juvenile. *The Telegraph.* London, England: Telegraph Media Group; photo © JOHNNY GREEN/PA Photos/Landov.

■ Summary

Saudi Arabia and Iran have two of the most traditional systems of criminal justice in the world because both states are theocracies and both have organized their systems of criminal justice on the basis of Shari'a Law and Islamic jurisprudence. There are, however, many differences in the way criminal justice systems are organized in Saudi Arabia and Iran and the way they interpret the nature of Shari'a Law and Islamic jurisprudence. These differences are rooted in the competing political perspectives of the ruling elites of these countries. Saudi Arabia is a kingdom born in 1932 based on the religious ideology of Wahhabism. The advocates of Wahhabism belong to the orthodox Hanbali school of Islamic jurisprudence, and they explicitly reject the role of *ijtihad* and *ijma* in the interpretation of the Quran and the Sunna. The Islamic judges and jurists of Saudi Arabia are mostly the adherents of Wahhabism and the Hanbali school of Islamic jurisprudence. The ruling monarchy of Saudi Arabia, however, is not a part of or extension of the Islamic judges and jurists in Saudi Arabia. They are an extension of the family of King Abdul Aziz ibn Saud—the creator of the Kingdom of Saudi Arabia who happened to be a believer in Wahhabism. The ruling monarchy of Saudi Arabia, from the days of the establishment of the kingdom, has been open to the West. The successive monarchs of the kingdom supported selective modernization of the kingdom in many areas including law and justice. It is for this relatively liberal perspective of the Saudi ruling monarchy that a number of law and justice institutions have recently grown to establish strict procedural guidelines in the implementation of Shari'a Law within the Islamic criminal justice system in Saudi Arabia. The Law of the Judiciary, promulgated by royal decree in 1975; the Law of the Board of Grievances, promulgated by royal decree in 1982; the Law and Regulations of the Bureau of Investigation and Public Prosecution, promulgated

TABLE 10-4 Criminal Justice in the United States, Saudi Arabia, and Iran: A Comparative Look

Criminal Justice	United States	Saudi Arabia	Iran
Systemic Profile	Modern	Traditional	Traditional
Legal Tradition	English common law; impact of British colonialism	Islamic law—Shari'a law; orthodox version of Hanbali school of Islamic jurisprudence; was never formally colonized	Islamic law—Shari'a law; extremely orthodox version-Jaafari school of Twelve Imams; was never formally colonized
Major Sources of Criminal Law	Constitutions: state and federal; federal and state statutes; federal and state judicial laws; local ordinances; and federal and state criminal codes	Quran and Sunna; royal decrees/ordinances; codification of Shari'a law began in 2010	Quran and Sunna; constitution; the 1982 Islamic Penal Code of Iran (as amended in 1991, 1996, and 2008); codification of Shari'a law began in the 1980s
Organizational Model	Decentralized; federal and state systems of criminal justice	Centralized; one single system of criminal justice	Centralized; one single system of criminal justice
Court Structure	Federal courts: U.S. Supreme Court; U.S. Court of Appeals; and U.S. District Courts; state supreme courts, state intermediary courts, and state lower courts; and state and local juvenile courts	Supreme court of Saudi Arabia (after the promulgation of the new Law of the Judiciary in 2007); Shari'a Court of Appeals; First Instance Shari'a courts (General Courts and Summary Courts); and the Board of Grievances	Revolutionary Courts; Public Courts; Courts of Peace; and Supreme Court of Cessation; criminal courts are mostly with the Public Courts (First-Class Criminal Courts and Second-Class Criminal Courts); Special Military Courts and the Special Courts for the Clergy
Police Organization	Decentralized; federal police, state police, city and local police, and county sheriffs; key federal law enforcement agencies are the FBI, U.S. Marshals Service, U.S. Secret Service, U.S. Capitol Police, and the Drug Enforcement Agency (DEA); and 18,000 state and local law enforcement agencies (20; police are much more professionalized and internationalized; 2008 data)	Highly centralized; two major types of policing: Public Security Police (two categories: regular police under the Ministry of the Interior and Special Investigation Police under the General Directorate of Investigation) and Religious Police (Mutaween) under the control of the Committee for the Promotion of Virtue and the Prevention of Vice; police are professionalized and partly militarized.	Highly centralized; multiple force structures (police forces): Islamic Revolutionary Guard Corps, national police under the Ministry of Intelligence and Security; the Qods force (an autonomous group of the Islamic Revolutionary Group); and Basij groups composed of military reservists, Boy Scouts, Hitler Youth, and clerical representatives of the Supreme Leader; there is also a group of police called "morality police"; police are militarized and ideologically mobilized

TABLE 10-4 (Continued)

Criminal Justice	United States	Saudi Arabia	Iran
Prison Organization	Decentralized; federal prisons under the U.S. Bureau of Prisons; state prisons mostly under the state departments of corrections; and incarceration rate is 743 per 100,000 population (2009 data)	The Shari'a law does not mention imprisonment, but there are prisons in Saudi Arabia; they are centralized and managed by a Director General of Prisons under the Ministry of Interior; and incarceration rate is 132 per 100,000 population (2007 data)	Prison system is centralized and managed by a director; total prison population is 220,000 (as of March, 2011); out of this number, 70,000 are not yet sentenced (as of March, 2011); will build 47 new prisons by 2014; and incarceration rate is 214 (2007 data)
Due Process	Based on the constitution and the laws made by the U.S. Supreme Court	Based on the constitution—Basic System of Governance, 1992, and the Law of Criminal Procedure, 2001	Based on the constitution of 1979 and the Code of Criminal Procedure, 1999
Juvenile Justice	Boundaries between juvenile and adult justice are clearly drawn and legally established	Boundaries between juvenile and adult justices are blurred and not legally and strictly enforced	Boundaries between juvenile and adult justice are blurred and not legally and strictly enforced
Science and Technology Orientation	Highly science and technology intensive, and extensive academic research on criminology and criminal justice	Limited science and technology orientations, and limited academic research on criminology and criminal justice	Limited science and technology orientations, and limited academic research on criminology and criminal justice

by royal decree in 1989; the Law of Procedure Before Shari'a Courts, promulgated by royal decree in 2000; the Law of Criminal Procedure, promulgated by royal decree in 2001; and the Code of Law Practice, promulgated by royal decree in 2001 described some of the major procedural guidelines in the implementation of Shari'a Law in Saudi Arabia. Some of the major due process issues have been addressed and codified particularly by the Law of Criminal Procedure, promulgated in 2001.

Islamic criminal justice in Iran was introduced after the establishment of the present theocratic state in Iran. The theocratic state of Iran was established by the ascendency of a Shiite Islamic clergy who captured the political power of Iran by overthrowing the modernist regime of Reza Shah Pahlavi in 1979. From the days of the rule of the Safavid dynasty in Iran in the 16th century, there began the gradual development of a special class of Shiite clergy in Iran different from the Sunni clergy of the Ottoman Empire. The doctrine of Shiism is based on two fundamental beliefs. The first is that the Islamic conception of justice can be realized only through the role of Imams (Islamic scholars and rulers). The second is called the doctrine of "Twelve Imam." The Iranian Shiism is based on the belief that after the Prophet Muhammad, Islam survived, progressed, and thrived because of the role of imams, particularly the role of Ali ibn Abu Talib. The Shiites of Iran believe that in an Islamic country, "temporal justice can be served only if the Shii Imams' heritage, particularly of the First Imam, Ali ibn Abu Talib, is emulated under the Shi'ite clergy's hegemonic control" (Kusha, 2002, p. 132). This political perspective is particularly visible in Islamic criminal justice in Iran. Since the Iranian ruling clergy came to power by destroying the modernist regime of Reza Shah Pahlavi, they were against the West and opposed to Western modernization from the early days of their ascendency to political power. The Islamic criminal justice system of Iran is based on the most conservative and most orthodox interpretations of Shari'a Law. In the case of Saudi Arabia, there are differences between the ruling monarchy and the system of Islamic justice governed by Islamic judges and jurists. In the case of Iran, those who govern the system of criminal justice are also those who govern the political system. The executive, legislative, and judicial branches of the state are in the same hands of the Islamic Shiite clergy.

The strict rules of evidence to establish *hudud* and *qisas* crimes, the public nature of criminal offenses, repeated revelations of the Quran to preserve the sanctity of life and search for repentance and forgiveness in dealing with human sin and evil, and the teachings of the Prophet Muhammad to "repeal Hudud to the extent you find a way for it" (Ahmed, 2009, p. 3) make Islamic jurisprudence highly flexible and compatible with modern criminal justice that is also based on the same principle of governing crime and punishment on the basis of preserving the sanctity and dignity of human life known as due process. But this perspective about Islamic jurisprudence is not clearly recognized within the traditional system of criminal justice in the Islamic Republic of Iran based on the Ja'fari school of Islamic jurisprudence and the Shi'ia Islam based on the doctrine of "Twelve Imams." The Islamic Penal Code of Iran has detailed hundreds of procedural laws related to the evidentiary rules and the rules of executing the *hudud* and *qisas* punishments. Some of the major issues that are widely debated about the criminal justice system of Iran, however, are not related to the internal rules of procedures based on Islamic jurisprudence and Shari'a Law. The major concerns are related to such problems as the limits on the independence of the judiciary, conduct of secret trials in the Revolutionary Courts, extension of capital punishment for a wide variety of statutory crimes (*ta'zir* crimes), extension of capital punishment for juveniles, mass executions, expansion of an unequal system of justice, and gross violations of the international standards of human rights.

■ Discussion Questions

1. Describe the nature of Islamic criminal justice in Saudi Arabia, focusing particularly on the ideological context of the kingdom: the Wahhabism. How is the Wahhabist interpretation of Islamic jurisprudence different from that of the Hanafi school of Islamic jurisprudence (i.e., the role of *ijtihad* and *ijma* in the interpretation of the Quran and Sunna)?

2. Describe the structure of the Shari'a judicial system in Saudi Arabia, focusing on the different types of courts and the role of the monarchy and the Supreme Court of Saudi Arabia (established after the promulgation of the Law of the Judiciary in 2007) in governance of criminal justice.

3. Describe the major institutions of criminal justice in Saudi Arabia, focusing of the role of the Consultative Council, the Ministry of Justice, the Senior Council of Ulema, the Board of Grievances, and the Committee for the Promotion of Virtue and the Prevention of Vice. Give examples of their respective roles and functions.

4. In 2007, the Kingdom of Saudi Arabia undertook a major initiative to reform Shari'a judiciary in particular and the system of criminal justice in general. Describe some of the key aspects of that reform in criminal justice in Saudi Arabia. In this context, comment on the nature of tensions in Islamic criminal justice in Saudi Arabia to make a balance between tradition and modernity.

5. Describe the nature of Islamic criminal justice in Iran, focusing particularly on the rise of a Shiite clergy in political power, reorganization of the Iranian judicial system, and the introduction of new substantive and procedural criminal laws based on a distinctive interpretation of Shari'a Law and Islamic jurisprudence by the ruling elite.

6. Make a comparative analysis of the theocratic nature of criminal justice in Saudi Arabia and Iran, focusing particularly on the role of the monarchy in Saudi Arabia and the Shi'ite clergy in power in Iran.

7. In the context of the rise of Shi'ite clergy in power and its role in shaping the nature of criminal justice in Iran, comment on the significance of understanding the history and the nature of the state in comparative analysis of criminal justice among the world's societies.

8. Describe the nature of procedural criminal law in Iran with particular reference to due process laws. How and to what extent has due process of law been integrated in the criminal justice system in Iran? (Hint: Examine the structure and functions of the Revolutionary Courts and Tribunals, and the nature of mass and public executions in Iran.)

9. On the basis of your understanding of the nature of Shari'a Law and its implementation in Saudi Arabia and Iran, comment on the possibility of some convergence between modern and Islamic systems of criminal justice. Give examples.

10. How is the Islamic criminal justice system of Saudi Arabia similar to or different from the Islamic criminal justice system of Iran? In what sense it is justified to say that the Islamic state of Iran is grossly violating not just the international standards of human rights, but also many of the divine commands of the Holy Quran?

■ References

Abdorrahman Boroumand Foundation. (2011a). *Islamic Republic's penal code* (S. A. R. Naqvi, Trans.). Retrieved from www.iranrights.org/english/document-139.php.

Abdorrahman Boroumand Foundation. (2011b). A letter from a juvenile inmate on death row (author Mohammad Fadaei, Iran Human Rights Voice, Trans.). Retrieved from www.iranrights.org /english/document-483.php.

Abrahamian, E. (1999). *Tortured confessions: Prisons and public recantations in modern Iran.* Los Angeles: University of California Press.

Ahmed, R. (2009, October). *Islamization of laws: A comparative study of Islamic and Pakistani laws regarding circumstantial evidence.* Ninth Annual IBER & TLC Conference Proceedings. Las Vegas, NV. Retrieved from www.cluteinstitute.com/proceedings/Las_Vegas_2009/Article%20220.pdf.

Al-Farsy, F. (1991). *Modernity and tradition: Saudi equation.* London, England: Kegan Paul International.

Al-Rasheed, M. (2002). *A history of Saudi Arabia.* Cambridge, England: Cambridge University Press.

Alasti, S. (2006). Cruel and unusual punishment: Comparative perspective in international conventions, and the United States and Iran. *Annual Survey of International and Comparative Law, 12*(1), 149–184.

Amnesty International. (2010). *Saudi Arabian court rejects 'sorcery' death sentence.* Retrieved from www.amnesty.org/en/news-and-updates/saudi-arabian-court-rejects-sorcery-death-sentence-2010-11-12.

Ansary, A. F. (2011). *A brief overview of the Saudi Arabian legal system.* Retrieved from www.nyulawglobal.org/Globalex/Saudi_Arabia.htm.

Arjomand, S. A. (1984). *The shadow of God and the hidden imam: Religion, political order, and societal change in Shi'ite Iran from the beginning to 1890.* Chicago, IL: The University of Chicago Press.

Arjomand, S. A. (1988). *The turban for the crown: The Islamic Revolution in Iran.* New York, NY: Oxford University Press.

Arjomand, S. A. (1992). Constitution of the Islamic Republic of Iran. *Encyclopedia Iranica.* Retrieved from www.iranicaonline.org/articles/constitution-of-the-islamic-republic.

Armstrong, K. (2002). *Islam: A short history.* New York, NY: Modern Library—A Division of the Random House.

Entessar, N. (1998). Criminal law and the legal system in revolutionary Iran. *Boston College Third World Law Journal, 8*(8), 91–102.

Floor, W. (2009). Judicial system from the advent of Islam through the 19th century. *Encyclopedia Iranica.* Retrieved from www.iranicaonline.org/articles/judicial-and-legal-systems-iv-judicial-system-from-the-advent-of-islam-through-the-19th-century.

Hegghammer, T. (2008). Islamist violence and regime stability in Saudi Arabia. *International Affairs, 84*(4), 701–715.

Human Rights Watch. (2005). *Saudi Arabia: Court orders eye to be gouged out.* Washington, DC: Author.

Human Rights Watch. (2010a). *Iran: 2010 annual report.* Washington, DC: Author.

Human Rights Watch. (2010b). *We are a buried generation: Discrimination and violence against sexual minorities in Iran.* Retrieved from www.hrw.org/sites/default/files/reports/iran1210webwcover_0.pdf.

International Federation for Human Rights. (2009). *Iran/death penalty: A state terror policy.* Retrieved from www.fidh.org/IMG/pdf/Rapport_Iran_final.pdf.

Janin, H., & Kahlmeyer, A. (2007). *Islamic law: The Sharia from Muhammad's time to the present.* Jefferson, NC: McFarland & Company.

Kusha, H. R. (2002). *The sacred law of Islam: A case study of women's treatment in the Islamic Republic of Iran's criminal justice system.* London, England: Ashgate.

Kusha, H. R. (2004). *Defendant rights: A reference handbook.* Santa Barbara, CA: ABC-CLIO.

Lawyers Committee for Human Rights. (1993). *The justice system of the Islamic Republic of Iran.* Retrieved from www.iranrights.org/english/document-93.php.

Middle East Constitutional Forum. (2012). *1979 Constitution of Iran.* Retrieved from www.righttononviolence.org/mecf/countries/iran/.

Mission for Establishment of Human Rights in Iran. (2012). *Islamic penal code of Iran.* Retrieved from http://mehr.org/Islamic_Penal_Code_of_Iran.pdf.

Nolan, L. (2011). *Managing reform? Saudi Arabia and the King's Dilemma* (policy briefing). Doha, Qatar: Brookings Doha Center.

Otto, J. M. (2010). *Sharia incorporated: A comparative overview of the legal systems of twelve Muslim countries in past and present.* Amsterdam, the Netherlands: Amsterdam University Press.

Project on Extra-Legal Executions in Iran. (2011). *Replies to the list of issues: Death penalty concerns* (Review of the third periodic review of Iran presented to the 103 session of the Human Rights Committee, Geneva). New York, NY: Author.

Raphael, J. C. (2009). *Mutawas: Saudi Arabia's dreaded religious police.* Mumbai, India: Turtle Books.

Redress Trust. (2003). *Reparation for torture: A survey of law and practice in thirty selected countries.* London, England: The Redress Trust. Retrieved from www.redress.org/downloads/publications/AuditReportText.pdf.

Royal Embassy of Saudi Arabia. (2012a). *The Law of the Judiciary* (Royal Decree No. M/64, July 1975). Washington, DC: Author.

Royal Embassy of Saudi Arabia. (2012b). *The Basic Law of Governance* (Royal Decree No. A/90, March 1992). Washington, DC: Author.

Royal Embassy of Saudi Arabia. (2012c). *Law of the Board of Grievances* (Royal Decree No. M/51, May 1982). Washington, DC: Author.

Royal Embassy of Saudi Arabia (2012d). *The Law of Criminal Procedure* (Royal Decree No. M/39, October 2001). Washington, DC: Author.

Royal Embassy of Saudi Arabia. (2012e). *Law and Regulations of the Bureau of Investigation and Prosecution* (Royal Decree No. M/56, May 1989). Washington, DC: Author.

Royal Embassy of Saudi Arabia. (2012f). *The Law of Procedure Before Shari'ah Courts* (Royal Decree M/21, August 2000). Washington, DC: Author.

Royal Embassy of Saudi Arabia. (2012g). *The Code of Law Practice* (Royal Decree No. M/38, October 2001). Washington, DC: Author.

Saeed, A., & Saeed. H. (2004). *Freedom of religion, apostasy and Islam.* London, England: Ashgate.

Shaheed, A. (2011). *The situation of human rights in the Islamic Republic of Iran.* New York, NY: The United Nations.

Sial, O. (2006). A guide to the legal system of the Islamic Republic of Iran. Retrieved from www.nyulawglobal.org/Globalex/Iran1.htm.

Teitelbaum, J. (2000). *Holier than thou: Saudi Arabia's Islamic opposition.* Washington, DC: The Washington Institute for Near Eastern Policy.

Vassiliev, A. (1998). *The history of Saudi Arabia.* London, England: Saqi Books.

Vogel, F. E. (2000). *Islamic law and legal system: Studies of Saudi Arabia.* Leiden, the Netherlands: Brill Academic Publishers.

Dual Systems of Criminal Justice: The Case of the People's Republic of China

CHAPTER **11**

▶ CHAPTER OUTLINE

■ Introduction

A large number of countries in Asia, Africa, and Latin America have dual systems of criminal justice. Dual systems of criminal justice exist in those countries that make deliberate political decisions to integrate law and justice institutions from different competing legal traditions such as common law, civil law, Islamic law, Hindu law, Catholic law, Talmudic law, and socialist law. In terms of the principle of the separation of church and state, which is one of the distinctive characteristics of modern criminal justice, these legal traditions can again be divided into two major categories: secular legal traditions (common law, civil law, and socialist law) and nonsecular legal traditions (Catholic law, Hindu law, Islamic law, and Talmudic law). Many scholars in comparative law argue that the laws of all nations are inherently plural in nature. There is no country in the world where there is purely a single system of law (Glenn, 2007; Menski, 2006; Riemann & Zimmermann, 2008).

There is, however, no denying that there is a modern system of law and justice that has evolved and has become dominant within the framework of the modern state in the West. It is this system of modern law and justice that is now the benchmark for a comparative understanding of different systems of law and justice among the world's societies. How different dual systems have been evolving in the context of the globalization of the modern system of law and justice—a process that began during the days of colonialism in the 18th and 19th centuries—is an intriguing problem in comparative criminal justice. It is an exciting project to examine how different countries, particularly those in the modernizing world of Asia, Africa, and Latin America, have been creating space for modern law and justice in their traditional (primarily nonsecular) legal systems, and the extent to which their traditional notions of law and justice are being changed and challenged as a result of intercivilizational debates and disputes with respect to tradition and modernity (Huntington, 1996; Nelson, 1981). It is in this context of the notion of legal pluralism and the spread of modern systems of law and justice as a dominant tradition that this chapter examines the growth and evolution of a dual system of criminal justice in China.

■ Criminal Justice in China: A Dual System of Tradition and Modernity

The law and justice system in China is based on some fundamental themes and core values that are more than 2,000 years old. However, the contemporary system of criminal justice in China is barely 30 years old. It began to grow from the beginning of socialist modernization in the early 1980s. During the progress of socialism (1949–1979), all modern institutions of criminal justice in China were deliberately destroyed. But China is one of the oldest civilizations in the world, and China inherited two of the oldest criminal codes of all civilizations: the Tang Code and the Great Qing Code (also known as the Qing Code). The Tang Code, completed in 624 at the time of the imperial rule of the Tang dynasty (618–907), is a remarkable example of an early medieval system of criminal justice based on elaborate descriptions of many substantive and procedural criminal laws. For more than 1,000 years, the Tang Code governed criminal justice in China. The Qing Code, completed in 1740 at the time of the imperial rule of the Qing dynasty (1644–1911), was the legal foundation of criminal justice in late medieval China for about 170 years. The Qing Code, which retained many of the substantive and procedural criminal laws of the Tang Code, was in force until the end of the

Chinese imperial dynasty and the beginning of the formation of the modern state in China in 1911.

Historians of criminal justice in China claim that understanding these two great legal traditions of China—the Tang Code and the Great Qing Code—is imperative for a comparative understanding of criminal justice in modern China. Muhlhahn (2009), a notable historian of Chinese criminal justice, wrote that in China the "basic notions of justice, crime and punishment as they were understood and applied in the twentieth century, were formed by the distinct legal traditions in China" (p. 14). Muhlhahn (2009) continued, saying, "It is virtually impossible to understand criminal justice in China's twentieth century without taking into account the ramification of premier legal language, practice and theory" (p. 14). The imperial legal codes of China outlined not only the nature of criminal law and justice—the intrasystemic issues—but also the social, political, moral, and philosophical contexts within which criminal justice was pursued and practiced. To reflect these historical contexts and understand their effects on contemporary developments, the following sections will discuss, in terms of five distinct phases, the evolution and nature of contemporary criminal justice in China: (1) criminal justice in early China and the legacy of the Tang Code; (2) criminal justice in late medieval China and the legacy of the Great Qing Code; (3) the beginning of modernization in criminal justice in China during the nationalist period, 1911–1949; (4) the breakdown of modernization in criminal justice in China during the communist era, 1949–1979; and (5) rebirth of modernization in criminal justice in contemporary China, 1979–2012. From the beginning of the formation of the modern state in China in 1911, reforms in criminal justice began with a debate about its transformation to modernity. Except the 3 decades of communist rule under Mao Zedong (1943–1976), transforming to modernity was central to Chinese vision throughout the 20th century, and has remained central to Chinese vision in the 21st century. China, however, has always seen its journey toward modernity in the context of its legal and cultural traditions. The core of China's position is to achieve modernity within the context of its cultural and civilizational traditions. This struggle for modernity within the context of tradition is more obvious in the realm of modernization in criminal justice in China.

■ Crime and Criminal Justice in Imperial China

The Legal Tradition of China: The Core Values

Two competing philosophies have remained at the core of Chinese law, justice, and penal philosophy since the beginning of Chinese civilization. These competing philosophies are known as Confucianism and legalism. Confucius was a Chinese philosopher (551–479 BC) who was older than Plato (429–347 BC) and Aristotle (384–322 BC)—two of the great Greek philosophers. Confucius, like Plato and Aristotle, was concerned with the nature of good governance and, hence, with the nature of law and justice. Confucius was born in an aristocratic family and worked for a short time as a minister of justice. Most of his life, however, was spent as an adviser to different imperial rulers. Just as Aristotle expanded the works of Plato, Mencius (390–305 BC), the grandson of Confucius, expanded the works of Confucius. The works of Confucius were compiled and recorded in a book called, *The Analects of*

Confucius, several hundred years after his death. During the rule of the Han dynasty, Emperor Gaozu (206–195 BC) made Confucianism a state ideology, and since then it has remained a dominant social and political philosophy in China and in the whole of East Asia. One of the studies on Confucianism noted that by end of the 19th century, "the whole East Asian region was thoroughly 'Confucianized.' That is Confucian values and practices informed the daily lives of people in China, Korea, Japan, and Vietnam, and the whole systems of governance were justified with reference to Confucian ideals" (Bell & Chaibong, 2003, p. 1). Another study (Nylan, 2001) on Confucianism observed that the "study of the Five Classics of the 'Confucian' canon—the *Odes,* the *Documents,* the *rites,* the *Changes,* and the *Spring and Autumn Annals*—was mandatory for Chinese imperial bureaucracy."

The Confucian classics "constitute a world view, a social ethic, a political ideology, a scholarly tradition, and a way of life in a China bound by tradition" (Nylan, 2001, p. 5). In understanding criminal justice in China, Confucianism becomes relevant because it is primarily a political philosophy and a blueprint for an ideal system of justice and an ideal polity. "Whatever insights there are in the classical writings of Confucianism, the substantive content of Confucian values lies in their concrete and distinctive influences on political and legal institutions in society" (Ho, 2003, p. 288). Confucius believed that an ideal polity and an ideal system of justice must be based on the dominance of morality and not on the dominance of formal law and legal codifications. A best system of justice is the one that is based on the normative principles of benevolence *(ren),* filial piety, reverence, fraternity, kindness, and humanness (Ho, 2003). A best system of justice must uphold the values of mediation rather than litigation (Chen, 2003). In the *Analects,* Confucius said that "in hearing litigation, I am no different from any other man. But if you insist on a difference, it is, perhaps, that I try to get the parties not to resort to litigation in the first place" (as quoted in Chen, 2003, p. 259). Mediation is better than litigation because litigation disrupts social harmony. "The construction of harmonious social order is one of the greatest Confucian ideals . . . . And the traditional Chinese approach to dispute resolution in society is inextricably linked to this vision of harmony" (Chen, 2003, p. 260).

Mediation, for Confucius, is not simply a matter of crime control and dispute resolution. It is also one of the greatest moral virtues. Through the practice of mediation, an individual can transcend the boundaries of selfishness, retribution, and retaliation, and reach to "higher moral demands" (Chen, 2003, p. 261). Whereas mediation comes from an inner sense of moral strength and a virtue of benevolence, litigation comes from a sense of retribution and profitability. Mediation is a way of searching and scrutinizing the moral failings of an offender or a victim. Litigation is a way of resorting to law and the court. "Indeed going to court would be an extremist act that is inconsistent with the Golden Mean advocated by Confucius" (Chen, 2003, p. 261). The court and the law, Confucius believed, are the end of morality. The court and the law will probably reduce crime, but the offenders and those who are punished will not be reformed and shameful. Confucius said that because of law and the court, and because of sanctions and punishments, "common people will stay out of trouble but will have no sense of shame. Guide them by virtue, keep them in line with rites, and they will, besides having a sense of shame, reform themselves" (*Analects,* II, 3 as quoted in Chen, 2003, p. 261).

Formal and codified law, according to Confucius, "is punitive, since it comes into action only when a crime has been committed and harm has been done. Penal laws are compulsive, coercive, and therefore indicate a tyrannical mode of government" (Muhlhahn, 2009, p. 17).

Confucius was not against punishment as a last resort for repeat and dangerous offenders who are incorrigible through moral teachings. "Penalties are meant to defend the moral order of society in an emergency" (Muhlhahn, 2009, p. 18). But even in the case of harsh punishments, he stressed that punishments must fit the crime and should "be used to demonstrate to the offender the nature of the mistake and let him repent. If the wicked person repents and changes his life, he can be redeemed" (Muhlhahn, 2009, p. 18). For Confucius, "the greatest danger lies in a ruler's inclination to use punishments excessively" (Muhlhahn, 2009, pp. 18–19). Good governance, for Confucius, is a form of governance where the rulers rule "in accordance with approved social norms (called *li* or rites) through persuasion and moral example, rather than governing in accordance with positive law and the threat of punishment" (Muhlhahn, 2009, p. 17).

The legalist school of thought, in contrast to the Confucian school of thought, is based on the notion that a good polity and a good system of justice must be based on codified law and rules, formal courts and adjudications, scope for litigations, a uniform system of justice, and willingness on the part of the rulers to impose punishments to control crime and violence. For the advocates of legalism, "the ruler is the center of gravity for all beings. The Legalists spoke of the ruler with 'Machiavellian straightforwardness' and elaborated principles for how the ruler could acquire and enhance his power for the sake of order and stability" (Muhlhahn, 2009, p. 19). The legalist school of thought is founded on the belief that "human nature is evil and human relationships are based on calculation of exchange of benefits.... Legalist political theory is based on the successful employment of three themes— political technique (shu), political authority (shi), and penal law (fa)" (Guo, 2002, p. xii). The penal law, particularly, "is deemed by Legalists as an effective tool to achieve social order and political rule" (Guo, 2002, p. xii). The legalists insist "that the ruler must rely on penal law and the imposition of heavy punishments as the main instrument of his government of the people" (MacCormack, 1996, p. 4). In contrast to the advocates of Confucianism, the advocates of the legalist philosophy believe that punishment is a deterrence and "punishment need not fit the crime. Instead the ruler should impose draconian punishment even for the slightest wrongdoing" (Muhlhahn, 2009, p. 20).

The third most important characteristic of the legal tradition of imperial China was the notion of the inseparability of law and morality. Confucius believed that the governing class should be governed by morality and the commoners should be governed by law. The dominant philosophy in traditional China was that a society is stable and in harmony when the governing class is guided by morality—an inner sense of benevolence, reverence, fraternity, decency, kindness, humanness, and filial piety. Social and political problems, and turbulence and escalation of crime and violence are the results of moral decay on the part of the ruling class. From the view of traditional Chinese philosophy, a society functioned "properly only when its members behaved in accordance with their social roles and that the state had an obligation to enforce the underlying moral prescriptions by punishing those who behaved improperly" (Muhlhahn, 2009, p. 55). It is, therefore, problematical to "decide where to draw the line between law and morality in imperial China" (Muhlhahn, 2009, p. 55). The beginning of a legal process, the Confucians believe, is the beginning of the end of morality. The Code was "regarded as the last means by which to protect society when all other attempts to promote desirable behavior in an individual or family had failed. Those who came before the county magistrate represented the failure of morality and education" (Johnson, 1997, p. 5). The advocates of the legalist school, however, in contrast to the Confucians, insist that "moral considerations should be rigorously excluded in the conduct of government" (MacCormack, 1996, p. 4).

Fourth, law in imperial China was conceived primarily as a set of rules to be used by the imperial bureaucracy. In the civil law and common law traditions, law is conceived primarily from the point of the individuals. The major concerns of law in these two Western legal traditions are to define the boundaries of the rights and obligations of the individuals. In imperial China, the major concerns of law were to define the boundaries of duties and obligations of the imperial bureaucracy and to protect the interest of the imperial state. In imperial China, "there was no notion that the individual had rights that were sacred and could be protected by law. Rather, the law was concerned with enforcing duties in order to maintain the social order" (Chow, 2003, p. 46). The primary focus of law was on the "activities of the bureaucrats in the performance of the duties, not the activities of ordinary human beings in their private lives" (Jones, 1994, p. 6). There were no distinctions between civil and criminal law and the legal code was "entirely administrative law" (Jones, 1994, p. 7). The law was codified to provide clear directions to the bureaucracy about what is and is not crime and how crime must be punished. The legal codes were essentially directives "to the magistrate to tell him when to punish and precisely what punishment to inflict in any circumstances that were perceived by the state as legally significant" (Jones, 1994, p. 9).The judicial system in imperial China was entirely in the hands of the imperial bureaucracy. "The Code was administered by the same civil servants who administered all other activities of the government, from collecting taxes to supervising examinations for the civil service . . . . It was entirely within the control of the magistrates (Jones, 1994, p. 11).

Another distinctive characteristic of law in traditional China was that it was strictly hierarchical in nature. There were separate laws and punishments for the ruler and the ruled, the young and the old, the men and the women, and the masters and the slaves. The hierarchical legal system was based on Confucian philosophy. In describing the Qing Code, Jones noted: "There seems to be no question that Confucianism did influence a large number of the Code provisions. Its influence is especially visible in the Code's recognition of the existence of social hierarchy and the importance of family relationships" (1994, p. 16). Torture, for example, was prohibited for members of the imperial family, members of the imperial bureaucracy, and members and families of old dynastic rulers. In describing the Tang Code, Johnson (1979) similarly observed that it "institutionalized the Confucian ethics by allowing family members to conceal each other's offenses. Offenses by superiors against inferiors should be punished less heavily . . . . Similarly, offenses against superiors by inferiors should be punished more heavily" (p. 12). The criminal justice system in imperial

China was a "system in which social status and moral judgments constitute the basis of law . . . . [It] produced a ranking of legally significant or punishable acts according to how morally reprehensible they were in the social status of the parties involved" (Muhlhahn, 2009, p. 55).

In pursuing comparative criminal justice in modern China and in understanding the contemporary Chinese struggle to modernize its criminal justice and to build a society based on the rule of law, some of these core values related to law and legal traditions in China need to be systematically examined. Confucianism is a great moral philosophy, but some of its core values are opposed to those of modernity. Confucians believe in the notions of hierarchy instead of equality, socialization instead of institutionalization, collectivism instead of individualism, informal justice instead of formal justice, and the role of morality instead of the role of law in crime control and prevention. Politically, Confucianism fosters authoritarianism rather than democracy. It believes not in judicial independence but in the dominance of the executive. An ideal polity, according to Confucianists, is the one that is based on the dominance of authority, centralization, and control, and not on the dominance of the rule of law, checks and balances, decentralization, and consensus. The inseparability of law and morality is also a notion that is opposed to legal positivism—the foundational philosophy of modern Western jurisprudence. The legal positivists assert that the social order of morality is different from the social order defined by law. All criminal laws are not necessarily moral in character, and all moral issues are not legally defined and conceptualized. Today's search for modernization in criminal justice in China is influenced in many complex ways by the enduring values of its imperial law and legal traditions.

Criminal Justice in Early Medieval China: The Legacy of the Tang Code

The Tang Code was completed about 2,400 years after the Code of Hammurabi (1772 BC) and about 1,000 years after the development of the Twelve Tables of the Roman Law (439 BC), which is the basis of the contemporary civil law tradition. There were many different imperial criminal codes in China even before the implementation of the Tang Code in 653. Penal historians found that in ancient China, five types of punishments were commonly used. Those were tattooing, amputation of the nose, amputation of one ear, castration, and decapitation. During the Zhou dynasty (1122–256 BC), the criminal justice system "was unified and highly sophisticated, with standard laws, detailed trial procedures, professional judges, and multitiered system of punishments" (Muhlhahn, 2009, p. 29). During the Han dynasty (206 BC–220 AD), all forms of mutilating punishments, however, were abolished. "The punishments to which criminals were then sentenced included exile, hard labor, flogging, castration, and death. Castration, the last remaining mutilating punishment, was ended around 220 AD. By then, all other mutilating corporal punishments had disappeared" (Muhlhahn, 2009, p. 30).

Criminal justice in China came to a new turning point during the Tang dynasty (618–907). Historians described the Tang dynasty as one of the most glorious periods in the history of China. During the Tang dynasty, China achieved remarkable progress in economic growth, political centralization, and administrative developments. The Tang Code was created to build a new system of codification of substantive and procedural criminal laws and, hence, a new universalistic system of justice throughout China. As Muhlhahn (2009) observed: "This systematic effort to maintain a universally applicable and comprehensive codification of law and administrative practice was essential to the uniform system of administration that the Tang succeeded in establishing throughout its diverse empire" (p. 31). This remarkable creation of the Tang Code was "considered authoritative as late as the fourteenth century . . . . It was also adopted with some modifications by Japan in the early eighteenth century and later by Korea and Vietnam" (Muhlhahn, 2009, p. 31). The Tang Code was divided into 12 books, 30 chapters, and 502 articles. The 12 books included descriptions of crime and punishment related to the sanctity of the imperial authority (Book 2), marriage and family (Book 4), unauthorized levies (Book 6), violence and robbery (Book 7), assault and accusations (Book 8), fraud and counterfeit (Book 9), and arrest and flight (Book 11). The Code also described the nature of convictions, sentencing, and prisons (Book 12).

The Code contained two sets of criminal provisions: substantive and procedural. One set of provisions "defined criminal acts by members of bureaucracy that affect the emperor or the state" (Johnson, 1997, p. 4). Another set of provisions defined the criminal activities of the general population. Out of 502 articles, about 205 defined criminal acts by members of the bureaucracy, 243 defined the criminal activities of the general population, and about 54 defined the nature of arrest and trial procedures. The Code was based also on two types of social controls: formal and informal. Informally, the Code preserved the right of settling disputes in terms of customary laws and the Confucian norms and ethics. "But once criminal activities were brought to the knowledge of the county magistrate, they would be dealt with under the rigid rules prescribed by the *Code* and punished harshly" (Johnson, 1997, p. 5). Six general principles that guided the development of the Tang Code were: (1) harmony of law and morality or law and nature; (2) criminalization of false accusations; (3) 10 types of serious crimes or 10 abominations; (4) adherence to the principle of personal status and hierarchy in defining crime and punishment; (5) the sanctity of family; and (6) criminal justice based on confessions. These general principles are related to the core values of law and justice in China: Confucianism, legalism, hierarchy, the protection of the sanctity of the family, and the dominance of morality.

One of the remarkable features of the Tang Code was its detailed descriptions of what constitutes crime and punishment. The Tang Code is one of the earliest examples of mandatory and determinate sentencing. Out of the 502 articles of the Code, 445 define "exactly what constitutes criminal behavior in a particular case" (Johnson, 1997, p. 3). Because of the promulgation of the Code, there was a relatively a clear and consistent understanding among the subjects of the empire about "what behavior was prohibited; a given crime received exactly the same punishment no matter where it was committed, and officials had little leeway in determining what act was a crime and what punishment should be sentenced for that act" (Johnson, 1997, p. 4). The Code prescribed punishment based on the nature of the crime, the severity of the criminal act, and the criminal intent. In the case of voluntary manslaughter, for example, punishment was severe: "Killing or wounding by intent is regarded much differently. Where the crime takes place because of a plot, or where the offense is committed intentionally, punishments are . . . severe" (Johnson, 1997, p. 8). Article 256 of the Code, for example, "punishes a plot to kill by three years of penal servitude. If the victim is even wounded, the punishment is strangulation. If the person is killed, the punishment is decapitation" (Johnson, 1997, p. 8). If a robbery was committed without the use of force, the punishment was 3 years of penal servitude. If a robbery was committed with the use of force and weapons, the punishment was life in exile at a distance of 3,000 miles.

The first general principle of the Code is based on the theme that social harmony is a deeply moral problem (yang). The breakdown of morality is the reason for the development of formal law and justice (yin). The first principle of the Code directly addressed the sanctity of Confucian values and ethics. The second principle is the criminalization of false accusations. "Article 351 punishes anonymous accusations severely. A person who concealed his or her name when making an accusation or who gave that of another person was punished by exile at a distance of 3,000 li (miles)" (Johnson, 1997, p. 6). The Code made provisions that all accusations must be submitted in written forms clearly mentioning where and when the crime was committed. The officials who accepted false accusations were punished by 2 years of penal servitude. The creators of the Code were also deeply concerned about wrongful conviction because there was a belief in traditional China that wrongful conviction and punishment of innocent people could cause natural disasters. People who were wrongfully convicted were entitled to reparations. "When the person who suffered unjustly was known and the facts were clear, such a person received reparation from the government" (Johnson, 1979, p. 15). The provision on false accusations included also the notion of the proportionality between crime and punishment. The Code made a provision of tax exemptions for people who received heavy sentences. "For each year of penal servitude either by someone who was, in fact, innocent or who was guilty but whose sentence was too heavy for his crime, two years of taxes and labor services would be remitted" (Johnson, 1979, p. 17).

The concerns in the Code about false accusations were closely related to the general principle of settling criminal trials and disputes through confessions. "Great efforts were made during the course of a trial to get the accused to confess his guilt to the charge pressed against him" (Johnson, 1979, p. 34). In some criminal cases, complete pardon could be gained by making truthful confessions before the start of a formal criminal trial based on written accusations. Various sections of Article 37 described the nature of acceptable confessions. Section 1a of Article 37 states that "in all cases where there is a confession of crimes that have not been discovered, the crime will be pardoned" (Johnson, 1979, p. 200). Section 3a of Article 37 stated that confessions made on behalf of an offender by his or her relative were acceptable: "Sending a representative to confess is the same as confessing oneself" (Johnson, 1979, p. 202).

One of the most important general principles at the core of the Tang Code is the 10 abominations—10 types of serious crimes. These are: (1) plotting rebellion against the ruler or the state; (2) plotting sedition—the destruction of ancestral temples, tombs, or places of the reigning house; (3) plotting treason; (4) killing or ploting to kill one's parents or grandparents, husband, wife, siblings, uncles, and other family members; (5) cruelty, violence, and involuntary manslaughter; (6) showing irreverence to the emperor, imperial symbols, imperial rites, imperial foods, and imperial possessions; (7) lack of filial piety—disobeying one's parents and/or elders; (8) discord—failure to live in peace and harmony with one's family members of various generations; (9) unrighteousness—to kill one's department head, prefect, or magistrate, or the teacher from whom one has received one's education; and (10) incest (Johnson, 1979).

The most serious crimes, according to the Code, are plotting rebellion against the ruler and the state and plotting sedition. For these two kinds of crimes, the Code prescribed mandatory punishment of death by decapitation. For rebellion and sedition, the Code also mandated collective prosecution. Punishment mandated by the Code "reached a great number of persons who had no involvement in the crime whatsoever. The father and sons of the criminals were strangled" (Johnson, 1979, p. 18). Provisions were also made for the enslavement of the offender's children, parents, grandparents, great grandparents, great-great grandparents, grandsons, great grandsons, great-great grandsons, and brothers and sisters and the confiscation by the state of their property. "Further, the offender's paternal uncles and nephews in the male line would be exiled for life to a distance of 3,000 li [miles]" (Johnson, 1979, p. 18). Unauthorized entry into the imperial palace, imperial pavilions, imperial gardens, or imperial kitchens was a serious crime. The punishment for entering an imperial palace or a pavilion with a military weapon was decapitation. Article 59 of the Code stated that "all cases of unauthorized entry of the gates of the imperial palace are punishable by two years of penal servitude" (Johnson, 1997, p. 17). Article 5 (2a) states that "entry into imperial pavilions is punishable by strangulation" (Johnson, 1997, p. 18).

Next are five categories of crimes that are related to offenses against the superior in the bureaucracy and the family. Under these five categories, a number of acts were defined as high crimes, such as showing disrespect to the emperor and the imperial symbols; assault or killing of superior officials, magistrates, and teachers; killing of family members; disobedience to parents; showing disrespect to the elderly; and inability to live in harmony with family members of multiple generations. The Code made provisions for severe punishments for the kinds of crimes related to the superior in the bureaucracy and the family. "A plot to kill a parent or paternal grandparent, or the chief of one's department in the government, was punishment by decapitation and life exile, respectively. Similarly, anyone who actually hit a parent or parental grandparent was decapitated" (Johnson, 1979, p. 21). Killing or plotting to kill a family member carried harsher punishments. A plot to "kill a person of non-kin status is at most sentenced to penal servitude, while a plot to kill a maternal uncle is punished by life exile" (Johnson, 1979, p. 205). According to the Code, children's abandonment of parents was a crime punishable by 2 years of penal servitude. "And a woman who struck her husband was punished by one year of penal servitude" (Johnson, 1979, p. 22). These kinds of differential punishments were prescribed for preserving the sanctity of family—a value that is central to Confucian ethics.

Closely related to the notion of preserving social order and the sanctity of family is the idea of hierarchy in defining crime and punishment. Crime and punishment are defined in the Tang Code strictly on the basis of the social status of the offender and the victim. "Crimes against each other by commoners and officials, by different ranks in the bureaucracy, and by relatives within five degrees of mourning as well as their slaves and personal retainers receive widely different punishment" based on their differences in status, rank, and prestige (Johnson, 1997, p. 9). Offenses committed by commoners against officials, officials of lower ranks against superiors, children against parents, and young against old "are punished more heavily than those against equals" (Johnson, 1997, p. 9). Article 312 of the Code stated that "even a single blow by a commoner against the prefect or county magistrate carries a minimum punishment of three years of penal servitude. If the victim is wounded, the punishment is life exile at a distance of 2,000 *li*" (Johnson, 1997, p. 9). The Code also stated how criminal offenses within the bureaucracy are to be punished in terms of divisions in rank and status, and that "these divisions are applicable not only to subordinate officials in an office who might commit a crime against their chief but also to officials of lower ranks who commit a crime against those of higher ranks" (Johnson, 1997, p. 10).

Devising punishments on the basis of hierarchy, however, is most clearly defined in cases of intrafamilial offenses: "Family relationships certainly form the most complex set of rules for increasing and decreasing punishment to be found in the *Code,* far more so than those involving crimes among different levels of officials" (Johnson, 1997, p. 10). Through its various provisions, the Tang Code wanted to protect the sanctity of family—the core of Confucian ethics. By criminalizing the desertion of parents and grandparents by their children, the establishment of separate households by children when their parents and grandparents are still alive, and the division of family property by children before the deaths of their parents and grandparents, and by allowing family members to conceal family crimes, the "*Code* shows its concern to preserve the family" (Johnson, 1979, p. 34).

The significance of studying the Tang Code for comparative criminal justice in China is that some of the principles that were dominant in organizing criminal justice during the Tang dynasty in the 7th century—the role of morality in society, the sanctity of preserving the social order of the state, the sanctity of preserving the social order of bureaucracy, the norms of bureaucratic responsibility, the norms of hierarchy, and the sanctity of preserving the family—are still the dominant themes in organizing criminal justice in China in the 21st century. Mandatory and determinate sentencing, differential sentencing based on the nature of the crime and the criminal intent, concerns about the proportionality between crime and punishment, victim compensation, and victim restitution are some of the notions that were surprisingly modern in the Tang Code that is more than 1,300 years old.

Criminal Justice in Late Medieval China: The Legacy of the Great Qing Code

After the demise of the Tang dynasty in the early 10th century, China was successively ruled until the beginning of the 20th century by four imperial dynasties: the Sung dynasty (960–1279), the Yuan dynasty (1279–1368), the Ming dynasty (1368–1644), and the Qing dynasty (1644–1911). With these different dynasties, the old legal traditions were not completely rejected. China's laws and legal traditions have gradually evolved. The Sung and the Yuan codes were extensions of the Tang Code. The legal code of the Ming dynasty was based on the cumulative traditions of the Tang, Sung, and Yuan dynasties. The Qing Code "was drawn directly from that of the Ming and generally only expanded upon it" (Hegel, 2007, p. 11). Throughout the evolution of Chinese legal philosophy and penal theory, two competing perspectives were dominant—the Confucian philosophy and the legalist perspective. The challenge for each and every succeeding dynasty since the 3rd century was to evolve a system of justice based on a balance between these two perspectives—the dominance of morality and education versus the dominance of law and punishment in the attainment of social order and harmony. Muhlhahn (2009) noted that "one of the most interesting theoretical accounts of punishment that tried to combine different Legalist and Confucian arguments (and actually preceded Han syncretism) was written by Xunzi (300–230 BC)" (p. 23). Xunzi presented his penal theory in his book, *Rectifying Theses* (Knoblock, 1994). Like Beccaria in *Crimes and Punishments*, Xunzi argued that law and punishment should not be seen as the end goal of justice. Law and punishment should be seen as tools to strengthen the moral fabric of a society. The end goal of justice is to strengthen the moral foundation of a society and the moral character of an individual. But to achieve this goal, the state needs a defined system of criminal law and punishment. Punishment should be used not as a method of revenge but as a method of deterrence, and the method of deterrence must be morally acceptable. Punishment should also fit the crime so that it is seen as fair and just. Punishment should be used at present for the withering away of punishment in future (Muhlhahn, 2009). This dualistic vision became an integral part of Chinese legal philosophy and penal theory through the theorizing of the duality between yin and yang by an ancient Chinese philosopher named Don Zhongshu (195–115 BC). Zhongshu "integrated Yin-Yang cosmology into a Confucian ethical framework, creating the theoretical foundation of the inchoate imperial state during the Han dynasty and the long-lasting official ideology of the Chinese imperial state" (Muhlhahn, 2009, p. 24).

By the time the Qing dynasty came to power in China in the early 17th century, Chinese society was going through some fundamental social and economic transformations. The rise of commercialization, the expansion of cities and urban life, the growth of population, and the increasing openness to the West through trade and commerce brought many new challenges for modernization in China in the 17th and 18th centuries. One of the remarkable achievements of the Qing dynasty was the creation of a series of institutions of modern criminal justice in China. The time of the Qing dynasty, many Chinese legal historians believe, was a time of "thoughtful reconsiderations of received philosophical and ethical teachings on the part of leading intellectuals. Judicial practices, too, were being refined during that period, partly in response to changing conceptions of the role of the government" (Hegel, 2009, p. 5). The Great Qing Code, completed in 1740, brought some significant transformations in criminal justice in China. No serious study of criminal justice in China is possible without examining the Great Qing Code and the criminal justice institutions that evolved in late imperial China under the control of the Qing dynasty.

The Qing Code and Qing rulers brought some significant changes in judicial administration in late imperial China, but there remained a great continuity in the core values and perspectives about law and justice in China. Like the Tang Code, the Great Qing Code was also a set of directives "to the district magistrate to tell him when to punish and precisely what punishment to inflict in any circumstances that were perceived by the state as legally significant" (Jones, 1994, p. 9). The dominant concern of the Code "was to make it clear to the magistrate what activities he was required to punish, and precisely what penalties he was to impose" (Jones, 1994, p. 9). Like the Tang Code, the Qing Code was also an imperial document that outlined the behavior and activities of bureaucratic officials that are improper and punishable. "The Code's point of view is shown by the fact that over half its provisions are devoted to the regulation of the official activities of government officials" (Jones, 1994, p. 6). The Code was not to protect the rights of the individuals but to enforce their duties for the interest of the whole society. "There were no parties. There might be an accuser and there was certainly an accused, but the magistrate was in immediate and total control, and he was concerned with protecting and advancing the interests of the society" (Jones, 1994, p. 9).

Like the Tang Code, the Qing Code was also based on the values of Confucianism. The ideas of moral education, protecting the sanctity of family, and defining crime and punishments on the basis of social and bureaucratic hierarchies were central to the Qing Code as they were to the Tang Code. The influence of Confucian values in the development of the Qing Code "is especially visible in the Code's recognition of the existence of a social hierarchy and the importance of family relationships, both key elements of Confucianism" (Jones, 1994, p. 16). Jones wrote that "the continuity between the Qing and the Tang Codes is so clear that there can be no doubt there was an active juristic tradition at the highest level of imperial bureaucracy for at least a thousand years" (1994, p. 28). The Qing Code contained 436 statutes and 1,049 substatutes. Muhlhahn estimated that "approximately 30 percent to 40 percent of the statutes were retained unchanged from the Tang Code of 653" (2009, p. 44). Because of this historical continuity in the legal tradition, the "definitions of severest crimes and punishment attached to them did not undergo any dramatic change" (Muhlhahn, 2009, p. 45) in China for more than 1,000 years. Out of 436 statutes, about 376 were devoted to defining the nature of different types of crimes, and about 60 were devoted to expanding procedural criminal law. Those 376 statutes of the Code named different kinds of crimes and punishments attached to them. They defined crimes against the emperor and the imperial state; crimes related to bureaucratic negligence; military crimes; family crimes; moral crimes; elderly crimes; crimes of violence, theft, and robbery; property crimes; public order crimes; and economic crimes.

Like the Tang Code, the Qing Code also divided serious crimes into 10 categories—the 10 abominations: plotting rebellion, plotting sedition, plotting treason, contumacy, depravity, great irreverence, lack of filial piety, discord, unrighteousness, and incest. Article 2 (the 10 Great Wrongs) of the Qing Code described these crimes as evil and serious in nature. Articles 254 and 255 of the Code stated that in cases of rebellion and high treason, the law does not distinguish between those who are directly and those who are indirectly involved. "Whether or not the plot has been carried out, all will be put to death by slicing" (Jones,

1994, p. 237). The Qing Code also kept the provision of collective prosecution in cases of rebellion and high treason. The definitions of the 10 abominations and their punishments have remained largely the same in the Tang Code of 653 and the Qing Code of 1740 (see **Table 11-1**). There also remained a remarkable continuity in defining crime and punishment in terms of one's social standing and one's location within the bureaucratic hierarchies. Article 3 in the Qing Code is called "The Eight Considered"—the eight categories of persons whose cases are to be especially considered (Jones, 1994, p. 36). The Tang Code called this provision the "The Eight Deliberations" (Johnson, 1979, p. 23). In both codes, the idea was that the relatives of the emperor, old retainers of the emperor, and guests of the emperor, people who are virtuous, and people who work in senior bureaucratic positions and have worked for a long time must receive special treatment within the system of criminal justice. The Tang Code stated that "if any one included within these eight categories

TABLE 11-1 Punishments for the 10 Abominations and the 10 Great Wrongs: The Tang Code and the Qing Code

Types of Serious Crimes	Punishment in the Tang Code, 653	Punishment in the Qing Code, 1740
Plotting rebellion	Death by decapitation and collective prosecution/confiscation of property	Death by decapitation and collective prosecution/confiscation of property
Plotting high treason	Death by decapitation and collective prosecution/confiscation of property	Death by decapitation and collective prosecution/confiscation of property
Plotting treason	Death by decapitation and collective prosecution/confiscation of property	Death by decapitation and collective prosecution/confiscation of property
Patricide and matricide	Death by decapitation/confiscation of property/exile	Death by decapitation/confiscation of property/exile
Depravity	Death by decapitation/confiscation of property/exile	Death by decapitation/confiscation of property/exile
Great irreverence	Beheading/100 strokes of the heavy bamboo/penal servitude/judicial tattooing	Beheading/100 strokes of the heavy bamboo/penal servitude/judicial tattooing
Lack of filial piety	Strangulation/100 strokes of the heavy bamboo/penal servitude	Strangulation/100 strokes of the heavy bamboo/penal servitude
Discord	Beheading/100-60 strokes of the heavy bamboo/exile	Beheading/100-60 strokes of the heavy bamboo/exile
Unrighteousness	Penal servitude/100-60-50 strokes of the heavy bamboo	Penal servitude/100-60-50 strokes of the heavy bamboo
Incest/family disorder	Beheading/100 strokes of the bamboo/penal servitude	Beheading/100 strokes of the bamboo/penal servitude

Sources: Data from Jones, W. C. (1994). *The great Qing Code.* Oxford, England: Oxford University Press; and Johnson, W. (1979). *The T'ang Code (Vol. I): General principles.* Princeton, NJ: Princeton University Press; Johnson, W. (1997). *The T'ang Code (Vol. II): Specific articles.* Princeton, NJ: Princeton University Press.

committed an offense punished by life exile or less, their punishment was automatically reduced one degree. For a capital offense they could not be punished through the ordinary criminal process" (Johnson, 1979, p. 24). Article 3 of the Qing Code similarly stated that the offenses committed by these categories of people must be treated outside the "normal processes of the law. Thus, the persons entitled to have their cases especially considered will be made to be conscious of their dignity" (Jones, 1994, p. 36). Like the Tang Code, the Qing Code was also "designed to promote and protect a social order based on naturalized hierarchies. It follows that the rights and interests of people with higher hierarchies were valued more highly than those of their hierarchical juniors" (Epstein, 2007, p. 28).

Like the Tang Code, the Qing Code was also designed to preserve the sanctity of family, and it criminalized a number of family and sex-related violence and behaviors such as fornication (Article 366), fornication between relatives (Article 368), spousal violence (Article 302, 315), the plotting to kill or killing paternal grandparents and parents (Article 284), killing a son (Article 294), killing a spouse (Article 298), establishing of separate households by children when their parents are still alive (Article 87), use of family property by young members of a family without the authorization of the superiors (Article 88), desertion of orphans and older persons (Article 89), use of fraud and deceit in establishing a marriage contract (Article 101), and hiring out of wives and daughters for prostitution (Article 102). About fornication, the Tang Code stated that "whoever engages in illicit sexual intercourse shall be sentenced to one-and-a-half years of penal servitude, if the woman has a husband, the penalty should be two years of penal servitude" (Sommer, 2000, p. 323). The Qing Code similarly stated: "Whoever commits consensual illicit sex (he jian) shall receive 80 blows of the heavy bamboo; if the woman has a husband, then the offender shall receive 90 blows of the heavy bamboo" (Sommer, 2000, p. 325). It went on to say that "if a man lures a woman to another place in order to have illicit sex (diao jian), they shall receive 100 blows regardless of whether the woman has a husband" (Sommer, 2000, p. 325). The punishment for attempted rape in the Qing Code was 100 blows and exile at a distance of 3,000 miles, and the punishment for completed rape was death by strangulation. In the Qing Code, the punishment for forced sodomy was death by beheading or strangulation. One of the Qing sodomy laws established that "whoever rapes (qiang jian) a young boy of between ten and twelve sui shall be sentenced to beheading" (Sommer, 2000, p. 329). Under the Qing Code, concealing the offenses of family members was permissible. Family members were even barred from reporting each other's crimes to law enforcement.

The system of criminal justice that evolved in China during the late imperial rule of the Qing dynasty in the 18th and 19th centuries, however, was remarkably different from that of the Tang dynasty in the 7th and 8th centuries. It was remarkably different not primarily because of the development of a new set of crimes and the rise of a new process of criminalization, but because of a series of institutional innovations made by the Qing rulers related to what we know as due process of law in modern criminal justice. During the Tang dynasty, the administration of criminal justice was largely in the hands of the local district and county magistrates. The Qing judicial administration was "hierarchically arranged, from the emperor at the apex to the 1,200 to 1,300 'county magistrates' . . . . Each magistrate was appointed in the name of the emperor and represented imperial authority on the local level (Hegel, 2007, p. 15).

The Qing rulers established a hierarchical system or an appealable system of criminal justice administration, a modern system of criminal investigation, public trial, procedures for judicial review, and the norms of judicial accountability. At the local level, the Qing judicial system was in the hands of the district magistrates. The district magistrates "were responsible for determining guilt and appropriate punishments" (Hegel, 2009, p. 10). In the criminal justice system of the Qing dynasty, "crime required complex official responses" (Hegel, 2007, p. 15). Criminal investigation required the gathering of crime-related information by the magistrate's staff, the collection of criminal evidence, the collection of forensic data, arrest and detention of the accused on the basis of defined procedures, and the assembling of the relevant witnesses. In cases of homicide, the magistrates were required to examine "the bodies of the . . . victims so as to verify the validity of the examiner's conclusions. Then [the] magistrate had to conduct a thorough review of all evidence" (Hegel, 2007, p. 15). In the case of petty crimes, the decisions of the district magistrate were final. The punishments imposed by the district magistrates in petty criminal cases "could not exceed beating or public humiliation in severity; magistrates were authorized to pass judgment only on relatively minor infractions such as attempted assault, or petty theft" (Hegel, 2009, p. 12).

But the decisions of the district magistrates in complex criminal cases, particularly in capital cases, were subject to reviews by higher-level prefectural and provincial authorities. The decisions of the district magistrates in capital cases had to be justified "to a series of reviewers stretching upward through the bureaucracy of the prefecture (*fy*), the province (*sheng*), central authorities in Beijing, and ultimately to the emperor himself" (Hegel, 2009, p. 10). Under the Qing Code, "all homicide cases had to be reviewed by (or in the name of) the emperor; only the emperor could authorize execution" (Hegel, 2009, p. 10). Even the investigation of serious crimes by the district magistrates at the local level "required approval from succeeding higher levels; where cases were retried as they passed upward through the judicial review system" (Hegel, 2009, p. 12). The typical structure of the institution of judicial review for serious criminal cases was composed of the district or prefectural administration, provincial judicial commissioners, provincial governors or governor-generals, provincial military commanders, and the emperor (Article 411). Before the recommendations were sent to the emperor, they were again reviewed by higher judicial authorities. The Code made it certain that "every capital case . . . was reexamined by some of the highest central authorities including the Three Judicial Officers (*Sanfasi*): the Censorate, the Board of Punishments, and the Court of Judicial Review" (Hegel, 2009, p. 13). The norms of judicial accountability and judicial integrity were enforced from the top of the judicial administration. Each stage of the judicial review system at the local and provincial levels was required to keep written documents of their deliberation procedures to show that "the process had been conducted properly" (Hegel, 2009, p. 12). The magistrates were legally obligated to conduct a fair trial and any "impropriety in procedure or unjustified penalties in any sort of legal action could lead to punishment for the magistrate" (Hegel, 2009, p. 12). Punishment of the magistrate included both beating and penal servitude. The threat of punishment "functioned as a strong inducement for magistrates to perform scrupulously and consciously as local magistrates, mediators, and judges" (Hegel, 2009, p. 12).

In the Qing Code, criminal procedural laws are scattered throughout the document, but 60 Articles (Articles 332–343; 387–423) are specifically focused on criminal procedural laws. In the Chinese legal tradition in general, criminal procedural laws are the laws that define not the rights of the offenders that need to be protected, but the duties of the governmental officials in the enforcement of the imperial law and the duties of the commoners to obey them. Article 1 of the Qing Code begins with the description of five types of punishment: (1) beating with a light bamboo, (2) beating with a heavy bamboo, (3) penal servitude, (4) exile, and (5) death penalty. Except for the death penalty, all other forms of punishments were divided into 5 grades. The death penalty was divided into 4 grades: "strangulation with or without delay and beheading with or without delay" (Muhlhahn, 2009, p. 33). The punishment of beating with a light bamboo had 5 grades: 10, 20, 30, 40, and 50 strokes. The punishment of beating with a heavy bamboo had also 5 grades: 60, 70, 80, 90, and 100 strokes. Penal servitude had 5 degrees of severity: 1 year and 60 strokes of the heavy bamboo, 1.5 years and 70 strokes of the heavy bamboo, 2 years and 80 strokes of the heavy bamboo, 2.5 years and 90 strokes of the heavy bamboo, and 3 years and 100 strokes of the heavy bamboo. These penalties were given for specific kinds of crimes, and they were mandatory. The judicial officials did not have much leeway for upward or downward sanctions. Changing these mandatory punishment guidelines was a punishable crime for the judicial officials. Article 401 of the Code imposed a penalty of 90 strokes of the heavy bamboo and 2.5 years of penal servitude for intentionally decreasing the penalty from penal servitude to strokes of the heavy bamboo.

Some of the procedural laws that were elaborated in the articles include procedures for of lodging a criminal complaint (Article 332), penalty for making anonymous accusations (Article 333), penalty for false accusations (Article 336), penalty for accepting a false accusation by the magistrates (Articles 315–317), arrest and detentions (Article 360), punishment for resisting an arrest (Article 388), for hiding an offender (Article 393), for wrongful incarceration (Article 396), for inflicting cruelty on prisoners (398), for not interrogating an accused according to the facts alleged (Article 406), for an official not releasing an accused after the conclusion of an interrogation (Article 407), for an official who deliberately increases or decreases statutory penalties (Article 409), for an official who deliberately increased strokes of the light bamboo to penal servitude (Article 409), and for increasing the penalty from a lower degree of penal servitude to a higher degree of penal servitude (Article 409). A close examination of many of these procedural laws contained in the Qing Code will suggest that although great emphasis was placed on describing the proper duties and responsibilities of officials, there were also serious concerns for the establishment of a just and fair system of criminal justice administration. Historically, there have been very few civilizations where a criminal code explicitly had so many different types of punishments for the lack of judicial accountability and judicial integrity as in the

Great Qing Code. The Qing Code, for example, states that "every official or clerk who, cherishing private enmity, intentionally incarcerates a law-abiding person will receive 80 strokes of the heavy bamboo" (Article 396). Article 401 states that if an official intentionally increases a punishment, he will receive 80 strokes of the heavy bamboo. The same Article adds that an official will receive a punishment of 100 strokes of the heavy bamboo and exile at a distance of 3,000 miles if he intentionally increases the penalty of a convicted offender from heavy strokes to exile.

What is evidenced from the previous brief descriptions of the Tang Code of 653 and the Qing Code of 1740 is that China has a legacy of a great legal culture and philosophy that has evolved over a period of more than 2,000 years. The first great systematic effort for the codification of criminal law came through the Tang Code of 653. But criminal laws of different types have been evolving in China since the beginning of the imperial power of the Qin dynasty (221–207 BC). Since the beginning of the Chinese legal tradition, two competing perspectives remained dominant: the Confucian perspective and the legalist perspective. The Confucian perspective is based on the idea of the dominance of morality and moral education in the organizing of a social order. For the Confucians, the dominance of law implies the failure of morality. The legalist advocates, on the other hand, take the Hobbesian perspective, which is that law and authority are absolutely critical for the maintenance of a social order. The evolution of the legal culture of China has been affected by both these perspectives. At different stages of the evolution of criminal law in China, efforts were made to strengthen Confucian values by emphasizing the moral role of the authority, bureaucracy, hierarchy, and familial piety. At the end of the imperial rule in 1911, China did not have a document like that of the Bill of Rights in the U.S. Constitution, but it had a system of criminal justice much more advanced than those of many countries, cultures, and civilizations. After the end of imperial rule, China entered into the age of modernity in the beginning of the 20th century with enormous legal and judicial competence and with a huge set of judicial institutions to be able to transform to a modern system of criminal justice. How this progress toward modernity in criminal justice in China has advanced in the 20th century will be discussed in the following sections.

■ Criminal Justice in the First Republic of China, 1911–1949

The criminal justice system of a country is an integral part of that state. The nature of criminal justice is intimately connected to the nature of the state. Any major transformations in the nature and ideology of the state are bound to bring major changes in the nature of its criminal justice. The rise of the institutions of modern criminal justice in England, France, the United States, and other countries of the West was possible only after the rise of the modern states. In Europe, the demise of feudalism and the medieval states set in motion the rise of the modern states, and the rise of the modern states set in motion the rise of the institutions of modern criminal justice. In China, the imperial rule of the medieval kingdom came to an end with the overthrowing of the last emperor of the Qing dynasty in 1911. A modern state—the Republic of China—was born in 1912 under the leadership of a new political party, Koumintang, and a new political leader, Sun Yat-sen (1866–1925). The first modern state of China, however, died in infancy. It was not quite 4 decades old when it was violently overthrown by a communist revolution led by Mao Zedong in 1949. The 37 years of the Republic of China were the best of times and also the worst of times. They were the best of times because China, after more than 2,000 years of imperial rule, began to dream of building a modern state based on the values of democracy, liberty, equality, and freedom. They were the best of times because China began to think of becoming a part of the modern world and participating in the process of the advancement of modernity. But those 37 years of the modern Republic of China were also the worst of times. It was a time of intense political turmoil and turbulence both internally and externally. Internally, it gave rise to various alternative structures of power controlled by different warlords of different regions who wanted to go back to imperial rule. The Beiyang army created during the last years of the Qing dynasty thwarted all political efforts by the new regime to establish a modern state and a strong central government on the basis of parliamentary democracy. Externally, there was the Japanese threat to colonize China in order to bring it to the vortex of the modern world. The most significant external event that shaped the political destiny of China in the whole of the 20th century, however, was the success of the Russian Revolution, the establishment of the Soviet Socialist regime, and the beginning of the Soviet Socialist expansion from 1917. Russia helped establish the Chinese Community Party (CCP) in the Republic of China under the leadership of Mao Zedong in 1921. After a series of political battles and uprisings that continued for more than 2 decades, the nationalist and the modernist forces of Sun Yat-sen and his deputy, Chiang Kai-shek, lost the power of the modern infant state of China to the communist regime of Mao Zedong in 1949.

Birth of Modernization in Criminal Justice in China: The New Policy Era

The first modern state of China collapsed in less than 4 decades. But it had some remarkable effects on criminal justice even within that short span of time. China came to a new turning point in its history in the last decade of the 19th century, particularly around the year 1898. Since the late 19th century, particularly after the defeat of China by the British and French forces in the second Opium War of 1860, there was a growing sense in both imperial political order and the emerging Chinese intelligentsia that the centuries of isolation of China from the West and the adamant refusal of Chinese imperial power to be a part of the emerging global economy where the reasons for the underdevelopment of China (even though Chinese technology in the 16th and 17th centuries was far superior to that of Europe). This growing sense of China's underdevelopment in comparison to Japan and the West culminated in the rise of a new modernist movement during the last days of the Qing dynasty. The ninth emperor of the Qing dynasty, Emperor Guangxu (1875–1908), through a series of imperial edicts, embarked on a major program of significant social and political transformations in China following the developmental model of Japan and the West (Karl & Zarrow, 2002). On January 20, 1901, an imperial edict nicely summarized the spirit of China's first modernist movement. The edict stated that China must "blend together the best of what is Chinese and what is foreign" (Xu, 2008, p. 1). The edict called upon the members of the Grand Council, the grand secretaries, the six boards and nine ministers, the Chinese ministers abroad, and the governor generals and the governors of the provinces to seriously study the Japanese and Western models of political and economic systems, administrations, education, science, and the military (Xu, 2008). Reforms for modern criminal justice began for the first time in China as a part of this modernist movement started by Emperor Guangxu. The major thrust of the movement survived only about 103 days—a historical event known in China as the Hundred Days' Reform. The key leaders of the movement were killed and exiled after a military coup led by Empress Dowager Cixi. But the effect of that modernist movement on the general society continued to grow even after the demise of the Qing dynasty in 1911. The political leadership of the new Republic of China ideologically followed the same path of modernization and westernization in China until the government of Chiang Kai-shek was overthrown by the communist revolution led by Mao Zedong in 1949.

During the expansion of modernist reforms by Qing Emperor Guangxu, through a project of modernization known as "New Policy" (Xu, 2008, p. 5), a series of criminal justice reforms were introduced to establish the rule of law, to create an independent judiciary, to develop a new criminal code, to expand professionalization in the practice of law and the judiciary, to build a professional police force, and to develop new penal laws. In 1902, the Law Codification Commission was established under the leadership of a number of legal experts trained and educated in the West for reforms in Chinese criminal law following the Japanese and Western models. In 1906, the Qing ruler established a new Ministry of Law and the Court of Judicial Review was renamed as the Supreme Court. In 1907, a commission on studying constitutional government was created, and it "served as the gate keeper for all reform proposals and counterproposals regarding the New Policy" (Xu, 2008, p. 28). The commission proposed "an independent judiciary" (Xu, 2008, p. 29) as a means for modernizing criminal justice based on the rule of law and the protection of human rights. The commission, in its exposition of Western models, "made it clear that the prerequisite for protecting human rights was the rule of law, and the institutional prerequisite for the rule of law was judicial independence" (Xu, 2008, p. 29). Although some of the leading legal reformers were trained and educated in the West, it was primarily by learning from the Japanese model of legal reforms in criminal justice that Chinese intellectuals became knowledgeable about the nature of modernization in law and justice in the West. "The fact that Japan had successfully transformed itself into a modern nation accepted by Western powers persuaded the Chinese (from Qing court to high officials to intellectuals) to take Japan as a copy of a Western model" (Xu, 2008, p. 32).

As a part of this process of modernization in criminal justice, the Law Codification Commission introduced a new code of criminal law in 1907 on the basis of the study of a number of foreign legal traditions. The commission by 1904 "had completed a large body of translations, and by 1907, it had translated a total of twenty-six foreign laws and legal works" (Xu, 2008, p. 35). Under the new criminal code, all forms of physical punishments were abolished, including torture, slow slicing, the public execution of heads, the beheading of a corpse, flogging, and the penalty of judicial tattooing. The imperial court also abolished the system of collective prosecution. The 1907 Code "limited punishments to three basic forms: fines, imprisonment, and the death penalty. Institutional confinement became the main form of punishment . . . public display of painful punishments disappeared. The death penalty, too, was no longer to be carried out in public" (Muhlhahn, 2009, p. 61). In 1908, a new prison law was also introduced. The new "law had twelve sections and 240 articles. It never came into effect because of the 1911 revolution, but like many other laws drafted in the late Qing period, it served as a basis for later legislation" (Muhlhahn, 2009, pp. 61–62). In 1910, the imperial court approved the Law on Organizing Courts proposed by the Law Codification Commission in 1907. The new law established a uniform judicial system—a hierarchical system of courts following the Western models.

Modernization in Criminal Justice in China: The New Policy Era

Modernization in criminal justice in the new Republic of China thus began not only in the context of a great era of social and political transformations but also with a rich legacy of modern institutional innovations in criminal justice that came from the New Policy era of the late Qing dynasty (Karl & Zarrow, 2002). The government of the new Republic of China, immediately after coming to power in 1912, embarked on a plan to continue with the process of modernization in criminal justice set in motion by the New Policy era. Sun Yat-sen's provisional government "enshrined the principle of judicial independence in the Provisional Constitution" (Xu, 2008, p. 55). In 1913, in the face of political turmoil created by some of the conservative military generals of the late Qing dynasty, Sun Yat-sen lost political power. From 1913 to 1927, China was governed by different regional military generals and warlords. But even during that period of intense political destabilization, known as the Beiyang era in Chinese political history, the Law Codification Commission continued to work with the progress of modernization in law and justice. Between 1912 and 1927, the Law Codification Commission "compiled several dozens of laws and ordinances" (Xu, 2008, p. 57). The Beiyang government renamed the Ministry of Law as the Ministry of Justice, and it was this Ministry of Justice that was a catalyst for modernizing the Chinese judicial system in the 1920s by creating a new system of courts proposed by the Law on Organizing Courts in 1910; by institutionalizing judicial independence; and by creating a new cadre of trained judicial personnel through the expansion of professional legal education. "The regulations of educational qualifications were enforced, so that in 1925, among 955 judges and procurators in the country, 211 were graduates from law schools in foreign countries and 770 had received higher education in China" (Xu, 2008, p. 61). During the Beiyang era, "judicial reform was pursued based on the principle of the rule of law, judicial independence, and due process, and even on the notions of human rights and civil rights" (Xu, 2008, p. 84).

At the end of the 1920s, a new political regime came to power in China under the leadership of Chiang Kai-shek and his political party—the Kuomintang. Chiang Kai-shek established a nationalist government, freed the country from the regional warlords, and re-unified the whole nation under a central leadership. The government of Chiang Kai-shek also continued with the project of modernizing the Chinese state and the Chinese system of criminal justice. But because of a host of competing political forces that were developing in the new state, a new process of politicization of the judiciary became an ideology of the government of Chiang Kai-shek, and that largely undermined the modernization process that started in the New Policy era. Under his government, the practice of appointing party officials "to judicial posts became the rule" (Xu, 2008, p. 89). "Partyizing of the judiciary required that judges apply party doctrines to adjudications and that judges be selected from among those who understood and would carry out party doctrines" (Xu, 2008, p. 92). The criminal code of the nationalist government introduced new crimes—"the crimes of being 'counterrevolutionaries', or local bullies and evil gentry" (Xu, 2008, p. 92). The government of Chiang Kai-shek was violently overthrown in 1949 by a revolution led by the Chinese Communist Party under the leadership of Mao Zedong. With the demise of the nationalist regime of Chiang Kai-shek, the movement for the modernization of the Chinese state and the Chinese criminal justice system that was started by Qing Emperor Guangxu came to a halt. The case of this movement for modernizing the Chinese criminal justice system in the first 4 decades of the 20th century is a glaring example of how changes and reforms in criminal justice are intimately connected with the political turns and turmoil of the state.

■ Criminal Justice in China During the Communist Era: The Breakdown of Modernization, 1949–1978

With the triumph of the socialist revolution in Russia in 1917 and the beginning of the expansion of socialist ideology across the world in the 1920s and 1930s, there emerged a bipolar political order in the world. One order was the political order of the West, born in the 18th and 19th centuries in the context of the Age of Enlightenment—the liberal capitalist political order. It is this liberal political order that gave birth to the modern state and the institutions of modern law and justice in the West. The second order was the political order of socialism and communism based on the ideology of Marxism. Under the direct support of the Soviet Socialist regime, a new political party—the Chinese Communist Party (CCP)—was established under the leadership of Mao Zedong in 1921. The CCP and Mao Zedong captured political power and established the state of the People's Republic of China by defeating the modernist political forces of Chiang Kai-shek in 1949. From 1949 to 1976, Mao Zedong was the architect of the socialist state of China.

Birth of the Socialist State in China

The history of China's criminal justice from 1949 to 1976 is the history of the destruction of almost all the institutions of modernity in law and justice that were built in the previous centuries. The socialist state of China under Mao Zedong deliberately pursued a policy regime sharply opposed to the capitalist and liberal system of the West. From the beginning, one of the major tasks of his socialist program was the complete overthrow and destruction of the core institutions of a modern state that had been slowly but steadily growing in China since the New Policy days of the Qing dynasty—parliamentary form of government, capitalist economic system, independent judiciary, political pluralism, professional bureaucracy, professional policing, and a modern system of law, justice, and judiciary. In 1949, the new socialist government of China introduced the Common Program of the People's Political Consultative Council. Article 17 of the Common Program "abolished all laws and legal institutions of Nationalist China. The judicial order that had been so high on the agenda of all administrations in the Chinese Republic came to an abrupt end" (Muhlhahn, 2009, p. 178). To pursue the path of socialism, the old criminal legal codes were removed, legal institutions were destroyed, judicial personnel were fired, and college and universities teaching the profession of modern law were permanently shut down. It is estimated that between 1952 and 1953, "at least 80 percent of the judicial personnel were removed from their posts" (Muhlhahn, 2009, p. 180). In 1959, the Ministry of Justice was dismantled. Within 3 decades of governance under socialism, the whole institution of criminal justice in China, which was based on more than 2,000 years of legacies of the great legal documents and discourses, collapsed from within and remained unrecognizable. The system "for a long time was very much in flux, and it became mixed up with many other governmental agencies and organizations" (Muhlhahn, 2009, p. 175). Immediately after Mao Zedong came to power, the task of destroying the prevailing system of criminal justice was taken up by the socialist government because it was "conceived as an instrument of the ruling class for the suppression and exploitation of the Chinese masses" (Muhlhahn, 2009, p. 147). For the CCP, "the system of criminal justice established in the Chinese Republic possessed a clear-cut 'class character.' For this reason, every effort to overthrow the Chinese Republic invariably also implied an attack against the criminal justice system" (Muhlhahn, 2009, p. 147). The socialist state of Mao Zedong looked not to the West, but to the Union of Soviet Socialist Republics (USSR) to borrow a model for a new system of criminal justice.

Socialist Theory of Crime, Law, and Justice

The perspective of moving away from the West's modern and liberal criminal justice system was based on the socialist theory of crime, law, and justice. Crime, according to Marxists and socialists, is a class phenomenon. The people who commit crimes are the people who are oppressed, debased, and dehumanized in the system of capitalism. The people who commit crimes are those who are alienated in the system of unequal distribution of wealth under capitalism. The system of capitalism is dominated by the bourgeoisie class—the owners of capital, wealth, and all major means of production. The working class, or the proletariat class, is economically exploited in the capitalist system, and this economic exploitation is the reason for increased crime and criminality under capitalism. The socialist theory of law is equally based on the perspective that law in a capitalist society is an instrument to perpetually dominate the working class and to keep them permanently subjugated. To make a society free from crime and criminality, argue the advocates of the socialist theory of crime and law, the economic system of capitalism and the legal institutions that bind the system together must be destroyed. A society will be free from crime and criminality under socialism because a socialist system is based on the collective ownership of property, and the dictatorship of the proletariat. In supporting the socialist theory of criminology and criminal justice, Mao Zedong said: "Such state apparatus as the army, the police and the courts are instruments with which one class oppresses another . . . these are instruments of oppression. They are violent and certainly not benevolent things" (as quoted in Leng & Chiu, 1985, p. 9).

Socialist penology is based on the theory of reeducation through hard labor. The social-ist theory of punishment "rested on one central element: the transformative role of labor" (Muhlhahn, 2009, p. 149). The Soviet Union created a new model of criminal justice based on the premise of the socialist theory of crime, law, and punishment (Cohen, 1968). Begin-ning in the 1930s, the prisoners in the Soviet Union were used, through coercions, in various industrial and construction projects. "The criminal justice system established in the Soviet Union was deliberately offered as a model to other socialist countries, with 'labor reforms' or 'corrective labor' as its central element" (Muhlhahn, 2009, p. 158). The new socialist gov-ernment of China saw the Soviet system of criminal justice "as the best and most valid way to deal with criminality in China" (Muhlhahn, 2009, p. 159). In 1954, Mao Zedong promul-gated the Act of Reform through Labor, and the program was adopted "in order to punish all counterrevolutionary and other criminal offenders and to compel them to reform through labor and become new persons" (Leng & Chiu, 1985, p. 26).

The new system of socialist criminal justice created in China in the late 1950s had the following four major institutions: (1) bureaus for public security; (2) the Office of the Proc-urator; (3) people's assessor; and (4) regular criminal courts. The regular criminal courts were composed of county courts, provincial courts, and the Supreme People's Courts. Among the most important extrajudicial institutions that were central to criminal justice in the first decade of the socialist government were the people's tribunals. People's tribunals were used primarily to punish those who were in defiance of the socialist order and labeled as counter-revolutionaries. The people's tribunals, composed mostly of local party workers, were used for mass trials, accusations meetings, and purging of class enemies—industrialists, bureau-crats, intellectuals, and landlords. It is estimated that in the early 1950s, about 4 million people were arrested "without any real involvement of the regular courts. Hundreds of thousands of 'class enemies' or 'enemies of the people' . . . were sentenced to death and executed. In mass trials, [the] death penalty was carried out immediately" (Muhlhahn, 2009, p. 183). Another observer of the Chinese criminal justice system during the communist era similarly noted that in the early 1950s, "the nationalist legal apparatus, including the bar, was formally abolished . . . yet it was not immediately replaced by a well-regulated system of criminal justice . . . . Much criminal punishment during these years was administered outside the courts" (Cohen, 1968, p. 10). It was further observed that during that time, "police had unfettered power to investigate, detain, prosecute, and convict. The police also conducted large-scale 'administrative' roundups of petty thieves, gamblers, opium addicts, whores, pimps, vagrants . . . and subjected them to 'non-criminal' reform measures during the course of long confinement" (Cohen, 1968, p. 10). Mao Zedong deliberately introduced a policy of "legalized" violence against those who opposed the communist revolution (Cohen, 1968, p. 10). The communist regime's "army, the police, and the regular and irregular courts imple-mented the directive of Chairman Mao to serve as instruments for oppressing the hostile classes and for inflicting 'legalized' violence" (Cohen, 1968, p. 10).

The first constitution of the socialist state of China was passed by the National People's Congress in 1954. The constitution was based on a translation of Soviet Russia's legal code. The constitution set up the Law Codification Commission, and the commission drafted a code of criminal law and a code of criminal procedure, but these were not implemented until the late 1970s—until the death of Mao Zedong. For almost 3 decades under the socialist regime of Mao Zedong, China remained without a code of criminal law and a code of criminal procedure: "For thirty years, no coherent, comprehensive law codes existed to regulate the criminal justice system in the People's Republic" (Muhlhahn, 2009, p. 188). Criminal justice under Mao Zedong was based on only two statutes: the 1951 Act for Punishment for Counterrevolutionaries and the 1952 Act of Punishment for Corruption. After the promulgation of the constitution of 1954, political control of the judiciary and the criminal justice system as a whole became much more pervasive. The criminal justice system of China in the late 1950s was politically more oppressive than that of the Stalinist time in the Soviet Union. Cohen observed that "under Stalin whatever the realities of practice, Party control over judicial decisions was not publicly advocated. . . . In China, since the antirightist movment, the model judge is one who consults the local Party apparatus about any important case" (1968, p. 16).

Criminal Justice in China During the Cultural Revolution, 1966–1978

From 1966 to 1978, China went through a fundamental process of socialist transformation known as the Great Proletarian Cultural Revolution. The Cultural Revolution was directed to completely destroy the vestiges of capitalism—the reactionary bureaucracy, the urban bourgeoisie, and the bourgeoisie intellectuals: "A . . . serious blow to the formal legal structure came during the Cultural Revolution . . . . Mao instructed the Red Guards to 'smash Gongjianfa (police, procuracy, and courts).' The procuracy was dissolved . . . law schools were closed and . . . judicial training was stopped" (Muhlhahn, 2009, p. 191). Scores of chief law enforcement officers were removed from their posts. "Among many law enforcement personnel, removed from office were President of the Supreme People's Court, the Chief Procurator, and the first Deputy Minister of Public Security" (Leng & Chiu 1985, p. 18).

The socialist criminal justice system was completely politicized during the Cultural Revolution. Between 1966 and 1976, case extermination groups were formed in all spheres of the government and the political party for the prosecution of the counterrevolutionaries and the political dissidents. Revolutionary committees and Red Guards composed of students, workers, and military personnel replaced the courts and the prosecutors. Petty crimes were prosecuted by local workgroups that included public security officers, a prosecutor, and a judge. "In this system, the administration of justice was viewed as an eminently political affair" (Muhlhahn, 2009, p. 195). By creating local and rural workgroups as the foundation for socialist criminal justice, the new socialist state of China abandoned even "the Soviet-inspired constitutional model of formal judicial procedure, which culminated in public trials before impartial judges who heard evidence and legal arguments presented by defense counsel as well as the prosecution" (Muhlhahn, 2009, p. 194). The socialist state of China under Mao Zedong successfully destroyed the institutions and the ethos of modern criminal justice that had begun to take shape in the last days of the Qing dynasty, and yet it failed to create any stable and sustainable alternative system of law and justice. For about 30 years, millions of people were tried, prosecuted, and executed in socialist China under Mao Zedong without the effective functioning of a formal system of law and justice, without a code of criminal law, and without a code of criminal procedure.

■ Criminal Justice in Contemporary China: Rebirth of Modernization, 1979–2011

After the death of Mao Zedong in 1976, China again came to a new crossroads of history. With his death came also the death of his philosophy and program of Cultural Revolution. The social and political institutions of the Cultural Revolution and the laws that legitimated them soon began to crumble. The death of about 40–70 million people during the socialist transformation of China under Mao Zedong; the total destruction of the social and legal institutions of China, some of which were more than 2,000 years old; and the destruction of the intellectual basis of a nation that glorified education (Confucian philosophy) more than any other world civilization of ancient and medieval times traumatized the Chinese mind. The same moment and the same perspective that were hovering along the horizons of the Chinese mind when Qing Emperor Guangxu almost unilaterally embarked on the path of modernization around the 1890s were again hovering along the horizons of the minds of a new generation of Chinese political leaders and intellectuals in the late 1970s after the death of Mao Zedong. This late 20th century moment was when the Chinese began to realize that China was incredibly isolated from, and lived on the periphery of the rest of the world's civilizations—the civilizations that were restlessly progressing toward the path of modernization and globalization.

This realization brought a paradigmatic shift in the minds of the Chinese political leaders who succeeded Mao Zedong. They came to power with an entirely new perspective—a perspective that did not abandon the socialist framework of the state of China, yet represented a path of socialist modernization that included a deep and intense engagement with the West. The leader who brought this perspective to the front of the Chinese mind was Deng Xiaoping (1904–1997). Under the leadership of Deng Xiaoping, a grand process of modernization and globalization began in China in 1979. The most visible parts of this process of modernization are the skylines of Beijing, Shanghai, Tianjin, Shantou, Guangzhou, Shenyang, Shenzhen, and other cities of China that grew in the wake of China's aggressive transition to a market economy. What is not most visible, but is far more fundamental, is China's equally aggressive process of transitioning to a system of modern law and justice and its deliberate policy of building a socialist nation within the framework of the rule of law. It is in this context that China has recently initiated a series of reforms for modernization in criminal justice. Any comparative criminal justice in contemporary China must be situated within its recent program of the rebirth of modernization in law, politics, and justice. It is a rebirth of the process of modernization because it was not the first time that China realized the significance of becoming a part of modernity and modern civilization. It was well conceived by Qing Emperor Guangxu and the generations of political leaders, intellectuals, jurists, and journalists who supported his program of modernization in law and justice during the New Policy era in China in 1898.

China's Transition Toward a Rule of Law and Constitutionalism

The rule of law, as discussed before, is a precondition for a modern system of criminal justice. A state that does not uphold and constitutionally protect the principle of the rule of law does not create a modern system of criminal justice. The rule of law is not merely a process of developing new laws. It is a distinctive philosophy of governance—a philosophy and a perspective that bind the ruler and the ruled within the same framework of law. In a state based on the principle of the rule of law, law not only protects the rights of citizens but also limits the power of the government. This notion of limiting the government's power has remained at the core of modernity since the days of the Magna Carta. The socialist state of Mao Zedong was based not on the rule *of* law but on rule *by* law. Mao Zedong said, "Depend on the rule of man, not the rule of law" (Leng & Chiu, 1985, p. 18). After the process of socialist modernization began in 1979, the issue of the rule of law, therefore, became a dominant concern for the political leadership in China. Den Xiaoping was a close associate of Mao Zedong, yet he never accepted Mao's legal nihilism. Den Xiaoping firmly believed that in China "there was an urgent need for an impersonal, highly institutionalized legal system with a complete set of legal codes" (Lo, 1995, p. 33). In the Third Plenum in 1978, Den Xiaoping said that "to ensure people's democracy, we must strengthen our legal system. Democracy has to be institutionalized and written into law, so as to make sure that institutions and laws do not change whenever the leadership changes" (as quoted in Lo, 1995, p. 33). In 1979, the Ministry of Justice was reestablished to reorganize the Chinese judiciary and to plan for the modernization of the Chinese police and the prison system. To advance this process of reforms in law and justice, "law schools were reopened, and a wide variety of legal journals commenced publication" (Peerenboom, 2002, p. 7), and the government began to "promote greater professionalization of judges, prosecutors, lawyers, and police. While in 1981, there were just 1,465 law offices and a mere 5,500 lawyers, by 1998 there were more than 8,300 law firms and 110,000 lawyers" (Peerenboom, 2002, p. 7).

Since the establishment of the People' Republic of China, China has had four constitutions promulgated in 1959, 1975, 1979, and 1982 (US–China Institute, 2007). It is the constitution of 1982 that, for the first time, recognized the centrality of the rule of law and the supremacy of the constitution in the construction of the socialist state of China (Kellogg, 2008; The Supreme People's Court of the People's Republic of China, 2003). The 1982 constitution states that the People's Republic of China will be governed "in accordance with the law and building a socialist country of law. All state organs, the armed forces, all political parties and public organizations and all enterprises and institutions must abide by the Constitution and the law" (Article 5). A more vigorous debate to uphold the rule of law began in the larger society in China in the middle of the 1990s, partly in the context of the expansion of the market economy, and partly in the context of the weakening "of the ideological control that the Chinese Communist Party (CCP) exercises over Chinese political reforms" (Lin, 2003, p. 261). It was in response to this growing discourse on the rule of law in the larger society of China that Jiang Zemin, who led the 15th CCP in 1997, further confirmed, in front of more than 2,000 party delegates, that China would not stop its long march toward the rule of law. He declared that the CCP amended "the party's character to include 'governing the country according to law' and 'establishing Socialist rule of law' as major goals for the country by the year 2010" (Lin, 2003, p. 261). The notion of the socialist rule of law "included the principle that all are equal before the law and no one is beyond the law: in particular, party members and government officials must act in accordance with the law" (Peerenboom, 2002, p. 60). Jiang Zemin, in his report to the 15th Congress, also outlined the need for an independent judiciary for the progress toward the rule of law. These directives were incorporated in the constitution in 1999, and after that, the meaning of the socialist rule of law became "a matter of constitutional interpretation" (Peerenboom, 2002, p. 62). China's rapid march toward the rule of law is evidenced by the fact that between 1996 and 1998, the National People's Congress (China's legislative body) and its standing committees "passed more than 337 laws and [the] local people's congress and governments issued more than 6,000 regulations. In contrast, only 134 laws were passed between 1949 and 1978, with only one law passed during the Cultural Revolution" (Peerenboom, 2002, p. 6). In the 16th Congress of the CCP in 2002, Jiang Zemin further upheld the notion of the rule of law and constitutionalism. He said: "No organization or individual enjoys any privilege above the constitution and laws" (as quoted in Lin, 2003, p. 261). A series of reforms in criminal justice in China have been introduced during the last 30 years as a part of this broader movement for the rule of law and constitutionalism in China (Hsu, 2003).

Reforms in Substantive Criminal Law

Reforms in criminal law began with the start of modernization under the leadership of Deng Xiaoping in 1979. In 1979, the National People's Congress enacted the first comprehensive criminal code of China—the Code of Criminal Law and the Criminal Procedural Law of 1979 that became effective in January 1980 (Luo, 1998; The Supreme People's Court of the People's Republic of China, 2003). At the inauguration of this new milestone in China's march toward the rule of law, Deng Xiaoping said: "For twenty nine-years since the founding of new China, we have had no criminal law . . . . Now a code of criminal law and a code of criminal procedure have been adopted" (as quoted in Lo, 1995, p. 39). The Code of Criminal Law of 1979 was substantially amended in 1997, and the Code of Criminal Procedural Law of 1979 was also substantially amended in 1997 and in 2001 (Jinwen, 2001). These amended versions of the Code of Criminal Law of

1997 and the Code of Criminal Procedural Law of 2001 are presently the key legal documents that govern the system of criminal justice in China. The 1997 Code of Criminal Law defines crime as:

> [an] act that endangers the sovereignty, territorial integrity and security of the State . . . undermines public and economic order, violates State-owned property, property collectively owned by the working people, or property privately owned by citizens, infringes on the citizens' rights of the person, their democratic or other rights, and any other act that endangers society (Article 13).

The important point to note is that under Article 13 of the 1997 Code of Criminal Law, the violation of the citizen's rights began to be defined as a crime for the first time in China. The constitutional recognition that individuals are entitled to certain rights, and that the violation of those rights by private individuals and the government is a crime, is a major step toward the implementation of the rule of law. Chapter II of the constitution of 1982 enumerates the fundamental rights of the citizens of China. The constitution guarantees that all citizens of China "are equal before the law" (Article 33). They have the right to vote (Article 34), the right of "freedom of speech, of the press, of assembly, of association, of procession and of demonstration" (Article 35). The constitution also protects the freedom of religion (Article 36), the right to education (Article 46), and the right to marriage and family (Article 49). The Criminal Code of 1997 defines the violation of these fundamental rights as a crime in China.

The 1997 Criminal Code identified 10 major categories of crimes (Articles 102–450), 5 types of principal punishments, and 3 types of supplementary punishments (Articles 33–86). The 10 types of crimes fall into 4 broad categories: national security crimes, public order crimes, economic crimes, and crimes of the dereliction of duty. The major national security crimes include armed rebellion, terrorism, and espionage. The major public order crimes include homicide, arson, kidnapping, spread of poison, terrorism, sabotaging a transportation system, sabotaging a telecommunications system, illegal ownership and manufacturing of guns, trafficking and transporting of narcotic drugs, hijacking of ships and aircrafts, engagement in prostitution, and producing and supplying pornographic materials. It is economic crime that is most extensively defined in the Code as crimes of disturbing the order of the socialist market economy. Some of the major economic crimes include marketing of fake commodities, smuggling, disruption of corporate administration, financial fraud, infringement on intellectual property rights, embezzlement, and bribery. Some of the crimes of the dereliction of duty include abuse of power, engagement in malpractice, deliberate divulgence of state secrets, corruption in the judiciary, corruption in law enforcement, environmental crimes, and crimes of servicemen's transgression of duties (see **Table 11-2**).

The five types of punishments are public surveillance, criminal detention, fixed-term imprisonment, life imprisonment, and death penalty (Article 33). The three types of supplementary punishments are fines, deprivation of political rights, and confiscation of property (Article 34). The punishment of public surveillance is close to the notions of GPS

TABLE 11-2 The 1997 Code of Criminal Law in China: Major Types of Crimes and Mandatory Punishments

Major Categories of Crimes	Major Types of Mandatory Punishments
Crimes of endangering national security	Life imprisonment or fixed-term imprisonment of not less than 10 years
Splitting the state or undermining the unity of the country	Life imprisonment or fixed-term imprisonment of not less than 10 years
Armed rebellion against the state	Life imprisonment or fixed-term imprisonment of not less than 10 years/deprivation of political rights
Joining an espionage organization	Fixed-term imprisonment of not less than 3 years, but not more than 10 years
Endangering public security	Fixed-term imprisonment of not less than 3 years, but not more than 10 years
Hijacking of an airplane	Fixed-term imprisonment of not less than 10 years or life imprisonment; if death results, death penalty
Hijacking a ship or motor vehicle by means of violence	Fixed-term imprisonment of not less than 5 years, but not more than 10 years; if there are serious consequences, fixed-term imprisonment of not less than 10 years or life imprisonment
Sabotaging telecommunication facilities	Fixed-term imprisonment of not less than 3 years, but not more than 7 years; if there are serious consequences, fixed-term imprisonment of not less than 7 years
Illegal manufacturing and selling of guns	Fixed-term imprisonment of not less than 5 years, but not more than 10 years; if the circumstances are especially serious, fixed-term imprisonment of not less than 10 years or life imprisonment
Producing fake commodities	Fixed-term imprisonment of 15 years or life imprisonment/confiscation of property
Crimes of smuggling	Fixed-term imprisonment of not less than 3 years, but not more than 7 years/fines
Disrupting the order of financial administration	Fixed-term imprisonment of not less than 10 years, life imprisonment, or death/fines
Financial fraud	Fixed-term imprisonment of not less than 5 years, but not more than 10 years/fines
Crimes of property violation	Fixed-term imprisonment of not less than 10 years, life imprisonment, or death/fines/confiscation of property
Intentional homicide	Death, life imprisonment, or fixed-term imprisonment of not less than 10 years
Raping a woman by violence or coercion	Fixed-term imprisonment of not less than 3 years, but not more than 10 years
Raping a girl under the age of 14	Fixed-term imprisonment of not less than 10 years, life imprisonment, or death
Insulting a woman by violence	Fixed-term imprisonment of not more than 5 years or criminal detention

Source: Data from the 1979 Chinese Code Criminal law as amended in 1997.

tracking and sex offender registration in the United States, Canada, and the United Kingdom. The Code states that an offender under public surveillance must:

> (1) observe laws and administrative rules and regulations, and submit to supervision; (2) exercise no right of freedom of speech, of the press, of assembly, of association, of procession or of demonstration; (3) report on his own activities as required by the organ executing the public surveillance; and (4) report to obtain approval from the organ executing the public surveillance for any departure from the city or county he lives in or for any change in residence (Chapter III, Section II, Article 39).

The punishments of fixed-term imprisonment and life-term imprisonment are based on mandatory guidelines as in the United States and the United Kingdom. The Code prohibited the imposition of the death penalty (Articles 48–51) on juveniles under the age of 18 (Article 49) and made a provision that "all death sentences, except for those that according to law should be decided by the Supreme People's Court, shall be submitted to the Supreme People's Court for verification and approval. Death sentences with a suspension of execution may be decided or verified and approved by a Higher People's Court" (Article 49). The punishment for the deprivation of political rights is what is known as felony disenfranchisement in the United States. Article 56 of the 1997 Criminal Code stated that:

> Anyone who commits the crime of endangering national security shall be sentenced to deprivation of political rights as a supplementary punishment; anyone who commits the crime of seriously undermining public order by intentional homicide, rape, arson, explosion, poisoning, or robbery may be sentenced to deprivation of political rights as a supplementary punishment (The Supreme People's Court of the People's Republic of China, 2003).

Offenders who are sentenced to life in prison are deprived of their political rights for life. For others, it cannot be imposed for more than 5 years (Article 55). What is noticeable is that the 1997 Criminal Code of China has prohibited all forms of physical punishments such as flogging, decapitation, torture, and judicial tattooing (see Table 11-2).

Reforms in Procedural Criminal Law and the Due Process

The present Chinese Code of Criminal Procedural Law was first established in 1979 by the Fifth National Congress, and it was later amended in 1997 by the Eighth National People's Congress. The 1997 Code of Criminal Procedure outlines the structure of criminal justice in China (The Supreme People's Court of the People's Republic of China, 2003). This structure is composed of three major sets of institutions: People's Courts, People's Procuratorates, and Public Safety Organs. There are four levels of People's Courts. In ascending order, they are the Basic People's Courts (courts of first instance), Intermediate People's Courts (courts of second instance), High People's Courts (provincial courts), and Supreme People's Court (final court of appeal). These four levels of the people's court system correspond to four levels of a procuratorate system comprised of local people's procuratorates, intermediate people's procuratorates, provincial procuratorates, and superior people's procuratorates (Trevaskes, 2007). The People's Courts and the procuratorates are functionally independent from the executive and the legislative branch—the National People's Congress. The 1997 Code of Criminal Procedure states: "The people's courts shall exercise independently the judicial powers . . . the people's procuratorates shall exercise independently the procuratorial powers as prescribed by the laws, and they shall be free from any interference from any administrative organ" (Article 5). But the courts are all under the supervision of the Chinese Ministry of Public Security and the Chinese Ministry of Justice.

The Chinese Ministry of Public Security is the national police agency of China with oversight authority on law enforcement. It is like the FBI of the United States, the National Police Agency of Japan, and the Federal Criminal Police of Germany. The Ministry of Public Security has regional, provincial, and municipal public security bureaus and sub-bureaus. The public security organizations can impose sanctions in emergency conditions, but they can also make an arrest without the approval of the court and the procuratorate. There are also public security stations at local and district levels. In addition to this mainstream police force under the Ministry of Public Security, there is also a state security police under the Ministry of State Security that was introduced in the early 1980s. The state security police is more militarized and is responsible for dealing with crimes against the state (i.e., espionage, conspiracy, and sabotage), and different forms of transnational crimes, such as human trafficking, drug trafficking, cyber crimes, and global terrorism. The other types of policing in China include judicial police and prison police. The judicial police are under the control of the Supreme People's Procuratorate, and the prison police are under the control of the Ministry of Justice (Terrill, 2009).

The Ministry of Public Security has the sole responsibility of developing an efficient and a competent police force for the maintenance of general law and order. There are three major institutions through which this function is performed: the University of Public Security, the University of Police Officers, and the Institute of Criminal Justice. There are police education and police training academies and organizations like that of the Federal Law Enforcement Training Center in the United States. China's Ministry of Justice is also an integral part of China's criminal justice system because it is responsible for the overall modernization of Chinese law and justice. The Chinese Ministry of Justice, which is like the U.S. Department of Justice, has a number of research institutes through which it ensures the development and modernization of Chinese law and justice and the efficient administration of criminal justice in China. Some of these include the Institute for Crime Prevention, the Institute for Judicial Administration, the Institute for Judicial Research, the Institute for Forensic Science, and the Central College for Judicial Affairs.

The description of the Chinese system of criminal justice, however, is incomplete without also looking at the role of the People's National Congress, which is like the Congress of the United States and Parliament of the United Kingdom—the main body for the making of criminal laws and statutes. The criminal justice of China is a complex network of institutions and organizations including the people's courts, the procuratorate system, the Ministry of Public Security, the Ministry of Justice, and the People's National Congress. The 1997 Code of Criminal Procedure defined the specific role and jurisdictions of these various branches of criminal justice. The 1997 Code of Criminal Procedural Law states that: "The public security organs shall be responsible for the investigation, detention, execution of arrests and pre-trial examination . . . . The people's procuratorates shall be responsible for the procuratorial work, the approving of arrests, and the investigation and initiation of public prosecution" (Article 3). Article 3 goes on to say that "the people's courts shall be responsible for the trial. No other organ, organization or person shall have the right to exercise such powers, unless the laws otherwise provide." The 1997 Code of Criminal Procedure Law also states that in conducting criminal proceedings, the people's courts, the people's procuratorates, and the public security organs "must rely on the masses, base themselves on facts and take law as the criterion. The law applies equally to all citizens and no privilege whatsoever is permissible before law" (Article 6).

One of the most intriguing areas of comparative research from the perspective modernization of criminal justice in contemporary China is to examine the provisions of the constitution, the Code of Criminal Law, and the Code of Criminal Procedural Law that are close to some of the due process laws in modern systems of criminal justice. Articles 37, 38, and 39 of the 1982 constitution of China resemble one of the key principles of the West's due process of law—the Fourth Amendment of the U.S. Constitution. Article 37 states that the freedom of the citizens of the People's Republic of China is inviolable: "No citizen may be arrested except with the approval or by decision of a people's procuratorate or by decision of a people's court . . . . Unlawful deprivation . . . of citizens' freedom . . . by detention . . . and unlawful search . . . is prohibited." Article 39 states that "the home of citizens of the People's Republic of China is inviolable. Unlawful search of, or intrusion into, a citizen's home is prohibited." The 1997 Code of Criminal Law determined that criminal detention shall be not less than 1 month but not more than 6 months (Article 42). Article 43 provides that "during the period of execution, a criminal sentenced to criminal detention may go home for one to two days each month; an appropriate remuneration may be given to those who participate in labor." Article 44 stipulates that "detention shall be counted from the date the judgment begins to be executed; if the criminal is held in custody before the execution of the judgment, one day in custody shall be considered one day of the term sentenced."

There are 225 articles in the 1997 Code of Criminal Procedure of China. They set forth the specific provisions related to searches and seizures, arrest and detention procedures, interrogation procedures, types of evidence, procedures of evidence collection, right to have counsel, right to know about the reasons of arrest and detention by the arrestees, procedures for questioning a witness, procedures for investigation and prosecution, rights of the juvenile under detention, and procedures for dealing with death penalty cases. A number of these articles explain issues related to due process of law (see **Table 11-3**). Article 11, for example, states that "all hearings in the people's courts shall be public, unless this Law provides otherwise. The defendants shall have the right to have access to defense, and the people's courts shall be obliged to guarantee their access to defense." Article 14 guarantees the rights of the parent of juveniles to be informed about the arrest of their children: "With regard to cases of crimes committed by minors under 18 years old, the legal representatives of the crime suspects and defendants may be notified to be present at the time of interrogation and trial."

TABLE 11-3 Provisions of the Chinese Code of Criminal Procedural Law of 1979, as Amended in 1997, Related to Due Process Issues

Article	Due Process Issues
Article 9	Citizens of any nationality shall have the right to use their respective native spoken and written language in the proceedings. The people's court, the people's procuratorate, or the public security organ shall provide translations for any party to the proceedings who is not familiar with the local spoken or written language. In a place where people of a minority nationality live in a concentrated community, hearings shall be conducted in the spoken language commonly used in the said place, and judgments, notices, and other documents shall be issued in the written language commonly used in the said place.
Article 14	The people's courts, the people's procuratorates, and the public security organs shall guarantee the rights to action for participants in the proceedings as they are so entitled according to law. Participants in proceedings shall have the right to file charges against judicial, procuratorial, and investigating personnel whose acts have infringed upon the citizens' rights to action or have caused personal insult thereto.
Article 32	In addition to exercising the right to defend himself, a crime suspect or defendant also may entrust one or two persons as his defender(s) including lawyers, guardians, friends, and relatives.
Article 46	In settling any case, stress and emphasis must be given to evidence, investigation, and study, and oral confessions shall not be readily depended on.
Article 64	When detaining a person, the public security organ must produce a warrant of detention. The public security organ shall, within 24 hours after detaining a person, notify his family or the unit to which he belongs of the reasons for the detention and the place of custody, unless such notification would hinder the investigation or there is no way for making such notification.
Article 65	The public security organ shall interrogate and question the person detained within 24 hours after detention.
Article 67	The decision on approval of arresting a crime suspect shall be made by the chief procurator of the people's procuratorate.
Article 71	The public security organ must produce a warrant of arrest when arresting a person. A public security organ shall, within 24 hours after arresting a person, notify his family or the unit to which he belongs of the reasons for the arrest and the place of custody.
Article 72	A person arrested respectively by the decision of a people's court or a people's procuratorate, or a person arrested by a public security organ with approval of the people's procuratorate, must be interrogated and questioned within 24 hours after the arrest.
Article 95	The written record of an interrogation shall be presented to the crime suspect for checking, or shall be read to the crime suspect if he cannot read. If the written record contains any omission or error, the crime suspect may make additions or corrections.
Article 111	When conducting a search, a search warrant must be produced to the person to be searched. Under emergency, a search may be carried out without a search warrant.

Source: Data from the 1979 Chinese Code of Criminal Procedure, as amended in 1997.

The Code of Criminal Procedural Law of 1997 has focused on many specific provisions that are related to due process laws such the presumption of innocence, burden of proof, existence of probable cause for arrest and detention, prohibition of torture for securing confessions, the exclusionary rule, and right to have counsel. Article 12 addresses the issue of the presumption of innocence: "Prior to a judgment rendered by the people's court according to law, no one may be convicted of guilty." According to the 1979 Code of Criminal Procedure, there were no differences between a suspect and a defendant. The 1997 Code of Criminal Procedure makes a distinction between a suspect and a defendant. Presently, one is a defendant only if he or she is charged by the prosecutor. Before an offender is indicted, he or she must be identified as a suspect. According to the 1997 Code of Criminal Procedure, the burden of proof is not on the defendant but on the prosecutors. The prosecutor must establish the guilt of the defendant on the basis of facts and evidence. These two provisions constitute the doctrine of the presumption of innocence. Closely related to this doctrine is the exclusionary principle—the inadmissibility of facts and evidence collected on the basis of torture or forced confessions or, as in the United States, in violation of the Fourth Amendment. Article 43 of the 1997 Code of Criminal Procedure prohibits the use of torture and forced confessions: "It shall be strictly forbidden to extort confessions by torture or to collect evidences by coercion, inducement, deceit or any other unlawful means."

In 2010, the People's Supreme Court, the Supreme People's Procuratorate, the Ministry of Public Security, and the Ministry of Justice issued two sets of rules. One set of rules was "Regulations on the Exclusion of Illegally Obtained Evidence in Criminal Cases" (Dui Hua Foundation, 2012a). Another set of rules was "Concerning Questions About Examining and Judging Evidence in Death Penalty Cases" (Dui Hua Foundation, 2012b). The preamble to these two sets of rules says: "The two sets of rules set higher standards and stricter demands on law enforcement organs' handling of criminal cases, especially death penalty cases. As such, they are extremely significant for the perfection of our nation's criminal procedure system" (Dui Hua Foundation, 2012c).

Article 1 of the first set of rules explains the nature of inadmissible oral evidence: "The category of illegal oral evidence includes statements by criminal . . . defendants obtained through illegal means such as coerced confession as well as witness testimony or victim statements obtained through illegal means such as use of violence or threats." It goes on to say that "if, prior to commencement of the trial or during the trial, a defendant or his or her defense counsel alleges that the defendant's pretrial confession was obtained illegally, the court should conduct an investigation" (Article 3). The first set of rules imposed on the prosecutor the responsibility to establish the legal validity of all forms of evidence: "If the prosecutor does not provide evidence to confirm the legality of the defendant's pretrial confession, or the evidence provided is not credible or sufficient enough, that confession may not serve as a basis for conviction" (Article 11). This rule is also applied in cases of material or documentary evidence (Article 14).

The exclusionary principle was interpreted in a much stricter way in the second set of rules concerning the examination and judging of evidence in death penalty cases (Dui Hua

Foundation, 2012b). The second set of rules states that the relevant provisions of the Code of Criminal Law and the Code of Criminal Procedural Law "must be strictly implemented in handling death penalty cases in order to ensure the case's quality and that the facts are clear, the evidence is credible and sufficient, procedures are legal, and the law is applied correctly" (Article 1). It goes on to say that in cases dealing with the death penalty, "determination of the facts of the defendant's crime must be based on credible, abundant evidence" (Article 5). In death penalty cases, "all facts used to convict a defendant must be based on evidence. Both physical and documentary evidence must be original in nature" (Article 5). Further more, the second set of rules explains: "Any physical or documentary evidence obtained through on-site investigation, inspection, search, or confiscation . . . may not serve as a basis for conviction if its origins cannot be verified" (Article 9). The rules also specified the conditions under which such evidence as photographs, videos, witness testimonies, expert opinions, victim statements, defendant statement, and electronic evidence are not admissible in death penalty cases.

The 1997 Code of Criminal Procedural Law also strengthened the defendant's right to have counsel. Under the 1979 Code of Criminal Procedural Law, the defendant was given the right to have an attorney in the trial phase. Under the 1997 Code of Criminal Procedural Law, the defendant has the right to have an attorney in all phases—at the time of arrest and interrogation, evidence collection, framing of the charges, bail hearings, trial, appeal, and convictions (Jinwen, 2001). The 1997 Code states that "a crime suspect may, after being interrogated for the first time or from the day on which compulsory measures are taken against him, hire a lawyer to offer him with legal consultancy" (Article 96). It also confirmed the same right to have an attorney during all phases of criminal investigation and trial (Article 36). In addition, the 1997 Code made a provision that legal aid must be given to indigent suspects and defendants: "If the defendant has not yet entrusted any defender due to financial difficulty or any other reasons, the people's court may appoint a lawyer undertaking the duty of legal aid to provide defense thereto" (Article 34).

With the advance of reforms in criminal law and the judiciary in China, an adversarial system of justice is also becoming increasingly prominent. For more than 2,000 years, the Chinese criminal justice system was inquisitorial in nature. The 1979 Code of Criminal Procedural Law preserved the inquisitorial system. Under the 1979 Code, the Chinese judiciary "resembled an inquisitorial system. The judge conducted the judicial proceedings and was also the fact finder. Judges initiated interrogations of the defendant and witnesses, including cross examination. The prosecutor and the defense attorney played a secondary role" (Jinwen, 2001, p. 5). Under the 1997 Code of Criminal Procedural Law, the prosecutor is the key actor in pretrial investigations and evidence collections. The police cannot make an arrest without the approval of the office of the prosecutor. Article 8 of the 1997 Code of Criminal Procedure said that "the People's Procuratorates shall, in accordance with law, exercise legal supervision over criminal proceedings."

The 1997 Code of Criminal Procedure made some significant changes to "ensure neutrality of judges in the trial process and to eliminate the phenomenon of 'first decide [the case], then have a trial'" (Belkin, 2011, p. 16). Under the 1997 Code, judges are not allowed to present the evidence at trial and procurators are not required to present the evidence to the judges before the trial (Belkin, 2007; 2011). In an empirical study of the process and functioning of criminal justice in China, McConville (2011) found that the prosecutors in the present system are much more visible, and they play many important roles. On the basis of interviews of 96 prosecutors and the examination of many case files, he found that

> the examination for prosecution stage of the criminal process is an apparently comprehensive affair in which prosecutors discharge numerous tasks. They include such preliminary and fundamental tasks as ensuring that the procuratorate has jurisdiction to handle the case, administrative tasks such as arranging for an interpreter where necessary and core legal tasks such as researching the law and ensuring that correct charges are preferred (McConville, 2011, p. 113).

In the present judicial system in China, "a trial begins with the presentation of evidence by the prosecution. Then the prosecution, the defendant, the victim (if any), and the defense attorney all have an opportunity to argue the case" (Belkin, 2011, p. 19). The 1997 Code of Procedural Law thus "introduced the concept of an adversarial system in which it was the prosecutor's responsibility (rather than the court's) to bring the evidence to court and prove the defendant's guilt" (Belkin, 2011, p. 22).

Carol Jones, another expert on criminal justice in China, made a similar observation: The 1997 Code of Criminal Procedural Law introduced a number of due process rights available in an adversarial system of justice. The trial process became more transparent and accountable to law by granting the new right for a defendant to have a legal representation from the beginning of the trial—that is, from the time the defendant is taken into custody. This right created more involvement for lawyers in the Chinese criminal courts (McConville, 2011).

There are two competing views about the progress of reforms in law and criminal justice in China. One group of scholars and legal experts, both from China and the West, argue that there are still significant limits to the progress of the rule of law and modernization in criminal justice in China (Peerenboom, 2002; Turner-Gottschang, Feinermann, & Guy, 2000). The fundamental problem in the reform for a modern system of law and justice in China, these groups of scholars believe, centers "on redefining a relationship between law and political authority" (Turner-Gottschang et al., 2000, p. 7). Within the existing socialist political system under the dominance of the CCP and the National People's Congress, the independence of the judiciary, they suggest, is a misleading notion (Sheng, 2004). They argue that without the independence of the judiciary and without the principle of judicial review, the progress of the rule of law is bound to be limited. In the criminal justice system of China, as one observer noted, the violation of the independence of the judiciary is manifested through the existence

> of party committees of political and legal affairs at all levels of government. Traditionally, the head of the committee has been the head of public security for the area, with the chief procurator and the chief judge beneath him. Thus, the Chinese Communist Party unquestionably still exercises

institutional influence over the operation of the legal system in general and the criminal justice system in particular (Belkin, 2011, p. 5).

Similar observations were also made by McConville (2011), who stated that the Code of Criminal Procedural Law of 1997 introduced a number of due process rights. However, he had concerns about the extent to which the members of the Chinese judiciary and the state officials will be able to function independently from the state ideology.

The second perspective is that within its philosophy of socialist modernization, China's progress toward the rule of law and a modern system of criminal justice has been remarkable (Clarke, 2008; Jinwen, 2001; Liang, 2008; Lo, 1995). The advocates of this perspective claim that the 1982 constitution of China, the 1979 Code of Criminal Law as amended in 1997, the 1979 Code of Criminal Procedural Law as amended in 1997, and the 2010 rules on judging and examining criminal evidence developed by the People's Supreme Court, the Supreme People's Procuratorate, the Ministry of Public Security, and the Ministry of Justice in China have brought some fundamental transformations in the structure and functions of the Chinese judiciary in general and the Chinese system of criminal justice in particular. This group of advocates argues that these fundamental transformations in the judiciary and in the broader arena of law and legal professions in China are irreversible. One Chinese legal expert claimed that China

> has entered an age characterized by the rule of law. A highly institutionalized system has been
> built up which functions on the basis of socialist legality. The Communist regime has undergone
> a legal awakening in which both Party leadership and popular masses have seen that the "rule of
> law" is a sound alternative to the former disastrous "rule of person" (Lo, 1995, p. 323).

"But more important," as another Chinese legal scholar argued, is that "traditional thinking has been challenged, ideological taboos have been broken, the relationship between the individual and government has been perceived in a new light, and the roles of the courts are under constant reassessment" (Lin, 2003, p. 258).

In balance, the perspective that can be more intriguing in pursuing comparative criminal justice in China is the perspective of modernization and globalization. Since the beginning of socialist modernization in 1979 by Deng Xiaoping, China is becoming increasingly integrated into the world system through the process of globalization. This process of globalization is not merely an economic phenomenon. It is also fundamentally social, political, and cultural in nature. Economic globalization has brought an enormous amount of economic wealth to China. But economic globalization in China has also brought an enormous number of economic crimes. Reforms in criminal law and criminal justice began partly in response to the process of economic globalization. However, reforms in criminal justice in China should not be seen merely from the perspective of economics and the socialist market economy (Liu, Zhang, & Messner, 2001). The movement for modernization in law and criminal justice that was started in 1898 by Qing Emperor Guangxu was not, in essence, an economic movement. It was rather a movement at that time for China to become a part of the global world—to join the process of globalization (Bakken, 2005; Liang, 2008). For about 4 decades during the socialist regime of Mao Zedong, China was cut off from this process of globalization. With the rebirth of reforms for modernization in 1979, China again became an integral part of the global world and the process of globalization. How the economic, political, social, and cultural forces of globalization will unfold in China and how the CCP will respond to some of the challenges posed by those forces in the next decades are hard to predict. But it is certain that the modernist reforms in law and justice in general and criminal justice in particular, which began in China in the late 1970s, are going to be more intensified and extended.

Due process of law in all countries of the West has evolved over a long period of time. The United States is an example. The concept of judicial review that became a part of American law and justice through the U.S. Supreme Court decision in *Marbury v. Madison* came 14 years after Congress passed the Bill of Rights Amendment in 1789. The due process rights were extended to juveniles in the U.S. justice system by the U.S. Supreme Court decision in *In re Gault* in 1967—178 years after the passing of the Bill of Rights by Congress. The Miranda rights became a part of the American criminal justice system after the U.S. Supreme Court decision in *Miranda v. Arizona* in 1966—177 years after the Bill of Rights. The death penalty punishment was abolished in the American juvenile justice system through the U.S. Supreme Court decision in *Roper v. Simmons* in 2005—216 years after the enactment of the Bill of Rights by Congress.

The present system of criminal justice in China is barely 3 decades old. Many due process laws are more likely to expand and improve with the evolution of the system of criminal justice in response to modernization and globalization. Peerenboom (2002), a long-time observer of law and justice in China, noted in his work that within the existing structure of the socialist polity, "the party is able to appoint or at least veto the appointment of the key members of the people's congress and undermine the legitimacy, independence, and authority of the legislature and the judiciary" (p. 8). In his recent work on the progress of judicial independence in China, he said that "decisional independence" is at the core of the notion of judicial independence, and in China in recent years, "notwithstanding problems in politically sensitive and socioeconomic cases or institutional weakness, particularly in lower level courts, there has been a significant increase in decisional independence of the courts overall as measured by various indicators" (Peerenboom, 2010, p. 86). He further added that "it is incorrect to conclude (or to assume) that the Chinese judiciary is unable to decide any case independently, especially commercial cases, and many other routine civil, administrative or criminal cases" (Peerenboom, 2010, p. 86). There is also a rapidly growing process of professionalization within the Chinese judiciary: "In 2004, 97.7 percent of the 20,000 candidates who passed the unified judicial exam had a bachelor degree or higher. The improvements in judicial competence and accountability have allowed for increases in independence and authority" (Peerenboom, 2010, p. 87).

Along with changes in the composition and functioning of the judges, prosecutors, and the police, many due process reforms in procedural law are also growing. The 2010 rules on "Regulations on the Exclusion of Illegally Obtained Evidence in Criminal Cases" and "Concerning Questions About Examining and Judging Evidence in Death Penalty Cases" developed jointly by the Supreme People's Court, the Supreme People's Procuratorate, the

Ministry of Public Security, and the Ministry of Justice are some of the examples of due process reforms in criminal procedural law. China's Strike Hard Campaign (*Yanda*) that was initiated in 1983 to control escalating crime, particularly economic crime in the wake of the transition to a market economy, rapidly increased the number of death penalty cases and human rights violations in China (Scott, 2010). The repressive measures enacted under the Strike Hard Campaign were severely criticized both inside and outside China. It was partly in response to these criticisms from the international world that many due process reforms have been initiated. Under the Strike Hard Campaign, the provincial courts were given the authority to review death penalty cases. This was one of the reasons why the number of executions grew so rapidly in the 1990s. In 2007, a new law was passed, and it abolished the authority of the provincial courts to review death penalty cases. The authority of reviewing death penalty cases, particularly those for immediate executions, now lies again with the Supreme People's Court. The 2010 rule, "Concerning Questions About Examining and Judging Evidence in Death Penalty Cases," was also directed to reform the procedures of investigating and adjudicating death penalty cases (Dui Hua Foundation, 2012b). This particular reform in death penalty cases is an example of how due process of law in general can grow and evolve more intensely with the further intensification of the process of globalization in China. The present system can still be called a dual system because its modernization is being defined and pursued within the framework of a socialist polity, and the traditional Confucian cultural framework of the values of authority, hierarchy, familial piety, and the moral sanctity of the official bureaucracy (see **Table 11-4**).

■ Summary

This chapter has examined the nature of the dual system of criminal justice in China. In comparative criminal justice, it is an exciting project to examine how criminal justice in many countries of the world is organized on the basis of legal pluralism or competing systems of law and justice. What is particularly significant is to explore the directionality of modernization in dual systems of criminal justice. In this chapter, the progress of modernization in China's criminal justice system in the context of its imperial legal heritage and the program of socialist modernization has been examined. The criminal justice system of China is as old as the Chinese Empire—it dates back more than 2,000 years. The Tang Code developed in 653 and the Qing Code developed in 1740 left a rich heritage and vast store of knowledge about law and justice in China. From its earlier days of imperial rule, two schools of thought were dominant in the understanding of law and justice in China: the Confucian school of thought and the legalist perspective. The Confucian school of thought was based on the notion that morality is at the core of law and justice. Confucius believed that an ideal polity and an ideal system of justice must be based on the dominance of morality and not on the dominance of formal law and legal codifications. The best system of justice is one that is based on the normative principles of benevolence (*ren*), filial piety, reverence, fraternity, kindness, compassion, and humanness. The best system of justice must uphold the values of mediation rather than litigation. The legalist school of thought, in contrast to the Confucian school of thought, was based on the notion that a good polity and a good system of justice must be based on codified laws and rules, formal courts and adjudications, scope for litigations, a uniform system of justice, and willingness on the part of the rulers to impose punishments to control crime and violence. The challenge of modernization in China is to achieve a balance between these two competing perspectives about law and justice.

Modernization in criminal justice in China began in the late 19th century, and the process was started by the ninth emperor of the Qing dynasty, Emperor Guangxu (1875–1908). Through a series of imperial edicts, Emperor Guangxu embarked on a major program of significant social and political transformations in China following the developmental model of Japan and the West. Reforms for modern criminal justice began for the first time in China as a part of this modernist movement started by Emperor Guangxu. Under the modernist New Policy project, a series of reforms were proposed and partly implemented in criminal justice, such as the creation of the rule of law, codification of law, introduction of an independent judiciary, development of a professional police force, introduction of Western legal education, and development of new penal laws. This process of modernization continued even after the collapse of imperial rule and the establishment of the new Republic of China in 1912. From 1912 to 1949, the process of modernization in criminal justice was slow, but it still continued even in the midst of enormous political crises and instabilities in the new Republic of China. The process of modernization collapsed after the communist revolution in China and the establishment of the People's Republic of China in 1949 under the leadership of Mao Zedong. The history of criminal justice from 1949 to 1978 is the history of the destruction of almost all the institutions of modernity in law and justice that were built in the previous decades and in previous centuries. During the Cultural Revolution of 1966–1978, most of the modern norms and institutions of criminal justice in China were completely destroyed and disbanded.

After the death of Mao Zedong, China came to a new turning point, and a new process of modernization in criminal justice began under the policy of socialist modernization introduced by Deng Xiaoping. Under the program of socialist modernization, a series of reforms in criminal justice were introduced by the Code of Criminal Law and the Code of Criminal Procedural Law of 1979 and their further amendments in 1997 and 2001. These amended versions of the Code of Criminal Law of 1997 and the Code of Criminal Procedural Law of 2001 are presently the key legal documents that govern the system of criminal justice in China.

There are two competing views about the progress of reforms in law and criminal justice in China. One group of scholars and legal experts, from both China and the West, argue that there are still significant limits to the progress of the rule of law and modernization in criminal justice in China. They argue that within the existing socialist political system under the dominance of the CCP and the National People's Congress, the rule of law and independence of the judiciary is a misleading notion. The second perspective is that within its philosophy of socialist modernization, China's progress toward the rule of law and a modern system of criminal justice has been remarkable. The advocates of this perspective claim that the 1982 constitution of China, the 1979 Code of Criminal Law as

TABLE 11-4 Criminal Justice Systems in the United States and China: A Comparative Look

Criminal Justice	United States	People's Republic of China
Time Dimensions	The evolution of modern criminal justice in the United States began with the evolution of the modern state and the first 10 Amendments to the U.S. Constitution, called the "Bill of Rights" (1791); 6 out of 10 Amendments are directly related to criminal justice	Institutions of modern criminal justice began to systematically grow from the days of the New Policy era in 1898 and continued to expand during the Nationalist era (1911–1948); the socialist regime of Mao Zedong (1949–1978) completely destroyed that process of evolution; modernization began in the early 1980s with the enactment of a comprehensive Code of Criminal Law and a Code of Criminal Procedural Law in 1979, as well as the promulgation of a new constitution in 1982
Modernization Period	Modern institutions of criminal justice rapidly evolved in the 1960s and 1970s (i.e., the Johnson era—the Challenge of Crime in a Free Society and Crime Control and Safe Street Act of 1968)	Institutions of modern criminal justice were completely disbanded within the period of 1966–1978; under the ideology of communism, China was completely isolated from the worldwide processes of modernization and globalization
Legal Traditions and the Sources of Law	English common law; statutory laws; judicial laws; a process of the replacement (or codification) of the common law through development of statutory laws began in the late 18th century (i.e., the Judiciary Act of 1791)	Civil law tradition reached China in the late 19th century using the Japanese/German model of criminal justice; expanded during the nationalist era (1911–1948); completely overthrown during the communist era (1949–1978); contemporary laws are drawn partly from civil law, partly from socialist law, and more prominently from the constitution and statutory laws made by the National People's Congress (NPC)
Organizational Model	Decentralized; federal system of government; federal and state systems of criminal justice; federal crimes and state crimes; federal laws and state laws; in case of conflicts, the federal constitution and federal laws, of course, prevail	Centralized; unitary system of government; one single system of criminal justice for all 33 provinces (about 1.3 billion people, 2012 estimate). The courts, police, and prisons, however, are administered, because of the vastness of the country, in decentralized ways
Court System	Federal Courts: U.S. Supreme Court; U.S. Court of Appeals; and U.S. District Courts; state supreme courts, state intermediary courts; and state lower courts; and state and local juvenile courts. Judges of the Supreme Court are nominated by the President and ratified by the Senate. In some states, judges are selected; in some states, they are elected; the Supreme Court is autonomous and is not directly responsible to Congress or the President	Four major tiers (in ascending order): the Supreme People's Court (SPC), Higher People's Courts; Intermediate People's Courts, and Basic People's Courts (presently about 3,000 courts); the SPC is directly responsible to the NPC; it is the highest court of appeal; the judges of the SPC and Higher People's Courts are directly appointed by the NPC; the SPC is headed by a president (elected for 5 years and renewable for another 5 years) and several vice-presidents; under the effect of present reforms in criminal justice, judicial independence and accountability have considerably increased

Judicial Model and the Prosecution System	Adversarial; the federal criminal prosecution is the responsibility of the federal prosecutors known as U.S. Attorneys; there is an Office of U.S. Attorneys within the Department of Justice; as of 2010, the U.S. Attorney system was comprised of 95 headquarters offices and 135 branch offices; U.S. Attorneys are appointed by the President; state attorneys (prosecutors), commonly called District Attorneys, are mostly elected	Increasingly becoming adversarial; corresponding to four tiers of the court system, there are four major tiers of procuratorates: Supreme People's Procuratorate, People's Procuratorates of the Provinces, People's Procuratorates of Prefectures and Cities, and People's Procuratorates of Counties and Municipal Districts; the Procuratorate-General of the Supreme People's Procuratorate is appointed by the NPC; the procuratorate system is administered by the constitution (Article 130) and the Public Procurator Law of 1995
Police Organization	Decentralized; federal police; state police; city and local police; and county sheriffs; key federal law enforcement agencies are the FBI, U.S. Marshals Service, U.S. Secret Service, U.S. Capitol Police, and the Drug Enforcement Agency (DEA); and 18,000 state and local law enforcement agencies	Centralized; four major types: national security police under the Ministry of Public Security; state security police under the Ministry of State security; judicial police under the Ministry of Justice; and prison police under the Ministry of Justice; roles and functions are determined by the constitutions and the Police Law of 1995; the state security police, somewhat like the FBI of the United States and the Mounted Police of Canada, are heavily armed and responsible for the control of crimes related to state security and transnational crimes; the rise of armed security policing in China is comparable to the rise of "super policing" in Germany; under present reforms for modernization and the rule of law, police accountability in China has considerably increased
Prison Organization	Decentralized; federal prisons under the U.S. Bureau of Prisons; state prisons mostly under the state departments of corrections; and incarceration rate is 754 per 100,000 population (2009 data)	The Prison Law of 1994 provides the guidelines for prison maintenance; supervised by the Bureau of Prison Administration of the Department of Justice; adult prisons are different from juvenile prisons; incarceration rate is 120 (2009 data)

amended in 1997, the 1979 Code of Criminal Procedural Law as amended in 1997 and 2001, and the 2010 rules on judging and examining criminal evidence developed by the People's Supreme Court, the Supreme People's Procuratorate, the Ministry of Public Security, and the Ministry of Justice in China have brought some fundamental transformations in the structures and functions of the Chinese judiciary in general and the Chinese system of criminal justice in particular. It seems, however, that the perspective that can be more intriguing in pursuing comparative criminal justice in China is the perspective of modernization and globalization. Since the beginning of the socialist modernization in 1979 by Deng Xiaoping, China is becoming increasingly integrated into the world system through the process of globalization. This process of globalization is not merely an economic phenomenon. It is also fundamentally political, social, and cultural in nature. How the economic, political, social, and cultural forces of globalization will unfold in China and how the CCP will respond to some of the challenges posed by those forces in the next decades are hard to predict. But it is certain that the modernist reforms that began in law and justice in general and criminal justice in particular in China in the late 1970s are going to be more intensified and extended.

■ Discussion Questions

1. What are two competing schools of thought that govern the understanding of law and justice in China? Describe the nature of these competing traditions expressed by the Tang Code and the Qing Code of China.

2. Explain the visions of Confucian philosophy with regard to crime and criminal justice. How are the Confucian visions of law and justice compatible with those of modern criminal justice? What role does morality play in understanding crime control and prevention in modern societies? Give examples.

3. Discuss the legalist philosophy visions of crime and criminal justice. How are the visions of the legalist perspective compatible with those of modern criminal justice? Explain the relations between the legalist philosophy and the ideas of the contemporary advocates of the new penology for crime control and prevention.

4. What are the 10 Great Wrongs identified by the Tang Code and the Qing Code? Which of those 10 Great Wrongs would not be punishable in a modern system of criminal justice? Give examples.

5. Explain the process of modernization in criminal justice that was started in China in the late 19th century. What major reforms are proposed and implemented by the New Policy project promulgated by Emperor Guangxu? What is the significance of the modernist movement of the late 19th century in understanding contemporary reforms in criminal justice in China?

6. Discuss the socialist theories of law, crime, and criminality and how they affected the development of law and justice in China during the rule of Mao Zedong, particularly during the time of the Cultural Revolution.

7. Name some of the provisions of the 1982 Constitution of China, and of the Code of Criminal Law and the Code of Criminal Procedural Law of China enacted in 1979 (amended in 1997 and 2001). How can some of those provisions be interpreted as significant steps toward the development of the rule of law in China and the progress of modernization in Chinese criminal justice? Give examples.

8. Based on the expansion of the rule of law in general and the development of the due process of law in particular, what are the competing views about China's emerging strategies of modernization in criminal justice? Why are some scholars skeptical about China's program of modernization within the socialist political framework? Give examples.

9. Since 1979, China has initiated a series of reforms in criminal justice by introducing of many new substantive and procedural criminal laws, and by creating of a new set of justice institutions. Discuss whether and how some of these laws and institutions are compatible with those of modern systems of criminal justice.

10. The contemporary processes of modernization and globalization are creating many homogenous sets of laws and institutions for reforms in criminal justice among the world's societies. In the context of this statement, comment on the possibility of the evolution of some of the modern institutions of criminal justice (e.g., secularization, rule of law, democracy, independent judiciary, and due process of law) in China.

■ References

Bakken, B. (Ed.). (2005). *Crime, punishment and policing in China.* Lanham, MD: Rowman & Littlefield.

Belkin, I. (2007). Criminal procedure: China. In C. M. Bradley (Ed.), *Criminal procedure: A worldwide study* (pp. 91–106). Durham: University of North Carolina Press.

Belkin, I. (2011). *China's criminal justice system: A work in progress.* Retrieved from www.law.yale.edu/documents/pdf/chinas_criminal_justice_system.pdf.

Bell, D. A., & Chaibong, H. (Eds.). (2003). *Confucianism for the modern world.* New York, NY: Cambridge University Press.

Chen, A. H. Y. (2003). Mediation, litigation, and justice: Confucian reflections in a modern liberal society. In D. A. Bell & H. Chaibong (Eds.), *Confucianism for the modern world* (pp. 257–287). New York, NY: Cambridge University Press.

Chow, D. C. K. (2003). *The legal system of the People's Republic of China: In a nutshell.* St. Paul, MN: Thomson West.

Clarke, D. C. (2008). *China's legal system: New developments, new challenges.* Cambridge, England: Oxford University Press.

Cohen, J. A. (1968). *The criminal process in the People's Republic of China, 1949–1963: An introduction.* Cambridge, MA: Harvard University Press.

Dui Hua Foundation. (2012a, June 25). China's new rules concerning questions about exclusion of illegal evidence in handling criminal cases. *Human Rights Journal: Current Issues in China's Criminal Justice System.* San Francisco, CA: Author.

Dui Hua Foundation. (2012b, June 29). China's new rules concerning questions about examining and judging evidence in death penalty cases. *Human Rights Journal: Current Issues in China's Criminal Justice System.* San Francisco, CA: Author.

Dui Hua Foundation. (2012c, June, 25). Translation: China's new rules on evidence in criminal trials. *Human Rights Journal: Current Issues in China's Criminal Justice System.* San Francisco, CA: Author.

Epstein, M. (2007). Making a case: Characterizing the filial son. In R. E. Hegel & K. Carlitz (Eds.), *Writing and law in late imperial China: Crime, conflict, and judgment* (pp. 27–43). Seattle: University of Washington Press.

Glenn, H. P. (2007). *Legal traditions of the world: Sustainable diversity in law.* New York, NY: Oxford University Press.

Guo, X. (2002). *The ideal Chinese political leader: A historical and cultural perspective.* Westport, CT: Praeger.

Hegel, R. E. (2007). Introduction: Writing and law. In R. E. Hegel & K. Carlitz (Eds.), *Writing and law in late imperial China: Crime, conflict, and judgment* (pp. 3–27). Seattle: University of Washington Press.

Hegel, R. E. (2009). *True crimes in eighteenth-century China: Twenty case histories.* Seattle: Washington University Press.

Ho, I. (2003). Traditional Confucian values and Western legal frameworks: The law of succession. In D. A. Bell & H. Chaibong (Eds.), *Confucianism for the modern world* (pp. 288–311). New York, NY: Cambridge University Press.

Hsu, C. S. (2003). *Understanding the Chinese legal system.* New York, NY: New York University Press.

Huntington, S. P. (1996). *The clash of civilizations and the remaking of world order.* New York, NY: Simon & Schuster.

In re Gault, 387 U.S. 1 (1967).

Jinwen, X. (2001). New development in 2001 Chinese criminal procedural law. *Annual Survey of International and Comparative Law, 7*(1), 1–6.

Johnson, W. (1979). *The T'ang Code (Vol. I): General principles.* Princeton, NJ: Princeton University Press.

Johnson, W. (1997). *The T'ang Code (Vol. II): Specific articles.* Princeton, NJ: Princeton University Press.

Jones, W. C. (1994). *The Great Qing Code.* Oxford, England: Oxford University Press.

Karl, R. E., & Zarrow, P. (Eds.). (2002). *Rethinking the 1898 reform period: Political and cultural change in the late Qing China.* Cambridge, MA: Harvard East Asia Monograph.

Kellogg, T. E. (2008). *Constitutionalism with Chinese characteristics? Constitutional development in civil litigation in China* (working paper No. 1). Bloomington, IN: Research Center for Chinese Politics & Business.

Knoblock, J. (1994). *Xunzi: A translation and study of the complete works.* Stanford, CA: Stanford University Press.

Leng, S., & Chiu, H. (1985). *Criminal justice in post-Mao China.* Albany: State University of New York at Albany Press.

Liang, B. (2008). *The changing Chinese legal systems, 1978–present: Centralization of power and the rationalization of the legal system.* Abingdon, England: Routledge.

Lin, C. X. (2003). A quiet revolution. An overview of China's judicial reform. *Asian-Pacific Law and Policy Journal, 4*(2), 256–319.

Liu, H., Zhang, L., & Messner, S. E. (2001). *Crime and social control in a changing China.* Westport, CT: Greenwood Press.

Lo, C. W. (1995). *China's legal awakening: Legal theory and criminal justice in Deng's era.* Hong Kong: Hong University Press.

Luo, W. (1998). *The 1997 Criminal Code of the People's Republic of China*. Buffalo, NY: William S. Hein & Co.

MacCormack, G. (1996). *The spirit of traditional Chinese law*. Athens, GA: University of Georgia Press.

McConville, M. (2011). *Criminal justice in China: An empirical inquiry*. Cheltenham, England: Edward Elgar.

Menski, W. F. (2006). *Comparative law in a global context: The legal systems of Asia and Africa*. Cambridge, England: Cambridge University Press.

Miranda v. Arizona, 384 U. S. 436 (1966).

Muhlhahn, K. (2009). *Criminal justice in China*. Cambridge, MA: Harvard University Press.

Marbury v. Madison, 5 U.S. 137 (1803).

Nelson, B. (1981). *On the roads to modernity: Conscience, science, and civilizations*. Totowa, NJ: Rowman & Littlefield.

Nylan, M. (2001). *The five "Confucian" classics*. New Haven, CT: Yale University Press.

Peerenboom, R. (2002). *China's long march toward the rule of law*. Cambridge, England: Cambridge University Press.

Peerenboom, R. (Ed.). (2010). *Judicial independence in China*. New York, NY: Cambridge University Press.

Riemann, M., & Zimmermann, R. (2008). *The Oxford handbook of comparative law*. New York, NY: Oxford University Press.

Roper v. Simmons, 543 U.S. 551 (2005).

Scott, K. (2010). Why did China reform its death penalty? *Pacific Rim Law and Policy Journal, 19*(1), 63–80.

Sheng, Y. (2004). A promise unfulfilled: The impact of China's 1996 criminal-procedure reform on China's criminal defense lawyers' role at the pretrial stage. *Perspectives, 4*(1), 1–27.

Sommer, M. H. (2000). *Sex, law, and society in late imperial China*. Stanford, CA: Stanford University Press.

The Supreme People's Court of the People's Republic of China. (2003). *Criminal procedural law of the People's Republic of China*. Beijing, China: Government of the People's Republic of China.

Terrill, R. J. (2009). *World criminal justice systems: A survey*. New Providence, NJ: Matthew Bender & Company.

Trevaskes, S. (2007). *Courts and criminal justice in contemporary China*. Lanham, MD: Rowman & Littlefield.

Turner-Gottschang, K., Feinerman, J. V., & Guy, R. K. (Eds.). (2000). *The limits of the rule of law in China*. Seattle: University of Washington Press.

US-China Institute. (2007). *Constitution of the People's Republic of China*. Los Angeles, CA: University of Southern California.

Xu, X. (2008). *Trial of modernity: Judicial reform in early twentieth-century China, 1901–1937*. Stanford, CA: Stanford University Press.

Dual Systems of Criminal Justice: The Case of the Islamic Republic of Pakistan

CHAPTER
12

■ Introduction

Pakistan is one of the most unique countries in the modern world. It was once a part of the great Indus Valley civilization. The cities of Mohenjo-Daro (presently in the Sind province of Pakistan) and Harappa (in the province of Punjab in Pakistan) were the centers of a great urban culture ruled by efficient governments more than 4,000 years ago. Pakistan became an independent country in 1947 in the wake of the decolonization of British India. At that time, Pakistan inherited a highly educated and secular group of political elites; an expanding group of industrial elites from India; a diverse culture of Muslims, Hindus, Christians, and Jews; a strong tradition of liberal and Western education introduced by the British colonial state; a huge reservoir of talented people; and a political landscape that was restless to establish a state compatible with the values of modernity. Quaid-e-Azam, the father of the nation of Pakistan, in his address to the constituent assembly on August 11, 1947, said, "The first duty of a government is to maintain law and order, so that the life, property and religious beliefs of its subjects are fully protected by the State" (Library of Congress, 2012a, p. 1).

Pakistan inherited the criminal justice system that was established by the British colonial state in India in the middle of the 19th century. The legal structure of Pakistan's criminal justice at that time was based on the same institutions that were at the core of criminal justice in India—the common law tradition, an adversarial system of justice, the Indian Police Act of 1861, the Indian Penal Code of 1862, the Indian Evidence Act of 1872, and the Indian Code of Criminal Procedure of 1898. In the formative years of the state of Pakistan, a modern system of criminal justice was rapidly expanding with the modernization of the police, courts, prisons, and profession of law and justice. In the 1950s and 1960s, Pakistan produced some of the most outstanding jurists of the subcontinent of India. During the decade of development in the 1960s, a modern infrastructure of criminal justice began to grow in all regions of Pakistan under the leadership of new cadres of bureaucrats of the Civil Service of Pakistan (CSP) and the Police Service of Pakistan (PSP). The first constitution of Pakistan, enacted in 1956, "guaranteed fundamental rights including rights such as equality of status and of opportunity, equality before law, freedom of thought, expression, belief, faith, worship, and association, and social, economic, and political justice, subject to law and public morality" (Choudhury, 1967). The constitution further said that "every citizen has the right to profess, practice and propagate any religion; and every religious denomination and every sect thereof has the right to establish, maintain and manage its religious institutions" (Choudhury, 1967). The constitution also set up the structure of the judiciary composed of the Supreme Court of Pakistan and the provincial high courts. Although the constitution said that all laws in Pakistan must conform to Islamic laws derived from the Quran and Sunna, English common law was still the foundation of criminal justice.

In the late 1970s, this process of modernization in criminal justice in Pakistan came to a new turning point. In 1978, the military government of President Muhammad Zia-ul-Haq introduced the Islamic system of justice. Influenced by the radical political Islam that was growing in Pakistan at that time, Zia-ul-Haq decided to introduce a new form of the Islamic system of governance (*Nizam-e-Mustafa*). After that, a new process of Islamization of criminal justice began in Pakistan. The common law system was not completely dismantled. Instead, a new dual system of criminal justice based on both English common law and Shari'a Law was introduced. From the beginning of Islamization in Pakistan in general and within its criminal justice system in particular, there was a rapid process of disintegration of the rule of law. Within 2 decades of the introduction of Islamic justice, radical Islamic fundamentalist movements rapidly spread in Pakistan. The spread of radical Islamic fundamentalism soon began to weaken the modernist foundation and the heritage of the state of Pakistan. In the late 1950s, a rapid process of militarization also began to engulf the political landscape of Pakistan after a military regime took over the political power led by Field Marshal Muhammad Ayub Khan in 1958. Out of its 65 years of existence, Pakistan was formally ruled by four military regimes led by four military generals (Ayub Khan, Yahya Khan, Zia-ul-Haq, and Pervez Musharraf) for about 33 years. The history of criminal justice in Pakistan is intimately connected to the dynamics of politics controlled by the Islamic fundamentalists on the one hand and the military on the other. Both these forces have significantly weakened the liberal basis of the state and hence the progress of the country toward a rule of law and a modern system of criminal justice. Any comparative study of criminal justice in Pakistan must be cast in the context of its increasing disintegration of the rule of law affected by the expansion of radical fundamentalist Islam and the continuing process of militarization in politics. Pakistan is unique because it is a country that has a great heritage of knowledge and education, as well as a huge reservoir of talented people. The country began as a model for modernity in the 1950s and 1960s. Today, Pakistan is widely perceived by the international world as a failed state and a failed system of criminal justice that does not hesitate to execute people for practicing freedom of expression and freedom of religion.

■ The Status of the Rule of Law and Criminal Justice in Pakistan

The World Bank's (Kaufmann, Kraay, & Mastruzzi, 2010) governance study that measured the status of governance in six indicators—voice and accountability; political stability and absence of violence; government effectiveness; regulatory quality; rule of law; and control of corruption—found that in the rule of law, Pakistan performed very poorly. Pakistan is below the 30th percentile. Pakistan is also seen as one of the most politically unstable and volatile countries in Southern Asia with a placement in the 0.5th percentile. In the ability of the government to control corruption, Pakistan is below the 15th percentile. In voice and accountability, Pakistan is below the 30th percentile. The World Justice Project's (WJP) 2011 *Rule of Law Index* that surveyed 66 countries similarly shows that Pakistan performed very poorly in all indicators of the rule of law (see **Table 12-1**). In the WJP's 2010 study, Pakistan scored

TABLE 12-1 World Justice Project (WJP) 2011 *Rule of Law Index*: The Status of the Rule of Law in Pakistan

WJP Rule of Law Index Factors	Score of Pakistan	Global Ranking of Pakistan
Limited government powers	0.37	60/66
Absence of corruption	0.21	65/66
Order and security	0.33	66/66
Fundamental rights	0.40	63/66
Open government	0.25	65/66
Regulatory enforcement	0.41	59/66
Access to civil justice	0.32	66/66
Effective criminal justice	0.36	61/66

Source: Data from World Justice Project. (2011). *Rule of Law Index, 2011.* Washington, DC: Author.

0.40 out of 1.00 in the effectiveness of its criminal justice. In the WJP's 2011 study, Pakistan scored 0.36 out of 1.00 in the effectiveness of its criminal justice. In the WJP's 2010 study, Pakistan scored 0.53 out of 1.00 in order and stability. In 2011, Pakistan scored 0.33 out of 1.00 in political order and stability. In the WJP's 2011 study, Pakistan was found to be the most politically unstable country in the world (World Justice Project, 2011, p. 85).

The Economist Intelligence Unit's (2011) *Democracy Index 2011,* which surveyed the status of democracy in 165 countries, identified Pakistan as a dual regime. A dual regime is defined as a regime in which serious weakness exists in "political culture, functioning of government and political participation. Corruption tends to be widespread and the rule of law is weak . . . and the judiciary is not independent" (Economist Intelligence Unit, 2011, p. 30). In the survey, on a 0 to 10 scale, Pakistan's overall score is 4.55. In the indicator of political participation, Pakistan's score is one of the lowest in the world (2.2 out of 10). The *Global Report 2009: Conflict, Governance, and State Fragility* (Marshall & Cole, 2009) described Pakistan as one of the weakest and most fragile states of the world. On a scale of 0 (no fragility) to 25 (extremely fragile), measuring social, economic, political, and security effectiveness and legitimacy, Pakistan received a score of 18. Pakistan's fragility score is below 136 countries of the world. Weaknesses in the rule of law and democracy and the fragile nature of the state in Pakistan have deeply affected its system of criminal justice.

In 2008, the United States Agency for International Development (USAID) conducted a major study on the rule of law and the nature of criminal justice in Pakistan. The study examined the nature of order and security, legitimacy, checks and balances, fairness in justice, and the effective application of law. The study is based on face-to-face interviews of more than 100 political leaders, judges and jurists, legal experts, representatives of the Pakistan Bar Association, and representatives of foreign embassies and international donor agencies in Pakistan. The study concluded that in Pakistan, "the lack of public confidence in the justice system undermines rule of law and contributes to rising violence" (Blue, Hoffman, & Berg, 2008, p. 7). The lack of public confidence is because of the development of a very confusing body of laws based on multiple sources—the common law tradition of the British colonial state, military ordinances, laws made by the civilian governments, and the Shari'a Law introduced in 1979. The report further explained that "the contrast between laws enacted by the parliamentary rule, and those ordinances proclaimed by military rulers has probably contributed to a perception of the Pakistani legal framework as confusing, inconsistent, and incoherent" (Blue et al., 2008, p. 8).

The system of criminal justice in Pakistan has some of the same characteristics that are common in all failed and fragile states—police brutality, widespread use of police torture, police corruption, lack of judicial independence, lack of judicial accountability, widespread judicial corruption, politicization of the judiciary, gross violation of human rights, and an archaic system of prisons. In Pakistan, some of these problems are more acute because of the state's continuing failure to control the rising tides of radical Islamic fundamentalism and militarization in politics. The 1973 constitution of Pakistan made a provision for independence of the judiciary and judicial review (Article 184). In reality, partly because of the entrenched role of the military in politics, Pakistan never saw an independent judiciary.

The aforementioned USAID report on the rule of law in Pakistan observed that from the earlier days:

> judicial independence has been strong in rhetoric but weak in implementation. Pakistan's superior courts have been reluctant to challenge the executive to enforce fundamental rights, and have not invalidated any major legislation on account of inconformity with fundamental rights provisions (Blue et al., 2008, p. 12).

The report further noted that "the Supreme Court has repeatedly legitimated interventions by the military into politics through coups d'etat and dissolution of parliament" (Blue et al., 2008, p. 12). The 18th amendment passed by the Parliament of Pakistan in 2010 (Library of Congress, 2012b) included provisions for an independent judiciary, strengthening of fundamental rights, and the right to a fair trial and due process. Under the 18th amendment, judicial appointments will not be under the control either of the president or the prime minister of Pakistan. They will be under the control of a seven-member Judicial Commission headed by the chief justice of the Supreme Court of Pakistan. To what extent the 18th amendment will restore the independence of the judiciary in Pakistan remains to be seen. A study by the International Crisis Group (2010) on criminal justice in Pakistan said that the 18th amendment "alone will not rebuild a deteriorating justice sector where conviction rates are 5 to ten percent, prisons are overcrowded and the capacity of courts stretched by backlogs" (p. 1). As of 2010, according to the Law and Justice Commission of Pakistan, "more than 1.1 million cases were pending with the country's lower courts, 150,000 cases awaited the four provincial high courts, and 17,500 cases awaited the Supreme Court" (United States Department of State, 2011, Section E).

The *2010 Human Rights Report* on Pakistan by the United States Department of State (2011) described the deplorable conditions of arrest and detention, the cruel nature of police torture in custody, the degrading nature of punishment, the denial of fair and public trial, and many forms of extrajudicial killings and human rights violations within the criminal justice system of Pakistan (International Crisis Group, 2010). The report noted that in 2010, there were many reports that police and "security forces, including intelligence services, tortured and abused individuals in custody" (United States Department of State, 2011, Section C). The report further noted that in 2010:

> a significant increase in the total number of torture and rape cases was observed, almost double the number compared with 2009 . . . There were accusations of security forces raping women during interrogations. The government rarely took action against those responsible (United States Department of State, 2011, Section C).

According to Pakistan's criminal procedural law, police can detain an individual for 24 hours, and a magistrate can order detention for 14 days. In reality, these procedural laws are widely violated. The *2010 Human Rights Report* further observed that "some police detained individuals arbitrarily without charge or on false charges to extort payment for their release. There were reports that some police also detained relatives of wanted individuals to compel suspects to surrender" (United States Department of State, 2011, Section D). A report from the International Crisis Group (2011) noted that "decades of manipulation by military and civilian governments alike have reduced the police to what a senior police officer referred to as the "hatchet men of whoever is in power" (p. 11). A report from the Commonwealth Human Rights Initiative and the Human Rights Commission of Pakistan (2010) on police organizations in Pakistan noted that "corruption in the administration of justice is rampant. Transparency International's National Corruption Perception Survey shows that the police are consistently perceived as the most corrupt institution in Pakistan with the judiciary never far behind" (p. 17).

Corruption in the lower judiciary is equally rampant. The *2010 Human Rights Report on Pakistan* by the United States Department of State (2011) found that "in some cases trials did not start until six months after the FIR (First Information Report), and in some cases individuals remained in pretrial detention for periods longer than the maximum sentence for the crime" (Section D). A report by the International Crisis Group (2011) on the prison system in Pakistan observed that "judges in subordinate courts, along with prison staff and police, also seek bribes to fix an early hearing. Fearing indefinite detention, many detainees feel compelled to pay off prison officials or even plead guilty to obtain lower sentences" (p. 12). Equally deplorable are the conditions of the juvenile justice system in Pakistan. The International Crisis Group's 2011 report observed that "children continue to be arrested for petty offences and illegally detained for days and even months; in the absence of adequate facilities, their exposure to hardened criminals, including jihadis, makes them more likely to embrace crime" (p. i). An empirical study of 200 children at the Youthful Offenders Industrial School in Karachi by a medical team found that "almost 6% of the boys had been subjected to torture and ill-treatment including severe beating, electric shock and hanging by the feet" (Amnesty International, 2005, p. 25). Pakistan issued a Juvenile Justice System Ordinance in 2000 to comply with the provisions of the United Nations Convention on the Rights of the Child (CRC). The United Nations Committee on the Rights of the Child expressed its concern "at the high number of children in prison who are detained in poor conditions, often together with adult offenders . . . . The very low minimum age of criminal responsibility (7 years) is also of concern" (Amnesty International, 2005, p. 3). There are also reports that juvenile offenders are "being sentenced to death and executed" (Amnesty International, 2005, p. 3).

More deplorable are the conditions of prisons in Pakistan. The U.S. Department of State's *2010 Human Rights Report* noted that "most prison facilities were of antiquated construction, without the capacity to control indoor temperatures . . . . Emergency medical care . . . did not always function effectively. Prisoners sometimes also had to pay bribes, and bureaucratic procedures slowed access to medical care" (United States Department of State, 2011, Section C). The 2011 report of the International Crisis Group noted that "Pakistan's prison system remains brutal, opaque and unaccountable" (p. ii). Police and judicial corruptions have further aggravated the problems of the prisons. Thousands of people are put in overcrowded prisons by corrupt police officials and judges "for crimes that never occurred" (p. 11). The report further added that "as a result, an unreformed justice sector, in which neither the government nor the higher judiciary have appeared ready to hold lower courts or prison staff and police accountable, continues to deny prisoners timely and impartial justice" (p. 12). The report concluded by saying that "a corrupt and dysfunctional prison system has contributed to—and is a manifestation of—the breakdown of the rule of law in Pakistan" (p. i). In 2011, the National Judicial Policy-Making Committee, Pakistan's highest body for policy-making in legal matters, observed in a report that "that issues regarding non-submission of *challans*, defective investigations and non-production of remand prisoners were continuing to impede justice" (International Crisis Group, 2011, p. 12). Justice Iftikhar Mohammed Chaudhry, former chief justice of the Supreme Court of Pakistan, described the deplorable status of criminal justice in Pakistan in the following way: "We have collected data from the courts, police, prosecution and the jail authorities and found that 40 percent of challans [offenders who are charged or indicted] are not produced in the court on one pretext or the other" (Associated Press of Pakistan, 2011, p. 1). He further said that "there was no effective prosecution and investigation of cases" (Associated Press of Pakistan, 2011, p. 1).

Legacies of Modern Law and the Judiciary in Pakistan

The criminal justice system of Pakistan was inherited from the criminal justice system created in British India. Before August 1947, there was no separate state in the name of Pakistan. The present landscape of Pakistan was a part of the subcontinent of India from the beginning of the Indus Valley civilization that flourished around 2600 BC. The early institutions of modern criminal justice in Pakistan—modern law, modern police, modern court, and modern prison—were created by the colonial government of British India. These earlier structures and the institutions of criminal justice in Pakistan were, therefore, similar to those of India. The modern structure of criminal justice in India was created based on a series of enactments by the British Colonial state in the middle and late 19th century. Some of the core enactments are the Indian Police Act of 1861, the Indian Penal Code of 1862, the Indian Evidence Act of 1872, the Indian Prison Act of 1894, the Indian Code of Criminal Procedure of 1898, and the Indian Prison Act of 1900. Thus Pakistan in 1947 was not without any system of criminal justice. From 1947 to 1978, some amended versions of these colonial acts and statutes, created on the basis of English common law tradition, remained at the core of criminal justice in Pakistan. The Indian Penal Code of 1862, the Indian Evidence Act of 1872, and the Indian Code of Criminal Procedure 1898 came to be known in 1947 as the Pakistan Penal Code of 1862, the Pakistan Evidence Act of 1872, and the Pakistan Criminal Procedure Act of 1898, respectively. The Pakistan Penal Code of 1862 has been amended several times since 1947, and many new categories of crimes and punishments were added through the enactment of the parliament and the promulgation of ordinances. The Penal Code of Pakistan (Section 53) named 18 major categories of offenses (see **Table 12-2**) and 10 major categories of punishments (United Nations High Commissioner for Refugees, 2012).

The major 10 categories of punishments include *hudud, qisas, diyat, arsh, daman, ta'zir,* death penalty, imprisonment for life (rigorous imprisonment with hard labor and simple imprisonment), forfeiture of property, and fine. These categories of offenses and punishments came through a series of amendments made to the Pakistan Penal Code of 1862 during the last 60 years of

TABLE 12-2 Various Categories of Offenses Named in the Penal Code of Pakistan, 1862–2012

Categories of Offenses	
Chapter 6: Offenses against the state	Chapter 15: Offenses relating to religion
Chapter 7: Offenses relating to army, navy, and air force	Chapter 16: Offenses affecting the human body
Chapter 8: Offenses against public tranquility	Chapter 17: Offenses against property
Chapter 9: Offenses relating to public servants	Chapter 18: Intellectual property crimes
Chapter 10: Contempt of lawful authority of public servants	Chapter 19: Breach of contractors of service
Chapter 11: False evidence and offenses against public justice	Chapter 20: Offenses relating to marriage
Chapter 12: Offenses relating to coins and stamps	Chapter 21: Defamation
Chapter 13: Offenses relating to weights and measures	Chapter 22: Criminal intimidation and insult
Chapter 14: Offenses affecting decency and morals	Chapter 23: Attempts to commit offenses

the existence of the state of Pakistan. All the amendments cannot be discussed within the scope of this chapter, but some examples can be given. Some of the major enactments and ordinances passed in recent years include the Abolition of the Punishment of Whipping Act of 1996, the Anti-Terrorism Act of 2001, the Juvenile Justice (Amendment) Act of 2002, the Anti-Terrorism Act of 2003, the Prevention and Control of Human Trafficking Act of 2004, the Criminal Law Amendment Act of 2005, the Criminal Law (Amendment) Act of 2006, the Anti-Money Laundering Act of 2007, the Prevention of Electronic Crimes Ordinance of 2007, the Criminal Law Amendment Act of 2009, and the Anti-Money Laundering Act of 2010. The Criminal Law Amendment Act of 2005 (The Gazette of Pakistan, 2005), for example, criminalized the tradition of offering a girl in marriage as a compensation (*badal-i-sulh*) for a crime. The law stated that "whoever gives a female in marriage or otherwise in Badal-i-Sulh shall be punished with rigorous imprisonment which may extend to ten years but shall not be less than three years" (The Gazette of Pakistan, 2005). The Protection of Women (Criminal Law Amendment) Act of 2006 (The Gazette of Pakistan, 2006) added many provisions in the Pakistan Penal Code of 1862 related to violence against women. The provisions criminalized kidnapping, abducting, or inducing a woman to compel for marriage (Section 365B); kidnapping or abducting in order to subject a person to unnatural lust (Section 367B); and selling and buying of a person for purposes of prostitution (Section 371A-B). The law also criminalized cohabitation caused by a man deceitfully inducing a belief of lawful marriage (Section 493A). For the abovementioned crimes, the Protection of Women (Criminal Law Amendment) Act of 2006 imposed a penalty of life imprisonment (The Gazette of Pakistan, 2006).

Another significant legislation enacted recently in Pakistan is the Criminal Law (Amendment) Act of 2009. The new law made sexual harassment of women a crime punishable by law; it was not defined as a crime in the original Pakistan Penal Code of 1862. The Criminal Law (Amendment) Act of 2009, by amending Section 509 of the Pakistan Penal Code, made a law that whoever commits a crime of sexual harassment shall receive a punishment of maximum 3 years in prison and shall be liable to pay a fine of 500,000 rupees. The act defined sexual harassment not just in terms of the creation of a hostile work environment for a woman by making unwanted sexual advances, asking for sexual favors, and making sexual favors as a condition for job retention and promotion, but also defined sexual harassment broadly as a set of unwanted sexual gestures, postures, and behaviors that constitute an invasion to the privacy of a woman (The Gazette of Pakistan, 2009).

The Code of Criminal Procedure of Pakistan (CrPC) is similarly based on the Indian Code of Criminal Procedure of 1898. The Code of Criminal Procedural of Pakistan, like that of the Criminal Procedural Code of India, includes two types of offenses: cognizable and noncognizable. Cognizable offenses are those offenses for which an offender can be arrested without a warrant, and noncognizable offenses are those for which an offender cannot be arrested without a warrant. Chapter II of Part II of the CrPC outlined the structure of the judicial system of Pakistan. The structure is composed of the Supreme Court of Pakistan (court of highest instance), the provincial high courts of Pakistan (courts of appeals), the Federal *Shariat* Court (court of highest instance for Shari'a crimes and Shari'a punishments), the court of sessions (first instance court at the local and district levels), and the court of magistrates (court of first instance at the local and district levels). There are also some specialized courts established by laws, such as the antiterrorism courts, juvenile courts, family courts, and drug courts. In a typical criminal case, the criminal justice process follows four major steps: (1) the preparation of the first written information report by the police (Section 154 of the CrPC) about the commission of a crime; (2) police investigation (searches and seizures, evidence collection, examination of witnesses and suspects, and arrests and interrogations); (3) the reporting of the crime to the concerned magistrates by the police; and (4) trial and conviction. After the charges are framed, the prosecution has the burden proof. Criminal cases must be established based on the principle of beyond reasonable doubt. Under the Police Act of 2002, all provinces have separate prosecution services controlled by the Ministry of Law (Commonwealth Human Rights Initiative and Human Rights Commission of Pakistan, 2010).

The Pakistan Criminal Procedural Code of 1898 has also gone through a series of amendments during the last 6 decades through various enactments made by the parliament and ordinances promulgated by military governments. Within the confines of this chapter, all of the amendments cannot be discussed, but examples can be given. The Code of Criminal Procedure (Second Amendment) Ordinance of 1994, for example, inserted a section in the Code indicating that military force can be used for the maintenance of public safety (The Gazette of Pakistan, 1994). The Code of Criminal Procedure (Third Amendment) Ordinance of 1993 authorized the provincial governments "to obtain the assistance of the armed forces, when satisfied that it is necessary for the public security, protection of life and property, public peace and the maintenance of law and order" (The Gazette of Pakistan, 1993). The Code of Criminal Procedure (Amendment) Ordinance of 2007 included a provision that female offenders shall be released on bail if they did not commit the crimes of terrorism, financial corruption, murder, and other forms of crimes that are punishable by death. The Code of Criminal Procedure (Amendment) Act of 2011 enacted major reforms in bail procedures (The Gazette of Pakistan, 2011). Under the new law, offenders under trial who did not commit a crime punishable by death and who were in detention for more than a year (or, for women, more than 6 months) are entitled to statutory bails. The offenders who committed a crime punishable by death and who were in detention for more than 2 years (or, for women, more than 1 year) are also entitled to statutory bail.

■ The Nature of Islamic Criminal Justice in Pakistan: Birth of the Dual System

Pakistan became a separate nation in 1947, comprising the Muslim majority areas of British India. As of 2012, Pakistan has 187 million people, about 95% of whom are Muslims. Of that 95%, about 75% are Sunnis and 20% are Shi'ites. The rest are mostly Hindus and Christians. Pakistan is the second largest Muslim majority country in the world, with about 11% of the world's 1.57 billion Muslims (2009 estimate). At the birth of Pakistan, there began a process of Islamization for carving out a separate identity for Muslims in South Asia, and Pakistan made a firm commitment to establish a modern state based on the values of modernity. From 1947 to 1978, the structure of governance in general and of criminal justice in particular was based on English common law. The 1956 constitution of Pakistan declared the nation to be the Islamic Republic of Pakistan, but it did not change the secular basis of law and justice. The constitution of 1973 declared that all laws of Pakistan shall be in accordance with Islam "but crucially, this article could not be enforced in a court" (Lau, 2007, p. 1294). During the 1950s and 1960s, Pakistan was one of the developing countries that were aggressively modernizing their economy, politics, science, technology, education, law, and justice. The number of British-educated barristers in Pakistan is probably much higher than that of any other postcolonial country in the world except India. Before 1978, reforms in criminal law and criminal procedures were conceived solely within the framework of English common law expressed through such enactments as the Pakistan Penal Code of 1862, the Pakistan Evidence Act of 1872, and the Pakistan Criminal Procedure Act of 1898. In 1978, during the military rule of General Zia-ul-Haq, the history of criminal justice in Pakistan came to a turning point. General Zia-ul-Haq, who was in power as president for 11 years, formally introduced the Islamic system of criminal justice in Pakistan. At that time in Pakistan, a dual system of criminal justice began to expand. For a student of comparative criminal justice, the most intriguing issues about contemporary criminal justice in Pakistan are not the ones about policing and prisons, but those concerning how the Islamic system of criminal justice is being conceived, how Islamic criminal justice is defining new crimes and criminality, how the Islamic system of punishment is being defined and devised, how the Islamic judiciary is organized, and what new problems and issues have been emerging within the criminal justice system of Pakistan as a result of the introduction of Islamic criminal law and jurisprudence (Lau, 2005).

The *Hudood* Ordinances of 1979

The introduction of Islamic criminal justice in Pakistan came first through the introduction of the *Hudood* Ordinances in 1979. Islamic criminal justice is based on three different forms of punishment, one for each of the following categories of crimes: *hudud* crimes, *qisas* crimes, and *ta'zir* crimes. The *hudud* crimes and *qisas* crimes and their punishments are defined and sanctioned by the Quran. In 1979, Zia-ul-Haq introduced five ordinances that are collectively known as the *Hudood* Ordinances (Kennedy, 1988). These ordinances are the Offences Against Property (Enforcement of *Hudood*) Ordinance; the Offence of *Zina* [rape] (Enforcement of *Hudood*) Ordinance; the Offence of *Qazf* [false imputation of *zina* or rape] (Enforcement of *Hudood*) Ordinance; the Prohibition (Enforcement of *Hudood*) Order; and the Execution of Punishment of Whipping Ordinance.

The Offence of *Zina* (Enforcement of *Hudood*) Ordinance of 1979 begins with a preamble that explains that this ordinance was being introduced "to bring in conformity with the injunctions of Islam the law relating to the Offence of Zina" (The Gazette of Pakistan, 1979a). Section 5 of the ordinance states that *zina* or rape will be treated as a *hudud* crime if (1) it is committed by a man who is an adult and is not insane with a woman to whom he is not, and does not suspect himself to be, married; or (2) it is committed by a woman who is an adult and is not insane with a man to whom she is not, and does not suspect herself to be, married (The Gazette of Pakistan, 1979a)." Section 5 of the ordinance also states that the crimes of *zina* or rape shall receive *hudud* punishments. It states that the punishment (1) if he or she is a *muhsan*, is to be stoned to death at a public place; or (2) if he or she is not a *mushan*, to be whipped in a public place with 100 lashes. The Offence of *Zina* (Enforcement of *Hudood*) Ordinance of 1979 amended the relevant portions of the Pakistan Penal Code of 1862 and the Pakistan Code of Criminal Procedure of 1898 (The Gazette of Pakistan, 1979a). The ordinance introduced Islamic criminal procedures related to the proof and evidence of *zina*. It states that there are two types of evidentiary rules for the establishment of rape (*zina*) as a *hudud* crime. The first is the confession by the accused in front of a court with appropriate jurisdictions. The second is the bringing by the victims of four trustworthy and socially reputed male Muslim eyewitnesses who observed the act of penetration, not by design, but by chance. The ordinance also said that if the accused is a non-Muslim, the eyewitnesses may be non-Muslims. About the process of execution of those who are convicted of *zina*, the ordinance said that stoning of the convict should begin by the eyewitnesses and then, "while stoning being carried on, he may be shot dead" (The Gazette of Pakistan, 1979a, p. 8).

The Offences Against Property (Enforcement of *Hudood*) Ordinance of 1979 made theft a *hudud* crime punishable by decapitation or life imprisonment. The ordinance states that the punishment for a first-time offender (theft) is amputation of the right hand from the joint of the wrist; for a second-time offender (theft), punishment is the decapitation of the left leg up to the ankle; and for a third-time offender (theft), the punishment is life in prison (The Gazette of Pakistan, 1979b). The Offence of *Qazf* (Enforcement of *Hudood*) Ordinance of 1979 made false accusation of *zina* or rape a *hudud* crime. The ordinance states that whoever brings false accusations of *zina*, by making a false reporting to the police, by filing a false case in the court, by spreading false rumors, or by publishing false reports and stories that are deliberately designed to hurt the feelings and harm the reputation of an individual, commits the crime of *qazf* (The Gazette of Pakistan, 1979c). The ordinance further adds that "whoever commits qazf liable to hadd shall be punished with whipping numbering eighty stripes" (The Gazette of Pakistan, 1979c). The Prohibition (Enforcement of *Hudood*) Order of 1979 made drinking a *hudud* crime. The ordinance stated: "Whoever being an adult Muslim takes intoxicating liquor by mouth is guilty of drinking liable to hadd and shall be punished with whipping numbering eighty stripes" (The Gazette of Pakistan, 1979d). The crime of drinking is established if the accused makes a confession in the court or evidence is given by two honest and pious Muslims. The prohibition ordinance also made the export, import, manufacturing, transportation, and possession of intoxicants illegal. They were made crimes punishable with imprisonment for 5 years and whipping not exceeding 30 stripes. The export, import, manufacturing, transportation, and possession of opium or coca derivatives were also made illegal and punishable with imprisonment for life and whipping not exceeding 30 stripes. The Execution of Punishment of Whipping Ordinance of 1979 made provisions for the punishment of whipping for persons convicted of *hudud* offenses.

The *Qisas* and *Diyat* Law of 1990

In 1990, there came another criminal law amendment that also vastly changed the landscape of criminal justice in Pakistan. The Criminal Law (Amendment) Ordinance promulgated in 1990 by the president of Pakistan introduced the *qisas* and *diyat* laws—laws that pertain to murder and the punishment of retaliation and blood money. The *qisas* crimes include willful and nonnegligent murder, aggravated assault, aggravated assault with a deadly weapon, and bodily injury. These crimes are seen as serious crimes and are prohibited by the Quran. *Qisas* and *diyat* laws have been further revised and amended through the Criminal Law (Amendment) Act of 1997 passed by the Parliament of Pakistan. After the promulgation of the *Hudood* Ordinances in 1979 and the introduction of *qisas* crimes and punishments in the criminal code by the parliament in 1997, most of the major categories of crimes such as rape, incest, adultery, fornication, cohabitation, homosexuality, murder, assault, kidnapping, theft, drinking, and the possession of drugs and intoxicants came to be defined and litigated in criminal justice in Pakistan in terms of the principles of Shari'a Law—the injunctions of Islam.

The Federal Shari'a Judiciary

The introduction of Islamic criminal justice in Pakistan also came through the creation of an Islamic judiciary. The birth of the Islamic judiciary was the beginning of the dual system of criminal justice in Pakistan. In 1980, President Zia-ul-Haq unilaterally brought an amendment to the constitution of Pakistan—Constitution (Amendment) Order of 1980 (The Gazette of Pakistan, 1980). This amendment (Chapter III-A) formally established the Federal *Shariat* Court in Pakistan. The amendment provided for the establishment of a *Shariat* court composed of five members including the chairman or the chief justice to be appointed by the president. The amendment also made a provision that the chairman of the Federal *Shariat* Court shall be a person who is capable of becoming a judge of the Supreme Court of Pakistan, and a member shall be a person who is capable of becoming a judge of a High Court of Pakistan. The amendment gave power to the Federal *Shariat* Court to examine whether any law made in Pakistan is repugnant to the principles or the "injunctions" of Islam (The Constitution Amendment Act of 1980, Article 203D , as cited in the Gazette of Pakistan, 1980). The Federal

Shariat Court, of course, is required to give the reasons for holding its opinions, on the basis of the majority vote, about a law that is repugnant to the principles of Islam. The amendment empowered the president to change the laws that are declared repugnant to Islam by the Federal *Shariat* Court. The amendment gave broad power to the Federal *Shariat* Court for issuing summons to anyone needed to testify in the *Shariat* court, anyone needed to produce or examine some evidentiary documents, and anyone needed for the cross-examination of witnesses. The Constitution (Amendment) Order of 1980 made the *Shariat* court constitutionally independent of the Supreme Court and the High Courts of Pakistan (The Gazette of Pakistan, 1980). The Federal *Shariat* Court was given original, revisional, appellate, and review jurisdictions. In its original jurisdiction, the constitution empowered the court "to examine and decide the question, whether or not any law is repugnant to the injunctions of Islam" (Haider, 2009, p. 1). During the last 30 years, the Federal *Shariat* Court examined 1,500 laws and found 55 federal laws and 212 provincial laws that are repugnant to the injunctions of Islam (Haider, 2009). In the case of *Muhammad Riaz v. the Federal Government* in 1980, the Federal *Shariat* Court "declares some provisions of *The Penal Code, 1862,* and the *Criminal Procedure Code, 1898,* pertaining to the law of culpable homicide and murder, as against the injunctions of Islam" (as quoted in Wasti, 2009, p. 293). In its revisional jurisdiction, the Federal *Shariat* Court is empowered to call for and examine the decisions of any criminal courts that are related to the enforcement of *hudud* punishments. With respect to its appellate jurisdiction, a separate *Shariat* Appellate Branch was created within the Supreme Court of Pakistan to hear appeals from the Federal *Shariat* Court. The *Shariat* Appellate Branch is composed of three judges of the Supreme Court and two ulemas selected by the president. The constitution also "empowers the court to review any decisions given or order made by it" (Haider, 2009, p. 2). The decisions of the Federal *Shariat* Court are "binding on a High Court and all courts subordinate to a High Court" (Haider, 2009, p. 3). Provisions were also made in the constitution to create a panel of jurisconsults by the Federal *Shariat* Court composed of the prominent ulema and religious scholars of different schools of Islamic jurisprudence. Islamabad—the capital of Pakistan—was designated as the permanent seat of the Federal *Shariat* Court. But the constitution made a provision for the establishment of provincial *Shariat* benches by the chief justice of the Federal *Shariat* Court with the approval of the president. Currently, there are four *Shariat* benches in the cities of Karachi, Lahore, Peshawar, and Quetta. In Karachi, Lahore, and Peshawar, the *Shariat* benches are located within the provincial High Court buildings. The functioning of the Federal *Shariat* Court and the provincial *Shariat* benches are guided by the Federal *Shariat* Court (Procedure) rules of 1981. Justice Syed Afzal Haider, a former judge of the Federal *Shariat* Court, said that the Federal *Shariat* Court of Pakistan "is a unique institution with no parallel in the entire Muslim World (see **Table 12-3**). It is backed by the powerful provisions of the constitution" (Haider, 2009, p. 1).

■ Islamic Criminal Justice in Pakistan: The Emerging Problems and Issues

After the introduction of the *Hudood* Ordinances in 1979, the promulgation of *qisas* and *diyat* laws through the Criminal Law (Amendment) Ordinance of 1990, and the establishment

TABLE 12-3 Organizational Structure of Criminal Justice in Pakistan, 2012

Criminal Justice System	Nature, Structure, and Functions
Dual System of Criminal Law	*Modern system of criminal justice is based on*: English common law; Pakistan Penal Code of 1862; Pakistan Police Act of 1861; Pakistan Evidence Act of 1872; Pakistan Code of Criminal Procedure of 1898; Police Rules of 1934; and parliamentary acts and statutes such as the Protection of Women (Criminal Law Amendment) Act of 2006 and the Code of Criminal Procedure (Amendment) Act of 2011
	Islamic system of criminal justice is based on: Shari'a Law codified through the following major ordinances (later passed by the parliament as statutes): Shari'a Law; Offence of Zina (Enforcement of *Hudood*) Ordinance of 1979; Offences Against Property (Enforcement of *Hudood*) Ordinance of 1979; Offence of *Qazf* (Enforcement of *Hudood*) Ordinance of 1979; Prohibition (Enforcement of *Hudood*) Order of 1979; and Quanun-e-Shahadat Order of 1984; these Shari'a laws deal with the offenses of adultery, fornication, rape, robbery, theft, slandering, false accusations, and drug trafficking
Dual System of Court Structures	*Modern Court Structure*: The higher judiciary is comprised of the Supreme Court of Pakistan, four Provincial High Courts (Lahore, Sind, Punjab, and Baluchistan), and one High Court in the capital of Islamabad; the lower judiciary is comprised of two classes of courts: civil and criminal; criminal courts are composed of session judge, additional session judge, and judicial magistrates class I, II, and III; there are also provisions for the creation of specialized courts and tribunals at federal and provincial levels such as Anti-Terrorism Courts and Anti-Corruption Courts; the judges of the higher judiciary including the chief justice of the Supreme Court of Pakistan are appointed by the president on the basis of recommendations of a judicial commission and the review those recommendations by a parliamentary committee and the prime minister (Constitution Amendment Act (18th Amendment of 2010); the Supreme Court is consisted of one chief justice and 16 justices; the administration of the lower judiciary is the responsibility of the four provincial high courts and the high court of Islamabad.
	Islamic Court Structure: Federal Shariat Court (1) established by the Constitution (Amendment) Order of 1980; the Federal Shari'a Court is composed of eight Muslim judges including the chief justice, and they are appointed for 3 years by the president on the basis of recommendations by the judicial commission; at least three out of eight judges of the Federal Shariat Court must be "ulema" who are experts in Islamic jurisprudence; regional benches of the Shari'a court (4): Lahore, Karachi, Peshawar, and Quetta; Shariat Appellate Bench (1) is created within the Supreme Court of Pakistan and it is composed of three judges of the Supreme Court of Pakistan and two ulemas appointed by the president. The Shariat Appellate Bench hears appeal from the Federal Shariat Court.

TABLE 12-3 (Continued)

Criminal Justice System	Nature, Structure, and Functions
Dual System of Prosecution	Prosecutions are conducted on the basis of both modern and Islamic laws depending on the nature of criminal offenses; one of the major developments has been the separation of the prosecuting agency from the police; a separate Office of District Prosecuting Agency was created in the mid-1980s, and prosecution at the provincial level is now the responsibility of the district attorneys and their assistants and deputies. The Office of the District Prosecuting Agencies is administered by the provincial Ministries of Law; federal prosecution is the responsibility of the federal office of the attorney general; the prosecution of public and government officials are done by two agencies: Federal Investigation Agency (like the FBI of the United States) and the Anti-Corruption Establishment.
Dual Systems of Policing	The Police Act of 1861 is still the legal foundation of organizing policing in Pakistan; there are two types of policing: federal policing and provincial policing; federal police are composed of 14 major types of police and police organizations, such as the Federal Investigating Agency (FIA), civil armed forces, frontier corps, Pakistan Rangers, anti-narcotic force, national police bureau, national public safety commission, Pakistan railway police, intelligence bureau, and capital territory police; four regional police forces (Punjab Police, Sindh Police, Balochistan Police, and Khyber Pakhtunkhwa Police); most of the senior cadres of police officers both in federal and provincial policing come from the Police Service of Pakistan (PSP); the Police Order of 2002 introduced some major reforms in policing in Pakistan in terms of autonomy and accountability.

Source: Hussain, F. (2011, February). *The judicial system of Pakistan.* Islamabad, Pakistan: The Supreme Court of Pakistan; Commonwealth Human Rights Initiative and Human Rights Commission of Pakistan. (2010). *Police Organization in Pakistan.* New Delhi, India, and Lahore, Pakistan: Author.

of a Shari'a judiciary through the Constitution (Amendment) Order of 1980, two new processes began to emerge within the criminal justice system of Pakistan (Kennedy, 1988). The first is that existing crimes, existing forms of punishments, and prevailing criminal procedural laws were redefined from a new perspective—the perspective of Shari'a Law. The second is a new process of criminalization. Acts and behaviors that were not previously defined as serious crimes were defined as serious crimes after the introduction of Shari'a Law. These include drinking, theft, adultery, fornication, and homosexuality. When the old crimes, old forms of punishments, and old criminal procedural laws were redefined, a number of intrasystemic issues began to emerge. The new perspective brought changes in the way crimes are reported, criminal cases are filed, criminal investigations are conducted, suspects are interrogated, proof and evidence are defined, witnesses are examined, trials are conducted, convictions and sentencing are imposed, and appeals are granted. The new perspective, in other words, brought many systemic challenges in criminal justice in Pakistan. There are four major schools of Islamic jurisprudence. The four schools can be divided into two major perspectives. There is a conservative perspective, based particularly on Wahhabism, that does not believe there is a space within Islamic criminal law for critical thinking, analytical reasoning (*ijtihad*), and judicial consensus (*ijma*). This is the strict constructionist perspective that is more common among the Shi'ite clergy in Iran, among some groups of religious scholars in Saudi Arabia, and among the *salafis* of Egypt. They are the followers of the Hanbali school of Islamic jurisprudence. The second is the perspective of the liberal constructionists. The liberal constructionists are those who belong to the Hanafi school of Islamic jurisprudence. They believe that Islamic jurisprudence is compatible with time and space based on the use of critical thinking, analytical reasoning, and consensus in the interpretation of Shari'a Law. In exploring comparative criminal justice in Pakistan, it would be exciting to examine how old crimes and punishments are being redefined and old criminal procedural laws are being revised in the context of Islamic criminal justice. Comparative criminal justice can explore how Shari'a laws related to crime and punishment are being examined and interpreted by the judges and jurists in the Shari'a judiciary in Pakistan. For the study of comparative criminal justice in Pakistan, equally significant is the issue of the expansion of the boundary of the definition of crime—the new process of criminalization. With the advent of Shari'a Law and the Shari'a judiciary, many new forms of crimes have been emerging in Pakistan. Two of the new crimes that have created huge tensions not only within the system of criminal justice but also in the larger social and cultural landscape of Pakistan are the crimes of blasphemy and apostasy. The following sections will briefly discuss and examine both issues—the nature of the interpretation of Shari'a Law in Pakistan with respect to *hudud* crimes (rape, fornication, and adultery) and *qisas* crimes (murder and physical assault), and the emerging debates and disputes with respect to the new crimes of blasphemy and apostasy.

The Interpretation and Effect of the *Hudood* Ordinances

The introduction of the *Hudood* Ordinances in 1979 and their further codification through the Criminal Law (Amendment) Act of 1997 created enormous complexities and confusion in Pakistan's system of criminal justice. The Offence of *Zina* (Enforcement of *Hudood*) Ordinance of 1979 and the Offence of *Qazf* (Enforcement of *Hudood*) Ordinance of 1979 have particularly created confusion about the right interpretation of the Shari'a Law. First, like Iran and Saudi Arabia, Pakistan did not inherit a class of Islamic judges and jurists competent to interpret Shari'a Law. Two of the most attractive professions in Pakistan today are the military and the civil service. Pakistan from its birth upheld the principles of Islam in all walks of life, but it never created and culturally legitimated the creation of a separate elite group of Islamic judges and jurists. Almost all judges and jurists of Pakistan are trained and educated in modern secular laws. Secondly, the Shari'a judiciary—the Federal *Shariat* Court and its provincial benches—was created as part of the modern judiciary of Pakistan inherited from British India. But it created vast complexities in the prevailing judicial system because the Federal *Shariat* Court was given the power to examine and review the laws of Pakistan that are in violation of the injunctions of Islam. The Federal *Shariat* Court found that the laws related to rape in Pakistan are in violation of the injunctions of Islam, and hence, beginning in the early 1980s, rape cases were litigated based on the Offence of *Zina* (Enforcement of *Hudood*) Ordinance of 1979. Adultery and fornication were not defined as crimes under the Pakistan Penal Code of 1862. After the Offence of *Zina* (Enforcement of *Hudood*) Ordinance of 1979, adultery and fornication were defined as *hudud* crimes. The judges of the lower courts and district courts, most of whom were not educated in Shari'a Law, began to adjudicate rape, adultery, and fornication cases in the early 1980s as *hudud* offenses, and that was the beginning of a new crisis in the criminal justice system in Pakistan (Ali, 2006; Imran, 2005; Lau, 2007; Mehdi, 2010; Usmani, 2006).

After the promulgation of the Offence of *Zina* (Enforcement of *Hudood*) Ordinance of 1979, the number of rape, adultery, and fornication cases began to rapidly increase in the lower courts (Imran, 2005). With the rapid increase in rape, adultery, and fornication cases, the number of women prisoners alarmingly went up in all provinces of Pakistan. One study found that "after the 1979 . . . Zina Hudood Ordinance, cases of reported fornication or adultery jumped from a handful to thousands. In 1980, seventy women were in prison in the Punjab province alone; by 1988 the figure jumped to 6,000" (Imran, 2005, p. 91). It is also reported that "from 1980 to 1987 the Federal Shari'a Court alone heard 3,399 appeals of *zina* involving female prisoners" (as quoted in Imran, 2005, p. 91). What is more intriguing is that since 1979, according to a former judge of the Federal *Shariat* Court, "no accused has been awarded a *hudud* punishment [and] all of those convicted were given *tazir* punishment" (Usmani, 2006, p. 289). The question that is still being researched is why so many women in Pakistan entered prison after the promulgation of the Offence of *Zina* (Enforcement of *Hudood*) Ordinance of 1979. Many studies have found that the misunderstanding and misinterpretation of the *hudud* laws, particularly by the judges of the lower courts, is one of the main reasons for the rapid increase of female prisoners (Ali, 2006; Imran, 2005). *Hudud* crimes in cases of rape, adultery, and fornication can be established, and *hudud* punishments can be given in cases of rape, adultery, and fornication, according to the injunctions of the Quran, only on the basis of four witnesses who are pious and socially reputable and who have seen the actual act of penetration not by choice but by chance. In almost all cases of rape, adultery, and fornication that came to the lower courts in Pakistan during the last 3 decades, these particular rules of evidence could not be established by the victims, most of whom were women. Because the women who brought those cases failed to produce four witnesses, the lower courts in a large number of cases charged them for the crime of false accusation under the Offence of *Qazf* (Enforcement of *Hudood*) Ordinance of 1979. The lower courts gave them the *ta'zir* punishment of imprisonment. Stories of such cases in Pakistan—where rape victims were unable to produce four eyewitnesses in support of their accusations and were, in turn, charged with false accusations and received imprisonment—are not few and far between (Imran, 2005).

In 1982, a blind girl named Safia Bibi, who came from the Punjab province of Pakistan, was raped by her employer and his son. She was working as a domestic servant. In the trial, the blind girl, who became pregnant from the rape, was asked to identify her accuser and bring four eyewitnesses. After she failed to identify her accuser and bring four witnesses, the court sentenced her to flogging and 3 years in prison on charges of adultery and false accusations. The presiding judge told her that because she was blind, her sentencing of flogging was reduced from 100 to 30 stripes in public. The verdict was overturned, after a massive domestic and international outcry for a miscarriage of justice, by the Federal *Shariat* Court of Pakistan in 1983. In another landmark case in 1982, a Pakistani lower court sentenced a couple (Allah Bux and Fehmida) to death by stoning for marrying without the consent of the woman's father. Fehmida's father brought a case of abduction, and the court sentenced both of them to death by stoning under the Offence of *Zina* (Enforcement of *Hudood*) Ordinance of 1979. The Supreme Court of Pakistan overturned the decision due to scarcity of evidence. In 1987, a lower court in Karachi sentenced a woman named Shahida Perveen who remarried after divorcing her first husband. Shahida was convicted of adultery because her divorce was not properly registered by her first husband, who was the complainant. Shahida was charged with adultery and was sentenced to death by stoning. The Supreme Court of Pakistan overturned the decision of the lower court due to the absence of evidence. In 2002, a Session Court in Kohat in North-West Frontier Province of Pakistan sentenced a woman named Zafran Bibi who was raped by her brother-in law when her husband was in prison. Because she failed to bring four witnesses in support of her accusation, she was, in return, charged with adultery because she became pregnant while her husband was in prison. Zafran Bibi was sentenced to death by stoning. The verdict of the lower court was overturned by the Federal *Shariat* Court in 2003.

During the last 2 decades, even more women were sent to prison as a result of the misinterpretation of the *zina* ordinance by the lower courts, and even more cases were invalidated by the Federal *Shariat* Court. It is estimated that as of 2006, about 7,000 women were in jails in Pakistan awaiting trial. A 2004 report from the Pakistan National Commission on the Status of Women found that about 80% of those women "are in jail because they failed to prove rape cases, and found themselves locked up on adultery convictions" (Daily Times, 2004, p. 1). Another study has found that about 95% of the women who are convicted of adultery for failing to prove rape charges by bringing four eyewitnesses were acquitted by the Federal *Shariat* Court and the Supreme Court of Pakistan. The implementation of the Offence of *Zina* (Enforcement of *Hudood*) Ordinance of 1979 and the Offence of *Qazf* (Enforcement of Hudood) Ordinance of 1979 thus created a major crisis of trust and legitimacy in the criminal justice system of Pakistan (Ali, 2006; Imran 2005; Lau, 2007; Mehdi, 2010; Shirkat Gah, 2004).

In 2006, Pakistan passed the Protection of Women (Criminal Law Amendment) Act of 2006, and it substantially amended the Offence of *Zina* (Enforcement of *Hudood*) Ordinance of 1979 and the Offence of *Qazf* (Enforcement of *Hudood*) Ordinance of 1979. The law was passed on the basis of a number of research studies, commission reports, and movements mobilized by different women's rights groups, national and international human rights groups, nongovernmental organizations, and civil society organizations such as the National Commission on the Status of Women and the Council of Islamic Ideology. As Lau (2007) noted:

> The first serious attempt to reform, though not abolish, the Zina Ordinance was initiated by General Pervez Musharraf, the President of Pakistan and the Chief of Staff of its armed forces. . . . Unlike Zia, who had used Islam to legitimize his usurpation of power, Musharraf has portrayed himself as an enlightened, benign, and progressive ruler. . . . An open admirer of Kemal Ataturk, the founder of secular Turkey, Musharraf has been the first Pakistani leader who has tried to reform the Zina Ordinance. At the end of 2006, he signed into law the Protection of Women (Criminal Laws Amendment) Act (p. 1300).

The Protection of Women (Criminal Law Amendment) Act invalidated the prosecution of rape, adultery, and fornication as a *hudud* crime to curb the abuse of women and the abuse of police power. The law is

> structured around three elements. The first element returns a number of offenses from the Zina Ordinance to the Pakistan Penal Code, where they had been prior to 1979. The second element reformulates and redefines the offenses of zina and qazf, the wrongful accusation of zina. The third element creates an entirely new set of procedures governing the prosecution of the offenses of adultery and fornication (Lau, 2007, p. 1308).

Lau (2007) observed that

> in pursuance of the first element, the following offenses have all been reinserted into the Pakistan Penal Code, 1860: kidnapping or abducting a woman in order to compel her to marry a person against her will or to force her to have illicit intercourse; kidnapping or abducting a person in order to subject him to 'unnatural lust;' and selling a person for the purposes of prostitution and related crimes (p. 1308).

The most significant change brought about by the law was that "the offense of rape has been removed from the Zina Ordinance and returned to the Pakistan Penal Code in the form of Section 375" (Lau, 2007, p. 1308). After the enactment of the Protection of Women (Criminal Law Amendment) Act of 2006, "Rape is therefore no longer governed by the Zina Ordinance or by any other Islamic criminal law" (Lau, 2007, p. 1309).

Secondly, the law defined an offense of fornication punishable by 5 years of imprisonment and a fine of 10,000 rupees. But the offense of fornication was removed from the *zina* ordinance, and it was inserted in the Pakistan Penal Code of 1862. The only offense that remained as part of the *zina* ordinance, after the enactment of the Protection of Women (Criminal Law Amendment) Act of 2006 was the offense of adultery—a *hudud* crime that can be established either on the basis of a confession or by the presentation of four pious and socially reputed eyewitnesses who have seen the actual act of penetration not by choice but by chance. The new act, however, also redefined the concept of confession. It described confession as "an oral statement, explicitly admitting the commission of the offence of zina, voluntarily made by the accused before a court of sessions . . . under section 203A of the Code of Criminal Procedure, 1898" (Lau, 2007, p. 1310). Amendments were also made to "prevent the overlap between the offenses of rape and adultery, where failed accusations of rape were converted into adultery charges on the basis that the woman had 'confessed' to sexual intercourse when she complained of rape" (Lau, 2007, p. 1310). The law created a provision (Section 5A) that ended the "overlap of cases of rape, adultery, and fornication, by providing that no complaint of adultery or rape can be converted into one of fornication and no complaint of fornication can be converted into one of adultery" (Lau, 2007, p. 1311). The third amendment brought by the Protection of Women (Criminal Law Amendment) Act of 2006 was about criminal procedures related to governing sexual offenses under both the *zina* ordinance and the Pakistan Penal Code. The new procedures mandated that a complaint of adultery has to be made not to local police agencies but directly in a court of sessions. The new procedures made it highly unlikely to prosecute the offense of adultery as a *hudud* crime and reduced the scope for false accusation of adultery. False accusation of adultery is punishable, according to the Offence of *Qazf* [false imputation of *zina* or rape] (Enforcement of *Hudood*) Ordinance of 1979, by whipping. Lau explained:

> The third element of reforms effected by the Protection of Women (Criminal Laws Amendment) Act relates to the procedure governing sexual offenses under both the amended Zina Ordinance and the Pakistan Penal Code. The procedure governing accusations of adultery makes the prospect of any prosecutions, let alone convictions, unlikely. A complaint of adultery has to be lodged directly in a court of sessions, thereby circumventing potentially corrupt police officers altogether. The judge hearing the complaint has to place under oath not only the complainant, but also at least four adult, male eyewitnesses, who have on examination satisfied the court that they are 'truthful persons and abstain from major sins.' These four witnesses have to testify under oath that they witnessed the act of penetration. Only then can the court issue a summons for the appearance of the accused (2007, pp. 1311–1312).

The Protection of Women (Criminal Law Amendment) Act of 2006 thus substantially amended the Offence of *Zina* (Enforcement of *Hudood*) Ordinance of 1979 promulgated by Zia-ul-Haq to Islamize the criminal law of Pakistan. The Protection of Women (Criminal Law Amendment) Act of 2006 did not repeal the *zina* ordinance but "instead, the Zina Ordinance has been hollowed out to its barest essentials. It only deals with one offense, namely adultery liable to a *hadd* punishment. The likelihood of such a prosecution succeeding is remote indeed" (Lau, 2007, p. 1314). In 2010, the Federal *Shariat* Court of Pakistan, however, declared many important provisions of the Protection of Women (Criminal Law Amendment) Act of 2006 unconstitutional (Federal Shariat Court, 2011). The Federal *Shariat* Court wants the reinstatement of the *Hudood* Ordinances of 1979 (Asian Human Rights Commission, 2010).

The Interpretation and Effect of the *Qisas* and *Diyat* Ordinance

In order to bring the crimes of and the punishments for murder, manslaughter, and physical injuries under the injunction of Islam and Islamic criminal justice, Pakistan promulgated the *Qisas* and *Diyat* Ordinance in 1990. In 1997, the *Qisas* and *Diyat* Ordinance became an act of the parliament through the enactment of the Criminal Law (Amendment) Act of 1997. The *Qisas* and *Diyat* Ordinance "re-conceptualized the offences relating to physical injury and murder in Islamic terms as understood in Pakistan and replaced about 40 relevant sections (299 to 338), of the Pakistan Penal Code, 1862 which were derived from British Common Law" (Hashmi, 2004, p. 1). The *qisas* and *diyat* law brought some fundamental changes in murder trials. Under the new law of *qisas* and *diyat*, murder or manslaughter became an act of offense not against the state but against the person of the victim. The new law "privatises justice by shifting the emphasis from homicide as a crime against the state to a private offence against the victim" (Knudsen, 2004, p. 8). It brought an entirely new notion to Pakistan's criminal justice that murders of family members are a family affair and that prosecution and redress are not inevitable but may be negotiated. Thus, "if a father, brother, or husband kills a woman of his family, the prosecution case collapses if any of the legal heirs of the deceased waives the right of Qisas or compounds the murder under the *Qisas* and *Diyat* Ordinance" (Hashmi, 2004, p. 1).

After the enactment of the *Qisas* and *Diyat* Ordinance, new forms of crimes and injustices in the criminal justice system of Pakistan rapidly escalated. Murder rates began to grow, appeals to reach a compromise in murder cases increased, the scope for police corruption in filing murder cases widened, honor killing began to explode, murder convictions declined, and many offenders of heinous murders began to roam the streets as free men taking advantage of *diyat* or blood money. One study, based on empirical research on cases from 10 districts of the province of Punjab, the Federal *Shariat* Court, and the Supreme Court of Pakistan, claimed that between 1981 and 2000, the murder rate in Pakistan increased, on average, at a rate of 6.5 per 100,000 population. The *qisas* and *diyat* laws were introduced through the Criminal Law (Amendment) Ordinance of 1990. Research has shown that between 1990 and 2010, not a single murderer was convicted under the *qisas* law. Research has also shown that during the same time period, the rate of murder prosecution and conviction remarkably declined, whereas the rate of out-of-court settlements for murder cases on the basis of the *diyat* laws (blood money) jumped almost 30%. Between 1984 and 2000, the acquittal rate in murder trials in the Supreme Court of Pakistan increased from 28% to 67%. During the same time period, the conviction rate declined from 79% to 35% (Saeed, 2010). Data from the Ministry of the Interior in Pakistan show that the rate of culpable homicide and murder in Pakistan in 1981 was 23 per 100,000 population. In 2000, the rate increased to 32 per 100,000 population. Between 1994 and 1998, the rate jumped to about 39 per 100,000 population. Data from the Ministry of the Interior also show that between 1981 and 1990, the average homicide rate in Pakistan was 50 per 100,000 population. Between 1991 and 2000, the average homicide rate increased to 61 per 100,000 population. This homicide rate in Pakistan in the decade of 1991–2000, in comparison to data on the intentional homicide rate in 2004 compiled by the United Nations Office on Drugs and Crime (UNODC), is the highest in the world.

Stories where compromise was reached and *diyat* was paid to get out of murder convictions are not few and far between. One of the earliest examples is the case of *Mushtaq v. State* in 1990 (as cited in Wasti, 2009. p. 183). Mushtaq murdered his grandfather, and the lower court sentenced him to death under the *qisas* and *diyat* law. In August 1990, a few days after the promulgation of the *Qisas* and *Diyat* Ordinance of 1990, the relatives of the victims "appeared before the High Court, stating that they had pardoned the accused in the name of Allah and applied for the Court's permission . . . [for] a compromise . . . . The compromise was allowed and the accused was acquitted immediately" (Wasti, 2009, p. 183). In another case in 1991—*Zulfiqar v. the State*—three people got out of murder convictions under the *Qisas* and *Diyat* Ordinance of 1990 (as cited in Wasti, 2009, p. 184). There were three people involved in the case. Zulfiqar killed a person named Yousaf. A relative of Yousaf, in retaliation, killed two of Zulfiqar's brothers. Both Zulfiqar and the relative of Yousaf won acquittal on the basis of compromise (Wasti, 2009, p. 184). In many instances, compromise applications were processed even before the beginning of a police investigation of a murder case, for murder cases committed before the promulgation of the *qisas* and *diyat* law, and for offenders who were absconding. In 1985, a man named Naheed stabbed to death his sister, Shaheen. The trial court sentenced Naheed to life in prison and a fine of 5,000 rupees under the Penal Code of 1862. After the *qisas* and *diyat* law came into effect, the High Court pardoned Naheed on the basis of a compromise deed signed by the legal heirs of the deceased— father, mother, four brothers, and one sister. "The deed affirmed that the heirs of the deceased had pardoned the accused . . . and waived the right of qisas" (Wasti, 2009, p. 211). In 1992, in the case of *Muhammad Ishaq v. the State*, a compromise deed was processed even before the start of a police investigation (as cited in Wasti, 2009. p. 211). Ishaq killed his sister for refusing to transfer ownership of the house she inherited from her deceased husband. Before the trial could formally proceed, her legal heirs—mother, four brothers, and two sisters— "appeared before the court and recorded statements to the effect that they have waived their rights of *qisas* and *diyat*" (Wasti, 2009, p. 211). Ishaq was sentenced to 5 years in prison by the lower court for not showing his remorse for the crime. On appeal, the High Court sent the case back to the lower court for retrial. In the retrial, the lower court acquitted the murder on the basis of the compromise reached earlier.

One of the most negative aspects of the introduction of the *qisas* and *diyat* law is that it increased the number of honor killings in Pakistan. Honor killing is a ritual that exists in many countries in Africa, the Middle East, and Southern Asia. In Southern Asia, it is more prevalent in Pakistan. It is a ritual of killing men and women, particularly young girls and women, by parents and family relatives for a range of offenses including disobeying parents, female adultery, falling in romantic love, refusing to agree to an arranged marriage, seeking divorce against parental consent, being a victim of rape or sexual assault, and dating. It is seen as revenge for bringing shame to a family and betraying family tradition and loyalty. The Human Rights Commission of Pakistan, in one of its studies, estimated that honor killings in Pakistan "averaged 412 victims per year during the five-year period 1998–2002 . . . About 60 percent of the victims were women and only about half of the incidents were reported to the police (226 cases)" (Knudsen, 2004, p. 12). The North-West Frontier Province of Pakistan is particularly notorious for honor killings: "The police records from the province for the period 1990–2002 estimate that about 1,844 women have been killed in the name of honour, the large majority of them (1,383) in the so-called 'tribal areas'" (Knudsen, 2004, p. 13).

Another study found that in the province of Punjab, between 1997 and 2003, there were 1707 cases of honor killings. Out of 1707, "only 1142 cases have been disposed off with 320 (28%) convictions and 822 (71.87%) acquittals" (Hashmi, 2004, p. 2). A study by the Human Rights Commission of Pakistan conducted on the basis of official statistics in 2006 found that on an average 1,000 men and women were killed in Pakistan in the name of honor killing (Austrian Red Cross, 2009, p. 3).

One of the major research studies (Nasrullah, Haqqi, & Cummings, 2009), which was based on 1,957 cases of honor killings of women in Pakistan that occurred between 2004 and 2007, found that 82% of the victims were under the age of 18, and 88% were married. "Alleged extramarital relation was the major reason for the killing (92%)" (p. 1). Among the perpetrators, 43% were husbands, 24% were brothers, and 12% were other relatives (see **Box 12-1**). The study reported that the mean annual rate of honor killing "in females (age 15–64) was found to be 15.0 per million" (Nasrullah et al., 2009, p. 1). After the promulgation of the *qisas* and *diyat* law, the number of honor killings went up in Pakistan because of the high rate of acquittal and low rate of convictions in murder trials, which, in turn, were based on the waiver of the right of *qisas* and the payment of blood money (*diyat*). In 2004, Pakistan enacted the Criminal Law (Amendment) Act of 2004. The law criminalized honor killing and increased its penalties. Section 302 of the law carries a maximum imprisonment of 25 years and not less than 10 years for the crime of honor killing. The law, however, has serious limitations. The law still allows the victim's heirs to waive the right of *qisas*, to pardon the offenders, and seek blood money (*diyat*). The general increase in the rate of culpable homicide and honor killings in Pakistan since the beginning of the 1980s bears the testimony that the introduction of the *qisas* and *diyat* law created enormous tensions and complexities in the criminal justice system of Pakistan with respect to murder trials and convictions. "The transplantation of the principles of Islamic law of *qisas* and *diyat*—essentially civil in nature—into the criminal justice system of Pakistan created an internal tension in its functioning, as well as causing conspicuous frictions in its administration" (Wasti, 2009, p. 236).

Criminalization of Free Speech in Pakistan: The Blasphemy Laws

The introduction of Shari'a Law and Islamic criminal justice in Pakistan brought amendments to the Pakistan Penal Code of 1862 and the Pakistan Code of Criminal Procedure of 1898 and criminalized not only adultery and fornication but also free speech with respect

BOX 12-1

Pakistani Artist, Poet Murdered in Shari'a "Honor" Killing

Honor killing is widely prevalent in Pakistan, particularly in the tribal region of the country. One episode that shocked the world is the killing of a Pakistani singer and artist by her own brothers for getting divorced and remarried. "Ayman Udas, a rising female vocalist in Peshawar [Pakistan] . . . was shot at her home, allegedly by her own brothers. Her death has rattled the city's jittery artistic community, as local musicians and dancers . . . face increasing pressure as the region falls under . . . Taliban influence. A beautiful woman in her 30s . . . Udas recently remarried after a divorce. Her two brothers . . . disapproved of her divorce, remarriage, and her artistic career, all of which disgrace a family's name" (Geller, 2009, p. 1). The Chief of the United Nations Human Rights Commission, Navi Pillay, recently said that "so-called 'honour killings' are an extreme symptom of discrimination against women, which—including other forms of domestic violence—is a plague that affects every country" (U.N. News Centre, 2010, p. 1). Navi further observed that about 5,000 women and girls every year, in the name of "honour killing," are "shot, stoned, burned, buried alive, strangled, smothered and knifed to death with horrifying regularity" (U.N. News Centre, 2010, p. 1). What is particularly shocking is that this horrifying crime is spreading all around the world, and North America is not an exception. On November 2, 2009, Noor Almaleki, a daughter of an Iraqi immigrant in Peoria, Arizona, was run over by her own father for allegedly divorcing her Iraqi husband and falling in love with another man. Maricopa County prosecutor Stephanie Low said that "by [the father's] own admission, this was an intentional act, and the reason was that his daughter had brought shame on him and his family" (as quoted in Dorell, 2009, p. 1). On June 30, an Afghani immigrant in Canada named Mohammad Shafia drowned and killed his three teenage daughters and his former wife. All four victims were found inside an SUV submerged in a canal in Kingston, Ontario. An Ontario Superior Court found him guilty of honor killing. "In a statement following the verdict, Canadian Justice Minister Rob Nicholson called honor killings a practice that is 'barbaric and unacceptable in Canada'" (as quoted in Huffpost World, 2012, p. 1). Although it is prevalent mostly in the Muslim countries of Asia, Africa, and the Middle East, Islam does not condone it, and the Quran does not have any injunction for honor killing. It is one of the ancient tribal beliefs still surviving in the midst of modernity in the 21st century. According to the Quran, it is rather a *qisas* crime, and it deserves *qisas* punishment. In Section 22 of Surah Al-Baqarah, the Quran said: "O men of understanding: There is security of life for you in the law of retaliation, so that you may become pious" (2:178–179).

Sources: UN News Centre (2010, March 4). *Impunity for domestic violence, 'honour killings' cannot continue – UN official.* New York, NY: The United Nations; Dorell, O. (2009, November 30). 'Honor killings' in USA raise concerns. *USA Today*, March 4; Huffpost World (2012, January, 29). *Canada honor killing trial verdict: Shafia family found guilty.* Retrieved from www.huffingtonpost.com/2012/01/29/canada -honor-killing-shafia-family-guilty_n_1240268.html; Geller. P. (2009, April 30). *Pakistani artist, poet murdered in Shariah "honor" killing.* Radio Free Europe. Retrieved from atlasshrugs2000.typepad.com/atlas_shrugs/2009/04/pakistani-artist-poet-murdered-in -shariah-honor-killing.html.

to Islam and alternative beliefs. The process of criminalization of free speech with respect to Islam, of course, began in the 1920s under the rule of British India. The Criminal Law (Amendment) Act (XXV) of 1927 introduced by the British colonial administration (Section 295 A-B) prohibited "deliberate/malicious acts intended to outrage religious feelings of any class by insulting its religion." In 1982, during the introduction of Islamic criminal justice in Pakistan, the government of Zia-ul-Haq brought the Pakistan Penal Code (Amendment) Ordinance of 1982. This ordinance further amended Section 295-B related to blasphemy and increased "penalty options to include life imprisonment." This ordinance also introduced Section 295-C, which outlaws the "use of derogatory remarks, etc., in respect of the Holy Prophet." In 1986, the Parliament of Pakistan further tightened the blasphemy law of Pakistan by passing the Criminal Law (Amendment) Act III of 1986. Section 2 of the Act introduced the death penalty for the crime of blasphemy (derogatory terms against the Prophet Muhammad) in addition to the punishment of life imprisonment. In 1992, the government of Nawaz Sharif removed the provision of life imprisonment from Section 295-C and made the death penalty mandatory for the crime of blasphemy (derogatory terms against the Prophet Muhammad). Like the introduction of the *Hudood* Ordinance in 1979 and the introduction of the *Qisas* and *Diyat* Ordinance of 1990, the new blasphemy laws of Pakistan unleashed an era of unprecedented confusion and complexities in the criminal justice system of Pakistan with respect to free speech about the religion of Islam as well as the practice of alternative faiths and beliefs. The blasphemy laws criminalized the act of apostasy—the act of rejecting Islam or conversion from Islam to other religions (see **Table 12-4**).

The first incident took place in Punjab immediately after the promulgation of the blasphemy laws in 1990. A report from the Jinnah Institute of Pakistan told of an incident during which "a Christian teacher and poet in Faisalabad, Punjab was accused of blaspheming against the Prophet (PBUH). He was subsequently stabbed to death by a member of the Anjuman-e-Sipah-e-Sahaba" (Jinnah Institute, 2010, p. 4). A study conducted on the implementation of the blasphemy laws in Pakistan between January and July of 2011 found that "scores of Pakistanis have been harassed and implicated in false cases instituted by misusing the country's blasphemy laws. Additionally, allegations of blasphemy have led to assassinations, extrajudicial killings and threats to life and property" (Imtiaz, 2011). Within the first 6 months of 2011, three men were killed by the supporters of blasphemy laws. In January 2011, the Governor of Punjab, Salman Taseer, was assassinated in Islamabad by his bodyguard, who shot the governor 26 times from close range. Salman Taseer was an advocate for repealing the blasphemy laws. Eight months after the killing of the governor, his son, Shahbaz Taseer, was kidnapped. In March 2011, Shahbaz Bhatti, the Federal Minister for Minorities Affairs and the only Christian minister in the cabinet of Pakistan, was assassinated. He was killed by two members of an extremist Islamic group who were recent converts from Christianity to Islam. Shahbaz Bhatti was an advocate for the rights of the religious minorities in Pakistan (see **Figure 12-1**). Two days after the killing of the federal minister, three unidentified gunmen killed a man named Mohammad Imran in Rawalpindi. Imran was arrested for blasphemy in 2010, but he was later released for lack of evidence. In 2011, two

TABLE 12-4 The Blasphemy Laws and Offenses Relating to Islam: Pakistan Penal Code

Penal Code	Description of the Offenses
295-A	Whoever, with deliberate and malicious intention of outraging the religious feelings of any class of the citizens of Pakistan, by words, either spoken or written, or by visible representations insults the religion or the religious beliefs of that class, shall be punished with imprisonment of either description for a term which may extend to ten years, or with fine, or with both.
295-B	Whoever willfully defiles, damages, or desecrates a copy of the Holy Qur'an or of an extract therefrom or uses it in any derogatory manner or for any unlawful purpose shall be punished with imprisonment for life.
295-C	Whoever by words, either spoken or written, or by visible representation or by any imputation, innuendo, or insinuation, directly or indirectly, defiles the sacred name of the Holy Prophet Muhammad (peace be upon him) shall be punished with death, or imprisonment for life, and shall also be liable to fine.
298	Whoever, with the deliberate intention of wounding the religious feelings of any person, utters any word or makes any sound in the hearing of that person or makes any gesture in the sight of that person or places any object in the sight of that person, shall be punished with imprisonment of either description for a term which may extend to one year or with fine, or with both.
298-A	Whoever by words, either spoken or written, or by visible representation, or by any imputation, innuendo, or insinuation, directly or indirectly, defiles the sacred name of any wife (Ummul Mumineen), or members of the family (Ahle-bait), of the Holy Prophet (peace be upon him), or any of the righteous Caliphs (Khulafa-e-Rashideen) or companions (Sahaaba) of the Holy Prophet (peace be upon him) shall be punished with imprisonment of either description for a term which may extend to three years, or with fine, or with both.
298-B	Any person of the Qadiani group or the Lahori group (who call themselves Ahmadis or by any other name) who by words, either spoken or written or by visible representation: (1) refers to or addresses, any person, other than a Caliph or companion of the Holy Prophet Mohammad (PBUH), as "Ameerul Momneen," "Khalifat-ul-Momneen," "Khalifat-ul-Muslimeen," "Sahaabi," or "Razi Allah Anho"; (2) refers to or addresses, any person, other than a wife of the Holy Prophet Mohammed (PBUH), as Ummul-Mumineen; (3) refers to, or names, or calls, his place of worship as Masjid; shall be punished with imprisonment or either description for a term which may extend to three years, and shall also be liable to fine. Any person of the Qadiani group or Lahore group (who call themselves Ahmadis or by any other names), who by words, either spoken or written, or by visible representations, refers to the mode or form of call to prayers followed by his faith as "Azan" or redites Azan as used by the Muslims, shall be punished with imprisonment of either description for a term which may extend to three years and shall also be liable to fine.
298-C	Persons of Qadiani group, etc., calling himself a Muslim or preaching or propagating his faith. Any person of the Qadiani group or the Lahori group (who call themselves Ahmadis or any other name), who directly or indirectly, passes himself as a Muslim, or calls, or refers to, his faith as Islam, or preaches or propagates his faith, or invites others to accept his faith, by words, either spoken or written, or by visible representation or in any manner whatsoever outrages the religious feelings of Muslims, shall be punished with imprisonment of either description for a term which may extend to three years and shall also be liable to fine.

Source: Data from the Pakistan Penal Code.

Figure 12-1 Students Protesting Against Any Attempts to Change the Blasphemy Laws in Pakistan

Source: © Fareed Khan/AP Photos.

men who were convicted of blasphemy died mysteriously in prisons. One was in Karachi and was a Christian (Qamar David), and another man (Sahukat Ali) died in a prison in Lahore (Imtiaz, 2011).

The blasphemy laws are said to be responsible not only for increased extrajudicial killings (see **Table 12-5**) but also for increased harassment of many Pakistanis, including the religious minorities. In January 2011, two Christian women in Lahore "were beaten and publicly humiliated by an angry mob in this city apparently over allegations of frivolous religious sacrilege" (Press Trust of India, 2011, p. 1). In April 30 of the same year, in the city of Gujranwala, "hundreds of people attacked a Christian seminary, a church and houses of Christians after police released two Christians who had been accused of blasphemy from protective custody" (Imtiaz, 2011, p. 3). On May 30, 2011, Jamiat Ulema-e-Islam (Samiul Haq) called "for the Bible to be banned on account of allegedly containing blasphemous material" (Imtiaz, 2011). One of the highly publicized cases is that of a Christian woman named Asia Bibi. She was a 45-year-old mother of five from the province of Punjab, and she was sentenced to death by a court in Lahore for defiling the sacred name of the Prophet Muhammad. Asia Bibi is still in prison, and her case is not likely to be heard by the upper court before 2015. Under the blasphemy laws, the criminal justice system of Pakistan is becoming increasingly burdened with cases of the prosecution of religious minorities (see **Figure 12-2**). A report from Freedom House published in 2010 noted that "a total of 697 people were accused of blasphemy in Pakistan between 1986 and 2006. Of those, 362 were Muslims, 239 were Ahmadis, 86 were Christians, and 10 were Hindus" (Freedom House, 2010, p. 69).

World Report 2012 from Human Rights Watch (2012) noted that in Pakistan, religious minorities are living in a culture of fear and terror: "Freedom of belief and expression came under severe threat as Islamist militant groups murdered Punjab Governor Salmaan Taseer and Federal Minorities' Minister Shahbaz Bhatti over their public support for amending

TABLE 12-5 Selected Extrajudicial Killing of People Under Claims of Blasphemy, 1990–2010

Year	Description of the Victim(s) and Killing	Religion	City
1992	Tahir Iqbal, poisoned to death in jail for converting to Christianity	Christian	Lahore
1994	Hafiz Farooq Sajad, murdered by mob	Muslim	Gujranwala
1994	Zahid Shah, stoned by mob	Muslim	Chak Jhumra
1995	Adnan Ahmad, murdered	Ahmadis	Sargodha
2000	Zafar Ahmad, murdered	Ahmadis	Dadu
2003	Mustaq Ahmad, murdered	Muslim	Lahore
2004	Samuel Masih, killed by a police constable	Christian	Lahore
2005	Place of worship of the Ahmadis attacked; 8 killed and 18 injured	Ahmadis	Phalian
2006	Mujubur Rehman-Pasha, murdered in his clinic	Ahmadis	Sindh
2006	Munawar Ahmad, murdered at home	Ahmadis	Gujrat
2007	Muhammad Ashraf, killed by a police officer for blasphemy	Ahmadis	Lahore
2008	Jagdesh Kumar, murdered by colleagues	Hindu	Karachi
2009	Seven Christians, burned alive	Christian	Punjab
2009	Mian Qasim Insari, murdered by police constable	Muslim	Gujrat
2010	Rashid Emmanuel and Sajid Emmanuel, shot dead by extremists	Christian	Faisalabad
2010	Muhammad Yusuf, a leader of the Ahmadi community, killed	Ahmadis	Lahore
2010	Terrorist attack on Ahmadis; 80 killed, 90 injured	Ahmadis	Lahore
2010	Sheikh Ashraf Parvez, Sheikh Masood Jawad, and Asif Masood, killed	Ahmadis	Faisalabad
2010	Naimatullah, stabbed to death by an assailant	Ahmadis	Narowal
2010	Sheikh Amir Raza, killed by a suicide bomber	Ahmadis	Mardan

Source: Data from Jinnah Institute. (2010). *Amendments to the Blasphemy Laws Act of 2010* (Jinnah Institute Briefing Pack). Karachi, Pakistan: Author.

the country's often abused blasphemy laws" (p. 1). The report further noted that "members of the Ahmadi religious community also continue to be a major target for blasphemy prosecutions . . . . In November, four Hindus, three of them doctors, were killed in an attack by religious extremists . . . sending shockwaves through the minority community" (Human Rights Watch, 2012, p. 2). A report from the Jinnah Institute made a similar observation. It said that in Pakistan, "the Blasphemy Laws as enshrined in the PPC have evolved in an excessively punitive manner and are being used to persecute religious minorities, settle vendettas and victimise the poor" (Jinnah Institute, 2010, p. 4).

Among the religious minorities, the Ahmadis are particularly victimized. The Freedom House (2010) report further noted that "while Pakistan's blasphemy laws affect the religious freedom of all minority groups, Ahmadis are singled out in Article 298 (A) through 298 (C),

Figure 12-2 Pakistan's Blasphemy Laws: A History of Violence
Source: © FAYAZ KABLI/Reuters/Landov.

which equate Ahmadi beliefs and practices with blasphemy against Islam" (p. 81). Although the Ahmadis claim themselves as Muslims, under the Penal Code of Pakistan (Section 298A-298C), they are prohibited from "using the Muslim call to prayer, quoting the Quran, participating in the pilgrimage to Mecca or the activities associated with the holy month of Ramadan" (Freedom House, 2010, p. 81). The 2011 annual report of the United States Commission on International Religious Freedom (2011), dedicated to the memory of Shahbaz Bhatti, similarly expressed serious concerns about the blasphemy laws in Pakistan. The report noted that "blasphemy laws are used against members of religious minority communities and dissenters within the majority Muslim community, and frequently result in imprisonment on account of religion or belief and/or vigilante violence" (p. 110). Currently, an amendment bill—Amendment to the Blasphemy Laws Act of 2010—is being considered by the National Assembly of Pakistan. The radical Islamic groups and the Sunni clerics, however, are vehemently opposed to any change in the blasphemy laws of Pakistan.

■ Summary

Pakistan inherited a modern system of criminal justice from British India. From 1947 to 1978, the criminal justice system of Pakistan was based on the common law tradition, an adversarial system of justice, the Indian Police Act of 1861, the Indian Penal Code of 1862, the India Evidence Act of 1872, and the Indian Code of Criminal Procedure of 1898. In the formative years of the state of Pakistan, a modern system of criminal justice was rapidly expanding with the modernization of the police, courts, prisons, and profession of law and justice. Pakistan's criminal justice system, however, came to a turning point after the introduction of Islamic criminal justice. The introduction of the *Hudood* Ordinances, the *Qisas* and *Diyat* Ordinance, and the blasphemy laws within the Pakistan Penal Code of 1862 and the Code of Criminal Procedure of 1898 created a dual system of criminal justice in Pakistan. This created enormous confusion and complexities not only about the meaning and interpretation of Islamic jurisprudence but also about the administration of criminal justice. The introduction of the *Hudood* Ordinances related to rape, adultery, and fornication created a new regime of discriminations and injustice for women. The judges of the lower courts were not sure how to interpret the Quranic laws related to *hudud* crimes and *qisas* crimes. The Criminal Law (Amendment) Act of 2006 substantially changed the Hudood Ordinances of 1979 by removing rape and fornication from the jurisdiction of the Shari'a judiciary and putting them back in the Pakistan Penal Code of 1862.

The *Qisas* and *Diyat* Ordinance created also a new culture of impunity through the legalization of the right to waive *qisas* and receive blood money (*diyat*). The blasphemy laws created more tensions and complexities in the system of criminal justice by escalating extra-judicial killings and violence against the religious minorities. The blasphemy laws criminalized free speech and the right to have alternative faiths. By introducing the blasphemy laws, Pakistan violated many international norms and standards of human rights.

The future direction of criminal justice in Pakistan will depend on the dynamics of politics in Pakistan. The nature and ideology of the state of Pakistan will mold the nature and ideology of its criminal justice. After 65 years of its independence, Pakistan is still in a process of state formation—searching for a stable political system. The two major competing political groups and elites are the modernists and the traditionalists. If the modernists come to control the state of Pakistan, Islamic criminal justice will be significantly changed and reformed, and there is a significant presence of modernists within the political and military elites of Pakistan. Modernity and religiosity are not incompatible. One of the core principles of modernity is to protect and preserve the right to religion, which the United States protects in its First Amendment. Pakistan is predominantly a Muslim country, but it is also a part of a civilization that is different from the civilization of the Middle East or the civilization of Iran. For more than 200 years, during the rule of the British colonial state, the regions that now constitute Pakistan were closely in touch with the modern civilization of the West. The progress of the state of Pakistan within the cultural demands of these competing civilizations will probably shape the nature of criminal justice in Pakistan in the 21st century. The future destinies and the directionalities of criminal justice in different countries of the world, particularly of the dual systems of criminal justice, will depend on the response of their political elites and masses to challenges posed by the processes of modernization and globalization.

■ Discussion Questions

1. What was the nature of criminal justice in Pakistan before the introduction of Shari'a Law? What were the key legal and judicial institutions on which an incipient system of modern criminal justice was growing in Pakistan in the 1960s and early 1970s? (Hint: Describe some of the selected provisions—the Pakistan Penal Code of 1862, and the Pakistan Criminal Procedure Act of 1898.)

2. What are the four different types of laws introduced by the *Hudood* Ordinances of 1979 in Pakistan? Describe the nature of the Offence of *Zina* (Enforcement of *Hudood*) Ordinance and the Offence of *Qazf* (Enforcement of *Hudood*) Ordinance. How are these Shari'a Laws different from those of the English common law tradition with respect to rape and adultery? Explain and give examples.

3. It is widely believed that the introduction of *Hudood* laws with respect to rape and adultery in Pakistan created a discriminatory system of justice for women. Explain how women are being disproportionately victimized by the introduction of the *Hudood* laws with respect to the litigation of rape and adultery cases. Give examples.

4. In 1990, Pakistan introduced the *Qisas* and *Diyat* laws through the introduction of the Criminal Law (Amendment) Ordinance of 1990. Describe the nature of *Qisas* and *Diyat* laws with respect to murder. What are the effects of these new Islamic laws on the litigation of murder cases in Pakistan? How are the *Qisas* and *Diyat* laws different from those of the English common law tradition with respect to the procedures of litigating murder cases?

5. In 2006, Pakistan passed the Protection of Women (Criminal Law Amendment) Act of 2006, and it substantially amended the Offence of *Zina* (Enforcement of *Hudood*) Ordinance of 1979 and the Offence of *Qazf* (Enforcement of *Hudood*) Ordinance of 1979. Describe the effect of this new legislation on the implementation of Shari'a Law with respect to rape and adultery.

6. What is the meaning of the ritual of honor killing? Describe some examples of honor killings in Pakistan. Explain why the promulgation of the *Qisas* and *Diyat* Ordinance contributed to the rise of the incidence of honor killings in Pakistan during the past 3 decades.

7. What are the different provisions of the blasphemy laws in Pakistan? How have the blasphemy laws criminalized free speech and the right to alternative faiths? Describe the stresses and strains that the promulgation of blasphemy laws has brought for criminal justice in Pakistan.

8. In the context of the nature of a failed state and growing radical Islamic fundamentalism within some sections of the Pakistani society, what is the future of modernization in criminal justice in Pakistan? What lessons can be drawn from the case of Pakistan with regard to the compatibility between Islamic and modern systems of criminal justice?

9. The nature of criminal justice in a country is intimately connected to the nature of its state and the ideology of its dominant political elites. Explain and expand this statement in terms of your understanding of the nature and implementation of Shari'a Law in Saudi Arabia, Iran, and Pakistan.

10. Read the USAID's, *Pakistan Rule of Law Assessment—Final Report*, and the U.S. Department of State's *2010 Human Rights Report: Pakistan*. Based on your reading of these two reports, describe the nature and status of criminal justice in Pakistan. Give examples.

■ References ■

Ali, S. S. (2006). *Applying Islamic criminal justice in plural legal systems: Exploring gender-sensitive judicial responses to* Hudood *laws in Pakistan*. Retrieved from www.supremecourt.gov.pk/ijc /Articles/11/2.pdf.

Amnesty International. (2005). *Pakistan: Protection of juveniles in the criminal justice system remains inadequate*. Retrieved from www.amnesty.org/en/library/info/ASA33/021/2005/en.

Asian Human Rights Commission. (2010, December). *Pakistan: Shari'a Court launches major challenges to Protection of Women Act*. Hong Kong: Author.

Associated Press of Pakistan. (2011). *Chief justice of Pakistan: Standard of investigation, prosecution deteriorating*. Retrieved from http://pakistanthinktank.org/islam/item/1127-chief-justice-of -pakistan-standard-of-investigation-prosecution-deteriorating.

Austrian Red Cross. (2009). *Pakistan: Honour killing of men; availability of state protection*. Retrieved from www.unhcr.org/refworld/pdfid/4a5604292.pdf.

Blue, R., Hoffman, R., & Berg, L., for Management Systems International. (2008). *Pakistan rule of law assessment—Final report*. Washington, DC: USAID.

Choudhury, G. W. (1967). *Documents and speeches on the constitution of Pakistan*. Dacca, East Pakistan: Book House.

Commonwealth Human Rights Initiative and Human Rights Commission of Pakistan. (2010). *Police organisations in Pakistan*. Delhi, India, and London, England: Authors.

Daily Times. (2004). *Laws victimising Pakistani women seen as 'divine' by hardline supporters*. Retrieved from www.dailytimes.com.pk/default.asp?page=story_3-5-2004_pg7_24.

Economist Intelligence Unit. (2011). *Democracy index 2011: Democracy under stress* (a report from the Economist Intelligence Unit). London, England: The Economist.

Federal Shariat Court of Pakistan. (2011). *Selected cases decided by the Federal* Shariat *Court in the year 2010*. Islamabad, Pakistan: The Government of Pakistan.

Freedom House. (2010). *Policing belief: The impact of blasphemy laws on human rights*. Washington, DC: Author.

Haider, S. A. (2009). *Powers, jurisdictions and functions of the Federal Shariat Court: Thirty years of its establishment*. Retrieved from www.qlc.edu.pk/publications/pdf/1%20-%20Powers%20 Jurisdiction%20&%20Functions%20of%20FSC.pdf.

Hashmi, S. V. (2004). *The concept of justice in Islam:* Qisas *&* diyat *law as a part of Pakistan Penal Code, 1860*. Retrieved from http://spaces.brad.ac.uk:8080/download/attachments/750/HR_ROWNC12. pdf.

Human Rights Watch. (2012). *World report 2012: Pakistan*. Retrieved from www.hrw.org/world -report-2012/world-report-2012-pakistan.

Imran, R. (2005). Legal injustices: The *Zina Hudood* ordinance of Pakistan and its implications. *Journal of International Women's Studies, 7* (2), 78–100.

Imtiaz, S. (2011). Timeline: Pakistan blasphemy law cases, Jan–July 2011. *International Herald Tribune*. Retrieved from http://tribune.com.pk/story/223353/timeline-pakistan-blasphemy-law-cases-jan -july-2011/.

International Crisis Group. (2010). *Reforming Pakistan's criminal justice system* (Asia Report No. 196). Washington, DC: Author.

International Crisis Group. (2011). *Reforming Pakistan's prison system* (Asia Report No. 212). Washington, DC: Author.

Jinnah Institute. (2010). *Amendments to the Blasphemy Laws Act of 2010* (Jinnah Institute Briefing Pack). Karachi, Pakistan: Author.

Kaufmann, D., Kraay, A., & Mastruzzi, M., for the World Bank. (2010). *The World Bank governance indicators: Methodology and analytical issues*. Washington, DC: World Bank Development Research Group.

Kennedy, C. H. (1988). Islamization in Pakistan: Implementation of the *Hudood* Ordinances. *Asian Survey, 8*(3), 307–316.

Knudsen, A. (2004). *License to kill: Honors killing in Pakistan*. Bergen, Norway: Michelsen Institute of Development Studies and Human Rights.

Lau, M. (2005). *Role of Islam in the legal system of Pakistan*. London, England: Martinus Nijhoff.

Lau, M. (2007). Twenty-five years of *Hudood* ordinances: A review. *Washington and Lee Law Review.* Retrieved from www.law.wlu.edu/deptimages/Law%20Review/64-4Lau.pdf.

Library of Congress. (2012a). *Mr. Jinnah's presidential address to the constituent assembly of Pakistan.* Washington, DC: Author.

Library of Congress. (2012b). *Constitution of the Islamic Republic of Pakistan.* Washington, DC: Author.

Marshall, M. G., & Cole, B. R. (2009). *Global report 2009: Conflict, governance, and state fragility.* Arlington, VA: George Mason University: Center for Global Policy.

Mehdi, R. (2010). *The Protection of Women (Criminal Law Amendment) Act of 2006 in Pakistan.* Retrieved from http://droitcultures.revues.org/2016.

Nasrullah, M., Haqqi, S., & Cummings, K. J. (2009). The epidemiological patterns of honour killing of women in Pakistan. *European Journal of Public Health, 19*(2), 193–197.

Press Trust of India. (2011, January 15). *Two Christian women beaten in Pak over blasphemy charges.* Retrieved from www.ndtv.com/article/world/two-christian-women-beaten-in-pak-over-blasphemy-charges-79523.

Saeed, S. (2010, September 18). Effect of *qisas* and *diyat* laws on criminal justice [Web log post]. Retrieved from http://secularpakistan.wordpress.com/2010/09/18/effect-of-qisas-and-diyat-laws-on-criminal-justice/.

Shirkat Gah (Women's Resource Center). (2004). *Why the* Hudood *Ordinances must be repealed.* Retrieved from www.apwld.org/pdf/Why_Hudood_Ordinances_must_be_Repealed.pdf.

The Gazette of Pakistan. (1979a, February). *Offence of Zina (Enforcement of Hudood) Ordinance* (Ordinance No. VII). Islamabad: The Government of Pakistan.

The Gazette of Pakistan. (1979b, February). *Offences Against Property (Enforcement of Hudood) Ordinance* (Ordinance No. VI). Islamabad: The Government of Pakistan.

The Gazette of Pakistan. (1979c, February). *The Offence of Qazf (Enforcement of Hudood) Ordinance* (Ordinance No. VIII). Islamabad: The Government of Pakistan.

The Gazette of Pakistan. (1979d, February). *Prohibition (Enforcement of Hudood) Order of 1979* (Ordinance No. IV). Islamabad: The Government of Pakistan.

The Gazette of Pakistan. (1980, May). *Constitution (Amendment) Order, 1980* (President's Order No.1). Islamabad: The Government of Pakistan.

The Gazette of Pakistan. (1993). *Code of Criminal Procedure (Third Amendment) Ordinance of 1993* (R 35689). Islamabad: The Government of Pakistan.

The Gazette of Pakistan. (1994). *The Code of Criminal Procedure (Second Amendment) Act of 1994.* Islamabad: The Government of Pakistan.

The Gazette of Pakistan. (2005, January). *Criminal Law Amendment Act of 2005* (M-302/L-7646). Islamabad: The Government of Pakistan.

The Gazette of Pakistan. (2006). *The Protection of Women (Criminal Law Amendment) Act of 2006.* Islamabad: The Government of Pakistan.

The Gazette of Pakistan. (2009, November). *The Criminal Law (Amendment) Act of 2009.* Islamabad: The Government of Pakistan.

The Gazette of Pakistan. (2011, April). *Code of Criminal Procedure (Amendment) Act of 2011* (M-302/L-7646). Islamabad: The Government of Pakistan.

United Nations High Commissioner for Refugees (UNCHR). (2012). *Pakistan Penal Code, 1860.* Retrieved from http://www.unhcr.org/refworld/docid/485231942.html.

United Nations Office on Drugs and Crime. (2004). *International homicide statistics.* Retrieved from http://www.unodc.org/documents/data-and-analysis/IHS-rates-05012009.pdf.

United States Commission on International Religious Freedom. (2011). *Annual report, 2011 (April 2010–March 31, 2011).* Washington, DC: Author.

United States Department of State. (2011). *2010 human rights report: Pakistan.* Washington, DC: USAID.

Usmani, M. T. (2006, April). The Islamization laws in Pakistan: The case of *Hudud* Ordinances. *The Muslim World, 90,* 287–304.

Wasti, T. (2009). *The application of Islamic criminal law in Pakistan: Sharia in practice.* Leiden, the Netherlands: Koninklijke Brill NV.

World Justice Project. (2010). *Rule of law index, 2010.* Washington, DC: Author.

World Justice Project. (2011). *Rule of law index, 2011.* Washington, DC: Author.

Index